THE NEGRO
IN
Twentieth Century America

THE NEGRO
IN
Twentieth Century America
A READER ON THE STRUGGLE FOR CIVIL RIGHTS

John Hope Franklin & Isidore Starr

VINTAGE BOOKS
A DIVISION OF RANDOM HOUSE
New York

The authors are grateful to the following for permission to reprint:

American Academy of Arts and Sciences, for excerpts from "The Goals of Integration," by Oscar Handlin (Daedalus, winter, 1966).

Beacon Press, for excerpts from Chapter I of SNCC: *The New Abolitionists,* by Howard Zinn. Copyright © 1964, 1965 by Howard Zinn.

The Bobbs-Merrill Company, Inc., for an excerpt from *On Being Negro in America,* by J. Saunders Redding. Copyright © 1951 by J. Saunders Redding.

Collins-Knowlton-Wing, Inc., for "The Coming Showdown in the Race Crisis," by Harry S. Ashmore (*Look,* July 16, 1963). Copyright © 1963 by Cowles Magazines and Broadcasting, Inc.

Joan Daves for "I Have a Dream," by Martin Luther King, Jr. Copyright © 1963 by Martin Luther King, Jr.

The Dial Press, Inc., for excerpts from *The Fire Next Time,* by James Baldwin. Copyright © 1962, 1963 by James Baldwin.

Doubleday & Company, Inc., for excerpts from *Following The Color Line,* by Ray Stannard Baker. Copyright 1904, 1905 by S. S. McClure Company; copyright 1907, 1908 by the Phillips Publishing Company; copyright 1908 by Doubleday & Company, Inc.

Fortune, for "The City and the Negro," by Charles E. Silberman (March 1962). Copyright © 1962 by Time, Inc.

Grove Press, Inc., for an excerpt from *The Autobiography of Malcolm X* (with the assistance of Alex Haley). Copyright © 1964 by Alex Haley and Malcolm X; copyright © 1965 by Alex Haley and Betty Shabazz.

Harper & Row, Publishers, Inc., for excerpts from *An American Dilemma,* by Gunnar Myrdal, *et al.* Copyright 1944 by Harper & Row, Publishers, Inc.

Johnson Publishing Company, Inc., for "The South Looks Ahead," by Ralph McGill (*Ebony,* September 1963).

Martin Luther King, Jr., for "Letter from a Birmingham City Jail," by Martin Luther King, Jr.

Alfred A. Knopf, Inc., for "Merry-Go-Round" and "Roland Hayes Beaten (Georgia: 1942)," from *Selected Poems,* by Langston Hughes. Copyright 1942 by Langston Hughes; copyright 1948 by Alfred A. Knopf, Inc.

McGraw-Hill Book Company, for an excerpt from *To Be Equal,* by Whitney M. Young. Copyright © 1964 by McGraw-Hill Book Company.

The *New York Post* for the column by Langston Hughes. Copyright © 1965 by the New York Post Corporation.

The *New York Times,* for "Civil Rights: Decade of Progress," by Anthony Lewis (December 20, 1964); "Civil Rights: South Slowly Yields," by John Herbers (December 20, 1964); "Alabama: Racism vs. Reason: (Editorial: March 14, 1965);

*To Whit and Larry
and their generation*

If there is no struggle, there is no progress. Those who profess to favor freedom, and yet deprecate agitation, are men who want crops without plowing up the ground. They want the ocean without the awful roar of its many waters.

Frederick Douglass—1857

Our Constitution is color-blind, and neither knows nor tolerates classes among citizens. In respect of civil rights, all citizens are equal before the law. The humblest is the peer of the most powerful. The law regards man as man, and takes no account of his sourroundings or of his color when his civil rights as guaranteed by the supreme law of the land are involved.

Supreme Court Justice Harlan in dissenting opinion
of *Plessy* v. *Ferguson,* 1896

It is true that the ultimate solution will not be found in laws, but in the dark places of men's minds and hearts. But it is also true that laws are the manifest of the national purpose, and when government is unwilling, or unable, to provide them, there is no standard to which the wise and just may repair.

Harry Ashmore—*Look,* July 16, 1963

The only thing necessary for the triumph of evil is for good men to do nothing.

Edmund Burke—*Thoughts on the Cause
of Present Discontent,* April 23, 1770

The Problem of the twentieth century is the problem of the color line.

W. E. B. Du Bois, 1903

CONTENTS

Part III: THE SEEDS OF PROTEST: THE NEGRO PROBLEM AT THE TURN OF THE CENTURY 1890–1910

BOOK TWO *A Struggle with Ideas: Means and Ends*

PART I: NEGRO LEADERS, ORGANIZATIONS, METHODS, AND GOALS

PART II: WHITE REACTION TO THE NEGRO PROTEST

Contents

BOOK THREE   *A Struggle with Issues*

PART I: EDUCATION FOR THE NEGRO

PART II: VOTING RIGHTS FOR THE NEGRO

PART III: JUSTICE FOR THE NEGRO

BOOK FOUR   *The Negro Today:*
Balance Sheet

FOREWORD

We had several ideas in mind in working on this book

. . .

The Negro problem was selected because it is one of the great case studies in man's never-ending fight for equal rights. The study of this problem forces us to compare our public ideals with our private practices. Our Declaration of Independence proclaims that "all men are created equal" and our Federal Constitution declares that all persons are entitled to "equal protection of the laws." Why does a gap exist between these public aims and our private deeds?

. . .

The focus of attention in this book is on the twentieth century because it is in the period 1900 to the present that the crusade for equality began to break through the curtain of public apathy. It is in this century that our country has fought two world wars and is now engaged in a Cold War. Slogans in each of these wars bear directly on the need to preserve those ways of life which are built upon the dignity and integrity of the individual. If we have fought and are fighting to preserve the democratic spirit abroad, then what prevents us from achieving it at home?

. . .

If the reader is looking for *the simple answer to the problem of the Negro* in twentieth century America, this is not the book for him. There can be no answers until we sense the nature of the problem and know which are the real questions. With this in mind, we have arranged documents, cartoons, charts, poems, selections from books, magazines, newspapers, and government documents to provide materials for thought. What the reader will find is a kaleidoscope of opinion bearing on a variety of subjects relating to the Negro's struggle for civil rights in twentieth century America. This kaleidoscope shows the dark side of human nature with its bigotry, hatred, and violence. It also shows the bright side of American decency, respect, and peaceful resolution of conflict. The story, as it unfolds, is more than a study in black and white. Negroes are not all of one mind concerning means and ends; whites are divided on what ought to be done.

To understand the complexity of the problems of the Negro is the first step in the search for solutions. To reject the problems and to throw up one's hands because of the many difficulties would result in an American tragedy for the whites, as well as for the Negroes.

The authors gratefully acknowledge the contribution of those who worked with them, and would like to thank especially Richard Fuke for his assistance in research, Jason Epstein for his encouragement, and Janice Eldon and Emily Lloyd for their enthusiastic help.

J.H.F. and I.S.

BOOK ONE

The Negro Problem

INTRODUCTION

Book One asks and tries to answer two questions: What is a Negro? and What is the nature of the Negro problem?

Obviously, when we speak of *The Negro in Twentieth Century America: A Reader on the Struggle for Civil Rights,* we ought to be able to define our terms. Part I begins with some of the provisions found in state constitutions and laws which attempt to define a Negro. A careful comparison of these statements raises some serious questions as to whether there is agreement on the meaning of the word "Negro." The fact that some Negroes may pass for whites continues to add complications for those who search for definitions.

Part II presents a wide range of viewpoints on the nature of the Negro problem. The readings create a kind of kaleidoscope as seen through the eyes of the young and the mature, the journalist and the scholar, and the white and the Negro man in the street.

PART I

WHAT IS A NEGRO?

Selection 1

STATE LAWS ON RACE AND COLOR*

State constitutions and laws concerning the Negro made it necessary for the state to define "Negro" (colored). This selection is concerned with the various legal definitions of "Negro" agreed upon for the purposes of upholding and enforcing the state constitutions and laws.

Alabama

Title 1, Sec. 2. Meaning of certain words and terms: . . . The word "Negro" includes mulatto. The word "mulatto" or the term "person of color" means a person of mixed blood descended on the part of the father or mother from Negro ancestors, without reference to or limit of time or number of generations removed. (1927, p. 716.)

* From *States' Laws on Race and Color,* Pauli Murray (editor), published by the Women's Division of Christian Service, Board of Missions and Church Extension, the Methodist Church, Cincinnati, Ohio: 1951.

Arkansas

41-808. "Person of Negro race" defined: . . . defines "person of Negro race" as "any person who has in his or her veins any Negro blood whatever." (Acts 1911, No. 320, Sec. 3, p. 295.)

Florida

Sec. 1.01. Definition: . . . The words "Negro," "colored," "colored persons," "mulatto," or "persons of color," when applied to persons, include every person having one-eighth or more of African or Negro blood. (Rev. Gen. St. 1920, Sec. 3939; Comp. Gen. Laws 1927, Sec. 5858.)

Georgia

Sec. 79-103. (2177) *Persons of color, who are:* All Negroes, mulattoes, mestizos and their descendants, having any ascertainable trace of either Negro or African, West Indian, or Asiatic Indian blood in their veins, and all descendants of any person having either Negro or African, West Indian, or Asiatic Indian blood in his or her veins shall be known in this State as persons of color. (Acts 1865-6, p. 239; 1927, p. 272.)

Sec. 53-312. "White person" defined: The term "white person" shall include only persons of the white or Caucasian race, who have no ascertainable trace of either Negro, African, West Indian, Asiatic Indian, Mongolian, Japanese or Chinese blood in their veins. No person, any one of whose ancestors has been duly registered with the State Bureau of Vital Statistics as a colored person or person of color, shall be deemed to be a white person. (Acts 1927, p. 277.)

Kentucky

(*Note:* "Colored children," within the meaning of Section 187 of Kentucky Constitution, include all children wholly or in part of Negro blood, or having any appreciable admixture thereof; and a child having one-sixteenth Negro blood may not attend a school for white children.)

Louisiana

(No statutory definition, but see *Lee* vs. *New Orleans Great Northern R. Co.* [1910] 125 La. 236, 239, 51 So. 182, which defines "colored persons" as "all persons with any appreciable mixture of Negro blood.")

Mississippi

(*Note:* Art. 14, Section 263 of the Constitution of Mississippi which prohibits marriage of a white person with a Negro or mulatto, or a person having one-eighth or more Negro blood, does not determine the status of a person as to whether he is white or colored under Art. 8, Section 207 of the Constitution, which provides for separate schools for children of the white and colored races. The word "white" under Section 207 means a member of the Caucasian race and the word "colored" includes not only Negroes but persons of mixed blood having any appreciable amount of Negro blood. ([*Moreau* vs. *Grandich,* (1917) 114 Miss. 560, 75 Sp 434].)

Oklahoma

Art. XXIII, Sec. 11. Colored race—Negro race—White race: Wherever in this Constitution and laws of this State, the word or words, "colored" or "colored race," "Negro" or "Negro race," are used, the same shall be construed to mean or apply to all persons of African descent. The term "white race" shall include all other persons. (Const. 1907 as amended Stat. 1931, Sec. 13724.)

Texas

Art. 2900. (2897-8): . . . The terms "colored race" and "colored children," as used in this title, include all persons of mixed blood descended from Negro ancestry. (Acts 1905, p. 263.)

Penal Code, Art. 493. (484) (347) (327) "Negro" and "white person": The term "Negro" includes also a person of mixed blood descended from Negro ancestry from the third generation inclusive, though one ancestor of each generation may have been a white person. Any person not included in the foregoing definition is deemed a white person within the meaning of this law. (Penal Code 1911, Art. 484, Acts 1887, p. 37.)

Tennessee

25: The word "Negro" includes mulattoes, mestizos and their descendants, having any blood of the African race in their veins.

8396. 417al (2745a) Persons of color defined: All Negroes, mulattoes, mestizos, and their descendants, having any African blood in their veins, shall be known as "persons of color." (1865-66, ch. 40, sec. 1, modified.)

Virginia

Sec. 1-14. Colored persons and Indians defined: Every person in whom there is ascertainable any Negro blood shall be deemed and taken to be a colored person, and every person not a colored person having one-fourth or more of American Indian blood shall be deemed an American Indian; except that members of Indian tribes living on reservations allotted them by the Commonwealth of Virginia having one-fourth or more of Indian blood and less than one-sixteenth of Negro blood shall be deemed tribal Indians so long as they are domiciled on such reservations. (Code 1887, Sec. 49; 1910, p. 581; 1930, p. 97; Michie Code 1942, Sec. 67.)

Sec. 20-54. Intermarriage prohibited; meaning of term "white persons": For the purpose of this chapter, the term "white person" shall apply only to such person as has no trace whatever of any blood other than Caucasian; but persons who have one-sixteenth or less of the American Indian and have no other non-Caucasic blood shall be deemed to be white persons. . . . (1924, p. 534; Michie Code, 5099a.)

Selection 2

WHAT IS A NEGRO?

RAY STANNARD BAKER*

Between 1906 and 1908, Ray Stannard Baker, a distinguished journalist, traveled throughout the South and the North and wrote a number of magazine articles on race relations at that time. These

---

* From Ray Stannard Baker, *Following the Color Line: American Negro Citizenship in the Progressive Era,* New York: Harper & Row, 1964, pp. 151-52. [Originally published in 1908 by Doubleday, Page & Co.]

articles were later published as a book entitled Following the Color
Line: American Negro Citizenship in the Progressive Era, *from
which the following selection is taken. In this selection we see the
difficulty faced by those who try to distinguish the Negro from
the white.*

I had not been long engaged in the study of the race problem
when I found myself face to face with a curious and seemingly
absurd question:

"What is a Negro?"

I saw plenty of men and women who were unquestionably Negroes, Negroes in every physical characteristic, black of countenance
with thick lips and kinky hair, but I also met men and women
as white as I am, whose assertion that they were really Negroes I
accepted in defiance of the evidence of my own senses. I have seen
blue-eyed Negroes and golden-haired Negroes; one Negro girl I
met had an abundance of soft straight red hair. I have seen Negroes I could not easily distinguish from the Jewish or French
types; I once talked with a man I took at first to be a Chinaman
but who told me he was a Negro. And I have met several people,
passing everywhere for white, who, I knew, had Negro blood.

Nothing, indeed, is more difficult to define than this curious
physical colour line in the individual human being. Legislatures
have repeatedly attempted to define where black leaves off and
white begins, especially in connection with laws prohibiting marriage between the races. Some of the statutes define a Negro as
a "person with one-eighth or more of Negro blood." Southern people, who take pride in their ability to distinguish the drop of dark
blood in the white face, are themselves frequently deceived. Several times I have heard police judges in the South ask concerning
a man brought before them:

"Is this man coloured or white?"

Just recently a case has arisen at Norfolk, Virginia, in which a
Mrs. Rosa Stone sued the Norfolk & Western Railroad Company
for being compelled by the white conductor, who thought her a
Negro, to ride in a "Jim Crow" car. Having been forced into the
Negro compartment, it remained for a real coloured woman, who
knew her personally, to draw the line against her. This coloured
woman is reported as saying:

"Lor, Miss Rosa, this ain't no place for you; you b'long in the
cars back yonder."

It appears that Mrs. Stone was tanned.

Curious Story of a White Man Who Was Expelled as a Negro

Here is a story well illustrating the difficulties sometimes encountered by Southerners in deciding who is white and who is coloured. On March 6, 1907, the Atlanta *Georgian* published this account of how a man who, it was said, was a Negro passing for a white man, was expelled by a crowd of white men from the town of Albany, Ga.:

Peter Zeigler, a Negro, was last night escorted out of town by a crowd of white men. Zeigler had been here for a month and palmed himself off as a white man. He has been boarding with one of the best white families in the city and has been associating with some of Albany's best people. A visiting lady recognized him as being a Negro who formerly lived in her city, and her assertion was investigated and found to be correct. Last night he was carried to Forester's Station, a few miles north or here, and ordered to board an outgoing train.

Zeigler has a fair education and polished manners, and his colour was such that he could easily pass for a white man where he was not known.

Immediately after suffering the indignity of being expelled from Albany, Mr. Zeigler communicated with his friends and relatives, a delegation of whom came from Charleston, Orangeburg, and Summerville, S.C. and proved to the satisfaction of everyone that Mr. Zeigler was, in reality, a white man connected with several old families of South Carolina. Of this return of Mr. Zeigler the Albany *Herald* says:

The *Herald* yesterday contained the account of the return to Albany of Peter B. Zeigler, the young man who was forced to leave Albany between suns on the night of March 4th. The young man upon his return was accompanied by a party composed of relatives and influential friends from his native state of South Carolina.

Nothing surely could throw a more vivid light on colour line confusions in the South than this story.

Selection 3

DEFINITION OF A NEGRO

GUNNAR MYRDAL*

An American Dilemma: The Negro Problem and Modern Democracy, *written by the distinguished Swedish scholar Gunnar
Myrdal, was published in 1944. The result of five years of study
by a number of scholars supported by the Carnegie Corporation,
this is one of the most important books on the Negro in American
society.*

The "Negro race" is defined in America by the white people. It
is defined in terms of parentage. Everybody having a *known* trace
of Negro blood in his veins—no matter how far back it was acquired—is classified as a Negro. No amount of white ancestry,
except one hundred per cent, will permit entrance to the white race.
As miscegenation has largely been an affair between white men
and Negro women, it is a fair approximation to characterize the
Negro race in America as the descendants of Negro women and
Negro or white men through the generations—minus the persons
having "passed" from the Negro into the white group and their
offspring.

This definition of the Negro race in the United States is at
variance with that held in the rest of the American continent. "In
Latin America whoever is not black is white: in teutonic America
whoever is not white is black." This definition differs also from that
of the British colonies and dominions, primarily South Africa,
where the hybrids (half-castes) are considered as a group distinct
from both whites and Negroes. Even in the United States many

* From Gunnar Myrdal, *An American Dilemma: The Negro Problem and Modern
Democracy*, New York: Harper & Brothers, 1944, pp. 113–16.

persons with a mixture of Indian and white blood are regarded as whites (for example, ex-Vice President Curtis and Will Rogers).

Legislation in this respect tends to conform to social usage, although often it is not so exclusive. In some states one Negro grandparent defines a person as a Negro for legal purposes, in other states any Negro ancestor—no matter how far removed—is sufficient. In the Southern states, definitions of who is a Negro are often conflicting. Since Reconstruction, there has been a tendency to broaden the definition. The Northeastern states generally have no definition of a Negro in law. These legal definitions and their changes and differences should not be taken too seriously, however. The more absolutistic "social" definition is, in most life situations, the decisive one.

This social definition of the Negro race, even if it does not change anything in the biological situation, increases the number of individuals actually included in the Negro race. It relegates a large number of individuals who look like white people, or almost so, to the Negro race and causes the Negro race to show a greater variability generally than it would show if the race were defined more narrowly in accordance with quantitative ethnological or biological criteria. "The farcical side of the color question in the States"—says Sir Harry H. Johnston—"is that at least a considerable proportion of the 'colored people' are almost white-skinned, and belong in the preponderance of their descent and in their mental associations to the white race." In the American white population the so-called Nordic type, which is popularly assumed to be the opposite extreme from the black Negro, is a rare phenomenon. This statement is especially true after the "new" immigration from Southern and Eastern Europe and from the Near East. But even the "Old American stock" was preponderantly "non-Nordic." There are, however, also American Negroes with the clearest of white skin, the bluest of blue eyes, and the long and narrow head which happens to be both a Negro and a "Nordic" trait.

. . .

The definition of the "Negro race" is thus a social and conventional, not a biological concept. The social definition and not the biological facts actually determines the status of an individual and his place in interracial relations. This also relieves us of the otherwise cumbersome duty of explaining exhaustively what we, in a scientific sense, could understand by "race" as an ethnological and biological entity. In modern biological or ethnological research "race" as a scientific concept has lost sharpness of meaning, and the term is disappearing in sober writings. In something even remotely approaching its strict sense, it applies only to exceptionally isolated population groups, usually with a backward culture, which thus seems to be the concomitant of "racial purity."

. . .

The common belief that the races could be ordered as higher or lower in an evolutionary series, so that Negroids could be deemed more ape-like than Caucasoids, is entirely discredited. It is now commonly assumed by expert opinion that man—the species *Homo sapiens*—evolved only once, and that such average differences as now exist between men are due to living under different geographic conditions after having separated from the common place of origin. Independent of this hypothesis, which, of course, can hardly be checked, it is a fact that the Negro is no more akin to the apes than the white man is. Of the four most noticeable characteristics generally ascribed to the average or typical Negro—dark skin, broad nose, woolly hair, thick lips—only the first two make him slightly more similar to the apes. The white man's thin lips and straight hair are, on the other hand, much nearer to the traits of the apes.

Selection 4

"PASSING"

GUNNAR MYRDAL*

Because of the American caste rule of classifying all hybrids as Negroes, it might be thought that no Negro blood would ever get into the white population. However, some extremely light Negroes—usually having more white ancestry than Negro—leave the Negro caste and become "white."

* From Gunnar Myrdal, *An American Dilemma: The Negro Problem and Modern Democracy,* New York: Harper & Brothers, 1944, p. 129.

"Passing" is the backwash of miscegenation, and one of its surest results. Passing must have been going on in America ever since the time when mulattoes first appeared. Passing may occur only for segmented areas of life—such as the occupational or recreational —or it may be complete; it may be temporary or permanent; it may be voluntary or involuntary; it may be with knowledge on the part of the passer or without his knowledge; it may be individual or collective. Usually the only kind that is important for the genetic composition of both the white and the Negro population is that kind which is complete and permanent.

Usually only the lighter colored Negroes pass in the United States. However, some of the darker do also by pretending to be Filipinos, Spaniards, Italians or Mexicans. [A] study further reveals how capable of passing are persons with one-fourth, three-eighths, and even one-half, Negro blood, not to speak of persons with even smaller admixtures. Because those who pass usually have more white ancestors than Negro, it is genetically less important that these people go over into the white world than if they were to remain in the Negro. Passing, therefore, involves far greater change in social definition of the individual than it does in his biological classification.

It is difficult to determine the extent of passing. Those who have passed conceal it, and some who have passed permanently are not even aware of it themselves because their parents or grandparents hid the knowledge from them. Census data and vital statistics are not accurate enough to permit of estimates within reasonable limits. The possible methods for estimating the extent of passing are: (1) getting at genealogies by direct questioning or other means; (2) noting discrepancies between the observed numbers of Negroes in the census and those which may be expected on the basis of the previous census and birth and death figures for the inter-censal years; (3) noting deviations from normal in the sex ratio of Negroes. All these methods have been employed, but—for one reason or another—have not permitted us to state the extent of passing.

PART II

WHAT IS THE NATURE OF THE NEGRO PROBLEM?

Selection 5

AS SEEN BY A CHILD

LANGSTON HUGHES*

Merry-Go-Round

Colored child at carnival:
Where is the Jim Crow section
On this merry-go-round,
Mister, 'Cause I want to ride?
Down South where I come from
White and colored
Can't sit side by side.
Down South on the train
There's a Jim Crow car.
On the bus we're put in the back—
But there ain't no back
To a merry-go-round!
Where's the horse
For a kid that's black?

* From *Selected Poems of Langston Hughes,* New York: Alfred A. Knopf, 1959, p. 194.

Selection 6

AS SEEN BY A BRIGHT SCHOOLBOY

MALCOLM X[*]

Malcolm X, born Malcolm Little, lived in the Midwest and in the "inner cities" of Boston and New York. He tells the story of his life and of his rise from the "dark ghetto" to leadership in the Black Muslim movement in The Autobiography of Malcolm X. *The excerpt which follows describes an incident that, in his words, became "the first major turning point" in his life.*

I kept close to the top of the class, though. The topmost scholastic standing, I remember, kept shifting between me, a girl named Audrey Slaugh, and a boy named Jimmy Cotton.

It went on that way, as I became increasingly restless and disturbed through the first semester. And then one day, just about when those of us who had passed were about to move up to 8-A, from which we would enter high school the next year, something happened which was to become the first major turning point of my life.

Somehow, I happened to be alone in the classroom with Mr. Ostrowski, my English teacher. He was a tall, rather reddish white man and he had a thick mustache. I had gotten some of my best marks under him, and he had always made me feel that he liked me. He was, as I have mentioned, a natural-born "advisor," about what you ought to read, to do, or think about any and everything. We used to make unkind jokes about him: why was he teaching

* From The Autboiography of Malcolm X, New York: Grove Press, Inc., 1964, pp. 36-37.

in Mason instead of somewhere else, getting for himself some of
the "success in life" that he kept telling us how to get?

I know that he probably meant well in what he happened to
advise me that day. I doubt that he meant any harm. It was just
in his nature as an American white man. I was one of his top
students, one of the school's top students—but all he could see for
me was the kind of future "in your place" that all white people
see for black people.

He told me, "Malcolm, you ought to be thinking about a career.
Have you been giving it thought?"

The truth is, I hadn't. I never have figured out why I told him,
"Well, yes, sir, I've been thinking I'd like to be a lawyer." Lansing
certainly had no Negro lawyers—or doctors either—in those days,
to hold up an image I might have aspired to. All I really knew for
certain was that a lawyer didn't wash dishes, as I was doing.

Mr. Ostrowski looked surprised, I remember, and leaned back
in his chair and clasped his hands behind his head. He kind of
half-smiled and said, "Malcolm, one of life's first needs is for us
to be realistic. Don't misunderstand me, now. We all here like you,
you know that. But you've got to be realistic about being a nigger.
A lawyer—that's no realistic goal for a nigger. You need to think
about something you *can* be. You're good with your hands—making
things. Everybody admires your carpentry shop work. Why don't
you plan on carpentry? People like you as a person—you'd get all
kinds of work."

The more I thought afterwards about what he said, the more
uneasy it made me. It just kept treading around in my mind.

What made it really begin to disturb me was Mr. Ostrowski's
advice to others in my class—all of them white. Most of them had
told him they were planning to become farmers, like their parents
—to one day take over their family farms. But those who wanted
to strike out on their own, to try something new, he had encouraged. Some, mostly girls, wanted to be teachers. A few wanted
other professions, such as one boy who wanted to become a county
agent; another, a veterinarian; and one girl wanted to be a nurse.
They all reported that Mr. Ostrowski had encouraged whatever
they had wanted. Yet nearly none of them had earned marks equal
to mine.

It was a surprising thing that I had never thought of it that way
before, but I realized that whatever I wasn't, I *was* smarter than
nearly all of those white kids. But apparently I was still not intelligent enough, in their eyes, to become whatever I wanted to be.

It was then that I began to change—inside.

Selection 7

AS SEEN BY A NEGRO EDUCATOR

BOOKER T. WASHINGTON*

Booker T. Washington's Up From Slavery *is one of the classics in American autobiography. Published in 1901, it is a great success story of the achievements of the son of a Negro slave and a white man, who founded the famous Tuskegee Institute.*

In those days, and later as a young man, I used to try to picture in my imagination the feelings and ambitions of a white boy with absolutely no limit placed upon his aspirations and activities. I used to envy the white boy who had no obstacles placed in the way of his becoming a Congressman, Governor, Bishop, or President by reason of the accident of his birth or race. I used to picture the way that I would act under such circumstances; how I would begin at the bottom and keep rising until I reached the highest round of success.

In later years, I confess that I do not envy the white boy as I once did. I have learned that success is to be measured not so much by the position that one has reached in life as by the obstacles which he has overcome while trying to succeed. Looked at from this standpoint, I almost reach the conclusion that often the Negro boy's birth and connection with an unpopular race is an advantage, so far as real life is concerned. With few exceptions, the Negro youth must work harder and must perform his task even better than a white youth in order to secure recognition. But out of the hard and

* From Booker T. Washington, *Up From Slavery,* in *Three Negro Classics,* New York: Avon Books, 1965, p. 50.

unusual struggle which he is compelled to pass, he gets a strength, a confidence, that one misses whose pathway is comparatively smooth by reason of birth and race.

From any point of view, I had rather be what I am, a member of the Negro race, than be able to claim membership with the most favored of any other race. I have always been made sad when I have heard members of any race claiming rights and privileges, or certain badges of distinction, on the ground simply that they were members of this or that race, regardless of their own individual worth or attainments. I have been made to feel sad for such persons because I am conscious of the fact that mere connection with what is known as a superior race will not permanently carry an individual forward unless he has individual worth, and mere connection with what is regarded as an inferior race will not finally hold an individual back if he possesses intrinsic, individual merit. Every persecuted individual and race should get much consolation out of the great human law, which is universal and eternal, that merit, no matter under what skin found, is in the long run, recognized and rewarded. This I have said here, not to call attention to myself as an individual, but to the race to which I am proud to belong.

Selections 8a–8b

AS SEEN BY A NEGRO HISTORIAN

W. E. B. DU BOIS*

The Souls of Black Folk *by William E. B. Du Bois, published in 1903, starts with this forethought:*
"Herein lie buried many things which if read with patience may show the strange meaning of being black here at the dawning of the Twentieth Century. This meaning is not without interest to

* From William E. B. Du Bois, *The Souls of Black Folk*, in *Three Negro Classics*, New York: Avon Books, 1965, pp. 213–16, 219–20.

you, Gentle Reader; for the problem of the Twentieth Century is
the problem of the color line."

Du Bois was a historian who participated actively in the organization of Negroes for a more militant program to achieve complete
equality. In 1905 he organized the Niagara Movement, and in 1910
he participated in the founding of the National Association for the
Advancement of Colored People. For many years he was editor of
The Crisis, the NAACP magazine. In his later years he became disillusioned with the slow progress made by Negroes. Toward the end
of his long life, he joined the Communist Party, renounced his
American citizenship, and became a citizen of Ghana. He died
there in 1963 at the age of 95.

8a. The Negro Problem

Between me and the other world there is ever an unasked question:
unasked by some through feelings of delicacy; by others through the
difficulty of rightly framing it. All, nevertheless, flutter round it.
They approach me in a half-hesitant sort of way, eye me curiously
or compassionately, and then, instead of saying directly, How does
it feel to be a problem? they say, I know an excellent colored man
in my town; or, I fought at Mechanicsville; or, Do not these Southern outrages make your blood boil? At these I smile, or am interested, or reduce the boiling to a simmer, as the occasion may require. To the real question, How does it feel to be a problem? I
answer seldom a word.

And yet, being a problem is a strange experience,—peculiar even
for one who has never been anything else, save perhaps in baby-
hood and in Europe. It is in the early days of rollicking boyhood
that the revelation first bursts upon one, all in a day, as it were.
I remember well when the shadow swept across me. I was a little
thing, away up in the hills of New England, where the dark
Housatonic winds between Hoosac and Taghkanic to the sea. In
a wee wooden schoolhouse, something put it into the boys' and
girls' heads to buy gorgeous visiting-cards—ten cents a package—
and exchange. The exchange was merry, till one girl, a tall new-
comer, refused my card,—refused it peremptorily, with a glance.
Then it dawned upon me with a certain suddenness that I was
different from the others; or like, mayhap, in heart and life and
longing, but shut out from their world by a vast veil. I had thereafter no desire to tear down that veil, to creep through; I held all
beyond it in common contempt, and lived above it in a region of
blue sky and great wandering shadows. That sky was bluest when
I could beat my mates at examination-time, or beat them at a foot-

race, or even beat their stringy heads. Alas, with the years all this fine contempt began to fade; for the worlds I longed for, and all their dazzling opportunities, were theirs, not mine. But they should not keep these prizes, I said; some, all, I would wrest from them. Just how I would do it I could never decide: by reading law, by healing the sick, by telling the wonderful tales that swarm in my head,— some way. With other black boys the strife was not so fiercely sunny: their youth shrunk into tasteless sycophancy, or into silent hatred of the pale world about them and mocking distrust of everything white; or wasted itself in a bitter cry. Why did God make me an outcast and a stranger in mine own house? The shades of the prison-house closed round about us all: walls straight and stubborn to the whitest, but relentlessly narrow, tall, and unscalable to sons of night who must plod darkly on in resignation, or beat unavailing palms against the stone, or steadily, half hopelessly, watch the streak of blue above.

After the Egyptian and Indian, the Greek and Roman, the Teuton and Mongolian, the Negro is a sort of seventh son, born with a veil, and gifted with second-sight in this American world,—a world which yields him no true self-consciousness, but only lets him see himself through the revelation of the other world. It is a peculiar sensation, this double-consciousness, this sense of always looking at one's self through the eyes of others, of measuring one's soul by the tape of a world that looks on in amused contempt and pity. One ever feels his twoness,—an American, a Negro; two souls, two thoughts, two unreconciled strivings; two warring ideals in one dark body, whose dogged strength alone keeps it from being torn asunder.

The history of the American Negro is the history of this strife,— this longing to attain self-conscious manhood, to merge his double self into a better and truer self. In this merging he wishes neither of the older selves to be lost. He would not Africanize America, for America has too much to teach the world and Africa. He would not bleach his Negro soul in a flood of white Americanism, for he knows that Negro blood has a message for the world. He simply wishes to make it possible for a man to be both a Negro and an American, without being cursed and spit upon by his fellows, without having the doors of Opportunity closed roughly in his face.

This, then, is the end of his striving; to be a co-worker in the kingdom of culture, to escape both death and isolation, to husband and use his best powers and his latent genius. These powers of body and mind have in the past been strangely wasted, dispersed, or forgotten. The shadow of a mighty Negro past flits through the tale of Ethiopia the Shadowy and of Egypt the Sphinx. Throughout history, the powers of single black men flash here and there like falling stars, and die sometimes before the world has rightly gauged their brightness. Here in America, in the few days since Emancipation, the black man's turning hither and thither in hesitant and doubtful striving has often made his very strength to lose effectiveness, to seem like absence of power, like weakness. And yet it is not weakness,—it is the contradiction of double aims. The double-aimed struggle of the black artisan—on the one hand to escape white contempt for a nation of mere hewers of wood and drawers of water, and on the other hand to plough and nail and dig for a poverty-striken horde—could only result in making him a poor craftsman, for he had but half a heart in either cause. By the poverty and ignorance of his people, the Negro minister or doctor was tempted toward quackery and demagogy; and by the criticism of the other world, toward ideals that made him ashamed of his lowly tasks. The would-be black *savant* was confronted by the paradox that the knowledge his people needed was a twice-told tale to his white neighbors, while the knowledge which would teach the white world was Greek to his own flesh and blood. The innate love of harmony and beauty that set the ruder souls of his people a-dancing and a-singing raised but confusion and doubt in the soul of the black artist; for the beauty revealed to him was the soul-beauty of a race which his larger audience despised, and he could not articulate the message of another people. This waste of double aims, this seeking to satisfy two unreconciled ideals, has wrought sad havoc with the courage and faith and deeds of ten thousand thousand people,—has sent them often wooing false gods and invoking false means of salvation, and at times has even seemed about to make them ashamed of themselves.

8b. The Negro Dream

. . . The bright ideals of the past,—physical freedom, political power, the training of brains and the training of hands,—all these in turn have waxed and waned, until even the last grows dim and overcast. Are they all wrong,—all false? No, not that, but each alone was over-simple and incomplete,—the dreams of a credulous race-childhood, or the fond imaginings of the other world which does not know and does not want to know our power. To be really true, all these ideals must be melted and welded into one. The training of the schools we need to-day more than ever,—the training of deft hands, quick eyes and ears, and above all the broader, deeper, higher culture of gifted minds and pure hearts. The power of the ballot we need in sheer self-defence,—else what shall save us from a second slavery? Freedom, too, the long-sought, we still seek,—the freedom of life and limb, the freedom to work and think, the freedom to love and aspire. Work, culture, liberty,—all these we need, not singly but together, not successively but together, each growing and aiding each, and all striving toward that vaster ideal that swims before the Negro people, the ideal of human brother-hood, gained through the unifying ideal of Race; the ideal of fos-tering and developing the traits and talents of the Negro, not in opposition to or contempt for other races, but rather in large con-formity to the greater ideals of the American Republic, in order that some day on American soil two world-races may give each to each those characteristics both so sadly lack. We the darker ones come even now not altogether empty-handed: there are to-day no truer exponents of the pure human spirit of the Declaration of In-dependence than the American Negroes; there is no true American music but the wild sweet melodies of the Negro slave; the Ameri-can fairy tales and folk-lore are Indian and African; and, all in all, we black men seem the sole oasis of a simple faith and reverence in a dusty desert of dollars and smartness. Will America be poorer if she replace her brutal dyspeptic blundering with light-hearted but determined Negro humility? or her coarse and cruel wit with loving jovial good-humor? or her vulgar music with the soul of the Sorrow Songs?

Merely a concrete test of the underlying principles of the great republic is the Negro Problem, and the spiritual striving of the freedmen's sons is the travail of souls whose burden is almost be-yond the measure of their strength, but who can bear it in the name of an historic race, in the name of this the land of their fathers' fathers, and in the name of human opportunity.

Selections 9a–9e

AS SEEN BY A JOURNALIST

RAY STANNARD BAKER*

These selections from Following the Color Line *give us a sense of the problem as it affected a journalist in the years 1906–1908.*

9a. A White Man's Problem

It keeps coming to me that this is more a white man's problem than it is a Negro problem. The white man as well as the black is being tried by fire. The white man is in full control of the South, politically, socially, industrially; the Negro, as ex-Governor Northen points out, is his helpless ward. What will he do with him? Speaking of the education of the Negro, and in direct reference to the conditions in Atlanta which I have already described, many men have said to me:

"Think of the large sums that the South has spent and is spending on the education of the Negro. The Negro does not begin to pay for his education in taxes."

Neither do the swarming Slavs, Italians, and Poles in our Northern cities. They pay little in taxes and yet enormous sums are expended in their improvement. For their benefit? Of course, but chiefly for ours. It is better to educate men in school than to let them so educate themselves as to become a menace to society. The present *kind* of education in the South may possibly be wrong; but for the protection of society it is as necessary to train every Negro as it is every white man.

When I saw the crowds of young Negroes being made criminal —through lack of proper training—I could not help thinking how

* From Ray Stannard Baker, *Following the Color Line: American Negro Citizenship in the Progressive Era,* New York: Harper & Row, 1964, pp. 65, 146–47, 84–86, 8–9, 84. [Originally published in 1908 by Doubleday, Page & Co.]

pitilessly ignorance finally revenges itself upon that society which neglects or exploits it.

9b.   Wherein Lies Success for Negroes

I have thus endeavoured to present the conditions of the Negro in the North and show his relationship with white people. I have tried to exhibit every factor, good or bad, which plays a part in racial conditions. Many sinister influences exist: the large increase of ignorant and unskilled Negroes from the South; the growing prejudice in the North, both social and industrial, against the Negro; the high death-rate and low birth-rate among the Negro population, which is due to poverty, ignorance, crime, and an unfriendly climate. On the other hand, many encouraging and hopeful tendencies are perceptible. Individual Negroes are forcing recognition in nearly all branches of human activity, entering business life and the professions. A new racial consciousness is growing up leading to organisations for self-help; and while white prejudice is increasing, so is white helpfulness as manifested in social settlements, industrial schools, and other useful philanthropies.

All these forces and counter forces—economic, social, religious, political—are at work. We can all see them plainly, but we cannot judge of their respective strength. It is a tremendous struggle that is going on—the struggle of a backward race for survival within the swift-moving civilisation of an advanced race. No one can look upon it without the most profound fascination for its interests as a human spectacle, nor without the deepest sympathy for the efforts of 10,000,000 human beings to surmount the obstacles which beset them on every hand.

And what a struggle it is! As I look out upon it and see this dark horde of men and women coming up, coming up, a few white men here and there cheering them on, a few bitterly holding them back, I feel that Port Arthur and the battles of Manchuria, bloody as they were, are not to be compared with such a conflict as this, for this is the silent, dogged, sanguinary, modern struggle in which the combatants never rest upon their arms. But the object is much the same: the effort of a backward race for a foothold upon this earth, for civilised respect and an opportunity to expand. And the Negro is not fighting Russians, but Americans—Germans, Irish, English, Italians, Jews, Slavs—all those mingling white races (each, indeed, engaged in the same sort of a struggle) which make up the nation we call America.

The more I see of the conflict the more I seem to see that victory or defeat lies with the Negro himself. As a wise Negro put it to me:

"Forty years ago the white man emancipated us: but we are only just now discovering that we must emancipate ourselves."

Whether the Negro can survive the conflict, how it will all come out, no man knows. For this is the making of life itself.

9c.   Vivid Illustration of Race Feeling

I have had innumerable illustrations of the extremes to which race feeling reaches among a certain class of Southerners. In a letter to the Atlanta *Constitution*, November 5, 1906, a writer who signs himself Mark Johnson, says:

The only use we have for the Negro is as a labourer. It is only as such that we need him; it is only as such that we can use him. If the North wants to take him and educate him we will bid him godspeed and contribute to his education if schools are located on the other side of the line.

And here are extracts from a remarkable letter from a Southern white working man signing himself Forrest Pope and published in the Atlanta *Georgian*, October 22, 1906:

When the skilled Negro appears and begins to elbow the white man in the struggle for existence, don't you know the white man rebels and won't have it so? If you don't it won't take you long to find it out; just go out and ask a few of them, those who tell you the whole truth, and see what you will find out about it.

What Is The Negro's Place?

All the genuine Southern people like the Negro as a servant, and so long as he remains the hewer of wood and carrier of water, and remains strictly in what we choose to call his place, everything is all right, but when ambition, prompted by real education, causes the Negro to grow restless and bestir himself to get out of that servile condition, then there is, or at least there will be, trouble, sure enough trouble, that all the great editors, parsons, and philosophers can no more check than they can now state the whole truth and nothing but the truth, about this all-absorbing, far-reaching miserable race question. There are those among Southern editors and other public men who have been shouting into the ears of the North for twenty-five years that education would solve the Negro question; there is not an honest, fearless, thinking man in the South but who knows that to be a bare-faced lie. Take a young Negro of little more than ordinary intelligence, even, get hold of him in time, train him thoroughly as to books, and finish him up with a good industrial education, send him out into the South with ever so good intentions both on the part of his benefactor and himself, send him to take my work away from me and I will kill him.

The writer says in another part of this remarkable letter, giving as it does a glimpse of the bare bones of the economic struggle for existence:

I am, I believe, a typical Southern white workingman of the skilled variety, and I'll tell the whole world, including Drs. Abbott and Eliot, that I don't want any educated property-owning Negro around me. The Negro would be desirable to me for what I could get out of him in the way of labour that I don't want to have to perform myself, and I have no other uses for him.

Who Will Do the Dirty Work?

One illustration more and I am through. I met at Montgomery, Alabama, a lawyer named Gustav Frederick Mertins. We were discussing the "problem" and Mr. Mertins finally made a striking remark, not at all expressing the view that I heard from some of the strongest citizens of Montgomery, but excellently voicing the position of many Southerners.

"It's a question," he said, "who will do the dirty work. In this country the white man won't: the Negro must. There's got to be a mudsill somewhere. If you educate the Negroes they won't stay where they belong; and you must consider them as a race, because if you let a few rise it makes the others discontented."

Mr. Mertins presented me with a copy of his novel called "The Storm Signal," in which he further develops the idea (p. 342):

> The Negro is the mudsill of the social and industrial South to-day. Upon his labour in the field, in the forest, and in the mind, the whole structure rests. Slip the mudsill out and the system must be reorganized. . . . Educate him and he quits the field. Instruct him in the trades and sciences and he enters into active competition with the white man in what are called the higher planes of life. That competition brings on friction, and that friction in the end means the Negro's undoing.

Is not this mudsill stirring to-day, and is not that the deep reason for many of the troubles in the South—and in the North as well, where the Negro has appeared in large numbers? The friction of competition has arrived, and despite the demand for justice by many of the best class of the Southern whites, the struggle is certainly of growing intensity.

And out of this economic struggle of whites and blacks grows an ethical struggle far more significant. It is the struggle of the white man with himself. How shall he, who is supreme in the South as in the North, treat the Negro? That is the *real* struggle.

9d. Fear

The better-class Negroes have two sources of fear: one of the criminals of their own race—such attacks are rarely given much space in the newspapers—and the other the fear of the white people. My very first impression of what this fear of the Negroes might be came, curiously enough, not from Negroes but from a fine white woman on whom I called shortly after going South. She told this story:

"I had a really terrible experience one evening a few days ago. I was walking along —— Street when I saw a rather good-looking young Negro come out of a hallway to the sidewalk. He was in a great hurry, and, in turning suddenly, as a person sometimes will do, he accidentally brushed my shoulder with his arm. He had not seen me before. When he turned and found it was a white woman he had touched, such a look of abject terror and fear came into his face as I hope never again to see on a human countenance. He knew what it meant if I was frightened, called for help, and accused him of insulting or attacking me. He stood still a moment, then turned and ran down the street, dodging into the first alley he came to. It shows, doesn't it, how little it might take to bring punishment upon an innocent man!"

The next view I got was through the eyes of one of the able Negroes of the South, Bishop Gaines of the African Methodist Episcopal Church. He is now an old man, but of imposing presence. Of wide attainments, he has travelled in Europe, he owns much property, and rents houses to white tenants. He told me of services he had held some time before in south Georgia. Approaching the church one day through the trees, he suddenly encountered a white woman carrying water from a spring. She dropped her pail instantly, screamed, and ran up the path toward her house.

"If I had been some Negroes," said Bishop Gaines, "I should have turned and fled in terror; the alarm would have been given, and it is not unlikely that I should have had a posse of white men with bloodhounds on my trail. If I had been caught what would my life have been worth? The woman would have identified me—and what could I have said? But I did not run. I stepped out in the path, held up one hand and said:

"'Don't worry, madam, I am Bishop Gaines, and I am holding services here in this church.' So she stopped running and I apologised for having startled her."

The Negro knows he has little chance to explain, if by accident or ignorance he insults a white woman or offends a white man. An educated Negro, one of the ablest of his race, telling me of how a friend of his who by merest chance had provoked a number of half-drunken white men, had been set upon and frightfully beaten, remarked: "It might have been me!"

Now, I am telling these things just as they look to the Negro;

it is quite as important, as a problem in human nature, to know how the Negro feels and what he says, as it is to know how the white man feels.

9e. Why Negroes Are Driven Out

Generally speaking, the race hatred in the South comes chiefly from the poorer class of whites who either own land which they work themselves or are tenant farmers in competition with Negroes and from politicians who seek to win the votes of this class of white men. The larger landowners and employers of labour, while they do not love the Negro, want him to work and work steadily, and will do almost anything to keep him on the land—so long as he is a faithful, obedient, unambitious worker. When he becomes prosperous, or educated, or owns land, many white people no longer "have any use for him" and turn upon him with hostility, but the best type of the Southern white men is not only glad to see the Negro become a prosperous and independent farmer but will do much to help him.

Selections 10a–10d

AS SEEN BY A SOCIAL ECONOMIST

GUNNAR MYRDAL*

Gunnar Myrdal, the Swedish sociologist, summarizes his views on the Negro problem as seen in 1944.

10a. The American Dilemma

The American Negro problem is a problem in the heart of the American. It is there that the interracial tension has its focus. It is

* From Gunnar Myrdal, *An American Dilemma: The Negro Problem and Modern Democracy*, New York: Harper & Brothers, 1944, pp. xlvii, lii, 1, 226–27.

there that the decisive struggle goes on. This is the central viewpoint of this treatise. Though our study includes economic, social, and political race relations, at bottom our problem is the moral dilemma of the American—the conflict between his moral valuations on various levels of consciousness and generality. The "American Dilemma," referred to in the title of this book, is the ever-raging conflict between, on the one hand, the valuations preserved on the general plane which we shall call the "American Creed," where the American thinks, talks, and acts under the influence of high national and Christian precepts, and, on the other hand, the valuations on specific planes of individual and group living, where personal and local interests; economic, social, and sexual jealousies; considerations of community prestige and conformity; group prejudice against particular persons or types of people; and all sorts of miscellaneous wants, impulses, and habits dominate his outlook.

10b.   The Negro Problem as a White Problem

The Negro was brought to America for the sake of the white man's profit. He was kept in slavery for generations in the same interest. A civil war was fought between two regional groups of white Americans. For two years no one wanted Negroes involved in the fighting. Later on some two hundred thousand Negro soldiers fought in the Northern army, in addition to all the Negro laborers, servants, spies, and helpers in both armies. But it was not the Negroes' war. As a result of the war, which took a toll of some half million killed and many more wounded, the four million Negro slaves were liberated. Since then the Negro's "place" in American society has been precarious, uncertain and changing; he was no longer so necessary and profitable to the white man as in slavery before the Civil War. In the main, however, the conflicting and vacillating valuations of the white majority have been decisive, whether the issue was segregation in the schools, discrimination with reference to public facilities, equal justice and protection under the laws, enjoyment of the franchise, or the freedom to enter a vocation and earn an honest living. The Negro, as a minority, and a poor and suppressed minority at that, in the final analysis, has had little other strategy open to him than to play on the conflicting values held in the white majority group. In so doing, he has been able to identify his cause with broader issues in American politics and social life and with moral principles held dear by the white Americans. This is the situation even today and will remain so in the foreseeable future. In that sense, "this is a white man's country."

10c. The Moral Problem

When we thus choose to view the Negro problem as primarily
a moral issue, we are in line with popular thinking. It is as a moral
issue that this problem presents itself in the daily life of ordinary
people; it is as a moral issue that they brood over it in their thoughtful moments. It is in terms of conflicting moral valuations that it
is discussed in church and school, in the family circle, in the work-
shop, on the street corner, as well as in the press, over the radio, in
trade union meetings, in the state legislatures, the Congress and the
Supreme Court. The social scientist, in his effort to lay bare con-
cealed truths and to become maximally useful in guiding practical
and political action, is prudent when, in the approach to a problem,
he sticks as closely as possible to the common man's ideas and
formulations, even though he knows that further investigation will
carry him into tracts uncharted in the popular consciousness. There
is a pragmatic common sense in people's ideas about themselves
and their worries, which we cannot afford to miss when we start
out to explore social reality. Otherwise we are often too easily dis-
tracted by our learned arbitrariness and our pet theories, concepts,
and hypotheses, not to mention our barbarous terminology, which
we generally are tempted to mistake for something more than mere
words. Throughout this study we will constantly take our starting
point in the ordinary man's own ideas, doctrines, theories and
mental constructs.

10d. Personal Story

The white South was, as has been said, for the most part violently
against any constructive program framed to raise the Negro freedmen to economic independence. A liberal Southerner of the older
generation with great political experience, Josephus Daniels, tells
this story:

> When I was eighteen I recall asking an old Confederate, "What was so bad
> about the promise to give every Negro head of a family forty acres and a
> mule? Wouldn't that have been better help than to turn the igonrant ex-slave
> without a dollar over to the mercy of Republican politicians, white and
> black, who made political slaves of them? And if each Negro had been given
> a piece of land, for which Uncle Sam would pay the Southern owner,
> wouldn't it have been better for the white man and the Negro?"
> The old man looked at me as if I were a curious individual to be raising
> such an unheard-of question. "No," he said emphatically, "for it would have
> made the Negro 'uppity,' and, besides, they don't know enough to farm
> without direction, and smart white men and Negroes would have gotten the

land away from them, and they'd have been worse off than ever . . . The real reason," pursued the old man, "why it wouldn't do, is that we are having a hard time now keeping the nigger in his place, and if he were a land-owner he'd think he was a bigger man than old Grant, and there would be no living with him in the Black District . . . Who'd work the land if the niggers had farms of their own . . . ?"

Selections 11a–11b

AS SEEN BY A CONTEMPORARY NEGRO WRITER

JAMES BALDWIN*

These two selections are from The Fire Next Time, *by a well known contemporary Negro writer, James Baldwin.*

11a. Fears of Negroes

. . . Negroes in this country—and Negroes do not, strictly or legally speaking, exist in any other—are taught really to despise themselves from the moment their eyes open on the world. This world is white and they are black. White people hold the power, which means that they are superior to blacks (intrinsically, that is: God decreed it so), and the world has innumerable ways of making this difference known and felt and feared. Long before the Negro child perceives this difference, and even longer before he under-stands it, he has begun to react to it, he has begun to be controlled by it. Every effort made by the child's elders to prepare him for a fate from which they cannot protect him causes him secretly, in terror, to begin to await, without knowing that he is doing so, his mysterious and inexorable punishment. He must be "good" not

* From James Baldwin, *The Fire Next Time,* New York: Dell, 1964, pp. 39–42, 93–96.

only in order to please his parents and not only to avoid being
punished by them; behind their authority stands another, nameless
and impersonal, infinitely harder to please, and bottomlessly cruel.
And this filters into the child's consciousness through his parents'
tone of voice as he is being exhorted, punished, or loved; in the
sudden, uncontrollable note of fear heard in his mother's or his
father's voice when he has strayed beyond some particular boundary. He does not know what the boundary is, and he can get no
explanation of it, which is frightening enough, but the fear he hears
in the voices of his elders is more frightening still. The fear that
I heard in my father's voice, for example, when he realized that I
really *believed* I could do anything a white boy could do, and had
every intention of proving it, was not at all like the fear I heard
when one of us was ill or had fallen down the stairs or strayed too
far from the house. It was another fear, a fear that the child, in
challenging the white world's assumptions, was putting himself in
the path of destruction. A child cannot, thank heaven, know how
vast and how merciless is the nature of power, with what unbelievable cruelty people treat each other. He reacts to the fear in
his parents' voices because his parents hold up the world for him
and he has no protection without them. I defended myself, as I
imagined, against the fear my father made me feel by remembering
that he was very old-fashioned. Also, I prided myself on the fact
that I already knew how to outwit him. To defend oneself against
a fear is simply to insure that one will, one day, be conquered by
it; fears must be faced.

11b.   How it Feels to be a Negro

. . . That sinners have always, for American Negroes, been white
is a truth we needn't labor, and every American Negro, therefore,
risks having the gates of paranoia close on him. In a society that is
entirely hostile, and, by its nature, seems determined to cut you
down—that has cut down so many in the past and cuts down so
many every day—it begins to be almost impossible to distinguish a
real from a fancied injury. One can very quickly cease to attempt this
distinction, and, what is worse, one usually ceases to attempt it
without realizing that one has done so. All doormen, for example,
and all policemen have by now, for me, become exactly the same,
and my style with them is designed simply to intimidate them before they can intimidate me. No doubt I am guilty of some injustice here, but it is irreducible, since I cannot risk assuming that
the humanity of these people is more real to them than their uniforms. Most Negroes cannot risk assuming that the humanity of

white people is more real to them than their color. And this leads, imperceptibly but inevitably, to a state of mind in which, having long ago learned to expect the worst, one finds it very easy to believe the worst. The brutality with which Negroes are treated in this country simply cannot be overstated, however unwilling white men may be to hear it. In the beginning—and neither can this be over-stated—a Negro just cannot *believe* that white people are treating him as they do; he does not know what he has done to merit it. And when he realizes that the treatment accorded him has nothing to do with anything he has done, that the attempt of white people to destroy him—for that is what it is—is utterly gratuitous, it is not hard for him to think of white people as devils. For the horrors of the American Negro's life there has been almost no language. The privacy of his experience, which is only beginning to be recognized in language, and which is denied or ignored in official and popular speech—hence the Negro idiom—lends credibility to any system that pretends to clarify it. And, in fact, the truth about the black man, as a historical entity and as a human being, *has* been hidden from him, deliberately and cruelly; the power of the white world is threatened whenever a black man refuses to accept the white world's definitions. So every attempt is made to cut that black man down—not only was made yesterday but is made today. Who, then, is to say with authority where the root of so much anguish and evil lies? Why, then, is it not possible that all things began with the black man and that he was perfect—especially since this is precisely the claim that white people have put forward for themselves all these years? Furthermore, it is now absolutely clear that white people are a minority in the world—so severe a minority that they now look rather more like an invention—and that they cannot possibly hope to rule it any longer. If this is so, why is it not also possible that they achieved their original dominance by stealth and cunning and bloodshed and in opposition to the will of Heaven, and not, as they claim, by Heaven's will? And if *this* is so, then the sword they have used so long against others can now, without mercy, be used against them.

Selection 12

AS SEEN BY WHITE PARTISANS*

The Ideology of White Supremacy

THE SOUTHERN SEGREGATIONIST CREDO. An integral component of the southern racial order is a body of ideas supporting and justifying the system. These can be summarized as follows:

I. *Segregation is part of a natural order and is instinctive in human nature.*

Segregation is a natural order—created by God, in His wisdom, who made black men black and white men white. Each man should be proud of his race and should constantly strive to preserve its purity.

Louisiana State Senator W. M. Rainach,
a segregationist leader

A. *Segregation is not a moral question.*

It is useless for me to argue whether the racial instinct [for segregation] is right or wrong—it exists.

Former Governor James F. Byrnes
of South Carolina

B. *Segregation is natural and best.*

. . . separateness of races is natural and best . . . members of each race prefer to associate with other members of their race and . . . they will do so naturally unless they are prodded and inflamed and controlled by outside pressures.

Report of the North Carolina
Advisory Committee on Education
(Pearsall Committee)

C. *We are not bigots.*

. . . racial segregation is not the off-spring of racial bigotry or racial prejudice. It results from the exercise of a funda-

---

* From James W. Vander Zanden, *American Minority Relations: The Sociology of Race and Ethnic Groups*, New York: The Ronald Press Co., 1963, pp. 131–35.

mental American freedom—the freedom to select one's associates. . . . This freedom is bottomed on a basic law of nature—the law that like seeks like . . . man finds his greatest happiness when he is among people of similar cultural, historical and social backgrounds.

U. S. Senator Sam J. Ervin
(D–N. C.)

II. *The Negro is a different kind of human being.*

A. There is a divergence of opinion among southern whites as to whether the Negro is necessarily biologically inferior to whites.

1. *The Negro is inferior to whites.*

History is not so much the record of the events of nations as a whole as it is the chronicle of the contributed civilizations of the superior races. . . . The Negro race, though one of the oldest, has never built a worthy civilization.

President D. M. Nelson,
of Mississippi College, Clinton, Miss.

2. *It is not necessarily a question of Negro inferiority or white superiority.*

I don't want to argue it [that Negroes are inherently inferior] with anybody, but I don't go along with that. It doesn't sound quite Christian to me. They're human beings, just like everybody else.

Mayor Kenneth Cass
of Greenville, S. C.

B. *But Negroes are different from whites.*

The traditions of the races are greatly different. The environment and background of the races are greatly different. Actually there are great social and emotional differences that quickly come to the surface when aroused. Their mental processes are different. . . .

U. S. Senator John C. Stennis
(D–Miss.)

C. *Negroes are more prone to violence and crime.*

Inquire of the wardens of State penitentiaries of Illinois, Michigan, Pennsylvania, Ohio, New Jersey, New York and California, or wherever the Negro has congregated, for what crimes he is incarcerated. You will find that murder, rape, sex crimes and aggravated assault are predominant ones.

Tom P. Brady,
Mississippi segregationist leader

D. *The moral standards of Negroes are lower than those of whites.*

One out of every 105 white births [in Mississippi] were illegitimate or less than 1%. 24.7% of the Negro births were illegitimate, which means that 247 out of every 1000 Negro births were born out of wedlock. . . . This is proof of the well-known fact that our Negroes as a race make a mockery of the white man's holy institution of matrimony.

Mississippi Citizens' Council leaflet

E. *The Negro has a lower capacity to learn.*

Now, the Negroes are—I think as a general proposition—generally more retarded in school than the white children. And I think this is rather important—it's probably one of the things you can't say in your paper—but a Negro of 14 may be in the fourth grade with a white girl of 10 or 11, and this Negro is a fully developed man, sexually. I think that is one of the things, I mean, there's a little fear in there.

C. P. Liter, editor of the
Baton Rouge (La.) Advocate & State Times

F. *The Negro is irresponsible.*

The Negro is irresponsible in every degree. I think it is a basic trait, although other conditions—environment, economics and education—contribute to his so-called lethargy.

A Charleston, S. C.,
utility executive

III. *Racial amalgamation or intermarriage is bad and dangerous.*

A. *Racial intermarriage will result in racial suicide.*

We publish to the world that we protest the attempts being made to desegregate the races, because we believe such would inevitably lead into a hybrid monstrosity that would defy the word and will of God.

Resolution of the Missionary
Baptist Association of Texas

B. *The Negro male has designs on white women.*

The average Negro who wants integration is not interested in equal educational and economic advantages with the white race, and when these things are dangled before him by the NAACP he is unmoved, but when they whisper in his ear that someday he will be able to live with a white woman he is very interested.

Rev. Leon C. Burns,
Pastor of the West Seventh Street Church
of Christ, Columbia, Tenn.

IV. *Our race relations are harmonious.*

 . . . our colored citizens are happy and they are proud of Jackson [Mississippi]. . . . There is no racial tension here. We are all living in harmony together.

> Mayor Allen Thompson,
> of Jackson, Miss.

A. *Look how much we are doing for our colored people!*

In the past 90 years—1865-1955—the Negro race has made the most amazing progress which has ever been made in the history of man in any comparative period of time.

That progress has been helped, in fact has been made possible, by the cooperation and assistance of the white race.

> Report of the North Carolina Advisory Committee on Education (Pearsall Committee)

B. *We don't hate Negroes—we're their friends.*

 . . . I'm not anti-black or anti-nigger. I work niggers. I still have five who have worked for me 32 years. But they're still niggers.

> David Hawkins, leader in the Mississippi Citizens' Councils

We love our colored folk, just love 'em. Why, we have a maid, worked for us 18 years, and when she went to the hospital last year I paid all bills—glad to do it.

> A white Mississippian

C. *The Negroes are contented.*

I have yet to meet one [Negro] who told me they wanted their children to go to school with white children.

> U. S. Congressman Charles E. Bennett (D–Fla.)

D. *Trouble is caused by outsiders.*

If there are racial tensions in Mississippi, it is an indisputable fact that the responsibility rests squarely on the political and pressure agitators from outside the South rather than upon the shoulders of our people.

> Governor Hugh White, of Miss.

E. *Northerners are hypocrites on the race issue.*

Schools in the North have to be pretty black before they'll hire a Negro teacher. There's a lot of hypocrisy about that. I resent too much admonition from the North.

> Superintendent of Wayne County Schools, Ky.

F. *The South is being persecuted by the rest of the nation.*

Propagandists and politicians have blown up stories about segregation until the rest of the country believes it is a dirty word. The Southern white man has been ridiculed and pilloried before the nation, and indeed throughout the world, until he is one of the underprivileged minorities of the earth.

> Thomas R. Waring, editor of
> the Charleston (S. C.) *News & Courier*

Selection 13

AS SEEN BY A WHITE JOURNALIST

CHARLES E. SILBERMAN*

The following selection is taken from Crisis in Black and White, *by Charles E. Silberman. While working on an assignment for* Fortune *magazine, Silberman began to probe the nature of the Negro problem and the deeper he probed, the more concerned he became about the nature of the* white *problem.*

What we are discovering . . . is that the United States—all of it, North as well as South, West as well as East—is a racist society in a sense and to a degree that we have refused so far to admit, much less face. Twenty years ago, Gunnar Myrdal concluded that "the American Negro problem is a problem in the heart of the American," and titled his monumental study of the Negro *An American Dilemma*. Myrdal was wrong. The tragedy of race relations in the United States is that there is no American Dilemma. White Americans are not torn and tortured by the conflict between their devotion to the American creed and their actual behavior. They are upset by the current state of race relations, to be sure. But what troubles them

* From Charles E. Silberman, *Crisis in Black and White*, New York: Random House, 1964, pp. 9–16.

is not that justice is being denied but that their peace is being shattered and their business interrupted.

It will take more than an appeal to the American conscience, therefore, to solve "the Negro problem," though such an appeal is long overdue. Nothing less than a radical reconstruction of American society is required if the Negro is to be able to take his rightful place in American life. And the reconstruction must begin not just in Oxford, Mississippi, or Birmingham, Alabama, but in New York, Philadelphia, Chicago, and other great cities of the North as well. For when Negroes leave the South, they don't move to New York —they move to Harlem; they don't move to Chicago—they move to the South Side. Without question, Harlem is a great improvement over Birmingham—but not nearly so great as white men assume. Northern discrimination is less brutal and less personal than the Southern variety, and it lacks the overt sanction of law. It hurts none the less. "What makes you think you are going to Heaven?" Langston Hughes asks his folk hero, Jesse B. Simple. "Because I have already been in Harlem," Simple replies.

The North must change for its own sake, therefore. It must change for the nation's sake as well, for the South will never change —and cannot be expected to change—until the North leads the way. At the moment, the North *is* leading, but in the wrong direction. It has shown the South that Negroes can be kept "in their place" without written laws. Southern cities are rapidly learning the de facto technique of the North. In the spring of 1963, for example, Albany, Georgia, removed all segregation ordinances from its city code in order to balk the Negro legal attack; the city remained as Jim Crow as ever.

It isn't enough for the white North or the white South to change, however; the black North and the black South must change as well. For "the Negro problem" is not just a white man's problem, as Myrdal thought; it is a black man's problem as well, because of what white prejudice and discrimination have done to the Negro's personality and self-esteem. In a recent *New Yorker* cartoon, one overstuffed tycoon grumbled to another, "Trouble is you start treating people like equals, they begin to believe it." The converse is also true: treat people as inferiors and they begin to believe *that,* too. White men began three and a half centuries ago to treat black men as inferiors, and they haven't stopped yet. A major part of "the Negro problem" in America lies in what these three hundred fifty years have done to the Negro's personality: the self-hatred, the sense of impotence and inferiority that destroys aspiration and keeps the Negro locked in a prison we have all made. Negroes are taught to despise themselves almost from the first moments of consciousness;

even without any direct experience with discrimination, they learn in earliest childhood of the stigma attached to color in the United States: "If you're white, you're right," a Negro folk saying goes: "if you're brown, stick around; if you're black, stay back." And they do stay back.

If whites were to stop all discriminatory practices tomorrow, this alone would not solve "the Negro problem." To be sure, an end to discrimination is a prerequisite to any solution. But too many Negroes are unable or unwilling to compete; segregation is an affliction, but for many it is a crutch as well.

The Negro will be unable to take his place in the main stream of American life until he stops despising himself and his fellows. The Negro will be unable to compete on equal terms until he has been able to purge from his mind all sense of white superiority and black inferiority—until he really believes, with all his being, that he is a free man, and acts accordingly. In this sense, therefore, only the Negro can solve the Negro problem. For freedom and equality, like power, cannot be given or handed down as a gift. They must be taken by people unwilling to settle for anything less.

This does not mean, however, that white Americans can simply toss the ball back to their Negro compatriots, as John Fischer of *Harper's* suggested a while ago. White Americans cannot duck their responsibility by placing the burden of change on Negroes themselves. On the contrary, the doctrine Fischer propounded represented but a slightly more sophisticated version of the old racist doctrine that Negroes "aren't ready" for equality. Writing from his chair as Editor-in-Chief of *Harper's,* Fischer called upon Negroes to redirect their energies from the field of civil rights to that of self-improvement. Since anti-Negro prejudice "is not altogether baseless," in Fischer's view, it cannot be eliminated by lecturing whites or by enacting new legislation. On the contrary, prejudice will disappear "only when a considerable majority of whites are convinced that they have nothing to fear from close, daily association with Negroes in jobs, schools, and neighborhoods." For that to happen, Fischer argued, Negro leaders will somehow have to arrange things so that "the average Negro is willing and able to carry the full responsibilities of good citizenship." But once this happy stage is reached, Fischer assured the Negroes of the United States, they will be "surprised to see how fast white prejudice begins to melt away."

Maybe; but there is little in the history of human bigotry—nothing, certainly, in the long history of anti-Semitism—to suggest that Fischer is right. Jews are as well-behaved as any other group; yet the calculated murder of six million Jews occurred not quite twenty years ago in the country in which Jews were proudest of their assimilation. And in our own country, Dr. Ralph Bunche, with whom Fischer presumably would not be afraid to associate, can be and has been denied hotel accommodations because of his race. What Fischer fails to see is that his own sense of superiority, his arrogant assumption that "the average Negro" has not yet earned the right to full citizenship, is responsible for the behavior he deplores! . . .

To be sure, the behavior of a good many Negroes does help perpetuate white prejudice; too many Negroes make it too easy for too many whites to rationalize their discrimination with a "they're all alike" attitude. Thus, white prejudice evokes Negro lawlessness, irresponsibility, and dependency—and these traits in turn nurture white prejudice. This is the real "American dilemma," and Tocqueville pointed it out two decades before the Civil War. "To induce whites to abandon the opinion they have conceived of the moral and intellectual inferiority of their former slaves," he wrote, "the Negroes must change; but as long as this opinion persists, they cannot change."

And so we are all, black and white together, trapped in a vicious circle from which no one seems able to escape. But we must escape, and it is up to the whites to lead the way; the guilt and the responsibility are theirs. To insist that Negroes must change before whites abandon their discriminatory practices is to deny the very essence of the Judaeo-Christian tradition: its insistence on the infinite worth of every human being. "Inasmuch as ye have done it unto one of the least of these my brethren," Jesus declared, "ye have done it unto me." "Whoever destroys a single soul," the Talmud warns, "should be considered the same as one who has destroyed a whole world."

"Divine Providence," declared Pope John XXIII in opening the Ecumenical Council, "is leading us to a new order of human relations." That new order must be based on justice—and we must understand that justice is neither an abstraction, nor a sentiment, nor a relationship, but an *act*. When the Prophets of old spoke of justice, their injunction was not to *be* just but to *do* justice; it is the act that counts. There has been far too much talk, for far too long, about the need to change men's hearts, about the difficulty of legislating morality. The truth of the matter is that men's hearts follow their actions at least as often as their actions follow their hearts. An old Hasidic legend tells of a man who asks his rabbi what he should do, since he does not believe in God. "Act each day as though you believe in God," the rabbi tells him—recite all the prayers and perform all the rituals required of the believer—"and before long you will find that you *do* believe." White Americans would do well to follow the same advice. We cannot wait for time or education to erase the prejudice that is ingrained so deeply in our hearts and minds; we must act as though we really do believe in the brotherhood of man, as though we really do love our black neighbors as ourselves. The belief and the love will follow.

There is no other choice. Out of the smoke and fire on Mount Sinai came a warning which white Americans have ignored for too long: ". . . I the Lord thy God am an impassioned God, visiting the guilt of the father upon the children, upon the third and fourth generations of those who reject Me, but showing kindness to the thousandth generation of those who love Me and keep My commandments." That warning represents not a spirit of vindictiveness but a basic law of human society: that while justice may be postponed, it cannot be denied. The longer justice is postponed, the greater the penalty, the more painful the inevitable confrontation. "I tremble for my country," Thomas Jefferson wrote, "when I reflect that God is just."

And that painful, inevitable confrontation is here and now. Ours is the fourth generation since the Civil War, and the sins of the last three generations (not to mention our own), are being visited upon us. We are just beginning to see how discrimination and indifference to discrimination have corrupted the souls of white men; in the general revulsion at pictures of white policemen unleashing dogs to keep Negroes from registering to vote, of vigilantes beating lunch-counter sit-ins while a crowd of white spectators grin and cheer, we are discovering the truth of Booker T. Washington's famous remark that the white man could not hold the Negro in the gutter without getting in there himself. White Americans are also discovering, to their surprise and horror, how deep is the store of anger and hatred three and a half centuries of humiliation have built up in the American Negro, and how quickly that anger can explode into violence. The real danger, however, is not violence but something deeper and far more corrosive: a sense of permanent alienation from American society. Unless the Negro position improves very quickly, Negroes of whatever class may come to regard their separation from American life as permanent, and so consider themselves outside the constraints and allegiances of American society. The Negro district of every large city could come to constitute an American Casbah, with its own values and controls and an implacable hatred of everything white that would poison American life.

It is not too much to say, therefore, that the plight of the Negro must become America's central concern, for he is the key to our mutual future. For one thing, the treatment of the Negro in America can affect this country's position in the world. What makes Red China loom so large a threat, for example—to the Russians as well as to us—is less its uncompromising totalitarianism than its evident desire to unite all the colored peoples of the world in holy war against the white race. It is in this context—not vague conversation about the importance of world public opinion—that what Africans and Asians think about the United States does matter. And what they think is clearly affected by Negro-white relations.

But the United States must solve "the Negro problem" out of more than political self-interest; it must accept the Negro as an equal and participating member of society because it is the only right thing, the only decent thing, to do. In the long run, the greatest threat to the United States is not political or military, but moral: the dehumanization of society that our awesome technology threatens, and that has been the central concern of theologians like Barth, Niebuhr, Buber, and Heschel, as well as of novelists and social critics.

The process is already too far advanced; man cannot deny the humanity of his fellow man without ultimately destroying his own. If we cannot learn now to reorder the relations between black and white—if we cannot allow the Negro to recover his lost identity by acknowledging his membership in America—we will never be able to handle the new problems of the age in which we find ourselves. In Camus' haunting phrase, "we are all condemned to live together." We must learn to live together in peace and in justice.

Selections 14a–14b

AS SEEN BY THE POLLS

The selection which follows is Gunnar Myrdal's summary in 1944 of what the white thinks the Negro wants in American society, as compared to the Negro's real demands.

The next selection is from a poll conducted by Newsweek magazine in 1966 to determine the nature and depth of the racial crisis in this country. This poll was based on the questioning of a representative sample of 1,059 Negroes and 1,088 whites. In addition, a selected list of 100 Negro leaders was interviewed to determine their attitudes. The results of the survey, from which this selection is taken, appeared in Newsweek *magazine.*

14a. The White Man's Rank Order of Discriminations (1944)

GUNNAR MYRDAL*

Rank 1. Highest in this order stands the bar against intermarriage. . . .

Rank 2. Next come the several etiquettes and discriminations, which specifically concern behavior in personal relations. (These are the barriers against dancing, bathing, eating, drinking together, and social intercourse generally; peculiar rules as to handshaking, hat lifting, use of titles, house entrance to be used, social forms when meeting on streets and in work, and so forth.) These patterns are sometimes referred to as the denial of "social equality" in the narrow meaning of the term.

Rank 3. Thereafter follow the segregations and discriminations in use of public facilities such as schools, churches and means of conveyance.

Rank 4. Next comes political disfranchisement.

Rank 5. Thereafter come discriminations in law courts, by the police, and by other public servants.

Rank 6. Finally comes the discriminations in securing land, credit, jobs, or other means of earning a living, and discriminations in public relief and other social welfare activities.

Next in importance to the fact of the white man's rank order of discriminations is the fact that *the Negro's own rank order is just about parallel, but inverse, to that of the white man.* The Negro resists least the discrimination on the ranks placed highest in the white man's evaluation and resents most any discrimination on the lowest level. This is in accord with the Negro's immediate interests. Negroes are in desperate need of jobs and bread, even more so than of justice in the courts, and of the vote. These latter needs are, in their turn, more urgent even than better schools and playgrounds, or, rather, they are primary means of reaching equality in the use of community facilities. Such facilities are, in turn, more important than civil courtesies. The marriage matter, finally, is of rather distant and doubtful interest.

* From Gunnar Myrdal, *An American Dilemma: The Negro Problem and Modern Democracy,* New York: Harper & Brothers, 1944, pp. 60, 61.

14b. *Newsweek* Poll of United States Racial Attitudes Today*

Where Whites and Negroes Disagree Most			
	NEGROES	WHITES	
Want integrated housing	68%	42%	Oppose
Think demonstrations helpful	73%	63%	Think harmful
Think riots helpful	34%	75%	Think harmful
Think police unfair	33%	58%	Think fair

* From *Newsweek*, August 22, 1966, p. 57.

Selection 15

AS SEEN IN SOME AMERICAN HISTORY TEXTBOOKS*

*A panel of six American historians, members of the History Depart-
ment at the University of California at Berkeley, was asked to review, from the standpoint of their treatment of the Negro, those
American history textbooks used most widely in California. The
following selection summarizes their findings.*

A panel of six American historians, members of the History Department of the University of California, Berkeley, have been asked to
review the American history textbooks that are most widely used in
California from the standpoint of their treatment of Negroes. . . .

* From *The Negro in American History textbooks: A Report of a Study of the
Treatment of Negroes in American History Textbooks Used in Grades Five and
Eight and in the High Schools of California's Public Schools,* Sacramento: Cali-
fornia State Department of Education, June 1964, pp. 1–6.

We are concerned first of all *as historians* that the history taught in our schools should accurately reflect the best findings of current scholarship. Professional scholars are aware that historical "truth" is an elusive quality. Well into the twentieth century professional scholars themselves were affected by the emotional aftermath of the Civil War, and there was a "Northern" and a "Southern" interpretation of such sensitive matters as slavery and Reconstruction. In the late nineteenth-century mood of national reconciliation, based on a widespread assumption of racial superiority among whites in both North and South, the "Southern" view tended to prevail; and the deference of textbook publishers to the special sensitivities of the Southern market has caused it to continue by and large to prevail in textbooks until this day. Meanwhile several generations of scholars, freer of sectional emotions and racist assumptions, through their researchers and writings developed a substantially different understanding of many of these matters. Most of the textbooks we have examined reflect views on racial and sectional themes that have been rejected or drastically modified by the best of current historical scholarship.

We are additionally concerned *as citizens* because these historical distortions help perpetuate and intensify the pattern of racial discrimination which is one of our society's most serious problems. We are concerned not only because much of the material in these books is bad history, but additionally because it is a kind of bad history that reinforces notions among whites of their superiority and among Negroes of their inferiority.

Admittedly there is a danger in assessing historical writing in terms of its social consequences. A laudable desire to combat racism, and especially to bolster self-respect among Negro students, might result in exaggerating Negro contributions and the heroic qualities of Negro figures. In our view this would be an equal distortion of historical truth, and in the long run would fail to have the desired social effects.

We do feel, however, that the seriousness of the problem of racism underscores the textbook author's responsibility to portray the Negro's role in American life fully, accurately, and without either sentimentality or condescension. There should be a conscious effort to portray outstanding Negro figures selected by the same criterion of historical significance applied to non-Negro figures. Even those textbooks that now make some effort in this direction tend to single out men like Booker T. Washington and the minor scientist George Washington Carver, whose attitudes about race relations are least disturbing to conservative whites. Equally or more worthy of inclusion by the standard of historical relevance are men like Denmark Vesey, Nat Turner, Frederick Douglass, W. E. B. Du Bois, and the Reverend Martin Luther King.

Always and everywhere our children should be told the truth, and the whole truth, as near as the best current scholarship can bring us to this elusive quality. This means, among other things, not obscuring the harsher aspects of the truth—the fact that Negroes entered American society as slaves, the brutalities of slavery, the racism of the Reconstruction and post-Reconstruction era, and the continuing depth and harshness of the problem of segregation and discrimination.

In the light of these general principles, the greatest defect in the textbooks we have examined is the virtual omission of the Negro. As several of the individual reports point out, the Negro does not "exist" in the books. The authors of the books must know that there are Negroes in America, and have been since 1619, but they evidently do not care to mention them too frequently. In one book there is no account of slavery in the colonial period; in a second, there is not a single word about Negroes after the Civil War; in a third (composed of documents and substantive chapters), the narrative does not mention Negroes in any connection.

As Ralph Ellison's novel, *Invisible Man,* demonstrates, whites frequently do not "see" Negroes. But Negroes are Americans; their history is part of American history. They need to be "seen" in textbooks. The space given Negro history will, of course, depend in part on the nature of the textbook, and minimum standards of coverage are proposed later in this report. What is especially important is that the discussions of Negroes appear as an integral part of the book. Perfunctory or casual treatment may imply that Negroes are not part of America.

Important aspects of Negro experience, of course, depart from that of many other groups in America. Negroes were not just another immigrant group; no other group could be so readily identified by its color, no other group was so systematically enslaved, and no other group has been subjected to as persistent and virulent discrimination. From the seventeenth century to our own day, Negro life has been filled with violence.

These facts highlight another failing of these textbooks that is almost as distressing as the invisibility of Negroes in them. All the texts play down or ignore the long history of violence between Negroes and whites, suggesting in different ways that racial contacts have been distinguished by a progressive harmony. The tone of a textbook is almost as important as anything it has to say. In their blandness and amoral optimism, these books implicitly deny the obvious deprivations suffered by Negroes. In several places they go further, implying approval for the repression of Negroes or patronizing them as being unqualified for life in a free society.

We should now like to suggest in some detail the substantive and interpretive elements relating to Negroes that should be included in textbooks covering the whole period of American history. These suggestions do not reflect any effort to give a special emphasis for the purpose of present-day social effects, but only what is necessary for portraying accurately the Negro's role as understood by current scholarship. We regard the suggested content as an indispensable minimum at the junior high level. Some compression would doubtless be necessary at the elementary level, while high school treatment should be expanded beyond our suggested content.

Early in the seventeenth century Negroes were brought by force from Africa to the English colonies, and over the next 50 years whites in the colonies reduced them to a slavery that was inherited and perpetual. The Negro incurred debasement because he was different, particularly because he was "heathen," black, and helpless. Other colonials entered types of servitude, but their arrangements were usually contractual, their rights were protected by the state, their physical and moral treatment was much better, and their status was temporary. Not even the American Indian, whose exploitation began in the seventeenth century, was reduced to slavery on a substantial scale. Textbooks should tell this story from its African beginnings, through the slave trade, to the enslavement of the Negro.

As the history of the origin of Negro slavery is important, so also is an understanding of slavery as a mature institution in the eighteenth and nineteenth centuries. Students should know that it existed in the North until after the Revolution. Textbooks should supply the most important statistics; for example, that in 1860 there were four million slaves in the United States, virtually all located in the South. Although a majority of Southern whites held no slaves, one out of every two persons in the South's fourteen million people was either a slave or a member of a slaveholding family.

There should be a full account of the life of the slave, starting from the fact that he was an article of property held for the profit that could be gained from his labor. Recent scholarship has shown that slaves labored in Southern factories as well as fields. They were often overworked, and customarily housed, clothed, and fed at only a subsistence level. As a result the slave was often ill, and his life expectancy was shorter than that of the whites around him. His master could punish or sell him at will, and could even kill him with near impunity, since slaves were not allowed to testify against white men. The informal character of slave marriages made for an unstable family life; and the whole pattern of debasement under slavery inflicted psychological and sociological scars from which Negroes still suffer.

Understandably the slave resented, even hated, his condition, though he usually disguised his real feelings by subservient behavior designed to protect him from the master's power. Students should be told that slaves often ran away, committed sabotage, and plotted revolts, and on one occasion a slave, Nat Turner, led a bloody general insurrection against the masters.

Slavery's moral and social evil did not go unremarked in the colonial period. The Quakers, for example, insisted that slavery violated both human dignity and divine law. Not until the Revolution, however, did most Americans become sensitive to the discrepancy between slavery and their professed ideals as embodied in the Declaration of Independence. All the states north of Delaware put the institution on the road to extinction, slavery was banned from the Old Northwest, and the Constitutional Convention opened the way for abolition of the slave trade after 1808. Even in the upper South, where the tobacco economy was languishing, liberal leaders hoped that the gradual operation of economic forces would eventually permit the abolition of slavery. Instead, the developing cotton market revived plantation agriculture. Slaves proved so productive in Southern cotton fields that slaveowners shut their ears to any criticism of the institution until the Civil War brought its demise.

Meanwhile antislavery sentiment was growing in the North. Even here racist assumptions caused free Negroes to be segregated and discriminated against, but after 1830 a vocal abolitionist movement had increasing effect. The efforts of the abolitionists, who included a substantial body of Northern free Negroes, deserve serious and sympathetic exposition in textbooks. They are often derided for their occasional extravagance and for their internal disagreements, yet the fact is that they performed an immense service in educating Americans to the moral evils of slavery.

Abolitionists are frequently blamed for the Civil War by people who also insist that slavery had nothing to do with the coming of the war, that indeed the South fought to preserve state rights. Most scholars today agree, however, that slavery, and especially the issue of extending slavery into the territories, was fundamental. Certainly a careful appraisal of the slavery issue in national politics should be included in any textbook covering this period.

When the Civil War came, some 200,000 Negroes participated in the fighting that resulted in their formal emancipation. Following the war they also took an important part in the struggle over Southern Reconstruction, which determined whether their emancipation was to be nominal or full. Reconstruction is a controversial issue in American history. The best scholarship today portrays sympathetically the radical Republicans in Congress, who opposed Lincoln's and later Johnson's plans for bringing the Southern states back into the Union as quickly and painlessly as possible under conservative white leadership. The radicals, this scholarship holds, operated from mixed motives: to be sure they were interested in maintaining their political advantage, but they also wished to reform the structure of Southern life. They especially wanted to help the Negro make himself a full partner in a free society.

It is in treating the Reconstruction state governments in the South that the older scholarship is most distorted by racist assumptions and most pernicious in its present-day effects. Modern scholarship overwhelmingly rejects the myth of Reconstruction as a saturnalia of misgovernment and corruption by ignorant and/or venal carpetbaggers, Negroes, and scalawags. Though the Reconstruction regimes had their quota of corruption, as did most other American governmental units in this period, the student needs to know that the radical Republican experiment for a time made progress toward a healthy reconstruction of Southern society, that many Negroes served ably in the Reconstruction governments, and that the Reconstruction governments had many constructive accomplishments, particularly the extension of the public school system, and the protection of equal civil and political rights of all.

The experiment in Reconstruction failed after a few years, owing to a growing Northern indifference which permitted conservative Southern whites to regain control by violence through such agencies as the Ku Klux Klan. Soon Negroes had been reduced to a kind of unofficial slavery. The vote was taken from them, first by trickery and intimidation and later by amendments to the state constitutions. Denied economic opportunity, many were exploited as sharecroppers, and others in menial jobs. By the end of the century, they were born and reared in segregated communities, and they lived and died in a state of inequality, isolated from the mainstream of American life. Southern state laws and a disastrous Supreme Court decision, *Plessy* vs. *Ferguson* (1896), helped encase them in segregation.

Segregation and violence continued to characterize race relations in the South during the first half of the twentieth century. The hundreds of lynchings which used to occur annually have almost disappeared, but bombings, burnings, and shootings have increased. A more important change has been the movement of millions of Negroes to the cities and to the North. Here repression has been somewhat more subtle but only somewhat less damaging. Employers and unions relegate most Negroes to menial jobs. They are segregated into ghettoes where they pay high rents for slum housing. Segregated housing means in turn segregated and inferior schools.

The other side of the story is the increasingly vigorous effort, especially by Negroes themselves, to change the situation. The growing Negro vote in crucial Northern cities and the cold-war campaign to win the support of the uncommitted nations of the world has made the federal government more responsive to the plight of Negroes. Prodded by the National Association for the Advancement of Colored People (NAACP), the federal courts began to declare in the 1930s and 1940s against racial discrimination in voting, jury service, and educational opportunities. This movement culminated in the Brown decision of 1954 (*Brown* vs. *Board of Education of Topeka*) outlawing racial segregation in the public schools. Meanwhile the executive branch of the federal government had begun to move against segregation and discrimination in the armed forces and in civil service employment. Some state legislatures acted against discrimination in housing and employment, and Congress took its first cautious steps since Reconstruction to advance civil rights.

In the years since the Brown decision, a civil rights mass movement has taken shape among Negroes, utilizing the tactics of non-violent direct action to demand immediate and full equality in all areas. The Reverend Martin Luther King led Negroes of Montgomery, Alabama, in a year-long boycott of the city's segregated bus system. Negro college students launched "sit-ins" throughout the South in a movement that ended segregation at lunch counters and other public facilities in hundreds of Southern communities. "Freedom riders" gave effect to court decisions outlawing segregation in transportation facilities. By 1963 mass demonstrations for equality in public facilities, jobs, education, and housing had spread from the South to many Northern cities, and over 200,000 people joined a "March on Washington" in support of former President John F. Kennedy's proposal that Congress pass a substantial civil rights bill. These efforts were pursued in the face of mob violence, the arrests of thousands of demonstrators, the assassination of an NAACP leader in Mississippi, and the death of four Negro girls in the bombing of a Birmingham church.

This civil rights revolution seems to us to be one of the major historical events of the mid-twentieth century and to demand full treatment in any American history textbook. The gains that have been made should be described realistically and not as an ode to the inevitable justice and progress of the democratic system. It should be made clear that the outcome of the civil rights struggle is still in doubt and that the inequalities are so great as to defy quick remedy by even the most vigorous effort.

In the midst of this civil rights revolution, historians and educators have a clear responsibility, at the very least, to see to it that the role of Negroes in American life is taught fully and accurately. We have tried to indicate what a minimally full and accurate textbook account should be.

Selection 16

AS SEEN BY AN INVESTIGATION COMMISSION IN 1965*

In the summer of 1965 a riot took place in the Watts district of Los Angeles. Why did it happen? Who was responsible?

The following selection has been taken from a report by the Governor's Commission on the Los Angeles Riots. The eight members of the Commission, distinguished Californians headed by John A. McCone, made the statement that the riots were a "symptom of a sickness in the center of our cities."

The Crisis—An Overview

The rioting in Los Angeles in the late, hot summer of 1965 took six days to run its full grievous course. In hindsight, the tinder-igniting incident is seen to have been the arrest of a drunken Negro youth about whose dangerous driving another Negro had complained to the Caucasian motorcycle officer who made the arrest. The arrest occurred under rather ordinary circumstances, near but not in the district known as Watts, at seven o'clock on the evening

* *Violence in the City—An End or a Beginning? A Report by the Governor's Commission on the Los Angeles Riots. December 2, 1965,* distributed by College Book Store, 3413 South Hoover Blvd., Los Angeles.

of 11 August, a Wednesday. The crisis ended in the afternoon of 17 August, a Tuesday, on Governor Brown's order to lift the curfew which had been imposed the Saturday before in an extensive area just south of the heart of the City.

In the ugliest interval, which lasted from Thursday through Saturday, perhaps as many as 10,000 Negroes took to the streets in marauding bands. They looted stores, set fires, beat up white passersby whom they hauled from stopped cars, many of which were turned upside down and burned, exchanged shots with law enforcement officers, and stoned and shot at firemen. The rioters seemed to have been caught up in an insensate rage of destruction. By Friday, the disorder spread to adjoining areas, and ultimately an area covering 46.5 square miles had to be controlled with the aid of military authority before public order was restored.

The entire Negro population of Los Angeles County, about two-thirds of whom live in this area, numbers more than 650,000. Observers estimate that only about two per cent were involved in the disorder. Nevertheless, this violent fraction, however minor, has given the face of community relations in Los Angeles a sinister cast.

When the spasm passed, thirty-four persons were dead, and the wounded and hurt numbered 1,032 more. Property damage was about $40,000,000. Arrested for one crime or another were 3,952 persons, women as well as men, including over 500 youths under eighteen. The lawlessness in this one segment of the metropolitan area had terrified the entire county and its 6,000,000 citizens.

Sowing the Wind

In the summer of 1964, Negro communities in seven eastern cities were stricken by riots.* Although in each situation there were unique contributing circumstances not existing elsewhere, the fundamental causes were largely the same:

—Not enough jobs to go around, and within this scarcity not enough by a wide margin of a character which the untrained Negro could fill.

* SUMMARY OF 1964 RIOTS

City	Date	Killed	Injured	Arrests	Stores Damaged
New York City	July 18–23	1	144	519	541
Rochester	July 24 25	4	350	976	204
Jersey City	August 2–4	0	46	52	71
Paterson	August 11–13	0	8	65	20
Elizabeth	August 11–13	0	6	18	17
Chicago (Dixmoor)	August 16–17	0	57	80	2
Philadelphia	August 28–30	0	341	774	225

—Not enough schooling designed to meet the special needs of the disadvantaged Negro child, whose environment from infancy onward places him under a serious handicap.

—A resentment, even hatred, of the police, as the symbol of authority.

These riots were each a symptom of a sickness in the center of our cities. In almost every major city, Negroes pressing ever more densely into the central city and occupying areas from which Caucasians have moved in their flight to the suburbs have developed an isolated existence with a feeling of separation from the community as a whole. Many have moved to the city only in the last generation and are totally unprepared to meet the conditions of modern city life. At the core of the cities where they cluster, law and order have only tenuous hold; the conditions of life itself are often marginal; idleness leads to despair and finally, mass violence supplies a momentary relief from the malaise.

Why Los Angeles?

In Los Angeles, before the summer's explosion, there was a tendency to believe, and with some reason, that the problems which caused the trouble elsewhere were not acute in this community. A "statistical portrait" drawn in 1964 by the Urban League which rated American cities in terms of ten basic aspects of Negro life—such as housing, employment, income—ranked Los Angeles first among the sixty-eight cities that were examined. ("There is no question about it, this is the best city in the world," a young Negro leader told us with respect to housing for Negroes.)

While the Negro districts of Los Angeles are not urban gems, neither are they slums. Watts, for example, is a community consisting mostly of one- and two-story houses, a third of which are owned by the occupants. In the riot area, most streets are wide and usually quite clean; there are trees, parks, and playgrounds. A Negro in Los Angeles has long been able to sit where he wants in a bus or a movie house, to shop where he wishes, to vote, and to use public facilities without discrimination. The opportunity to succeed is probably unequaled in any other major American city.

Yet the riot did happen here, and there are special circumstances here which explain in part why it did. Perhaps the people of Los Angeles should have seen trouble gathering under the surface calm. In the last quarter century, the Negro population here has exploded. While the County's population has trebled, the Negro population has increased almost tenfold from 75,000 in 1940 to 650,000 in 1965.

Much of the increase came through migration from Southern states and many arrived with the anticipation that this dynamic city would somehow spell the end of life's endless problems. To those who have come with high hopes and great expectations and see the success of others so close at hand, failure brings a special measure of frustration and disillusionment. Moreover, the fundamental problems, which are the same here as in the cities which were racked by the 1964 riots, are intensified by what may well be the least adequate network of public transportation in any major city in America.

Looking back, we can also see that there was a series of aggravating events in the twelve months prior to the riots.

—Publicity given to the glowing promise of the Federal poverty program was paralleled by reports of controversy and bickering over the mechanism to handle the program here in Los Angeles, and when the projects did arrive, they did not live up to their press notices.

—Throughout the nation, unpunished violence and disobedience to law were widely reported, and almost daily there were exhortations, here and elsewhere, to take the most extreme and even illegal remedies to right a wide variety of wrongs, real and supposed.

—In addition, many Negroes here felt and were encouraged to feel that they had been affronted by the passage of Proposition 14—an initiative measure passed by two-thirds of the voters in November 1964 which repealed the Rumford Fair Housing Act and unless modified by the voters or invalidated by the courts will bar any attempt by state or local governments to enact similar laws.

When the rioting came to Los Angeles, it was not a race riot in the usual sense. What happened was an explosion—a formless, quite senseless, all but hopeless violent protest—engaged in by a few but bringing great distress to all.

Nor was the rioting exclusively a projection of the Negro problem. It is part of an American problem which involves Negroes but which equally concerns other disadvantaged groups. In this report, our major conclusions and recommendations regarding the Negro problem in Los Angeles apply with equal force to the Mexican-Americans, a community which is almost equal in size to the Negro community and whose circumstances are similarly disadvantageous and demand equally urgent treatment. That the Mexican-American community did not riot is to its credit; it should not be to its disadvantage.

The Dull Devastating Spiral of Failure

In examining the sickness in the center of our city, what has depressed and stunned us most is the dull, devastating spiral of failure that awaits the average disadvantaged child in the urban core. His home life all too often fails to give him the incentive and the elementary experience with words and ideas which prepares most children for school. Unprepared and unready, he may not learn to read or write at all; and because he shares his problem with 30 or more in the same classroom, even the efforts of the most dedicated teachers are unavailing. Age, not achievement, passes him on to higher grades, but in most cases he is unable to cope with courses in the upper grades because they demand basic skills which he does not possess. ("Try," a teacher said to us, "to teach history to a child who cannot read.")

Frustrated and disillusioned, the child becomes a discipline problem. Often he leaves school, sometimes before the end of junior high school. (About two-thirds of those who enter the three high schools in the center of the curfew area do not graduate.) He slips into the ranks of the permanent jobless, illiterate and untrained, unemployed and unemployable. All the talk about the millions which the government is spending to aid him raise his expectations but the benefits seldom reach him.

Reflecting this spiral of failure, unemployment in the disadvantaged areas runs two to three times the county average, and the employment available is too often intermittent. A family whose breadwinner is chronically out of work is almost invariably a disintegrating family. Crime rates soar and welfare rolls increase, even faster than the population.

This spiral of failure has a most damaging side effect. Because of the low standard of achievement in the schools in the urban core and adjacent areas, parents of the better students from advantaged backgrounds remove them from these schools, either by changing the location of the family home or by sending the children to private school. In turn, the average achievement level of the schools in the disadvantaged area sinks lower and lower. The evidence is that this chain reaction is one of the principal factors in maintaining de facto school segregation in the urban core and producing it in the adjacent areas where the Negro population is expanding. From our study, we are persuaded that there is a reasonable possibility that raising the achievement levels of the disadvantaged Negro child will materially lessen the tendency towards de facto segregation in education, and that this might possibly also make a substantial contribution to ending all de facto segregation.

All Segments of Society

Perhaps for the first time our report will bring into clear focus, for all the citizens to see, the economic and sociological conditions in our city that underlay the gathering anger which impelled the rioters to escalate the routine arrest of a drunken driver into six days of violence. Yet, however powerful their grievances, the rioters had no legal or moral justification for the wounds they inflicted. Many crimes, a great many felonies, were committed. Even more dismaying, as we studied the record, was the large number of brutal exhortations to violence which were uttered by some Negroes. Rather than making proposals, they laid down ultimatums with the alternative being violence. All this nullified the admirable efforts of hundreds, if not thousands, both Negro and white, to quiet the situation and restore order.

What can be done to prevent a recurrence of the nightmare of August? It stands to reason that what we and other cities have been doing, costly as it all has been, is not enough. Improving the conditions of Negro life will demand adjustments on a scale unknown to any great society. The programs that we are recommending will be expensive and burdensome. And the burden, along with the expense, will fall on all segments of our society—on the public and private sectors, on industry and labor, on company presidents and hourly employees, and most indispensably, upon the members and leaders of the Negro community. For unless the disadvantaged are resolved to help themselves, whatever else is done by others is bound to fail.

The consequences of inaction, indifference, and inadequacy, we can all be sure now, would be far costlier in the long run than the cost of correction. If the city were to elect to stand aside, the walls of segregation would rise ever higher. The disadvantaged community would become more and more estranged and the risk of violence would rise. The cost of police protection would increase, and yet would never be adequate. Unemployment would climb; welfare costs would mount apace. And the preachers of division and demagoguery would have a matchless opportunity to tear our nation asunder.

Of Fundamental and Durable Import

As a Commission, we are seriously concerned that the existing breach, if allowed to persist, could in time split our society irretrievably. So serious and so explosive is the situation that, unless it is checked, the August riots may seem by comparison to be only a curtain-raiser for what could blow up one day in the future.

Our recommendations will concern many areas where improvement can be made but three we consider to be of highest prority and greatest importance.

1. Because idleness brings a harvest of distressing problems, employment for those in the Negro community who are unemployed and able to work is a first priority. Our metropolitan area employs upwards of three millions of men and women in industry and in the service trades, and we face a shortage of skilled and semi-skilled workers as our economy expands. We recommend that our robust community take immediate steps to relieve the lack of job opportunity for Negroes by cooperative programs for employment and training, participated in by the Negro community, by governmental agencies, by employers and by organized labor.

2. In education, we recommend a new and costly approach to educating the Negro child who has been deprived of the early training that customarily starts at infancy and who because of early deficiencies advances through school on a basis of age rather than scholastic attainment. What is clearly needed and what we recommend is an emergency program designed to raise the level of scholastic attainment of those who would otherwise fall behind. This requires pre-school education, intensive instruction in small classes, remedial courses and other special treatment. The cost will be great but until the level of scholastic achievement of the disadvantaged child is raised, we cannot expect to overcome the existing spiral of failure.

3. We recommend that law enforcement agencies place greater emphasis on their responsibilities for crime prevention as an essential element of the law enforcement task, and that they institute improved means for handling citizen complaints and community relationships.

The road to the improvement of the condition of the disadvantaged Negro which lies through education and employment is hard and long, but there is no shorter route. The avenue of violence and lawlessness leads to a dead end. To travel the long and difficult road will require courageous leadership and determined participation by all parts of our community, but no task in our times is more important. Of what shall it avail our nation if we can place a man on the moon but cannot cure the sickness in our cities? . . .

PART III

THE SEEDS
OF PROTEST:
THE NEGRO PROBLEM
AT THE TURN
OF THE CENTURY

INTRODUCTION

The end of the Civil War brought with it three great amendments to the United States Constitution. The Thirteenth Amendment freed the slaves; the Fourteenth made the former slave a citizen and extended to him equal protection under the law and protection against state interference with his life, liberty, and property; the Fifteenth Amendment declared that no one could be deprived of the right to vote because of his color.

It is no secret that the Fourteenth and Fifteenth Amendments were disregarded in many communities, especially in the South. By the turn of the century—in the years 1890 to 1910—the Negro was subjected to a variety of forms of discrimination in his social, economic, and political life. It is those critical twenty years that furnish in large part the immediate backdrop for the present protest movement or revolution.

Selections 17–21 provide a cross section of views on the Negro problem as it was seen at the turn of the century, beginning with an important interpretation of the rise of Jim Crowism in the South and a journalist's reporting of the Negro's feeling toward segregation during the early years of the twentieth century. Senator Tillman's extremist position is included because he represents a type of political figure who was said to have been kind to Negroes in private life, but who made political capital of the issue in public life. The case of *Plessy* vs. *Ferguson* deserves to be read with care because it offers an insight into the nature of our judicial process. The dissent of Justice Harlan with its prophetic overtones is a classic piece of writing. The thinking of President Theodore Roosevelt, a progressive, on the status of the Negro offers us a clue to liberal thought at the time.

In Selections 22 and 23 Booker T. Washington and W. E. B. Du Bois present dissenting opinions on what has become a major issue of civil rights—whether the Negro should pursue his goals through cooperation or vigorous protest. Selection 25 describes the origins and early goals of the NAACP, the first group organized to protest unjust treatment of Negroes.

Selection 17

AS SEEN BY AN HISTORIAN

C. VANN WOODWARD*

When and why did the Southern states pass Jim Crow laws segregating the races? The noted historian, C. Vann Woodward, offers us his explanation in The Strange Career of Jim Crow.

Capitulation to Racism

Up to the year 1898 South Carolina had resisted the Jim Crow car movement which had swept the western states of the South completely by that time. In that year, however, after several attempts,

* From C. Vann Woodward, *The Strange Career of Jim Crow,* New York: Oxford University Press, 1966, pp. 67–70, 81–82, 105–107.

the proponents of the Jim Crow law were on the eve of victory. The Charleston *News and Courier,* the oldest newspaper in the South and a consistent spokesman of conservatism, fired a final broadside against extremists in behalf of the conservative creed of race policy.

"As we have got on fairly well for a third of a century, including a long period of reconstruction, without such a measure," wrote the editor, "we can probably get on as well hereafter without it, and certainly so extreme a measure should not be adopted and enforced without added and urgent cause." He then called attention to what he considered the absurd consequences to which such a law might lead once the principle of the thing were conceded. "If there must be Jim Crow cars on the railroads, there should be Jim Crow cars on the street railways. Also on all passenger boats. . . . If there are to be Jim Crow cars, moreover, there should be Jim Crow waiting saloons at all stations and Jim Crow eating houses. . . . There should be Jim Crow sections of the jury box, and a separate Jim Crow dock and witness stand in every court—and a Jim Crow Bible for colored witnesses to kiss. It would be advisable also to have a Jim Crow section in county auditors' and treasurers' offices for the accommodation of colored taxpayers. The two races are dreadfully mixed in these offices for weeks every year, especially about Christmas. . . . There should be a Jim Crow department for making returns and paying for the privileges and blessings of citizenship. Perhaps, the best plan would be, after all, to take the short cut to the general end . . . by establishing two or three Jim Crow counties at once, and turning them over to our colored citizens for their special and exclusive accommodation."

In resorting to the tactics of *reductio ad absurdum* the editor doubtless believed that he had dealt the Jim Crow principle a telling blow with his heavy irony. But there is now apparent to us an irony in his argument of which the author was unconscious. For what he intended as a *reductio ad absurdum* and obviously regarded as an absurdity became in a very short time a reality, and not only that but a reality that was regarded as the only sensible solution to a vexing problem, a solution having the sanction of tradition and long usage. Apart from the Jim Crow counties and the Jim Crow witness stand, all the improbable applications of the principle suggested by the editor in derision had been put into practice—down to and including the Jim Crow Bible.

The South's adoption of extreme racism was due not so much to a conversion as it was to a relaxation of the opposition. All the elements of fear, jealousy, proscription, hatred, and fanaticism had long been present, as they are present in various degrees of intensity in any society. What enabled them to rise to dominance was not so much cleverness or ingenuity as it was a general weakening and discrediting of the numerous forces that had hitherto kept them in check. The restraining forces included not only Northern liberal opinion in the press, the courts, and the government, but also internal checks imposed by the prestige and influence of the Southern conservatives, as well as by the idealism and zeal of the Southern radicals. What happened toward the end of the century was an almost simultaneous—and sometimes not unrelated—decline in the effectiveness of restraint that had been exercised by all three forces: Northern liberalism, Southern conservatism, and Southern radicalism. . . . Just as the Negro gained his emancipation and new rights through a falling out between white men, he now stood to lose his rights through the reconciliation of white men.

* * *

If the psychologists are correct in their hypothesis that aggression is always the result of frustration, then the South toward the end of the 'nineties was the perfect cultural seedbed for aggression against the minority race. Economic, political, and social frustrations had pyramided to a climax of social tensions. No real relief was in sight from the long cyclical depression of the 'nineties, an acute period of suffering that had only intensified the distress of the much longer agricultural depression. Hopes for reform and the political means employed in defiance of tradition and at great cost to emotional attachments to effect reform had likewise met with cruel disappointments and frustration. There had to be a scapegoat. And all along the line signals were going up to indicate that the Negro was an approved object of aggression. These "permissions-to-hate" came from sources that had formerly denied such permission. They came from the federal courts in numerous opinions, from Northern liberals eager to conciliate the South, from Southern conservatives who had abandoned their race policy of moderation in their struggle against the Populists, from the Populists in their mood of disillusionment with their former Negro allies, and from a national temper suddenly expressed by imperialistic adventures and aggressions against colored peoples in distant lands.

* * *

At any rate, the findings of the present investigation tend to bear out the testimony of Negroes from various parts of the South, as reported by the Swedish writer Gunnar Myrdal, to the effect that "the Jim Crow statutes were effective means of tightening and freezing—in many cases instigating—segregation and discrimination." The evidence has indicated that under conditions prevailing in the earlier part of the period reviewed the Negro could and did do many things in the South that in the latter part of the period, under different conditions, he was prevented from doing.

We have seen that in the 'seventies, 'eighties, and 'nineties, the Negroes voted in large numbers. White leaders of opposing parties encouraged them to vote and earnestly solicited their votes. Qualified and acknowledged leaders of Southern white opinion were on record as saying that it was proper, inevitable, and desirable that they should vote. Yet after the disfranchisement measures were passed around 1900 the Negroes ceased to vote. And at that time qualified and acknowledged leaders of white opinion said that it was unthinkable that they should ever be permitted to vote. In the earlier decades Negroes still took an active, if modest, part in public life. They held offices, served on the jury, the bench, and were represented in local councils, state legislatures and the national Congress. Later on these things were simply not so, and the last of the Negroes disappeared from these forums.

It has also been seen that their presence on trains upon equal terms with white men was once regarded as normal, acceptable, and unobjectionable. Whether railways qualify as folkways or stateways, black man and white man once rode them together and without a partition between them. Later on the stateways apparently changed the folkways—or at any rate the railways—for the partitions and Jim Crow cars became universal. And the new seating arrangement came to seem as normal, unchangeable, and inevitable as the old ways. And so it was with the soda fountains, eating places, bars, waiting rooms, street cars, and circuses. And so it probably was with the parks in Atlanta, and with cemeteries in Mississippi. There must even have been a time in Oklahoma when a colored man could walk into any old telephone booth he took a notion to and pick up the receiver . . . the Jim Crow laws applied to *all* Negroes—not merely to the rowdy, or drunken, or surly, or ignorant ones. The new laws did not countenance the old conservative tendency to distinguish between classes of the race, to encourage the "better" element, and to draw it into a white alliance. Those laws backed up the Alabamian who told the disfranchising convention of his state that no Negro in the world was the equal of "the least, poorest, lowest-down white man I ever knew"; but not ex-Governor Oates, who replied: "I would not trust him as quickly as I would a Negro of intelligence and good character." The Jim Crow laws put the authority of the state or city in the voice of the street-car conductor, the railway brakeman, the bus driver, the theater usher, and also into the voice of the hoodlum of the public parks and playgrounds. They gave free rein and the majesty of the law to mass aggressions that might otherwise have been curbed, blunted, or deflected.

The Jim Crow laws, unlike feudal laws, did not assign the subordinate group a fixed status in society. They were constantly pushing the Negro farther down.

Selections 18a–18b

AS SEEN BY A JOURNALIST

RAY STANNARD BAKER*

The two selections which follow are taken from Ray Stannard Baker's interviews with Negroes in 1906–1908.

18a. The Negroes' Struggle for Survival in Northern Cities

One of the questions I asked of Negroes whom I met both North and South was this:

"What is your chief cause of complaint?"

In the South the first answer nearly always referred to the Jim Crow cars or the Jim Crow railroad stations; after that, the complaint was of political disfranchisement, the difficulty of getting justice in the courts, the lack of good school facilities, and in some localities, of the danger of actual physical violence.

But in the North the first answer invariably referred to working conditions.

* From Ray Stannard Baker, *Following the Color Line: American Negro Citizenship in the Progressive Era,* New York: Harper and Row, 1964, pp. 130, 31–32. [Originally published in 1908 by Doubleday, Page & Co.]

"The Negro isn't given a fair opportunity to get employment. He is discriminated against because he is coloured."

Professor Kelly Miller, one of the acutest of Negro writers, has said:

"The Negro (in the North) is compelled to loiter around the edges of industry."

18b. Jim Crow

No other one point of race contact is so much and so bitterly discussed among the Negroes as the Jim Crow car. I don't know how many Negroes replied to my question: "What is the chief cause of friction down here?" with a complaint of their treatment on street cars and in railroad trains.

Why the Negro Objects to the Jim Crow Car

Fundamentally, of course they object to any separation which gives them inferior accommodations. This point of view—and I am trying to set down every point of view, both coloured and white, exactly as I find it, is expressed in many ways.

"We pay first-class fare," said one of the leading Negroes in Atlanta, "exactly as the white man does, but we don't get first-class service. I say it isn't fair."

In answer to this complaint, the white man says: "The Negro is inferior, he must be made to keep his place. Give him a chance and he assumes social equality, and that will lead to an effort at intermarriage and amalgamation of the races. The Anglo-Saxon will never stand for that."

Selections 19a–19b

AS SEEN BY A SOUTHERN
WHITE PARTISAN

SENATOR BEN TILLMAN*

These two selections are excerpts from speeches delivered by Senator Ben Tillman from South Carolina in the United States Senate.

19a. Speech Before the Senate, March 29, 1900

Mr. President, I regret that I feel the necessity of bringing up again some parts of the speech of the Senator who has just taken his seat. However, he would not allow me to answer or interject an objection as he went along. It has reference to the race question in the South, the question which has been the cause of more sorrow, more misery, more loss of life, more expenditure of treasure than any and all questions which have confronted the American people from the foundation of the Government to the present day. Out of it grew the war, and after the war came the results of the war, and those results are with us now. The South has this question always with it. It can not get rid of it. It is there. It is like Banquo's ghost, and will not down. If I have felt called on to attack the Republican policy of this day and time and to accuse the Republicans in this Chamber with being hypocrites in regard to that issue, I have felt constrained to do so by reason of facts and of the events of the past few years. . . .

There were numerous instances, possibly too numerous, of cruelty and wrongdoing, and I shall not apologize for the system, for, thank God, it is gone—torn up by the roots at a great cost of life and

* From *The Congressional Record,* March 23, 1900 and February 24, 1903.

sacrifice of property. I would not restore it if I could by the waving
of a hand. But I say to him when he parades that as a reason why
we ought to be grateful—and I acknowledge that we ought—he at
once convicts himself and those of his fellows who went on that
crusade of blood and destruction for the purpose of liberating those
people of having been misled and of having given Harriet Beecher
Stowe's *Uncle Tom's Cabin* undue weight in inaugurating that
crusade. I have already given due credit on this floor to the North
for patriotism and honesty of purpose, and I realize that the love
of the Union was a mighty factor in that great struggle. But it can
not be denied that the slaves of the South were a superior set of
men and women to freedmen of to-day, and that the poison in their
minds—the race hatred of the whites—is the result of the teachings
of Northern fanatics. Ravishing a woman, white or black, was
never known to occur in the South till after the Reconstruction era.
So much for that phase of the subject. . . .

Mr. President, I have not the facts and figures here, but I want
the country to get the full view of the Southern side of this question
and the justification for anything we did. We were sorry we had
the necessity forced upon us, but we could not help it, and as white
men we are not sorry for it, and we do not propose to apologize
for anything we have done in connection with it. We took the
government away from [the carpetbag Negro government] in 1876.
We did take it. If no other Senator has come here previous to this
time who would acknowledge it, more is the pity. We have had
no fraud in our elections in South Carolina since 1884. There has
been no organized Republican party in the State.

We did not disfranchise the Negroes until 1895. Then we had
a constitutional convention convened which took the matter up
calmly, deliberately, and avowedly with the purpose of disfranchising as many of them as we could under the Fourteenth and Fifteenth
Amendments. We adopted the educational qualification as the only
means left to us, and the Negro is as contented and as prosperous
and as well protected in South Carolina to-day as in any State of
the Union south of the Potomac. He is not meddling with politics,
for he found that the more he meddled with them the worse off he
got. As to his "rights"—I will not discuss them now. We of the
South have never recognized the right of the Negro to govern
white men, and we never will. We have never believed him to be
equal to the white man, and we will not submit to his gratifying
his lust on our wives and daughters without lynching him. I would
to God the last one of them was in Africa, and that none of them
had ever been brought to our shores. . . .

19b. Speech Before the Senate, February 24, 1903

Some people have been ready to believe and to contend that the Negro is a white man with a black skin. All history disproves that. Go to Africa. What do you find there? From one hundred and fifty million to two hundred million savages.

I happened in my boyhood, when I was about 12 years old, to see some real Africans fresh from their native jungles. The last cargo of slaves imported into this country were brought here in 1858 on the yacht Wanderer, landed on an island below Savannah, and sneaked by the United States marshal up the Savannah River and landed a little distance below Augusta, and my family bought some thirty of them.

Therefore I had a chance to see just what kind of people these were, and to compare the African as he is to-day in Africa with the African who, after two centuries of slavery, was brought side by side to be judged. The difference was as "Hyperion to a satyr." Those poor wretches, half starved as they had been on their voyage across the Atlantic, shut down and battened under the hatches and fed a little rice, several hundred of them, were the most miserable lot of human beings—the nearest to the missing link with the monkey—I have ever put my eyes on. . . .

Then if God in His providence ordained slavery and had these people transported over here for the purpose of civilizing enough of them to form a nucleus and to become missionaries back to their native heath, that is a question. . . . But the thing I want to call your attention to is that slavery was not an unmitigated evil for the Negro, because whatever of progress the colored race has shown itself capable of achieving has come from slavery; and whether among those four million there were not more good men and women than could be found among the nine million now is to my mind a question. I would not like to assert it; but I am strongly of that belief from the facts I know in regard to the demoralization that has come to those people down there by having liberty thrust upon them in the way it was, and then having the ballot and the burdens of government, and being subjected to the strain of being tempted and misled and duped and used as tools by designing white men who went there among them. . . .

Well, Mr. President, I am done. I have treated this subject but imperfectly, but I have spoken from the soul, from my very heart, to tell you the truth, so help me God. I warn you that in proportion as you arouse false hopes in these people's minds as to their future, keeping the door of hope open by giving them offices, you are only sowing the wind which will whirl up into a whirlwind later on.

You cannot keep that door open without shutting it on the whites. The Northern millions which have gone down there have gone into Negro colleges and schools to equip these people to compete with their white neighbors.

All of the millions that are being sent there by Northern philanthropy has been but to create an antagonism between the poorer classes of our citizens and these people upon whose level they are in the labor market. There has been no contribution to elevate the white people in the South, to aid and assist the Anglo-Saxon Americans, the men who are descended from the people who fought with Marion and Sumter. They are allowed to struggle in poverty and in ignorance, and to do everything they can to get along, and they see Northern people pouring in thousands and thousands to help build up an African domination.

Senators, I leave the subject with you. May God give you wisdom and light to "do as you would have others do unto you."

Selections 20a–20b

AS SEEN BY THE SUPREME COURT

PLESSY *vs.* FERGUSON*

This famous Supreme Court case, decided May 18, 1896, established the "separate but equal" rule. Homer Adolph Plessy, the plaintiff, was so fair-skinned that he was not recognizably a Negro.

20a. Majority Opinion by Mr. Justice Brown

This was a petition . . . by Plessy, the plaintiff, against the Hon. John H. Ferguson, judge of the criminal district court for the parish of Orleans, and setting forth in substance the following facts:

* *Homer Adolph Plessy vs. John H. Ferguson.*

That petitioner was a citizen of the United States; and a resident of the state of Louisiana, of mixed descent, in the proportion of seven eighths Caucasian and one eighth African blood; that the mixture of colored blood was not discernible in him, and that he was entitled to every recognition, right, privilege, and immunity secured to the citizens of the United States of the white race by its Constitution and laws; that on June 7, 1892, he engaged and paid for a first-class passage on the East Louisiana Railway from New Orleans to Covington, in the same state, and thereupon entered a passenger train and took possession of a vacant seat in a coach where passengers of the white race were accommodated: that such railroad company was incorporated by the laws of Louisiana as a common carrier, and was not authorized to distinguish between citizens according to their race. But, notwithstanding this, petitioner was required by the conductor, under penalty of ejection from said train and imprisonment, to vacate said coach and occupy another seat in a coach assigned by said company for persons not of the white race, and for no other reason than that petitioner was of the colored race; that upon petitioner's refusal to comply with such order, he was, with the aid of a police officer, forcibly ejected from said coach and hurried off to and imprisoned in the parish jail of New Orleans, and there held to answer a charge made by such officer to the effect that he was guilty of having criminally violated an act of the general assembly of the state, approved July 10, 1890, in such case made and provided. . . .

Mr. Justice Brown delivered the opinion of the court:

This case turns upon the constitutionality of an act of the general assembly of the state of Louisiana, passed in 1890, providing for separate railway carriages for the white and colored races. . . .

The 1st section of the statute enacts "that all railway companies carrying passengers in their coaches in this state shall provide equal but separate accommodations for the white and colored races, by providing two or more passenger coaches for each passenger train, or by dividing the passenger coaches by a partition so as to secure separate accommodations: *Provided,* That this section shall not be construed to apply to street railroads. No person or persons shall be permitted to occupy seats in coaches other than the ones assigned to them, on account of the race they belong to."

By the 2d section it was enacted "that the officers of such passenger trains shall have power and are hereby required to assign each passenger to the coach or compartment used for the race to which such passenger belongs; any passenger insisting on going into a coach or compartment to which by race he does not belong, shall be liable to a fine of $25 or in lieu thereof to imprisonment for a period of not more than twenty days in the parish prison, and any officer of any railroad insisting on assigning a passenger to a coach or compartment other than the one set aside for the race to which said passenger belongs, shall be liable to a fine of $25, or in lieu thereof to imprisonment for a period of not more than twenty days in the parish prison; and should any passenger refuse to occupy the coach or compartment to which he or she is assigned by the officer of such railway, said officer shall have power to refuse to carry such passenger on his train, and for such refusal neither he nor the railway company which he represents shall be liable for damages in any of the courts of this state."

The 3d section provides penalties for the refusal or neglect of the officers, directors, conductors, and employees of railway companies to comply with the act, with a proviso that "nothing in this act shall be construed as applying to nurses attending children of the other race." The 4th section is immaterial.

The information filed in the criminal district court charged in substance that Plessy, being a passenger between two stations within the state of Louisiana, was assigned by officers of the company to the coach used for the race to which he belonged, but he insisted upon going into a coach used by the race to which he did not belong. Neither in the information nor plea was his particular race or color averred.

The petition . . . averred that petitioner was seven eighths Caucasian and one eighth African blood; that the mixture of colored blood was not discernible in him, and that he was entitled to every right, privilege, and immunity secured to citizens of the United States of the white race; and that, upon such theory he took possession of a vacant seat in a coach where passengers of the white race were accommodated, and was ordered by the conductor to vacate said coach and take a seat in another assigned to persons of the colored race, and having refused to comply with such demand he was forcibly ejected with the aid of a police officer, and imprisoned in the parish jail to answer a charge of having violated the above act.

The constitutionality of this act is attacked upon the ground that it conflicts both with the 13th Amendment of the Constitution, abolishing slavery, and the 14th Amendment, which prohibits certain restrictive legislation on the part of the states.

1. That it does not conflict with the 13th Amendment, which abolished slavery and involuntary servitude, except as a punishment for crime, is too clear for argument. Slavery implies involuntary servitude—a state of bondage; the ownership of mankind as a chattel, or at least the control of the labor and services of one man for

the benefit of another, and the absence of a legal right to the disposal of his own person, property, and services. . . .

A statute which implies merely a legal distinction between the white and colored races—a distinction which is founded in the color of the two races, and which must always exist so long as white men are distinguished from the other race by color—has no tendency to destroy the legal equality of the two races, or re-establish a state of involuntary servitude. Indeed, we do not understand that the 13th Amendment is strenuously relied upon by the plaintiff in error in this connection.

2. By the 14th Amendment, all persons born or naturalized in the United States, and subject to the jurisdiction thereof, are made citizens of the United States and of the state wherein they reside; and the states are forbidden from making or enforcing any law which shall abridge the privileges or immunities of citizens of the United States, or shall deprive any person of life, liberty, or property without due process of law, or deny to any person within their jurisdiction the equal protection of the laws. . . .

The object of the amendment was undoubtedly to enforce the absolute equality of the two races before the law, but in the nature of things it could not have been intended to abolish distinctions based upon color, or to enforce social, as distinguished from political, equality, or a commingling of the two races upon terms unsatisfactory to either. Laws permitting, and even requiring their separation in places where they are liable to be brought into contact do not necessarily imply the inferiority of either race to the other, and have been generally, if not universally, recognized as within the competency of the state legislatures in the exercise of their police power. The most common instance of this is connected with the establishment of separate schools for white and colored children, which have been held to be a valid exercise of the legislative power even by courts of states where the political rights of the colored race have been longest and most earnestly enforced. . . .

In the present case no question of interference with interstate commerce can possibly arise, since the East Louisiana Railway appears to have been purely a local line with both its termini within the state of Louisiana. . . .

In this connection it is also suggested by the learned counsel for the plaintiff . . . that the same argument that will justify the state legislature in requiring railways to provide separate accommodations for the two races will also authorize them to require separate cars to be provided for people whose hair is of a certain color, or who are aliens, or who belong to certain nationalities, or to enact laws requiring colored people to walk upon one side of the street, and white people upon the other, or requiring white men's houses to be painted white, and colored men's black, or their vehicles or business signs to be of different colors, upon the theory that one side of the street is as good as the other, or that a house or vehicle of one color is as good as one of another color. The reply to all this is that every exercise of the police power must be reasonable, and extend only to such laws as are enacted in good faith for the promotion of the public good, and not for the annoyance or oppression of a particular class. . . .

So far, then, as a conflict with the 14th Amendment is concerned, the case reduces itself to the question whether the statute of Louisiana is a reasonable regulation, and with respect to this there must necessarily be a large discretion on the part of the legislature. In determining the question of reasonableness it is at liberty to act with reference to the established usages, customs, and traditions of the people, and with a view to the promotion of their comfort, and the preservation of the public peace and good order. Gauged by this standard, we cannot say that a law which authorizes or even requires the separation of the races in public conveyances is unreasonable or more obnoxious to the 14th Amendment than the acts of Congress requiring separate schools for colored children in the District of Columbia, the constitutionality of which does not seem to have been questioned, or the corresponding acts of state legislatures.

We consider the underlying fallacy of the plaintiff's argument to consist in the assumption that the enforced separation of the two races stamps the colored race with a badge of inferiority. If this be so, it is not by reason of anything found in the act, but solely because the colored race chooses to put that construction upon it. The argument necessarily assumes that if . . . the colored race should become the dominant power in the state legislature, and should enact a law in precisely similar terms, it would thereby relegate the white race to an inferior position. We imagine that the white race, at least, would not acquiesce in this assumption. The argument also assumes that social prejudice may be overcome by legislation, and that equal rights cannot be secured to the Negro except by an enforced commingling of the two races. We cannot accept this position. If the two races are to meet on terms of social equality, it must be the result of natural affinities, a mutual appreciation of each other's merits and a voluntary consent of individuals. . . . Legislation is powerless to eradicate racial instincts or to abolish distinctions based upon physical differences, and the attempt to do so can only result in accentuating the difficulties of the present situation. If the civil and political rights of both races be equal, one cannot be inferior to the other civilly or politically. If one race be inferior to the other socially, the Constitution of the United States cannot put them upon the same plane. . . .

20b. Mr. Justice Harlan Dissenting

By the Louisiana statute, the validity of which is here involved, all railway companies (other than street railway companies) carrying passengers in that state are required to have separate but equal accommodations for white and colored persons, "by providing two or more passenger coaches for each passenger train, *or* by dividing the passenger coaches by *partition* so as to secure separate accommodations." Under this statute, no colored person is permitted to occupy a seat in a coach assigned to white persons; nor any white person to occupy a seat in a coach assigned to colored persons. The managers of the railroad are not allowed to exercise any discretion in the premises, but are required to assign each passenger to some coach or compartment set apart for the exclusive use of his race. If a passenger insists upon going into a coach or compartment not set apart for persons of his race, he is subject to be fined, or to be imprisoned in the parish jail. Penalties are prescribed for the refusal or neglect of the officers, directors, conductors, and employees of railroad companies to comply with the provisions of the act.

Only "nurses attending children of the other race" are excepted from the operation of the statute. No exception is made of colored attendants traveling with adults. A white man is not permitted to have his colored servant with him in the same coach, even if his condition of health requires the constant personal assistance of such servant. If a colored maid insists upon riding in the same coach with a white woman whom she has been employed to serve, and who may need her personal attention while traveling, she is subject to be fined or imprisoned for such an exhibition of zeal in the discharge of duty.

While there may be in Louisiana persons of different races who are not citizens of the United States, the words in the act, "white and colored races" necessarily include all citizens of the United States of both races residing in that state. So that we have before us a state enactment that compels, under penalties, the separation of the two races in railroad passenger coaches, and makes it a crime for a citizen of either race to enter a coach that has been assigned to citizens of the other race.

Thus the state regulates the use of a public highway by citizens of the United States solely upon the basis of race. . . .

In respect of civil rights, common to all citizens, the Constitution of the United States does not, I think, permit any public authority to know the race of those entitled to be protected in the enjoyment of such rights. Every true man has pride of race, and under appropriate circumstances, when the rights of others, his equals before the law, are not to be affected, it is his privilege to express such pride and to take such action based upon it as to him seems proper. But I deny that any legislative body or judicial tribunal may have regard to the race of citizens when the civil rights of those citizens are involved. Indeed such legislation as that here in question is inconsistent, not only with that equality of rights which pertains to citizenship, national and state, but with the personal liberty enjoyed by every one within the United States.

The 13th Amendment does not permit the withholding or the deprivation of any right necessarily inhering in freedom. It not only struck down the institution of slavery as previously existing in the United States, but it prevents the imposition of any burdens or disabilities that constitute badges of slavery or servitude. It decreed universal civil freedom in this country. This court has so adjudged. But that amendment having been found inadequate to the protection of the rights of those who had been in slavery, was followed by the 14th Amendment, which added greatly to the dignity and glory of American citizenship, and to the security of personal liberty, by declaring that "all persons born or naturalized in the United States, and subject to the jurisdiction thereof, are citizens of the United States and of the state wherein they reside," and that "no state shall make or enforce any law which shall abridge the privileges or immunities of citizens of the United States; nor shall any state deprive any person of life, liberty, or property without due process of law, nor deny to any person within its jurisdiction the equal protection of the laws." These two amendments, if enforced according to their true intent and meaning, will protect all the civil rights that pertain to freedom and citizenship. Finally, and to the end that no citizen should be denied, on account of his race, the privilege of participating in the political control of his country, it was declared by the 15th Amendment that "the right of citizens of the United States to vote shall not be denied or abridged by the United States or by any state on account of race, color, or previous condition of servitude."

These notable additions to the fundamental law were welcomed by the friends of liberty throughout the world. They removed the race line from our governmental systems. They had, as this court has said, a common purpose, namely, to secure "to a race recently emancipated, a race that through many generations has been held in slavery, all the civil rights that the superior race enjoy." They declared, in legal effect, this court has further said, "that the law in the states shall be the same for the black as for the white: that all persons, whether colored or white, shall stand equal before the laws of the states, and, in regard to the colored race, for whose protection the amendment was primarily designed, that no discrimination shall be made against them by law because of their color." We also said: "The words of the amendment, it is true, are prohibitory, but they contain a necessary implication of a positive immunity, or right, most valuable to the colored race—the right to exemption from unfriendly legislation against them distinctively as colored—exemption from legal discriminations, implying inferiority in civil society, lessening the security of their enjoyment of the rights which others enjoy, and discriminations which are steps towards reducing them to the condition of a subject race." It was consequently adjudged that a state law that excluded citizens of the colored race from juries because of their race and however well qualified in other respects to discharge the duties of jurymen was repugnant to the 14th Amendment. . . .

It was said in argument that the statute of Louisiana does not discriminate against either race, but prescribes a rule applicable alike to white and colored citizens. But this argument does not meet the difficulty. Everyone knows that the statute in question had its origin in the purpose, not so much to exclude white persons from railroad cars occupied by blacks, as to exclude colored people from coaches occupied by or assigned to white persons. Railroad corporations of Louisiana did not make discrimination among whites in the matter of accommodation for travelers. The thing to accomplish was, under the guise of giving equal accommodation for whites and blacks, to compel the latter to keep to themselves while traveling in railroad passenger coaches. No one would be so wanting in candor as to assert the contrary. The fundamental objection, therefore, to the statute, is that it interferes with the personal freedom of citizens. "Personal liberty," it has been well said, "consists in the power of locomotion, of changing situation, or removing one's person to whatsoever places one's own inclination may direct, without imprisonment or restraint, unless by due course of law." . . . If a white man and a black man choose to occupy the same public conveyance on a public highway, it is their right to do so, and no government, proceeding alone on grounds of race, can prevent it without infringing the personal liberty of each.

It is one thing for railroad carriers to furnish, or to be required by law to furnish, equal accommodations for all whom they are under a legal duty to carry. It is quite another thing for the government to forbid citizens of the white and black races from traveling in the same public conveyance, and to punish officers of railroad companies for permitting persons of the two races to occupy the same passenger coach. If a state can prescribe as a rule of civil conduct, that whites and blacks shall not travel as passengers in the same railroad coach, why may it not so regulate the use of the streets of its cities and towns as to compel white citizens to keep on one side of the street and black citizens to keep on the other? Why may it not, upon like grounds, punish whites and blacks who ride together in street cars or in open vehicles on a public road or street? Why may it not require sheriffs to assign whites to one side of a court-room and blacks to the other? And why may it not also prohibit the commingling of the two races in the galleries of legislative halls or in public assemblages convened for the political questions of the day? Further, if this statute of Louisiana is consistent with the personal liberty of citizens, why may not the state require the separation in railroad coaches of native and naturalized citizens of the United States, or of Protestants and Roman Catholics? . . .

The white race deems itself to be the dominant race in this country. And so it is, in prestige, in achievements, in education, in wealth, and in power. So, I doubt not that it will continue to be for all time, if it remains true to its great heritage and holds fast to the principles of constitutional liberty. But in view of the Constitution, in the eye of the law, there is in this country no superior dominant, ruling class of citizens. There is no caste here. Our Constitution is color-blind, and neither knows nor tolerates classes among citizens. In respect of civil rights, all citizens are equal before the law. The humblest is the peer of the most powerful. The law regards man as man, and takes no account of his surroundings or of his color when his civil rights as guaranteed by the supreme law of the land are involved. It is therefore to be regretted that this high tribunal, the final expositor of the fundamental law of the land, has reached the conclusion that it is competent for a state to regulate the enjoyment by citizens of their civil rights solely upon the basis of race.

In my opinion, the judgment this day rendered, will, in time, prove to be quite as pernicious as the decision made by this tribunal in the *Dred Scott Case.* It was adjudged in that case that the descendants of Africans who were imported into this country and sold as slaves were not included nor intended to be included under the word "citizens" in the Constitution, and could not claim any of the rights and privileges which that instrument provided for and secured to citizens of the United States; that at the time of the adoption of the Constitution they were "considered as a subordinate and inferior class of beings, who had been subjugated by the dominant race, and, whether emancipated or not, yet remained subject to their authority, and had no rights or privileges but such as those who held the power and the government might choose to grant them." . . . The recent amendments of the Constitution, it was supposed, had eradicated these principles from our institutions. But it seems that we have yet, in some of the states a dominant race, a superior class of citizens, which assumes to regulate the enjoyment of civil rights, common to all citizens, upon the basis of race. The present decision, it may well be apprehended, will not stimulate aggressions, more or less brutal and irritating, upon the admitted rights of colored citizens, but will encourage the belief that it is possible, by means of state enactments, to defeat the beneficent purposes which the people of the United States had in view when they adopted the recent amendments of the Constitution, by one of which the blacks of this country were made citizens of the United States and of the states in which they respectively reside and whose privileges and immunities, as citizens, the states are forbidden to abridge. Sixty millions of whites are in no danger from the presence here of eight millions of blacks. The destinies of the two races in this country are indissolubly linked together, and the interests of both require that the common government of all shall not permit the seeds of race hate to be planted under the sanction of law. What can more certainly arouse race hate, what more certainly create and perpetuate a feeling of distrust between these races, than state enactments which in fact proceed on the ground that colored citizens are so inferior and degraded that they cannot be allowed to sit in public coaches occupied by white citizens? That, as all will admit, is the real meaning of such legislation as was enacted in Louisiana.

The sure guaranty of the peace and security of each race is the clear, distinct, unconditional recognition by our governments, national and state, of every right that inheres in civil freedom, and of the equality before the law of all citizens of the United States without regard to race. State enactments, regulating the enjoyment of civil rights, upon the basis of race, and cunningly devised to defeat legitimate results of the war under the pretense of recognizing equality of rights, can have no other result than to render permanent peace impossible and to keep alive a conflict of races, the continuance of which must do harm to all concerned. This question is not met by the suggestion that social equality cannot exist between the white and black races in this country. That argument, if it can be properly regarded as one, is scarcely worthy of consideration, for social equality no more exists between two races when traveling in a passenger coach or a public highway than when members of the same races sit by each other in a street car or in the jury box, or stand or sit with each other in a political assembly, or when they use in common the streets of a city or town, or when they are in the same room for the purpose of having their names placed on the registry of voters, or when they approach the ballot box in order to exercise the high privilege of voting.

There is a race so different from our own that we do not permit those belonging to it to become citizens of the United States. Persons belonging to it are, with few exceptions, absolutely excluded from our country. I allude to the Chinese race. But by the statute in question a Chinaman can ride in the same passenger coach with white citizens of the United States, while citizens of the black race in Louisiana, many of whom, perhaps, risked their lives for the preservation of the Union, who are entitled by law to participate in the political control of the state and nation, who are not excluded, by law or by reason of their race, from public stations of any kind, and who have all the legal rights that belong to white citizens, are yet declared to be criminals, liable to imprisonment, if they ride in a public coach occupied by citizens of the white race. It is scarcely just to say that a colored citizen should not object to occupying a public coach assigned to his own race. He does not object, nor, perhaps, would he object to separate coaches for his race, if his rights under the law were recognized. But he does object, and he ought never to cease objecting, that citizens of the white and black races can be adjudged criminals because they sit, or claim the right to sit, in the same public coach on a public highway.

The arbitrary separation of citizens, on the basis of race, while they are on a public highway, is a badge of servitude wholly inconsistent with the civil freedom and the equality before the law established by the Constitution. It cannot be justified upon any legal grounds.

If evils will result from the commingling of the two races upon public highways established for the benefit of all, they will be infinitely less than those that will surely come from state legislation regulating the enjoyment of civil rights upon the basis of race. We boast of the freedom enjoyed by our people above all other peoples. But it is difficult to reconcile that boast with a state of the law which, practically, puts the brand of servitude and degradation upon a large class of our fellow citizens, our equals before the law. The thin disguise of "equal" accommodations for passengers in railroad coaches will not mislead anyone, or atone for the wrong this day done.

The result of the whole matter is that while this court has frequently adjudged, and at the present term has recognized the doctrine, that a state cannot, consistently with the Constitution of the

United States, prevent white and black citizens, having the required qualifications for jury service, from sitting in the same jury box, it is now solemnly held that a state may prohibit white and black citizens from sitting in the same passenger coach on a public highway, or may require that they be separated by a "partition," when in the same passenger coach. May it not now be reasonably expected that astute men of the dominant race, who affect to be disturbed at the possibility that the integrity of the white race may be corrupted, or that its supremacy will be imperiled, by contact on public highways with black people, will endeavor to procure statutes requiring white and black jurors to be separated in the jury box by a "partition" and that, upon retiring from the court room to consult as to their verdict, such partition, if it be a movable one, shall be taken to their consultation room, and set up in such way as to prevent black jurors from coming too close to their brother jurors of the white race. If the "partition" used in the court room happens to be stationary, provision could be made for screens with openings through which jurors of the two races could confer as to their verdict without coming into personal contact with each other. I cannot see but that, according to the principles this day announced, such state legislation, although conceived in hostility to, and enacted for the purpose of humiliating citizens of the United States of a particular race, would be held to be consistent with the Constitution. . . .

I am of opinion that the statute of Louisiana is inconsistent with the personal liberty of citizens, white and black, in that state, and hostile to both the spirit and letter of the Constitution of the United States. If laws of like character should be enacted in the several states of the Union, the effect would be in the highest degree mischievous. Slavery as an institution tolerated by law would, it is true, have disappeared from our country, but there would remain a power in the states, by sinister legislation, to interfere with the full enjoyment of the blessings of freedom; to regulate civil rights, common to all citizens, upon the basis of race; and to place in a condition of legal inferiority a large body of American citizens, now constituting a part of the political community called the people of the United States, for whom and by whom, through representatives, our government is administered. Such a system is inconsistent with the guarantee given by the Constitution to each state of a republican form of government, and may be stricken down by congressional action, or by the courts in the discharge of their solemn duty to maintain the supreme law of the land, anything in the Constitution or laws of any state to the contrary notwithstanding.

For the reasons stated, I am constrained to withhold my assent from the opinion and judgment of the majority.

Selections 21a–21f

AS SEEN BY PRESIDENT
THEODORE ROOSEVELT*

The following selections consist of excerpts from the speeches of Theodore Roosevelt.

21a. Duty of the Educated Negro

Remember . . . that no help can permanently avail you save as you yourselves develop capacity for self-help. You young colored men and women educated at Tuskegee must by precept and example lead your fellows toward sober, industrious, law-abiding lives. You are in honor bound to join hands in favor of law and order and to war against all crime, and especially against all crime by men of your own race; for the heaviest wrong done by the criminal is the wrong to his own race. You must teach the people of your race that they must scrupulously observe any contract into which they in good faith enter, no matter whether it is hard to keep or not. If you save money, secure homes, become taxpayers, and lead clean, decent, modest lives, you will win the respect of your neighbors of both races. Let each man strive to excel his fellows only by rendering substantial service to the community in which he lives. The colored people have many difficulties to pass through, but these difficulties will be surmounted if only the policy of reason and common sense is pursued. You have made real and great progress. [At Tuskegee Institute, Tuskegee, Ala., October 24, 1905.]

21b. Education of the Negro

The white man, if he is wise, will decline to allow the Negroes in a mass to grow to manhood and womanhood without education.

* From *Theodore Roosevelt Cyclopedia*, Albert Bushnell Hart and Herbert Ronald Ferleger (editors), New York: Roosevelt Memorial Assn., 1941, pp. 378, 379, 380, 381.

Unquestionably education such as is obtained in our public schools does not do everything toward making a man a good citizen; but it does much.

. . . Of course the best type of education for the colored man, taken as a whole, is such education as is conferred in schools like Hampton and Tuskegee; where the boys and girls, the young men and young women, are trained industrially as well as in the ordinary public-school branches. The graduates of these schools turn out well in the great majority of cases, and hardly any of them become criminals, while what little criminality there is never takes the form of that brutal violence which invites lynch-law. Every graduate of these schools—and for the matter of that every other colored man or woman—who leads a life so useful and honorable as to win the good-will and respect of those whites whose neighbor he or she is, thereby helps the whole colored race as it can be helped in no other way; for next to the Negro himself, the man who can do most to help the Negro is his white neighbor. . . . [Sixth Annual Message, Washington, December 3, 1906.]

21c. Future of the Negro

It is true of the colored man, as it is true of the white man, that in the long run his fate must depend far more upon his own effort than upon the efforts of any outside friend. Every vicious, venal, or ignorant colored man is an even greater foe to his own race than to the community as a whole. The colored man's self-respect entitles him to do that share in the political work of the country which is warranted by his individual ability and integrity and the position he has won for himself. But the prime requisite of the race is moral and industrial uplifting.

Laziness and shiftlessness, these, and above all, vice and criminality of every kind, are evils more potent for harm to the black race than all acts of oppression of white men put together. The colored man who fails to condemn crime in another colored man, who fails to co-operate in all lawful ways in bringing colored criminals to justice, is the worst enemy of his own people, as well as an enemy to all the people. Law-abiding black men should, for the sake of their race, be foremost in relentless and unceasing warfare against law-breaking black men. If the standards of private morality and industrial efficiency can be raised high enough among the black race, then its future on this continent is secure. The stability and purity of the home is vital to the welfare of the black race, as it is to the welfare of every race. [At Lincoln dinner, Republican Club of New York City, February 13, 1905.]

21d.   Square Deal for the Negro

It is a good thing that the guard around the tomb of Lincoln should be composed of colored soldiers. It was my own good fortune at Santiago to serve beside colored troops. A man who is good enough to shed his blood for the country is good enough to be given a square deal afterward. More than that no man is entitled to, and less than that no man shall have. [At Lincoln Monument, Springfield, Ill., June 4, 1903.]

21e.   The Negro in the North

The attitude of the North toward the Negro is far from what it should be and there is need that the North also should act in good faith upon the principle of giving to each man what is justly due him, of treating him on his worth as a man, granting him no special favors, but denying him no proper opportunity for labor and the reward of labor. [At Lincoln dinner, Republican Club of New York City, February 13, 1905.]

21f.   Solution of the Negro Problem

The Negroes were formerly held in slavery. This was a wrong which legislation could remedy, and which could not be remedied except by legislation. Accordingly they were set free by law. This having been done, many of their friends believed that in some way, by additional legislation, we could at once put them on an intellectual, social, and business equality with the whites. The effort has failed completely. In large sections of the country the Negroes are not treated as they should be treated, and politically in particular the frauds upon them have been so gross and shameful as to awaken not merely indignation but bitter wrath; yet the best friends of the Negro admit that his hope lies, not in legislation, but in the constant working of those often unseen forces of the national life which are greater than all legislation. [*Reviews of Reviews,* January 1897.]

. . . I have not been able to think out any solution of the terrible problem offered by the presence of the Negro on this continent, but of one thing I am sure, and that is that inasmuch as he is here and can neither be killed nor driven away, the only wise and honorable and Christian thing to do is to treat each black man and each white man strictly on his merits as a man, giving him no more and no less than he shows himself worthy to have. I say I am "sure" that this

is the right solution. Of course I know that we see through a glass
dimly, and, after all, it may be that I am wrong; but if I am, then
all my thoughts and beliefs are wrong, and my whole way of looking at life is wrong. At any rate, while I am in public life, however
short a time that may be, I am in honor bound to act up to my beliefs and convictions. I do not intend to offend the prejudices of any
one else, but neither do I intend to allow their prejudices to make
me false to my principles. [To Albion W. Tourgee, November 8,
1901.]

Selection 22

THE ATLANTA EXPOSITION
ADDRESS, 1895

BOOKER T. WASHINGTON*

*Booker T. Washington, the Negro educator, was one of the most
distinguished citizens in the United States. His reputation as
an educator, leader, and a man of enormous influence among Negroes and whites was recognized by President Theodore Roosevelt,
who invited him to dine at the White House, and William Howard
Taft, as well as by industrialists and philanthropists.*

The Atlanta Exposition, at which I had been asked to make an
address as a representative of the Negro race, was opened with a
short address from Governor Bullock. After other interesting exercises, including an invocation from Bishop Nelson, of Georgia, a
dedicatory ode by Albert Howell, Jr., and addresses by the president
of the Exposition and Mrs. Joseph Thompson, the president of the
Women's Board, Governor Bullock introduced me with the words,

* From Booker T. Washington, *Up From Slavery*, New York: Avon Books, 1965,
pp. 145–57.

"We have with us today a representative of Negro enterprise and Negro civilization."

When I arose to speak, there was considerable cheering, especially from the colored people. As I remember it now, the thing that was uppermost in my mind was the desire to say something that would cement the friendship of the races and bring about hearty cooperation between them. So far as my outward surroundings were concerned, the only thing that I recall distinctly now is that when I got up, I saw thousands of eyes looking intently into my face. The following is the address which I delivered:

Mr. President and Gentlemen of the Board of Directors and Citizens:

One-third of the population of the South is of the Negro race. No enterprise seeking the material, civil, or moral welfare of this section can disregard this element of our population and reach the highest success. I but convey to you, Mr. President and Directors, the sentiment of the masses of my race when I say that in no way have the value and manhood of the American Negro been more fittingly and generously recognized than by the managers of this magnificent exposition at every stage of its progress. It is a recognition that will do more to cement the friendship of the two races than any occurrence since the dawn of our freedom.

Not only this, but the opportunity here afforded will awaken among us a new era of industrial progress. Ignorant and inexperienced, it is not strange that in the first years of our new life we began at the top instead of at the bottom; that a seat in Congress or the state legislature was more sought than real estate or industrial skill; that the political convention or stump speaking had more attractions than starting a dairy farm or truck garden.

A ship lost at sea for many days suddenly sighted a friendly vessel. From the mast of the unfortunate vessel was seen a signal, "Water, water; we die of thirst!" The answer from the friendly vessel at once came back, "Cast down your bucket where you are." A second time the signal, "Water, water; send us water!" ran up from the distressed vessel, and was answered, "Cast down your bucket where you are." And a third and fourth signal for water was answered, "Cast down your bucket where you are." The captain of the distressed vessel, at last heeding the injunction, cast down his bucket, and it came up full of fresh, sparkling water from the mouth of the Amazon River. To those of my race who depend on bettering their condition in a foreign land or who underestimate the importance of cultivating friendly relations with the Southern white man, who is their next-door neighbor, I would say: "Cast down your bucket where you are"—cast it down in making friends in every manly way of the people of all races by whom we are surrounded.

Cast it down in agriculture, mechanics, in commerce, in domestic service, and in the professions. And in this connection it is well to bear in mind that whatever other sins the South may be called to bear, when it comes to business, pure and simple, it is in the South that the Negro is given a man's chance in the commercial world, and in nothing is this exposition more eloquent than in emphasizing this chance. Our greatest danger is that in the great leap from slavery to freedom we may overlook the fact that the masses of us are to live by the productions of our hands, and fail to keep in mind that we shall prosper in proportion as we learn to dignify and glorify common labor and put brains and skill into the common occupations of life; shall prosper in proportion as we learn to draw the line between the superficial and the substantial, the ornamental gewgaws of life and the useful. No race can prosper till it learns that there is as much dignity in tilling a field as in writing a poem. It is at the bottom of life we must begin, and not at the top. Nor should we permit our grievances to overshadow our opportunities.

To those of the white race who look to the incoming of those of foreign birth and strange tongue and habits for the prosperity of the South, were I permitted I would repeat what I say to my own race, "Cast down your bucket where you are." Cast it down among the eight millions of Negroes whose habits you know, whose fidelity and love you have tested in days when to have proved treacherous meant the ruin of your firesides. Cast down your bucket among these people who have, without strikes and labor wars, tilled your fields, cleared your forests, builded your railroads and cities, and brought forth treasures from the bowels of the earth, and helped make possible this magnificent representation of the progress of the South. Casting down your bucket among my people, helping and encouraging them as you are doing on these grounds, and to education of head, hand, and heart, you will find that they will buy your surplus land, make blossom the waste places in your fields, and run your factories. While doing this, you can be sure in the future, as in the past, that you and your families will be surrounded by the most patient, faithful, law-abiding, and unresentful people that the world has seen. As we have proved our loyalty to you in the past, in nursing your children, watching by the sickbed of your mothers and fathers, and often following them with tear-dimmed eyes to their graves, so in the future, in our humble way, we shall stand by you with a devotion that no foreigner can approach, ready to lay down our lives, if need be, in defense of yours, interlacing our industrial, commercial, civil, and religious life with yours in a way that shall make the interests of both races one. In all things that are purely social we can be as separate as the fingers, yet one as the hand in all things essential to mutual progress.

There is no defense or security for any of us except in the highest intelligence and development of all. If anywhere there are efforts tending to curtail the fullest growth of the Negro, let these efforts be turned into stimulating, encouraging, and making him the most useful and intelligent citizen. Effort or means so invested will pay a thousand per cent interest. These efforts will be twice blessed—"blessing him that gives and him that takes."

There is no escape through law of man or God from the inevitable:—

> The laws of changeless justice bind
> Oppressor with oppressed;
> And close as sin and suffering joined
> We march to fate abreast.

Nearly sixteen millions of hands will aid you in pulling the load upward, or they will pull against you the load downward. We shall constitute one-third and more of the ignorance and crime of the South, or one-third its intelligence and progress; we shall contribute one-third to the business and industrial prosperity of the South, or we shall prove a veritable body of death, stagnating, depressing, retarding every effort to advance the body politic.

Gentlemen of the Exposition, as we present to you our humble effort at an exhibition of our progress, you must not expect over much. Starting thirty years ago with ownership here and there in a few quilts and pumpkins and chickens (gathered from miscellaneous sources), remember the path that has led from these to the inventions and production of agricultural implements, buggies, steam-engines, newspapers, books, statuary, carving, paintings, the management of drugstores and banks, has not been trodden without contact with thorns and thistles. While we take pride in what we exhibit as a result of our independent efforts, we do not for a moment forget that our part in this exhibition would fall far short of your expectations but for the constant help that has come to our educational life, not only from the southern states, but especially from northern philanthropists, who have made their gifts a constant stream of blessing and encouragement.

The wisest among my race understand that the agitation of questions of social equality is the extremest folly, and that progress in the enjoyment of all the privileges that will come to us must be the result of severe and constant struggle rather than of artificial forcing. No race that has anything to contribute to the markets of the world is long in any degree ostracized. It is important and right that all privileges of the law be ours, but it is vastly more important that we be prepared for the exercises of these privileges. The opportunity to earn a dollar in a factory just now is worth infinitely more than the opportunity to spend a dollar in an opera house.

In conclusion, may I repeat that nothing in thirty years has given us more hope and encouragement and drawn us so near to you of the white race, as this opportunity offered by the Exposition; and here bending, as it were, over the altar that represents the results of the struggles of your race and mine, both starting practically empty-handed three decades ago, I pledge that in your effort to work out the great and intricate problem which God has laid at the doors of the South, you shall have at all times the patient, sympathetic help of my race. Only let this be constantly in mind: that, while from representations in these buildings of the product of field, of forest, of mine, of factory, letters, and art much good will come, yet far above and beyond material benefits will be that higher good, that, let us pray God, will come, in a blotting out of sectional differences and racial animosities and suspicions, in a determination to administer absolute justice, in a willing obedience among all classes to the mandates of law. This, coupled with our material prosperity, will bring into our beloved South a new heaven and a new earth.

. . . The colored people and the colored newspapers at first seemed to be greatly pleased with the character of my Atlanta address, as well as with its reception. But after the first burst of enthusiasm began to die away, and the colored people began reading the speech in cold type, some of them seemed to feel that they had been hypnotized. They seemed to feel that I had been too liberal in my remarks toward the southern whites, and that I had not spoken out strongly enough for what they termed the "rights" of the race. For a while there was a reaction, so far as a certain element of my own race was concerned, but later these reactionary ones seemed to have been won over to my way of believing and acting.

. . . I am often asked to express myself more freely than I do upon the political condition and the political future of my race. These recollections of my experience in Atlanta give me the opportunity to do so briefly. My own belief is, although I have never before said so in so many words, that the time will come when the Negro in the South will be accorded all the political rights which his ability, character, and material possessions entitle him to. I think, though, that the opportunity to freely exercise such political rights will not come in any large degree through outside or artificial forcing, but will be accorded to the Negro by the southern white people themselves, and that they will protect him in the exercise of those rights. Just as soon as the South gets over the old feeling that it is being forced by "foreigners," or "aliens," to do something which it does not want to do, I believe that the change in the direction that I have indicated is going to begin. In fact, there are indications that it is already beginning in a slight degree.

Let me illustrate my meaning. Suppose that some months before the opening of the Atlanta Exposition there had been a general demand from the press and public platform outside the South that a Negro be given a place on the opening program, and that a Negro be placed upon the board of jurors of award. Would any such recognition of the race have taken place? I do not think so. The Atlanta officials went as far as they did because they felt it to be a pleasure, as well as a duty, to reward what they considered merit in the Negro race. Say what we will, there is something in human nature which we cannot blot out, which makes one man, in the end, recognize and reward merit in another, regardless of color or race.

I believe it is the duty of the Negro—as the greater part of the race is already doing—to deport himself modestly in regard to political claims, depending upon the slow but sure influences that proceed from the possession of property, intelligence, and high character for the full recognition of his political rights. I think that the according of the full exercise of political rights is going to be a matter of natural, slow growth, not an overnight, gourd-vine affair. I do not believe that the Negro should cease voting, for a man cannot learn the exercise of self-government by ceasing to vote, any more than a boy can learn to swim by keeping out of the water, but I do believe that in his voting he should more and more be influenced by those of intelligence and character who are his next-door neighbors.

I know colored men who, through the encouragement, help, and advice of southern white people, have accumulated thousands of dollars' worth of property, but who, at the same time, would never think of going to those same persons for advice concerning the casting of their ballots. This, it seems to me, is unwise and unreasonable, and should cease. In saying this I do not mean that the Negro should truckle, or not vote from principle, for the instant he ceases to vote from principle he loses the confidence and respect of the southern white man even.

I do not believe that any state should make a law that permits an ignorant and poverty-stricken white man to vote, and prevents a black man in the same condition from voting. Such a law is not only unjust, but it will react, as all unjust laws do, in time; for the effect of such a law is to encourage the Negro to secure education and property, and at the same time it encourages the white man to remain in ignorance and poverty. I believe that in time, through the operation of intelligence and friendly race relations, all cheating at the ballot-box in the South will cease. It will become apparent that the white man who begins by cheating a Negro out of his ballot soon learns to cheat a white man out of his, and that the man who does this ends his career of dishonesty by the theft of property or by some equally serious crime. In my opinion, the time will come when the South will encourage all of its citizens to vote. It will see that it pays better, from every standpoint, to have healthy, vigorous life than to have that political stagnation which always results when one-half of the population has no share and no interest in the government.

As a rule, I believe in universal, free suffrage, but I believe that in the South we are confronted with peculiar conditions that justify the protection of the ballot in many of the states, for a while at least, whether by an educational test, a property test, or by both combined; but whatever tests are required, they should be made to apply with equal and exact justice to both races.

Selection 23

NEGRO LEADERS

W. E. B. DU BOIS*

W. E. B. Du Bois opposed the Washington position as being too much concerned with work and money and too little concerned with higher education and suffrage. Labeling the Atlanta Exposition Speech as the "Atlanta Compromise," he proposed a program of vigorous action to achieve equality and full citizenship.

Those Negroes who agreed with Du Bois met in 1905 at Niagara Falls, Canada and drew up a program of action. This Niagara move-

* From William E. B. Du Bois, *The Souls of Black Folk*, in *Three Negro Classics*, New York: Avon Books, 1965, pp. 245–50.

*ment served as the first important step in a movement which led to
the formation of the NAACP in 1910.*

. . . Then came the new leader. Nearly all the former ones had become leaders by the silent suffrage of their fellows, had sought to
lead their own people alone, and were usually, save Douglass, little
known outside their race. But Booker T. Washington arose as essentially the leader not of one race but of two,—a compromiser between the South, the North, and the Negro. Naturally the Negroes
resented, at first bitterly, signs of a compromise which surrendered
their civil and political rights, even though this was to be exchanged
for larger chances of economic development. The rich and dominat-
ing North, however, was not only weary of the race problem, but
was investing largely in Southern enterprises, and welcomed any
method of peaceful cooperation. Thus, by national opinion, the
Negroes began to recognize Mr. Washington's leadership; and the
voice of criticism was hushed.

Mr. Washington represents in Negro thought the old attitude of
adjustment and submission; but adjustment at such a peculiar time
as to make his programme unique. This is an age of unusual economic development, and Mr. Washington's programme naturally
takes an economic cast, becoming a gospel of Work and Money to
such an extent as apparently almost completely to overshadow the
higher aims of life. Moreover, this is an age when the more advanced races are coming in closer contact with the less developed
races, and the race-feeling is therefore intensified; and Mr. Washington's programme practically accepts the alleged inferiority of the
Negro races. Again, in our own land, the reaction from the sentiment of war time has given impetus to race-prejudice against Negroes, and Mr. Washington withdraws many of the high demands
of Negroes as men and American citizens. In other periods of intensified prejudice all the Negro's tendency to self-assertion has been
called forth; at this period a policy of submission is advocated. In
the history of nearly all other races and peoples the doctrine preached
at such crises has been that manly self-respect is worth more than
lands and houses, and that a people who voluntarily surrender such
respect, or cease striving for it, are not worth civilizing.

In answer to this, it has been claimed that the Negro can survive
only through submission. Mr. Washington distinctly asks that black
people give up, at least for the present, three things,—

First, political power,

Second, insistence on civil rights,

Third, higher education of Negro youth,—
and concentrate all their energies on industrial education, the accumulation of wealth, and the conciliation of the South. This policy has been courageously and insistently advocated for over fifteen years, and has been triumphant for perhaps ten years. As a result of this tender of the palm-branch, what has been the return? In these years there have occurred:

1. The disfranchisement of the Negro.
2. The legal creation of a distinct status of civil inferiority for the Negro.
3. The steady withdrawal of aid from institutions for the higher training of the Negro.

These movements are not, to be sure, direct results of Mr. Washington's teachings; but his propaganda has, without a shadow of doubt, helped their speedier accomplishment. The question then comes: Is it possible, and probable, that nine millions of men can make effective progress in economic lines if they are deprived of political rights, made a servile caste, and allowed only the most meagre chance for developing their exceptional men? If history and reason give any distinct answer to these questions, it is an emphatic *No.* And Mr. Washington thus faces the triple paradox of his career:

1. He is striving nobly to make Negro artisans businessmen and property-owners; but it is utterly impossible, under modern competitive methods, for workingmen and property-owners to defend their rights and exist without the right of suffrage.
2. He insists on thrift and self-respect, but at the same time counsels a silent submission to civic inferiority such as is bound to sap the manhood of any race in the long run.
3. He advocates common-school and industrial training, and depreciates institutions of higher learning; but neither the Negro common-schools, nor Tuskegee itself, could remain open a day were it not for teachers trained in Negro colleges, or trained by their graduates.

This triple paradox in Mr. Washington's position is the object of criticism by two classes of colored Americans. One class is spiritually descended from Toussaint the Savior, through Gabriel, Vesey, and Turner, and they represent the attitude of revolt and revenge; they hate the white South blindly and distrust the white race generally, and so far as they agree on definite action, think that the Negro's only hope lies in emigration beyond the borders of the United States. And yet, by the irony of fate, nothing has more effectually made this programme seem hopeless than the recent course of the United States toward weaker and

darker peoples in the West Indies, Hawaii, and the Philippines,—
for where in the world may we go and be safe from lying and
brute force?

The other class of Negroes who cannot agree with Mr. Washington has hitherto said little aloud. They deprecate the sight of
scattered counsels, of internal disagreement; and especially they
dislike making their criticism of a useful and earnest man an excuse
for a general discharge of venom from small-minded opponents.
Nevertheless, the questions involved are so fundamental and serious that it is difficult to see how men like Grimkes, Kelly Miller,
J. W. E. Bowen, and other representatives of this group, can
much longer be silent. Such men feel in conscience bound to ask
of this nation three things:

1. The right to vote.
2. Civic equality.
3. The education of youth according to ability.

They acknowledge Mr. Washington's invaluable service in counselling patience and courtesy in such demands; they do not ask
that ignorant black men vote when ignorant whites are debarred,
or that any reasonable restrictions in the suffrage should not be
applied; they know that the low social level of the mass of the
race is responsible for much discrimination against it, but they also
know, and the nation knows, that relentless color-prejudice is
more often a cause than a result of the Negro's degradation; they
seek the abatement of this relic of barbarism, and not its systematic
encouragement and pampering by all agencies of social power from
the Associated Press to the Church of Christ. They advocate, with
Mr. Washington, a broad system of Negro common schools supplemented by thorough industrial training; but they are surprised
that a man of Mr. Washington's insight cannot see that no such
educational system ever has rested or can rest on any other basis
than that of the well-equipped college and university, and they
insist that there is a demand for a few such institutions throughout
the South to train the best of the Negro youth as teachers, professional men, and leaders.

This group of men honor Mr. Washington for his attitude of
conciliation toward the white South; they accept the "Atlanta
Compromise" in its broadest interpretation; they recognize, with
him, many signs of promise, many men of high purpose and fair
judgment, in this section; they know that no easy task has been
laid upon a region already tottering under heavy burdens. But,
nevertheless, they insist that the way to truth and right lies in
straightforward honesty, not in indiscriminate flattery; in praising
those of the South who do well and criticising uncompromisingly

those who do ill; in taking advantage of the opportunities at hand and urging their fellows to do the same, but at the same time in remembering that only a firm adherence to their higher ideals and aspirations will ever keep those ideals within the realm of possibility. They do not expect that the free right to vote, to enjoy civic rights, and to be educated, will come in a moment; they do not expect to see the bias and prejudices of years disappear at the blast of a trumpet; but they are absolutely certain that the way for a people to gain their reasonable rights is not by voluntarily throwing them away and insisting that they do not want them; that the way for a people to gain respect is not by continually belittling and ridiculing themselves; that, on the contrary, Negroes must insist continually, in season and out of season, that voting is necessary to modern manhood, that color discrimination is barbarism, and that black boys need education as well as white boys.

In failing thus to state plainly and unequivocally the legitimate demands of their people, even at the cost of opposing an honored leader, the thinking classes of American Negroes would shirk a heavy responsibility,—a responsibility to themselves, a responsibility to the struggling masses, a responsibility to the darker races of men whose future depends so largely on this American experiment, but especially a responsibility to this nation,—this common Fatherland. It is wrong to encourage a man or a people in evil-doing; it is wrong to aid and abet a national crime simply because it is unpopular not to do so. The growing spirit of kindliness and reconciliation between the North and South after the frightful difference of a generation ago ought to be a source of deep congratulation to all, and especially to those whose mistreatment caused the war; but if that reconciliation is to be marked by the industrial slavery and civic death of those same black men, with permanent legislation into a position of inferiority, then those black men, if they are really men, are called upon by every consideration of patriotism and loyalty to oppose such a course by all civilized methods, even though such opposition involves disagreement with Mr. Booker T. Washington. We have no right to sit silently by while the inevitable seeds are sown for a harvest of disaster to our children, black and white.

Selection 24

HOW THE NAACP BEGAN

MARY WHITE OVINGTON *

*Mary White Ovington, a social worker in New York, was very
much interested in the problems of the Negro. After reading an
article about the terrible Springfield, Ohio riot of 1908 in which
two Negroes had been lynched, four white men had been killed,
and more than seventy persons had been injured, she decided to
contact some friends and call a meeting of persons interested in trying to achieve civil and political liberty for all Americans. The conference was called for Lincoln's Birthday in 1909, and in the following months the NAACP was launched.*

The National Association for the Advancement of Colored People
is five years old—old enough, it is believed, to have a history; and
I, who am perhaps its first member, have been chosen as the person
to recite it. As its work since 1910 has been set forth in its annual
reports, I shall make it my task to show how it came into existence
and to tell of its first months of work.

In the summer of 1908, the country was shocked by the account
of the race riots at Springfield, Illinois. Here, in the home of
Abraham Lincoln, a mob containing many of the town's "best
citizens," raged for two days, killed and wounded scores of Negroes, and drove thousands from the city. Articles on the subject
appeared in newspapers and magazines. Among them was one in
the *Independent* of September 3d, by William English Walling,
entitled "Race War in the North." After describing the atrocities
committed against the colored people, Mr. Walling declared:

"Either the spirit of the abolitionists, of Lincoln and of Lovejoy

* Mary White Ovington, *How the National Association for the Advancement of
Colored People Began*, New York: NAACP, as originally printed in 1914.

must be revived and we must come to treat the Negro on a plane of absolute political and social equality, or Vardaman and Tillman will soon have transferred the race war to the North." And he ended with these words, "Yet who realizes the seriousness of the situation, and what large and powerful body of citizens is ready to come to their aid?"

It so happened that one of Mr. Walling's readers accepted his question and answered it. For four years I had been studying the status of the Negro in New York. I had investigated his housing conditions, his health, his opportunities for work. I had spent many months in the South, and at the time of Mr. Walling's article, I was living in a New York Negro tenement on a Negro street. And my investigations and my surroundings led me to believe with the writer of the article that "the spirit of the abolitionists must be revived."

So I wrote to Mr. Walling, and after some time, for he was in the West, we met in New York in the first week of the year 1909. With us was Dr. Henry Moskowitz, now prominent in the administration of John Purroy Mitchell, Mayor of New York. It was then that the National Association for the Advancement of Colored People was born.

It was born in a little room of a New York apartment. It is to be regretted that there are no minutes of the first meeting, for they would make interesting if unparliamentary reading. Mr. Walling had spent some years in Russia where his wife, working in the cause of the revolutionists, had suffered imprisonment; and he expressed his belief that the Negro was treated with greater inhumanity in the United States than the Jew was treated in Russia. As Mr. Walling is a Southerner we listened with conviction. I knew something of the Negro's difficulty in securing decent employment in the North and of the insolent treatment awarded him at Northern hotels and restaurants, and I voiced my protest. Dr. Moskowitz, with his broad knowledge of conditions among New York's helpless immigrants, aided us in properly interpreting our facts. And so we talked and talked voicing our indignation.

Of course, we wanted to do something at once that should move the country. It was January. Why not choose Lincoln's birthday, February 12, to open our campaign? We decided, therefore, that a wise, immediate action would be the issuing on Lincoln's birthday of a call for a national conference on the Negro question. At this conference we might discover the beginnings, at least, of that "large and powerful body of citizens" of which Mr. Walling had written.

And so the meeting adjourned. Something definite was determined upon, and our next step was to call others into our councils. We at once turned to Mr. Oswald Garrison Villard, president of the N. Y. Evening Post Company. He received our suggestions with enthusiasm, and aided us in securing the co-operation of able and representative men and women. It was he who drafted the Lincoln's birthday call and helped to give it wide publicity. I give the Call in its entirety with the signatures since it expresses, I think, better than anything else we have published, the spirit of those who are active in the Association's cause.

"The celebration of the Centennial of the birth of Abraham Lincoln, wide-spread and grateful as it may be, will fail to justify itself if it takes no note of and makes no recognition of the colored men and women for whom the great Emancipator labored to assure freedom. Besides a day of rejoicing, Lincoln's birthday in 1909 should be one of taking stock of the nation's progress since 1865.

"How far has it lived up to the obligations imposed upon it by the Emancipation Proclamation? How far has it gone in assuring to each and every citizen, irrespective of color, the equality of opportunity and equality before the law, which underlie our American institutions and are guaranteed by the Constitution?

"If Mr. Lincoln could revisit this country in the flesh, he would be disheartened and discouraged. He would learn that on January 1, 1909, Georgia had rounded out a new confederacy by disfranchising the Negro, after the manner of all the other Southern States. He would learn that the Supreme Court of the United States, supposedly a bulwark of American liberties, had refused every opportunity to pass squarely upon this disfranchisement of millions, by laws avowedly discriminatory and openly enforced in such manner that the white men may vote and black men be without a vote in their government; he would discover, therefore, that taxation without representation is the lot of millions of wealth-producing American citizens, in whose hands rests the economic progress and welfare of an entire section of the country.

"He would learn that the Supreme Court, according to the official statement of one of its own judges in the Berea College case, has laid down the principle that if an individual State chooses, it may 'make it a crime for white and colored persons to frequent the same market place at the same time, or appear in an assemblage of citizens convened to consider questions of a public or political nature in which all citizens, without regard to race, are equally interested.'

"In many states Lincoln would find justice enforced, if at all, by judges elected by one element in a community to pass upon the liberties and lives of another. He would see the black men and women, for whose freedom a hundred thousand of soldiers gave their lives, set apart in trains, in which they pay first-class fares for third-class service, and segregated in railway stations and in places of entertainment; he would observe that State after State declines to do its elementary duty in preparing the Negro through education for the best exercise of citizenship.

"Added to this, the spread of lawless attacks upon the Negro, North, South, and West—even in the Springfield made famous by Lincoln—often accompanied by revolting brutalities, sparing neither sex nor age nor youth, could but shock the author of the sentiment that 'government of the people, by the people, for the people, shall not perish from the earth.'

"Silence under these conditions means tacit approval. The indifference of the North is already responsible for more than one assault upon democracy, and every such attack reacts as unfavorably upon whites as upon blacks. Discrimination once permitted cannot be bridled; recent history in the South shows that in forging chains for the Negroes the white voters are forging chains for themselves. 'A house divided against itself cannot stand'; this government cannot exist half-slave and half-free any better to-day than it could in 1861.

"Hence we call upon all the believers in democracy to join in a national conference for the discussion of present evils, the voicing of protests, and the renewal of the struggle for civil and political liberty."

. . .

It was thus decided that we should hold a conference, and the next two months were busily spent arranging for it. . . . It was agreed that the conference should be by invitation only, with the one open meeting at Cooper Union. Over a thousand people were invited, the Charity Organization Hall was secured, and, on the evening of May 30th, the conference opened with an informal reception at the Henry Street Settlement. . . . The next morning our deliberations began.

We have had five conferences since 1909, but I doubt whether any have been so full of a questioning surprise, amounting swiftly to enthusiasm, on the part of the white people in attendance. These men and women, engaged in religious, social and educational work, for the first time met the Negro who demands, not a pittance, but his full rights in the commonwealth. They received a stimulating shock and one which they enjoyed. They did not want to leave the meeting. We conferred all the time, formally and informally, and the Association gained in those days many of the earnest and uncompromising men and women who have since worked unfalteringly in its cause. Mr. William Hayes Ward, senior editor of the *Independent,* opened the conference, and Mr. Charles Edward Russell, always the friend of those who struggle for opportunity, presided at the stormy session at the close. The full proceedings have been published by the Association.

Out of this conference we formed a committee of forty. . . . We were greatly hampered by lack of funds. Important national work would present itself which we were unable to handle. But our secertary was an excellent organizer, and at the end of a year we had held four mass meetings, had distributed thousands of pamphlets, and numbered our membership in the hundreds. In May, 1910, we held our second conference in New York, and again our meetings were attended by earnest, interested people. It was then that we organized a permanent body to be known as the National Association for the Advancement of Colored People. Its officers were:

National President, Moorfield Storey, Boston; Chairman of the Executive Committee, William English Walling; Treasurer, John E. Milholland; Disbursing Treasurer, Oswald Garrison Villard; Executive Secretary, Frances Blascoer; Director of Publicity and Research, Dr. W. E. B. Du Bois.

The securing of a sufficient financial support to warrant our calling Dr. Du Bois from Atlanta University into an executive office in the Association was the most important work of the second conference.

When Dr. Du Bois came to us we were brought closely in touch with an organization of colored people, formed in 1905 at Niagara and known as the Niagara Movement. This organization had held important conferences at Niagara, Harpers Ferry, and Boston, and had attempted a work of legal redress along very much the lines upon which the National Association for the Advancement of Colored People was working. Its platform, as presented in a statement in 1905, ran as follows:

Freedom of speech and criticism.

An unfettered and unsubsidized press.

Manhood suffrage.

The abolition of all caste distinctions based simply on race and color.

The recognition of the principle of human brotherhood as a practical present creed.

The recognition of the highest and best training as the monopoly of no class or race.

A belief in the dignity of labor.

United effort to realize these ideals under wise and courageous leadership.

In 1910 it had conducted important civil rights cases and had in its membership some of the ablest colored lawyers in the country, with Mr. W. Ashbie Hawkins, who has since worked with our Association, on the Baltimore Segregation acts, as its treasurer.

The Niagara Movement, hampered as it was by lack of funds and by a membership confined to one race only, continued to push slowly on, but when the larger possibilities of this new Association were clear, the members of the Niagara Movement were advised to join, as the platforms were practically identical. Many of the most prominent members of the Niagara Movement thus brought their energy and ability into the service of the Association, and eight are now serving on its Board of Directors.

Our history, after 1910, may be read in our annual reports, and in the numbers of THE CRISIS. We opened two offices in the *Evening Post* building. With Dr. Du Bois came Mr. Frank M. Turner, a Wilberforce graduate, who has shown great efficiency in handling our books. In November of 1910 appeared the first number of THE CRISIS, with Dr. Du Bois as editor, and Mary Dunlop MacLean, whose death has been the greatest loss the Association has known, as managing editor. Our propaganda work was put on a national footing, our legal work was well under way and we were in truth, a National Association, pledged to a nation-wide work for justice to the Negro race.

I remember the afternoon that THE CRISIS received its name. We were sitting around the conventional table that seems a necessary adjunct to every Board, and were having an informal talk regarding the new magazine. We touched the subject of poetry.

"There is a poem of Lowell's," I said, "that means more to me to-day than any other poem in the world—'The Present Crisis.'"

Mr. Walling looked up. "The Crisis," he said. "There is the name for your magazine, THE CRISIS."

And if we had a creed to which our members, black and white, our branches North and South and East and West, our college societies, our children's circles, should all subscribe, it should be the lines of Lowell's noble verse, lines that are as true to-day as when they were written seventy years ago:

Once to every man and nation comes the moment to decide,
In the strife of Truth with Falsehood for the good or evil side;
Some great Cause, God's New Messiah, offering each the bloom or blight,

Parts the goats upon the left hand, and the sheep upon the right,
And the choice goes by forever 'twixt that darkness and that light.

Then to side with Truth is noble when we share her wretched crust,
Ere her cause bring fame and profit, and 'tis prosperous to be just;
Then it is the brave man chooses, while the coward stands aside,
Doubting in his abject spirit, till his Lord is crucified,
And the multitude make virtue of the faith they had denied.

BOOK TWO

A Struggle with Ideas:

Means and Ends

PART I

NEGRO LEADERS, ORGANIZATIONS, METHODS, AND GOALS

Selections 1a–1b

THE ROOTS OF NEGRO LEADERSHIP

RAY STANNARD BAKER*

These two selections show the torment the Negro faced in trying to achieve dignity for himself. The time is the early part of the twentieth century.

1a. The New Racial Consciousness Among Negroes

One of the natural and inevitable results of the effort of the white man to set the Negro off, as a race, by himself, is to awaken in him a new consciousness—a sort of racial consciousness. It drives the Negroes together for defence and offence. Many able Negroes, some largely of white blood, cut off from all opportunity of suc-

---

* From Ray Stannard Baker, *Following the Color Line: American Negro Citizenship in the Progressive Era*, New York: Harper & Row, 1964, pp. 38–39, 216. [Originally published in 1908 by Doubleday, Page & Co.]

cess in the greater life of the white man, become of necessity leaders of their own people. And one of their chief efforts consists in urging Negroes to work together and to stand together. In this they are only developing the instinct of defence against the white man which has always been latent in the race. This instinct exhibits itself in the way in which the mass of Negroes sometimes refuse to turn over a criminal of their colour to white justice; it is like the instinctive clannishness of the Highland Scotch or the peasant Irish. I don't know how many Southern people have told me in different ways of how extremely difficult it is to get at the real feeling of a Negro, to make him tell what goes on in his clubs and churches or in his innumerable societies.

1b. An Ostracised Race in Ferment

*The Conflict of Negro Parties and Negro Leaders Over Methods
of Dealing with Their Own Problem*

One of the things that has interested me most of all in studying Negro communities, especially in the North, has been to find them so torn by cliques and divided by such wide differences of opinion.

No other element of our population presents a similar condition; the Italians, the Jews, the Germans and especially the Chinese and Japanese are held together not only by a different language, but by ingrained and ancient national habits. They group themselves naturally. But the Negro is an American in language and customs; he knows no other traditions and he has no other conscious history; a large proportion indeed, possess varying degrees of white American blood (restless blood!) and yet the Negro is not accepted as an American. Instead of losing himself gradually in the dominant race, as the Germans, Irish, and Italians are doing, adding those traits or qualities with which Time fashions and modifies this human mosaic called the American nation, the Negro is set apart as a peculiar people.

With every Negro, then, an essential question is: "How shall I meet this attempt to put me off by myself?"

That question in one form or another—politically, industrially, socially—is being met daily, almost hourly, by every Negro in this country. It colours his very life.

"You don't know, and you can't know," a Negro said to me, "what it is to be a problem, to understand that everyone is watching you and studying you, to have your mind constantly on your own actions. It has made us think and talk about ourselves more than other people do. It has made us self-conscious and sensitive."

Selection 2

ORGANIZED PROTEST— THE NAACP AND THE URBAN LEAGUE*

In the opening years of the twentieth century, two important organizations were formed to help the Negro.

The new National Association for the Advancement of Colored People (NAACP) [organized in 1910] states its purpose to be:

To promote equality of rights and eradicate caste or race prejudice among the citizens of the United States; to advance the interest of colored citizens; to secure for them impartial suffrage; and to increase their opportunities for securing justice in the courts, education for their children, employment according to their ability, and complete equality before the law.

Shortly after its organization, the NAACP formed a Legal Committee which, four years later, was to come under the chairmanship of Arthur B. Spingarn of New York. Within five years, committee activity grew from the filing of a petition of pardon for a Negro sharecropper in South Carolina to the filing of a friend-of-the-court brief in the Supreme Court of the United States attacking the constitutionality of Oklahoma's "grandfather clause." From then on it was only a matter of time before NAACP lawyers were arguing civil rights before the highest court in the land.

During this period another private organization dedicated to the eradication of racial discrimination was in its formative years. In 1905, an organization called the League for the Protection of

* From *Freedom to the Free, A Report to the President by the United States Commission on Civil Rights,* Washington, D. C.: U. S. Government Printing Office, 1963, pp. 79–82.

Colored Women was founded by Frances Keller and Mrs. William
H. Baldwin, Jr., to help penniless and homeless Negroes from
southern rural areas, particularly women, to find employment and
homes in New York. The League, which gave industrial training
and offered employment opportunities to both men and women,
inspired the formation of the Committee on Industrial Relations
Among Negroes. By 1910, Mrs. Baldwin and a young doctor of
philosophy named George Edmund Haynes organized the Committee on Urban Conditions Among Negroes because they believed that the problem of adapting the rural, southern Negro to
his new, urban, industrial, northern environment was broader
than just finding jobs. The new committee arranged for the education and training of social workers to organize local Leagues
across the country. The following year a merger of the three
interracial agencies was effected and the new organization subsequently became known as the National Urban League. In the
words of Eugene Kinckle Jones, its executive secretary for thirty
years, the ultimate goal of the Urban League was, "To work itself
out of a job."

Selection 3

THE NEGRO'S PLACE IN
WORLD REORGANIZATION

MARCUS GARVEY*

*Founder of the Universal Negro Improvement Association, Marcus
Garvey came to this country from Jamaica in 1916. An estimated
half million Negroes joined his organization during the 1920s. Garvey ran into financial difficulties and was found guilty of using the
mails to defraud in raising money for his Black Star Line. After*

* From Marcus Garvey, *Philosophy and Opinions of Marcus Garvey, compiled by*
Amy Jacques-Garvey, New York: Universal Publishing House, 1926, Vol. II,
pp. 34–36.

serving a part of his sentence, he was pardoned by President Cool-
idge and deported in 1927 as an undesirable alien.

Gradually we are approaching the time when the Negro peoples
of the world will have either to consciously, through their own
organization, go forward to the point of destiny as laid out by
themselves, or must sit quiescently and see themselves pushed back
into the mire of economic serfdom, to be ultimately crushed by
the grinding mill of exploitation and be exterminated ultimately
by the strong hand of prejudice.

There is no doubt about it that we are living in the age of
world reorganization out of which will come a set program for
the organized races of mankind that will admit of no sympathy
in human affairs, in that we are planning for the great gigantic
struggle of the survival of the fittest group. It becomes each and
every one engaged in this great race for place and position to use
whatsoever influence possible to divert the other fellow's attention
from the real object. In our own sphere in America and the western world we find that we are being camouflaged, not so much
by those with whom we are competing for our economic, political
existence, but by men from within our own race, either as agents
of the opposition or as unconscious fools who are endeavoring
to flatter us into believing that our future should rest with chance
and with Providence, believing that through these agencies will
come the solution of the restless problem. Such leadership is but
preparing us for the time that is bound to befall us if we do not
exert ourselves now toward our own creative purpose. The mission
of the Universal Negro Improvement Association is to arouse
the sleeping consciousness of Negroes everywhere to the point
where we will, as one concerted body, act for our own preservation. By laying the foundation for such we will be able to work
toward the glorious realization of an emancipated race and a constructed nation. Nationhood is the strongest security of any people
and it is for that the Universal Negro Improvement Association
strives at this time. With the clamor of other peoples for a similar
purpose, we raise a noise even to high heaven for the admission
of the Negro into the plan of autonomy.

On every side we hear the cry of white supremacy—in America,
Canada, Australia, Europe, and even South America. There is
no white supremacy beyond the power and strength of the white
man to hold himself against the others. The supremacy of any
race is not permanent; it is a thing only of the time in which the

race finds itself powerful. The whole world of white men is becoming nervous as touching its own future and that of other races. With the desire of self-preservation, which naturally is the first law of nature, they raise the hue and cry that the white race must be first in government and in control. What must the Negro do in the face of such a universal attitude but to align all his forces in the direction of protecting himself from the threatened disaster of race domination and ultimate extermination?

Without a desire to harm anyone, the Universal Negro Improvement Association feels that the Negro should without compromise or any apology appeal to the same spirit of racial pride and love as the great white race is doing for its own preservation, so that while others are raising the cry of a white America, a white Canada, a white Australia, we also without reservation raise the cry of a "Black Africa." The critic asks, "Is this possible?" and the four hundred million courageous Negroes of the world answer, "Yes."

Out of this very reconstruction of world affairs will come the glorious opportunity for Africa's freedom. Out of the present chaos and European confusion will come an opportunity for the Negro never enjoyed in any other age, for the expansion of himself and the consolidation of his manhood in the direction of building himself a national power in Africa.

The germ of European malice, revenge and antagonism is so deeply rooted among certain of the contending powers that in a short while we feel sure they will present to Negroes the opportunity for which we are organized.

No one believes in the permanent disablement of Germany, but all thoughtful minds realize that France is but laying the foundation through revenge for a greater conflict than has as yet been seen. With such another upheaval, there is absolutely no reason why organized Negro opinion could not be felt and directed in the channel of their own independence in Africa.

To fight for African redemption does not mean that we must give up our domestic fights for political justice and industrial rights. It does not mean that we must become disloyal to any government or to any country wherein we were born. Each and every race outside of its domestic national loyalty has a loyalty to itself; therefore, it is foolish for the Negro to talk about not being interested in his own racial, political, social and industrial destiny. We can be as loyal American citizens or British subjects as the Irishman or the Jew, and yet fight for the redemption of Africa, a complete emancipation of the race.

Fighting for the establishment of Palestine does not make the

American Jew disloyal; fighting for the independence of Ireland does not make the Irish-American a bad citizen. Why should fighting for the freedom of Africa make the Afro-American disloyal or a bad citizen?

The Universal Negro Improvement Association teaches loyalty to all governments outside of Africa; but when it comes to Africa, we feel that the Negro has absolutely no obligation to any one but himself.

Out of the unsettled state and condition of the world will come such revolutions that will give each and every race that is oppressed the opportunity to march forward. The last world war brought the opportunity to many heretofore subject races to regain their freedom. The next world war will give Africa the opportunity for which we are preparing. We are going to have wars and rumors of wars. In another twenty or thirty years we will have a changed world, politically, and Africa will not be one of the most backward nations, but Africa shall be, I feel sure, one of the greatest commonwealths that will once more hold up the torchlight of civilization and bestow the blessings of freedom, liberty and democracy upon all mankind.

Generally the public is kept misinformed of the truth surrounding new movements of reform. Very seldom, if ever, reformers get the truth told about them and their movements. Because of this natural attitude, the Universal Negro Improvement Association has been greatly handicapped in its work, causing thereby one of the most liberal and helpful movements of the twentieth century to be held up to ridicule by those who take pride in poking fun at anything not already established.

The white man of America has become the natural leader of the world. He, because of his exalted position, is called upon to help in all human efforts. From nations to individuals the appeal is made to him for aid in all things affecting humanity, so, naturally, there can be no great mass movement or change without first acquainting the leader on whose sympathy and advice the world moves.

It is because of this, and more so because of a desire to be Christian friends with the white race, why I explain the aims and objects of the Universal Negro Improvement Association.

The Universal Negro Improvement Association is an organization among Negroes that is seeking to improve the condition of the race, with the view of establishing a nation in Africa where Negroes will be given the opportunity to develop by themselves, without creating the hatred and animosity that now exists in countries of the white race through Negroes rivaling them for the highest and best positions in government, politics, society and industry. The organization believes in the rights of all men, yellow, white and black. To us, the white race has a right to the peaceful possession and occupation of countries of its own and in like manner the yellow and black races have their rights. It is only by an honest and liberal consideration of such rights can the world be blessed with the peace that is sought by Christian teachers and leaders.

The following preamble to the constitution of the organization speaks for itself: "The Universal Negro Improvement Association and African Communities' League is a social, friendly, humanitarian, charitable, educational, institutional, constructive, and expansive society, and is founded by persons, desiring to the utmost to work for the general uplift of the Negro peoples of the world. And the members pledge themselves to do all in their power to conserve the rights of their noble race and to respect the rights of all mankind, believing always in the Brotherhood of Man and the Fatherhood of God. The motto of the organization is: One God! One Aim! One Destiny! Therefore, let justice be done to all mankind, realizing that if the strong oppresses the weak confusion and discontent will ever mark the path of men, but with love, faith and charity toward all the reign of peace and plenty will be heralded into the world and the generation of men shall be called Blessed."

The declared objects of the association are:

"To establish a universal Confraternity among the race; to promote the spirit of pride and love; to reclaim the fallen; to administer to and assist the needy; to assist in civilizing the backward tribes of Africa; to assist in the development of Independent Negro Nations and Communities; to establish a central nation for the race; to establish Commissaries or Agencies in the principal countries and cities of the world for the representation of all Negroes; to promote a conscientious Spiritual worship among the native tribes of Africa; to establish Universities, Colleges, Academies and Schools for the racial education and culture of the people; to work for better conditions among Negroes everywhere."

Selection 4

THE METHODS

SAUNDERS REDDING*

A well known Negro writer describes the contradictions and conflicts in the Negro protest movement as of 1951.

Names have been given to the advocates and promoters of various racial policies. There are gradualists (and they are black and white), who feel that somehow by a process of mechanical progression everything will work out, though to what concrete ends they do not say. The race chauvinists advocate a self-sustaining Negro economic, social and cultural island, and seem to have no fear of a destructive typhoon roaring in from the surrounding sea of the white world. The educationists believe that intellectual competence as indicated by the number of Negro Phi Beta Kappas, doctors of philosophy and various experts will win for the race the respect it does not now receive. There are the individualists who urge that each man work out for himself the compromises that will bring the self-fulfillment he seeks. Finally there are the radicals (there are no degrees of radicalism among them), who, because they seem to see destruction as an end and would first uproot everything, are actually nihilists.

Various racial and biracial institutions look on themselves as representing and implementing one or the other of these policies. The Southern Regional Council, for instance, is gradualist. The Negro press is chauvinist. Most Negro Greek-letter organizations (of which there are seven national and many dozen sectional and local) are educationist. Howard University—though not its president—and the best-known private Negro colleges are individualistic

* From Saunders Redding, *On Being Negro in America*, New York: Bantam Books, 1964, pp. 16–20.

in their approach. Until its demise, the National Negro Congress was radical.

But none of these is seamless, pure and undefiled. Into each of them have seeped influences from one or more of the others. In so far as the Southern Regional Council believes in segregation (and that is very far indeed), it is chauvinistic, and in as much as it sets a premium on intellectual growth as measured by scholarly achievement, it is also educationistic. By the very circumstances of their founding, private Negro colleges lean toward chauvinism, and they encourage this tendency further by courses in "Negro" history, art, literature, business and life. Recently, moreover, some Negro colleges have spoken in favor of the South's segregated regional education plan—the private ones for reasons not quite clear; the public ones because only segregation will save them from extinction. The radicals who, anyway, take the position that radicalism is the highest, brightest star in the ideological heavens, are very proud of the intellectual caliber of Paul Robeson, Ben Davis, and that other Davis, John, erstwhile president of the National Negro Congress. The Negro press, of course, reflects these conflicts and inconsistencies.

But something more fundamental than the contradictions accounts for the failure of these policies. Gradualism, a habit of thought that marks interracial activities in the South, is geared to the historic-compulsion idea mentioned earlier. It is mostly faith without works, thunder without God, and lengthy, frequently fraudulent reports of "victories" as represented in the decline of lynching and the "long step forward" (nearly a generation in the taking) from the Holcutt case (1932) to the Sweatt case (1950). As a principle, gradualism is very flattering to the Negro people. It ascribes to them superhuman patience, fortitude and humility in the face of very great social evils. Gradualism is laissez faire—a proscription of planning and foresight in the dynamics of society.

Chauvinism is as impractical for the Negro in America as it is fundamentally dangerous for any people anywhere. Even if Negroes could duplicate the social and economic machinery—and I doubt that they could—the material resources on which their racial island must then depend would have to come from somewhere outside. In a constantly shrinking world, complete independence and isolation are impossible. And even if they were not impossible for the Negro in America, would not the achieving of them result in permanent relegation to secondary status? The very numbers involved—that is, the popular ratio—would assure it. I cannot imagine the white majority saying, "Sure, come on and set up your self-sustaining household in a corner of my house."

There is still a great deal of race chauvinism, and the fact should surprise no one. Negro organs of expression, including scholarly journals, document it: *Phylon:* [A] *Review of Race & Culture,* published by Atlanta University; the *Journal of Negro Education,* published by Howard University; the *Journal of Negro Higher Education,* published by Johnson C. Smith University; the *Journal of Negro History,* published by the Association for the Study of Negro Life and History; and a spate of lesser publications. A purely emotional conviction informs chauvinism. It is partly the frustrated pride that is expressed in "Negro History Week" observances, which dichotomize United States history, and in courses in "Negro" literature and art, which turn out to be valiant but thin trickles forcibly and ingenuously diverted from the mainstream of American life. Chauvinism springs from a natural desire to find remission from the unequal struggle between black and white, and surcease of discrimination.

The philosophy of the educationist is only superficially different from that of the individualist. The concepts in which they are hallowed seem only to obscure the fact that no man is completely the master of his fate. Only the immature fail to recognize that individual wishes now have almost no authority in the world. Educationists and individualists acknowledge the existence of co-operative evils but deny the necessity to act co-operatively against them. This is also, it seems to me, a denial of brotherhood—a principle which must be made to operate in increasingly wider and wider arcs of human endeavor. Any statement of the individualist's ideals would sound like a throwback to the time before theories of social compact, or better, social contract, evolved.

The contradictions and conflicts in all this go deeper, much deeper than any short and general analysis can indicate. They plunge their iron tentacles into the minds of individual Negroes, raggedly fragmenting them, scoring them into oversensitized compartments. It is this that we must understand when we think, for instance, of Paul Robeson; and when we hear a Negro college president declare himself opposed to segregation, while at the same time he urges the state to add graduate courses to his already sub-standard curriculum, so that Negro aspirants to graduate degree will not embarrass the state's white university; and when we read on page one of a Negro paper a vilification of white women who "run after" Negro men and on the next page an encomium of a successful mixed marriage. This is more than simply resiliency and accommodation, and there is more than just Negro heart and mind involved. For the Negro is not the problem *in toto,* nor a problem *in vacuo.* His behavior, the patterns of his multiple personality, the ebb and flow of action and counteraction and the agonizing ruptures in his group life result from the ill-usage to which he is subject at the hands of American white people.

Selections 5a–5b

NEW ORGANIZATIONS AND NEW METHODS

The following selection describes some of the methods utilized by participants in the civil rights movement.

5a. "Sit-ins" and Freedom Riders*

In 1955, a group of Montgomery, Alabama, Negroes under the leadership of the Reverend Martin Luther King protested segregated seating on city bus lines. When Mrs. Rosa Parks was arrested for refusing to move to the rear of a bus, the group instituted a boycott. For 12 months makeshift car-pools substituted for public transportation. Many persons walked several miles to and from their jobs. The bus company at first scoffed at the Negro protest. But as the economic effects of the boycott began to be felt, the company sought a settlement. When negotiations broke down, legal action was brought to end bus segregation. On June 5, 1956, a Federal district court ruled that segregation on local public transportation violated the due process and equal protection clauses of the 14th Amendment. Later that year, the Supreme Court, citing the *School Segregation Cases,* affirmed the judgment. The boycott was ended.

The success in Montgomery gave new stimulus to organizations committed to nonviolent action. The Congress of Racial Equality and the Southern Christian Leadership Conference intensified their

* From *Freedom to the Free: A Report to the President by the United States Commission on Civil Rights,* Washington, D. C.: U. S. Government Printing Office, 1963, pp. 175–80.

efforts. Created in 1943, the Congress on Racial Equality (CORE) from its early beginnings utilized the nonviolent protest to achieve its goals. The Southern Christian Leadership Conference (SCLC), a direct outgrowth of the Montgomery bus boycott, was formed to serve as a coordinating agency for those employing the technique and philosophy of nonviolent protest. At its organizational meeting in Atlanta in 1957, the Reverend Martin Luther King was elected as its president. The NAACP, itself a participant in direct action, the Southern Regional Council, religious groups, and various labor and civic organizations gave support and aid to those involved in direct action.

Then on February 1, 1960, four students from the Negro Agricultural and Technical College of Greensboro, North Carolina, entered a variety store, made several purchases, sat down at the lunch counter, ordered coffee, and were refused service because they were Negroes. They remained in their seats until the store closed.

In the spring and summer of 1960, young people, both white and Negro, participated in similar protests against segregation and discrimination wherever it was to be found. They sat in white libraries, waded at white beaches, and slept in the lobbies of white hotels. Many were arrested for trespassing, disturbing the peace, and disobeying police officers who ordered them off the premises. As a result of the sit-ins, literally hundreds of lunch counters began to serve Negroes for the first time and other facilities were opened to them.

Thus began a sweeping protest movement against entrenched practices of segregation. In summing up the movement, Reverend King said that legislation and court orders tend to declare rights but can never thoroughly deliver them. "Only when people themselves begin to act are rights on paper given life blood. . . . Nonviolent resistance also makes it possible for the individual to struggle to secure moral ends through moral means." By 1962, the sit-in movement had achieved considerable success. As a result of the sit-ins and negotiations undertaken because of them, department store lunch counters and other facilities had been desegregated in more than 100 cities in 14 states in various parts of the Nation.

The sit-in movement did not escape Executive attention. On March 16, 1960, President Eisenhower commented that he was "deeply sympathetic with efforts of any group to enjoy the rights . . . of equality that they are guaranteed by the Constitution" and that "if a person is expressing such an aspiration as this in a perfectly legal way," the President did not see any reason why he should not do so. On June 1, Attorney General William P. Rogers met with representatives of several national variety stores and secured their promises to have their local managers confer with public officials and citizens' committees to work out means of desegregating their lunch counters. On August 10, the Attorney General announced that the national chains had made good on their promises by desegregating lunch counters in 69 southern communities.

The judiciary was soon to become involved in the sit-ins. For while some of the sit-in demonstrators voluntarily went to jail, many appealed their convictions on the ground that the ejections, arrests, and convictions by local government officials constituted enforcement of the private proprietor's discrimination and therefore constituted State action in violation of the 14th Amendment. Three cases involving 16 students reached the Supreme Court from Louisiana in the fall of 1961. On December 11, 1961, without reaching the broader constitutional questions, the Court reversed the convictions because of lack of evidence that the sit-ins disturbed the peace either by outwardly boisterous conduct or by passive conduct likely to cause a public disturbance.

In November 1962, the Supreme Court heard arguments in six cases in which the arrest of sit-in demonstrators was attacked as unconstitutional. The Solicitor General of the United States, appearing as a friend of the Court, maintained that four of the criminal convictions were based on unconstitutional State laws, and the fifth on a pervasive State policy of segregation, and that the sixth should be reversed because the agent who evicted the defendants also served as the arresting officer. . . .

One of the most dramatic attacks on segregation and discrimination was undertaken in May 1961 by the Congress of Racial Equality. A group of CORE-sponsored "freedom riders" toured the South to test segregation laws and practices in interstate transportation and terminal facilities. The "freedom riders" encountered no difficulties until they arrived in Alabama and Mississippi. In Montgomery, Alabama, 20 persons were injured on May 20, 1961, by mob action. When local police failed to restore order, 400 Federal marshals were brought in to maintain order. President Kennedy said the situation was "the source of the deepest concern to me as it must be to the vast majority of the citizens of Alabama and all Americans." On May 21, after initially resisting Federal authority, Governor Patterson called out the National Guard and order was quickly restored. The Department of Justice secured a temporary restraining order from the Federal district court prohibiting any further attempt by force to stop "freedom riders" from continuing their test of bus segregation. On June 2, Montgomery city officials, together with several private individuals and organizations were enjoined by the court from interfering with travel of passengers in interstate commerce. The city officials were also enjoined from refusing to provide protection for such travelers.

When the "freedom riders" rode into Mississippi, the Governor called out the National Guard to escort them into Jackson. On May 24, 1961, the first contingent was arrested for refusing to obey a police officer's command to move from segregated terminal waiting room facilities. In the following months, more than 300 "freedom riders" were arrested and convicted. On July 10, the Department of Justice intervened before a three-judge Federal court to halt the arrest of the riders in Mississippi. The Attorney General charged that local authorities had gone "beyond the scope of their lawful power" in making the arrests. On November 17, the court ruled that the arrests must be challenged in State courts. An application to the Supreme Court for an injunction to stay State criminal prosecutions was denied. President Kennedy, in reply to a question at his July 19 news conference, upheld the right of American citizens to move in interstate commerce "for whatever reasons they travel."

By the summer of 1962, the leaders of the direct action movements could see results in the form of Government response to their demands and favorable changes in business attitudes and policies.

5b.   Modern Freedom Songs

We Shall Overcome

We shall overcome
We shall overcome
We shall overcome someday.
Deep in my heart I do believe
We shall overcome someday.

The truth shall make us free
The truth shall make us free
The truth shall make us free someday.
Deep in my heart I do believe
The truth shall make us free someday.

from *Sing Out* magazine, March–April, 1963.

Freedom Is a Constant Struggle

Freedom is a constant struggle
Freedom is a constant struggle
Freedom is a constant struggle
      Lord we've struggled so long

We must be free
We must be free
                    from *Sing Out* magazine, January, 1965.

It Isn't Nice

It isn't nice to block the door-way
It isn't nice to go to jail
There are nicer ways to do it
But the nice ways always fail

You told us once
You told us twice
Thanks buddy for your advice
Well if that's Freedom's price
We don't mind.
                    from *Sing Out* magazine, October, 1964.

Selection 6

THE MESSENGER OF ALLAH PRESENTS THE MUSLIM PROGRAM*

Since 1960 the Nation of Islam—commonly called the Black Muslims—has pushed its program of separation among urban Negroes. By 1967 its leader, Elijah Muhammed, has succeeded in building a militant organization with members numbering in the scores of thousands.

What the Muslims Want

This is the question asked most frequently by both the whites and the blacks. The answers to this question I shall state as simply as possible.

* From *Muhammad Speaks* [the official newspaper of the Black Muslims], Vol. 4, No. 32, July 2, 1965.

1. We want freedom. We want a full and complete freedom.

2. We want justice. Equal justice under the law. We want justice applied equally to all, regardless of creed or class or color.

3. We want equality of opportunity. We want equal membership in society with the best in civilized society.

4. We want our people in America whose parents or grandparents were descendants from slaves, to be allowed to establish a separate state or territory of their own—either on this continent or elsewhere. We believe that our former slave masters are obligated to provide such land and that the area must be fertile and minerally rich. We believe that our former slave masters are obligated to maintain and supply our needs in this separate territory for the next 20 to 25 years—until we are able to produce and supply our own needs.

Since we cannot get along with them in peace and equality, after giving them 400 years of our sweat and blood and receiving in return some of the worst treatment human beings have ever experienced, we believe our contributions to this land and the suffering forced upon us by white America, justifies our demand for complete separation in a state or territory of our own.

5. We want freedom for all Believers of Islam now held in federal prisons. We want freedom for all black men and women now under death sentence in innumerable prisons in the North as well as the South.

We want every black man and woman to have the freedom to accept or reject being separated from the slave master's children and establish a land of their own.

We know that the above plan for the solution of the black and white conflict is the best and only answer to the problem between two people.

6. We want an immediate end to the police brutality and mob attacks against the so-called Negro throughout the United States.

We believe that the federal government should intercede to see that black men and women tried in white courts receive justice in accordance with the laws of the land—or allow us to build a new nation for ourselves, dedicated to justice, freedom and liberty.

7. As long as we are not allowed to establish a state or territory of our own, we demand not only equal justice under the laws of the United States, but equal employment opportunities NOW!

We do not believe that after 400 years of free or nearly free labor, sweat and blood, which has helped America become rich and powerful, that so many thousands of black people should have to subsist on relief, charity or live in poor houses.

8. We want the government of the United States to exempt our

people from ALL taxation as long as we are deprived of equal justice under the laws of the land.

9. We want equal education—but separate schools up to 16 for boys and 18 for girls on the condition that the girls be sent to women's colleges and universities. We want all black children educated, taught and trained by their own teachers.

Under such schooling system we believe we will make a better nation of people. The United States government should provide free, all necessary textbooks and equipment, schools and college buildings. The Muslim teachers shall be left free to teach and train their people in the way of righteousness, decency and self-respect.

10. We believe that intermarriage or race mixing should be prohibited. We want the religion of Islam taught without hindrance or suppression.

These are some of the things that we, the Muslims, want for our people in North America.

What the Muslims Believe

1. WE BELIEVE in the One God Whose proper Name is Allah.

2. WE BELIEVE in the Holy Qur-an and in the Scriptures of all the Prophets of God.

3. WE BELIEVE in the truth of the Bible, but we believe that it has been tampered with and must be reinterpreted so that mankind will not be snared by the falsehoods that have been added to it.

4. WE BELIEVE in Allah's Prophets and the Scriptures they brought to the people.

5. WE BELIEVE in the resurrection of the dead—not in physical resurrection—but in mental resurrection. We believe that the so-called Negroes are most in need of mental resurrection; therefore, they will be resurrected first.

Furthermore, we believe we are the people of God's choice, as it has been written, that God would choose the rejected and the despised. We can find no other persons fitting this description in these last days more than the so-called Negroes in America. We believe in the resurrection of the righteous.

6. WE BELIEVE in the judgment; we believe this first judgment will take place, as God revealed, in America. . . .

7. WE BELIEVE this is the time in history for the separation of the so-called Negroes and the so-called white Americans. We believe the black man should be freed in name as well as in fact. By this we mean that he should be freed from the names imposed upon him by his former slave masters. Names which identified him as being the slave master's slave. We believe that if we are free indeed, we

should go in our own people's names—the black peoples of the earth.

8. WE BELIEVE in justice for all, whether in God or not; we believe as others, that we are due equal justice as human beings. We believe in equality—as a nation—of equals. We do not believe that we are equal with our slave masters in the status of "freed slaves."

We recognize and respect American citizens as independent peoples and we respect their laws which govern this nation.

Selections 7a–7d

PROPOSED SOLUTIONS

These selections present a wide variety of methods available to solve some of the Negro's problems. Myrdal is a well-known Swedish economist, and Golden is a well-known humorist.

7a. Remuneration Theme

GUNNAR MYRDAL*

After the Civil War, the overwhelming majority of Negroes were concentrated in Southern agriculture. Consequently, the greatest problem was what to do with these great masses of Southern Negroes, most of whom were former slaves. Even the Negroes not in Southern agriculture were influenced by the patterns set, since the Northern Negro laborer was recruited, in later decades, from the rural South.

A rational economic reform of Southern plantation economy, which would preserve individual property rights to the maximum (always of greatest importance for a smooth readjustment) but also utilize the revolutionary situation for carrying into effect the

* From Gunnar Myrdal, *An American Dilemma: The Negro Problem and Modern Democracy*, New York: Harper & Brothers, 1944, p. 225.

aims of Reconstruction, could have included the following points besides freeing the slaves:

1. Remunerating fully the slave owners out of federal funds.

2. Expropriating the slave plantations or a larger part of them and remunerating fully their owners out of federal funds.

3. Distributing this land in small parcels to the cultivators who wished it, against mortgaged claims of their new property, and requiring them to pay for the land in yearly installments over a long period.

4. Creating for a transition period a rather close public supervision over the freedmen and also certain safeguards against their disposition of their property; also instituting an effective vocational education of Negro farmers, somewhat along the lines of the F.S.A. [Federal Security Administration] of the 1930's.

5. Instituting a scheme of taxation to pay off the former slave and land-owners and, perhaps, to allow repayments for the land by the new owners to be kept down under the actual expropriation costs.

6. As a partial alternative, in order to relieve the Negro population pressure in the South and in order to help keep down the scope of the Reconstruction program: helping Negroes take part in the westward rural migration.

7b. A Carolina Humorist: A Quick Solution

HARRY GOLDEN[*]

Those who love North Carolina will jump at the chance to share in the great responsibility confronting our Governor and the State Legislature. A special session of the Legislature (July 25–28, 1956) passed a series of amendments to the State Constitution. These proposals submitted by the Governor and his Advisory Education Committee included the following:

(A) The elimination of the compulsory attendance law, "to prevent any child from being forced to attend a school with a child of another race."
(B) The establishment of "Education Expense Grants" for education in a private school, "in the case of a child assigned to a public school attended by a child of another race."
(C) A "uniform system of local option" whereby a majority of the folks in a school district may suspend or close a school if the situation becomes "intolerable."

But suppose a Negro child applies for this "Education Expense Grant" and says he wants to go to the private school too? There

* From Harry Golden, *Only in America,* New York and Cleveland: World Publishing Co., 1958, pp. 121–23.

are fourteen Supreme Court decisions involving the use of public funds; there are only two "decisions" involving the elimination of racial discrimination in the public schools.

The Governor has said that critics of these proposals have not offered any constructive advice or alternatives. Permit me, therefore, to offer an idea for the consideration of the members of the regular sessions. A careful study of my plan, I believe, will show that it will save millions of dollars in tax funds and eliminate forever the danger to our public education system. Before I outline my plan, I would like to give you a little background.

One of the factors involved in our tremendous industrial growth and economic prosperity is the fact that the South, voluntarily, has all but eliminated VERTICAL SEGREGATION. The tremendous buying power of the twelve million Negroes in the South has been based wholly on the absence of racial segregation. The white and Negro stand at the same grocery and supermarket counters; deposit money at the same bank teller's window; pay phone and light bills to the same clerk; walk through the same dime and department stores, and stand at the same drugstore counters.

It is only when the Negro "sets" that the fur begins to fly.

Now, since we are not even thinking about restoring VERTICAL SEGREGATION, I think my plan would not only comply with the Supreme Court decisions, but would maintain "sitting-down" segregation. Now here is the GOLDEN VERTICAL NEGRO PLAN. Instead of all those complicated proposals, all the next session needs to do is pass one small amendment which would provide *only* desks in all the public schools of our state—*no seats*.

The desks should be those standing-up jobs, like the old-fashioned bookkeeping desk. Since no one in the South pays the slightest attention to a VERTICAL NEGRO, this will completely solve our problem. And it is not such a terrible inconvenience for young people to stand up during their classroom studies. In fact, this may be a blessing in disguise. They are not learning to read sitting down, anyway; maybe standing up will help. This will save more millions of dollars in the cost of our remedial English course when the kids enter college. In whatever direction you look with the GOLDEN VERTICAL NEGRO PLAN, you save millions of dollars, to say nothing of eliminating forever any danger to our public education system upon which rests the destiny, hopes and happiness of this society. . . .

7c. Needed Now: A Special Effort

WHITNEY M. YOUNG, JR.*

Whitney M. Young has been Executive Director of the National Urban League since 1961. In his book, To Be Equal, *he presents a comprehensive program for overcoming the "discrimination gap."*

1. Our basic definition of equal opportunity must include recognition of the need for special effort to overcome serious disabilities resulting from historic handicaps. When you find a man in the wilderness dying from malnutrition you don't just bring him to civilization and turn him loose with a pat on the back saying, "We've saved you, now you're on your own; lots of luck!" He is on the point of starvation. He requires special attention, careful diet and rest, and psychological and physical aid to readjust to civilization.

The Negro has been starving, not in the wilderness, but in the midst of the world's richest nation in the period of its greatest prosperity in history. He has been sighted, but whether his true condition has been "diagnosed" accurately and will be corrected by the majority is yet to be seen.

2. America must recognize and assess at a higher value than ever before the human potential of its Negro citizens, and then our society must move positively to develop that potential.

It is no accident that the U. S. Department of Labor and economists such as Gunnar Myrdal, Eli Ginzberg and others agree that the Negro population is America's greatest undeveloped natural resource. The extraordinary contributions to America of those Negro citizens who have overcome incredible handicaps merely hint at the tremendous benefits that will be ours when Negroes can participate freely in our society.

3. The best schools and the best teachers are needed:
—to instill in Negro children and other educationally disadvantaged youth a desire for excellence;
—to motivate them to achieve and prepare them to advance up the economic ladder with full understanding of the rewards they will receive.

We do not need more examples of school boards treating ghetto schools as the Siberias of their system, relegating to them largely

* From Whitney M. Young, Jr., *To Be Equal,* New York: McGraw-Hill Book Co., 1964, pp. 28–31.

the problem teachers, probational teachers, neophyte teachers on a "make or break" basis. We need insight, courage, understanding, and an educational value system which parallels that of the medical profession, where doctors and nurses who selflessly devote themselves to combatting an epidemic, for example, earn greater prestige than those who dispense pills for allergies and colds in the suburbs.

4. A conscious, planned effort must be made to bring qualified Negroes into "entrance jobs" in *all* types of employment, to upgrade them and aid them to qualify for advancement, and to place them in positions of responsibility, including the full range of management positions. The day is past when token integration and pilot placement of Negroes in business and industry, labor and government can be considered solutions. These devices never were acceptable nor adequate, except to white Americans.

For employers the special effort, domestic Marshall Plan approach means exercising the same creative zeal and imagination to include Negro workers at all levels that management has used throughout the years in excluding them. And incorporating Negroes into the work force will not happen automatically by taking down a sign, pasting up a poster, or autographing the President's Plans for Progress Program—a statement of fair-hiring practices. It means honest, realistic seeking out of workers, for fillable jobs, not just positions for which industry can't find whites—such as nuclear physicists, or secretaries who look like Lena Horne and can type 120 words per minute.

Special effort means not hiding behind lame excuses. Any employer who does not want to hire can find excuses. This approach suggests that if a business has never hired Negroes in its offices or plants and two equally qualified people apply, it should hire the Negro to redress the injustice previously visited upon him. Such action has double virtue; it gives Negro youth a new role model and promotes the image of a truly American company.

5. Effective, positive action must be taken to destroy the racial ghetto and to open housing opportunities of all types on the basis of need and ability to buy or rent. Too long the cancerous sore of the ghetto has festered in our urban communities, spewing forth human wreckage and the major portion of criminal offenders; draining our body politic of treasure; robbing us of the meaningful contributions of hundreds of thousands of citizens whose lives and ambitions have been thwarted and truncated.

6. Health and welfare agencies, both public and private, must bring to the ghettoized population their best services and most competent personnel. Needed are trained workers who understand the myriad ills that afflict ghetto dwellers—unstable family patterns,

illegitimate births, the direct relationship between low socio-economic status and social problems—and how to rehabilitate urban Negro families.

7. Qualified Negroes should be sought and named to all public and private boards and commissions, particularly those that shape policy in the areas of employment, housing, education, and health and welfare services. These are the key areas in which the racial differential is greatest and the need for dramatic change—meaning the inclusion of Negro citizens in decision-making—is most urgent.

To achieve this, strong leadership in the Negro community must be encouraged and developed. This leadership will then be ready to step into the vanguard of the teamwork effort so imperative in resolving the smoldering problems of civil rights. The experiences of 1963 should have made clear, if it was not evident before, that the era of paternalistic handling by whites of the needs and ambitions of Negro citizens is gone. American Negroes are done with being "done for"; they demand the right to participate, to do for themselves and determine their own destiny.

8. Every opportunity to acquire education and technical skills must be utilized to the fullest. Every means of strengthening the social and economic fabric of the Negro community must be employed.

Negro citizens, adults as well as young people, must maintain and even accelerate the sense of urgency that now characterizes the drive for first-class citizenship.

9. It is vital that government at all levels, philanthropic foundations, labor, business, and industry reassess their financial support of, and cooperation with, established organizations committed to securing equal opportunity for Negro citizens to share in the fundamental privileges and rights of American democracy.

It is imperative that all of these major sources of support increase substantially their contributions, both financial and non-financial, to the preventive and remedial programs carried on by responsible Negro leadership organizations. These agencies aid Negroes to help themselves by staying in school, registering and voting, making use of adult education classes and retraining centers. For far too long the agencies that have seen the needs and attempted unspectacularly but effectively to meet them have suffered from a crippling anemia of finances, caused by the acute myopia of government, philanthropy, business, and labor.

10. Negro citizens must exert themselves energetically in constructive efforts to carry their full share of responsibilities and to participate in a meaningful way in every phase of community life. It is not enough to man the machinery of protest. Equally impor-

tant today and twice as important tomorrow is participation in the responsibilities and opportunities of full citizenship in our democracy. This means Negroes moving not only onto the picket lines but also into PTA meetings, moving not only into lunch counters but also into libraries, moving into both community facilities and committee rooms, into both public accommodations and public hearings, and, finally, moving onto the commissions and boards to exercise their rights and insure their fair share.

Selection 7d

A LEADER OF CORE PROPOSES A PROGRAM*

James Farmer helped to found CORE, Congress of Racial Equality, in 1942. Since then he has served as Program Director of NAACP and as National Director of CORE from 1961 to 1966. In the following selection from his book, Freedom—When? *he sets forth his program for achieving freedom.*

One measure of how much the civil rights movement has achieved in the decade since the school desegregation decision of the Supreme Court is that we are now beginning to think and plan "beyond civil rights." If we need to designate a turning point, we might mention the March on Washington in the summer of 1963 which, too few people noticed, was not only for "freedom" but for "jobs" as well. Until then we understood the race problem as a problem of discrimination and segregation. If only the nation would lift the unnatural barriers to economic, social, and political opportunity for Negroes, we thought; if only Negroes had full protection and equal privileges and immunities, in law and social fact, our task would be complete.

* From James Farmer, *Freedom—When?* New York: Random House, 1965, pp. 170–97.

Today, when much, though by no means all, of the civil rights legislation we have worked for is on the books, we are beginning to realize that civil rights alone may not be enough. Freedom is an art demanding practice, and too many of us are unpracticed. Some of the programs we now project—mobilizing local and national political action, voter registration and education, local community-development and self-help programs, cultural enrichment—are designed to encourage such practice. The fact that Negroes *can* vote, to put the matter most simply, does not mean that they will or that they will do justice to themselves and their interests when they do.

Then, too, we have come to understand that a blind, broken horse will not move smartly out of an open gate. Perhaps being deprived of civil rights is the explanation for the pervasive impoverishment of Negroes, and certainly the Negro will not rise from poverty until his rights are secure, but the simple fact is that he *is* poor and does suffer all the impoverishment of soul and spirit that chronic poverty implies in America. Offering him equal rights, even equal opportunity, at this late date, without giving him a special boost, is the kind of cruel joke American individualism has played on the poor throughout American history. And so CORE and the movement of which we are part plan compensatory and remedial programs to provide the necessary boost.

And "beyond" these considerations we have come to realize that Negro poverty is a special case of the general problem of poverty in America. The fact that Negroes who are one tenth of the population comprise one fourth of the nation's poor leads one to conclude not only that Negroes are uniquely victimized, but also that three quarters of the forty million or so poor in this country are white. As cybernetics and automation proceed apace the problem may become more acute. Obviously, Negro poverty will be eliminated only when all poverty is eliminated; accordingly, we are glimpsing programs and policies which will force the nation to deal radically with this radical condition.

It is inviting to think exclusively from a perspective beyond civil rights but it is dangerous too, for we may be seduced into forgetting the remaining workaday tasks. Already the ideologues are telling the movement that civil rights are outmoded; that demonstrations and other forms of direct action are a dead letter or at best a mopping-up exercise, and that the movement must suddenly rethink all its assumptions. To a movement made up of people who ask constantly, What, concretely, can we do now, at this meeting, in this particular season of our discontent? this can be cruel and irresponsible advice. Unless, of course, one has some specific program to offer. It is easy to dream bold dreams, it is harder to translate them into a program. Actually, civil rights, while no longer our exclusive concern, are not as anachronistic as the ideologues suggest, and it seems to me wise, in this discussion of the future of the movement, to look first at the civil rights tasks which remain before turning to new vistas.

Civil Rights

One rule of thumb Negroes have learned well, from having their thumbs smashed so often, is that a law on the books means nothing when it is not vigorously implemented. Many of the Northern states in which Negroes dwell in sizeable numbers have strong fair housing, fair employment, fair labor practices legislation; yet landlords and realtors still contrive to keep desirable areas lily-white, and employers and some union officials still keep Negroes out of jobs and apprenticeship programs.

There are several things we will do about this. For one, we can bring vigorous anti-discrimination suits under appropriate state and local ordinances which have fallen into disuse—partly, we must confess, because of our own emphasis on federal action. As always, these suits will be more speedily implemented in a climate of direct action and specific protest. We will continue to persuade individuals and groups guilty of discrimination to mend their ways if not their hearts. A real estate agency guilty of illegal discrimination will suffer the inconvenience of pickets and the humiliation of public disclosure, as will a derelict landlord or employer or union. When circumstances warrant, we will organize economic boycotts. We will, of course, continue to enlist the support and co-operation of sympathetic groups in the North—while demanding that Kennedy's weak Executive Order on housing be made stronger.

· · ·

Eventually, we will succeed in bringing the South to the point where it will face the problems the North faces now. One of the things this will mean is that civil rights in the South will become a local matter, hammered out among Southerners. We cannot expect and should not wish to have a federal presence forever, though we don't want federal attentions to end one minute before the Negro has the power to cope with the South as an equal among equals. There is a mythology which holds that the South will "solve its problems" more quickly than the North, because unlike the fractured and anguished cities of the North, Southern towns are tied in "love and community." Reconciliation, the myth runs, will be swift and dramatic. This sentiment is usually uttered by whites trying to persuade the government to cease and desist its attentions, though I have heard militant Negroes say the same thing. I doubt this strongly. As legal segregation in the South becomes *de facto* segregation, as Negroes get some money and education and the mobility these bring, as the South industrializes and new Northern-like cities emerge and the Negro moves from the land to the city, it seems to me that the South will become more and more like the North and the problems of the sections will be the same.

Northern civil rights workers will continue to exert pressure on the South. One of the techniques we shall exploit is the national economic boycott. There has been considerable discussion of Martin Luther King's calls for a boycott of Alabama and Mississippi. While national boycotts are a sound idea, I feel that the buckshot method of dealing with an entire state may be unsound, hurting everyone in general and no one in particular. The boycotts should be more selective. Perhaps against products of a particular factory, demonstrably discriminatory in its hiring practices, or against bonds floated by a particular school district which is obdurately segregationist. The purpose of the boycott is to add another dimension of pressure on the South and to help develop a national sense of responsibility for conditions in the South. Many Northerners are incredulous when we tell them that they are responsible for segregation in the South and can do something about it. The boycott pinpoints their responsibility and their opportunities.*

I am often asked what would constitute a successful boycott. Many feel that the national boycotts have been a total failure. Their definition of a success, I might say, invokes images of a beleaguered fort, utterly surrounded by hostile Indians who are cutting them off from food and water. When the last living soldier staggers out, surrendering the fort for a crust of bread, the boycott is deemed a success. Nothing so dramatic will happen. But there are subtler effects: a factory all set to move into a Southern town thinks twice and delays its decision; interest on bonds for a new school goes a point higher. Businessmen and the politicians they talk to can be very sensitive to these things. The very threat of a boycott is enough

* For the record, in the spring of 1965 the Childs Security Corporation, a subsidiary of C. F. Childs & Co., sent a letter to Governor George C. Wallace stating that the concern would not deal in the state's bonds. When Wallace had announced that the State of Alabama did not have enough money to protect the marchers from Selma to Montgomery, the Childs people wrote, saying the state was obviously in terrible financial shape and a poor investment risk. Also, since the time of the civil rights murders in Philadelphia, Mississippi, in June, 1964, Baxter & Co. of New York and Cleveland has refused to handle Mississippi and Alabama bonds.

to make a businessman uneasy. There will be no apocalypse, but the boycott technique will be very useful.

*   *   *

. . . CORE believes open political action, partisan and direct, is dictated.

There are several reasons for this new policy. Partly it is the outgrowth of an insight which has dawned on us in the midst of struggling these past years . . . the civil rights movement, we now know, is not simply a means to achieve the status of abstract equality; it is also a form of self-expression and self-determination for America's Negroes and their brothers in spirit. Negroes are passionately and self-interestedly devoted to civil rights for themselves —and, of course, for all men. Without knowing it, the civil rights movement has always been a political movement of Negroes, and when we at CORE realized this, we decided that if we were to be political we might as well do it in the most effective way—by entering politics.

Until now, we have tended to make our political demands from outside of what we call the power structure. "Do something for us, oh mighty power structure!"—this in sum is what we said. And undeniably a lot of things happened that way, including the expanding opportunity to enter the political system as participants rather than beseechers.

Many of our objectives—job training and retraining, elimination of slums, city planning for desegregation in housing and schools, the elimination of political, educational, and cultural inequities—clearly will depend ultimately upon the political machinery, local, state, and federal. Men in motion, we have learned, generate power, but there comes a time when pure motion must consolidate into something more tangible and permanent. This consolidation will produce self-conscious, purposive, well-organized political structures. We must back up our cajolery with inside muscle.

This means much more than endorsing candidates on a national level, though we must do that too, and endorse and propose specific programs as well. More crucially, it means endorsing candidates, *and running our own people* on the local and state level (as an example, we can point to the election of Archibald Hill, chairman of our Oklahoma City CORE chapter, to the state legislature). It also means placing the right people in decision-making and planning positions in local, state, and federal agencies, and "infiltrating" party politics on a ward and precinct level.

I have spoken of "community organization" and CORE's determination to enter the Negro community—the ghettos of the North, the segregated towns of the South—and organize block by block, house by house. Inevitably, these community organizations must take a political form, for political action always results when people develop a collective sense of themselves and a collective will to achieve a better life. It is essential that these community organizations be truly local, with local leadership and a program which emanates from local needs. The field worker who sets out to organize a local group must learn not to superimpose his own idea of what the people ought to want upon their own idea of what they actually want. One cannot predict what set of priorities a community will establish. Better pavement, perhaps, or improved sewage disposal; a new playground, a safer street; a new traffic light; an alteration in school curriculum; more Negro policemen; honest housing inspectors; stricter supervision of cut-throat landlords; better-designed public housing; public works; a lessening of police brutality and a civilian review board (this is a blood-and-guts issue in every Negro settlement I know of). What is important is that whatever the program, it will be the expression of the people themselves, wishing, in the classic democratic tradition, a strong voice in governing themselves.

I emphasize local politics here because I believe that we are entering an era when local politics will be increasingly important. The government poverty program is committed to working within existing community institutions and organizations, and CORE must work to keep money which could be well spent from ending up in the pork barrel of some petty politico. Everywhere we will be registering voters, and with the swift enfranchisement of Negroes we can expect politicians to zero in on new voters. CORE will be an inside force resisting the inevitable graft and corruption, dismantling and paralyzing the oppressive political machines which will begin to emerge, helping develop sound leaders, challenging local tyrants.

Students of the modern city are now saying that city governments are outmoded instruments for dealing with local problems. Metropolitan New York, for example, functions as one huge economic unit, yet it is governed by three states, hundreds of towns, and other overlapping authorities. Rationally, there should be no New York City, and in two or three decades we may witness, as Peter Drucker has predicted, a veritable revolution in local government. At the same time, if present trends continue, we shall see Negroes comprising the majority or near majority of several Northern cities: Philadelphia, New York, Detroit, Chicago, Newark, Los Angeles, Cleveland. Will the politicians seek to take power away from the

center city just as Negroes come into prominence? It could happen.
The fact is that there will be no major urban problem which will
not touch the lives of Negroes and command their political attention.
Clearly, we must be party to all local change.

CORE intends to mount political action in the South as well as
the North. . . .

Community Development

Political action, as we use the term, is a method of self-help. The
kind of community organization and mobilization politics require
will also provide the framework for CORE programs in remedial
education, economic development, cultural enrichment.

Take remedial education. Many educators have commented about
the low level of reading and mathematical skills among young Negroes sequestered in the ghetto. From these skills all educational
things follow; without them the child falls helplessly behind. If
expertise and professional technique alone could mend broken hearts
and hopes, we might look to the educational establishment to upgrade the capacities of these youngsters. But it is clear to us that they
suffer from that total conspiracy which has ripped so much of the
fabric of American Negro life, and since the ghetto will be with us
for a while, that they will not be mended until the ghetto is mended.
Even if there were teachers available for them, the problem would
remain that they distrust teachers and institutions.

In the next year there will be initiated a pilot program in remedial
reading, using whatever buildings are available and non-teachers
who are known in the community to instruct. We are now engaged
in training ghetto personnel to master the Accelerated Progressive
Choice Reading Program, developed by Myron Woolman of the
Institute of Educational Research in Washington. The method developed by Dr. Woolman was designed specifically for use by relatively untrained personnel. It incorporates the learning-by-teaching
approach. The content of the reading material can be tailored to
meet the special vocabulary and requirements of the particular
neighborhood, and it allows the student to advance as rapidly as his
capabilities permit. I have seen this method in operation and was
amazed at the interest, involvement, discipline, and motivation of
both instructors and students.

The initial cadre of instructors will come from the active membership of community organizations. They will recruit their own students. Later, other community volunteers will be utilized; eventually
we will use older students to instruct others. I observed student
helpers giving instruction in a junior high school in North Carolina.
The eighth-graders were almost as effective as the teachers, and if

eighth-graders can teach reading to others, it becomes obvious that with proper supervision the number of potential teachers is enormous. Many bright ghetto youngsters have shown an eagerness to help.

We are extremely excited about prospects for this program throughout the country. But one point needs emphasis. The remedial-reading program can be effective only in the context of other community programs. It recommends itself not only as an effective technique but as one form of community expression in the context of a community learning to express itself. Our task will be to begin building that larger context. A remedial-reading program will have limited effect if there is no literacy course to permit the parent to keep up with his child. Both programs will have limited effect if the parents have no marketable skills and live in squalor. Relentlessly we will seek out local people to staff or at least assist in the projects the community chooses to mount.

What kind of programs can be developed within communities? Here is a list of some of the programs pursued by CORE community action projects throughout the country.

1. Remedial education, with particular emphasis on reading, writing, and arithmetic, comprehension and oral expression.
2. Academic counseling and vocational guidance.
3. Provision of after-school study centers, after-school tutoring, summer, weekend, and after-school classes.
4. Establishment of programs for preschool children.
5. Special services for disoriented migrant and transient families.
6. Provision of medical examinations and health education.
7. Rehabilitation and retraining of physically or mentally handicapped persons.
8. Provision of health, rehabilitation, employment, educational and related services to young men not qualified for military service.
9. Community child-care centers and youth activity centers.
10. Improvement of housing and living facilities and home-management skills.
11. Provision of recreation and physical-fitness services and facilities.

The impetus which will mount these programs, I repeat, must be part and parcel of the same impetus which will lead Negroes to vote or to protest and picket. I make no idle connection. The social-service mentality, enamored of its own techniques, filled with a lust to serve, invariably fails in the ghetto. We need people helping themselves, made healthy by the knowledge that the world is theirs, invigorated by their effort to make it just.

I stress the inalienability of political action from the total picture, because local communities will certainly be under heavy pressure to drop their political activities. Much of the money for community development will come from the government and foundations, and as much as the anti-poverty program and other programs may be committed to the ideal of community self-help, no government will be able to subsidize for too long what a congressman will call subversive. Most assuredly, the phone call will come into a CORE office: "Be practical, you know I'm on your side, you know how hard I've fought to preserve your independence. Call off the garbage-dump." "I can't," the answer must be, "it's not my decision, it's theirs." It's a desperate dilemma. We need outside money, but not outside advice. And to complicate matters further, there will be Negroes and Negro organizations which will court favor with municipal and state and federal officials, angling for power, angling for approval. There is no simple solution, though there are some useful platitudes. We must be cautious and not be compromised by accepting support with strings attached. We must try to remain as self-sufficient as possible. We must not betray the people, not only because betrayal is dishonorable but because it undermines the freedom we are trying to build. There is no freedom without political self-expression.

And here I would speak of the cultural dimension of our efforts. I have spoken of the burgeoning sense of pride and self-identity among American Negroes—the identification with Africa, the sense of roots. Education is not simply a collection of skills; it must have a solid substance which resounds with meaning for the learner. When there is something to learn which, in the fullest sense, is about ourselves and for ourselves, we will learn. Until recently very little a ghetto child was asked to learn academically related in a valid way to his life. Not being free, he could make no history; unable to make history, he had no reason to learn it, or to learn anything. CORE intends to teach Negro history; and to study the world with an eye to the history our brothers are making; we will build libraries filled with *our* books, and we will write new ones. And recite *our* poetry, and write great new poems. We will produce plays, and exhibit our art, and dance as only we can dance. And we will make the American music, the Negro music, which is jazz, as Americans, as Negroes. We will be for ourselves, but not only for ourselves, for America, for mankind. And all of this is possible because we are making ourselves free.

The title of this book asks the question, Freedom—When? In a way it is an outmoded question. A relic of those days when we dreamed of some apocalyptic end to our struggles. A flash of light perhaps, singing and weeping, the heavenly kingdom. But freedom is not an end: it is a beginning and a process. We feel further from the end now than we did before a decade's progress was wrought. We have settled down for a long haul. Things are not so clear as they once seemed, but the complexity is splendid; perhaps that is freedom too. We are overcoming. Maybe that is the sum of my reflections.

7e. Why Should We March?

A. PHILIP RANDOLPH*

Though I have found no Negroes who want to see the United Nations[1] lose this war [World War II], I have found many who, before the war ends, want to see the stuffing knocked out of white supremacy and of empire over subject peoples. American Negroes, involved as we are in the general issues of the conflict, are confronted not with a choice but with the challenge both to win democracy for ourselves at home and to help win the war for democracy the world over.

There is no escape from the horns of this dilemma. There ought not to be escape. For if the war for democracy is not won abroad, the fight for democracy cannot be won at home. If this war cannot be won for the white peoples, it will not be won for the darker races.

Conversely, if freedom and equality are not vouchsafed the peoples of color, the war for democracy will not be won. Unless this double-barreled thesis is accepted and applied, the darker races will never wholeheartedly fight for the victory of the United Nations. That is why those familiar with the thinking of the American Negro have sensed his lack of enthusiasm, whether among the educated or uneducated, rich or poor, professional or nonprofessional, religious or secular, rural or urban, North, South, East or West.

That is why questions are being raised by Negroes in church, labor union, and fraternal society; in poolroom, barbershop, schoolroom, hospital, hair-dressing parlor; on college campus, railroad, and bus. One can hear such questions asked as these: What have Negroes to fight for? What's the difference between Hitler and that "cracker" Talmadge of Georgia? Why has a man got to be Jim-Crowed to die for democracy? If you haven't got democracy yourself, how can you carry it to somebody else?

What are the reasons for this state of mind? The answer is: dis-

* From *Survey Graphic*, Vol. 31, November 1942, pp. 488-89.
    [1] The Allies.

crimination, segregation, Jim Crow. Witness the navy, the army, the air corps; and also government services at Washington. In many parts of the South, Negroes in Uncle Sam's uniform are being put upon, mobbed, sometimes even shot down by civilian and military police, and on occasion lynched. Vested political interests in race prejudice are so deeply entrenched that to them winning the war against Hitler is secondary to preventing Negroes from winning democracy for themselves. This is worth many divisions to Hitler and Hirohito. While labor, business, and farm are subjected to ceilings and doors and not allowed to carry on as usual, these interests trade in the dangerous business of race hate as usual.

When the defense program began and billions of the taxpayers' money were appropriated for guns, ships, tanks, and bombs, Negroes presented themselves for work only to be given the cold shoulder, North as well as South; and despite their qualifications, Negroes were denied skilled employment. Not until their wrath and indignation took the form of a proposed protest march on Washington, scheduled for July 1, 1941, did things begin to move in the form of defense jobs for Negroes. The march was postponed by the timely issuance (June 25, 1941) of the famous Executive Order No. 8802 by President Roosevelt. But this order and the President's Committee on Fair Employment Practice, established thereunder, have as yet only scratched the surface by way of eliminating discriminations on account of race or color in war industry. Both management and labor unions in too many places and in too many ways are still drawing the color line.

It is to meet this situation squarely with direct action that the March on Washington Movement launched its present program of protest mass meetings. Twenty thousand were in attendance at Madison Square Garden, June 16; sixteen thousand in the Coliseum in Chicago, June 26; nine thousand in the City Auditorium of St. Louis, August 14. Meetings of such magnitude were unprecedented among Negroes.[2] The vast throngs were drawn from all walks and levels of Negro life—businessmen, teachers, laundry workers, Pullman porters, waiters, and red caps; preachers, crapshooters, and social workers; jitterbugs and Ph.D.'s. They came and sat in silence, thinking, applauding only when they considered the truth was told, when they felt strongly that something was going to be done about it.

The March on Washington Movement is essentially a movement

[2] In view of charges made that they were subsidized by Nazi funds, it may not be amiss to point out that of the $8,000 expenses of the Madison Square meeting every dime was contributed by Negroes themselves, except for tickets bought by some liberal white organizations.

of the people. It is all Negro and pro-Negro, but not for that reason anti-white or anti-Semitic, or anti-Catholic, or anti-foreign, or anti-labor. Its major weapon is the nonviolent demonstration of Negro mass power. Negro leadership has united back of its drive for jobs and justice. "Whether Negroes should march on Washington, and if so, when?" will be the focus of a forthcoming national conference. For the plan of a protest march has not been abandoned. Its purpose would be to demonstrate that American Negroes are in deadly earnest, and all out for their full rights. No power on earth can cause them today to abandon their fight to wipe out every vestige of second class citizenship and the dual standards that plague them.

A community is democratic only when the humblest and weakest person can enjoy the highest civil, economic, and social rights that the biggest and most powerful possess. To trample on these rights of both Negroes and poor whites is such a commonplace in the South that it takes readily to anti-social, anti-labor, anti-Semitic, and anti-Catholic propaganda. It was because of laxness in enforcing the Weimar constitution in republican Germany that Nazism made headway. Oppression of the Negroes in the United States, like suppression of the Jews in Germany, may open the way for a fascist dictatorship.

By fighting for their rights now, American Negroes are helping to make America a moral and spiritual arsenal of democracy. Their fight against the poll tax, against lynch law, segregation, and Jim Crow, their fight for economic, political, and social equality, thus becomes part of the global war for freedom.

Program of the March on Washington Movement

1. We demand, in the interest of national unity, the abrogation of every law which makes a distinction in treatment between citizens based on religion, creed, color, or national origin. This means an end to Jim Crow in education, in housing, in transportation, and in every other social, economic, and political privilege; and especially, we demand, in the capital of the nation, an end to all segregation in public places and in public institutions.

2. We demand legislation to enforce the Fifth and Fourteenth Amendments guaranteeing that no person shall be deprived of life, liberty, or property without due process of law, so that the full weight of the national government may be used for the protection of life and thereby may end the disgrace of lynching.

3. We demand the enforcement of the Fourteenth and Fifteenth Amendments and the enactment of the Pepper Poll Tax bill so that all barriers in the exercise of the suffrage are eliminated.

4. We demand the abolition of segregation and discrimination in the army, navy, marine corps, air corps, and all other branches of national defense.

5. We demand an end to discrimination in jobs and job training. Further, we demand that the FEPC be made a permanent administrative agency of the U. S. Government and that it be given power to enforce its decisions based on its findings.

6. We demand that federal funds be withheld from any agency which practices discrimination in the use of such funds.

7. We demand colored and minority group representation on all administrative agencies so that these groups may have recognition of their democratic right to participate in formulating policies.

8. We demand representation for the colored and minority racial groups on all missions, political and technical, which will be sent to the peace conference so that the interests of all people everywhere may be fully recognized and justly provided for in the post-war settlement.

Selections 8a–8c

THE MARCH ON WASHINGTON, 1963

The following selections include the statement by the leaders of the March on Washington, August 28, 1963, stating the purpose and calling for discipline; Martin Luther King's famous speech during the March; and President Kennedy's reaction to this historic event which took place one hundred years after the Emancipation Proclamation.

8a.   Statement by the Leaders*

The Washington March of August 28th is more than just a demonstration.

It was conceived as an outpouring of the deep feeling of millions of white and colored American citizens that the time has come for the government of the United States of America, and particularly for the Congress of that government, to grant and guarantee complete equality in citizenship to the Negro minority of our population.

As such, the Washington March is a living petition—in the flesh —of the scores of thousands of citizens of both races who will be present from all parts of our country.

It will be orderly, but not subservient. It will be proud, but not arrogant. It will be nonviolent, but not timid. It will be unified in purposes and behavior, not splintered into groups and individual competitors. It will be outspoken, but not raucous.

It will have the dignity befitting a demonstration in behalf of the human rights of twenty millions of people, with the eye and the judgment of the world focused upon Washington, D. C., on August 28, 1963.

In a neighborhood dispute there may be stunts, rough words and even hot insults; but when a whole people speaks to its government, the dialogue and the action must be on a level reflecting the worth of that people and the responsibility of that government.

We, the undersigned, who see the Washington March as wrapping up the dreams, hopes, ambitions, tears, and prayers of millions who have lived for this day, call upon the members, followers and wellwishers of our several organizations to make the March a disciplined and purposeful demonstration.

We call upon them all, black and white, to resist provocations to disorder and to violence.

We ask them to remember that evil persons are determined to smear this March and to discredit the cause of equality by deliberate efforts to stir disorder.

We call for self-discipline, so that no one in our own ranks, however enthusiastic, shall be the spark for disorder.

We call for resistance to the efforts of those who, while not enemies of the March as such, might seek to use it to advance causes not dedicated primarily to civil rights or to the welfare of our country.

We ask each and every one in attendance in Washington or in spiritual attendance back home to place the Cause above all else.

* From *Speeches by the Leaders: The March on Washington for Jobs and Freedom, August 28, 1963*, New York: NAACP, n.d.

Do not permit a few irresponsible people to hang a new problem around our necks as we return home. Let's do what we came to do —place the national human rights problem squarely on the doorstep of the national Congress and of the Federal Government.

Let's win at Washington.

Signed:

MATHEW AHMANN, Executive Director of the National Catholic Conference for Interracial Justice.

REVEREND EUGENE CARSON BLAKE, Vice-Chairman of the Commission on Race Relations of the National Council of Churches of Christ in America.

JAMES FARMER, National Director of the Congress of Racial Equality.

REVEREND MARTIN LUTHER KING, JR., President of the Southern Christian Leadership Conference.

JOHN LEWIS, Chairman of the Student Nonviolent Coordinating Committee.

RABBI JOACHIM PRINZ, President of the American Jewish Congress.

A. PHILIP RANDOLPH, President of the Negro American Labor Council.

WALTER REUTHER, President of the United Automobile, Aerospace and Agricultural Implement Workers of America, AFL–CIO, and Chairman, Industrial Union Department, AFL–CIO.

ROY WILKINS, Executive Secretary of the National Association for the Advancement of Colored People.

WHITNEY M. YOUNG, JR., Executive Director of the National Urban League.

In addition, the March has been endorsed by major religious, fraternal, labor and civil rights organizations.

8b. I Have a Dream

MARTIN LUTHER KING, JR.*

I am happy to join with you today in what will go down in history as the greatest demonstration for freedom in the history of our nation.

* From *Speeches by the Leaders: The March on Washington for Jobs and Freedom,* *August 28, 1963,* New York: NAACP, n.d.

Five score years ago, a great American, in whose symbolic shadow we stand today, signed the Emancipation Proclamation. This momentous decree came as the great beacon light of hope for millions of Negro slaves who had been seared in the flames of withering injustice. It came as the joyous daybreak to end the long night of their captivity.

But one hundred years later the Negro still is not free. One hundred years later, the life of the Negro is still badly crippled by the manacles of segregation and the chains of discrimination. One hundred years later, the Negro lives on a lonely island of poverty in the midst of a vast ocean of material prosperity. One hundred years later, the Negro is still languished in the corners of American society and finds himself an exile in his own land. So we have come here today to dramatize the shameful condition.

In a sense we've come to our Nation's Capital to cash a check. When the architects of our republic wrote the magnificent words of the Constitution and the Declaration of Independence, they were signing a promissory note to which every American was to fall heir. This note was a promise that all men, yes, black men as well as white men, should be guaranteed the unalienable rights of life, liberty and the pursuit of happiness.

It is obvious today that America has defaulted on this promissory note insofar as her citizens of color are concerned. Instead of honoring this sacred obligation, America has given the Negro people a bad check, a check which has come back marked "Insufficient Funds." But we refuse to believe the bank of justice is bankrupt. We refuse to believe that there are insufficient funds in the great vaults of opportunity of this nation. So we have come to cash this check, a check that will give us upon demand, the riches of freedom and the security of justice. We have also come to this hallowed spot to remind America of the fierce urgency of now.

This is no time to engage in the luxury of cooling off or to take the tranquilizing drug of gradualism. Now is the time to make real the promises of democracy. Now is the time to rise from the dark and desolate valley of segregation to the sunlit path of racial justice. Now is the time to lift our nation from the quicksands of racial injustice to the solid rock of brotherhood. Now is the time to make justice a reality for all of God's children.

It would be fatal for the nation to overlook the urgency of the moment. This sweltering summer of the Negro's legitimate discontent will not pass until there is an invigorating autumn of freedom and equality. Nineteen sixty-three is not an end but a beginning. Those who hoped that the Negro needed to blow off steam and will now be content will have a rude awakening if the nation returns to business as usual. There will be neither rest nor tranquility in America until the Negro is guaranteed his citizenship rights. The whirlwinds of revolt will continue to shake the foundations of our nation until the bright day of justice emerges.

But there is something I must say to my people who stand on the warm threshold which leads them to the palace of justice. In the process of gaining our rightful place we must not be guilty of wrongful deeds. Let us not seek to satisfy our thirst for freedom by drinking from the cup of bitterness and hatred. We must forever conduct our struggle on the high plane of dignity and discipline. We must not allow our creative protest to degenerate into physical violence. Again and again we must rise to the majestic heights of meeting physical force with soul force.

The marvelous new militancy which has engulfed the Negro community must not lead us to a distrust of all white people, for many of our white brothers, as evidenced by their presence here today, have come to realize that their destiny is tied up with our destiny. They have come to realize that their freedom is inextricably bound to our freedom. We cannot walk alone.

And as we walk we must make the pledge that we shall always march ahead. We cannot turn back. There are those who are asking the devotees of civil rights: "When will you be satisfied?" We can never be satisfied as long as our bodies, heavy with the fatigue of travel, cannot gain lodging in the motels of the highways and the hotels of the cities. We cannot be satisfied as long as the Negro's basic mobility is from a smaller ghetto to a larger one. We can never be satisfied as long as our children are stripped of their self-hood and robbed of their dignity by signs stating: "For Whites Only." We cannot be satisfied as long as the Negro in Mississippi cannot vote and the Negro in New York believes he has nothing for which to vote. No, no, we are not satisfied and we will not be satisfied until justice rolls down like the waters and righteousness like a mighty stream.

I am not unmindful that some of you have come here out of great trials and tribulations, some of you have come fresh from narrow jail cells, some of you have come from areas where your quest for freedom left you battered by the storms of persecution and staggered by the winds of police brutality. You have been the veterans of creative suffering. Continue to work with the faith that unearned suffering is redemptive.

Go back to Mississippi, go back to Alabama, go back to South Carolina, go back to Georgia, go back to Louisiana, go back to the slums and ghettos of our northern cities, knowing that somehow this situation can and will be changed. Let us not wallow in the valley of despair.

I say to you today, my friends, even though we face the difficulties of today and tomorrow, I still have a dream. It is a dream deeply rooted in the American dream. I have a dream that one day this nation will rise up and live out the true meaning of its creed: "We hold these truths to be self-evident that all men are created equal."

I have a dream that one day on the red hills of Georgia the sons of former slaves and the sons of former slaveowners will be able to sit down together at the table of brotherhood.

I have a dream that one day even the State of Mississippi, a state sweltering with the heat of injustice, sweltering with the heat of oppression, will be transformed into an oasis of freedom and justice. I have a dream that my four little children will one day live in a nation where they will not be judged by the color of their skin but by the content of their character. I have a dream today.

I have a dream that one day down in Alabama with its vicious racists, with its Governor having his lips dripping with the words of interposition and nullification—one day right there in Alabama, little black boys and black girls will be able to join hands with little white boys and white girls as sisters and brothers.

I have a dream today.

I have a dream that one day every valley shall be exalted, every hill and mountain shall be made low, the rough places will be made plain and the crooked places will be made straight, and the glory of the Lord shall be revealed, and all flesh shall see it together.

This is our hope. This is the faith that I go back to the South with. With this faith we will be able to hew out of the mountain of despair a stone of hope. With this faith we will be able to transform the jangling discords of our nation into a beautiful symphony of brotherhood. With this faith we will be able to work together, to pray together, to struggle together, to go to jail together, to stand up for freedom together, knowing that we will be free one day.

This will be the day when all of God's children will be able to sing with new meaning:

> My country 'tis of thee,
> Sweet land of liberty,
> Of thee I sing:
> Land where my fathers died,
> Land of the pilgrims' pride,
> From every mountain-side
> Let Freedom ring.

And if America is to be a great nation, this must become true. So, let freedom ring from the prodigious hill tops of New Hampshire. Let freedom ring from the mighty mountains of New York. Let freedom ring from the heightening Alleghenies of Pennsylvania. Let freedom ring from the snowcapped Rockies of Colorado. Let freedom ring from the curvaceous slopes of California. But not only that, let freedom ring from Stone Mountain of Georgia.

Let freedom ring from Lookout Mountain of Tennessee.

Let freedom ring from every hill and molehill of Mississippi. From every mountainside, let freedom ring. And when we allow freedom to ring, when we let it ring from every village, from every hamlet, from every state and every city, we will be able to speed up that day when all of God's children, black men and white men, Jews and Gentiles, Protestants and Catholics, will be able to join hands and sing in the words of the old Negro spiritual: "Free at last! free at last! thank God almighty, we are free at last!"

8c. Statement by President Kennedy on the March on Washington*

We have witnessed today in Washington tens of thousands of Americans—both Negro and white—exercising their right to assemble peaceably and direct the widest possible attention to a great national issue. Efforts to secure equal treatment and equal opportunity for all without regard to race, color, creed, or nationality are neither novel nor difficult to understand. What is different today is the intensified and widespread public awareness of the need to move forward in achieving these objectives—objectives which are older than this Nation.

Although this summer has seen remarkable progress in translating civil rights from principles into practices, we have a very long way yet to travel. One cannot help but be impressed with the deep fervor and the quiet dignity that characterizes the thousands who have gathered in the Nation's Capital from across the country to demonstrate their faith and confidence in our democratic form of government. History has seen many demonstrations—of widely varying character and for a whole host of reasons. As our thoughts travel to other demonstrations that have occurred in different parts of the world, this Nation can properly be proud of the demonstration that has occurred here today. The leaders of the organizations sponsoring the March and all who have participated in it deserve our apprecia-

* From *Public Papers of the President of the United States, John F. Kennedy,* Vol. III, 1963, Washington, D. C.: U. S. Government Printing Office, 1964.

tion for the detailed preparations that made it possible and for the orderly manner in which it has been conducted.

The executive branch of the Federal Government will continue its efforts to obtain increased employment and to eliminate discrimination in employment practices, two of the prime goals of the March. In addition, our efforts to secure enactment of the legislative proposals made to the Congress will be maintained, including not only the civil rights bill, but also proposals to broaden and strengthen the manpower development and training program, the youth employment bill, amendments to the vocational education program, the establishment of a work-study program for high school age youth, strengthening of the adult basic education provisions in the administration's education program, and the amendments proposed to the public welfare work-relief and training program. This Nation can afford to achieve the goals of a full employment policy— it cannot afford to permit the potential skills and educational capacity of its citizens to be unrealized.

The cause of 20 million Negroes has been advanced by the program conducted so appropriately before the Nation's shrine to the Great Emancipator, but even more significant is the contribution to all mankind.

Note: The statement was released at 6:15 P.M. after the President had met in his office with the leaders of the March on Washington for Jobs and Freedom.

Selection 9

A FAMOUS NEGRO WRITER LOOKS AT THE PROBLEMS OF MEANS AND ENDS

LANGSTON HUGHES*

Langston Hughes' well known character, Simple, discusses the methods he would use to solve The Problem.

"If I was white," said Simple, "I would be wondering what in God's name to do with the Negroes."

"That is exactly what white Americans are wondering these days," I replied.

"Yes," said Simple, "because every time the white folks give Negroes a little something, the Negroes want *more*."

"A little civil rights is not enough," I said, "just like a crust of bread will hardly do for a meal."

"Whoever made up that old saying about 'A half loaf is better than none,' was wrong," said Simple. "A half a loaf just whets the appetite for more. When Negroes did not have no civil rights at all in Alabama, nobody agitated for *more* civil rights. 'Give a Negro an inch, and he'll want an el,' is a true saying for true. Take me, now, I don't want to be treated *half* right, I want to be *right*."

"The sit-in kids in Greensboro, North Carolina, back in 1960 certainly started something which spread all across the country—Negroes marching, picketing, boycotting everywhere."

"Something really got started," said Simple, "but the white folks are too slow. Just decreeing decrees and passing bills is not enough on their part. Results is what colored folks want to see, *results*. Let

* From *New York Post*, August 6, 1965.

us in them Jim Crow unions. Let us out of these Jim Crow schools. Give us a decent house at rent folks can pay. Tear down the slums. Let my people vote in Alabama."

. . .

"You don't want much, do you?"

"I wants everything anybody else in this American country has that's all. My ancestries worked three hundred years without pay to help build this country up. Why shouldn't I have everything white Americans has? We earned it. My grandpa and my grandma and my great-grandpa and great-grandma, and their pa and ma before them on back to when the first slave ship came, earned it. If white folks don't intend to pay us our back wages then they can at least give us our back civil rights, and cut the red tape. If they is just going to keep on handing out civil rights *bills* instead of dollar bills, they better make some of them civil rights bills *work*. Am I right or wrong?"

"That is why Negroes keep on agitating," I said, "since nothing much works."

"We have got to think up some new ways of agitating, though," said Simple, "because the old ways is about worn out. Speech making is not enough. The young Negroes is impatient. Now, if they have to go in a draft to Viet Nam, who knows what is going to happen? The young Negroes is liable to say, 'Gimme my gun right here in Harlem and Selma and Chicago and Cambridge, Maryland.' That is what they is liable to say, these kids nowadays. And what answer will the white folks have for that?"

. . .

"You know all them Southern draft boards is going to draft the colored boys first, just to get them off the picket lines and far away somewhere where Sheriff Clark won't have to be bothered with them, and Governor Wallace can sleep in peace. You know Sheriff Clark and Governor Wallace and Faubus and folks like that is not going to no Viet Nam war themselves. I think the draft ought to start with *old* folks and work down to the young, myself. Draft all the old heads that vote for war, and see how they would like being out there in Viet Nam in the rice swamps and jungles with snakes and moccasins that bite even with your boots laced. Let them run from bombs and bullets a little. Then they won't be so quick as to want to send young folks over there."

"You are getting into international questions of vast proportions,"

I said. "What I am wondering, for instance, is what should Negroes do now *right here* in Harlem."

"Turn on the water, some of them is saying, and let it run all day and all night during the water shortage," said Simple. "All over Harlem and Brooklyn and the Bronx, 'Let the water run,' some kids on Lenox Av. these days is saying. Their idea is since New York has got a water shortage, dry it out a little more. If white folks get dried out dry enough, they will settle this Negro Problem *now*. If all the white folks in New York could not get a drink of water in the morning, neither take a bath on Saturday night, and the laundries couldn't wash nobody's clothes at all, and Mayor Wagner could not even wash his hands because his face bowl were dry at Gracie Mansion, something would be done. A water-wasting protest! Only thing about running off all the water in New York, is that I might get thirsty myself some hot day. Of course, if my bar is still open, I could drink beer."

"But you forget, my good man," I said, "if there were no water, there would be no ice to keep the beer cold."

"Then call off the protest," said Simple, "because hot beer would just make the race problem worse."

Selection 10

LETTER FROM BIRMINGHAM CITY JAIL

MARTIN LUTHER KING, JR.*

This selection begins with a letter from eight Alabama clergymen to Reverend Martin Luther King, and gives his famous reply in his Letter from Birmingham City Jail, *explaining why he had engaged in civil disobedience.*

* Martin Luther King, Jr., *Letter from Birmingham City Jail*, Philadelphia: American Friends Service Committee, May, 1963.

April 12, 1963

We the undersigned clergymen are among those who, in January, issued "An Appeal for Law and Order and Common Sense," in dealing with racial problems in Alabama. We expressed understanding that honest convictions in racial matters could properly be pursued in the courts, but urged that decisions of those courts should in the meantime be peacefully obeyed.

Since that time there had been some evidence of increased forbearance and a willingness to face facts. Responsible citizens have undertaken to work on various problems which cause racial friction and unrest. In Birmingham, recent public events have given indication that we all have opportunity for a new constructive and realistic approach to racial problems.

However, we are now confronted by a series of demonstrations by some of our Negro citizens, directed and led in part by outsiders. We recognize the natural impatience of people who feel that their hopes are slow in being realized. But we are convinced that these demonstrations are unwise and untimely.

We agree rather with certain local Negro leadership which has called for honest and open negotiation of racial issues in our area. And we believe this kind of facing of issues can best be accomplished by citizens of our own metropolitan area, white and Negro, meeting with their knowledge and experience of the local situation. All of us need to face that responsibility and find proper channels for its accomplishment.

Just as we formerly pointed out that "hatred and violence have no sanction in our religious and political traditions," we also point out that such actions as incite to hatred and violence, however technically peaceful those actions may be, have not contributed to the resolution of our local problems. We do not believe that these days of new hope are days when extreme measures are justified in Birmingham.

We commend the community as a whole, and the local news media and law enforcement officials in particular, on the calm manner in which these demonstrations have been handled. We urge the public to continue to show restraint should the demonstrations continue, and the law enforcement officials to remain calm and continue to protect our city from violence.

We further strongly urge our own Negro community to withdraw support from these demonstrations, and to unite locally in working peacefully for a better Birmingham. When rights are consistently denied, a cause should be pressed in the courts and in negotiations among local leaders, and not in the streets. We appeal to both our white and Negro citizenry to observe the principles of law and order and common sense.

Signed by:

C. C. J. CARPENTER, D.D., LL.D., Bishop of Alabama

JOSEPH A. DURICK, D.D., Auxiliary Bishop, Diocese of Mobile-Birmingham

RABBI MILTON L. GRAFMAN, Temple Emanu-El, Birmingham, Alabama

BISHOP PAUL HARDIN, Bishop of the Alabama-West Florida Conference of the Methodist Church

BISHOP NOLAN B. HARMON, Bishop of the North Alabama Conference of the Methodist Church

GEORGE M. MURRAY, DD., LL.D., Bishop Coadjutor, Episcopal Diocese of Alabama

EDWARD V. RAMAGE, Moderator, Synod of the Alabama Presbyterian Church in the United States

EARL STALLINGS, Pastor, First Baptist Church, Birmingham, Alabama

> MARTIN LUTHER KING, JR.
> Birmingham City Jail
> April 16, 1963

My dear Fellow Clergymen,

While confined here in the Birmingham City Jail, I came across your recent statement calling our present activities "unwise and untimely." Seldom, if ever, do I pause to answer criticism of my work and ideas. If I sought to answer all of the criticisms that cross my desk, my secretaries would be engaged in little else in the course of the day and I would have no time for constructive work. But since I feel that you are men of genuine goodwill and your criticisms are sincerely set forth, I would like to answer your statement in what I hope will be patient and reasonable terms.

I think I should give the reason for my being in Birmingham, since you have been influenced by the argument of "outsiders coming in." I have the honor of serving as president of the Southern Christian Leadership Conference, an organization operating in every Southern state with headquarters in Atlanta, Georgia. We have some eighty-five affiliate organizations all across the South— one being the Alabama Christian Movement for Human Rights. Whenever necessary and possible we share staff, educational, and financial resources with our affiliates. Several months ago our local affiliate here in Birmingham invited us to be on call to engage in a nonviolent direct action program if such were deemed necessary. We readily consented and when the hour came we lived up to our promises. So I am here, along with several members of my staff, because we were invited here. I am here because I have basic organizational ties here. Beyond this, I am in Birmingham because injustice is here. Just as the eighth century prophets left their little villages and carried their "thus saith the Lord" far beyond the boundaries of their home town, and just as the Apostle Paul left his little village of Tarsus and carried the gospel of Jesus Christ to practically every hamlet and city of the Graeco-Roman world, I too am compelled to carry the gospel of freedom beyond my particular home town. Like Paul, I must constantly respond to the Macedonian call for aid.

Moreover, I am cognizant of the interrelatedness of all communities and states. I cannot sit idly by in Atlanta and not be concerned about what happens in Birmingham. Injustice anywhere is a threat to justice everywhere. We are caught in an inescapable network of mutuality tied in a single garment of destiny. Whatever affects one directly affects all indirectly. Never again can we afford to live with the narrow, provincial "outside agitator" idea. Anyone who lives inside the United States can never be considered an outsider anywhere in this country.

You deplore the demonstrations that are presently taking place in Birmingham. But I am sorry that your statement did not express a similar concern for the conditions that brought the demonstrations into being. I am sure that each of you would want to go beyond the superficial social analyst who looks merely at effects, and does not grapple with underlying causes. I would not hesitate to say that it is unfortunate that so-called demonstrations are taking place in Birmingham at this time, but I would say in more emphatic terms that it is even more unfortunate that the white power structure of this city left the Negro community with no other alternative.

In any nonviolent campaign there are four basic steps: (1) collection of the facts to determine whether injustices are alive; (2) negotiation; (3) self-purification; and (4) direct action. We have gone through all of these steps in Birmingham. There can be no gainsaying of the fact that racial injustice engulfs this community. Birmingham is probably the most thoroughly segregated city in the United States. Its ugly record of police brutality is known in every section of this country. Its unjust treatment of Negroes in the courts is a notorious reality. There have been more unsolved bombings of Negro homes and churches in Birmingham than any city in this nation. These are the hard, brutal, and unbelievable facts. On the basis of these conditions Negro leaders sought to negotiate with the city fathers. But the political leaders consistently refused to engage in good faith negotiation.

Then came the opportunity last September to talk with some of the leaders of the economic community. In these negotiating sessions certain promises were made by the merchants—such as the promise to remove the humiliating racial signs from the stores. On the basis of these promises Rev. Shuttlesworth and the leaders of the Alabama Christian Movement for Human Rights agreed to call a moratorium on any type of demonstrations. As the weeks and months unfolded we realized that we were the victims of a broken promise. The signs remained. As in so many experiences of the past we were confronted with blasted hopes, and the dark shadow of a deep disappointment settled upon us. So we had no alternative except that of preparing for direct action, whereby we would present our very bodies as a means of laying our case before the conscience of the local and national community. We were not unmindful of the difficulties involved. So we decided to go through a process of self-purification. We started having workshops on nonviolence and repeatedly asked ourselves the questions, "Are you able to accept blows without retaliating?" "Are you able to endure the ordeals of jail?"

We decided to set our direct action program around the Easter season, realizing that with the exception of Christmas, this was the largest shopping period of the year. Knowing that a strong economic withdrawal program would be the by-product of direct action, we felt that this was the best time to bring pressure on the merchants for the needed changes. Then it occurred to us that the March election was ahead, and so we speedily decided to postpone action until after election day. When we discovered that Mr. Connor was in the run-off, we decided again to postpone action so that the demonstrations could not be used to cloud the issues. At this time we agreed to begin our nonviolent witness the day after the run-off.

This reveals that we did not move irresponsibly into direct action. We too wanted to see Mr. Connor defeated; so we went through postponement after postponement to aid in this community need. After this we felt that direct action could be delayed no longer.

You may well ask, "Why direct action? Why sit-ins, marches, etc.? Isn't negotiation a better path?" You are exactly right in your call for negotiation. Indeed, this is the purpose of direct action. Nonviolent direct action seeks to create such a crisis and establish such creative tension that a community that has constantly refused to negotiate is forced to confront the issue. It seeks so to dramatize the issue that it can no longer be ignored. I just referred to the creation of tension as a part of the work of the nonviolent resister. This may sound rather shocking. But I must confess that I am not afraid of the word tension. I have earnestly worked and preached against violent tension, but there is a type of constructive nonviolent tension that is necessary for growth. Just as Socrates felt that it was necessary to create a tension in the mind so that individuals could rise from the bondage of myths and half-truths to the unfettered realm of creative analysis and objective appraisal, we must see the need of having nonviolent gadflies to create the kind of tension in society that will help men rise from the dark depths of prejudice and racism to the majestic heights of understanding and brotherhood. So the purpose of the direct action is to create a situation so crisis-packed that it will inevitably open the door to negotiation. We, therefore, concur with you in your call for negotiation. Too long has our beloved Southland been bogged down in the tragic attempt to live in monologue rather than dialogue.

One of the basic points in your statement is that our acts are untimely. Some have asked, "Why didn't you give the new administration time to act?" The only answer that I can give to this inquiry is that the new administration must be prodded about us, much as the outgoing one before it acts. We will be sadly mistaken if we feel that the election of Mr. Boutwell will bring the millennium to Birmingham. While Mr. Boutwell is much more articulate and gentle than Mr. Connor, they are both segregationists dedicated to the task of maintaining the status quo. The hope I see in Mr. Boutwell is that he will be reasonable enough to see the futility of massive resistance to desegregation. But he will not see this without pressure from the devotees of civil rights. My friends, I must say to you that we have not made a single gain in civil rights without determined legal and nonviolent pressure. History is the long and tragic story of the fact that privileged groups seldom give up their privileges voluntarily. Individuals may see the moral light and voluntarily give up their unjust posture; but as Reinhold

Niebuhr has reminded us, groups are more immoral than individuals.

We know through painful experience that freedom is never voluntarily given by the oppressor; it must be demanded by the oppressed. Frankly I have never yet engaged in a direct action movement that was "well timed," according to the timetable of those who have not suffered unduly from the disease of segregation. For years now I have heard the word "Wait!" It rings in the ear of every Negro with a piercing familiarity. This "wait" has almost always meant "never." It has been a tranquilizing thalidomide, relieving the emotional stress for a moment, only to give birth to an ill-formed infant of frustration. We must come to see with the distinguished jurist of yesterday that "justice too long delayed is justice denied." We have waited for more than three hundred and forty years for our constitutional and God-given rights. The nations of Asia and Africa are moving with jet-like speed toward the goal of political independence, and we still creep at horse and buggy pace toward the gaining of a cup of coffee at a lunch counter.

I guess it is easy for those who have never felt the stinging darts of segregation to say wait. But when you have seen vicious mobs lynch your mothers and fathers at will and drown your sisters and brothers at whim; when you have seen hate filled policemen curse, kick, brutalize, and even kill your black brothers and sisters with impunity; when you see the vast majority of your twenty million Negro brothers smothering in an air-tight cage of poverty in the midst of an affluent society; when you suddenly find your tongue twisted and your speech stammering as you seek to explain to your six-year-old daughter why she can't go to the public amusement park that has just been advertised on television, and see tears welling up in her little eyes when she is told that Funtown is closed to colored children, and see the depressing clouds of inferiority begin to form in her little mental sky, and see her begin to distort her little personality by unconsciously developing a bitterness toward white people; when you have to concoct an answer for a five-year-old son asking in agonizing pathos: "Daddy, why do white people treat colored people so mean?"; when you take a cross country drive and find it necessary to sleep night after night in the uncomfortable corners of your automobile because no motel will accept you; when you are humiliated day in and day out by nagging signs reading "white" men and "colored"; when your first name becomes "nigger" and your middle name becomes "boy" (however old you are) and your last name becomes "John," and when your wife and mother are never given the respected title "Mrs."; when you are harried by day and haunted by night by the fact that you are a Negro, living constantly at tip-toe stance never quite knowing what to expect next, and plagued with inner fears and outer resentments; when you are forever fighting a degenerating sense of "nobodiness";—then you will understand why we find it difficult to wait. There comes a time when the cup of endurance runs over, and men are no longer willing to be plunged into an abyss of injustice where they experience the bleakness of corroding despair. I hope, sirs, you can understand our legitimate and unavoidable impatience.

You express a great deal of anxiety over our willingness to break laws. This is certainly a legitimate concern. Since we so diligently urge people to obey the Supreme Court's decision of 1954 outlawing segregation in the public schools, it is rather strange and paradoxical to find us consciously breaking laws. One may well ask, "How can you advocate breaking some laws and obeying others?" The answer is found in the fact that there are two types of laws: There are *just* laws and there are *unjust* laws. I would be the first to advocate obeying just laws. One has not only a legal but moral responsibility to obey just laws. Conversely, one has a moral responsibility to disobey unjust laws. I would agree with Saint Augustine that "An unjust law is no law at all."

Now what is the difference between the two? How does one determine when a law is just or unjust? A just law is a man-made code that squares with the moral law or the law of God. An unjust law is a code that is out of harmony with the moral law. To put it in the terms of Saint Thomas Aquinas, an unjust law is a human law that is not rooted in eternal and natural law. Any law that uplifts human personality is just. Any law that degrades human personality is unjust. All segregation statutes are unjust because segregation distorts the soul and damages the personality. It gives the segregator a false sense of superiority and the segregated a false sense of inferiority. To use the words of Martin Buber, the great Jewish philosopher, segregation substitutes an "I-it" relationship for the "I-thou" relationship, and ends up relegating persons to the status of things. So segregation is not only politically, economically, and sociologically unsound, but it is morally wrong and sinful. Paul Tillich has said that sin is separation. Isn't segregation an existential expression of man's tragic separation, an expression of his awful estrangement, his terrible sinfulness? So I can urge men to obey the 1954 decision of the Supreme Court because it is morally right, and I can urge them to disobey segregation ordinances because they are morally wrong.

Let us turn to a more concrete example of just and unjust laws. An unjust law is a code that a majority inflicts on a minority that is not binding on itself. This is *difference* made legal. On the other hand a just law is a code that a majority compels a minority to follow that it is willing to follow itself. This is *sameness* made legal.

Let me give another explanation. An unjust law is a code inflicted upon a minority which that minority had no part in enacting or creating because they did not have the unhampered right to vote. Who can say the legislature of Alabama which set up the segregation laws was democratically elected? Throughout the state of Alabama all types of conniving methods are used to prevent Negroes from becoming registered voters and there are some counties without a single Negro registered to vote despite the fact that the Negro constitutes a majority of the population. Can any law set up in such a state be considered democratically structured?

These are just a few examples of unjust and just laws. There are some instances when a law is just on its face but unjust in its application. For instance, I was arrested Friday on a charge of parading without a permit. Now there is nothing wrong with an ordinance which requires a permit for a parade, but when the ordinance is used to preserve segregation and to deny citizens the First Amendment privilege of peaceful assembly and peaceful protest, then it becomes unjust.

I hope you can see the distinction I am trying to point out. In no sense do I advocate evading or defying the law as the rabid segregationist would do. This would lead to anarchy. One who breaks an unjust law must do it *openly, lovingly* (not hatefully as the white mothers did in New Orleans when they were seen on television screaming "nigger, nigger, nigger") and with a willingness to accept the penalty. I submit that an individual who breaks a law that conscience tells him is unjust, and willingly accepts the penalty by staying in jail to arouse the conscience of the community over its injustice, is in reality expressing the very highest respect for law.

Of course there is nothing new about this kind of civil disobedience. It was seen sublimely in the refusal of Shadrach, Meshach, and Abednego to obey the laws of Nebuchadnezzar because a higher moral law was involved. It was practiced superbly by the early Christians who were willing to face hungry lions and the excruciating pain of chopping blocks, before submitting to certain unjust laws of the Roman Empire. To a degree academic freedom is a reality today because Socrates practiced civil disobedience.

We can never forget that everything Hitler did in Germany was "legal" and everything the Hungarian freedom fighters did in Hungary was "illegal." It was "illegal" to aid and comfort a Jew in Hitler's Germany. But I am sure that, if I had lived in Germany during that time, I would have aided and comforted my Jewish brothers even though it was illegal. If I lived in a communist country today where certain principles dear to the Christian faith are suppressed, I believe I would openly advocate disobeying these anti-religious laws.

I must make two honest confessions to you, my Christian and Jewish brothers. First I must confess that over the last few years I have been gravely disappointed with the white moderate. I have almost reached the regrettable conclusion that the Negroes' great stumbling block in the stride toward freedom is not the White Citizens' "Counciler" or the Ku Klux Klanner, but the white moderate who is more devoted to "order" than to justice; who prefers a negative peace which is the absence of tension to a positive peace which is the presence of justice; who constantly says "I agree with you in the goal you seek, but I can't agree with your methods of direct action"; who paternalistically feels that he can set the time-table for another man's freedom; who lives by the myth of time and who constantly advises the Negro to wait until a "more convenient season." Shallow understanding from people of good will is more frustrating than absolute misunderstanding from people of ill will. Lukewarm acceptance is much more bewildering than outright rejection.

I had hoped that the white moderate would understand that law and order exist for the purpose of establishing justice, and that when they fail to do this they become the dangerously structured dams that block the flow of social progress. I had hoped that the white moderate would understand that the present tension in the South is merely a necessary phase of the transition from an obnoxious negative peace, where the Negro passively accepted his unjust plight, to a substance-filled positive peace, where all men will respect the dignity and worth of human personality. Actually, we who engage in nonviolent direct action are not the creators of tension. We merely bring to the surface the hidden tension that is already alive. We bring it out in the open where it can be seen and dealt with. Like a boil that can never be cured as long as it is covered up but must be opened with all its pus-flowing ugliness to the natural medicines of air and light, injustice must likewise be exposed, with all of the tension its exposing creates, to the light of human conscience and the air of national opinion before it can be cured.

In your statement you asserted that our actions, even though peaceful, must be condemned because they precipitate violence. But can this assertion be logically made? Isn't this like condemning the robbed man because his possession of money precipitated the evil act of robbery? Isn't this like condemning Socrates because his unswerving commitment to truth and his philosophical delvings precipitated the misguided popular mind to make him drink the hemlock? Isn't this like condemning Jesus because His unique God consciousness and never-ceasing devotion to His will precipitated the evil act of crucifixion? We must come to see, as federal courts have consistently affirmed, that it is immoral to urge an individual to withdraw his efforts to gain his basic constitutional rights because the quest precipitates violence. Society must protect the robbed and punish the robber.

I had also hoped that the white moderate would reject the myth of time. I received a letter this morning from a white brother in Texas which said: "All Christians know that the colored people will receive equal rights eventually, but is it possible that you are in too great of a religious hurry? It has taken Christianity almost 2000 years to accomplish what it has. The teachings of Christ take time to come to earth." All that is said here grows out of a tragic misconception of time. It is the strangely irrational notion that there is something in the very flow of time that will inevitably cure all ills. Actually time is neutral. It can be used either destructively or constructively. I am coming to feel that the people of ill will have used time much more effectively than the people of good will. We will have to repent in this generation not merely for the vitriolic words and actions of the bad people, but for the appalling silence of the good people. We must come to see that human progress never rolls in on wheels of inevitability. It comes through the tireless efforts and persistent work of men willing to be co-workers with God, and without this hard work time itself becomes an ally of the forces of social stagnation.

We must use time creatively, and forever realize that the time is always ripe to do right. Now is the time to make real the promise of democracy, and transform our pending national elegy into a creative psalm of brotherhood. Now is the time to lift our national policy from the quicksand of racial injustice to the solid rock of human dignity.

You spoke of our activity in Birmingham as extreme. At first I was rather disappointed that fellow clergymen would see my non-violent efforts as those of the extremist. I started thinking about the fact that I stand in the middle of two opposing forces in the Negro community. One is a force of complacency made up of

Negroes who, as a result of long years of oppression, have been so completely drained of self-respect and a sense of "somebodiness" that they have adjusted to segregation, and of a few Negroes in the middle class who, because of a degree of academic and economic security, and because at points they profit by segregation, have unconsciously become insensitive to the problems of the masses. The other force is one of bitterness and hatred and comes perilously close to advocating violence. It is expressed in the various black nationalist groups that are springing up over the nation, the largest and best known being Elijah Muhammad's Muslim movement. This movement is nourished by the contemporary frustration over the continued existence of racial discrimination. It is made up of people who have lost faith in America, who have absolutely repudiated Christianity, and who have concluded that the white man is an incurable "devil." I have tried to stand between these two forces saying that we need not follow the "do-nothingism" of the complacent or the hatred and despair of the black nationalist. There is the more excellent way of love and nonviolent protest. I'm grateful to God that, through the Negro church, the dimension of nonviolence entered our struggle. If this philosophy had not emerged I am convinced that by now many streets of the South would be flowing with floods of blood. And I am further convinced that if our white brothers dismiss us as "rabble rousers" and "outside agitators"—those of us who are working through the channels of nonviolent direct action—and refuse to support our nonviolent efforts, millions of Negroes, out of frustration and despair, will seek solace and security in black nationalist ideologies, a development that will lead inevitably to a frightening racial nightmare.

Oppressed people cannot remain oppressed forever. The urge for freedom will eventually come. This is what has happened to the American Negro. Something within has reminded him of his birthright of freedom; something without has reminded him that he can gain it. Consciously and unconsciously, he has been swept in by what the Germans call the *Zeitgeist,* and with his black brothers of Africa, and his brown and yellow brothers of Asia, South America, and the Caribbean, he is moving with a sense of cosmic urgency toward the promised land of racial justice. Recognizing this vital urge that has engulfed the Negro community, one should readily understand public demonstrations. The Negro has many pent-up resentments and latent frustrations. He has to get them out. So let him march sometime; let him have his prayer pilgrimages to the city hall; understand why he must have sit-ins and freedom rides. If his repressed emotions do not come out in these nonviolent ways, they will come out in ominous expressions of violence. This is not a threat; it is a fact of history. So I have not said to my people, "Get rid of your discontent." But I have tried to say that this normal and healthy discontent can be channeled through the creative outlet of nonviolent direct action. Now this approach is being dismissed as extremist. I must admit that I was initially disappointed in being so categorized.

But as I continued to think about the matter I gradually gained a bit of satisfaction from being considered an extremist. Was not Jesus an extremist in love? "Love your enemies, bless them that curse you, pray for them that despitefully use you." Was not Amos an extremist for justice—"Let justice roll down like waters and righteousness like a mighty stream." Was not Paul an extremist for the gospel of Jesus Christ—"I bear in my body the marks of the Lord Jesus." Was not Martin Luther an extremist—"Here I stand; I can do none other so help me God." Was not John Bunyan an extremist—"I will stay in jail to the end of my days before I make a butchery of my conscience." Was not Abraham Lincoln an extremist—"This nation cannot survive half slave and half free." Was not Thomas Jefferson an extremist—"We hold these truths to be self-evident; that all men are created equal." So the question is not whether we will be extremist but what kind of extremist will we be. Will we be extremists for hate or will we be extremists for love? Will we be extremists for the preservation of injustice—or will we be extremists for the cause of justice? In that dramatic scene on Calvary's hill three men were crucified. We must never forget that all three were crucified for the same crime—the crime of extremism. Two were extremists for immorality, and thus fell below their environment. The other, Jesus Christ, was an extremist for love, truth, and goodness, and thereby rose above His environment. So, after all, maybe the South, the nation, and the world are in dire need of creative extremists.

I had hoped that the white moderate would see this. Maybe I was too optimistic. Maybe I expected too much. I guess I should have realized that few members of a race that has oppressed another race can understand or appreciate the deep groans and passionate yearnings of those that have been oppressed, and still fewer have the vision to see that injustice must be rooted out by strong, persistent, and determined action. I am thankful, however, that some of our white brothers have grasped the meaning of this social revolution and committed themselves to it. They are still all too small in quantity, but they are big in quality. Some like Ralph McGill, Lillian Smith, Harry Golden, and James Dabbs have written about our struggle in eloquent, prophetic, and understanding terms. Others have marched with us down nameless streets of the South. They have languished in filthy, roach-infested jails, suffering the abuse and brutality of angry policemen who see them as "dirty nigger lovers." They, unlike so many of their moderate brothers and sisters, have recognized the urgency of the moment and sensed the need for powerful "action" antidotes to combat the disease of segregation.

Let me rush on to mention my other disappointment. I have been so greatly disappointed with the white Church and its leadership. Of course there are some notable exceptions. I am not unmindful of the fact that each of you has taken some significant stands on this issue. I commend you, Rev. Stallings, for your Christian stand on this past Sunday, in welcoming Negroes to your worship service on a non-segregated basis. I commend the Catholic leaders of this state for integrating Springhill College several years ago.

But despite these notable exceptions I must honestly reiterate that I have been disappointed with the Church. I do not say that as one of those negative critics who can always find something wrong with the Church. I say it as a minister of the gospel, who loves the Church; who was nurtured in its bosom; who has been sustained by its spiritual blessings and who will remain true to it as long as the cord of life shall lengthen.

I had the strange feeling when I was suddenly catapulted into the leadership of the bus protest in Montgomery several years ago that we would have the support of the white Church. I felt that the white ministers, priests, and rabbis of the South would be some of our strongest allies. Instead, some have been outright opponents, refusing to understand the freedom movement and misrepresenting its leaders; all too many others have been more cautious than courageous and have remained silent behind the anesthetizing security of stained glass windows.

In spite of my shattered dreams of the past, I came to Birmingham with the hope that the white religious leadership of this community would see the justice of our cause and, with deep moral concern, serve as the channel through which our just grievances could get to the power structure. I had hoped that each of you would understand. But again I have been disappointed.

I have heard numerous religious leaders of the South call upon their worshippers to comply with a desegregation decision because it is the law, but I have longed to hear white ministers say follow this decree because integration is morally right and the Negro is your brother. In the midst of blatant injustices inflicted upon the Negro, I have watched white churches stand on the sideline and merely mouth pious irrelevancies and sanctimonious trivialities. In the midst of a mighty struggle to rid our nation of racial and economic injustice, I have heard so many ministers say, "Those are social issues with which the Gospel has no real concern," and I have watched so many churches commit themselves to a completely other-worldly religion which made a strange distinction between body and soul, the sacred and the secular.

So here we are moving toward the exit of the twentieth century with a religious community largely adjusted to the status quo, standing as a tail light behind other community agencies rather than a headlight leading men to higher levels of justice.

I have travelled the length and breadth of Alabama, Mississippi, and all the other Southern states. On sweltering summer days and crisp autumn mornings I have looked at her beautiful churches with their spires pointing heavenward. I have beheld the impressive outlay of her massive religious education buildings. Over and over again I have found myself asking: "Who worships here? Who is their God? Where were their voices when the lips of Governor Barnett dripped with words of interposition and nullification? Where were they when Governor Wallace gave the clarion call for defiance and hatred? Where were their voices of support when tired, bruised, and weary Negro men and women decided to rise from the dark dungeons of complacency to the bright hills of creative protest?"

Yes, these questions are still in my mind. In deep disappointment, I have wept over the laxity of the Church. But be assured that my tears have been tears of love. There can be no deep disappointment where there is not deep love. Yes, I love the Church; I love her sacred walls. How could I do otherwise? I am in the rather unique position of being the son, the grandson, and the great grandson of preachers. Yes, I see the Church as the body of Christ. But, oh! How we have blemished and scarred that body through social neglect and fear of being nonconformist.

There was a time when the Church was very powerful. It was during that period when the early Christians rejoiced when they were deemed worthy to suffer for what they believed. In those days the Church was not merely a thermometer that recorded the ideas and principles of popular opinion; it was a thermostat that transformed the mores of society. Wherever the early Christians entered a town the power structure got disturbed and immediately sought to convict them for being "disturbers of the peace" and "outside agitators." But they went on with the conviction that they were a "colony of heaven" and had to obey God rather than man. They were small in number but big in commitment. They were too God-intoxicated to be "astronomically intimidated." They brought an end to such ancient evils as infanticide and gladiatorial contest.

Things are different now. The contemporary Church is so often a weak, ineffectual voice with an uncertain sound. It is so often the arch-supporter of the status quo. Far from being disturbed by the presence of the Church, the power structure of the average community is consoled by the Church's silent and often vocal sanction of things as they are.

But the judgment of God is upon the Church as never before. If the Church of today does not recapture the sacrificial spirit of the early Church, it will lose its authentic ring, forfeit the loyalty of millions, and be dismissed as an irrelevant social club with no meaning for the twentieth century. I am meeting young people every day whose disappointment with the Church has risen to outright disgust.

Maybe again I have been too optimistic. Is organized religion too inextricably bound to the status quo to save our nation and the world? Maybe I must turn my faith to the inner spiritual Church, the church within the Church, as the true *ecclesia* and the hope of the world. But again I am thankful to God that some noble souls from the ranks of organized religion have broken loose from the paralyzing chains of conformity and joined us as active partners in the struggle for freedom. They have left their secure congregations and walked the streets of Albany, Georgia, with us. They have gone through the highways of the South on torturous rides for freedom. Yes, they have gone to jail with us. Some have been kicked out of their churches and lost the support of their bishops and fellow ministers. But they have gone with the faith that right defeated is stronger than evil triumphant. These men have been the leaven in the lump of the race. Their witness has been the spiritual salt that has preserved the true meaning of the Gospel in these troubled times. They have carved a tunnel of hope through the dark mountain of disappointment.

I hope the Church as a whole will meet the challenge of this decisive hour. But even if the Church does not come to the aid of justice, I have no despair about the future. I have no fear about the outcome of our struggle in Birmingham, even if our motives are presently misunderstood. We will reach the goal of freedom in Birmingham and all over the nation, because the goal of America is freedom. Abused and scorned though we may be, our destiny is tied up with the destiny of America. Before the pilgrims landed at Plymouth, we were here. Before the pen of Jefferson etched across the pages of history the majestic words of the Declaration of Independence, we were here. For more than two centuries our foreparents labored in this country without wages; they made cotton "king"; and they built the homes of their masters in the midst of brutal injustice and shameful humiliation—and yet out of a bottomless vitality they continued to thrive and develop. If the inexpressible cruelties of slavery could not stop us, the opposition we now face will surely fail. We will win our freedom because the sacred heritage of our nation and the eternal will of God are embodied in our echoing demands.

I must close now. But before closing I am impelled to mention one other point in your statement that troubled me profoundly. You warmly commended the Birmingham police force for keeping "order" and "preventing violence." I don't believe you would have so warmly commended the police force if you had seen its angry violent dogs literally biting six unarmed, nonviolent Negroes. I don't believe you would so quickly commend the policemen if you would observe their ugly and inhuman treatment of Negroes here in the city jail; if you would watch them push and curse old Negro women and young Negro girls; if you would see them slap and kick old Negro men and young Negro boys; if you will observe them, as they did on two occasions, refuse to give us food because we wanted to sing our grace together. I'm sorry that I can't join you in your praise for the police department.

It is true that they have been rather disciplined in their public handling of the demonstrators. In this sense they have been rather publicly "nonviolent." But for what purpose? To preserve the evil system of segregation. Over the last few years I have consistently preached that nonviolence demands that the means we use must be as pure as the ends we seek. So I have tried to make it clear that it is wrong to use immoral means to attain moral ends. But now I must affirm that it is just as wrong, or even more so, to use moral means to preserve immoral ends. Maybe Mr. Connor and his policemen have been rather publicly nonviolent, as Chief Prichett was in Albany, Georgia, but they have used the moral means of nonviolence to maintain the immoral end of flagrant racial injustice. T. S. Eliot has said that there is no greater treason than to do the right deed for the wrong reason.

I wish you had commended the Negro sit-inners and demonstrators of Birmingham for their sublime courage, their willingness to suffer, and their amazing discipline in the midst of the most inhuman provocation. One day the South will recognize its real heroes. They will be the James Merediths, courageously and with a majestic sense of purpose, facing jeering and hostile mobs and the agonizing loneliness that characterizes the life of the pioneer.

They will be old, oppressed, battered Negro women, symbolized in a seventy-two year old woman of Montgomery, Alabama, who rose up with a sense of dignity and with her people decided not to ride the segregated buses, and responded to one who inquired about her tiredness with ungrammatical profundity: "My feets is tired, but my soul is rested." They will be young high school and college students, young ministers of the gospel and a host of the elders, courageously and nonviolently sitting in at lunch counters and willingly going to jail for conscience sake. One day the South will know that when these disinherited children of God sat down at lunch counters they were in reality standing up for the best in the American dream and the most sacred values in our Judeo-Christian heritage, and thus carrying our whole nation back to great wells of democracy which were dug deep by the founding fathers in the formulation of the Constitution and the Declaration of Independence.

Never before have I written a letter this long (or should I say a book?). I'm afraid that it is much too long to take your precious time. I can assure you that it would have been much shorter if I had been writing from a comfortable desk, but what else is there to do when you are alone for days in the dull monotony of a narrow jail cell other than write long letters, think strange thoughts, and pray long prayers?

If I have said anything in this letter that is an overstatement of the truth and is indicative of an unreasonable impatience, I beg you to forgive me. If I have said anything in this letter that is an understatement of the truth and is indicative of my having a patience that makes me patient with anything less than brotherhood, I beg God to forgive me.

I hope this letter finds you strong in the faith. I also hope that circumstances will soon make it possible for me to meet each of you, not as an integrationist or a civil rights leader, but as a fellow clergyman and a Christian brother. Let us all hope that the dark clouds of racial prejudice will soon pass away and the deep fog of misunderstanding will be lifted from our fear-drenched communities and in some not too distant tomorrow the radiant stars of love and brotherhood will shine over our great nation with all of their scintillating beauty.

Yours for the cause of Peace and Brotherhood

MARTIN LUTHER KING, JR.

Selections 11a–11b

SNCC

SNCC, Student Nonviolent Coordinating Committee, is an organization of young people that has emerged as an important force in the movement for civil rights. Selection 11a is taken from Howard Zinn's SNCC: The New Abolitionists.

Stokely Carmichael, National Chairman of the Student Nonviolent Coordinating Committee, used the term Black Power *during the March on Mississippi in the summer of 1966. In Selection 11b, published in the* New York Review of Books, *he clarifies the meaning of this term, as well as his position in the racial crisis.*

11a. The New Abolitionists

HOWARD ZINN*

For the first time in our history a major social movement, shaking the nation to its bones, is being led by youngsters. This is not to deny the inspirational leadership of a handful of adults (Martin Luther King and James Farmer), the organizational direction by veterans in the struggle (Roy Wilkins and A. Philip Randolph), or the participation of hundreds of thousands of older people in the current Negro revolt. But that revolt, a long time marching out of the American past, its way suddenly lit up by the Supreme Court decision, and beginning to rumble in earnest when thousands of people took to the streets of Montgomery in the bus boycott, first flared into a national excitement with the sit-ins by college students that started the decade of the 1960's.

And since then, those same youngsters, hardened by countless jailings and beatings, now out of school and living in ramshackle headquarters all over the Deep South, have been striking the

* From Howard Zinn, *SNCC: The New Abolitionists*, Boston: Beacon Press, 1964. pp. 1–15.

sparks, again and again, for that fire of change spreading through the South and searing the whole country.

These young rebels call themselves the Student Nonviolent Coordinating Committee, but they are more a movement than an organization, for no bureaucratized structure can contain their spirit, no printed program capture the fierce and elusive quality of their thinking. And while they have no famous leaders, very little money, no inner access to the seats of national authority, they are clearly the front line of the Negro assault on the moral comfort of white America.

To be with them, walking a picket line in the rain in Hattiesburg, Mississippi or sleeping on a cot in a cramped "office" in Greenville, Mississippi; to watch them walk out of the stone jailhouse in Albany, Georgia; to see them jabbed by electric prod poles and flung into paddy wagons in Selma, Alabama, or link arms and sing at the close of a church meeting in the Delta—is to feel the presence of greatness. It is a greatness that comes from their relationship to history, and it does not diminish when they are discovered to be human: to make mistakes or feel fear, to act with envy, or hostility or even violence.

All Americans owe them a debt for—if nothing else—releasing the idealism locked so long inside a nation that has not recently tasted the drama of a social upheaval. And for making us look on the young people of the country with a new respect. Theirs was the silent generation until they spoke, the complacent generation until they marched and sang, the money-seeking generation until they renounced comfort and security to fight for justice in the dank and dangerous hamlets of the Black Belt.

· · ·

. . . Sixteen college youngsters . . . in the fall of 1961, decided to drop everything—school and family and approved ambition—and move into the Deep South to become the first guerrilla fighters of the Student Nonviolent Coordinating Committee.

By early 1964, the number was up to 150. In the most heated days of abolitionism before the Civil War, there were never that many dedicated people who turned their backs on ordinary pursuits and gave their lives wholly to the movement. There were William Lloyd Garrison and Wendell Phillips and Theodore Weld and Frederick Douglass and Sojourner Truth and a handful of others, and there were hundreds of part-time abolitionists and thousands of followers. But for 150 youngsters today to turn on their pasts, to decide to live and work twenty-four hours a day in the most dangerous region of the United States, is cause for wonder. And wherever they have come from—the Negro colleges of the South, the Ivy League universities of the North, the small and medium colleges all over the country—they have left ripples of astonishment behind. This college generation as a whole is not committed, by any means. But it has been shaken.

These 150—who next year will be 250 or more, because the excitement grows daily on the college campuses—are the new abolitionists. It is not fanciful to invest them with a name that has the ring of history; we are always shy about recognizing the historic worth of events when they take place before our eyes, about recognizing heroes when they are still flesh and blood and not yet transfixed in marble. But there is no doubt about it: we have in this country today a movement which will take its place alongside that of the abolitionists, the Populists, the Progressives—and may outdo them all.

Their youth makes us hesitant to recognize their depth. But the great social upsurge of post-war America is the Negro revolt, and this revolt has gotten its most powerful impetus from young people, who gave it a new turn in 1960 and today, as anonymous as infantrymen everywhere, form the first rank in a nonviolent but ferocious war against the old order.

It would be easy to romanticize them, but they are too young, too vulnerable, too humanly frail to fit the stereotype of heroes. They don't match the storybook martyrs who face death with silent stoicism; the young fellows sometimes cry out when they are beaten; the girls may weep when abused in prison. Most often, however, they sing. This was true of the farmer and labor movements in this country, and of all the wars; but there has never been a singing movement like this one. Perhaps it is because most of them were brought up on the gospel songs and hymns of the Negro church in the South, perhaps also because they are young, probably most of all because what they are doing inspires song. They have created a new gospel music out of the old, made up of songs adapted or written in jail or on the picket line. Every battle station in the Deep South now has its Freedom Chorus, and the mass meetings there end with everyone standing, led by the youngsters of SNCC, linking arms, and singing "We Shall Overcome."

• • •

Yet they are the most serious social force in the nation today. They are not playing; it is no casual act of defiance, no irresponsible whim of adolescence, when young people of sixteen or twenty or twenty-five turn away from school, job, family, all the tokens of success in modern America, to take up new lives, hungry and hunted, in the hinterland of the Deep South. Jim Forman was a teacher in Chicago before he joined the SNCC, and an aspiring novelist; Bob Moses was a graduate of Harvard, teaching in New York; Charles Sherrod was a divinity school graduate in Virginia; Mendy Samstein, a graduate of Brandeis University, was on the faculty of a Negro college, working for his Ph.D. in history at the University of Chicago. Others found it easier—and harder—for they came right out of the Black Belt and, even though they tasted college, they had nowhere then to go but back towards danger and freedom: John Lewis, Sam Block, Willie Peacock, Lafayette Surney, MacArthur Cotton, Lawrence Guyot and too many more to name.

. . .

These new abolitionists are different from the earlier ones. The movement of the 1830's and 1840's was led by white New Englanders, bombarding the South and the nation with words. The present movement is planted firmly in the deepest furrows of the Deep South, and it consists mostly of Negroes who make their pleas to the nation more by physical acts of sacrifice than by verbal declamation. Their task is made easier by modern mass communication, for the nation, indeed the whole world, can *see* them, on the television screen or in newspaper photos—marching, praying, singing, *demonstrating* their message. The white people of America, to whom Negroes were always a dark, amorphous mass, are forced to see them for the first time sharply etched as individuals, their features—both physical and moral—stark, clear, and troubling.

But in one important way these young people are very much like the abolitionists of old: they have a healthy disrespect for respectability; they are not ashamed of being agitators and troublemakers; they see it as the essence of democracy. In defense of William Lloyd Garrison, against the accusation that he was too harsh, a friend replied that the nation was in a sleep so deep "nothing but a rude and almost ruffian-like shake could rouse her." The same deliberate harshness lies behind the activities of James Forman, John Lewis, Bob Moses, and other leaders of SNCC. What Samuel May once said of Garrison and slavery might be said today of each of these people and segregation: "He will shake our nation to its center, but he will shake slavery out of it."

. . .

Yet the staff member of the Student Nonviolent Coordinating Committee can never be isolated as was the New England abolitionist of the 1830's, who was far from slave territory, and surrounded by whites unconcerned for the slave. The SNCC youngster is in the midst of his people, surrounded by them, protected by them. To be cut off, by harsh criticism of his "extremism," from Northern white intellectuals or from those in national political power is a minor blow, cushioned by a popularity based on the poor and the powerless, but perhaps even more comforting because of that.

. . .

There is another striking contrast to Garrison and Phillips, Lewis Tappan and Theodore Weld: these young people are not middle-class reformers who became somehow concerned about others. They come themselves from the ranks of the victims, not just because they are mostly Negroes, but because for the most part their fathers are janitors and laborers, their mothers maids and factory workers.

In late 1963 I checked the backgrounds of forty-one field workers for SNCC in Mississippi (roughly one-third of the total SNCC force in the Deep South). Thirty-five of them were Negro, and twenty-five of them came from the Deep South. Of the six white staff members two were from the Deep South. The white youngsters and most of the Northern Negroes came from middle-class homes; their fathers were ministers or teachers or civil service workers. All of the Southern Negroes, and some of the Northern Negroes (twenty-one out of thirty-five) came from homes where the mothers were maids or domestics, the fathers factory workers, truck drivers, farmers, bricklayers, carpenters. Twenty-nine (about three-fourths) of the total SNCC Mississippi staff were between fifteen and twenty-two years old. There were twelve between twenty-two and twenty-nine, and one person each in his thirties, forties, and fifties. Twenty-six, or about two thirds, of the Mississippi SNCC staff were either college graduates or had some college education. Ten had finished high school or had some high school education and two had no more than part of an elementary school education. If one were to generalize roughly about the SNCC staff in the Deep South, one would say they are young, they are Negro, they come from the South, their families are poor and of the working class, but they have been to college. Northern middle-class whites and Negroes are a minority.

As of mid-1964, about 150 people worked full-time for SNCC, roughly 80 percent of them Negro. Of the whites, most were Northerners, but the few white Southerners played important roles (Jane Stembridge, the first office secretary in Atlanta; Bob Zellner and Sam Shirah, assigned to white college campuses; Sandra Hayden, in the Jackson, Mississippi office). Of the Negro staff people, most were Southern born; more and more, young Negroes were being recruited out of Deep South towns to become SNCC field secretaries right there at home.

By 1963, the annual budget of SNCC was about $250,000, almost all of this coming from the contributions of individuals and organizations (churches, colleges, foundations). About one-fourth of this income was being used to pay the salaries of field secretaries, $10 a week for most of them, with a few married people in the Atlanta office receiving $50 or $60 a week. Most of the remaining income went to pay for field operations in Mississippi, southwest Georgia, and the other areas of concentration.

• • •

These are young radicals; the word "revolution" occurs again and again in their speech. Yet they have no party, no ideology, no creed. They have no clear idea of a blueprint for a future society. But they do know clearly that the values of present American society—and this goes beyond racism to class distinction, to commercialism, to profit-seeking, to the setting of religious or national barriers against human contact—are not for them.

They are prepared to use revolutionary means against the old order. They believe in civil disobedience. They are reluctant to rely completely on the niceties of negotiation and conciliation, distrustful of those who hold political and economic power. They have a tremendous respect for the potency of the demonstration, an eagerness to move out of the political maze of normal parliamentary procedure and to confront policy-makers directly with a power beyond orthodox politics—the power of people in the streets and on the picket line.

They are nonviolent in that they suffer beatings with folded arms and will not strike back. There have been one or two rare exceptions of discipline being broken, yet this must be laid against hundreds of instances of astounding self-control in the face of unspeakable brutality.

Next to the phrase "nonviolence," however, what you hear most often among SNCC workers is "direct action." They believe, without inflicting violence, and while opening themselves to attack, in confronting a community boldly with the sounds and sights of protest. When it is argued that this will inevitably bring trouble, even

violence, the answer is likely to be that given by James Bevel, who
in his activity with the Southern Christian Leadership Conference
works closely with SNCC in Alabama and Mississippi: "Maybe
the Devil has got to come out of these people before we will have
peace. . . ."

. . .

The nation has suddenly become aware that the initiative today
is in the hands of these 150 young people who have moved into the
Deep South to transform it. Everyone waits on their next action:
the local police, the state officials, the national government, the mass
media of the country, Negroes and whites sitting at their radios and
television sets across the land. Meanwhile, these people are living,
hour by hour, the very ideals which this country has often thought
about, but not yet managed to practice: they are courageous, though
afraid, they live and work together in a brotherhood of black and
white. Southerner and Northerner, Jew and Christian and agnostic,
the likes of which this country has not yet seen. They are creating
new definitions of success, of happiness, of democracy.

It is just possible that the momentum created by their enormous
energy—now directed against racial separation—may surge, before
it can be contained, against other barriers which keep people apart
in the world: poverty, and nationalism, and all tyranny over the
minds and bodies of men. If so, the United States may truly be on
the verge of a revolution—nonviolent, but sweeping in its consequences—and led by those who, perhaps, are most dependable in a
revolution: the young.

11b. What We Want

STOKELY CARMICHAEL[*]

One of the tragedies of the struggle against racism is that up to
now there has been no national organization which could speak to
the growing militancy of young black people in the urban ghetto.
There has been only a civil rights movement, whose tone of voice
was adapted to an audience of liberal whites. It served as a sort of
buffer zone between them and angry young blacks. None of its so-
called leaders could go into a rioting community and be listened
to. In a sense, I blame ourselves—together with the mass media—
for what has happened in Watts, Harlem, Chicago, Cleveland,
Omaha. Each time the people in those cities saw Martin Luther

[*] From *The New York Review of Books*, Vol. VII, No. 4, September 22, 1966.

King get slapped, they became angry; when they saw four little black girls bombed to death, they were angrier; and when nothing happened, they were steaming. We had nothing to offer that they could see, except to go out and be beaten again. We helped to build their frustration.

For too many years, black Americans marched and had their heads broken and got shot. They were saying to the country, "Look, you guys are supposed to be nice guys and we are only going to do what we are supposed to do—why do you beat us up, why don't you give us what we ask, why don't you straighten yourselves out?" After years of this, we are at almost the same point—because we demonstrated from a position of weakness. We cannot be expected any longer to march and have our heads broken in order to say to whites: come on, you're nice guys. For you are not nice guys. We have found you out.

An organization which claims to speak for the needs of a community—as does the Student Nonviolent Coordinating Committee —must speak in the tone of that community, not as somebody else's buffer zone. This is the significance of black power as a slogan. For once, black people are going to use the words they want to use— not just the words whites want to hear. And they will do this no matter how often the press tries to stop the use of the slogan by equating it with racism or separatism.

An organization which claims to be working for the needs of a community—as SNCC does—must work to provide that community with a position of strength from which to make its voice heard. This is the significance of black power beyond the slogan.

· · ·

Black power can be clearly defined for those who do not attach the fears of white America to their questions about it. We should begin with the basic fact that black Americans have two problems: they are poor and they are black. All other problems arise from this two-sided reality: lack of education, the so-called apathy of black men. Any program to end racism must address itself to that double reality.

Almost from its beginning, SNCC sought to address itself to both conditions with a program aimed at winning political power for impoverished Southern blacks. We had to begin with politics be- cause black Americans are a propertyless people in a country where property is valued above all. We had to work for power, because this country does not function by morality, love, and nonviolence, but by power. Thus we determined to win political power, with the idea of moving on from there into activity that would have economic effects. With power, the masses could *make or participate in making* the decisions which govern their destinies, and thus create basic change in their day-to-day lives.

. . . The concept of "black power" is not a recent or isolated phenomenon: It has grown out of the ferment of agitation and activity by different people and organizations in many black communities over the years. Our last year of work in Alabama added a new concrete possibility. In Lowndes county, for example, black power will mean that if a Negro is elected sheriff, he can end police brutality. If a black man is elected tax assessor, he can collect and channel funds for the building of better roads and schools serving black people—thus advancing the move from political power into the economic arena. In such areas as Lowndes, where black men have a majority, they will attempt to use it to exercise control. This is what they seek: control. Where Negroes lack a majority, black power means proper representation and sharing of control. It means the creation of power bases from which black people can work to change statewide or nationwide patterns of oppression through pressure from strength—instead of weakness. Politically, black power means what it has always meant to SNCC: the coming-together of black people to elect representatives and *to force those representatives to speak to their needs.* It does not mean merely putting black faces into office. A man or woman who is black and from the slums cannot be automatically expected to speak to the needs of black people. Most of the black politicians we see around the country today are not what SNCC means by black power. The power must be that of a community, and emanate from there.

SNCC today is working in both North and South on programs of voter registration and independent political organizing. In some places, such as Alabama, Los Angeles, New York, Philadelphia, and New Jersey, independent organizing under the black panther symbol is in progress. The creation of a national "black panther party" must come about; it will take time to build, and it is much too early to predict its success. We have no infallible master plan and we make no claim to exclusive knowledge of how to end racism; different groups will work in their own different ways. SNCC cannot spell out the full logistics of self-determination but it can address itself to the problem by helping black communities define their needs, realize their strength, and go into action along a variety of lines which they must choose for themselves. Without knowing all the answers, it can address itself to the basic problem of poverty; to the fact that in Lowndes County, 86 white families own 90 per cent of the land. What are black people in that county going to do for jobs, where are they going to get money? There must be reallocation of land, of money.

• • •

. . . Integration speaks not at all to the problem of poverty, only to the problem of blackness. Integration today means the man who "makes it," leaving his black brothers behind in the ghetto as fast as his new sports car will take him. It has no relevance to the Harlem wino or to the cottonpicker making three dollars a day. As a lady I know in Alabama once said, "the food that Ralph Bunche eats doesn't fill my stomach."

Integration, moreover, speaks to the problem of blackness in a despicable way. As a goal, it has been based on complete acceptance of the fact that *in order to have* a decent house or education, blacks must move into a white neighborhood or send their children to a white school. This reinforces, among both black and white, the idea that "white" is automatically better and "black" is by definition inferior. This is why integration is a subterfuge for the maintenance of white supremacy. It allows the nation to focus on a handful of Southern children who get into white schools, at great price, and to ignore the 94 per cent who are left behind in unimproved all-black schools. Such situations will not change until black people have power—to control their own school boards, in this case. Then Negroes become equal in a way that means something, and integration ceases to be a one-way street. Then integration doesn't mean draining skills and energies from the ghetto into white neighborhoods; then it can mean white people moving from Beverly Hills into Watts, white people joining the Lowndes County Freedom Organization. Then integration becomes relevant.

• • •

. . . America's anti-poverty program has been a sick farce in both North and South. In the South, it is clearly racism which prevents the poor from running their own programs; in the North, it more often seems to be politicking and bureaucracy. But the results are not so different: In the North, non-whites make up 42 per cent of all families in metropolitan "poverty areas" and only 6 per cent of families in areas classified as not poor. SNCC has been working with local residents in Arkansas, Alabama, and Mississippi to achieve control by the poor of the program and its funds; it has also been working with groups in the North, and the struggle is no less difficult. Behind it all is a federal government which cares far more about winning the war on the Vietnamese than the war on poverty; which has put the poverty program in the hands of self-serving politicians and bureaucrats rather than the poor themselves; which is unwilling to curb the misuse of white power but quick to condemn black power.

To most whites, black power seems to mean that the Mau Mau are coming to the suburbs at night. The Mau Mau are coming, and whites must stop them. Articles appear about plots to "get Whitey," creating an atmosphere in which "law and order must be maintained." Once again, responsibility is shifted from the oppressor to the oppressed. Other whites chide, "Don't forget—you're only 10 per cent of the population; if you get too smart, we'll wipe you out." If they are liberals, they complain, "What about me?—don't you want my help any more?" These are people supposedly concerned about black Americans, but today they think first of themselves, of their feelings of rejection. Or they admonish, "you can't get anywhere without coalitions," when there is in fact no group at present with whom to form a coalition in which blacks will not be absorbed and betrayed. Or they accuse us of "polarizing the races" by our calls for black unity, when the true responsibility for polarization lies with whites who will not accept their responsibility as the majority power for making the democratic process work.

. . .

Whites will not see that I, for example, as a person oppressed because of my blackness, have common cause with other blacks who are oppressed because of blackness. This is not to say that there are no white people who see things as I do, but that it is black people I must speak to first. It must be the oppressed to whom SNCC addresses itself primarily, not to friends from the oppressing group.

From birth, black people are told a set of lies about themselves. We are told that we are lazy—yet I drive through the Delta area of Mississippi and watch black people picking cotton in the hot sun for fourteen hours. We are told, "If you work hard, you'll succeed" —but if that were true, black people would own this country. We are oppressed because we are black—not because we are ignorant, not because we are lazy, not because we're stupid (and got good rhythm), but because we're black.

I remember that when I was a boy, I used to go to see Tarzan movies on Saturday. White Tarzan used to beat up the black natives. I would sit there yelling, "Kill the beasts, kill the savages, kill 'em!" I was saying: Kill *me*. It was as if a Jewish boy watched Nazis taking Jews off to concentration camps and cheered them on.

Today, I want the chief to beat hell out of Tarzan and send him back to Europe. But it takes time to become free of the lies and their shaming effect on black minds. It takes time to reject the most important lie: that black people inherently can't do the same things white people can do, unless white people help them.

The need for psychological equality is the reason why SNCC today believes that blacks must organize in the black community. Only black people can convey the revolutionary idea that black people are able to do things themselves. Only they can help create in the community an aroused and continuing black consciousness that will provide the basis for political strength. In the past, white allies have furthered white supremacy without the whites involved realizing it—or wanting it, I think. Black people must do things for themselves; they must get poverty money they will control and spend themselves, they must conduct tutorial programs themselves so that black children can identify with black people. This is one reason Africa has such importance: The reality of black men ruling their own natives gives blacks elsewhere a sense of possibility, of power, which they do not now have.

This does not mean we don't welcome help, or friends. But we want the right to decide whether anyone is, in fact, our friend. In the past, black Americans have been almost the only people whom everybody and his momma could jump up and call their friends. We have been tokens, symbols, objects—as I was in high school to many young whites, who liked having "a Negro friend." We want to decide who is our friend, and we will not accept someone who comes to us and says: "If you do X, Y, and Z, then I'll help you." We will not be told whom we should choose as allies. We will not be isolated from any group or nation except by our own choice. We cannot have the oppressors telling the oppressed how to rid themselves of the oppressor.

•   •   •

I have said that most liberal whites react to "black power" with the question, What about me? rather than saying: Tell me what you want me to do and I'll see if I can do it. There are answers to the right question. One of the most disturbing things about almost all white supporters of the movement has been that they are afraid to go into their own communities—which is where the racism exists—and work to get rid of it. They want to run from Berkeley to tell us what to do in Mississippi; let them look instead at Berkeley. They admonish blacks to be nonviolent; let them preach nonviolence in the white community. They come to teach me Negro history; let them go to the suburbs and open up freedom schools for whites. Let them work to stop America's racist foreign policy; let them press this government to cease supporting the economy of South Africa.

There is a vital job to be done among poor whites. We hope to see, eventually, a coalition between poor blacks and poor whites. That is the only coalition which seems acceptable to us, and we see such a coalition as the major internal instrument of change in American society. SNCC has tried several times to organize poor whites; we are trying again now, with an initial training program in Tennessee. It is purely academic today to talk about bringing poor blacks and whites together, but the job of creating a poor-white power bloc must be attempted. The main responsibility for it falls upon whites. Black and white can work together in the white community where possible; it is not possible, however, to go into a poor Southern town and talk about integration. Poor whites every-where are becoming more hostile—not less—partly because they see the nation's attention focused on black poverty and nobody com-ing to them. Too many young middle-class Americans, like some sort of Pepsi generation, have wanted to come alive through the black community; they've wanted to be where the action is—and the action has been in the black community. . . .

But our vision is not merely of a society in which all black men have enough to buy the good things of life. When we urge that black money go into black pockets, we mean the communal pocket. We want to see money go back into the community and used to benefit it. We want to see the cooperative concept applied in busi-ness and banking. We want to see black ghetto residents demand that an exploiting landlord or store keeper sell them, at minimal cost, a building or a shop that they will own and improve coopera-tively; they can back their demand with a rent strike, or a boycott, and a community so unified behind them that no one else will move into the building or buy at the store. The society we seek to build among black people, then, is not a capitalist one. It is a society in which the spirit of community and humanistic love prevail. The word love is suspect; black expectations of what it might produce have been betrayed too often. But those were expectations of a re-sponse from the white community, which failed us. The love we seek to encourage is within the black community, the only American community where men call each other "brother" when they meet. We can build a community of love only where we have the ability and power to do so: among blacks.

Selection 12

THE NEWSWEEK POLL*

These charts are taken from a poll conducted by Newsweek *magazine in 1963, and again in 1966. (The 1963 survey was subsequently published in William Brink and Louis Harris'* The Negro Revolution in America, *New York: Simon & Schuster, 1964.) The 1966 poll was based on the questioning of a representative sample of 1,059 Negroes and 1,088 whites. In addition, a selected list of 100 Negro leaders was interviewed to determine their attitudes.*

How Negroes Rank Their Leaders				
RANK-AND-FILE			LEADERSHIP GROUP	
% approve			% approve	
1966	1963		1966	1963
88	88	Martin Luther King Jr.	87	95
71	79	James Meredith	35	81
66	80	Jackie Robinson	58	82
64	68	Roy Wilkins	62	92
56	60	Dick Gregory	65	80
54	X	Charles Evers	68	X
53	62	Ralph Bunche	49	87
48	64	Thurgood Marshall	81	94
47	X	James Farmer	70	X
44	51	Adam Clayton Powell	49	52
35	X	A. Philip Randolph	83	X
33	X	Whitney Young Jr.	70	X
22	X	Bayard Rustin	53	X
19	X	Floyd McKissick	35	X
19	X	Stokely Carmichael	33	X
12	15	Elijah Muhammad	15	17

X—not on 1963 list

* From *Newsweek,* August 22, 1966, pp. 22, 34.

How Negroes Feel About Riots				
	Total Rank-and-File	Non-South	South	Leadership Group
Would join a riot	15%	13%	18%	1%
Would not join	61	62	59	75
Not sure	24	25	23	24
Think there will be more riots	61	62	61	79
Will not be	8	7	8	2
Not sure	31	31	31	19

Selections 13a–13b

TWO POEMS
BY LANGSTON HUGHES*

The noted Negro poet reflects on the future of the racial crisis in our country.

13a.   Harlem

What happens to a dream deferred?

Does it dry up
like a raisin in the sun?
Or fester like a sore—
And then run?
Does it stink like rotten meat?
Or crust and sugar over—
like a syrupy sweet?

* From *Selected Poems of Langston Hughes*, New York: Alfred A. Knopf, 1959, pp. 268, 167.

Maybe it just sags
like a heavy load.

Or does it explode?

13b.   Roland Hayes Beaten (Georgia: 1942)

Negroes,
Sweet and docile,
Meek, humble, and kind:
Beware the day
They change their minds!

Wind
In the cotton fields,
Gentle breeze:
Beware the hour
It uproots trees!

PART II

WHITE REACTION TO THE NEGRO PROTEST

What has been the reaction of whites to the civil rights movement? Violence continues to play its part in the South, although there is white opinion that urges moderation. In the North there is a considerable segment of white opinion which supports the movement toward equality, but there is also some strong opposition.

Selections 14a–14b

LYNCHING

14a. Lynching in This Country
RAY STANNARD BAKER*

Lynching in this country is peculiarly the white man's burden. The white man has taken all the responsibility of government; he really governs in the North as well as in the South, in the North disfran-

---

* From Ray Stannard Baker, *Following the Color Line: American Negro Leadership in the Progressive Era,* New York: Harper & Row, 1964, p. 215. [Originally published in 1908 by Doubleday, Page & Co.]

chising the Negro with cash, in the South by law or by intimidation. All the machinery of justice is in his hands. How keen is the need, then, of calmness and strict justice in dealing with the Negro! Nothing more surely tends to bring the white man down to the lowest level of the criminal Negro than yielding to those blind instincts of savagery which find expression in the mob. The man who joins a mob, by his very acts, puts himself on a level with the Negro criminal: both have given way wholly to brute passion. For, if civilisation means anything, it means self-restraint; casting away self-restraint the white man becomes as savage as the criminal Negro.

If the white man sets an example of non-obedience to law, of non-enforcement of law, and of unequal justice, what can be expected of the Negro? A criminal father is a poor preacher of homilies to a wayward son. The Negro sees a man, white or black, commit murder and go free, over and over again in all these lynching counties. Why should he fear to murder? Every passion of the white man is reflected and emphasised in the criminal Negro.

14b. Lynchings by State and Race, 1882–1951[*]

State	Whites	Negroes	Total
Alabama	48	299	347
Arizona	31	0	31
Arkansas	58	226	284
California	41	2	43
Colorado	66	2	68
Delaware	0	1	1
Florida	25	257	282
Georgia	39	491	530
Idaho	20	0	20
Illinois	15	19	34
Indiana	33	14	47
Iowa	17	2	19
Kansas	35	19	54
Kentucky	63	142	205
Louisiana	56	335	391
Maryland	2	27	29
Michigan	7	1	8
Minnesota	5	4	9
Mississippi	40	534	574
Missouri	53	69	122
Montana	82	2	84
Nebraska	52	5	57

[*] From *Negro Year Book*, New York: William H. Wise and Co., Inc., 1952, p. 277.

State	Whites	Negroes	Total
Nevada	6	0	6
New Jersey	0	3	1
New Mexico	33	1	36
New York	1	1	2
N. Carolina	15	84	99
N. Dakota	13	3	16
Ohio	10	16	26
Oklahoma	82	40	122
Oregon	20	1	21
Pennsylvania	2	6	8
S. Carolina	4	156	160
S. Dakota	27	0	27
Tennessee	47	204	251
Texas	141	352	493
Utah	6	2	8
Virginia	17	83	100
Washington	25	1	26
W. Virginia	20	28	48
Wisconsin	6	0	6
Wyoming	30	5	35
TOTAL	1,293	3,437	4,730

Selection 15

THE VARIOUS SHADY LIVES
OF THE KU KLUX KLAN*

The following selection describes the activities of the Ku Klux Klan.

It started as something of a lark, just 100 years ago. On Dec. 24, 1865, in Pulaski, Tenn., six young ex-Confederate officers, looking

* From *Time*, April 9, 1965, pp. 24–25.

for something to occupy their time, got together to form a club. Like college kids, they gave the club all the trappings of a fraternity —mysterious rites, initiations, secret words. For a name, they hit on the Greek word for circle, *kyklos,* gave it a few twists and came up with Ku Klux Klan. For kicks, they made robes and hoods out of bedsheets and pillowcases, and took to riding sheet-draped horses solemnly through the town at night. Soon they discovered that their frolics frightened superstitious Negroes, and that was reason enough for scores of others to join in the fun.

To fight Reconstruction, Klansmen decided to organize nationally. In Nashville, in 1867, they drew up a constitution, picked for their Imperial Wizard the Confederate general Nathan Bedford Forrest, and turned their talents to terrorism. Cloaked in their sheets and masks, they rode the countryside thirsting for violence. Anyone— white or black—who cooperated with Reconstruction was fair game for barbarism. White men who taught in Negro schools were lashed, and their schools were set afire and reduced to ashes. Negroes who refused to work for white men, or who seemed to flourish on their own, were thrashed with whips; some were hanged, some castrated, some burned to death, some murdered and quartered like animals.

For the most part, the Klan's outrages were applauded by Southerners who felt that the K.K.K. was the last best hope for the South's lily-white cause. But in 1869, Nathan Forrest himself ordered the Klan to disband. As University of Florida Professor David Chalmers writes in his book, *Hooded Americanism,* "A secret masked society, composed of autonomous units, dedicated to the use of force, operating in unsettled times, proved impossible to control. The better citizens were dropping out and the quality of membership in many of the states was declining."

"Practical Fraternity"

The Klan mentality, however, never died; it merely lay quiescent, while apologists fed it intravenously with myths. Thomas Dixon Jr.'s 1905 book, *The Clansman,* idealized the K.K.K. as a righteous crusade led by noble men, and D. W. Griffith immortalized the book in 1914 with his film, *The Birth of a Nation.*

An itinerant Methodist preacher named William Joseph Simmons started up the Klan again in Atlanta in 1915. Simmons, an ascetic-looking man, was a fetishist on fraternal organizations. He was already a "colonel" in the Woodmen of the World, but he decided to build an organization all his own. He was an effective speaker, with an affinity for alliteration; he had preached on "Women, Weddings and Wives," "Red Heads, Dead Heads and No Heads," and the "Kinship of Kourtship and Kissing." On Thanksgiving Eve

1915, Simmons took 15 friends to the top of Stone Mountain, near Atlanta, built an altar on which he placed an American flag, a Bible and an unsheathed sword, set fire to a crude wooden cross, muttered a few incantations about a "practical fraternity among men," and declared himself Imperial Wizard of the Invisible Empire of the Knights of the Ku Klux Klan.

Publicity & Politics

Under Simmons, the Klan drifted along for four years, collecting a membership of a few thousand people (using such come-on slogans as "a high-class order for men of intelligence and character," and "a classy order of the highest class") and a small treasury. Then, to breathe greater life into the organization, Simmons hired Edward Clark Young, a press-agent who specialized in fund raising, and Young's partner, a well-to-do widow named Elizabeth Tyler. Young set forth the Klan's goal in terms of Christian morality *v.* sin. The enemies of America, the Klan proclaimed, were booze, loose women, Jews, Negroes, Roman Catholics (whose "dago" Pope was bent on taking over the U. S.), and anybody else who was not a native-born white Protestant Anglo-Saxon. Many churchmen across the nation acclaimed the Klan's program, and in the South especially, Methodist and Baptist clergymen lent the K.K.K. massive support. It was not long before it blossomed into a mighty nationwide organization that claimed to number in its hooded ranks about 4,000,000 members.

As a political force, the Klan was incredibly effective. It was a key issue in the 1924 and 1928 presidential conventions and campaigns, as well as in hundreds of local elections. Klan organizations elected judges, mayors and other city officials, sheriffs, state legislators, and even some governors, senators and congressmen. Many politicians joined the K.K.K. out of fierce conviction, others merely in order to survive. Alabama's Hugo Black became a member, but he quit in 1925, a year before he was elected a Democratic U. S. senator; in 1934, after F.D.R. named him to the Supreme Court, Black repudiated racism and religious intolerance on a nationwide radio speech.

Klanonyms

Klansmen appeared as self-appointed judges, juries and executioners. They resumed the reign of terror against Negroes. They tarred and feathered men and women—white and black—whom they suspected of illicit sexual relations, and lynched, mutilated or lashed hundreds of others. They tortured Jewish shopkeepers, whom they accused of massive international financial conspiracies; they published a spurious Knights of Columbus "oath" that portrayed Roman Catholics as villainous conspirators against the U. S. Their bedsheets became robes emblazoned with ornate embroidery, and they invented a whole new thesaurus of Klanonyms. There were the Kleagle and the Klabee, the Kladd and the Klaliff, the Klectoken and the Klexter, the Kligrapp and the Klokan, the Klokard and the Kloncilium, the Klonklave and the Klonvokation, the Kloran and the Klarogo, the Klorero and the Kludd.* In the Klan Kalendar, the days of the week were named Dark, Deadly, Dismal, Doleful, Desolate, Dreadful and Desperate; the weeks of the month were Woeful, Weeping, Wailing, Wonderful and Weird, and the months Bloody, Gloomy, Hideous, Fearful, Furious, Alarming, Terrible, Horrible, Mournful, Sorowful, Frightful and Appalling.

The Injured Image

The Klan's operations provided tidy profits for Imperial Wizard Simmons and the publicity team of Young and Tyler, but by 1924 the Klan's great days were ending. Several states invoked anti-Klan laws; others forbade the Klan to wear masks. Corruption among the bosses and internecine battles for leadership further weakened the organization. In 1926 David Stephenson, the posturing Grand Dragon of the Indiana Realm, was convicted of murder after the lower-berth Pullman-car rape of a young woman. The Indiana affair hurt the Klan image considerably more than the castrations and lynchings that Klansmen had perpetrated in all the years before. Members resigned by the hundreds. In the '30s the Klan cuddled up to U. S. Nazis, and continued all the while to murder Negroes and "immoral" whites, chiefly in the South.

During World War II, the Klan slept again. But in 1954 the U. S. Supreme Court's school desegregation decision awakened it once more. As in the beginning, the Klan made the Southern Negro— and civil rights "agitators"—its target, and turned to dynamite bombings as its chief form of violence. Much of the Klan's terrorism is handled by goon squads with such picturesque names as "The Holy Terrors" and "The Secret Six." Such groups were held responsible for the mutilation and murder of three civil rights workers who were found in an earthen dam in Mississippi last June, for the killing of Washington, D. C., Educator Lemuel Penn in Georgia

* Kleagle, Klabee, Kladd, Klaliff, Klexter, Kligrapp, Klarogo, Klokan and Klokard are officials of various sorts; Klectoken is the initiation fee; Kloran is Klan bible; Klonvokation is the Imperial legislature; Kloncilium is the Klonvokation's advisory group; Klonklave is the Klan's monthly meeting; Klorero is a state meeting; and Kludd is the chaplain.

last July, and for the death of Mrs. Viola Liuzzo in Selma last month.

The Mentality

No longer a monolithic organization, the Klan today consists of several ragtag independent groups, the best known of which is the United Klans of America, Knights of the Ku Klux Klan, Inc., headquartered in Tuscaloosa, Ala., with an ex-tire salesman named Robert Shelton as its Imperial Wizard. Estimates of Klan strength range from 10,000 to 40,000 members, many of whom for some peculiar reason seem to be rural service-station attendants. Most members, in any case, are deluded rednecks whose only skill is sharpshooting. That the FBI has infiltrated deeply into their ranks is indicated by the speed with which agents rounded up the four suspected killers of Mrs. Liuzzo.

Crushing the Klan is tougher than infiltrating it. Local Southern juries ordinarily let Klansmen off no matter what the accusation. The only federal charge that can be leveled in most cases—such as in the Liuzzo murder—deals with "denying the civil rights" of the victim, and the maximum penalty for the crime is only ten years in prison. Even though Congress might now enact legislation outlawing the Klan, the deeper problem is that the law alone can never erase the Klan mentality.

Selection 16

THREE LIVES FOR MISSISSIPPI

WILLIAM BRADFORD HUIE*

On June 21, 1964, three young Americans—a Negro and two whites —were murdered in Philadelphia, Mississippi while engaged in the civil rights movement. James Chaney, age twenty-two, was a native of Mississippi; Michael Schwerner, age twenty-five, and Andrew Goodman, age twenty-one, were from New York. The bodies of

* From William Bradford Huie, *Three Lives for Mississippi*, New York: WCC Books, 1965, pp. 212-17, 239-41, 251-52.

*these victims were so well hidden that it took federal officials forty-
four days to uncover them.*

*William Bradford Huie, a native of Alabama, an author and
journalist, was sent by the* New York Herald Tribune *to do a series
of articles on the story. The following selections are from his book,*
Three Lives for Mississipi.

A Personal Word

I am a Southerner and I hate what the Wallaces and the Barnetts
and the Klansmen, and all the white supremacy terrorists are doing
to Negroes, to the South, and to the United States. I have often
been asked why I continue to live where there is one Ku Klux
group four miles to the north of my home and another four miles
to the east, and it is only a four-hour drive from Neshoba County,
Mississippi.

My answer is that I belong in the Tennessee Valley in North
Alabama. I was born here, as were seven generations of my fore-
bears. Across North Alabama and North Georgia there must be
two thousand people who call me Cousin. I'm an agrarian who
may reside temporarily in New York, Washington, Los Angeles,
London, or Zürich but who still feels "at home" only near the
ancient churchyards where the generations are sleeping. Even in
the jet age a man, to remain sane and in good digestion, must *belong* somewhere.

Moreover, in all the world I know of no better place to live than
the Tennessee Valley. Nothing I have seen in a lifetime of travel
has lifted my heart like watching the transformation of this valley
since I cast my first ballot in 1932. All that Franklin Delano Roosevelt dreamed for America has been realized in the Tennessee Valley.
Today we are even becoming more international in outlook, with
hundreds of European intellectuals living among us, their eyes on
the stars and outer space.

It must not be imagined that all the white people in Alabama
and Mississippi support the George Wallaces, the Ross Barnetts, the
Lawrence Raineys and the Cecil Prices. When Wallace ran for Governor in 1962, my home county voted two to one against him. In
the urban counties of Alabama Wallace was badly beaten. He became Governor only with massive support in our backward counties where few or no Negroes voted. There is nothing wrong with
Alabama or Mississippi that 300,000 Negro votes in each state can't
help cure.

Even those citizens who fear Negroes voting are beginning to understand that the Nobel Prize was won for Martin Luther King by Bull Connor and George Wallace . . . that passage of the Civil Rights Bill of 1964 was helped by George Wallace and Byron de la Beckwith . . . and that the Civil Rights Bill of 1965 is the handiwork of Wallace, Sheriff Jim Clark's posse, and the murderers of Michael Schwerner, James Chaney, and Andrew Goodman.

Successful revolutions, it appears, are made as much by their opponents as by their proponents.

I wrote this book for those citizens of Alabama and Mississippi, white and Negro, who hate intimidation and terrorism as much as I do. And I wrote it for three young men I never met whose lives were good, and who, in the manner of their death, served the cause of liberty for all men.

The day is coming, and soon, in Alabama and Mississippi, when good men and women such as Jimmie Lee Jackson, James Reeb and Mrs. Viola Gregg Liuzzo can walk safely under the magnolias in Selma; and when good men like Michael Schwerner, James Chaney, and Andrew Goodman need not fear the sight of a police car behind them in Mississippi. . . .

· · ·

In a murder case where every knowledgeable survivor is guilty, and where every living witness is a murderer, you obtain information from informers, and you obtain evidence by inducing one murderer to witness against another. And where every witness is under a real threat of death from his fellows if he talks, a witness can be a problem.

In this Mississippi is, in fact, no different from New York. When, because they fear involvement, thirty-eight "decent" New Yorkers neglect to call the police while an innocent woman is murdered before their eyes, how can "decent" Mississippians be expected to witness against terrorists? Bodies hidden by the Mafia and other gangsters are as hard to find as those hidden by Mississippi gangsters; and a thousand murders committed by gangsters have gone unpunished in the United States because "decent" citizens declined to take the risks of giving testimony.

I thought something might be gained by my talking with two or three secure, honorable, sophisticated men in the power structure of Philadelphia [Mississippi]—men who were not politicians or preachers, but business or professional men, capable of some degree of objectivity, and with whom I might have mutual friends. It is well known in Mississippi that in order to publish the truth about the Emmett Till murder, I paid those murderers with the assistance of reputable alumni of the Ole Miss Law School. It is also known that in both the Mack Parker case and in the Beckwith case, I had the assistance of Mississippi lawyers and of Mississippi police investigators. For my talks with citizens of Philadelphia to be effective, the talks had to be held away from Philadelphia. I arranged such talks, which went on at some length. I thought I might persuade one of these men to assist at least in finding the bodies if not in obtaining information or evidence.

"Well," one man said, "I'll say this. I'm sorry about the murders. Of course I'm sorry. They were wrong, stupid, and very bad for business in Mississippi. I'm capable of sympathy for the victims. I'm sorry for the families. I'm sure that Schwerner and Goodman were decent, well-meaning young men. They wanted to ride white horses and, right or wrong, they were riding their horses in Mississippi. But here is a fact. On both sides everybody knew that at least one of these young people coming to Mississippi was going to be murdered. I knew it. I assume the fathers of Schwerner and Goodman knew it. I know the instigators of this 'March on Mississippi' expected at least one murder. Joe Alsop wrote that murder was expected, and that the provoking of violence was a tactic deliberately being adopted by the militant Negro organizations."

"But the fact that murder may have been expected doesn't justify it," I said.

"No, but it helps explain it. Mississippi has been a white-supremacy state since its beginning. These rednecks are capable of violence. That's why they make good soldiers; why we use them to lead night patrols in our wars; why so many of them have won Congressional Medals of Honor. They may not read much, but they now own television sets. And when they hear on TV every day that everybody in Mississippi is a stupid, tobacco-chewing bigot, then a murder case like this one here is as predictable as sunrise."

"How about helping find the bodies? For humanitarian reasons if no other?"

"Well," he said, "I'll have to think about that. I suppose I might induce one of these jokers to tell me where they are if I really set my hand to it. But what good can come of it? Maybe the best course for everybody is just to let the bodies lie and let the excitement gradually die down. Once the bodies are found, then there is a great hue and cry to convict somebody . . . to put somebody in jail. And that's a power I don't have. That power doesn't exist in Mississippi. Not even Paul Johnson has any such power. There is no way in the world, in open court, where a twelve-man jury verdict must be unanimous, and where every juror can be polled in

open court and made to say how he voted—there's no possible way
to ever put anybody in jail. Instead of reducing hate, all a trial can
do is spread it. So why should we have all that hue and cry, and a
big circus trial. . . . What's the use of it? Since a murder like this
was expected, why don't we all just admit that we got what we
expected and devote ourselves to trying to prevent another one?"

"How do we prevent another one by letting this one go unpunished?"

"This one is going unpunished in any case. That is, the murderers
are going unpunished. Mississippi has already been punished, and
will continue to be punished."

"So you refuse to help find the bodies?"

"I haven't said that," he answered. "I'll have to think about it. It's
a tough question. It's *right* that the bodies should be found. But
nothing good can come of finding them."

"Well, here is another of your realities," I said. "The bodies *will*
be found. You know it as well as I do. The pressure is great and
will get greater. Too many people know where the bodies are. One
of them is sure to sell out. There is too much money available."

"How much money?"

"I'd say twenty-five thousand dollars. More if necessary."

"You mean twenty-five thousand dollars for nothing more than
the *information* as to where the bodies are? No confession? No
public identification of the informer? No signed statement identifying and accusing the others?"

"I think that can be arranged," I said. "If all we can get is the
bodies. Naturally, a signed confession which implicates the others
would be best, but if we can't get that let's at least get the evidence
of murder. The deal will have to be COD. Nobody will pay an
informer that amount of money just for an unproved tip. The informer has to pass the information, then wait two or three days
while the FBI finds the bodies and identifies them. The informer
has to take the calculated risk that he will get his money, but ways
can be devised to reduce the risk to a minimum."

"Christ," he said, "maybe I ought to stop what I'm doing and
get in the business of finding and selling the bodies of civil rights
workers."

"Well, what I'm telling you is no secret," I said. "The FBI has
always paid informers. So does every effective police agency on
earth. How else could these bodies ever be found? Or these murderers identified? I think the bodies will be found, and I think that
many, perhaps most, of the murderers will eventually be identified
even if they are never convicted."

In addition to such talks with substantial citizens of Philadelphia,

I spread my Alabama and Mississippi telephone numbers around and let it be widely known that I would pay for information. The FBI agents were doing the same thing. I told them most of what I was doing. They didn't tell me what they were doing: they quite properly never tell anybody.

By July 20 I believed I knew the identity of three of the young men who were in the actual murder and burial parties. I had been told that the bodies had been buried, not submerged; and I had the information that the graves were southwest of Philadelphia. I told one of my publishers that the bodies would be found "not later than August tenth," and I wrote the first draft of a story titled *How the Bodies Were Found in Mississippi.*

*   *   *

I think it can be said truly that the white-supremacy society of Mississippi has been shaken. Murder helped to shake it. And since most men will call this shaking process good, I believe most men of good will will agree that James Chaney, Andrew Goodman, and Michael Schwerner did not die in vain. Their deaths served the cause of freedom for all people, white and Negro, in Mississippi, in the United States, and, hopefully, throughout the world.

*   *   *

One of the murderers said: "We couldn't get at them South-haters in Washington. But we could get at them three we had. So we showed 'em." Every one of the murderers seems to believe that "we showed" somebody something.

In his book *Mississippi: The Closed Society,* Professor James W. Silver describes the white-supremacy terrorists in these words:

[There is] an anxious, fearful, frustrated group of marginal white men, who exist in every Mississippi community. It makes no difference whether these people are suffering from their own personal inadequacies or whether they are overwhelmed by circumstances: they escape from their troubles periodically into the excitement of racial conflict. They are impelled to keep the Negro down in order to look up to themselves. . . . Racial bigotry trancends reason in Mississippi because, for varying motives, so many leaders are willing to exploit the nameless dreads and alarms that have taken possession of most white people. The poor whites may not raise their low standard of living by blaming it on Negroes, but they do release an aggressive energy upon a socially accepted scapegoat. Themselves last in everything else, they can still rejoice in having the "nigger" beneath them. At least in the short run, nearly every white man does stand to derive economic, political, or social status from keeping Negroes in their place.

. . .

The statement by President Lyndon B. Johnson on March 25, 1965, after four Klansmen were arrested for "conspiracy to violate the civil rights" of Mrs. Viola Gregg Liuzzo, the murdered woman, read in part:

The four members of the United Klans of America, Inc., Knights of the Ku Klux Klan, will, of course, be arraigned immediately. They will later stand trial.

Mrs. Liuzzo went to Alabama to serve the struggle for justice. She was murdered by the enemies of justice, who for decades have used the rope and the gun, the tar and the feathers to terrorize their neighbors.

They struck by night, as they generally do, for their purposes cannot stand the light of day.

My father fought them in Texas. I have fought them all my life, because I believe them to threaten the peace of every community where they exist.

I shall continue to fight them because I know their loyalty is not to the United States, but to a hooded society of bigots.

Men and women have stood against the Klan at times and places where to do so required a continuous act of courage. If Klansmen hear my voice today, let it be both an appeal—and a warning—to get out of the Klan *now* and return to a decent society—before it is too late.

I call on every law enforcement officer in our land to insist on obedience to the law and respect for justice. No nation can long endure, either in history's judgment or in its own national conscience, if hoodlums or bigots can defy the law and get away with it. Justice must be done, in the largest city as well as the smallest village—on the dirt road as well as the interstate highway.

Selection 17

THE SELMA MARCH

This selection deals with conditions in Alabama that culminated with the March from Selma to Montgomery, Alabama, in March, 1965. The purpose of the March from Selma to Montgomery,

*according to its leaders, was to demonstrate to the American people
the need for reform in voter registration procedures in the South.
Many whites joined the Negroes in this March.*

Alabama: Racism *vs.* Reason*

The past week in Alabama has been a time of dangerous competition between the forces of racism and reason, of violence and
law, of the defeated past and the struggling future. By his dec-
larations yesterday President Johnson has improved the prospect
for a peaceful and prompt triumph of reason on this crucial battleground.

Gov. George C. Wallace and Sheriff James Clark symbolize a
reactionary, racist cause that is already defeated and dying. In its
final stage it has nothing to fall back upon except the desperate
tactic of brutal force. The Rev. Martin Luther King symbolizes
the cause of the Southern Negro who at the beginning of this
second century of emancipation, is struggling to achieve his rights
by legal, peaceful means. By law and by moral commitment, the
overwhelming majority of Americans have taken their stand in
this contest. There can be no doubt about the outcome.

The nation has thus far been fortunate in averting a castastrophic
confrontation between these contending forces, but there have been
losses, most recently the brutal killing of the Rev. James J. Reeb,
a young white minister. The task now before the nation is to
make sure that confrontation never occurs.

This view was well set forth by the President in his televised
remarks to the nation. What is now needed is a convincing demonstration by him, Congress and the courts that the side of law
and reason is going to win—not only in the long run but in the
short run—and in ways that are immediate, sure and visible.

President Johnson has been widely criticized in recent days for
failing to send Federal troops to Selma. This criticism seems to
us unmerited. The armed forces ought not to be used until all
other solutions have failed. Mr. Johnson can more accurately be
criticized for his slowness in sending a new voting rights bill to
Congress. He promised such a measure more than a month ago.
Now the delay is ended. The President has promised that a bill
intended to establish a simple uniform voting standard will go to
Congress tomorrow. Where discriminatory state policies continue
to block full and free exercise of the voting right, Federal registrars
will be empowered to see to it that Negroes are enrolled. The duty

* Editorial, *The New York Times,* March 14, 1965.

of Congress will be to move swiftly to translate the President's pledge into a law without the stultifying new delay of a cruel and hopeless filibuster.

The President has made it plain to Governor Wallace that the Federal Government intends to protect the right of citizens to exercise their constitutional right of peaceful assembly and protest, whether the Alabama authorities like it or not. The sound way for Mr. Wallace and the other champions of states' rights to guard against such direct Federal intervention is—and always has been— the one suggested to him by the President of taking independent action to guarantee that every citizen, Negro or white, will enjoy full protection in availing himself of his rights.

The United States has been extremely fortunate that the struggle for Negro rights has remained up to now under mature responsible leadership which always seeks peaceful solutions by legal and political means. If that leadership is to be vindicated, then those means must be seen to be working. Otherwise the young Negro hotheads thirsting for a dramatic showdown for its own sake will be encouraged, and the white demagogues and their police henchmen will be emboldened to new acts of violence and repression.

The nation cannot afford to run either of these risks. The President's non-bellicose but forceful words at his news conference provide encouragement that law and political leadership will master this crisis—effectively and quickly.

Selection 18

STRIFE IN SELMA*

Following are some views from the South on the violence which accompanied demonstrations for Negro voter registration in Selma and the neighboring Alabama Black Belt.

RICHMOND FLOWERS, ATTORNEY GENERAL OF ALABAMA: In Alabama there is so much hate that it just hurts you to see it. . . . I have

* From *The New York Times*, March 14, 1965.

been at tremendous odds with George Wallace and I have always taken a strong stand for law and order. Race hatred and the defiance of law is wrong in the eyes of the law and it is wrong in the eyes of God.

ATLANTA JOURNAL: Before the year is out, in all probability, there will be breakthroughs in Negro voting registration in the South like none seen before. We soon will see a strong voter registration bill in Congress. . . . Educational and interpretation "tests" used for racial suppression have no proper place in a democracy. We do think, however, that a basic education requirement—just basic—should remain for voters, to be used in a completely nondiscriminatory manner.

NASHVILLE TENNESSEAN: It would take a distorted interpretation of the law to argue that the marching Negroes would pose a threat to the safety of the people of Alabama. . . . If Governor Wallace had been interested in reducing racial tensions arising from the voter registration efforts at Selma, he would have made arrangements for the Negroes to present their grievances to him in an orderly way.

BIRMINGHAM NEWS: Federal District Judge Frank M. Johnson Jr., acted in great wisdom and human helpfulness in barring a second Selma-to-Montgomery march attempt by Negroes. Rev. Martin Luther King's decision to "march anyway" was a callous disregard of the court order. . . . But if Negroes are to be led to a decision not to march, then the state of Alabama must do more . . . to convince Negroes . . . that this state will fully defend and sincerely will advance their just cause of the vote for all qualified.

THE [COLUMBIA, S. C.] STATE: The march has little to do with the registration of Negro voters in Alabama. It is a propaganda spectacular, and it has within it the seeds of real violence.

SAVANNAH MORNING NEWS: Alabama police have acted shamefully in their brutal tactics against Negro demonstrators. But the Negroes themselves, in search of national publicity at any cost, haven't helped by provoking an already bad situation. Outsiders who only worsen a bad situation are moving into the Selma, Ala., area under their pseudo-cloaks of righteousness. . . . There is an urgent need for all parties to back up and pursue a more reasonable course.

Selection 19

A SOUTHERN LAWYER TRIES TO HELP HIS COMMUNITY*

Racial Peacemaker Who Failed

Atlanta, Sept. 15—Confronted with hostility and hatred at virtually every turn, Warren C. Fortson and his family have left Americus, Ga., where the 39-year-old white lawyer had tried to bring about racial harmony.

Mr. Fortson essayed the role of peacemaker early in August when Americus Negroes and whites clashed during demonstrations. He unsuccessfully sought creation of a bi-racial committee to study the issues.

When whites who disagreed with his moderate views attempted to get him dismissed as attorney for Sumter County, he said:

"This is a time when the voice of reason is very weak in our community. This is a human problem that requires a human solution. Sooner or later the community will sit down and talk."

Assistant Named

Mr. Fortson was not dismissed, but associate counsel was appointed to "assist" him with the county's business.

In just over a month Mr. Fortson, who was born in Georgia, found himself "ruined" in his law practice, relieved of Sunday-school teaching duties, called a Communist and atheist, ostracized by former friends, threatened by telephone. His children were harassed in school.

Last Saturday Mr. Fortson moved his wife, Betty, and their five children out of their 19-room home in Americus and into a three-bedroom apartment in Atlanta.

Yesterday, on the 12th birthday of his oldest daughter, Jane, he

* From *The New York Times,* September 16, 1965.

returned to Americus to begin closing his office and make the move permanent.

In Atlanta, Mrs. Fortson and Jane sat in the living room of their new home, a birthday cake unopened on the table nearby, and talked of the move and the reasons for it.

Some clients had stood by Mr. Fortson, but he referred to the animosity toward him and asked them, "How could I win a jury trial for you?"

The animosity was what hurt Mrs. Fortson. Suddenly the family was strangely alone in a town where they had been leading citizens. Old friends chilled, and stopped speaking when they met on the street.

"The most tragic thing of all," Mrs. Fortson said, "was what happened to other people. There would be these two friends. Either would speak to me in private, but not in front of each other."

One day recently Mrs. Fortson answered a telephone call. She heard a quiet voice say, "Leave. I am your friend, and I've loved you since you came here. But for your own sake, leave."

On two occasions when racial fever was high in Americus, the Fortsons were advised by loyal friends to spend the night outside of their home. As the hostility intensified, they sent the children to visit relatives in the country. They began to make routine checks to make sure that bombs had not been planted in the family cars.

Trouble in School

When school opened, the children were exposed to harassment. "A few of them called me a 'nigger-lover,'" Jane said.

"What did you do?" she was asked.

"I turned around and walked away."

Mr. Fortson was born in Washington, Ga. He attended the University of Georgia and Emory University, Atlanta. He has never lived outside the South.

He is from a family of lawyers. His brother is Georgia's Secretary of State, Ben W. Fortson Jr.

Despite this background, the tide rolled against him from the time he argued for a bi-racial committee.

So the Fortsons left. Without a job, the young lawyer moved his family, hoping to find in another city the peace he failed to achieve in Americus.

Selection 20

CONTEMPORARY RELIGIOUS LEADERS*

The following speeches were delivered at the March on Washington ceremonies, in August, 1963.

Rev. Eugene Carson Blake:

I wish, indeed, that I were able to speak for all Protestant, Anglican and Orthodox Christians as I speak here today in behalf of full justice and freedom for all who are born or living under the American flag. But that is precisely the point. If all the members and all the ministers of the constituency I represent here today were ready to stand and march with you for jobs and freedom for the Negro community together with those of the Roman Catholic Church and of the synagogues in America, then the battle for full civil rights and dignity would be already won.

I do, however, in fact represent officially the Commission on Religion and Race of the National Council of Churches. And I am honored to be here in the highest tradition of that council and of the churches that constitute it, thus to represent one of the sponsoring bodies of this march for jobs and freedom.

For many years now the National Council of Churches and most of its constituent communions have said all the right things about civil rights. Our official pronouncements for years have called for a non-segregated church in a non-segregated society but as of August

---

* Statements by Rev. Eugene Carson Blake, Vice-Chairman of the Commission on Race Relations of the National Council of Churches of Christ in America; Mathew Ahmann, Executive Director of the National Catholic Conference for Interracial Justice; and Rabbi Joachim Prinz, President of the American Jewish Congress, in *Speeches by the Leaders: The March on Washington for Jobs and Freedom,* New York: NAACP, n.d.

28, 1963, we have achieved neither a non-segregated church nor a non-segregated society and it is partly because the churches of America have failed to put their own houses in order, that 100 years after the Emancipation Proclamation, 175 years after the adoption of the Constitution, 173 years after the adoption of the Bill of Rights, the United States of America still faces a racial crisis.

We do not, therefore, come to this Lincoln Memorial in any arrogant spirit of moral or spiritual superiority to set the Congress or the nation straight or to judge or to denounce the American people in whole or in part. Rather we come—late, late we come—in the reconciling and repentant spirit in which Abraham Lincoln of Illinois once replied to a delegation of morally arrogant churchmen who came to see him. He said: "Never say God is on our side, rather pray that we may be found on God's side." We come in the fear of God that moved Thomas Jefferson of Virginia, whose memorial stands across the lagoon, once to say: "Indeed I tremble for my country, when I reflect that God is just."

Yes, we come to march behind and with these amazingly able leaders of the Negro American who, to the shame of almost every white American, have alone and without us mirrored the suffering of the cross of Jesus Christ. They have offered their bodies to arrest and violence, to the hurt and indignity of firehoses and dogs, of derisions and of poverty and some death for this just cause.

We come and late we come, but we come to present ourselves this day, our souls and bodies, to be a living sacrifice holy and acceptable to God which is our reasonable service in a kind of tangible, visible sacrament which alone in times like these can manifest to a troubled world the grace that is available at communion table or high altar. We come in prayer that we in our time may be more worthy to bear the name our tongues so fluently profess. We come in faith that the God who made us and gave His Son for us and for our salvation will overrule the fears and hatred that so far have prevented the establishment of full racial justice in our beloved country. We come in hope that those who have marched today are but a token of a new and massive, high determination of all men of religion and patriotism to win in this nation under God liberty and justice for all. And we come—late we come—we come in that love revealed in Jesus Christ which reconciles into true community all men of every color, race and nation who respond in faith and obedience to Him.

Mathew Ahmann:

Who can call himself a man, say he is created by God and at the same time take part in a system of segregation which destroys the livelihood, the citizenship, the family life and the very heart of the Negro citizens of the United States? Who can call himself a man and take part in a system of segregation which frightens the white man into denying what he knows to be right, into denying the law of his God? The wind of the racial revolution has finally bent the reeds of the conscience of our people. Never before has the direction we must take been so clear, yet many bend before the winds of injustice and confusion. The balance yet lies with the silent and fearful American. It is he who sees the direction of the future dimly before his conscience, who must act if a wholesome and integrated community of Negro and white Americans is to be built without violence and without rending this country's spirit.

We are gathered a long 100 years after Lincoln declared slavery at an end in the United States. Yet, slavery is all too close to us as we demonstrate for equality and freedom today. We live together in a country which has shown remarkable capacity for social change, an ability to absorb people from all over the world and produce out of their unified efforts a strong economic order, glistening ideals, an ability to operate its spirit, its resources, its sons, for the freedom of all mankind. Yet we have tolerated a great blindspot, we have permitted racial discrimination to remain with us too long. The United States of America is a country which produced the Marshall Plan, helped resurrect the spirit and economy of Europe with great dedication and billions of dollars. We have come to the aid of the refugees of the world. What man can say that this great country with its democratic ideals, its vital and resilient spirit, its sophisticated resources, cannot bring an end to racial discrimination at home now and within a decade or two and the other disabilities under which for so long so many Negro citizens have labored?

We dedicate ourselves today to secure federal civil rights legislation which will guarantee every man a job based on his talents and training, legislation which will do away with the myth that the ownership of a public place of business carries the moral or legal right to reject a customer because of the color of his hair or of his skin. We dedicate ourselves to guarantee by legislation that all American citizens have integrated education and the right to vote on reaching legal age. We dedicate ourselves today to secure a minimum wage which will guarantee a man or a woman the resources for a vital and healthy family life, unencumbered by uncertainty and by racial discrimination. A good job for every man is a just demand and it becomes our motto. But we are gathered, too, to dedicate ourselves to building a people, a nation, a world, which is free of the sin of discrimination based on race, creed, color or national origin, a world of the sons of God, equal in all important respects, a world dedicated to justice and to fraternal bonds between men.

These are the goals the Catholic community shares with all other Americans. Those of us who are gathered here before the Lincoln Memorial and those of us gathered in witness around the nation pledge ourselves that now is the time to respond to the demands of our conscience, pledge ourselves that now is the time we grasp the ideals our faith and our Constitution hold before us. There is no turning back. In a decade or less we will have done our utmost to have secured a community of justice and fraternity and love among us or we will have laid the seeds of our own destruction.

Rabbi Joachim Prinz:

I speak to you as an American Jew. As Americans we share the profound concern of millions of people about the shame and disgrace of inequality and injustice which make a mockery of the great American idea.

As Jews we bring to this great demonstration, in which thousands of us proudly participate, a twofold experience—one of the spirit and one of our history.

In the realm of the spirit, our fathers taught us thousands of years ago that when God created man, He created him as everybody's neighbor. Neighbor is not a geographic term. It is a moral concept. It means our collective responsibility for the preservation of man's dignity and integrity.

From our Jewish historic experience of three and a half thousand years we say:

Our ancient history began with slavery and the yearning for freedom. During the Middle Ages my people lived for a thousand years in the ghettos of Europe. Our modern history begins with a proclamation of emancipation.

It is for these reasons that it is not merely sympathy and compassion for the black people of America that motivates us. It is above all and beyond all such sympathies and emotions a sense of complete identification and solidarity born of our own painful historic experience.

When I was the rabbi of the Jewish community in Berlin under the Hitler regime, I learned many things. The most important thing that I learned under those tragic circumstances was that bigotry and hatred are not the most urgent problem. The most urgent, the disgraceful, the most shameful and the most tragic problem is silence.

A great people which had created a great civilization had become a nation of silent onlookers. They remained silent in the face of hate, in the face of brutality and in the face of mass murder.

America must not become a nation of onlookers. America must not remain silent. Not merely black America, but all of America. It must speak up and act, from the President down to the humblest of us, and not for the sake of the Negro, not for the sake of the black community but for the sake of the image, the dream, the idea and the aspiration of America itself.

Our children, yours and mine, in every school across the land, every morning pledge allegiance to the flag of the United States and to the republic for which it stands and then, they, the children, speak fervently and innocently of this land as the land of "liberty and justice for all."

The time, I believe, has come to work together—for it is not enough to hope together, and it is not enough to pray together—to work together that this children's oath, pronounced every morning from Maine to California, from North to South, that this oath will become a glorious, unshakeable reality in a morally renewed and united America.

Selection 21a

© 1965 Herblock in the *Washington Post*

"You Don't Understand, Boy — You're Supposed To Just Shuffle Along"

From *Straight Herblock* (Simon & Schuster, Inc., 1964), p. 199

"I Got One Of 'Em Just As She Almost Made It Back To The Church"

Selection 21b

REACTION OF WHITE NEW YORKERS TO NEGRO PROTEST*

Following are results of key questions asked in *The New York Times* survey of white attitudes. In some tables the figures will not add up to 100 per cent. This is because some respondents gave more than one answer and others did not reply.

National, State and Local Affairs

For whom did you vote in the 1960 Presidential election?

	Per Cent
Kennedy	57
Nixon	17
Didn't vote	23

If you had to decide right now, would you vote for President Johnson or for Senator Goldwater in the 1964 Presidential election?

	Per Cent
Johnson	61
Goldwater	18
Not sure	20

If you had to decide right now, who would you vote for in the United States Senate race in New York State: Robert F. Kennedy, Kenneth B. Keating, or Mrs. Clare Booth Luce? (Mrs. Luce decided not to run as a Conservative candidate while the survey was in progress.)

	Per Cent
Keating	32
Kennedy	38
Luce	2
Not sure	27

* From *The New York Times*, September 21, 1964.

Considering everything that's been happening in the last couple of months, how have President Johnson and his Administration handled the civil rights situation? Has the President gone too far in supporting Negro interests, or hasn't he gone far enough, or has he handled it about the way it should be handled?

	Per Cent
Gone too far	24
Not far enough	6
Just right	57
Not sure	13

How do you feel Mayor Wagner and the city government have handled the civil rights situation?

	Per Cent
Gone too far	27
Not far enough	16
Just right	35
Not sure	22

Familiarity With Negro Movement

A number of Negro leaders have been talked about in the last couple of months. Which of these have you heard of?

	Per Cent
Rev. Martin Luther King	94
Adam Clayton Powell	93
Malcolm X	82
James Farmer	74
Roy Wilkins	64
Rev. Milton A. Galamison	63
Jesse Gray	46
James Baldwin	46
Bayard Rustin	33
Whitney M. Young Jr.	26
Kenneth Clark	18
Livingston Wingate	9
John Lewis	9
None, don't know	4
Lincoln Williams*	3

*Lincoln Williams is an artificial name used to determine credibility of answers.

	Per Cent Approve	Per Cent Disapprove
King	52	14
Wilkins	33	7
Farmer	26	25
Baldwin	18	8
Galamison	14	24
Rustin	11	10
Young	9	4
Powell	6	60
Clark	6	3
Gray	4	29
Lewis	4	1
Malcolm X	2	60
Williams	1	1
Wingate	1	1
None, not sure	39	26

Relations With Negroes

When you were in school, were there any Negroes in your classes?

	Per Cent
Yes	57
No	42

Did you have a lot of chances to get to know Negroes, a few chances, or no chances at all?

	Per Cent
Lot	20
Few	38
None	42

As of right now, do you know any Negroes by name?

	Per Cent
Yes	69
No	31

Are there any Negro families living in your neighborhood—right near you?

	Per Cent
Yes	42
No	58

Do you think most Negroes dislike white people, like whites, or are neutral and don't care much one way or the other?

	Per Cent
Dislike whites	45
Like whites	4
Are neutral	39
Not sure, it depends	12

How do you yourself feel about Negroes, and how do you suppose most other white people feel about them? Do you like them as well as other people you know, do you like them less, or are you neutral?

	Per Cent Self	Per Cent Others
Like as well	40	15
Like less	11	37
Neutral	45	36
Not sure	4	12

How long do you think it will be before whites and Negroes can live together without friction?

	Per Cent
Less than one year	1
1–3 years	2
3–5 years	4
5–10 years	9
Over 10 years	49
Never	21
They do now	1
Not sure	13

Employment

Is the employment section of the Civil Rights Act, which prohibits discrimination in the hiring of workers, a good thing or a bad thing?

	Per Cent
Good	66
Bad	27
Not sure	7

Housing

Would you feel uncomfortable about having a number of Negro families living near you?

	Per Cent
Yes	40
Not if they were nice	20
No	40

Would you feel uncomfortable about having one or two Negro families living near you?

	Per Cent
Yes	18
Not if they were nice	25
No	57

Would it bother you if you were the only white person living on a block made up of Negroes?

	Per Cent
Yes	66
No	15
Not sure	19

School Pairing

What do you think of the school board's plan to further school integration by "pairing" nearby white and Negro schools?

	Per Cent
Good idea	11
Bad idea	80
Not sure	9

If it happened, what would you do? (Asked of the 80 per cent opposed to pairing.)

	Per Cent
Let children go	17
Send to private schools	45
Other	6
Not sure	11

Attitudes Toward Movement

Is the civil rights movement proceeding at the right pace, or is more speed needed, or is it moving too quickly?

	Per Cent
Right pace	23
More speed needed	12
Should slow down	54
Not sure	11

Have the nonviolent demonstrations, such as sit-ins and picketing, helped the Negro's cause, hurt it, or produced no change?

	Per Cent
Helped	42
Hurt	49
No change	4
Not sure	5

Do most of the Negro leaders approve of the summer's rioting, do they oppose it, or are they neutral?

	Per Cent
Favor	22
Oppose	69
Neutral	6
Not sure, it depends	3

Have you been affected in any way by a "white backlash?" Have you changed your thinking during the last couple of months? Which category describes your feelings?

	Per Cent
More strongly in favor of what Negroes want	6
More opposed to what Negroes want	27
Pretty much the same as you always felt	62

Selections 22a-22e

PRESIDENT KENNEDY'S VIEWS ON THE PROBLEMS OF CIVIL RIGHTS*

President John F. Kennedy eloquently expresses his feelings on the civil rights issue in general, and his horror at the tragic violence which it has engendered.

22a. Radio and Television Report to the American People on Civil Rights
June 11, 1963

Good evening, my fellow citizens:

This afternoon, following a series of threats and defiant statements, the presence of Alabama National Guardsmen was required on the University of Alabama to carry out the final and unequivocal order of the United States District Court of the Northern District of Alabama. That order called for the admission of two clearly qualified young Alabama residents who happened to have been born Negro.

That they were admitted peacefully on the campus is due in good measure to the conduct of the students of the University of Alabama, who met their responsibilities in a constructive way.

I hope that every American, regardless of where he lives, will stop and examine his conscience about this and other related incidents. This Nation was founded by men of many nations and backgrounds. It was founded on the principle that all men are

---

* *Public Papers of the President of the United States, John F. Kennedy,* Vol. III, 1963, Washington, D. C.: U. S. Government Printing Office, 1964.

created equal, and that the rights of every man are diminished when the rights of one man are threatened.

Today we are committed to a worldwide struggle to promote and protect the rights of all who wish to be free. And when Americans are sent to Viet-Nam or West Berlin, we do not ask for whites only. It ought to be possible, therefore, for American students of any color to attend any public institution they select without having to be backed up by troops.

It ought to be possible for American consumers of any color to receive equal service in places of public accommodation, such as hotels and restaurants and theaters and retail stores, without being forced to resort to demonstrations in the street, and it ought to be possible for American citizens of any color to register and to vote in a free election without interference or fear of reprisal.

It ought to be possible, in short, for every American to enjoy the privileges of being American without regard to his race or his color. In short, every American ought to have the right to be treated as he would wish to be treated, as one would wish his children to be treated. But this is not the case.

The Negro baby born in America today, regardless of the section of the Nation in which he is born, has about one-half as much chance of completing a high school as a white baby born in the same place on the same day, one-third as much chance of completing college, one-third as much chance of becoming a professional man, twice as much chance of becoming unemployed, about one-seventh as much chance of earning $10,000 a year, a life expectancy which is 7 years shorter, and the prospects of earning only half as much.

This is not a sectional issue. Difficulties over segregation and discrimination exist in every city, in every State of the Union, producing in many cities a rising tide of discontent that threatens the public safety. Nor is this a partisan issue. In a time of domestic crisis men of good will and generosity should be able to unite regardless of party or politics. This is not even a legal or legislative issue alone. It is better to settle these matters in the courts than on the streets, and new laws are needed at every level, but law alone cannot make men see right.

We are confronted primarily with a moral issue. It is as old as the scriptures and is as clear as the American Constitution.

The heart of the question is whether all Americans are to be afforded equal rights and equal opportunities, whether we are going to treat our fellow Americans as we want to be treated. If an American, because his skin is dark, cannot eat lunch in a restaurant open to the public, if he cannot send his children to the best public school available, if he cannot vote for the public officials who represent him, if, in short, he cannot enjoy the full and free life which all of us want, then who among us would be content to have the color of his skin changed and stand in his place? Who among us would then be content with the counsels of patience and delay?

One hundred years of delay have passed since President Lincoln freed the slaves, yet their heirs, their grandsons, are not fully free. They are not yet freed from the bonds of injustice. They are not yet freed from social and economic oppression. And this Nation, for all its hopes and all its boasts, will not be fully free until all its citizens are free.

We preach freedom around the world, and we mean it, and we cherish our freedom here at home, but are we to say to the world, and much more importantly, to each other that this is a land of the free except for the Negroes; that we have no second-class citizens except Negroes; that we have no class or caste system, no ghettoes, no master race except with respect to Negroes?

Now the time has come for this Nation to fulfill its promise. The events in Birmingham and elsewhere have so increased the cries for equality that no city or State or legislative body can prudently choose to ignore them.

The fires of frustration and discord are burning in every city, North and South, where legal remedies are not at hand. Redress is sought in the streets, in demonstrations, parades, and protests which create tensions and threaten violence and threaten lives.

We face, therefore, a moral crisis as a country and as a people. It cannot be met by repressive police action. It cannot be left to increased demonstrations in the streets. It cannot be quieted by token moves or talk. It is a time to act in the Congress, in your State and local legislative body and, above all, in all of our daily lives.

It is not enough to pin the blame on others, to say this is a problem of one section of the country or another, or deplore the fact that we face. A great change is at hand, and our task, our obligation, is to make that revolution, that change, peaceful and constructive for all.

Those who do nothing are inviting shame as well as violence. Those who act boldly are recognizing right as well as reality.

Next week I shall ask the Congress of the United States to act, to make a commitment it has not fully made in this century to the proposition that race has no place in American life or law. The Federal judiciary has upheld that proposition in a series of forthright cases. The executive branch has adopted that proposition in the conduct of its affairs, including the employment of Federal personnel, the use of Federal facilities, and the sale of federally financed housing.

But there are other necessary measures which only the Congress can provide, and they must be provided at this session. The old code of equity law under which we live commands for every wrong a remedy, but in too many communities, in too many parts of the country, wrongs are inflicted on Negro citizens and there are no remedies at law. Unless the Congress acts, their only remedy is in the street.

I am, therefore, asking the Congress to enact legislation giving all Americans the right to be served in facilities which are open to the public—hotels, restaurants, theaters, retail stores, and similar establishments.

This seems to me to be an elementary right. Its denial is an arbitrary indignity that no American in 1963 should have to endure, but many do.

I have recently met with scores of business leaders urging them to take voluntary action to end this discrimination and I have been encouraged by their response, and in the last two weeks over 75 cities have seen progress made in desegregating these kinds of facilities. But many are unwilling to act alone, and for this reason, nationwide legislation is needed if we are to move this problem from the streets to the courts.

I am also asking Congress to authorize the Federal Government to participate more fully in lawsuits designed to end segregation in public education. We have succeeded in persuading many districts to desegregate voluntarily. Dozens have admitted Negroes without violence. Today a Negro is attending a State-supported institution in every one of our 50 States, but the pace is very slow.

Too many Negro children entering segregated grade schools at the time of the Supreme Court's decision 9 years ago will enter segregated high schools this fall, having suffered a loss which can never be restored. The lack of an adequate education denies the Negro a chance to get a decent job.

The orderly implementation of the Supreme Court decision, therefore, cannot be left solely to those who may not have the economic resources to carry the legal action or who may be subject to harassment.

Other features will be also requested, including greater protection for the right to vote. But legislation, I repeat, cannot solve this problem alone. It must be solved in the homes of every American in every community across our country.

In this respect, I want to pay tribute to those citizens North and

South who have been working in their communities to make life better for all. They are acting not out of a sense of legal duty but out of a sense of human decency.

Like our soldiers and sailors in all parts of the world they are meeting freedom's challenge on the firing line, and I salute them for their honor and their courage.

My fellow Americans, this is a problem which faces us all—in every city of the North as well as the South. Today there are Negroes unemployed, two or three times as many compared to whites, inadequate in education, moving into the large cities, unable to find work, young people particularly out of work without hope, denied equal rights, denied the opportunity to eat at a restaurant or lunch counter or go to a movie theater, denied the right to a decent education, denied almost today the right to attend a State university even though qualified. It seems to me that these are matters which concern us all, not merely Presidents or Congressmen or Governors, but every citizen of the United States.

This is one country. It has become one country because all of us and all the people who came here had an equal chance to develop their talents.

We cannot say to 10 percent of the population that you can't have that right; that your children can't have the chance to develop whatever talents they have; that the only way that they are going to get their rights is to go into the streets and demonstrate. I think we owe them and we owe ourselves a better country than that.

Therefore, I am asking for your help in making it easier for us to move ahead and to provide the kind of equality of treatment which we would want ourselves; to give a chance for every child to be educated to the limit of his talents.

As I have said before, not every child has an equal talent or an equal ability or an equal motivation, but they should have the equal right to develop their talent and their ability and their motivation, to make something of themselves.

We have a right to expect that the Negro community will be responsible, will uphold the law, but they have a right to expect that the law will be fair, that the Constitution will be color blind, as Justice Harlan said at the turn of the century.

This is what we are talking about and this is a matter which concerns this country and what it stands for, and in meeting it I ask the support of all our citizens.

Thank you very much.

22b.   Statement by the President on Desegregation in the Schools of Alabama

September 9, 1963

It should be clear that United States Government action regarding the Alabama schools will come only if Governor Wallace compels it.

In 144 school districts in 11 Southern and border States, desegregation was carried out for the first time this month in an orderly and peaceful manner. Parents, students, citizens, school officials, and public officials of these areas met their responsibilities in a dignified, law-abiding way. It was not necessary for the Federal Government to become involved in any of those States.

In the State of Alabama, however, where local authorities repeatedly stated they were prepared to carry out court directives and maintain public peace, Governor Wallace has refused to respect either the law or the authority of local officials. For his own personal and political reasons—so that he may later charge Federal interference—he is desperately anxious to have the Federal Government intervene in a situation in which we have no desire to intervene.

The Governor knows that the United States Government is obligated to carry out the orders of the United States court. He knows that the great majority of the citizens in Birmingham, Mobile, Tuskegee, and Huntsville were willing to face this difficult transition with the same courage and respect for the law as did the communities in neighboring States. And he knows that there was and is no reason or necessity for intervention by the Federal Government, unless he wishes and forces that result.

This Government will do whatever must be done to see that the orders of the court are implemented—but I am hopeful that Governor Wallace will enable the local officials and communities to meet their responsibilities in this regard, as they are willing to do.

[*Note:* On the following day the President signed and the White House released the following papers:

1. Proclamation 3554 ordering all persons engaged in obstructing justice in Alabama to cease and desist therefrom and to disperse and retire peaceably forthwith (28 F. R. 9861; 3 CFR, 1963 Supp.).

2. Executive Order 11118 directing the Secretary of Defense to take all appropriate steps to enforce the orders of United States courts, including the calling into active service of units of the Alabama National Guard (28 F. R. 9863; 3 CFR, 1963 Supp.).]

22c. Statement by the President on the Sunday Bombing in Birmingham
September 16, 1963

I know I speak on behalf of all Americans in expressing a deep sense of outrage and grief over the killing of the children yesterday in Birmingham, Alabama. It is regrettable that public disparagement of law and order has encouraged violence which has fallen on the innocent. If these cruel and tragic events can only awaken that city and State—if they can only awaken this entire Nation—to a realization of the folly of racial injustice and hatred and violence, then it is not too late for all concerned to unite in steps toward peaceful progress before more lives are lost.

The Negro leaders of Birmingham who are counselling restraint instead of violence are bravely serving their ideals in their most difficult task—for the principles of peaceful self-control are least appealing when most needed.

Assistant Attorney General Burke Marshall has returned to Birmingham to be of assistance to community leaders and law enforcement officials—and bomb specialists of the Federal Bureau of Investigation are there to lend every assistance in the detection of those responsible for yesterday's crime. This Nation is committed to a course of domestic justice and tranquility—and I call upon every citizen, white and Negro, North and South, to put passions and prejudices aside and to join in this effort.

22d. Further Statement by the President on the Sunday Bombing in Birmingham
September 19, 1963

The tragic death of the Negro children in Birmingham last Sunday has given rise to fears and distrust which require the cooperation and restraint of all the citizens of that city.

I have received reports from the leading Negro citizens concerning the situation this afternoon. Next Monday I will confer at the request of Mayor Boutwell with white civic leaders who want to give us information concerning the steps which the city has taken and plans to take to reestablish the confidence of everyone that law and order in Birmingham will be maintained.

In addition, I have today appointed Gen. Kenneth Royall and Col. Earl Blaik as a committee to represent me personally in helping the city to work as a unit in overcoming the fears and suspicions which now exist. They will go to Birmingham in the next few days to start on this work of great importance.

In the meantime the Federal Bureau of Investigation, as well as the local authorities, is making massive efforts to bring to justice the persons responsible for the bombing on Sunday and previous incidents.

I urge everyone to cooperate with them in this effort and that all citizens of Birmingham and Alabama will give these processes of law enforcement a full opportunity to work. I urge all citizens in these next days to conduct themselves with restraint and responsibility.

22e. Statement by the President Following Meetings With Civic Leaders and Members of the Clergy of Birmingham

September 23, 1963

Today I met with two groups from the City of Birmingham—one a group selected by Mayor Boutwell who were representative of the city administration and the business community, and the other a group of clergymen who are representative of the major faiths.

All of the persons at these meetings expressed a desire to meet Birmingham's problems within the city itself, and to make progress to restore the confidence of the citizens of Birmingham, both Negroes and white, in its ability to keep the peace and to make progress on the problems which confront that troubled city.

Both groups also expressed hope that General Royall and Colonel Blaik will be able to contribute to easing the situation and stated that these representatives would be welcome to the city, as did the group of Negro leaders last week.

General Royall and Colonel Blaik intend to proceed to Birmingham tomorrow. Their mission is to be of whatever assistance they can in restoring good communications between the white and Negro communities in that city and in easing the racial tensions which now exist. We have now had expression from all the major elements in the city that this committee will be welcome and I ask everyone to cooperate with them.

All the groups have expressed confidence that these matters can be settled on a local level. That is also my strong belief. I am hopeful that all groups will work vigorously to that end in the coming days.

Selection 23

TO FULFILL THESE RIGHTS

LYNDON B. JOHNSON*

The speech of President Johnson at Howard University is regarded as one of his best statements on the issue of inequality in this country.

Our earth is the home of revolution.

In every corner of every continent men charged with hope contend with ancient ways in the pursuit of justice. They reach for the newest of weapons to realize the oldest of dreams; that each may walk in freedom and pride, stretching his talents, enjoying the fruits of the earth.

Our enemies may occasionally seize the day of change. But it is the banner of our revolution they take. And our own future is linked to this process of swift and turbulent change in many lands in the world. But nothing in any country touches us more profoundly, nothing is more freighted with meaning for our own destiny, than the revolution of the Negro American.

In far too many ways American Negroes have been another nation: deprived of freedom, crippled by hatred, the doors of opportunity closed to hope.

In our time change has come to this Nation too. The American Negro, acting with impressive restraint, has peacefully protested and marched, entered the courtrooms and the seats of government, demanding a justice that has long been denied. The voice of the Negro was the call to action. But it is a tribute to America that, once aroused, the courts and the Congress, the President and most of the people, have been the allies of progress.

* Remarks of the President at Howard University, Washington, D. C., June 4, 1965.

Legal Protection for Human Rights

Thus we have seen the high court of the country declare that discrimination based on race was repugnant to the Constitution, and therefore void. We have seen in 1957, 1960, and again in 1964, the first civil rights legislation in this Nation in almost an entire century.

As majority leader of the United States Senate, I helped to guide two of these bills through the Senate. As your President, I was proud to sign the third. And now very soon we will have the fourth—a new law guaranteeing every American the right to vote.

No act of my entire administration will give me greater satisfaction than the day when my signature makes this bill too the law of this land.

The voting rights bill will be the latest, and among the most important, in a long series of victories. But this victory—as Winston Churchill said of another triumph for freedom—"is not the end. It is not even the beginning of the end. But it is perhaps, the end of the beginning."

That beginning is freedom. And the barriers to that freedom are tumbling down. Freedom is the right to share fully and equally in American society—to vote, to hold a job, to enter a public place, to go to school. It is the right to be treated in every part of our national life as a person equal in dignity and promise to all others.

Freedom Is Not Enough

But freedom is not enough. You do not wipe away the scars of centuries by saying: Now you are free to go where you want, do as you desire, and choose the leaders you please.

You do not take a person who, for years, has been hobbled by chains and liberate him, bring him up to the starting line of a race and then say, "You are free to compete with all the others," and still justly believe that you have been completely fair.

Thus it is not enough just to open the gates of opportunity. All of our citizens must have the ability to walk through those gates.

This is the next and more profound stage of the battle for civil rights. We seek not just freedom but opportunity—not just legal equity but human ability—not just equality as a right and a theory, but equality as a fact and as a result.

For the task is to give 20 million Negroes the same chance as every other American to learn and grow, to work and share in society, to develop their abilities—physical, mental and spiritual, and to pursue their individual happiness.

To this end equal opportunity is essential, but not enough. Men and women of all races are born with the same range of abilities. But ability is not just the product of birth. Ability is stretched or stunted by the family you live with, and the neighborhood you live in, by the school you go to and the poverty or the richness of your surroundings. It is the product of a hundred unseen forces playing upon the infant, the child, and the man.

Progress for Some

This graduating class at Howard University is witness to the indomitable determination of the Negro American to win his way in American life.

The number of Negroes in schools of higher learning has almost doubled in 15 years. The number of nonwhite professional workers has more than doubled in 10 years. The median income of Negro college women exceeds that of white college women. And there are also the enormous accomplishments of distinguished individual Negroes—many of them graduates of this institution, and one of them the first lady ambassador in the history of the United States.

There are proud and impressive achievements. But they tell only the story of a growing middle-class minority, steadily narrowing the gap between them and their white counterparts.

A Widening Gulf

But for the great majority of Negro Americans—the poor, the unemployed, the uprooted and the dispossessed—there is a much grimmer story. They still are another nation. Despite the court orders and the laws, despite the legislative victories and the speeches, for them the walls are rising and the gulf is widening.

Here are some of the facts of this American failure.

Thirty-five years ago the rate of unemployment for Negroes and whites was about the same. Today the Negro rate is twice as high.

In 1948 the 8 percent unemployment rate for Negro teenage boys was actually less than that of whites. By last year that rate had grown to 23 percent, as against 13 percent for whites.

Between 1949 and 1959, the income of Negro men relative to white men declined in every section of this country. From 1952 to 1963 the median income of Negro families compared to white actually dropped from 57 percent to 53 percent.

In the years 1955 through 1957, 22 percent of experienced Negro workers were out of work at some time during the year. In 1961 through 1963 that proportion had soared to 29 percent.

Since 1947 the number of white families living in poverty has decreased 27 percent, while the number of poor nonwhite families decreased only 3 percent.

The infant mortality of nonwhites in 1940 was 70 percent greater than whites. Twenty-two years later it was 90 percent greater.

Moreover, the isolation of Negro from white communities is increasing, rather than decreasing, as Negroes crowd into the central cities and become a city within a city.

Of course Negro Americans as well as white Americans have shared in our rising national abundance. But the harsh fact of the matter is that in the battle for true equality too many are losing ground every day.

The Causes of Inequality

We are not completely sure why this is. The causes are complex and subtle. But we do know the two broad basic reasons. And we do know that we have to act.

First, Negroes are trapped—as many whites are trapped—in inherited, gateless poverty. They lack training and skills. They are shut in slums, without decent medical care. Private and public poverty combine to cripple their capacities.

We are trying to attack these evils through our poverty program, through our education program, through our medical care and our other health programs and a dozen more of the Great Society programs that are aimed at the root causes of this poverty.

We will increase, and accelerate, and broaden this attack in years to come until this most enduring of foes finally yields to our unyielding will. But there is a second cause—much more difficult to explain, more deeply grounded, more desperate in its force. It is the devastating heritage of long years of slavery; and a century of oppression, hatred and injustice.

Special Nature of Negro Poverty

For Negro poverty is not white poverty. Many of its causes and many of its cures are the same. But there are differences—deep, corrosive, obstinate differences—radiating painful roots into the community, the family, and the nature of the individual.

These differences are not racial differences. They are solely and simply the consequence of ancient brutality, past injustice, and present prejudice. They are anguishing to observe. For the Negro they are a constant reminder of oppression. For the white they are a constant reminder of guilt. But they must be faced and dealt with and overcome, if we are ever to reach the time when the only difference between Negroes and whites is the color of their skin.

Nor can we find a complete answer in the experience of other

American minorities. They made a valiant and a largely successful effort to emerge from poverty and prejudice. The Negro, like these others, will have to rely mostly on his own efforts. But he just can not do it alone. For they did not have the heritage of centuries to overcome. They did not have a cultural tradition which had been twisted and battered by endless years of hatred and hopelessness. Nor were they excluded because of race or color—a feeling whose dark intensity is matched by no other prejudice in our society.

Nor can these differences be understood as isolated infirmities. They are a seamless web. They cause each other. They result from each other. They reinforce each other. Much of the Negro community is buried under a blanket of history and circumstance. It is not a lasting solution to lift just one corner of that blanket. We must stand on all sides and raise the entire cover if we are to liberate our fellow citizens.

The Roots of Injustice

One of the differences is the increased concentration of Negroes in our cities. More than 73 percent of all Negroes live in urban areas compared with less than 70 percent of the whites. Most of these Negroes live in slums. Most of them live together—separated people. Men are shaped by their world. When it is a world of decay, ringed by an invisible wall—when escape is arduous and uncertain, and the saving pressures of a more hopeful society are unknown—it can cripple the youth and desolate the man.

There is also the burden that a dark skin can add to the search for a productive place in society. Unemployment strikes most swiftly and broadly at the Negro. This burden erodes hope. Blighted hope breeds despair. Despair brings indifference to the learning which offers a way out. And despair, coupled with indifference, is often the source of destructive rebellion against the fabric of society.

There is also the lacerating hurt of early collision with white hatred or prejudice, distaste, or condescension. Other groups have felt similar intolerance. But success and achievement could wipe it away. They do not change the color of a man's skin. I have seen this uncomprehending pain in the eyes of the little Mexican-American schoolchildren that I taught many years ago. It can be overcome. But, for many, the wounds are always open.

Family Breakdown

Perhaps most important—its influence radiating to every part of life—is the breakdown of the Negro family structure. For this, most of all, white America must accept responsibility. It flows from centuries of oppression and persecution of the Negro man. It flows from long years of degradation and discrimination, which have attacked his dignity and assaulted his ability to provide for his family.

This, too, is not pleasant to look upon. But it must be faced by those whose serious intent is to improve the life of all Americans.

Only a minority—less than half—of all Negro children reach the age of 18 having lived all their lives with both of their parents. At this moment little less than two-thirds are living with both of their parents. Probably a majority of all Negro children receive federally aided public assistance sometime during their childhood.

The family is the cornerstone of our society. More than any other force it shapes the attitude, the hopes, the ambitions, and the values of the child. When the family collapses it is the children that are usually damaged. When it happens on a massive scale the community itself is crippled.

So, unless we work to strengthen the family, to create conditions under which most parents will stay together—all the rest: schools and playgrounds, public assistance and private concern, will never be enough to cut completely the circle of despair and deprivation.

To Fulfill These Rights

There is no single easy answer to all of these problems.

Jobs are part of the answer. They bring the income which permits a man to provide for his family.

Decent homes in decent surroundings, and a chance to learn— an equal chance to learn—are part of the answer.

Welfare and social programs better designed to hold families together are part of the answer.

Care of the sick is part of the answer.

An understanding heart by all Americans is also a large part of the answer.

To all these fronts—and a dozen more—I will dedicate the expanding efforts of the Johnson Administration.

But there are other answers still to be found. Nor do we fully understand all of the problems. Therefore, I want to announce tonight that this fall I intend to call a White House conference of scholars, and experts, and outstanding Negro leaders—men of both races—and officials of government at every level.

This White House conference's theme and title will be "To Fulfill These Rights."

Its object will be to help the American Negro fulfill the rights which, after the long time of injustice, he is finally about to secure.

To move beyond opportunity to achievement.

To shatter forever not only the barriers of law and public practice, but the walls which bound the condition of man by the color of his skin.

To dissolve, as best we can, the antique enmities of the heart which diminish the holder, divide the great democracy, and do wrong—great wrong—to the children of God.

I pledge you tonight this will be a chief goal of my Administration, and of my program next year, and in years to come. And I hope, and I pray, and I believe, it will be a part of the program of all America.

What Is Justice?

For what is justice?

It is to fulfill the fair expectations of man.

Thus, American justice is a very special thing. For, from the first, this has been a land of towering expectations. It was to be a nation where each man could be ruled by the common consent of all—enshrined in law, given life by institutions, guided by men themselves subject to its rule. And all—all of every station and origin—would be touched equally in obligation and in liberty.

Beyond the law lay the land. It was a rich land, glowing with more abundant promise than man had ever seen. Here, unlike any place yet known, all were to share the harvest.

And beyond this was the dignity of man. Each could become whatever his qualities of mind and spirit would permit—to strive, to seek, and, if he could, to find his happiness.

This is American justice. We have pursued it faithfully to the edge of our imperfections. And we have failed to find it for the American Negro.

It is the glorious opportunity of this generation to end the one huge wrong of the American Nation and, in so doing, to find America for ourselves, with the same immense thrill of discovery which gripped those who first began to realize that here, at last, was a home for freedom.

All it will take is for all of us to understand what this country is and what this country must become.

The Scripture promises: "I shall light a candle of understanding in thine heart, which shall not be put out."

Together, and with millions more, we can light that candle of understanding in the heart of all America.

And, once lit, it will never again go out.

Selection 24

WHITE AND NEGRO "EXTREMISM"

HARRY S. ASHMORE*

Harry S. Ashmore is a well-known newspaperman and writer. Editor of the Arkansas Gazette *at the time of the Little Rock crisis, he was critical of the policies of Governor Faubus, who was opposed to the desegregation policies of federal government.*

. . . Negroes have moved, in less than a generation, from the passive role of supplicants to active participation in a mass crusade against the form and substance of inequality. To this point, the tide of history has run with them, and they have been supported by the national conscience. Even in the South, the devotion of most whites to the *status quo* has been countered by a sense of personal guilt. At the ethical operating level, the United States Supreme Court has systematically translated the Constitution's libertarian spirit into the law of the land. Having won every critical test before the bar, Negroes can now carry their protest onto the sidewalks of the deep South with the full protection of the federal presence.

The parallel between Southern white resistance and the Negro crusade is striking and significant. One begot the other, and, substituting black for white, the language, the symbols, even the characteristics of the most conspicuous leaders and organizations are interchangeable.

At the far limits are the Ku Klux Klan and the Black Muslims—both ostensibly committed to the same declared aim, absolute seg-

---

* Harry Ashmore, "Coming Showdown in the Race Crisis," *Look*, July 6, 1963, pp. 62–67.

regation of the races. Both are secret societies that indulge in mystical, quasi-religious activities and rig up the faithful in uniforms. Both are ardent dues collectors. Both have a great fondness for parades and rallies and unbounded faith in their ability to intimidate their enemies. Both preach unbridled racial hatred and covertly encourage violence. Many of the past national leaders of the Klan have wound up in prison, usually on fraud charges, and Malcolm X, (once) the most active of the Muslim apostles, is a former jailbird.

Or consider General Walker and James Baldwin. Both are men of education and attainment, fully endowed with the status symbols of their respective trades. Both came late to the racial battlefield, and have long been isolated from the rank and file for whom they now profess to speak—General Walker in the course of a distinguished military career, Baldwin in the years of literary exile that brought him deserved recognition as a writer. General Walker is unable to turn his back completely on his red-necked followers, or Baldwin on the Black Muslims, although both are obviously socially discomfited. Both deal with the race problem in stirring terms of personal, apocalyptic visions: General Walker sees the Visigoths of Communism already over the walls, and Baldwin thinks a dark-skinned host has assembled at Armageddon. These revelations give each an exclusive patent on the verities. General Walker finds even so stalwart an anti-Communist as Senator Dodd "blind" on home-grown subversion, and Baldwin believes Martin Luther King has reached the end of his rope.

The most notable political leaders also pair out neatly. Orval Faubus of Arkansas and Adam Clayton Powell of Harlem are wily old professionals who have found in the race issue the key to what appears to be permanent office. When he needs to be re-elected, Governor Faubus simply hollers, "Nigger!" When Congressman Powell faces similar necessities, he cries, "Discrimination!" If this tends to cut them off from their political colleagues, who can't afford to say so, but with reason consider each a liability to his cause, it has its compensations. Powell is able to travel at public expense, and Faubus has the pleasure of operating the most comprehensive state political machine since the late Huey Long's.

These and men like them have made most of the headlines that mark the steady progress of the Negro crusade. They are eternally ready to provide reporters with a harsh word and a dire prediction. They are in fact prime figures in the action and reaction, and the history of the period doubtless would have been different without them. Yet they are symbols, not leaders. They have been able to unleash powerful emotions, but the task of controlling the resulting force for coherent purpose has been left to others. For the white Southern leadership, the failure is clear and final; segregation cannot endure. For the Negro leadership, the test is only beginning.

It is at least possible that recovery from the emotional excesses of the recent past will serve to further reduce the incidence and virulence of Southern bigotry. In the period of convalescence ahead, white Southerners will be required to form new institutions and arrangements to replace those they can no longer doubt are unacceptable to their Negro neighbors. They have no real choice except to examine the possibility that they have nothing to lose and much to gain by seeing to it that Negroes reach their declared goals of increased economic opportunity and unlimited access to the facilities and amenities of the community. Not the least of the benefits could be the restoration of the bonds of genuine affection between whites and Negroes that enriched the older Southern tradition.

An increasing share of the burden of creating the necessary conditions for this development in the South, and for maintaining them in the North, is passing to the Negro leadership. The process that has contained the manifestations of white bigotry has encouraged the expression of Negro bigotry—and this has had inevitable response among a people whose grievances are real.

There has emerged a set of Negro myths as dangerous and as debilitating as their white Southern counterparts. The basic proposition here is that no white man can really understand how a Negro feels. This, in effect, accepts the argument of white racists that Negroes are inherently different. Since Negroes can hardly be expected to equate racial difference with inferiority, the result is the spurious doctrine of black supremacy long preached on the street corners of Harlem and now heard in more respectable precincts.

At its crudest, the Negro mythology has produced the Black Muslims and their effort to exploit the emotional response of American Negroes to the racial unrest that doomed colonialism in Africa and Asia. The identification of the Black Muslims with the true sons of Allah is about as valid as the Ku Klux Klan's claim to the traditions of the Scottish Highlands. Negroes have been in this country as long as any other Americans, and there has been no mass immigration since the slave trade was banned more than a century ago. The historic relationship of American Negroes to Africa is now devoid of cultural or religious significance. It is purely a matter of pigmentation, and this, as they discover at every point of contact with genuine African nationalists, is of minor consequence.

At a more sophisticated level, it is argued that the unique Negro experience under slavery and enforced segregation has had a purifying effect on those who suffered it. Baldwin, who occasionally seems to confuse himself with Job, gives the proposition a religious cast, contending that the black man represents a kind of original white sin, which, by means never made entirely clear, must be purged. Norman Mailer, Jack Kerouac, and other avant-garde white novelists have attempted to distill out of the jazz, marijuana, and uninhibited sex of the Negro Bohemian fringe the thesis that only alienation reveals ultimate truth.

These fantasies have led to public seizures of emotional segregation and have produced an outright attack on the older heroes of the Negro movement. Roy Wilkins of the NAACP is accused of selling his people down the river because there are white members on his board of directors. Adam Clayton Powell proclaims that Negroes cannot support any interracial organization that has white leadership. Attorney General Robert F. Kennedy, who with considerable effect has been devoting his time to service as advocate and negotiator for the Negro cause, is treated to derisive laughter simply because he is white. William Worthy, Jr., the controversial Negro journalist, has reached the remarkable conclusion that no white man can support the American Negro unless he also supports Fidel Castro. Here, as in the white South, passionate irrationality precludes effective discussion of the issue and of the practical means of resolving it. A leading Negro entertainer, shaken by the excesses of his peers, has privately confessed that he nevertheless has found it necessary to remain silent in order to avoid the dread epithet, "Uncle Tom."

The Negro mythology, like the white, constitutes a mirror image of reality. The degradation of the slums has crushed far more spirits than it has purified. Only the strongest members of any race emerge without crippling scars from a lifetime of deprivation, callous mistreatment, and scornful abuse. That such individuals have now appeared in significant number to lead the marching columns of protest is a tribute to the older generation of white and colored leaders they have impatiently shouldered aside. It was the lonely battlers of the Urban League, the NAACP, the New Deal, and the labor movement who brought the reforms that freed many of the new generation from the ghetto and unshackled their militant spirit.

These dedicated young men and women, armed with pride and

dignity, will find, if they look back, that they are still a minority among their own people. For most Negroes, the weight of oppression has eroded away the will and the capacity to seize the new opportunities and face the new risks. A high proportion have slipped irrevocably into the sloth and crime of slum life and constitute a social problem that is not affected by the argument that the fault is the community's, not theirs.

The Negro crusade, like any other, is fueled by emotion and does not welcome the dampening strictures of logic. As the only domestic social movement of current consequence, it has magnetic attraction for the sort of radicals and reformers who gave vent to their general protest against society by supporting the labor movement before the unions went flabby with success and affluence. For these, proud in their moral fervor, thrilled by vicarious martyrdom, and comfortably removed from the scene of battle, the outcome of a given engagement is of little consequence. The situation is somewhat different for the tacticians in the field.

The most successful of these by far is the Reverend Martin Luther King, Jr. Upon the solid base of the legal successes won by the now-eclipsed NAACP, he has promoted the mass demonstrations that have penetrated Southern resistance even in the final redoubts of Alabama and Mississippi. For the front-line leaders, it has been, and will continue to be, a delicate balancing act.

Dr. King needs the emotional voltage, and the financial support, generated by the firebrands at the great rallies in the North and West. But he also needs an open line, usually routed through the Department of Justice, to the white men who must issue the orders to desegregate. He can hardly file a public dissent when Professor Kenneth Clark of City College of New York takes issue with Attorney General Kennedy and proclaims that the Negro people are no longer going to beg favors from the white power structure. But Dr. King is in Birmingham, and Professor Clark isn't, and it is Dr. King who in the end will sit down and negotiate the compromise settlement that will mark another step forward for the Negro people.

Considerations of strategy as well as his Christian devotion to nonviolence sent Dr. King into the pool halls of Birmingham to remind the boys in the back rooms that switchblade knives provide no answer to the dynamite of white hoodlums. So long as violence is directed against Negro demonstrators, elemental standards of justice and federal guns automatically are on their side. Let Negroes initiate the attack or even reply in kind, and the balance will shift —and without this essential support, Negroes again will be a helpless minority in an aroused white community.

Martin Luther King not only subscribes to, but has given real meaning to, the battle cry of the movement: No white man has a right to ask a Negro to wait any longer for equality. But, as a practicing Christian, Dr. King also has to recognize that every white man has a right to insist that the quest for equality not be marked by a trail of blood.

It is on this critical point that Dr. King has had to part company with a good many of those who have lately swung aboard the freedom train. He speaks for justice. They cry out for vengeance. There was a moving, simple eloquence in the statement Dr. King's followers issued after a truce had been worked out in Birmingham: "The city of Birmingham has reached an accord with its conscience." All his adult life, Dr. King has preached and practiced in the service of a mission to unite a national community put asunder by the inhumanity of slavery and segregation. He could no more accept the mad design of the Muslims for a separate Negro state, or the admonition of the intellectuals who urge that bitterness be nurtured in the ghettos of the mind, than he could join forces with George Wallace, Ross Barnett, and Orval Faubus.

These are the surface elements of a racial crisis moving inexorably toward a showdown. All are the product of the tragic American failure to resolve the great moral issue that has tainted the Nation's free institutions and truncated its ideals—the failure that once before led to fratricide.

It is, as Gunnar Myrdal has said, a peculiarly American dilemma. The Negro crusade has the sound of revolution, and many frightened whites and a few loquacious Negroes see it as such. Yet its goal is the opposite of that set by dark-skinned revolutionaries abroad, who seek to drive out their white rulers and shape their destiny on their terms. Here, Negroes are demanding only admission to a closed white society that has imposed its standards while callously denying full access to its protections and benefits.

The demand is made as a matter of right, not as a device to create a new social order. It cannot be rejected, or further postponed, without still more damage to our diminished libertarian tradition and to our tarnished religious ethic. The high price the South has paid for intransigence is now being levied against the nation as a whole. The white community's effective abdication of moral purpose has produced a paralyzing failure of will on the part of the political leadership. Only now is there recognition that we can't get on with the nation's urgent business until we have begun, at least, to take care of the Negro's needs.

The Supreme Court, in splendid isolation, has discharged its responsibilities. The Court has defined the national policy forbidding racial discrimination and laid down the ground rules for its implementation. This should have brought Congress to the necessary business of fashioning new laws to replace those that have been swept off the statute books. Tangled in its antiquated rules, intimidated by the uncertain temper of its constituency, Congress has indulged instead in a fruitless decade of angry recrimination.

Eisenhower hoped until the end of his term that the race problem somehow would go away. Kennedy . . . understood that it will not, but he [gave] it low priority—and only [in 1963 did he bring] himself to use the full weight of his office to force the issue upon the lawmakers. . . .

It is true that the ultimate solution will not be found in laws, but in the dark places of men's minds and hearts. But it is also true that laws are the manifest of the national purpose, and when government is unwilling, or unable, to provide them, there is no standard to which the wise and just may repair.

It is argued that the moderates have failed, and this is so. But it does not follow that moderation as a policy has failed. The fact is that it has not yet been tried. White, and now Negro, extremists have successfully blocked the scattered efforts to bring the leaderless mass of Americans to the kind of accommodations that will achieve harmony as well as justice. Yet this, surely, is the minimum essential, since Negroes and whites somehow must fashion the future on terms acceptable to both.

History and the peculiarities of our political system provide explanations, and even excuses, for our failure to live up to the moral imperative we have never denied. And the realities of the depressed Negro community make it clear that there will be no neat and orderly solution to social problems compounded by racial prejudice on both sides. But we have run out of options. The restoration of domestic tranquillity demands nothing less than a renewed national commitment to the guarantees of life, liberty, and the pursuit of happiness, this time without reservations.

Selection 25

IF I WERE A NEGRO

WILLIAM FAULKNER *

The writer of the following article, which first appeared in Ebony *magazine, was William Faulkner. Born in Mississippi, he became one of our greatest novelists and in 1949 was awarded the Nobel prize in literature. He died in 1962.*

I quote the following from a piece of mine printed in *Life* magazine, March 5, 1956, entitled *A Letter to the North,* this part of the *Letter* addressed specifically to the NAACP and the other organizations working actively for the abolishment of segregation: "Go slow now. Stop now for a time, a moment. You have the power now; you can afford to withhold for a moment the use of it as a force. You have done a good job, you have jolted your opponent off-balance and he is now vulnerable. But stop there for a moment; don't give him the advantage of a chance to cloud the issue by that purely automatic sympathy for the underdog simply because he is under. . . . You have shown the Southerner what you can do and what you will do if necessary; give him a space in which to get his breath and assimilate that knowledge; to look about and see that (1) Nobody is going to force integration on him from the outside; (2) That he himself faces an obsolescence in his own land which only he can cure; a moral condition which not only must be cured but a physical condition which has got to be cured if he, the white Southerner, is to have any peace, is not to be faced with another legal process or maneuver every year, year after year, for the rest of his life."

By "Go slow, pause for a moment," I meant, "Be flexible." When

* From Era Bell Thompson and Herbert Thompson (editors), *White on Black,* Chicago: Johnson Publishing Co., 1963, pp. 69–75.

I wrote the letter and then used every means I knew to get it printed in time, Autherine Lucy had just been compelled to withdraw temporarily from the University of Alabama by a local violence already of dangerous proportions. I believed that when the judge validated her claim to be re-admitted, which he would have to do, that the forces supporting her would send her back for re-admission, and that when that happened she would probably lose her life. That didn't happen. I want to believe that the forces supporting Miss Lucy were wise enough themselves not to send her back—not merely wise enough to save her life, but wise enough to foresee that even her martyrdom would in the long run be less effective than the simple, prolonged, endless nuisance-value of her threat, which was what I meant by ". . . a physical condition which has got to be cured if he, the white Southerner, is to have any peace, is not to be faced with another Miss Lucy every year . . . for the rest of his life."

Not the individual Negro to abandon or lower one jot his hope and will for equality, but his leaders and organizations to be always flexible and adaptable to circumstance and locality in their methods of gaining it. If I were a Negro in America today, that is the course I would advise the leaders of my race to follow: to send every day to the white school to which he was entitled by his ability and capacity to go, a student of my race, fresh and cleanly dressed, courteous, without threat or violence, to seek admission; when he was refused I would forget about him as an individual, but tomorrow I would send another one, still fresh and clean and courteous, to be refused in his turn, until at last the white man himself must recognize that there will be no peace for him until he himself has solved the dilemma.

This was Gandhi's way. If I were a Negro, I would advise our elders and leaders to make this our undeviating and inflexible course—a course of inflexible and unviolent flexibility directed against not just the schools but against all the public institutions from which we are interdict, as is being done against the Montgomery, Alabama, bus lines. But always with flexibility: inflexible and undeviable only in hope and will but flexible always to adapt to time and place and circumstance.

I would be a member of NAACP, since nothing else in our United States culture has yet held out to my race that much of hope. But I would remain only under conditions: That it recognize the most serious quantity in our problem which, so far as I know, it has not publicly recognized yet: That it make that same flexibility the watchword of its methods. I would say to others of my race that we must never curb our hopes and demands for equal rights, but merely to curb with flexibility our methods of demanding them. I would say to other members of my race that I do not know how long "slow" will take, but if you will grant me to mean by "going slow," being flexible, I do not believe that anything else save "going slow" will advance our hopes. I would say to my race, "The watchword of our flexibility must be decency, quietness, courtesy, dignity; if violence and unreason come, it must not be from us." I would say that all the Negroes in Montgomery *should* support the bus line boycott, but never that all of them *must,* since by that *must,* we will descend to the same methods which those opposing us are using to oppress us, and our victory will be worth nothing until it is willed and not compelled. I would say that our race must adjust itself psychologically, not to an indefinite continuation of a segregated society, but rather to a continuation as long as necessary of that inflexible unflagging flexibility which in the end will make the white man himself sick and tired of fighting it.

It is easy enough to say glibly, "If I were a Negro, I would do this or that." But a white man can only imagine himself for the moment a Negro; he cannot be that man of another race and griefs and problems. So there are some questions he can put to himself but cannot answer, for instance:

Q. Would you lower your sights on your life's goals and reduce your aspirations for reasons of realism?

A. No. I would impose flexibility on the methods.

Q. Would this apply to your children?

A. I would teach them both the aspirations and the flexibility. But there is hope, since life itself is hope in simply being alive since living is change and change must be either advancement or death.

Q. How would you conduct yourself so as to avoid controversy and hostility and make friends for your people instead of enemies?

A. By decency, dignity, moral and social responsibility.

Q. How would you pray to God for human justice and racial salvation?

A. I don't believe man prays to God for human justice and racial salvation. I believe he affirms to God that immortal individual human dignity which has always outlasted injustice and before which families and clans and tribes talking of themselves as a race of men and not the race of Man, rise and pass and vanish like so much dust. He merely affirms his own belief in the grace and dignity and immortality of individual man, as Dostoevski's Ivan did when he repudiated any heaven whose order was founded on the anguished cry of one single child.

Q. Surrounded by antagonistic white people, would you find it hard not to hate them?

A. I would repeat to myself Booker T. Washington's words when he said: "I will let no man, no matter what his color, ever make me hate him."

So if I were a Negro, I would say to my people: "Let us be always unflaggingly and inflexibly flexible. But always decently, quietly, courteously, with dignity and without violence. And above all, with patience. The white man has devoted three hundred years to teaching us to be patient; that is one thing at least in which we are his superiors. Let us turn it into a weapon against him. Let us use this patience not as a passive quality, but as an active weapon. But always, let us practice cleanliness and decency and courtesy and dignity in our contacts with him. He has already taught us to be more patient and courteous with him than he is with us; let us be his superior in the others too."

But above all, I would say this to the leaders of our race: "We must learn to deserve equality so that we can hold and keep it after we get it. We must learn responsibility, the responsibility of equality. We must learn that there is no such thing as a 'right' without any ties to it, since anything given to one free for nothing is worth exactly that: nothing. We must learn that our inalienable right to equality, to freedom and liberty and the pursuit of happiness, means exactly what our founding fathers meant by it: the right to *opportunity* to be free and equal provided one is worthy of it, will work to gain it and then work to keep it. And not only the right to that opportunity, but the willingness and the capacity to accept the responsibility of that opportunity—the responsibilities of physical cleanliness and of moral rectitude, of a conscience capable of choosing between right and wrong and a will capable of obeying it, or reliability toward other men, the pride of independence of charity or relief.

"The white man has not taught us that. He taught us only patience and courtesy. He did not even see that we had the environment in which we could teach ourselves cleanliness and independence and rectitude and reliability. So we must teach ourselves that. Our leaders must teach us that. We as a race must lift ourselves by our own bootstraps to where we are competent for the responsibilities of equality, so that we can hold on to it when we get it. Our tragedy is that these virtues of responsibility are the white man's virtues of which he boasts, yet we, the Negro, must be his superior in them. Our hope is that, having beaten him in patience and courtesy, we can probably beat him in these others too."

Selection 26

THE GOALS OF INTEGRATION

OSCAR HANDLIN*

Oscar Handlin, Professor of History at Harvard University, has written books and articles on immigration, education, and other important historical subjects. As a thoughtful observer of the civil rights movement, he raises a number of important questions concerning the nature of the ultimate goals of this struggle.

The following selection consists of excerpts from his article, "The Goals of Integration," in Daedalus.

. . . Recent demonstrations of solidarity on behalf of civil rights have been impressive. The march on Washington in 1963 and from Selma in 1965 showed the extent to which diverse elements in American society coalesced in support of a common cause. These occasions have ceremonial significance; they manifest the extent to which a variety of people affirm their dislike of brutality and their faith in the orderly methods of democracy. There is no difficulty in eliciting unanimity of support for the slogan of equal rights as man and citizen as long as the terms remain vague and undefined.

But it is erroneous to regard these events or professions of sentiment as expressions of unity with reference to a program of action. The calls for brotherly love sounded on the platforms do not reduce the intensity of the hatreds in Harlem. White resentment at black demands is also stiffening. . . .

Insofar as the civil rights movement has proceeded beyond the call for brotherly love or for equality, it has ventured upon unsure ground. Civil rights demands in Alabama and Mississippi are com-

* From Oscar Handlin, "The Goals of Integration," in *Daedalus: Journal of the American Academy of Arts and Sciences*, V. 95, 1, winter 1966, 268–86.

prehensible; the promises of personal security, the ballot, and decent schools are familiar and long overdue. But the issues blur in the newer context of New York or Chicago or Atlanta where these minimal gains are well on the way to attainment. There the failure to define appropriate goals has created future difficulties, the shape of which is already apparent. The new problems are important not only because an increasing percentage of American Negroes live in an urban environment, but also because the range of decisions involved will confront the nation long after the difficulties of the rural South are resolved.

In the earlier stages of the struggle for equality, it was enough to ask that the government be color-blind. The barriers that confined the Negro were the products of law, and it was necessary to demand only the equal treatment that the Constitution guaranteed. Desegregation was the response to segregation; and it was a response that attracted the support not only of other underprivileged minorities but also of many Americans who found it in accord with their own creed of individual dignity and equality of opportunity.

In the past decade, emphasis has gradually and imperceptibly shifted from desegregation to integration, but without adequate awareness of the consequences and often with a profound ambiguity about the nature of the desirable goal.

The term integration sometimes refers to the openness of society, to a condition in which every individual can make the maximum number of voluntary contacts with others without regard to qualifications of ancestry. In that sense, the objective is a leveling of all barriers to association other than those based on ability, taste, and personal preference.

But integration sometimes also refers to a condition in which individuals of each racial or ethnic group are randomly distributed through the society so that every realm of activity contains a representative cross section of the population. In that sense, the object is the attainment, in every occupational, educational, and residential distribution, of a balance among the constituent elements in the society.

In crucial matters of public policy, antithetical consequences follow from the two positions. The one calls for improvements in the Negroes' opportunities for jobs, housing, and schooling even though the group may remain as separate as before; the other puts a primary emphasis upon racial balance.

The civil rights movement has never made a clear choice between these alternatives, nor has any spokesman fully articulated the implications of the two points of view. But increasingly in the past five years, the thrust has been in the latter direction, toward an organization in which every sector of society is racially balanced; and it is in that sense that the term integration will be used in the discussion which follows.

. . .

The view of integration as racial balance rests on two fallacious assumptions—that the position of the Negro is absolutely unique in the American experience and that racist prejudice is so thoroughly ingrained in the people of the United States that only positive exertions by the government will assure the colored man his rights. Neither proposition conforms to the evidence.

. . .

Neither in the North nor in the South is integration in the sense of racial balance a meaningful guide to proximate future action. Desegregation is likely soon to eliminate the vestiges of discrimination inherited from the Jim Crow era; and it may open the way to full participation by Negroes in the political and economic life of the nation, but it will do so within the terms of some approximation of the group life already developed. Integration, defined as the elimination of differences, on the other hand, demands of both Negroes and whites an impossible surrender of identity. The deletion of all memory of antecedents, the severance of all ties to the past, and the liquidation of all particularistic associations is not only unfeasible but undesirable. It would curtail the capacity of this society to deal with its problems under the conditions of freedom; and significantly some of its advocates are either altogether nihilistic or else do not flinch from the totalitarian methods and consequences that would be involved in achieving this version of integration.

Only a small minority of Negroes, however, think in these terms. The vast majority understand that they are a group and will remain so; they seek an expansion of their rights and opportunities, but show neither a desire to merge with the whites nor any expectation that that will soon happen. Desegregation is a genuine issue; racial balance is a vague and confusing abstraction that turns their attention away from the genuine political, economic, and social problems they and other Americans confront.

. . .

Integration in the sense of the elimination of distinctiveness is no more relevant to the economic plight than to the political plight of the mass of Negroes. The demands for preferential hiring, for assigned quotas of desirable jobs, and for a Black Man's Marshall Plan are sometimes presented as if they were the means of attaining racial balance and therefore of furthering integration. Actually, they are calls for the recognition of the special character of the group; and to the extent that they are heeded, they strengthen identification with it.

• • •

In the last analysis, the welfare of the Negroes depends upon the health of the whole economy and its capacity to produce and distribute goods according to an acceptable pattern. But the last analysis is remote indeed. In the interim, the Negroes will use what power they can muster as a group for their own advantage. Preferential treatment in some high-prestige forms of employment will be justified not because it will improve the lot of the great mass of the unskilled, but because it is a means of opening some avenues of escape for the most qualified. At relatively little cost in efficiency, this device can create a pool of potential leaders with a stake in social order and at the same time break the identification of the race with poverty.

• • •

The demand for racial balance has sometimes had a blackmail effect; it has forced concessions on municipal authorities willing to spend more heavily on slum schools than they might otherwise have in order to stave off the drive for bussing. But this tactic has also had the adverse effect of exaggerating the deficiencies of schools in Negro neighborhoods and thus of frightening away experienced teachers, of hastening the flight to the suburbs and increasing the rate of withdrawal to private and parochial schools. The insistence upon integration is thus self-frustrating, as the experience of Washington, D. C., shows. Further pressure toward racial balance will certainly weaken the public schools and leave the Negroes the greatest sufferers.

The dilemma is unnecessary. There is no evidence that racial balance itself improves the capacity of the underprivileged to learn; nor that the *enforced* contact of dissimilar children has significant educational advantages. There is abundant evidence that deprived children have distinctive needs that require the special attention of the school. Yet the drive for integration has obscured, and sometimes actually impeded, the task of providing for those needs. Indeed the argument is now often being made that racial balance is desirable to meet the needs of white children.

Here, too, an awareness of the groups' identity and a determination to deal with its problems is the most promising path to equality. The Negro deserves preferential treatment in education because his needs are great. But to receive it calls for the recognition of the special character of his situation, not for costly efforts artificially to commingle his children with others in the interest of the ideal of balance.

• • •

Integration is a false issue. The problem is housing—how can adequate space up to present-day standards of decency be made available to the poor? How can all other colored families get fair value up to the level of their incomes, without being penalized for their race? For most Negroes these are the primary issues. They are difficult enough without the complications of racial balance. The control of the urban renewal process, the role of government as entrepreneur, and problems of design and form will set the framework within which the character of the Negroes' future housing will be determined. And group cohesiveness will be of great importance in influencing decisions in these matters.

The development and strengthening of Negro communal institutions may also help normalize the situation of the colored family. The disorderly features of that position are well known—the absence of a male head, frequent illegitimacy and dependence—as well as their relationship to juvenile delinquency, crime, and narcotic addiction. But these characteristics have been too readily associated with the effects of the slave heritage. The servitude of the plantation may have left elements of weakness in the families of the freedmen; but the extent to which sound family life developed among the Negroes between 1865 and 1915 is impressive, as is the extent to which it still prevails in the rural South closest to the slave setting.

A more plausible source of disorder is the effect of rural-urban migration with low income and slum housing at its destination. That correlation conforms to what is known about the changes in family life in other societies in which slavery has not been a factor. It conforms also to the experience of earlier groups of migrants to American cities. Less than a half-century ago, the foreign-born residents of Irish, Jewish, or Polish slums faced comparable problems of matriarchal households and delinquency.

It was not alone the tradition of solidarity and discipline that contained the damage among these peoples, but also the fact that their families were encased in social and cultural institutions which imposed restraints upon recalcitrant individuals, established norms of behavior, and disposed of weighty sanctions for conformity. Negroes have been slower to develop similar institutions, partly because this migration came at a moment when government absorbed some of these functions, but also because in their experience separation meant segregation and bore the imputation of inferiority. Yet those men who, in the name of integration, deny that there is a significant role for the Negro press, or for Negro churches, or for Negro associations are also denying the group of its media for understanding, for expression, and for action. They would thereby weaken the capacity of the people who need those media to act on their own behalf.

It is the ultimate illogic of integration to deny the separateness of the Negro and therefore to inhibit him from creating the communal institutions which can help cope with his problems. Delinquency, poverty, slums, and inadequate housing of course concern all Americans; and the attempt to eradicate them calls for common efforts from every part of the nation. But history has given the Negroes a special involvement in these matters; and to deny the actualities of the group's existence is to diminish its ability to deal with them. To confuse segregation, the function of which is to establish Negro inferiority, with the awareness of separate identity, the function of which is to generate the power for voluntary action, hopelessly confuses the struggle for equality.

Clarification of the goals of the civil rights movement has immediate tactical implications. Desegregation is not the same as integration; Selma is not Harlem, Bogalusa, not Chicago.

Where violence, exclusion from the ballot, or state power has deprived the Negro of his equal rights as a man and a citizen, it is his obligation and that of all other Americans to demand an immediate end to the discriminatory measures that aim at his subordination.

Desegregation will not solve any of the other important economic, social, and political problems of American life; it will only offer a starting point from which to confront them. The inadequacies of the political system, unemployment, inferior education, poor housing, and delinquency will still call for attention. In some of these matters the peculiarities of the Negroes' situation call for special treatment. But with reference to none of them is integration a meaningful mode of action; and the call for it which echoes from a different struggle on a different battleground only produces confusion.

Whatever may happen in the more distant future, Negroes will not merge into the rest of the population in the next few decades. Those who desire to eliminate every difference so that all Americans will more nearly resemble each other, those who imagine that there is a mainstream into which every element in the society will be swept, are deceived about the character of the country in which they live. As long as common memories, experience, and interests make the Negroes a group, they will find it advantageous to organize and act as such. And the society will better be able to accommodate them as equals on those terms than it could under the pretense that integration could wipe out the past.

Selection 27

THE AMERICAN DREAM AND THE AMERICAN NEGRO: THE BALDWIN-BUCKLEY DEBATE*

At Cambridge University in England, there is a debating club which examines the important issues of the day. In February, 1965, the club invited two Americans to join two British students in debating the issue: "The American Dream is at the expense of the American Negro." Taking the affirmative position was James Baldwin, the novelist. Opposing him was William F. Buckley, Jr., editor of The National Review *and a prominent leader of the conservative movement in this country.*

James Baldwin:

I find myself, not for the first time, in the position of a kind of Jeremiah. It would seem to me that the question before the house is

* From *The New York Times Magazine*, March 7, 1965.

a proposition horribly loaded, that one's response to that question depends on where you find yourself in the world, what your sense of reality is. That is, it depends on assumptions we hold so deeply as to be scarcely aware of them.

The white South African or Mississippi sharecropper or Alabama sheriff has at bottom a system of reality which compels them really to believe when they face the Negro that this woman, this man, this child must be insane to attack the system to which he owes his entire identity. For such a person, the proposition which we are trying to discuss here does not exist.

On the other hand, I have to speak as one of the people who have been most attacked by the Western system of reality. It comes from Europe. That is how it got to America. It raises the question of whether or not civilizations can be considered equal, or whether one civilization has a right to subjugate—in fact, to destroy—another.

Now, leaving aside all the physical factors one can quote—leaving aside the rape or murder, leaving aside the bloody catalogue of oppression which we are too familiar with anyway—what the system does to the subjugated is to destroy his sense of reality. It destroys his father's authority over him. His father can no longer tell him anything because his past has disappeared.

In the case of the American Negro, from the moment you are born every stick and stone, every face, is white. Since you have not yet seen a mirror, you suppose you are, too. It comes as a great shock around the age of 5, 6 or 7 to discover that the flag to which you have pledged allegiance, along with everybody else, has not pledged allegiance to you. It comes as a great shock to see Gary Cooper killing off the Indians and, although you are rooting for Gary Cooper, that the Indians are you.

It comes as a great shock to discover that the country which is your birthplace and to which you owe your life and identity has not, in its whole system of reality, evolved any place for you. The disaffection and the gap between people, only on the basis of their skins, begins there and accelerates throughout your whole lifetime. You realize that you are 30 and you are having a terrible time. You have been through a certain kind of mill and the most serious effect is again not the catalogue of disaster—the policeman, the taxi driver, the waiters, the landlady, the banks, the insurance companies, the millions of details 24 hours of every day which spell out to you that you are a worthless human being. It is not that. By that time you have begun to see it happening in your daughter, your son or your niece or your nephew. You are 30 by now and nothing you have done has helped you to escape the trap. But what is worse is that nothing you have done, and as far as you can tell nothing you *can* do, will save your son or your daughter from having the same disaster and from coming to the same end.

We speak about expense. There are several ways of addressing oneself to some attempt to find out what that word means here. From a very literal point of view, the harbors and the ports and the railroads of the country—the economy, especially in the South —could not conceivably be what they are if it had not been (and this is still so) for cheap labor. I am speaking very seriously, and this is not an overstatement: I picked cotton, I carried it to the market, I built the railroads under someone else's whip for nothing. For nothing.

The Southern oligarchy which has still today so very much power in Washington, and therefore some power in the world, was created by my labor and my sweat and the violation of my women and the murder of my children. This in the land of the free, the home of the brave. None can challenge that statement. It is a matter of historical record.

In the Deep South you are dealing with a sheriff or a landlord or a landlady or the girl at the Western Union desk. She doesn't know quite whom she is dealing with—by which I mean, if you are not part of a town and if you are a Northern nigger, it shows in millions of ways. She simply knows that it is an unknown quantity and she wants to have nothing to do with it. You have to wait a while to get your telegram. We have all been through it. By the time you get to be a man it is fairly easy to deal with.

But what happens to the poor white man's, the poor white woman's, mind? It is this: they have been raised to believe, and by now they helplessly believe, that no matter how terrible some of their lives may be and no matter what disaster overtakes them, there is one consolation like a heavenly revelation—at least they are not black. I suggest that of all the terrible things that could happen to a human being that is one of the worst. I suggest that what has happened to the white Southerner is in some ways much worse than what has happened to the Negroes there.

Sheriff Clark in Selma, Ala., cannot be dismissed as a total monster; I am sure he loves his wife and children and likes to get drunk. One has to assume that he is a man like me. But he does not know what drives him to use the club, to menace with the gun and to use the cattle prod. Something awful must have happened to a human being to be able to put a cattle prod against a woman's breasts.

What happens to the woman is ghastly. What happens to the man who does it is in some ways much, much worse. Their moral lives have been destroyed by the plague called color.

This is not being done 100 years ago, but in 1965 and in a country which is pleased with what we call prosperity, with a certain amount of social coherence, which calls itself a civilized nation and which espouses the notion of freedom in the world. If it were white people being murdered, the Government would find some way of doing something about it. We have a civil rights bill now. We had the 15th Amendment nearly 100 years ago. If it was not honored then, I have no reason to believe that the civil rights bill will be honored now.

The American soil is full of the corpses of my ancestors, through 400 years and at least three wars. Why is my freedom, my citizenship, in question now? What one begs the American people to do, for all our sakes, is simply to accept our history.

It seems to me when I watch Americans in Europe that what they don't know about Europeans is what they don't know about me. They were not trying to be nasty to the French girl, rude to the French waiter. They did not know that they hurt their feelings; they didn't have any sense that this particular man and woman were human beings. They walked over them with the same sort of bland ignorance and condescension, the charm and cheerfulness, with which they had patted me on the head and which made them upset when I was upset.

When I was brought up I was taught in American history books that Africa had no history and that neither had I. I was a savage about whom the least said the better, who had been saved by Europe and who had been brought to America. Of course, I believed it. I didn't have much choice. These were the only books there were. Everyone else seemed to agree. If you went out of Harlem the whole world agreed. What you saw was much bigger, whiter, cleaner, safer. The garbage was collected, the children were happy. You would go back home and it would seem, of course, that this was an act of God. You belonged where white people put you.

It is only since World War II that there has been a counter-image in the world. That image has not come about because of any legislation by any American Government, but because Africa was suddenly on the stage of the world and Africans had to be dealt with in a way they had never been dealt with before. This gave the American Negro, for the first time, a sense of himself not as a savage. It has created and will create a great many conundrums.

One of the things the white world does not know, but I think I know, is that black people are just like everybody else. We are also mercenaries, dictators, murderers, liars. We are human, too. Unless we can establish some kind of dialogue between those people who enjoy the American dream and those other people who have not achieved it, we will be in terrible trouble. This is what concerns me most. We are sitting in this room and we are all civilized; we can talk to each other, at least on certain levels, so that we can walk out of here assuming that the measure of our politeness has some effect on the world.

I remember when the ex-Attorney General, Mr. Robert Kennedy, said it was conceivable that in 40 years in America we might have a Negro President. That sounded like a very emancipated statement to white people. They were not in Harlem when this statement was first heard. They did not hear the laughter and bitterness and scorn with which this statement was greeted. From the point of view of the man in the Harlem barber shop, Bobby Kennedy only got here yesterday and now he is already on his way to the Presidency. We were here for 400 years and now he tells us that maybe in 40 years, if you are good, we may let you become President.

Perhaps I can be reasoned with, but I don't know—neither does Martin Luther King—none of us knows how to deal with people whom the white world has so long ignored, who don't believe anything the white world says and don't entirely believe anything I or Martin say. You can't blame them.

It seems to me that the City of New York has had, for example, Negroes in it for a very long time. The City of New York was able in the last 15 years to reconstruct itself, to tear down buildings and raise great new ones and has done nothing whatever except build housing projects, mainly in the ghettoes, for the Negroes. And of course the Negroes hate it. The children can't bear it. They want to move out of the ghettoes. If American pretensions were based on more honest assessments of life, it would not mean for Negroes that when someone says "urban renewal" some Negroes are going to be thrown out into the streets, which is what it means now.

It is a terrible thing for an entire people to surrender to the notion that one-ninth of its population is beneath them. Until the moment comes when we, the Americans, are able to accept the fact that my ancestors are both black and white, that on that continent we are trying to forge a new identity, that we need each other, that I am not a ward of America, I am not an object of missionary charity, I am one of the people who built the country—until this moment comes there is scarcely any hope for the American dream. If the people are denied participation in it, by their very presence they will wreck it. And if that happens it is a very grave moment for the West.

William Buckley:

It seems to me that of all the indictments Mr. Baldwin has made of America here tonight, and in his copious literature of protest, the one that is most striking involves, in effect, the refusal of the American community to treat him other than as a Negro. The American community has refused to do this. The American community, almost everywhere he goes, treats him with the kind of unction, with the kind of satisfaction that a posturing hero gets for his flagellations of our civilization, so that he quite properly commands the contempt he so eloquently showers upon us.

It is quite impossible in my judgment to deal with the indictments of Mr. Baldwin unless one is prepared to deal with him as a white man, unless one is prepared to say to him that the fact that your skin is black is utterly irrelevant to the arguments you raise. The fact that you sit here, carrying the entire weight of the Negro ordeal on your own shoulders, is irrelevant to the argument we are here to discuss.

I am treating you as a fellow American, as a man whose indictments of our civilization are unjustified, as an American who—if his counsels were listened to—would be cursed by all his grandchildren's grandchildren.

About 125 years ago this house was bitterly divided over the question of whether or not some people in England who practiced the faith of Erasmus, your most distinguished lecturer, should be allowed to vote. By a slim margin it was decided that they ought to be allowed to do so. We know that there was more blood shed trying to emancipate the Irish here in the British Isles than has been shed by 10 times the number of people who have been lynched as a result of the delirium of race consciousness, race supremacy, in the United States. Shall we devote the night to these luridities? Shall we devote the evening to examining the sociological facts of human nature? Shall we discuss these class antagonisms in terms of race, in terms of economic standing? Shall we discuss the existential dilemma of humankind?

It is a fact that the position in America is as it is, that the situation in Africa is as it is. The question before the house is not whether we should have purchased slaves generations ago, or ought the blacks to have sold us those slaves. The question, rather, is this: Is there anything in the American dream which intrinsically argues against some kind of deliverance from the system that we all recognize as evil? What shall we do about it? What shall we in

America do to eliminate these psychic humiliations which I join Mr. Baldwin in believing are the very worst aspects of this discrimination?

It is the case that seven-tenths of the average white's income in the United States is equal to the entire income of the average Negro. But my great-grandparents worked hard. I do not know of anything which has ever been created without the expense of something. We have a dastardly situation. But I am going to ask you not to make politics as the crow flies.

What is it that we Americans ought to do? I wonder. What is it we should do, for instance, to avoid the humiliations mentioned by Mr. Baldwin as having been part of his own experiences? At the age of 12 he trespassed outside the ghetto of Harlem and was taken by the scruff of his neck by a policeman on 42d Street and Madison Avenue and told, "Here, you nigger, go back to where you belong." Fifteen to 20 years later he asks for a Scotch whisky in Chicago and is told by the white barman that he is obviously under age and under the circumstances cannot be served. I know from your faces that you share with me a feeling of compassion and a feeling of outrage that this kind of thing should have happened. How are we going to avoid the kind of humiliations which are visited perpetually upon members of the minority race?

Obviously, the first element is concern. We have got to care that it happens. We have got to do what we can to change the warp and woof of moral feelings and society to make it happen less and less.

The proposition before us tonight as elaborated by Mr. Baldwin is that we ought precisely to recognize that the American civilization, and indeed the Western civilization, has failed him and his people, that we ought to throw it over. He tells us that our civilization rests on the rantings of the Hebrew, sunbaked fanatic called Jesus—not, says he, truly the founder of the Christian religion. The founder of the Christian religion was actually Paul, whom he describes as a merciless fanatic. And as a result of these teachings of Jesus and Paul, we have Dachau.

If we assume that Dachau was the natural consequence of the teachings of St. Paul and Jesus, what shall we do with the library around here? Shall we descend on it and uproot all the literature that depends in any way on the teachings of Plato and Aristotle because they justified slavery? The primary question before the house is whether or not our civilization has shown itself so flawed as the result of the failure of its response to the Negro problem of the United States that it ought to be jettisoned.

Now I suggest that anyone who argued that English civilization ought to have been jettisoned because Catholics were not allowed to vote in England as late as 1829 and Jews not until 1832 should consider the other possibility. Precisely the reason they *did* get the vote was because English civilization was not jettisoned. The whole point of our philosophical concern ought never to make that terrible fault made so frequently by the positivists, that we should rush forward and overthrow our civilization because we don't live up to our high ideals.

It may be that there has been some sort of sunburst of moral enlightenment that has hit this community so as to make it predictable that if you were the governors of the United States the situation would change overnight. The engines of concern in the United States are working. The presence of Mr. Baldwin here is, in part, a reflection of that concern.

You cannot go to any university in the United States in which practically every other problem of public policy is not pre-empted by the primary concern for the Negro. I challenge you to name me another civilization in the history of the world in which the problems of the minority, which have been showing considerable material and political advancement, are as much a subject of dramatic concern as in the United States.

Americans are not willing, as a result of Mr. Baldwin's aspirations, to say that the whole American proposition was an unfortunate experiment. They are not willing to say that because we have not accelerated Negro progress faster, we are going to desert the constitutional system, the idea of the rule of law, the idea of individual rights of the American citizen, that we are going to burn all the Bibles, burn our books, that we want to reject our entire Judaeo-Christian civilization because of the continued persistence of the kind of evil that has been so eloquently described by Mr. Baldwin.

There is no instant cure for the race problem in America. Anyone who tells you that there is a quick solution is a charlatan and ultimately a boring man—a boring man because he is then speaking in the kind of abstractions which do not relate to human experience. The Negro problem is a very complicated one. I urge those of you who have an actual interest in the problem to read "Beyond the Melting Pot," by Nathan Glazer and Daniel Moynihan. They say that in 1900 there were 3,500 Negro doctors in America. In 1960 there were 3,900, an increase of 400. Is this because there were no opportunities? No, they say. There are a great many medical schools which by no means practice discrimination. It is because the Negro's particular energy is not directed toward that goal.

What should James Baldwin be doing other than telling us to renounce our civilization? He should be addressing his own people and urging them to take advantage of those opportunities which do exist. And urging us to make those opportunities wider.

Where Negroes are concerned, the danger, as far as I can see at this moment, is that they will seek to reach out for some sort of radical solutions, on the basis of which the true problem is obscured. They have done a great deal to focus on the facts of white discrimination against Negroes. They have done a great deal to agitate a moral concern. But where in fact do they go now? They seem to be slipping into some sort of Procrustean formulation which ends up by urging the advancement of the Negro less than the regression of white people.

[Interjection from an American undergraduate: "Mr. Buckley, one thing you can do is to let them vote in Mississippi."

[Buckley: "I agree. Except, lest I appear too ingratiating, I think actually what is wrong in Mississippi is not that not enough Negroes have the vote but that too many white people are voting."]

What we need is a considerable amount of frankness that acknowledges there are two sets of difficulties. We must recognize the difficulty that brown people, white people, black people have all over the world to protect their own vested interests. They suffer from a kind of racial narcissism which tends always to convert every contingency in such a way as to maximize their own power. We must acknowledge that problem, but we must also reach through to the Negro people and tell them that their best chances are in a mobile society and the most mobile society in the world today is in the United States.

It is precisely that mobility which can give opportunities to the Negroes, which they must be encouraged to take. But they must not be encouraged to adopt the kind of cynicism, the kind of despair, the kind of iconoclasm that is urged by Mr. Baldwin.

For one thing I believe—that the fundamental trend in the United States is to the good nature, the generosity and good wishes, the decency that do lie in the spirit of the American people. These qualities must not be laughed at, and under no circumstances must America be told that the only alternative is the overthrow of that civilization which we consider to be the faith of our fathers, the faith of your fathers.

If it finally does come to a confrontation between giving up the best features of the American way of life and fighting for them, then we will fight the issue. We will fight the issue not only in the Cambridge Union, but we will fight as you were once asked to fight—on the beaches, in the hills, in the mountains. And just as you waged war to save civilization, you also waged war for the benefit of the Germans, your enemies. We, too, are convinced that if it should ever come to that kind of confrontation, then our determination will be to wage war not only for the whites, but also for the Negroes.

[*The motion supported by Mr. Baldwin was carried overwhelmingly. The vote: 544 for the motion, 164 against.*]

BOOK THREE

A
Struggle with Issues

INTRODUCTION

The Negro problem has its roots deep in the history of our country and its branches spread into the social, political, and economic life of our time. To speak of the Negro problem is to invoke a number of issues, each of which is connected with the tissue of the major question: What do we really mean when we speak of liberty, equality, and justice? Do these great historic ideals apply only to some Americans or to all Americans?

The selections in Book Three explore the gap between principle and practice in American life. The principles that are so proudly recited in our great public documents are often disregarded in our local communities and in our private lives. To praise equality and justice and to practice discrimination raises serious questions about the sincerity of a people.

PART I

EDUCATION FOR THE NEGRO

Selections 1a–1b

THE GOALS OF EDUCATION

In these selections Booker T. Washington and W. E. B. Du Bois offer two views on the goals of education. Washington's position is taken from Up From Slavery, *originally published in 1901, while the Du Bois selection appeared in* The Negro Problem *in 1903.*

1a. Booker T. Washington on Education*

Of one thing I felt more strongly convinced than ever, after spending this month in seeing the actual life of the coloured people, and that was that, in order to lift them up, something must be done more than merely to imitate New England education as it then existed. I saw more clearly than ever the wisdom of the system which General Armstrong had inaugurated at Hampton. To take the children of such people as I had been among for a month, and each day give them a few hours of mere book education, I felt would be almost a waste of time.

After consultation with the citizens of Tuskegee, I set July 4, 1881,

---

* From Booker T. Washington, *Up From Slavery* in *Three Negro Classics*, New York: Avon Books, 1965, pp. 1, 92, 96, 108, 199–200.

as the day for the opening of the school in the little shanty and church which had been secured for its accommodation. The white people, as well as the coloured, were greatly interested in the starting of the new school, and the opening day was looked forward to with much earnest discussion. There were not a few white people in the vicinity of Tuskegee who looked with some disfavour upon the project. They questioned its value to the coloured people, and had a fear that it might result in bringing about trouble between the races. Some had the feeling that in proportion as the Negro received education, in the same proportion would his value decrease as an economic factor in the state. These people feared the result of education would be that the Negroes would leave the farms, and that it would be difficult to secure them for domestic service.

The white people who questioned the wisdom of starting this new school had in their minds pictures of what was called an educated Negro, with a high hat, imitation gold eye glasses, a showy walking-stick, kid gloves, fancy boots, and what not—in a word, a man who was determined to live by his wits. It was difficult for these people to see how education would produce any other kind of a coloured man. . . .

Miss Davidson and I began consulting as to the future of the school from the first. The students were making progress in learning books and in developing their minds; but it became apparent at once that, if we were to make any permanent impression upon those who had come to us for training, we must do something besides teach them mere books. The students had come from homes where they had had no opportunities for lessons which would teach them how to care for their bodies. With few exceptions, the homes in Tuskegee in which the students boarded were but little improvement upon those from which they had come. We wanted to teach the students how to bathe; how to care for their teeth and clothing. We wanted to teach them what to eat, and how to eat it properly, and how to care for their rooms. Aside from this, we wanted to give them such a practical knowledge of some one industry, together with the spirit of industry, thrift, and economy, that they would be sure of knowing how to make a living after they had left us. We wanted to teach them to study actual things instead of mere books alone. . . .

. . .

From the very beginning, at Tuskegee, I was determined to have the students do not only the agricultural and domestic work, but to have them, while performing this service, taught the latest and best methods of labour, so that the school would not only get the benefit of their efforts, but the students themselves would be taught to see not only utility in labour, but beauty and dignity, would be taught, in fact, how to lift labour up from mere drudgery and toil, and would learn to love work for its own sake. My plan was not to teach them to work in the old way but to show them how to make the forces of nature—air, water, steam, electricity, horse-power—assist them in their labour.

At first many advised against the experiment of having the buildings erected by the labour of the students, but I was determined to stick to it. I told those who doubted the wisdom of the plan that I knew that our first buildings would not be so comfortable or so complete in their finish as buildings erected by the experienced hands of outside workmen, but that in the teaching of civilization, self-help, and self-reliance, the erection of the buildings by the students themselves would more than compensate for any lack of comfort or fine finish.

. . .

Twenty years have now passed since I made the first humble effort at Tuskegee, in a broken-down shanty and an old hen-house, without owning a dollar's worth of property, and with but one teacher and thirty students. At the present time the institution owns twenty-three hundred acres of land, one thousand of which are under cultivation each year, entirely by student labour. There are now upon the grounds, counting large and small, sixty-six buildings; and all except four of these have been almost wholly erected by the labour of our students. While the students are at work upon the land and in erecting buildings, they are taught, by competent instructors, the latest methods of agriculture and the trades connected with building.

There are in constant operation at the school, in connection with thorough academic and religious training, thirty industrial departments. All of these teach industries at which our men and women can find immediate employment as soon as they leave the institution. The only difficulty now is that the demand for our graduates from both white and black people in the South is so great that we cannot supply more than one-half the persons for whom applications come to us. Neither have we the buildings nor the money for current expenses to enable us to admit to the school more than one-half the young men and women who apply to us for admission.

In our industrial teaching we keep three things in mind: first, that the student shall be so educated that he shall be enabled to meet conditions as they exist *now,* in the part of the South where he lives —in a word, to be able to do the thing which the world wants done; second, that every student who graduates from the school shall have enough skill, coupled with intelligence and moral character, to enable him to make a living for himself and others; third, to send every graduate out feeling and knowing that labour is dignified and beautiful—to make each one love labour instead of trying to escape it. In addition to the agricultural training which we give to young men, and the training given to our girls in all the usual domestic employments, we now train a number of girls in agriculture each year. These girls are taught gardening, fruit-growing, dairying, bee-culture, and poultry-raising.

1b.   The Talented Tenth

W. E. B. DU BOIS*

The Negro race, like all races, is going to be saved by its exceptional men. The problem of education, then, among Negroes must first of all deal with the Talented Tenth; it is the problem of developing the Best of this race that they may guide the Mass away from the contamination and death of the Worst, in their own and other races. Now the training of men is a difficult and intricate task. Its technique is a matter for educational experts, but its object is for the vision of seers. If we make money the object of man-training, we shall develop money-makers but not necessarily men; if we make technical skill the object of education, we may possess artisans but not, in nature, men. Men we shall have only as we make manhood the object of the work of the schools—intelligence, broad sympathy, knowledge of the world that was and is, and of the relation of men to it—this is the curriculum of that Higher Education which must underlie true life. On this foundation we may build bread-winning skill of hand and quickness of brain, with never a fear lest the child and man mistake the means of living for the object of life. . . .

You misjudge us because you do not know us. From the very first it has been the educated and intelligent of the Negro people that have led and elevated the mass, and the sole obstacles that nullified and retarded their efforts were slavery and race prejudice; for what is slavery but the legalized survival of the unfit and the nullification of the work of natural internal leadership? Negro leadership, therefore, sought from the first to rid the race of this awful incubus that

* From W. E. B. Du Bois, *The Negro Problem,* New York: James Pott, 1903, pp. 31–75.

it might make way for natural selection and the survival of the fittest. In colonial days came Phillis Wheatley and Paul Cuffe striving against the bars of prejudice; and Benjamin Banneker, the almanac maker, voiced their longings. . . .

Where were these black abolitionists trained? Some, like Frederick Douglass, were self-trained, but yet trained liberally; others, like Alexander Crummell and McCune Smith, graduated from famous foreign universities. Most of them rose up through the colored schools of New York and Philadelphia and Boston, taught by college-bred men like Russworm, of Dartmouth, and college-bred white men like Neau and Benezet.

After emancipation came a new group of educated and gifted leaders: Langston, Bruce and Elliot, Greener, Williams and Payne. Through political organization, historical and polemic writing, and moral regeneration, these men strove to uplift their people. It is the fashion of today to sneer at them and to say that with freedom Negro leadership should have begun at the plow and not in the Senate—a foolish and mischievous lie; two hundred and fifty years that black serf toiled at the plow and yet that toiling was in vain till the Senate passed the war amendments; and two hundred and fifty years more the half-free serf of today may toil at his plow, but unless he have political rights and righteously guarded civic status, he will still remain the poverty-stricken and ignorant plaything of rascals, that he now is. This all sane men know even if they dare not say it.

And so we come to the present—a day of cowardice and vacillation, of strident wide-voiced wrong and faint-hearted compromise; of double-faced dallying with the Truth and Right. Who are today guiding the work of the Negro people? The "exceptions" of course. And yet so sure as this Talented Tenth is pointed out, the blind worshippers of the Average cry out in alarm: "These are exceptions, look here at death, disease and crime—these are the happy rule." Of course they are the rule, because a silly nation made them the rule: Because for three long centuries this people lynched Negroes who dared to be brave, raped black women who dared to be virtuous, crushed dark-hued youth who dared to be ambitious, and encouraged and made to flourish servility and lewdness and apathy. But not even this was able to crush all manhood and chastity and aspiration from black folk. A saving remnant continually survives and persists, continually aspires, continually shows itself in thrift and ability and character. Exceptional it is to be sure, but this is its chiefest promise; it shows the capability of Negro blood, the promise of black men. Do Americans ever stop to reflect that there are in this land a million men of Negro blood, well-educated, owners of homes, against the honor of whose womanhood no breath was ever raised, whose men occupy positions of trust and usefulness, and who, judged by any standard, have reached the full measure of the best type of modern European culture? Is it fair, is it decent, is it Christian to ignore these facts of the Negro problem, to belittle such aspiration, to nullify such leadership and seek to crush these people back into the mass out of which by toil and travail, they and their fathers have raised themselves? . . .

How then shall the leaders of a struggling people be trained and the hands of the risen few strengthened? There can be but one answer: The best and most capable of their youth must be schooled in the colleges and universities of the land. We will not quarrel as to just what the university of the Negro should teach or how it should teach it—I willingly admit that each soul and each race-soul needs its own peculiar curriculum. But this is true: A university is a human invention for the transmission of knowledge and culture from generation to generation, through the training of quick minds and pure hearts, and for this work no other human invention will suffice, not even trade and industrial schools.

All men cannot go to college but some men must; every isolated group or nation must have its yeast, must have for the talented few centers of training where men are not so mystified and befuddled by the hard and necessary toil of earning a living, as to have no aims higher than their bellies, and no God greater than Gold. This is true training, and thus in the beginning were the favored sons of the freedmen trained. . . . Where ought they to have begun to build? At the bottom, of course, quibbles the mole with his eyes in the earth. Aye! truly at the bottom, at the very bottom; at the bottom of knowledge, down in the very depths of knowledge there where the roots of justice strike into the lowest soil of Truth. And so they did begin; they founded colleges, and up from the colleges shot normal schools, and out from the normal schools went teachers, and around the normal teachers clustered other teachers to teach the public schools; the college trained in Greek and Latin and mathematics, 2,000 men; and these men trained full 50,000 others in morals and manners, and they in turn taught thrift and the alphabet to nine millions of men, who today hold $300,000,000 of property. It was a miracle—the most wonderful peace-battle of the nineteenth century, and yet today men smile at it, and in fine superiority tell us that it was all a strange mistake; that a proper way to found a system of education is first to gather the children and buy them spelling books and hoes; afterward men may look about for teachers, if haply they may find them; or again they would teach men Work, but as for Life—why, what has Work to do with Life, they ask vacantly.

Was the work of these college founders successful; did it stand the test of time? Did the college graduates, with all their fine theories of life, really live? Are they useful men helping to civilize and elevate their less fortunate fellows? Let us see. Omitting all institutions which have not actually graduated students from a college course, there are today in the United States thirty-four institutions giving something above high school training to Negroes and designed especially for this race.

Three of these were established in border states before the war; thirteen were planted by the Freedmen's Bureau in the years 1864–1869; nine were established between 1870 and 1880 by various church bodies; five were established after 1881 by Negro churches, and four are state institutions supported by United States agricultural funds. In most cases the college departments are small adjuncts to high- and common-school work. As a matter of fact six institutions— Atlanta, Fisk, Howard, Shaw, Wilberforce, and Leland, are the important Negro colleges so far as actual work and number of students are concerned. In all these institutions, seven hundred and fifty Negro college students are enrolled. In grade the best of these colleges are about a year behind the smaller New England colleges and a typical curriculum is that of Atlanta University. Here students from the grammar grades, after a three years' high-school course, take a college course of 136 weeks. One-fourth of this time is given to Latin and Greek; one-fifth, to English and modern languages; one-sixth, to history and social science; one-seventh, to natural science; one-eighth to mathematics, and one-eighth to philosophy and pedagogy.

In addition to these students in the South, Negroes have attended Northern colleges for many years. As early as 1826 one was graduated from Bowdoin College, and from that time till today nearly every year has seen elsewhere other such graduates. They have, of course, met much color prejudice. Fifty years ago very few colleges would admit them at all. Even today no Negro has ever been admitted to Princeton, and at some other leading institutions they are rather endured than encouraged. Oberlin was the great pioneer in the work of blotting out the color line in colleges, and has more Negro graduates by far than any other Northern college.

The total number of Negro college graduates up to 1899 (several of the graduates of that year not being reported) is indicated. Of these graduates 2,079 were men and 252 were women; 50 per cent of Northern-born college men come south to work among the masses of their people, at a sacrifice which few people realize; nearly 90 per cent of the Southern-born graduates instead of seeking that personal freedom and broader intellectual atmosphere which their training has led them, in some degree, to conceive, stay and

	Negro Colleges	White Colleges
Before '76	137	75
'75–80	143	22
'80–85	250	31
'85–90	413	43
'90–95	465	66
'95–99	475	88
Class Unknown	57	64
Total	1940	389

labor and wait in the midst of their black neighbors and relatives.

The most interesting question, and in many respects the crucial question, to be asked concerning college-bred Negroes, is: Do they earn a living? It has been intimated more than once that the higher training of Negroes has resulted in sending into the world of work men who could find nothing to do suitable to their talents. Now and then there comes a rumor of a colored college man working at menial service, etc. Fortunately, returns as to occupations of college-bred Negroes, gathered by the Atlanta conference, are quite full— nearly 60 per cent of the total number of graduates.

This enables us to reach fairly certain conclusions as to the occupations of all college-bred Negroes. Of 1,312 persons reported, there were:

	Per Cent
Teachers	53.4
Clergymen	16.8
Physicians, etc.	6.3
Students	5.6
Lawyers	4.7
In Govt. Service	4.0
In Business	3.6
Farmers and Artisans	2.7
Editors, Secretaries, and Clerks	2.4
Miscellaneous	.5

Over half are teachers, a sixth are preachers, another sixth are students and professional men; over 6 per cent are farmers, artisans, and merchants, and 4 per cent are in government service. . . .

These figures illustrate vividly the function of the college-bred Negro. He is, as he ought to be, the group leader, the man who sets the ideals of the community where he lives, directs its thoughts, and heads its social movements. It need hardly be argued that the Negro people need social leadership more than most groups; that they have no traditions to fall back upon, no long-established customs, no strong family ties, no well-defined social classes. All these things must be slowly and painfully evolved. The preacher was, even before the war, the group leader of the Negroes, and the church their greatest social institution. Naturally this preacher was ignorant and often immoral, and the problem of replacing the older type by better educated men has been a difficult one. Both by direct work and by direct influence on other preachers, and on congregations, the college-bred preacher has an opportunity for reformatory work and moral inspiration, the value of which cannot be overestimated.

It has, however, been in the furnishing of teachers that the Negro college has found its peculiar function. Few persons realize how vast a work, how mighty a revolution has been thus accomplished. To furnish five millions and more of ignorant people with teachers of their own race and blood, in one generation, was not only a very difficult undertaking, but a very important one, in that it placed before the eyes of almost every Negro child an attainable ideal. It brought the masses of the blacks in contact with modern civilization, made black men the leaders of their communities and trainers of the new generation. In this work college-bred Negroes were first teachers, and then teachers of teachers. And here it is that the broad culture of college work has been of peculiar value. Knowledge of life and its wider meaning has been the point of Negroes' deepest ignorance, and the sending out of teachers whose training has not been simply for breadwinning, but also for human culture, has been of inestimable value in the training of these men.

In earlier years the two occupations of preacher and teacher were practically the only ones open to the black college graduate. Of later years a larger diversity of life among his people has opened new avenues of employment. Nor have these college men been paupers and spendthrifts; 557 college-bred Negroes owned, in 1899, $1,342,-862.50 worth of real estate (assessed value) or $2,411 per family. The real value of the total accumulations of the whole group is perhaps about $10,000,000 or $5,000 apiece. Pitiful, is it not, beside the fortunes of oil kings and steel trusts, but after all is the fortune of the millionaire the only stamp of true and successful living? Alas! it is, with many, and there's the rub.

The problem of training the Negro is today immensely complicated by the fact that the whole question of the efficiency and appropriateness of our present systems of education, for any kind of child, is a matter of active debate, in which final settlement seems still afar off. Consequently it often happens that persons arguing for or against certain systems of education for Negroes have these controversies in mind and miss the real question at issue. The main question, so far as the Southern Negro is concerned, is: What, under the present circumstance, must a system of education do in order to raise the Negro as quickly as possible in the scale of civilization? The answer to this question seems to me clear: It must strengthen the Negro's character, increase his knowledge, and teach him to earn a living. Now it goes without saying, that it is hard to do all these things simultaneously or suddenly, and that at the same time it will not do to give all the attention to one and neglect the others; we could give black boys trades, but that alone will not civilize a race of ex-slaves; we might simply increase their knowledge of the world, but this would not necessarily make them wish to use this knowledge honestly; we might seek to strengthen character and purpose, but to what end if this people have nothing to eat or to wear? . . . Schoolhouses do not teach themselves—piles of brick and mortar and machinery do not send out *men*. It is the trained, living human soul, cultivated and strengthened by long study and thought, that breathes the real breath of life into boys and girls and makes them human, whether they be black or white, Greek, Russian, or American. Nothing, in these latter days, has so dampened the faith of thinking Negroes in recent educational movements as the fact that such movements have been accompanied by ridicule and denouncement and decrying of those very institutions of higher training which made the Negro public school possible, and make Negro industrial schools thinkable. It was Fisk, Atlanta, Howard, and Straight, those colleges born of the faith and sacrifice of the abolitionists, that placed in the black schools of the South the 30,000 teachers and more, which some, who depreciate the work of these higher schools, are using to teach their own new experiments. If Hampton, Tuskegee, and the hundred other industrial schools prove in the future to be as successful as they deserve to be, then their success in training black artisans for the South will be due primarily to the white colleges of the North and the black colleges of the South, which trained the teachers who today conduct these institutions. There was a time when the American people believed pretty devoutly that a log of wood with a boy at one end and Mark Hopkins [a famous 19th century American educator] at the other represented the highest ideal of human training. But in these eager days it would seem that we have changed all that and think it necessary to add a couple of saw mills and a hammer to this outfit, and, at a pinch, to dispense with the services of Mark Hopkins.

I would not deny, or for a moment seem to deny, the paramount necessity of teaching the Negro to work, and to work steadily and skillfully; or seem to depreciate in the slightest degree the important part industrial schools must play in the accomplishment of these ends, but I *do* say, and insist upon it, that it is industrialism drunk with its vision of success to imagine that its work can be accomplished without providing for the training of broadly cultured men and women to teach its own teachers, and to teach the teachers of the public schools. . . .

I am an earnest advocate of manual training and trade teaching for black boys, and for white boys, too. I believe that next to the founding of Negro colleges the most valuable addition to Negro education since the war has been industrial training for black boys. Nevertheless, I insist that the object of all true education is not to make men carpenters, it is to make carpenters men; there are two means of making the carpenter a man, each equally important; the first is to give the group and community in which he works liberally trained teachers and leaders to teach him and his family what life means; the second is to give him sufficient intelligence and technical skill to make him an efficient workman; the first object demands the Negro college and college-bred men—not a quantity of such colleges, but a few of excellent quality; not too many college-bred men, but enough to leaven the lump, to inspire the masses, to raise the Talented Tenth to leadership; the second object demands a good system of common schools, well-taught, conveniently located, and properly equipped. . . .

What is the chief need for the building up of the Negro public school in the South? The Negro race in the South needs teachers today above all else. This is the concurrent testimony of all who know the situation. For the supply of this great demand two things are needed—institutions of higher education and money for schoolhouses and salaries. It is usually assumed that a hundred or more institutions for Negro training are today turning out so many teachers and college-bred men that the race is threatened with an oversupply. This is sheer nonsense. There are today less than 3,000 living Negro college graduates in the United States, and less than 1,000 Negroes in college. Moreover, in the 164 schools for Negroes, 95 per cent of their students are doing elementary and secondary work, work which should be done in the public schools. Over half the remaining 2,157 students are taking high-school studies. The mass of so-called "normal" schools for the Negro are simply doing elementary common-school work, or, at most, high-school work, with a little instruction in methods. The Negro colleges and the postgraduate courses at other institutions are the only agencies for the broader and more careful training of teachers. The work of these institutions is hampered for lack of funds. It is getting increasingly difficult to get funds for training teachers in the best modern methods, and yet all over the South, from state superintendents, county officials, city boards, and school principals, comes the wail, "We need TEACHERS!" and teachers must be trained. As the fairest minded of all white Southerners, Atticus G. Haygood, once said: "The defects of colored teachers are so great as to create an urgent necessity for training better ones. Their excellences and their successes are sufficient to justify the best hopes of success in the effort, and to vindicate the judgment of those who make large investments of money and service, to give to colored students opportunity for preparing themselves for the work of teaching children of their people."

The truth of this has been strikingly shown in the marked improvement of white teachers in the South. Twenty years ago the rank and file of white public-school teachers were not as good as the Negro teachers. But they, by scholarships and good salaries, have been encouraged to thorough normal and collegiate preparation, while the Negro teachers have been discouraged by starvation wages and the idea that any training will do for a black teacher. . . .

Further than this, after being provided with group leaders of civilization, and a foundation of intelligence in the public schools, the carpenter, in order to be a man, needs technical skill. This calls for trade schools. Now trade schools are not nearly such simple things as people once thought. The original idea was that the "industrial" school was to furnish education, practically free, to those willing to work for it; it was to "do" things—i.e.: become a center of productive industry, it was to be partially, if not wholly, self-supporting, and it was to teach trades. Admirable as were some of the ideas underlying this scheme, the whole thing simply would not work in practice; it was found that if you were to use time and material to teach trades thoroughly, you could not at the same time keep the industries on a commercial basis and make them pay. Many schools started out to do this on a large scale and went into virtual bankruptcy. Moreover, it was found also that it was possible to teach a boy a trade mechanically, without giving him the full educative benefit of the process, and, vice versa, that there was a distinctive educative value in teaching a boy to use his hands and eyes in carrying out certain physical processes, even though he did not actually learn a trade. It has happened, therefore, in the last decade, that a noticeable change has come over the industrial schools. In the first place the idea of commercially remunerative industry in a school is being pushed rapidly to the background. There are still schools with shops and farms that bring an income, and schools that use student labor partially for the erection of their buildings and the furnishing of equipment. It is coming to be seen, however, in the education of the Negro, as clearly as it has been seen in the education of the youths the world over, that it is the *boy,* and not the material product, that is the true object of education. Consequently the object of the industrial school came to be the thorough training of boys regardless of the cost of the training, so long as it was thoroughly well done.

Even at this point, however, the difficulties were not surmounted. In the first place modern industry has taken great strides since the war, and the teaching of trades is no longer a simple matter. Machinery and long processes of work have greatly changed the work of the carpenter, the ironworker, and the shoemaker. A really efficient workman must be today an intelligent man who has had good technical training in addition to thorough common-school, and perhaps even higher, training. To meet this situation the industrial schools began a further development; they established distinct trade schools for the thorough training of better-class artisans, and at the same time they sought to preserve, for the purposes of general education, such of the simpler processes of elementary trade learning as were best suited therefor. In this differentiation of the trade school and manual training, the best of the industrial schools simply followed the plain trend of the present educational epoch. A prominent educator tells us that, in Sweden, "In the beginning the economic conception was generally adopted, and everywhere manual training was looked upon as a means of preparing the children of the common people to earn their living. But gradually it came to be recognized that manual training has a more elevated purpose, and one, indeed, more useful in the deeper meaning of the term. It came to be considered as an educative process for the complete moral, physical and intellectual development of the child."

Thus, again, in the manning of trade schools and manual-training schools we are thrown back upon the higher training as its source and chief support. There was a time when any aged and wornout carpenter could teach in a trade school. But not so today. Indeed the demand for college-bred men by a school like Tuskegee ought to make Mr. Booker T. Washington the firmest friend of higher training. Here he has as helpers the son of a Negro senator, trained in Greek and the humanities, and graduated at Harvard; the son of a Negro congressman and lawyer, trained in Latin and mathematics, and graduated at Oberlin; he has as his wife a woman who read Virgil and Homer in the same classroom with me; he has as college chaplain a classical graduate of Atlanta University; as teacher of science, a graduate of Fisk; as teacher of history, a graduate of Smith—indeed some thirty of his chief teachers are college graduates, and instead of studying French grammars in the midst of weeds, or buying pianos for dirty cabins, they are at Mr. Washington's right hand helping him in a noble work. And yet one of the effects of Mr. Washington's propaganda has been to throw doubt upon the expediency of such training for Negroes as these persons have had.

Men of America, the problem is plain before you. Here is a race transplanted through the criminal foolishness of your fathers. Whether you like it or not the millions are here, and here they will remain. If you do not lift them up, they will pull you down. Education and work are the levers to uplift a people. Work alone will not do it unless inspired by the right ideals and guided by intelligence. Education must not simply teach work—it must teach Life. The Talented Tenth of the Negro race must be made leaders of thought and missionaries of culture among their people. No others can do this work and Negro colleges must train men for it. The Negro race, like all other races, is going to be saved by its exceptional men.

Selection 2

WHY NEGRO CHILDREN ARE NOT IN SCHOOL

RAY STANNARD BAKER*

Ray Stannard Baker adds a journalist's view of the problem as seen in 1906–1908.

My curiosity, aroused by the very large number of young prisoners, led me next to inquire why these children were not in school. I visited a number of schools and I talked with L. M. Landrum, the

---

* From Ray Stannard Baker, *Following the Color Line: American Negro Citizenship in the Progressive Era*, New York: Harper and Row, 1964, p. 52. [Originally published in 1908 by Doubleday, Page & Co.]

assistant superintendent. Compulsory education is not enforced anywhere in the South, so that children may run the streets unless their parents insist upon sending them to school.* I found more than this, however, that Atlanta did not begin to have enough school facilities for the children who wanted to go. Like many rapidly growing cities, both South and North, it has been difficult to keep up with the demand. Just as in the North the tenement classes are often neglected, so in the South the lowest class—which is the Negro—is neglected. Several new schools have been built for white children, but there has been no new school for coloured children in fifteen or twenty years (though one Negro private school has been taken over within the last few years by the city). So crowded are the coloured schools that they have two sessions a day, one squad of children coming in the forenoon, another in the afternoon. The coloured teachers, therefore, do double work, for which they receive about two-thirds as much salary as the white teachers.

* Before 1900 only Kentucky among the southern states required compulsory school attendance. North Carolina in 1907 and several other southern states during the next few years enacted modest compulsory education statutes.

Selections 3a–3c

THREE LEGAL CASES

These selections present the great Supreme Court decisions which ruled that segregated education is unequal education and violates both the Fifth and the Fourteenth Amendments of the Constitution of the United States.

3a.   Brown *vs*. Board of Education, 1954*

These cases come to us from the States of Kansas, South Carolina, Virginia, and Delaware. They are premised on different facts and

* *Brown* vs. *Board of Education, Briggs* vs. *Elliot, Davis* vs. *County School Board, Gebhart* vs. *Belton*, May 17, 1954 (347 U.S. 483).

different local conditions, but a common legal question justifies their consideration together in this consolidated opinion.

In each of the cases, minors of the Negro race, through their legal representatives, seek the aid of the courts in obtaining admission to the public schools of their community on a nonsegregated basis. In each instance, they had been denied admission to schools attended by white children under laws requiring or permitting segregation according to race. This segregation was alleged to deprive the plaintiffs of the equal protection of the laws under the Fourteenth Amendment. In each of the cases other than the Delaware case, a three-judge federal district court denied relief to the plaintiffs on the so-called "separate but equal" doctrine announced by this Court in *Plessy* vs. *Ferguson,* 163 U.S. 537. Under that doctrine, equality of treatment is accorded when the races are provided substantially equal facilities, even though these facilities be separate. In the Delaware case, the Supreme Court of Delaware adhered to that doctrine, but ordered that the plaintiffs be admitted to the white schools because of their superiority to the Negro schools.

The plaintiffs contend that segregated public schools are not "equal" and cannot be made "equal" and that hence they are deprived of the equal protection of the laws. Because of the obvious importance of the question presented, the Court took jurisdiction. Argument was heard in the 1952 Term, and reargument was heard this Term on certain questions propounded by the Court.

Reargument was largely devoted to the circumstances surrounding the adoption of the Fourteenth Amendment in 1868. It covered exhaustively consideration of the Amendment in Congress, ratification by the states, then existing practices in racial segregation, and the views of the proponents and opponents of the Amendment. This discussion and our own investigation convince us that, although these sources cast some light, it is not enough to resolve the problem with which we are faced. At best, they are inconclusive. The most avid proponents of the post-War Amendments undoubtedly intended them to remove all legal distinctions among "all persons born or naturalized in the United States." Their opponents, just as certainly, were antagonistic to both the letter and the spirit of the Amendments and wished them to have the most limited effect. What others in Congress and the state legislatures had in mind cannot be determined with any degree of certainty.

An additional reason for the inconclusive nature of the Amendment's history, with respect to segregated schools, is the status of public education at that time. In the South, the movement toward free common schools, supported by general taxation, had not yet taken hold. Education of white children was largely in the hands of private groups. Education of Negroes was almost non-existent, and practically all of the race were illiterate. In fact, any education of Negroes was forbidden by law in some states. Today, in contrast, many Negroes have achieved outstanding success in the arts and sciences as well as in the business and professional world. It is true that public school education at the time of the Amendment had advanced further in the North, but the effect of the Amendment on Northern States was generally ignored in the congressional debates. Even in the North, the conditions of public education did not approximate those existing today. The curriculum was usually rudimentary; ungraded schools were common in rural areas; the school term was but three months a year in many states; and compulsory school attendance was virtually unknown. As a consequence, it is not surprising that there should be so little in the history of the Fourteenth Amendment relating to its intended effect on public education.

In the first cases in this Court construing the Fourteenth Amendment, decided shortly after its adoption, the Court interpreted it as proscribing all state-imposed discriminations against the Negro race. The doctrine of "separate but equal" did not make its appearance in this Court until 1896 in the case of *Plessy* vs. *Ferguson, supra,* involving not education but transportation. American courts have since labored with the doctrine for over half a century. In this Court, there have been six cases involving the "separate but equal" doctrine in the field of public education. In *Cumming* vs. *County Board of Education,* 175 U.S. 528, and *Gong Lum* vs. *Rice,* 275 U.S. 78, the validity of the doctrine itself was not challenged. In more recent cases, all on the graduate school level, inequality was found in that specific benefits enjoyed by white students were denied to Negro students of the same educational qualifications. *Missouri ex rel. Gaines* vs. *Canada,* 305 U.S. 337; *Sipuel* vs. *Oklahoma,* 332 U.S. 631; *Sweatt* vs. *Painter,* 339 U.S. 629; *McLaurin* vs. *Oklahoma State Regents,* 339 U.S. 637. In none of these cases was it necessary to re-examine the doctrine to grant relief to the Negro plaintiffs. And in *Sweatt* vs. *Painter, supra,* the Court expressly reserved decision on the question whether *Plessy* vs. *Ferguson* should be held inapplicable to public education.

In the instant cases, that question is directly presented. Here, unlike *Sweatt* vs. *Painter,* there are findings below that the Negro and white schools involved have been equalized, or are being equalized, with respect to buildings, curricula, qualifications and salaries of teachers, and other "tangible" factors. Our decision, therefore, cannot turn on merely a comparison of these tangible factors in the Negro and white schools involved in each of the cases. We must look instead to the effect of segregation itself on public education.

In approaching this problem, we cannot turn the clock back to 1868 when the Amendment was adopted, or even to 1896 when *Plessy* vs. *Ferguson* was written. We must consider public education in the light of its full development and its present place in American life throughout the Nation. Only in this way can it be determined if segregation in public schools deprives these plaintiffs of the equal protection of the laws.

Today, education is perhaps the most important function of state and local governments. Compulsory school attendance laws and the great expenditures for education both demonstrate our recognition of the importance of education to our democratic society. It is required in the performance of our most basic public responsibilities, even service in the armed forces. It is the very foundation of good citizenship. Today it is a principal instrument in awakening the child to cultural values, in preparing him for later professional training, and in helping him to adjust normally to his environment. In these days, it is doubtful that any child may reasonably be expected to succeed in life if he is denied the opportunity of an education. Such an opportunity, where the state has undertaken to provide it, is a right which must be made available to all on equal terms.

We come then to the question presented: Does segregation of children in public schools solely on the basis of race, even though the physical facilities and other "tangible" factors may be equal, deprive the children of the minority group of equal educational opportunities? We believe that it does.

In *Sweatt* vs. *Painter, supra,* in finding that a segregated law school for Negroes could not provide them equal educational opportunities, this Court relied in large part on "those equalities which are incapable of objective measurement but which make for greatness in a law school." In *McLaurin* vs. *Oklahoma State Regents, supra,* the Court, in requiring that a Negro admitted to a white graduate school be treated like all other students, again resorted to intangible considerations: ". . . his ability to study, to engage in discussions and exchange views with other students, and, in general, to learn his profession." Such considerations apply with added force to children in grade and high schools. To separate them from others of similar age and qualifications solely because of their race generates a feeling of inferiority as to their status in the community that may affect their hearts and minds in a way unlikely ever to be undone. The effect of this separation on their educational opportunities was well stated by a finding in the Kansas case by a court which nevertheless felt compelled to rule against the Negro plaintiffs:

Segregation of white and colored children in public schools has a detrimental effect upon the colored children. The impact is greater when it has the sanction of the law; for the policy of separating the races is usually interpreted as denoting the inferiority of the Negro group. A sense of inferiority affects the motivation of a child to learn. Segregation with the sanction of law, therefore has a tendency to [retard] the educational and mental development of Negro children and to deprive them of some of the benefits they would receive in a racial[ly] integrated school system.

Whatever may have been the extent of psychological knowledge at the time of *Plessy* vs. *Ferguson,* this finding is amply supported by modern authority. Any language in *Plessy* vs. *Ferguson* contrary to this finding is rejected. We conclude that in the field of public education the doctrine of "separate but equal" has no place. Separate educational facilities are inherently unequal. Therefore, we hold that the plaintiffs and others similarly situated for whom the actions have been brought are, by reason of the segregation complained of, deprived of the equal protection of the laws guaranteed by the Fourteenth Amendment. This disposition makes unnecessary any discussion whether such segregation also violates the Due Process Clause of the Fourteenth Amendment.

Because these are class actions, because of the wide applicability of this decision, and because of the great variety of local conditions, the formulation of decrees in these cases presents problems of considerable complexity. On reargument, the consideration of appropriate relief was necessarily subordinated to the primary question—the constitutionality of segregation in public education. We have now announced that such segregation is a denial of the equal protection of the laws. In order that we may have the full assistance of the parties in formulating decrees, the cases will be restored to the docket, and the parties are requested to present further argument on Questions 4 and 5 previously propounded by the Court for the reargument of this Term. The Attorney General of the United States is again invited to participate. The Attorneys General of the states requiring or permitting segregation in public education will also be permitted to appear as *amici curiae* upon request to do so by September 15, 1954, and submission of briefs by October 1, 1954.

It is so ordered.

3b. Bolling *vs.* Sharpe, 1954*

This case challenges the validity of segregation in the public schools of the District of Columbia. The petitioners, minors of the Negro race, allege that such segregation deprives them of due process of

* *Bolling et al.* vs. *Sharpe et al.,* May 17, 1954 (347 U.S. 483).

law under the Fifth Amendment. They were refused admission to a public school attended by white children solely because of their race. They sought the aid of the District Court for the District of Columbia in obtaining admission. That court dismissed their complaint. The Court granted a writ of certiorari before judgment in the Court of Appeals because of the importance of the constitutional question presented. (344 U.S. 873.)

We have this day held that the Equal Protection Clause of the Fourteenth Amendment prohibits the states from maintaining racially segregated public schools. The legal problem in the District of Columbia is somewhat different, however. The Fifth Amendment, which is applicable in the District of Columbia, does not contain an equal protection clause as does the Fourteenth Amendment which applies only to the states. But the concepts of equal protection and due process, both stemming from our equal American ideal of fairness, are not mutually exclusive. The "equal protection of the laws" is a more explicit safeguard of prohibited unfairness than "due process of law," and, therefore, we do not imply that the two are always interchangeable phrases. But, as this Court has recognized, discrimination may be so unjustifiable as to be violative of due process.

Classifications based solely upon race must be scrutinized with particular care, since they are contrary to our traditions and hence constitutionally suspect. As long ago as 1896, this Court declared the principle "that the Constitution of the United States, in its present form, forbids, so far as civil and political rights are concerned, discrimination by the General Government, or by the States, against any citizen because of his race." And in *Buchanan* vs. *Warley*, 245 U.S. 60, the Court held that a statute which limited the right of a property owner to convey his property to a person of another race was, as an unreasonable discrimination, a denial of due process of law.

Although the Court has not assumed to define "liberty" with any great precision, that term is not confined to mere freedom from bodily restraint. Liberty under law extends to the full range of conduct which the individual is free to pursue, and it cannot be restricted except for a proper governmental objective. Segregation in public education is not reasonably related to any proper governmental objective, and thus it imposes on Negro children of the District of Columbia a burden that constitutes an arbitrary deprivation of their liberty in violation of the Due Process Clause.

In view of our decision that the Constitution prohibits the states from maintaining racially segregated public schools, it would be unthinkable that the same Constitution would impose a lesser duty on the Federal Government. We hold that racial segregation in the public schools of the District of Columbia is a denial of the due process of law guaranteed by the Fifth Amendment to the Constitution.

For the reasons set out in *Brown* vs. *Board of Education,* this case will be restored to the docket for reargument on Questions 4 and 5 previously propounded by the Court. (345 U.S. 972.)

It is so ordered.

3c.   Brown *vs.* Board of Education, 1955*

These cases were decided on May 17, 1954. The opinions of that date, declaring the fundamental principle that racial discrimination in public education is unconstitutional, are incorporated herein by reference. All provisions of federal, state, or local law requiring or permitting such discrimination must yield to this principle. There remains for consideration the manner in which relief is to be accorded.

Because these cases arose under different local conditions and their dispositions will involve a variety of local problems, we requested further argument on the question of relief. In view of the nation-wide importance of the decision, we invited the Attorney General of the United States and the Attorneys General of all states requiring or permitting racial discrimination in public education to present their views on that question. The parties, the United States, and the States of Florida, North Carolina, Arkansas, Oklahoma, Maryland, and Texas filed briefs and participated in the oral argument.

These presentations were informative and helpful to the Court in its consideration of the complexities arising from the transition to a system of public education freed of racial discrimination. The presentations also demonstrated that substantial steps to eliminate racial discrimination in public schools have already been taken, not only in some of the communities in which these cases arose, but in some of the states appearing as *amici curiae,* and in other states as well. Substantial progress has been made in the District of Columbia and in the communities in Kansas and Delaware involved in this litigation. The defendants in the cases coming to us from South Carolina and Virginia are awaiting the decision of this Court concerning relief.

Full implementation of these constitutional principles may require solution of varied local school problems. School authorities have the primary responsibility for elucidating, assessing, and solving these problems; courts will have to consider whether the action of school authorities constitutes good faith implementation of the governing constitutional principles. Because of their proximity to local condi-

* *Brown et al.* vs. *Board of Education et al.,* May 31, 1955 (349 U.S. 294).

tions and the possible need for further hearings, the courts which originally heard these cases can best perform this judicial appraisal. Accordingly, we believe it appropriate to remand the cases to those courts.

In fashioning and effectuating the decrees, the courts will be guided by equitable principles. Traditionally, equity has been characterized by a practical flexibility in shaping its remedies and by a facility for adjusting and reconciling public and private needs. These cases call for the exercise of these traditional attributes of equity power. At stake is the personal interest of the plaintiffs in admission to public schools as soon as practicable on a nondiscriminatory basis. To effectuate this interest may call for elimination of a variety of obstacles in making the transition to school systems operated in accordance with the constitutional principles set forth in our May 17, 1954, decision. Courts of equity may properly take into account the public interest in the elimination of such obstacles in a systematic and effective manner. But it should go without saying that the vitality of these constitutional principles cannot be allowed to yield simply because of disagreement with them.

While giving weight to these public and private considerations, the courts will require that the defendants make a prompt and reasonable start toward full compliance with our May 17, 1954, ruling. Once such a start has been made, the courts may find that additional time is necessary to carry out the ruling in an effective manner. The burden rests upon the defendants to establish that such time is necessary in the public interest and is consistent with good faith compliance at the earliest practicable date. To that end, the courts may consider problems related to administration, arising from the physical condition of the school plant, the school transportation system, personnel, revision of school districts and attendance areas into compact units to achieve a system of determining admission to public schools on a nonracial basis, and revision of local laws and regulations which may be necessary in solving the foregoing problems. They will also consider the adequacy of any plans the defendants may propose to meet these problems and to effectuate a transition to a racially nondiscriminatory school system. During this period of transition, the courts will retain jurisdiction of these cases.

The judgments below, except that in the Delaware case, are accordingly reversed and the cases are remanded to the District Courts to take such proceedings and enter such orders and decrees consistent with this opinion as are necessary and proper to admit to public schools on a racial nondiscriminatory basis with all deliberate speed the parties to these cases. The judgment in the Delaware case —ordering the immediate admission of the plaintiffs to schools previously attended only by white children—is affirmed on the basis of the principles stated in our May 17, 1954, opinion, but the case is remanded to the Supreme Court of Delaware for such further proceedings as that Court may deem necessary in light of this opinion.

It is so ordered.

Selection 4

THE SOUTHERN MANIFESTO*

This was signed by nineteen Senators and eighty-two House members.

The unwarranted decision of the Supreme Court in the public school cases is now bearing the fruit always produced when men substitute naked power for established law.

The founding fathers gave us a constitution of checks and balances because they realized the inescapable lesson of history that no man or group of men can be safely entrusted with unlimited power. They framed this constitution with its provisions for change by amendment in order to secure the fundamentals of government against the dangers of temporary popular passion or the personal predilections of public office holders.

We regard the decision of the Supreme Court in the school cases as a clear abuse of judicial power. It climaxes a trend in the federal judiciary undertaking to legislate, in derogation of the authority of Congress, and to encroach upon the reserved rights of the states and the people.

The original Constitution does not mention education. Neither does the Fourteenth Amendment nor any other amendment. The debates preceding the submission of the Fourteenth Amendment clearly show that there was no intent that it should affect the systems of education maintained by the states.

* From *Southern School News*, April, 1956, p. 2.

The very Congress which proposed the amendment subsequently provided for segregated schools in the District of Columbia.

When the amendment was adopted in 1868, there were 37 states of the union. Every one of the 26 states that had any substantial racial differences among its people either approved the operation of segregated schools already in existence or subsequently established such schools by action of the same law-making body which considered the Fourteenth Amendment.

As admitted by the Supreme Court in the public school case (*Brown* vs. *Board of Education*), the doctrine of separate but equal schools "apparently originated in *Roberts* vs. *City of Boston* . . . (1849), upholding school segregation against attack as being violative of a state constitutional guarantee of equality." This constitutional doctrine began in the North—not in the South, and it was followed not only in Massachusetts, but in Connecticut, New York, Illinois, Indiana, Michigan, Minnesota, New Jersey, Ohio, Pennsylvania and other northern states until they, exercising their rights as states through the constitutional processes of local self-government, changed their school systems.

In the case of *Plessy* vs. *Ferguson* in 1896 the Supreme Court expressly declared that under the Fourteenth Amendment no person was denied any of his rights if the states provided separate but equal public facilities. This decision has been followed in many other cases. It is notable that the Supreme Court, speaking through Chief Justice Taft, a former president of the United States, unanimously declared in 1927 in *Lum* vs. *Rice* that the "separate but equal" principle is ". . . within the discretion of the state in regulating its public schools and does not conflict with the Fourteenth Amendment."

This interpretation, restated time and again, became a part of the life of the people of many of the states and confirmed their habits, customs, tradition and way of life. It is founded on elemental humanity and common sense, for parents should not be deprived by government of the right to direct the lives and education of their own children.

Though there has been no constitutional amendment or act of Congress changing this established legal principle almost a century old, the Supreme Court of the United States, with no legal basis for such action, undertook to exercise their naked judicial power and substituted their personal political and social ideas for the established law of the land.

This unwarranted exercise of power by the court, contrary to the Constitution, is creating chaos and confusion in the states principally affected. It is destroying the amicable relations between the white and Negro races that have been created through 90 years of patient effort by the good people of both races. It has planted hatred and suspicion where there has been heretofore friendship and understanding.

Without regard to the consent of the governed, outside agitators are threatening immediate and revolutionary changes in our public school systems. If done, this is certain to destroy the system of public education in some of the states.

With the gravest concern for the explosive and dangerous condition created by this decision and inflamed by outside meddlers:

We reaffirm our reliance on the Constitution as the fundamental law of the land.

We decry the Supreme Court's encroachments on rights reserved to the states and to the people, contrary to established law and to the Constitution.

We commend the motives of those states which have declared the intention to resist forced integration by any lawful means.

We appeal to the states and people who are not directly affected by these decisions to consider the constitutional principles involved against the time when they too, on issues vital to them, may be the victims of judicial encroachment.

Even though we constitute a minority in the present Congress, we have full faith that a majority of the American people believe in the dual system of government which has enabled us to achieve our greatness and will in time demand that the reserved rights of the states and of the people be made secure against judicial usurpation.

We pledge ourselves to use all lawful means to bring about a reversal of this decision which is contrary to the Constitution and to prevent the use of force in its implementation.

In this trying period, as we all seek to right this wrong, we appeal to our people not to be provoked by the agitators and troublemakers invading our states and to scrupulously refrain from disorder and lawless acts.

Selections 5a–5f

THE LITTLE ROCK CRISIS:
A CASE STUDY

The following selections tell the Little Rock story from a variety of points of view.

Selection 5d is taken from the transcript of an interview conducted for the National Broadcasting Company by Mrs. Jorunn Ricketts, a Norwegian correspondent. On October 14, 1957, Mrs. Ricketts interviewed several students at Little Rock's Central High School. The students were: a Negro girl, Minnijean Brown; a Negro boy, Ernest Green; a white boy, Joseph Fox; and three white girls, Sammy Dean Parker, Kay Bacon, and Robin Woods. The interview took place one month after 1000 federal troops had to be used to support nine Negro students in their legal right to attend the school.

5a. The Governor's Explanation*
September 2, 1957

. . . This is a decision I have reached prayerfully. It has been made after conferences with dozens of people and after the checking and the verification of as many of the reports as possible.

The mission of the State Militia is to maintain or restore order and to protect the lives and property of citizens. They will act not as segregationists or integrationists, but as soldiers called to active duty to carry out their assigned tasks.

But I must state here in all sincerity, that it is my opinion—yes, even a conviction, that it will not be possible to restore or to main-

---

* From *Southern School News*, October 1957, p. 1; part of report of Faubus' television speech explaining his reasons for sending the National Guard to Central High School.

tain order and protect the lives and property of the citizens if forcible integration is carried out tomorrow in the schools of this community. The inevitable conclusion, therefore, must be that the schools in Pulaski County, for the time being, must be operated on the same basis as they have been operated in the past. . . .

5b. Interview with a Student Leader in Central High School*
September 1957

Q. How long do you think this tension is going to last?

A. It's up to Governor Faubus.

Q. If you had your say, speaking personally, the Negro students could come to the school tomorrow?

A. Sir, it's the law. We are going to have to face it sometime.

Q. Do you think the day is going to come when your school is going to be integrated?

A. Yes.

Q. Are you opposed to integration yourself?

A. If it's a court order we have to follow it and abide by the law.

Q. Would you mind sitting next to a Negro in school?

A. No. . . .

Q. Do you have any Negro friends?

A. No, sir.

Q. Have you done any soul searching at all about the segregation problem as a whole?

A. Not particularly.

Q. Would it make a big difference to you if you saw a white girl dating a Negro boy?

A. I believe it would.

Q. It would?

A. Yes, sir.

Q. Why?

A. I don't know. I just was brought up that way.

Q. Do you think Negroes are equal in intelligence and physically to white people?

A. That's just a matter of opinion.

Q. What's yours? You are [a] person of some significance. You are the president of the student body.

* From a Mike Wallace television interview with Ralph Brodie, president of Little Rock's Central High School student body, as reprinted in the *Arkansas Gazette,* September 10, 1957, p. 4A.

A. If they have had the same benefits and advantages, I think they're equally as smart.

Q. Do you respect the Supreme Court?

A. I certainly do.

Q. Do you believe all Southerners should live by the law of the land?

A. I don't see why we shouldn't. We've been living under it all our lives.

5c. Speech by President Eisenhower Explaining Why Troops Were Being Sent to Little Rock*
September 24, 1957

For a few minutes this evening I want to talk to you about the serious situation that has arisen in Little Rock. To make this talk I have come to the President's office in the White House. I could have spoken from Rhode Island, where I have been staying recently, but I felt that, in speaking from the house of Lincoln, of Jackson, and of Wilson, my words would better convey both the sadness I feel in the action I was compelled today to take and the firmness with which I intend to pursue this course until the orders of the Federal Court at Little Rock can be executed without unlawful interference.

In that city, under the leadership of demagogic extremists, disorderly mobs have deliberately prevented the carrying out of proper orders from a Federal Court. Local authorities have not eliminated that violent opposition and, under the law, I yesterday issued a Proclamation calling upon the mob to disperse.

This morning the mob again gathered in front of the Central High School of Little Rock, obviously for the purpose of again preventing the carrying out of the Court's order relating to the admission of Negro children to that school.

Whenever normal agencies prove inadequate to the task and it becomes necessary for the Executive Branch of the Federal Government to use its powers and authority to uphold Federal Courts, the President's responsibility is inescapable.

In accordance with that responsibility, I have today issued an Executive Order directing the use of troops under Federal authority to aid in the execution of Federal law at Little Rock, Arkansas.

* From *Vital Speeches*, XXIV, 11–12 (October 15, 1957–October 1, 1958), New York: City News Publishing Co.

This became necessary when my Proclamation of yesterday was not observed, and the obstruction of justice still continues. . . .

Our personal opinions about the decision have no bearing on the matter of enforcement; the responsibility and authority of the Supreme Court to interpret the Constitution are very clear. . . .

Mob rule cannot be allowed to override the decisions of our courts.

Now, let me make it very clear that Federal troops are not being used to relieve local and state authorities of their primary duty to preserve the peace and order of the community. Nor are the troops there for the purpose of taking over the responsibility of the School Board and the other responsible local officials in running Central High School. The running of our school system and the maintenance of peace and order in each of our states are strictly local affairs, and the Federal Government does not interfere, except in very special cases and when requested by one of the several states. In the present case the troops are there, pursuant to law, solely for the purpose of preventing interference with the orders of the Court. . . .

In the South, as elsewhere, citizens are keenly aware of the tremendous disservice that has been done to the people of Arkansas in the eyes of the nation, and that has been done to the nation in the eyes of the world.

At a time when we face grave situations abroad because of the hatred that Communism bears toward a system of government based on human rights, it would be difficult to exaggerate the harm that is being done to the prestige and influence and, indeed, to the safety of our nation and the world.

Our enemies are gloating over this incident and using it everywhere to misrepresent our whole nation. We are portrayed as a violator of those standards of conduct which the peoples of the world united to proclaim in the Charter of the United Nations. There they affirmed "faith in fundamental human rights" and "in the dignity and worth of the human person," and they did so "without distinction as to race, sex, language, or religion."

And so, with deep confidence, I call upon citizens of the State of Arkansas to assist in bringing to an immediate end all interference with the law and its processes. If resistance to the Federal Court order ceases at once, the further presence of Federal troops will be unnecessary and the city of Little Rock will return to its normal habits of peace and order—and a blot upon the fair name and high honor of our nation will be removed.

Thus will be restored the image of America and of all its parts as one nation, indivisible, with liberty and justice for all.

5d. Interview with Little Rock Students*

A Norwegian correspondent interviews on the National Broadcasting System six Little Rock Central High School students: three white girls (Sammy, Kay and Robin), one white boy (Joseph), one Negro boy (Ernest) and one Negro girl (Minnijean).

MRS. RICKETTS: Do you think it is possible to start working this out on a more sensible basis than violent demonstration?

SAMMY: No, I don't because the South has always been against racial mixing and I think they will fight this thing to the end. . . . We fight for our freedom that's one thing. And we don't have any freedom any more.

ERNEST: Sammy, you said that you don't have freedom. I wonder what do you mean by it—that you don't have freedom? You are guaranteed your freedoms in the Bill of Rights and your Constitution. You have the freedom of speech—I noticed that has been exercised a whole lot in Little Rock. The freedom of petition, the freedom of religion and the other freedoms are guaranteed to you. As far as freedom, I think that if anybody should kick about freedoms, it should be us. Because I think we have been given a pretty bad side on this thing as far as freedoms.

SAMMY: Do you call those troops freedom? I don't. And I also do not call free when you are being escorted into the school every morning.

ERNEST: You say why did the troops come here? It is because our government—our state government—went against the federal law. . . . Our country is set up so that we have forty-eight states and no one state has the ability to overrule our nation's government. I thought that was what our country was built around. I mean, that is why we fight. We fought in World War II together—the fellows that I know died in World War II, they died in the Korean War. I mean, why should my friends get out there and die for a cause called "democracy" when I can't exercise my rights—tell me that.

ROBIN: I agree with Ernest.

JOE: Well, Sammy, I don't know what freedom has been taken away from you because the truth there—I know as a senior myself —the troops haven't kept me from going to my classes or participating in any school activity. I mean, they're there just to keep order in case—I might use term "hotheads"—get riled up. But I think as long as—if parents would just stay out of it and let the children

* From *Anthony Lewis and the New York Times—Portrait of a Decade,* New York: Random House, 1964, pp. 63–66.

of the school at Central High figure it out for themselves, I think it would be a whole lot better. I think the students are mature enough to figure it out for themselves. . . . As far as I'm concerned, I'll lay the whole blame of this trouble in Governor Faubus's lap.

SAMMY: I think we knew before this ever started that some day we were going to have to integrate the schools. And I think that our Governor was trying to protect all of us when he called out the National Guard—and he was trying to prepare us, I think.

ERNEST: . . . Well, I have to disagree. . . . I know a student that's over there with us, Elizabeth, and that young lady, she walked two blocks, I guess—as you all know—and the mob was behind her. Did the troops break up the mob?

ROBIN: . . . And when Elizabeth had to walk down in front of the school I was there and I saw that. And may I say, I was very ashamed—I felt like crying—because she was so brave when she did that. And we just weren't behaving ourselves—just jeering her. I think if we had had any sort of decency, we wouldn't have acted that way. But I think if everybody would just obey the Golden Rule—do unto others as you would have others do unto you—might be the solution. How would you like to have to . . . walk down the street with everybody yelling behind you like they yelled behind Elizabeth?

MRS. RICKETTS: Sammy, why do these children not want to go to school with Negroes?

SAMMY: Well, I think it is mostly race mixing.

MRS. RICKETTS: Race mixing? What do you mean?

SAMMY: Well, marrying each other.

MINNIJEAN: Hold your hand up. I'm brown, you are white. What's the difference? We are all of the same thoughts. You're thinking about your boy—he's going to the Navy. I'm thinking about mine—he's in the Air Force. We think about the same thing.

SAMMY: I'll have to agree with you.

ERNEST: Well, getting back to this intermarriage and all that. I don't know [where] people get all that. Why do I want to go to school? To marry with someone? I mean, school's not a marriage bureau. . . . I'm going there for an education. Really, if I'm going there to socialize, I don't need to be going to school. I can stand out on the corner and socialize, as far as that.

MINNIJEAN: Kay, Joe and Robin—do you know anything about me, or is it just that your mother has told you about Negroes? . . .

MRS. RICKETTS: . . . Have you ever really made an effort to try to find out what they're like?

KAY: Not until today.

SAMMY: Not until today.

MRS. RICKETTS. And what do you think about it after today?

KAY: Well, you know that my parents and a lot of the other students and their parents think that the Negroes aren't equal to us. But—I don't know. It seems like they are, to me.

SAMMY: These people are—we'll have to admit that.

ERNEST: I think, like we're doing today, discussing our different views . . . if the people of Little Rock . . . would get together I believe they would find out a different story—and try to discuss the thing instead of getting out in the street and kicking people around and calling names—and all that sort of thing. If . . . people got together it would be smoothed over.

KAY: I think that if . . . our friends had been getting in this discussion today, I think that maybe some of them—not all of them —in time, they would change their mind. But probably some of them would change their mind today.

SAMMY: I know now that it isn't as bad as I thought it was— after we got together and discussed it.

KAY: [Sammy and I] We both came down here today with our mind set on it [that] we weren't going to change our mind that we were fully against integration. But I know now that we're going to change our mind.

MRS. RICKETTS: What do your parents say to that?

KAY: I think I'm going to have a long talk with my parents.

5e. The *Arkansas Democrat* Protests

KARR SHANNON*

Little Rock's Central High School is still under military occupation. The troops are still there—on the campus, in the building.

The troops are still there, despite the fact that their presence is resented by the big majority of the students, the parents, and the people in general throughout the South.

The troops continue to stand guard during school hours, on the grounds and within the corridors and classrooms, despite the fact that there is no law or precedent—Federal or State—that permits them to do so.

There is not even an order, or so much as a sanction, from the U. S. Supreme Court that makes its own "laws" on mixing of races in the public schools.

Federal troops continue to occupy Central High—in defiance of

* From *Arkansas Democrat*, Little Rock, March 10, 1958.

the Constitution, law, and precedent—while the Congress of the United States sits out the sessions and does nothing.

Never before in the history of America has any area of our so-called Free Republic been so shamefully treated.

When two sections of this country were at war with each other, no troops ever patrolled the public school buildings and grounds from day to day. After the South had been beaten down, Federal forces kept the vanquished under the iron heel for the duration of the "Reconstruction" period. But not once did they molest the public schools with troop occupation.

Education, or attempted education, under the scrutiny of armed troops is un-American, un-Godly.

It is not even Communistic. Russia, in all her cruelty, has never bothered school children in occupied territory by stationing armed soldiers on the grounds and in the buildings. Germany never did it.

No other nation, however barbaric and cruel and relentless, ever —in the history of the human race—resorted to such tactics—only the United States, which sets itself up as a world example of peace, freedom, and democracy, forces the military upon a free school.

How much longer will Congress sit idly by and let such brazen violation of American principle and law continue on and on and on?

5f.   A Negro Newspaper Praises Courage*

Few incidents in recent American history can match the courage shown by the nine teen-age Negroes of Little Rock. They risked their lives for the sake of establishing a principle: the right to attend an integrated high school. They did it in the face of ugly and determined opposition; they did it under circumstances that would have caused many stout-hearted grownups to withdraw behind the protective shield of their own homes.

This was the most severe test of the law. The Federal courts paved the way; Federal troops held the angry mob at bay. But the nine Negro pupils did not have to march through the guardsmen to enter Little Rock's Central High School. They could have waited until public indignation had subsided; or they could have decided to attend a nearby Negro school rather than avail themselves of their legal rights. They didn't. Instead they went ahead, despite jeers and bitter invectives.

How many of us would have had the fortitude to do what these youngsters have done? How often have we failed to take advantage

* From Chicago *Daily Defender*, May 28, 1958.

of victories won for us? It is therefore the more remarkable that these young Negroes, living in the Deep South, fearlessly implemented the Court's action by their daily presence at Central High School.

Though their lot was not a happy one even inside the high school building, though they were pushed around, insulted, and beaten by some of the white students, the Negro pupils held their ground. The Supreme Court's integration ruling would have been meaningless had these Negro boys and girls failed to follow the course mapped out for them by the law. They should be applauded by all of us.

Selection 6

PROPOSED TALMADGE AMENDMENT TO THE CONSTITUTION*

The following is the text of remarks of U. S. Sen. Herman E. Talmadge (Ga.) upon introducing in the U. S. Senate, Jan. 28, 1960 a revised version of his proposed constitutional amendment to restore to the states exclusive control over public education. Joining him as co-sponsors were Senators Harry F. Byrd and A. Willis Robertson (Va.), Olin D. Johnston (S. Car.), Lister Hill and John J. Sparkman (Ala.), James O. Eastland and John C. Stennis (Miss.), and Russell B. Long (La.).

Mr. President, last January eight colleagues and I introduced a proposed constitutional amendment which we sincerely felt offered a reasonable and realistic solution to the worsening educational

* *Speech by Herman Talmadge,* Congressional Record, *January 28, 1960, 86th Congress, 2nd session, Vol. 106, Part 2, pp. 1499–1501.*

crisis growing out of the Supreme Court's 1954 decision prohibiting separate schools for the races.

The proposal was widely acclaimed not only in the South but also in all other sections of the country. Many newspapers carried editorials commenting favorably upon it and I had a number of them printed in the Congressional Record. I received hundreds of letters from individuals throughout the nation endorsing the approach proposed by the Talmadge School Amendment as fair, sound and workable.

Extensive public hearings were held last May by the Subcommittee on Constitutional Amendments at which an impressive number of responsible and respected leaders—including some of the country's best legal scholars—testified in support of so amending the Constitution of the United States. The 282-page printed transcript of testimony taken at those hearings stands as irrefutable proof of the fact that support of the Talmadge School Amendment is not limited to any one region but is national in scope.

Unfortunately the resolution embodying the proposed amendment was tabled in the Subcommittee by a vote of 3-to-2 as the result of some of the specious objections which were raised to it.

There were some who contended that the language was too broad.

There were others who maintained that it opened the door to economic, religious and racial discrimination.

There were others who insisted that it would nullify the guarantee of "equal protection of the laws" contained in the Fourteenth Amendment.

There were others who charged that it would result in all manner of lowered standards, capricious regulations and restricted educational opportunity.

Of course, Mr. President, all of those fears were completely groundless and those of us sponsoring the proposed amendment sought so to assure the members of the Subcommittee. As the principal author, I advised them that the sponsors would welcome any clarifying language which they felt was needed to allay the various apprehensions which had been expressed.

It was disappointing, therefore, that the Subcommittee decided to table the proposal rather than revise its wording and give the full Committee on the Judiciary an opportunity to pass on it.

Consequently, the other sponsors and I have endeavored to re-write the original resolution in an effort to satisfy the objections which have been raised to it while at the same time striving to preserve the original objective of restoring control over public education to the states as intended by the framers of the Constitution.

The result of our efforts is contained in a new resolution which I shall offer for introduction and appropriate reference at the close of my remarks.

Our revised amendment would read as follows:

"Notwithstanding any other provision of this Constitution, every State shall have exclusive control of its public schools, public educational institutions and public educational systems, whether operated by the State or by political or other subdivisions of the State or by instrumentalities or agencies of the State; Provided, however, that nothing contained in this Article shall be construed to authorize any State to deny to any pupil because of race, color, national origin or religious belief the right to attend schools equal in respect to the quality and ability of the teachers, curriculum and physical facilities to those attended by other pupils attending schools in the same school system."

Mr. President, it is my firm belief that this new language for the Talmadge School Amendment would serve to set at rest all the fears of those who have had doubts either as to the motives of its sponsors or as to the ultimate result of its application.

Nothing in that language, Mr. President, would relieve any state of its obligation within the context and intent of the Fourteenth Amendment to guarantee to all of its citizens equal protection of the laws. It would merely assure for all time to come that, insofar as public education is concerned, no state could be deprived of its constitutional right to operate its public schools in accordance with the wishes of its citizens within the limits of constitutional guarantees.

Let me point out and emphasize, Mr. President, that the Talmadge School Amendment is neither a segregation nor an integration measure. It rather is a proposal to reassert affirmatively the time-honored right of local people to administer their schools on the state and local levels in accordance with prevailing conditions, circumstances and attitudes. Under it school patrons in each state would be free to determine for themselves through their elected representatives whether segregation, integration or some median procedure would best serve the interests of their children and state.

The basic question involved is far more fundamental than the mere matter of who attends what school. It goes to the very heart of our concept of constitutional republican government; that is, the right of local self-determination.

The bedrock of our form of government is, in the words of the Declaration of Independence, that it derives its "just powers from the consent of the governed." And whenever we in this country get away from that foundation of our freedom, as of that moment we will have ceased to be a nation in which the people govern themselves.

Now, Mr. President, I recognize that on the issue of separation of the races in the schools of the nation there is a wide divergence of opinion and individual feelings are strong and inflamed on both sides. Many false emotional factors have been injected and those undoubtedly account for the fact that the Talmadge School Amendment to date has not been considered on its merits.

As I endeavored to stress when I introduced the original version of the amendment last year, Mr. President, the constitutional and sociological ramifications of the Supreme Court's school ruling have stirred a continuing controversy which has divided the best minds of the country.

There are two opposing camps of opinion—those who consider the decision to be the law of the land and who are determined to force its implementation regardless of the results and those, like myself, who consider the decision to be outside the scope of the Constitution and who are dedicated to seeking its reversal by every lawful means.

On one hand there is the accomplished fact of a Supreme Court edict while on the other hand the overwhelming majority of the people of the South will neither accept nor submit to the forced implementation of it.

The only realistic, constitutional way by which the public schools in many areas of the South can be spared the fate of being crushed between those two millstones, lies in recognizing that public schools are local institutions which must be operated by local people on the state and local levels if they are to survive.

It was with the view of affording such a solution that the original Talmadge School Amendment was proposed last year and it is with that same objective in mind that the revised version is being presented at this Session.

I ask unanimous consent, Mr. President, to have the text of my statement before the Senate upon the introduction of the original amendment on January 27, 1959, printed at this juncture in my remarks.

The argument that the Talmadge School Amendment would result in lowered standards, capricious regulations, restricted educational opportunity and various fancied forms of racial, religious and economic descrimination is a gross insult to the intelligence, vision, aspirations and humanity of all Americans of all regions.

No responsible individual would advocate or condone any backward step in the quality or quantity of American education. All thinking citizens recognize that the great need of our nation in this era of scientific and technological revolution is for more and better education and the extraordinary efforts which the citizens of the South presently are making to provide such education for all children of all races, national origins and religions bespeaks more eloquently of their sincerity and good faith in this regard than anything I might say.

There would be no curtailment or infringement of educational opportunity for children of any race in the South as the result of the incorporation of the Talmadge School Amendment into the Constitution of the United States. To the contrary the actual result would be an acceleration of the present effort to improve the educational opportunity of all children to justify the confidence of the remainder of the nation in giving specific constitutional recognition to the right of the people of the South to work out solutions to their problems in accordance with the prevailing situation in each particular state.

Mr. President, the American people will have degenerated to a sad state indeed when, as some opponents of the Talmadge School Amendment contended last year, the Supreme Court and its strained interpretations of the Fourteenth Amendment are the only remaining safeguards against inferior education in this country.

Fortunately for the nation, Mr. President, the American people do not have so low an opinion of their conscience, sense of justice and fair play and ability to manage their own affairs as do some of their detractors on the national scene.

And it is to give the American people the opportunity to prove that point, Mr. President, that I herewith introduce for myself and the Senators from Virginia (Mr. Byrd and Mr. Robertson), South Carolina (Mr. Johnston), Alabama (Mr. Hill and Mr. Sparkman), Mississippi (Mr. Eastland and Mr. Stennis), and Louisiana (Mr. Long), a proposed constitutional amendment and ask unanimous consent that it be read twice, appropriately referred and printed herewith in the Record at the conclusion of my remarks.

"...SURE WE'VE COMPLIED. HERE'S OUR NEGRO!"

Selections 8a–8d

STATISTICS ON SCHOOL DESEGREGATION

8a. Status in the Southern and Border States as of June 1965*

	Districts With Negroes and			Enrollment		Enrollment in Desegregated Districts		Negroes in Schools with Whites	
	Total	Whites	Deseg.	White	Negro	White	Negro	No.	%
Alabama	118	118	9	549,593**	293,426**	131,241**	87,457**	101	.034
Arkansas	411	220	24	333,630†	114,551†	93,072	28,943	930	.811
Delaware	79	45	45	83,164	19,357	78,942	14,064	12,051	62.2
District of Columbia	1	1	1	17,487	123,906	17,487	123,906	106,578	86.0
Florida	67	67	22	1,014,920	247,475	817,842	175,969	6,612	2.67
Georgia	196	180	12	686,761	334,126	200,127	133,454	1,337	.400
Kentucky	204	165	165	607,522	55,215	540,000*	55,215	37,585	68.1
Louisiana	67	67	3	472,923*	313,314*	63,591	88,677	3,581	1.14
Maryland	24	23	23	566,375	169,207	561,300	169,207	86,205	50.9
Mississippi	163	163	4	299,748	279,106	34,620	21,929	57	.020
Missouri	1,056	212*	203*	818,000*	104,000*	NA	95,000	44,000*	42.3
North Carolina	170	170	86	828,638	349,282	555,997	207,551	4,963	1.42
Oklahoma	1,090	321	211	555,000*	45,000*	334,000*	38,000*	14,000*	31.1
South Carolina	108	108	18	371,921	260,667	173,833	96,196	265	.102
Tennessee	152	141	65	724,327	173,673	475,877	136,936	9,289	5.35
Texas	1,379	862	450*	2,086,752*	344,312*	1,600,000*	245,000*	27,000*	7.84
Virginia	130	127	81	736,017	233,270	600,000*	200,000*	12,000*	5.15
West Virginia	55	54	54	426,500*	21,200*	426,500*	21,300*	13,500	63.4
TOTAL	5,470	3,044	1,476	11,179,278	3,481,297	6,704,429††	1,938,804	380,054	10.9

* Estimated   ** 1963–64   † 1962–63   †† Missouri not included

* From *Southern School News*, June 1965.

8b. Percentage of Biracial School Districts Desegregated in 11 Southern States, 1956–62

State	Academic year					
	1956–57	*1957–58*	*1958–59*	*1959–60*	*1960–61*	*1961–62*
Mississippi	0	0	0	0	0	0
Alabama	0	0	0	0	0	0
South Carolina	0	0	0	0	0	0
Georgia	0	0	0	0	0	0.5%
Louisiana	0	0	0	0	0	1.5
Florida	0	0	0	0.5%	0.5%	7.5
Virginia	0	0	2.3%	4.7	8.6	14.7
North Carolina	0	1.7%	2.3	4.0	5.8	6.4
Tennessee	0.7%	1.4	2.1	2.8	4.2	9.1
Arkansas	1.8	3.1	2.6	3.5	4.4	4.4
Texas	12.3	14.6	17.3	17.6	18.1	23.0

Sources: This and the following two tables are taken from *Essays on the American Constitution,* Gottfried Dietze (editor), "Stateways Versus Folkways: Critical Factors in Southern Reactions to *Brown* versus *Board of Educaion,*" by Donald R. Matthews and James W. Prothro, New Jersey: Prentice-Hall, 1964, pp. 143–45.

Sources: Derived from statistics in Southern Education Reporting Service, *Status of School Segregation-Desegregation in the Southern and Border States,* Nashville, Tenn., 1960; *Southern School News,* December 1960, p. 1; *ibid.,* December 1961, p. 1; Southern Regional Council, *School Desegregation: The First Six Years,* Atlanta, Ga., 1960.

8c. Estimated Number of Negroes in Public Schools with Whites in 11 Southern States, 1956–62

State	Academic year					
	1956–57	*1957–58*	*1958–59*	*1959–60*	*1960–61*	*1961–62*
Mississippi	0	0	0	0	0	0
Alabama	0	0	0	0	0	0
South Carolina	0	0	0	0	0	0
Georgia	0	0	0	0	0	9
Louisiana	0	0	0	0	4	12
Florida	0	0	0	22*	27	552
Virginia	0	0	30	103	208	533
North Carolina	0	11	14	34	82	203
Tennessee	6**	19**	82	169	342	1,142
Arkansas	34	91	73	94	113	152
Texas***	3,400	3,600	3,750	3,300	3,500	4,300
TOTALS	3,440	3,721	3,449	3,722	4,276	6,903

* These 22 Negroes were attending the Homestead Air Force Base school with 745 whites. In Orchard Villa (Dade County) school 8 whites also attended classes with 490 Negroes; these are omitted from the table.

** These figures exclude Negroes attending school in Oak Ridge, which was operated during these years by the federal government on a desegregated basis.

*** Texas figures are estimates. The decline between 1958 and 1961 is apparently the result of more accurate estimates in recent times.

Sources: Same as for Table 1.

8d. Per Cent of Negro Schoolchildren in Public School with Whites, December, 1961

State	Per cent
Mississippi	0
Alabama	0
South Carolina	0
Georgia	0.003%
Louisiana	0.004
Florida	0.258
Virginia	0.246
North Carolina	0.061
Tennessee	0.734
Arkansas	0.142
Texas	1.420

Source: Southern School News, Dec. 1961, p. 7.

Selection 9

THE FACTS OF DE FACTO*

De facto segregation is separation of races based on fact or reality, whereas de jure segregation is segregation based on laws, such as the Jim Crow laws. De facto segregation most frequently arises out of housing patterns where people of the same color, for whatever reasons, move into the same neighborhood.

In 1960 most of the 77,000 citizens of New Rochelle, N. Y. viewed school segregation as a disease confined to the distant likes of Little Rock, Ark. The town's ethnic mix—14 per cent Negro, 30 per cent Jewish, 45 per cent Irish and Italian Catholic—was so faithfully reflected in the high school that the Voice of America once touted it as a shining example of integrated education. Only a year later, New Rochelle became the "Little Rock of the North," convicted in a federal court of gerrymandering to promote segregation. Case in point: Lincoln Elementary School, 94 per cent Negro.

More in hurt than anger, New Rochelle defended Lincoln as a typical "neighborhood school" that, like Topsy, just grew that way. The trial told a different story. Back in 1930, the school board redrew lines to make the Lincoln district match the Negro area. It also allowed whites to transfer out—and they did. By 1949 the school was 100 per cent Negro.

The board tried to bring resident whites back to the school by revoking transfers. Instead, whites switched to private and parochial schools or moved away, making the district more Negro than ever. By 1960 Lincoln's pupils in general were academically behind every other elementary school in town. The board, nobly it thought, got a city-wide vote to build a fine new Lincoln on the same spot. Negro parents countered with a federal suit on then-novel grounds:

* From *Time*, August 2, 1963, pp. 30–31.

it is just as unconstitutional to compel Negroes to attend a *de facto* segregated school in the North as a *de jure* segregated school in the South.

Federal Judge Irving R. Kaufman did not decide that question (nor has any other federal court so far). He ruled only that gerrymandering had violated equal protection under the 14th Amendment. The outcome jogged white minds all over the North. Given free access to other schools, Lincoln's pupils on the whole did better, except for some who landed in a white school that overwhelmed them. Because two-fifths of Lincoln's pupils chose to remain, New Rochelle is now closing the 65-year-old building, assigning the children to balanced schools, and launching an extensive bus service to help keep the entire city desegregated.

On the Attack

The experience of New Rochelle is a case history in a development that is spreading across the Northern U. S.: a movement against *de facto* segregation of schools. Victory in New Rochelle spurred the N.A.A.C.P. to a successful attack on *de facto* school segregation last year (1962) in a dozen Northern communities, from Coatesville, Pa., to Eloy, Ariz. This summer (1963) it is "mobilizing direct action" in 70 cities throughout 18 Northern and Western states. School boards are responding, and many a change will have been made by September. All kinds of tools are being tried. Samples:

Open Enrollment. The most widely used method so far, it modifies the neighborhood-school concept enough to let students of mostly Negro schools transfer to mostly white schools that have sufficient room. Open enrollment was pioneered in New York City, is used or will be starting in some form next September (1963) in Baltimore, Detroit, Pittsburgh, Buffalo, San Francisco and many smaller cities. Usually only a fraction of the eligible Negro students take advantage of it.

Rezoning—which is often the same as ungerrymandering. In San Francisco, mostly white Grant School lies near mostly Negro Emerson School in a rectangular area cut by a horizontal attendance line; made vertical, the line would integrate both schools. New York City's school zoning boss, Assistant Superintendent Francis A. Turner, a Negro, is such a skilled mixmaster that balanced schools are rapidly increasing.

The Princeton Plan, so called for the New Jersey town that devised it. Formerly segregated schools are rematched, so that one school accommodates all children of perhaps three grades, a second school the next three, and so on. This works well in small communities, might do in big cities by clustering each grade group in several nearby schools to avoid long bus trips.

Recombination. An example: A Negro elementary school can be turned into a junior high school serving a wider area, or into a school for gifted or retarded children, while the original pupils are sent to other schools.

School Spotting. New schools are built only in areas of integrated housing. For fast-changing big cities, the latest idea is "educational parks," putting all new schools in one or several central clusters. Last week a New York City Board of Education member suggested a perfect site: the World's Fair grounds, where after 1965 an education center could accommodate 15 public schools and a teachers' college, enrolling a total of 31,000 students.

Fears and Illusions

All these changes stir deep fears and emotions. Negroes, demanding more than token integration, have lately attacked *de facto* segregation by street-marching protests in Los Angeles and Philadelphia, "study-ins" at the white schools of Englewood, N. J., sit-ins at the boards of education of New York and Chicago. Whites envision their neighborhood being flooded with poorly prepared Negro pupils or their own children being forced to integrate Negro slum schools. A feeling of "discrimination against the majority" has sparked reactions like that of white parents in Montclair, N. J., who filed a federal suit under the 14th Amendment, claiming that Negro children were allowed free transfers while theirs were not. The long-honored concept of the neighborhood school—a homey place that children can walk to, a living symbol of local pride and progress—seems in danger.

Yet behind the stresses and strains is a consensus, by many school authorities, some courts and most Negroes, that *de facto* segregation must go. The problem is to break the low-income Negro's vicious circle of slum birth to slum school to bad education to low-paid job and parenthood of more slum children. The widely accepted premise is that the circle can and must be broken at the school stage. Equally important is that segregated neighborhood schools refute the original aim of Horace Mann's "common school," strengthening democracy by serving all races, creeds and classes. Integrationists believe that schools can help to heal U. S. race relations by returning to Mann's ideal.

Segregated Equals Bad

Nothing in theory prevents the hundreds of predominantly Negro schools in the North from excelling, but in practice a school that becomes 30 per cent to 50 per cent Negro is in for trouble. Whites pull out and it "tips" toward 100 per cent. Gone are the "motivated" bright white children who might have been models for slum kids to copy and compete with. Good teachers become hard to get (although the "spirit of the Peace Corps" is diminishing this problem, according to Cleveland's School Superintendent William B. Levenson). "Once we become concentrated, we become ignored," says a Boston Negro leader. Most of Los Angeles' 53 Negro schools are on double sessions. Chicago's Urban League calculates that in operating expenses Negro schools get only two-thirds as much per pupil as white schools.

The result is unsurprising. In Boston, where special high schools require entrance exams, one Negro boy typically complains: "I never saw that kind of math before I went for the exam." In his recent (1963) civil-rights speech, President Kennedy said: "The Negro baby born in America today has about one-half as much chance of completing a high school as a white baby, born in the same place, on the same day; one-third as much chance of completing college; one-third as much chance of becoming a professional man; twice as much chance of becoming unemployed."

Big-City Problems

While small Northern cities may attack the situation in the manner of New Rochelle, big cities, with miles of Negro ghettoes, have problems that range up to hopeless. Washington, where even the most civil-righteous New Frontiersmen are prone to send their children to private schools, can hardly give classes a desegregated look when 85 per cent of public school students are Negro. Chicago, Boston and Philadelphia are marking time. A measure of New York's quandary is that some integration crusaders have proposed mass transfer of whites into Harlem schools, although few officials see it as a workable solution.

Nonetheless, the Nation's biggest city school system is also the most enterprising. New York is trying to make slum schools so good that Negroes can rise more easily into an integrated society. It devised the famed Higher Horizons program, heavy on culture and counseling, which now involves 64,000 students in 76 schools. At state level, New York's Commissioner of Education James E. Allen, Jr. recently requested school boards to report by September (1963) on what steps they intend to take to balance schools with more than 50 per cent Negro enrollment.

"In the minds of Negro pupils and parents," says New Jersey's State Commissioner of Education Frederick M. Raubinger, "a stigma is attached to attending a school whose enrollment is completely or exclusively Negro, and this sense of stigma and resulting feeling of inferiority has an undesirable effect on attitudes related to successful training." Raubinger has issued orders to end *de facto* segregation in three New Jersey communities. In the same vein, a former foe of "social engineering via bussing," Dr. John Fischer, president of Columbia's Teachers College, warns that schools must "take positive action to bring Negro children into the mainstream of American cultural activity." And in California, the State Supreme Court in June came close to outlawing *de facto* segregation. Where it exists, ruled the court, "it is not enough for a school board to refrain from affirmative discriminatory conduct." No exact racial ratio is required, but schools must take "corrective measures."

The ideal integration situation, says psychiatrist Robert Coles after studying Southern schools, is apparently a middle-class school with diverse ethnic groups and high teaching standards. In a forthcoming report, sponsored by the Southern Regional Council and the Anti-Defamation League of B'nai B'rith, Coles adds that young children mix naturally, ignoring adult tensions. Teen-agers take longer, but in the course of a year begin to see "them" as individuals to be judged on personal merit. As for standards, both races generally work as hard as ever. Says Coles: "We have yet to hear a Southern teacher complain of any drop in intellectual or moral climate in a desegregated room or school."

While the pressures for integration bring a troublesome measure of controversy, reaction and disillusionment, it is a fact that every sensible effort to desegregate schools—alarmists to the contrary— is likely to improve the general level of U. S. education.

Selection 10

THE NORTH AND WEST HAVE PROBLEMS, TOO

G. W. FOSTER, JR. *

By the beginning of 1963, the attack on public school segregation had become nationwide. In more than sixty communities of the North and West there were active and organized pressures for desegregation programs.

The drive in the North and West differs in many respects from the efforts which continue in the South. The problems are different. So are the tactics, the demands, and—inevitably—the legal issues raised when conflict ripens into court action.

In the years after the 1954 Supreme Court decision in the school segregation cases national attention focused largely upon the South. There the attack was against a whole legal structure which compelled segregation. Negroes, insisting that state officials must be color-blind, sought removal of racial classifications and demanded reorganization of schools without regard to race.

By the 1960s a drive developed against what is called "de facto" segregation in the public schools of the North and West. De facto segregation does not result from any formal, legal classifications based on race. Rather, it arises from the effect of residential segregation upon patterns of neighborhood school attendance districts.

The problems raised by de facto segregation are more sophisticated and more subtle, and they stem from complex causes. The Negro fortunate enough to find housing in predominantly white neighborhoods usually has little difficulty in obtaining access to schools that serve those areas. Most Negroes in the North and West, however, live in crowded urban slum areas that racially are almost

* From *Saturday Review*, April 20, 1963.

or entirely homogeneous. Even those with resources adequate to acquire housing elsewhere encounter private discrimination that discourages and often prevents their escape from segregated neighborhoods. Still more Negroes, caught by discrimination in employment and having few developed skills, simply lack the resources to escape.

School officials, accused of being responsible for de facto segregation in the schools, usually counter by insisting that residential patterns and not racial bias on their part produced the result. An attorney representing Negroes who commenced judicial action against Philadelphia school officials gave his answer to that position:

> The position of the board is that it does not consider race at all in the operation of the school system, either in setting boundaries or in administrative practices. This is not enough. The board cannot be color-blind. It is the affirmative responsibility of the board to work toward integration. Every choice which may arise in making decisions about school matters must be made in such a way as to accomplish results leading to the integration goal.

This concept of color-consciousness marks a sharp break, tactically and legally, with the thrust of school desegregation efforts in the South. It poses for many educators troublesome questions in attempting to provide adequate education for academically and culturally handicapped children in slum schools. And finally, the demand for color-consciousness raises some serious legal questions of Constitutional proportion.

Assignment by race was of course the historic basis for the dual school systems of the South. Outside the South, school assignment is typically based on geography. The school system is divided into a single set of zones and each child is initially assigned to the school in his zone of residence. Frequently some provision exists for attending school outside the zone of residence, either by permitting transfer under specified conditions or by allowing a free choice of any uncrowded school in the system. A few communities do little or no zoning and simply permit a choice among all or some of the schools in the district.

The predominant pattern, however, involves geographic zoning with rather stringent restrictions against transfer on attendance outside the zone of residence. Often this is referred to as a "neighborhood" school pattern, although there is much variation in defining the characteristics of a neighborhood. The school in a particular "neighborhood" may be large or small and it may be located near the center, or close to the edge, of the area it serves.

The neighborhood school is particularly characteristic of the organization of elementary schools in urban areas. There, with younger children involved, concern is felt for having the schools close at hand and available along safe routes which avoid major traffic problems. In more sparsely populated areas the neighborhood concept tends to break down. Buses are then provided to bring children in from greater distances, and convenience in fixing bus routes may be a major factor in determining the attendance area of a school.

At the level of secondary schools the neighborhood concept tends to be somewhat less important. These schools are generally larger and serve more extensive geographic areas. Where a high school does not offer a comprehensive curriculum, but instead is specialized and offers either a vocational or college preparatory curriculum, it may serve quite a large area of the community. In communities with two or more high schools the student populations in each are derived from a group of "feeder" elementary schools and thus a high school acquires the population characteristics of the "feeder" schools.

A neighborhood school—however defined—reflects the economic, social, cultural, and racial characteristics of the area served. Since most Negroes in the North and West live in densely populated, racially homogeneous slum areas, the schools available to them are largely or entirely segregated. Negro discontent, then, grows largely out of the problems of these slum schools.

Slum schools have traditionally had their problems. Poverty, squalid and congested housing, and social and economic discrimination combine to produce higher rates of adult crime, juvenile delinquency, general disorder, and disease. Yet the successive waves of white immigrants who once filled the slums in time found ways to escape into the white mainstream of America. The fact that escape was possible supplied motivation for many who finally succeeded in getting away.

A great fraction of the slum dwellers in the 1960s, however, are not white and they face additional handicaps which stem from their race and the peculiar problems of their cultural isolation from the whites. Oriental minorities, principally on the West Coast, with more stable family organization, higher levels of motivation, and tighter self-discipline, are steadily finding it easier to become assimilated into the community at large. But the Spanish-speaking Puerto Ricans and Mexicans and the English-speaking American Negroes, burdened after centuries of slavery and peonage with far greater rates of family disorganization and illegitimacy, and lower levels of motivation and discipline, are still finding it difficult to escape.

Many Negroes in the North and West are recent immigrants from the South and they bring with them the inherited educational and social handicaps of their rural Southern background. Hoped-for employment does not always materialize and the combination of job discrimination and their own limited skills relegate them generally to the lowest-paying jobs or, worse yet, to chronic unemployment.

Other school problems grow out of housing. Population densities in areas occupied by Negroes in the cities of the North and West rise sharply above the levels in the same neighborhoods when earlier occupied by whites. Schools become overcrowded and in many instances operate on double shifts, providing each child with only a half-day of education. Elsewhere in the community, school populations drop in older white neighborhoods because the children have grown up and left. The result is that there are often empty classrooms and smaller classes in many white sections of a city and overcrowded and sometimes double-shift classes in others which are all or largely Negro.

Still other difficulties grow out of employment barriers faced by minority groups. Racial discrimination, particularly by many of the skilled craft unions, seriously affects vocational training programs. Pupils, seeing few prospects for employment after being specially trained for it, shun vocational programs. And job discrimination generally contributes to higher rates of dropping school altogether since there is little incentive to acquire an education when it cannot be gainfully used.

The problem of obtaining an adequate supply of interested and competent teachers for the overcrowded slum schools also haunts school administrators. A Baltimore school official admitted the use of some 1,100 uncertified elementary teachers, largely in the slum schools, during the 1961–62 school year. On Manhattan in the same year more than one-third of the teachers newly appointed to the schools rejected their assignments and looked for jobs elsewhere.

The hesitation of many teachers to serve in slum schools grows out of a variety of causes. Most teachers, middle-class in aspiration if not in fact, are under many pressures which direct them away from teaching in culturally disadvantaged schools. Schools of education generally train teachers on the assumption that "a child is a child"—and use the middle-class white child as the model to be taught. As a result many teachers are but little equipped to deal with the distinctive problems of communication barriers, economic deprivation, and social and cultural disadvantages of children in depressed-area schools. This, and factors of teacher aspiration to work in the "better" schools close to where the teacher lives, create attitudes which minimize the desire or willingness to teach in the slum schools.

Physical facilities in the slum school, too, are often inferior. Many buildings tend to be old and the pressures from excessive enrollments add further burdens on the physical plant and the educational program. Major programs to rehabilitate and enlarge facilities in crowded slum areas are to be found in most large cities today. Too often, however, it has remained true that the demands for additional classrooms have continued to outrun the rising supply.

The slum schools, then, are handicapped in many serious ways and protests on behalf of those forced to attend them can commonly be grounded on objections that they furnish inadequate educational opportunities. Since the troubles are often linked with segregation as well, many of the protests take the form of demands for increased integration.

The demands for school integration in the North and West have taken a variety of forms depending upon the particular situation on which attention focused. Understandably, some of the demands have been inconsistent with one another. At New Rochelle, for example, Negroes won a court order permitting free transfer from a largely Negro elementary school to predominantly white schools elsewhere in the city. A year later, groups at Philadelphia were opposing a free transfer policy on the ground that it permitted too many whites to run away from schools in which Negroes were enrolled.

Protests against segregation in schools around the periphery of Negro neighborhoods generally suggested one or more of three alternatives:

1) *Rezoning of attendance areas.* In some instances, it has been possible to show that school officials have apparently zoned schools to "contain" Negroes once they moved into a particular neighborhood. In other instances, zone lines remained unchanged from the days that whites occupied the entire area. In both these situations it is occasionally possible to show that existing zone lines may reasonably be changed to promote integration. Thus, it has been insisted that school authorities have a duty to rezone whether the resulting segregation has been the product of intentional board policy or merely a refusal to deal with the charging character of the neighborhoods involved.

2) *The Princeton Plan.* Another suggestion, taken from a plan installed at Princeton, New Jersey, in 1948, calls for reclassification of schools to handle fewer grades and thus serve larger geographic areas. This is accomplished by pairing two adjacent schools both of which cover grades from, say, kindergarten through the sixth. On reclassification, one of the "sister" schools handles all pupils in both attendance areas from kindergarten through third grade and

the other school serves both areas for grades four through six. By doubling the geographic area of each school it is occasionally possible to promote integration around the edges of segregated neighborhoods.

3) *Location of new school facilities.* The location of new facilities, either to replace over-age buildings or to handle the needs of increased enrollments, has frequently provoked much controversy. Obviously, the location of facilities can have substantial short-run effects upon the racial composition of a school.

These suggestions for promoting integration along boundaries between segregated neighborhoods often have only temporary effect. Boundaries between racial groups tend to be unstable, holding only where freeways, rivers, or railroad tracks block expansion. Elsewhere the segregated areas expand, sometimes abetted by "block-busting" techniques of unscrupulous realtors who panic whites into moving out as Negroes begin to move in. Integrated schools in these areas frequently become segregated again in relatively brief periods of time.

For schools deeper within segregated neighborhoods, other plans are suggested. Rezoning or reclassification of schools in these cases produces no change because of the homogeneous neighborhood patterns. In such situations the proposals involve moving some of the children out to uncrowded, predominantly white schools elsewhere in the city. Occasionally, protests have led to complete abandonment of a school, with resulting reassignment of all pupils to less segregated schools in other areas. The demands for transfers out of segregated areas are frequently coupled with insistence that bus service be provided without charge.

These open enrollment and free transfer policies merely scratch the surface. They provide means of escape for relatively small numbers of minority-group children who are strongly enough motivated to seek transfer. Most children, however, are left behind in congested, segregated schools.

To alleviate congestion, the urban school systems are busy with vast programs of new construction. Because of the high costs of acquiring additional land, much of this is going on at the sites of existing schools. Some systems—Chicago and Philadelphia are examples—are also using so-called mobile-unit classrooms, carried to a site on a trailer. These units are attractive and air-conditioned, but in Chicago particularly many Negroes regard them as symbols of a settled intent on the part of school officials to preserve segregation. And indeed, new school construction in segregated areas is increasingly coming under fire everywhere because of its failure to mitigate the effects of residential segregation.

There is broad agreement among educators that a policy of providing integrated experience for all children is a desirable objective if equality of educational opportunity is to be achieved. From this point on, however, there is real dispute among them over how much weight integration should be given in shaping school organization and educational practices.

Even in desegregated schools there are wide differences in classroom organization and teaching methods. These grow primarily out of the problem of dealing with differences in motivation, ability, and achievement among children at the same grade level. Most school systems make some efforts to group children according to one or more of these characteristics. In some instances, achievement grouping occurs within the classroom, with the teacher devoting attention to each group in turn. In other instances, achievement groups are isolated in separate classrooms. Less frequently, no achievement grouping is attempted and the entire class is considered as a heterogeneous unit.

The cultural deficiencies and poorer educational backgrounds among minority-group children tend to separate them at one end of the grouping scale. This means that many wind up in the "slow" group within the classroom or off in a separate classroom by themselves. There is much disagreement over the extent of damage which this kind of isolation does to social adjustment and ability to learn.

Some, placing greatest weight on the damage done by isolation, argue that properly trained teachers can handle heterogeneous classes without grouping. Others disagree, laying stress on the need to expand the horizons of the gifted child and to protect slow learners from situations in which the goals are beyond their reach.

The same sorts of differences grow out of discussing what to do about children in segregated schools. Those who strongly support policies of open enrollment and free transfer stress the value of an integrated education. They are met, however, by others who argue on behalf of strengthening the neighborhood school. The case for the neighborhood school is supported by a wide range of arguments.

Experimental programs in a number of school systems have produced striking results in upgrading the performance levels of disadvantaged children. A feature common to many of these is a concern for the child not only during the school day but in his neighborhood and his home. Social workers, school psychologists, and teachers deal with families and others with whom the child associates. Special efforts are made to enlist those around the child to encourage and support him in seeking an education. The child himself is placed in situations designed to expand his horizons and motivate him to set his own sights higher. The Banneker Group program at St. Louis and the Higher Horizons project in New York are notable examples of such endeavors. The "Great Cities" project sponsored by the Fund for the Advancement of Education has also launched experimental programs in a number of cities designed to improve educational opportunities for deprived children.

An interesting program at Hunter College in New York attacks the problems of segregated and culturally deprived schools on another front, that of training teachers for the job. This, a voluntary program open to education majors while still at the undergraduate level, places them in slum schools for their practice teaching.

Attacks are being made on still other fronts, among them on the kind of teaching materials furnished children in depressed-area schools. Beginning with the "Look, look, look. See, see, see" elementary readers, the conventional teaching materials describe a white, middle-class world which is as foreign to that of the slum child as the back of the moon. He never sees himself in that world except incidentally as a servant or some other distantly viewed figure. He does not understand that world and cannot see himself becoming part of it. In a few places, Detroit and New York among them, efforts are being made to create teaching materials that give the disadvantaged child a chance to identify himself and see a way to goals beyond anything he or his family ever experienced.

The disagreements among educators suggest that there is much to be learned before any specific program can be imposed with much more than a hunch that it would be better than some competing alternative. Whether or not open enrollment or free transfer programs are adopted, most children will remain in their neighborhood schools. And the neighborhood schools in depressed areas will require much more understanding and attention before many of the children in them can acquire the skills, confidence, and motivation that will be needed to move into middle-class status.

Indeed, programs to increase integration by siphoning off some small fraction of these children through open enrollment and free transfer mechanisms create other problems. Placing the child in a school far removed from his home environment makes it virtually impossible for the school to work closely with his family and neighborhood problems. Again, as happened in New Rochelle during the 1961–62 school year, if the child is too far out of step with the motivation and achievement of the other children in the school to which he transfers, the result can be a humiliating failure for the disadvantaged youngster and a hardening of attitudes against him among those who make the grade and see him fail.

There are questions, too, about the effects of open enrollment on the children who remain behind in the neighborhood schools. The children who transfer are likely to be the more strongly motivated, better achievers. Their absence only makes it more difficult to create good neighborhood schools with a wide range of goals to spur everyone along more rapidly.

The concept that public officials should become conscious of race —provided they do so benignly—represents a substantial departure from the position long asserted by and on behalf of Negroes in their fight against racial restrictions. They have fought for, and won in a number of states, legislation that prohibits keeping public records by race. They have insisted that colleges and universities not require photographs as a condition to admission and that job application forms contain no reference to race.

Indeed, the principal argument advanced in the Supreme Court in the cases which led to the school segregation decision of 1954 was that classifications based on race have no place in public education. "That the Constitution is color-blind is our dedicated belief," reads a key sentence in the brief submitted to the court on behalf of the Negro plaintiffs in the school segregation cases.

Yet the basic issue before the Supreme Court in 1954 was quite different from the question whether state officials could take racial considerations benignly into account. The question at that time was whether states could require separation of public schools by race in view of the obligation under the Fourteenth Amendment to provide all persons "equal protection of the laws." The court's answer was that public school segregation could not be required. "Separate educational facilities are inherently unequal," the court held. Neither then nor later did the court speak specifically to the question whether the Constitution required public officials to be color-blind, although the concept of color blindness was implied in a series of cryptic decisions which the court handed down thereafter that invalidated laws requiring segregation of parks, buses, restaurants, and the like.

Many questions remain to be decided in determining how far and in what manner state authority may—or perhaps must—constitutionally take race into account in shaping public policy.

It was abundantly clear by the beginning of 1963 that the process of doing away with the dual school systems in the South has endlessly taken racial considerations into account. Everyone involved in the process has done so—the community at large, school officials, even the courts. The patterns and practices of school operation have to be understood before solutions can be worked out. In this respect the actions of public authority are not color-blind.

It is also reasonably clear that, while racial considerations can be taken into account, they cannot be used invidiously against any racial group. Thus, school zone lines cannot be gerrymandered to contain Negroes. And even with racial considerations not in the picture, substantial questions of equal protection are raised by claims of serious overcrowding or that schools are badly deficient in physical plant, quality of teaching, or curricular offerings. Where any such questions develop, the Constitution probably affords a basis for judicial relief.

Other questions, however, are more difficult. As long as private discrimination produces residential segregation, it will affect the racial composition of the schools themselves. The state, whether it likes it or not, must take the community as it finds it. Since segregation cannot under the circumstances be erased, racial considerations must be taken into account. What is needed, it seems, is some flexibility of choice among reasonable educational alternatives to avoid placing any group at a disadvantage because of its race.

Where it can be shown that the practices of school authorities operate purposely to place Negroes at a racial disadvantage, judicial relief can be expected. There are, however, difficult and delicate problems in fixing the Constitutional line that measures the extent to which judicial relief may be forthcoming. Several illustrations suffice to make the point. San Francisco closed down a junior high school after protests that its student population would be 60 per cent Negro. Was this a "separate"—or "segregated"—and hence "unequal" school in the sense that the Constitution would require judicial action to put it out of business or to require alteration of its racial composition? Or was the action merely one which the political processes of the community are free to take—or not take? Again, it has been suggested that Negroes may be entitled to compensatory educational benefits because of damage done by past practices of racial segregation. It hardly seems constitutionally possible that the state can establish a compensatory program exclusively for Negroes and bar similarly handicapped whites who attend the same school.

Yet the controversy over de facto segregation in the schools of the North and West is reaching the federal courts under a wide range of claimed Constitutional deprivations. The most celebrated case thus far came out of New Rochelle, New York, where the court found that school board practices more than a decade earlier caused the development of a segregated elementary school. This produced a court order permitting pupils in that school to transfer to any uncrowded school in the district. Cases like this one, which produce findings of intentional segregation practices, manifestly demonstrate a need for some corrective action. The far harder question is that of determining what kind of relief is appropriate; a number of Negro children in New Rochelle suffered serious setbacks when they transferred to classes maintaining higher academic standards.

For wholly understandable reasons, Negroes continue to insist that school authorities have the duty to mitigate the effects of residential segregation. The farthest reach of judicial language on this point came from the case in Hempstead, Long Island, in April 1962. The school board moved to dismiss the case before trial on the ground that residential patterns, not school board practices, produced the school segregation. The court denied the motion to dismiss, indicating the board had an obligation to mitigate the effects of segregation, whatever its cause. The board's obligation, the court said, could be discharged either by doing something to relieve segregation or by "a conclusive demonstration that no circumstantially possible effort can effect any significant mitigation." Thus, where the Hempstead case departed from earlier cases was in the court's insistence that the state, in operating its schools, has a Constitutional obligation to mitigate the effects of private discrimination.

So far as the drive against school segregation in the North and West insists that school authorities become benignly color-conscious, it raises many questions still to be resolved. In a great many situations public authority is not, and cannot be, color-blind. The earlier insistence by Negroes that the Constitution required the state to be color-blind seems clearly inconsistent with the minimum need of the state at least to be sufficiently color conscious to make sure that invidious racial discrimination is not being practiced in its name.

The courts, too, in passing on claims of racial discrimination, have to take race into account. That the Fourteenth Amendment requires judicial relief against intentional segregation of public schools has been settled. Whether the courts are required by the Constitution to insist upon maximum integration where segregation is attributable to private discrimination is another question. Particularly is it another question in light of the deep differences among educators about methods for overcoming social, cultural, and educational disadvantages suffered by those isolated from the mainstream of American life.

Merely that judicial action may not be available to compel maximum integration, however, does not suggest that the state cannot experiment with such educational programs. Nor does it suggest any impropriety in having Negroes and others make political demands for these things. It does suggest that there are certain questions which must be addressed to the political processes of the community and state rather than to the courts. And where state legislation requires affirmative integration programs, courts could be looked to for enforcement of the statutes; but judicial action in such cases would flow from legislation rather than from the federal Constitution.

Manifestly, public education has a great burden to discharge in helping disadvantaged children develop their abilities to the fullest extent possible. But public education seems hardly equipped to carry the whole load of mitigating and ending all the disadvantages minority groups suffer from private discrimination. Other efforts, both public and private, must continue on many fronts if America is to make good on its Constitutional commitment to equality for all its people. Fortunately, more and more Americans are aware of this. And while much more effort is still required, significant changes are taking place in lessening job discrimination, in breaking up patterns of housing discrimination, and in generally providing more and more reasons for hope among the nation's minority groups that they can share our democratic ideals on equal terms.

Selection 11

EDUCATIONAL PROVISIONS OF THE CIVIL RIGHTS ACT OF 1964*

Title IV: Public Education

Under this title the U.S. Office of Education is authorized to:

a. conduct a national survey to determine the availability of equal educational opportunity;

b. provide technical assistance, upon request, to help States, political subdivisions or school districts carry out school desegregation plans;

---

* From *Civil Rights Digest*, Washington, D.C.: special bulletin by U. S. Commission on Civil Rights, August, 1964.

c. arrange training institutes to prepare teachers and other school personnel to deal with desegregation problems;

d. make grants enabling school boards to employ specialists for in-service training programs.

In addition, the Attorney General is authorized to file civil suits seeking to compel desegregation of public schools, including public colleges.

Before filing such a suit the Attorney General must have received a signed complaint from a pupil or parent and must have determined that the complainant, according to standards set forth in the Act, is unable to bring the action. The Attorney General is also required to notify the school board and give it a reasonable period of time to correct the alleged condition before filing suit.

Title VI: Federally Assisted Programs

Under this title every Federal agency which provides financial assistance through grants, loans or contracts is required to eliminate discrimination on the grounds of race, color or national origin in these programs.

For example, this title would require the following:

a. hospitals constructed with Federal funds would have to serve all patients without regard to race, color or national origin;

b. elementary and secondary schools constructed, maintained and operated with Federal funds would have to admit children without regard to race, color or national origin;

c. State employment services financed by Federal funds would have to refer qualified job applicants for employment without discrimination;

d. schools for the deaf and the blind operated with Federal funds would have to serve the deaf and blind of any color;

e. colleges and universities receiving funds for their general operation or for the construction of special facilities, such as research centers, would have to admit students without discrimination;

f. construction contractors receiving funds under Federal public works programs would have to hire employees without discrimination.

Action by a Federal agency to carry out the requirements of this title may include the terminating of programs where discrimination is taking place or refusal to grant assistance to such a program.

Each agency is required to publish rules or regulations to carry out the purposes of the title. These rules and regulations are subject to the approval of the President.

PART II

VOTING RIGHTS FOR THE NEGRO

In our country, ballots not bullets decide issues. The right to vote is precious because it gives a citizen the power to select the officials who make and carry out the laws. Those who are deprived of the right to vote because of their color or religion or national origin become a type of second-class citizen. They cannot influence the decisions of government.

The Negro's drive for suffrage is connected with his demand for the right to participate in the selection of his representatives. Southern white partisan opposition to Negro suffrage is based on practice and prejudice, as well as fear that the Negro's vote will give him the power to improve his competitive position in the community and to end the pattern of racial segregation.

The Fifteenth Amendment, ratified in 1870, declared that the right to vote shall not be denied because of race, color, or previous condition of servitude. Southern states, however, managed to deny the Negro this right by a variety of methods.

Selections 12a–12d

VOTING IN MISSISSIPPI: A CASE STUDY*

The United States Commission on Civil Rights, established by the Civil Rights Act of 1957, is empowered to investigate and report

* From *Voting in Mississippi: A Report of the U. S. Civil Rights Commission*, Washington, D. C.: 1965.

on racial discrimination. The following excerpts from the Commission's report on Voting in Mississippi: A Case Study, *is representative of interference with the right to vote.*

12a. History of Mississippi Voting Legislation

At the time of the Presidential election of 1964 it was estimated that more than 70 percent of the white voting age population of Mississippi, but less than 7 percent of its Negro voting age population, were registered to vote. Mississippi had by far the lowest rate of Negro registration and the greatest disparity between the rates of white and Negro registration of any Southern State. The causes of this disparity are rooted in history. An examination of the development of voting laws in Mississippi indicates that disfranchisement of the Negro is the result of a deliberate State policy pursued over many years. . . .

Reconstruction

Negroes first began to register and vote in Mississippi under the military government established at the conclusion of the [Civil] War. Following the passage of the Reconstruction Act of 1867, an election was held to select delegates to a constitutional convention. Negroes were permitted to register and vote freely in this election and they participated in large numbers. The Black and Tan Convention (as it was known), which assembled in 1868, numbered 16 Negroes among its 100 members. It drew up a constitution eliminating most qualifications for voting and extending the franchise to Negroes on the same basis as whites. This constitution was ratified in 1869. For the first time Negroes were permitted by State law to vote, and, in fact, comprised a majority of the electorate.

The peak of Negro political participation was reached between 1870 and 1873. In 1870 there were five Negro State senators, and the representatives from Adams, Washington, Warren, and the other river counties were all Negroes. The legislature met in January and promptly ratified both the 14th and 15th amendments to the United States Constitution, thus clearing the way for readmission to the Union. It also chose United States Senators, one of whom, Hiram R. Revels, became the first Negro to sit in the Senate. In February 1870 Mississippi was readmitted by Act of Congress upon the condition that the constitution of the State "shall never be so amended or changed as to deprive any citizen or class of citizens of the United States of the right to vote who are entitled to vote by the constitution herein recognized . . ."

In 1871 the first elections of local officials were held under the new constitution. Some Negroes were chosen as county officers in these elections, and their number was increased after the local elections of 1873.

1875–1890

During this period, white opposition to Negro political activity began to organize. Its principal weapons were economic intimidation and violence. In the election of 1875 local Democratic political clubs announced that no Negro who voted for a Republican could hope for any form of employment the following year. Checkers were stationed at the polls, and groups of armed men intercepted Negroes on their way to register. Negro political leaders were threatened that continued activity would result in death. As a result of these tactics, Negro voting diminished throughout the State and the Democrats returned to power.

The election of 1875 resulted in the defeat of the Radical government in Mississippi. In the words of a Congressional investigating committee in 1876, the new political leaders "secured power by fraud and force, and, if left to themselves, they will by fraud and force retain it."

The period between 1876 and 1890 was marked by enactment of the first of modern laws to discourage Negro voting. The Election Law of 1876 placed registration of voters in the hands of local registration officers appointed by the Governor. A prospective voter was required to give detailed information about his residence, including the election district, township, and ward of the town in which he lived and worked. Any error or confusion in his response was used as a basis for rejection. Despite this, Negroes continued to comprise a majority of the electorate. But after 1876 they were allowed to vote and hold office only under the direction and control of the white minority.

During these years white dominance was maintained by fraud and violence. Corruption became so pervasive that demands were raised to substitute a legalized disfranchisement of the Negro. In the words of one prominent white Mississippian:

Sir, it is no secret that there has not been a full vote and a fair count in Mississippi since 1875—that we have been preserving the ascendancy of the white people by revolutionary methods. In plain words, we have been stuffing ballot boxes, committing perjury and here and there in the State carrying the elections by fraud and violence until the whole machinery for elections was about to rot down.

The Convention of 1890

Early in 1890 the Mississippi legislature called for a convention to prepare a new constitution. The State of Mississippi, whose population at that time was almost 58 percent Negro, elected 134 delegates: 133 white men and 1 Negro. When the convention met in August 1890, its purpose, candidly stated by the delegates, was to secure white supremacy. . . .

The first device chosen was a $2 poll tax. . . .

Although poll tax receipts were designated for educational purposes, it is clear that the primary purpose of the tax was to restrict the franchise. According to one writer, it was adopted because

the leaders of the black counties were eventually able to persuade the convention that educational and property qualifications, with the addition of a poll tax, would be the best means of eliminating the negro vote.

As a delegate observed: "The very idea of a poll qualification is tantamount to the State of Mississippi, saying to the Negro: 'We will give you two dollars not to vote.'"

• • •

In 1934 the poll tax requirement was extended to primary elections. It is currently required both for State primary and general elections in Mississipi.

As the second major instrument of disfranchisement, the convention adopted a "literacy" test for registration. The test adopted required an applicant for registration either to read a section of the constitution *or* to understand the same when read to him *or* to give a reasonable interpretation thereof. The reading clause would, one delegate noted, take advantage of the fact that "in Mississippi at least 10 percent of the white, and 60 percent of the colored population can neither read nor write." The understanding and interpretation clauses were, according to proponents, "designed to furnish a loophole to qualify illiterate whites. . . ."

No standards were provided to control the registrar's choice of constitutional section. In fact, at least one delegate commented that the registrar could determine who would qualify by choosing hard or easy sections of the constitution.

The constitution of 1890 adopted by the convention was never submitted to or ratified by the people of Mississippi. The Judiciary Committee of the convention determined that such ratification was not required for lawful adoption.

The new constitutional provisions had quick and lasting effect.

While in 1867 almost 70 percent of the Negro voting age population was registered, by 1892, two years after the adoption of the new constitution, less than 6 percent of the Negro voting age population was registered. In 1946 United States Senator Theodore Bilbo summed up the role of section 244:

> The poll tax won't keep 'em from voting. What keeps 'em from voting is section 244 of the Constitution of 1890 that Senator George wrote. It says that a man to register must be able to read and explain the Constitution or explain the Constitution when read to him. . . . And then Senator George wrote a Constitution that damn few white men and no niggers at all can explain. . . .

Section 244 remained unchanged until the early 1950s. . . .

The legislature met next in 1954, during a period of heightened racial feeling following the Supreme Court's school desegregation decision. It again adopted a resolution to amend section 244 similar to the one rejected in 1952. This time the resolution also required the applicant to demonstrate "a reasonable understanding of the duties and obligations of citizenship under a constitutional form of government." Exempted from its requirements were all persons registered before January 1, 1954, *i.e.,* about one-twentieth of the eligible Negroes and roughly two-thirds of the adult white population. . . .

Other provisions of the constitution of 1890 furthered Negro disfranchisement. Various disabilities to voting were imposed which were thought to reflect the racial characteristics of Negroes. The requirement of long residency, two years in the State and one year in the election district, was aimed at the supposed "disposition of young Negroes . . . to change their homes and precincts every year." The disfranchising crimes were those to which Negroes were thought to be particularly prone: burglary, theft, arson, and obtaining money or goods under false pretenses. The more serious felonies of murder, rape, or assault were not included. . . .

The White Primary

Section 244 and the other provisions of the 1890 constitution did not long remain the sole legal barrier to Negro political participation. Even in 1890 State leaders foresaw that the number of Negroes educationally qualified for the franchise would continue to increase. Many feared that:

> It may be only a question of time when there will again be a majority of qualified negro voters in the State, and when it will become necessary to place further limitations on the elective franchise in order to secure the proper administration of the public affairs of the State.

Prior to 1902 candidates for office were selected at a party convention. In that year the legislature provided that party nominations for State and local offices should thereafter be made by primary election. The State executive committee of any party was authorized to exclude any person from its primary. . . . Since nomination by the Democratic Party in Mississippi was tantamount to election in all statewide, county, and most local elections, exclusion from the primary was, in effect, total disfranchisement.

Party elections remained closed to Negroes until 1944, when the Supreme Court held the white primary unconstitutional in *Smith* vs. *Allwright*. . . .

During the next two years the Mississippi legislature enacted measures to put the exclusion of Negroes from primaries on a basis designed to survive challenge under *Smith* vs. *Allwright*. . . .

Recent Developments

The success with which this system of election laws has operated to exclude Negroes is reflected in the following table of Negro and white registration at various times up to 1955.

Year	Negro voting age population[a]	Negro registration	Percent of Negro voting age population registered	White voting age population[a]	White registration	Percent of white voting age population registered
1867	98,926	[b] 60,167	66.9	84,784	[b] 46,636	55.0
1892	150,409	[c] 8,615	5.7	120,611	[c] 68,127	56.5
1896	198,647	[d] 16,234	8.2	150,530	[d] 108,998	72.4
1899	198,647	[e] 18,170	9.1	150,530	[e] 122,724	81.5
1955	495,138	[f] 21,502	4.3	710,639	[f] 423,456	59.6

[a] Nearest decennial census is used for each voting age population figure, male only for the census years 1870–1900; thereafter male and female.

[b] *Jackson Weekly Clarion,* Sept. 19, 1867, p. 2, col. 1.

[c] Wharton, *op. cit. supra* note 14, at 215.

[d] *Biennial Report of Secretary of State to Legislature of Mississippi for the Years 1896 and 1897,* 68.

[e] *Biennial Report of Secretary of State to Legislature of Mississippi for the Years 1898 and 1899,* 171.

[f] U. S. Department of Justice figures, statement of Burke Marshall, T. 257.

In 1957 Congress enacted legislation authorizing the Attorney General to bring suit to prevent denial of the right to vote based on race, color, or national origin. This authority was strengthened by the Civil Rights Act of 1960 which required the maintenance and production of registration and voting records and authorized the appointment of voting referees where a pattern or practice of discrimination was found. With this authority, the Department of Justice in 1960 began a program of investigation and litigation in Mississippi.

The Mississippi legislature responded by enacting laws imposing new qualifications for electors and by creating new obstacles to Federal litigation. . . .

The litigation program of the Department of Justice first bore fruit on April 10, 1962, when the Court of Appeals issued a temporary injunction directing the registrar of Forrest County to assist Negro applicants as he had previously assisted whites, to ignore insignificant errors and omissions on Negroes' forms, and to cease requiring that each unsuccessful Negro applicant wait six months before reapplying. . . .

This case was widely publicized in Mississippi and the legislature reacted promptly. On April 17 bills were introduced. . . .

Registration Procedure

The registration procedure created by these and earlier laws currently operates in the following manner. An applicant for registration must go to the office of the registrar, which is usually in the county courthouse. The registrar gives him an application blank, the form of which is dictated by the State Election Commission, but the format of which varies considerably among the counties. (Page 329 shows a sample form). The applicant must then complete the form perfectly without any assistance.

Questions 1 through 17 request such information as the applicant's name, age, occupation, residence, citizenship, and criminal record. Question 18 requires him to copy a section of the Mississippi constitution selected by the registrar. Question 19 requires him to write an interpretation of the section he has copied. Question 20 calls for a description of the duties of citizenship under a constitutional form of government. Finally, he must sign the form in two places: under the appropriate oath and at the foot of the application.

After completing this test the applicant waits at least 30 days, during which time his name and address are published twice in a local newspaper. He is not notified at the end of the waiting period whether he has passed or failed. In order to determine this, he must return to the registrar's office. If he qualifies, he signs the registration book and becomes a registered voter. If he fails to qualify, he may take the test again.

It is a characteristic of this system that the registrar in each county has extremely broad discretion in determining the qualifications of applicants. He must determine whether the applicant is of good moral character, has demonstrated a reasonable understanding of the duties and obligations of citizenship under a constitutional form of government, and has properly interpreted a section of the Mississippi constitution. The statutes do not prescribe any standards to control or guide the registrar in making these determinations.

The history of Mississippi voting legislation makes it clear that stringent registration requirements were established and broad discretion vested in local registrars for one reason—to disfranchise Negro citizens. When barriers against Negro voting were threatened by new Federal laws in the 1950's, the Mississippi legislature reacted by making registration even more difficult. . . .

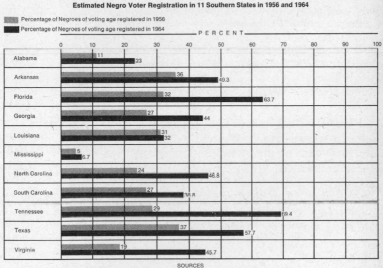

Estimated Negro Voter Registration in 11 Southern States in 1956 and 1964

Percentage of Negroes of voting age registered in 1956
Percentage of Negroes of voting age registered in 1964

State	1956	1964
Alabama	11	23
Arkansas	36	40.3
Florida	32	63.7
Georgia	27	44
Louisiana	31	32
Mississippi	5	6.7
North Carolina	24	46.8
South Carolina	27	38.8
Tennessee	29	69.4
Texas	37	57.7
Virginia	19	45.7

SOURCES
1956 percentages: Price, **The Negro and The Ballot in the South 9** (Southern Regional Council, 1959).
1964 percentages: Testimony of Wiley A. Branton, Director, Voter Education Project, Southern Regional Council, T 177-81.

12b.   Intimidation, Reprisal, and Fear

In all but a few Mississippi counties the number of Negroes registered to vote is so low that registration and voting are acts rendering the individual Negro conspicuous. In such counties the Commission found that fear of economic or physical reprisal influenced the individual Negro in determining whether to attempt to register or to vote. According to one Negro leader testifying before the Commission, Negroes "are afraid of physical violence, economic reprisals, losing jobs, or not getting jobs" as a result of such attempts. The Commission's purpose in exploring this subject was to evaluate the extent to which such fears have inhibited Negro registration and voting.

Interference by Public Officials

Incidents of violence at registration or polling places appear to affect seriously the willingness of Negroes to attempt to register or vote. Reprisal after attempted registration may produce a similar result. The Commission investigated allegations that such incidents had occurred in Humphreys, Tallahatchie, and Jefferson Counties.

In Humphreys County two elderly Negro women testified at the hearing that G. H. Hood, registrar of the county, abused them verbally when they attempted to register. Mrs. Mary Oliver Welsh, a woman in her 70's, described her conversation with the registrar:

MRS. WELSH. Well, when I went to register, the registrar asked me what did I come down there for. I told him "to register."

He said, "register? For what?"

I told him, "to vote."

He said, "vote? For what?"

And I told him I didn't know what I was coming to vote for.

He hollered at me and scared me so, I told him I didn't know what I came to vote for. I was just going to vote.

Both Mrs. Welsh and Mrs. Daisy Griffin, her companion, rely upon government surplus commodities, such as flour, meal, and rice, for some of their food. Before going to the courthouse they had expressed concern to civil rights workers in Belzoni that an attempt to register would cost them their commodities. They both testified that when they attempted to register Mr. Hood warned them about commodities. In the words of Mrs. Welsh: "Well, he told me I was going to get in trouble, and he wasn't going to give me no commodities. That's what he said." Mrs. Griffin corroborated this testimony.

When asked if she had passed the test, Mrs. Welsh replied: "Well, I didn't go back there. I didn't go back. After I went there and he scared me so bad, I didn't go back to see was I passed or no."

Other Negro witnesses testified that this registrar had referred to commodities, questioned them about their motives in seeking to vote, or harassed them by tapping on the table with a pencil while they completed their forms. In his testimony, Mr. Hood denied he had made the statements attributed to him.

The Commission also investigated the conduct of the sheriff of Humphreys County towards Negroes who attempted to register. Negro witnesses testified that their pictures had been taken as they left the registration office. The sheriff admitted he and his deputies had taken such pictures and submitted six prints of Negroes in response to the Commission's subpena. He had not taken pictures of white applicants. He justified the photography by claiming that he wanted to show how peaceful Humphreys County had been in spite of the adverse publicity which the county and the State had received. Also, he said: "I wanted them for my own use. I take a lot of pictures." When asked whether he considered the effect which taking these photographs outside the registrar's office might have on Negro applicants, Sheriff Purvis replied, "I didn't consider it; no."

In two cases the sheriff's office arrested Negroes shortly after they had attempted to register. In the first case, Mrs. Mary Thomas of Belzoni, a grocery store owner, applied for registration in September 1964. As she was leaving the registration office, someone snapped her picture. Fifteen minutes after arriving home she was arrested by a deputy sheriff, pursuant to a warrant issued that day. The charge against her was selling beer without a State license. She was taken to jail and bond was set at $1,000. The following week she pleaded guilty and was fined $365.71; in addition, county officials suspended her permit to sell beer for one year.

The cost of the missing license was $15. Mrs. Thomas had been selling beer for eight years without such a license prior to attempting to register. During this time and at the time of her arrest, she possessed a current Federal Tax Stamp, as well as State and municipal beer permits. Sheriff Purvis testified he did not know at the time Mrs. Thomas was arrested that she had applied for registration. Several weeks earlier he had sent out notices to some 40 persons that licenses were required. According to him, all except Mrs. Thomas paid the tax or stopped selling beer. He further testified that once, years ago, he had arrested a white man for selling beer without a license in connection with a prosecution for selling whiskey in violation of the prohibition law.

The second case involved Mrs. Alene Hunter of Belzoni, who attempted to register on January 4, 1965. Pursuant to law, her name was published in the *Belzoni Banner,* a local newspaper, on the seventh of January. The next day she was arrested at her home by a deputy sheriff on a charge of passing a bad check in the amount of $5.15. It is a practice in some rural communities to secure a sale on credit by requiring the purchaser to sign a check for the amount of the credit even though the merchant knows his customer has no bank account. The storekeeper may then initiate criminal proceedings against the customer for passing a bad check in the event the bill is not paid. It appears that the check signed by Mrs. Hunter was of this character, since it was made out by the store owner and drawn on a bank at which Mrs. Hunter had never had an account. Mrs. Hunter testified concerning her arrest, as follows:

MRS. HUNTER. On January the 8th I was at home making bed; the deputy sheriff came to my house and he asked me was I Alene Hunter; I told him yes.

He said, "Well, Alene, I came after you."

I said, "What for?"

He said, "Well, I didn't exactly come after you," he said, "but I have a warrant to pick you up for $5.15." He said, "You owe it." I said, "Yes." I said, "I owe $5.15 to the store." He said, "Do you have it?"

I said I had the $5. But he said, "It's more now; it's $12.15."

I said, "Well, I don't have the $12."

"Well," he said, "you have to go with me."

* * *

MR. TAYLOR. Where did he take you?

MRS. HUNTER. To the jail. And when I got inside the jail he sit at a desk, so he wrote something down on the book and he said, "Alene," he said, "when I turn this key on you it will be $14.50. Do you know it?"

I said, "I'm going by what you say." So he put me in jail.

Mrs. Hunter was released 15 minutes after she had been locked up. The deputy sheriff advised her that her fine had been paid but refused to say by whom. She felt she knew why she had been arrested:

MR. TAYLOR. Why do you think you were arrested, Mrs. Hunter?

MRS. HUNTER. Because I registered.

Intimidation and reprisal by registrars or local officials against Negroes who have attempted to register is not confined to Humphreys County. There is a history of such practices in various parts of the State. In addition to reports of such incidents received by the Commission some of these cases have been the subject of judicial inquiry. In Walthall County in 1961 a voter registration worker accompanying Negro applicants for registration was struck by the registrar with the butt of a gun. Later that day he was arrested and charged with breach of the peace. When the Federal Government intervened, the prosecution was dropped. In Rankin County in 1963 the sheriff, armed with a blackjack, and several deputy sheriffs assaulted and beat several Negroes waiting in the registrar's office. In Holmes County in 1963 two firebombs were thrown into the house of Hartman Turnbow, a local Negro farmer and a leader in the registration effort, a few weeks after he and others had attempted to register. Turnbow and four voter registration workers were arrested the next day on suspicion of arson. The grand jury returned a "no bill" on the arson charge, but indicted Turnbow and his wife for unlawful cohabitation. They pleaded guilty and paid the fine.

Private Violence

In Tallahatchie County, the Commission investigated the effect of threats of violence by private citizens on the registration and voting process. Tallahatchie is an agricultural county at the eastern edge of the Delta with a population of 30,000, of which approximately 53 percent is Negro. The county is particularly significant because of the contrasting progress of registration in neighboring Panola County. In both counties the Department of Justice had been successful in simplifying the registration test.

On October 16, 1961, the Department of Justice brought an action against the Panola County registrar and a month later, a similar suit was instituted against the Tallahatchie registrar. At the time, there was one Negro registered in Panola County and none in Tallahatchie.

In May 1964 the District Court directed the Panola County registrar to cease using the constitutional interpretation test. The Court further directed him to register Negroes who demonstrated literacy by completing the preliminary questions concerning name, age, and residence, and by copying a brief section of the Mississippi constitution. Under the decree they were entitled to such help as they might need. A month later a Federal District Judge ordered the Tallahatchie County registrar to register all applicants who were able to complete the preliminary questions. Under this decree, applicants were not required to copy or interpret any constitutional section.

By the end of November 1964, about a thousand Negroes had succeeded in registering in Panola County while only 64 Negroes in Tallahatchie County had attempted to register. The Commission sought to determine the factors producing such a wide difference in Negro registration attempts under similar circumstances.

In August 1964, the first group of Negroes in Tallahatchie attempted to register under the new court-imposed system. They were accompanied by civil rights workers and Justice Department representatives. When they reached the county courthouse, 25 to 30 white spectators were standing outside with several county law officers. The Negroes were directed to stand on the lawn outside the courthouse and permitted to enter four at a time to register. Each applicant was photographed as he approached the registrar's office. While the second group of four was taking the test, those who had finished were directed to stand outside in the yard. A Negro witness, Mr. Jesse Brewer, described the scene:

When we got back out there, there were about 65 gathered around there. A lot more white people drove up there in pickup trucks with gun racks on them. They had guns on them and one ranch wagon comes with three white men with guns and they told us, "you niggers get away from the courthouse. You don't have any business up here." They circled the courthouse about three or four times and when they registered all the people who were up there, the sheriff told us, we did what we came up there to do and to get out of town. . . .

As the Negroes drove away, they were followed by the ranch wagon and cursed by its occupants. The Justice Department attorneys who had accompanied Mr. Brewer left him at the entrance to the dead-end road leading to his home. Shortly thereafter, two pickup trucks drove up.

MR. BREWER. After they passed the house they stopped, parked, got out and turned around and came back and drove around slow, and between that time and night I reckon seven, eight cars came in, pickups, and all of them had these same gun racks in the back of them and the guns, and these two to three guns, in the back window of the truck where you could see. . . . All night after twelve o'clock they would come in. Sometime they would have the lights off, two or three at a time . . . so when they got up near the house they would flash the lights on, go on by and cut them back off. That went on regularly for 3 weeks, I know.

• • •

COMMISSIONER HESBURGH. Mr. Brewer, were you afraid when all of this was going on?

MR. BREWER. Yes, sure was.

According to Mr. Brewer this experience was directly responsible for the failure of at least one group of Negroes to attempt to register.

MR. TAYLOR. Is what happened to you known to other people in your community?

MR. BREWER. Well, no sir. Well, they know I went down to register. I didn't tell them the bad part of it. I told them the good part because 35 or 40 had promised they would go the next day.

MR. TAYLOR. You don't think the word got around about the cars around your house, the trucks around your house?

MR. BREWER. That was the reason why they didn't go the next day because they seen all them cars and guns and everybody. They got scared and in fact they didn't go into the fields for about the next week. They stayed hid in the woods, everybody.

In Panola County there were few reported incidents of violence or intimidation accompanying Negro registration. Civil rights workers were able to operate effectively and the success of the registration drive was attributed by witnesses to their activities. A similar drive did not occur in Tallahatchie because the workers were reportedly "afraid to come to Tallahatchie and work" and because local Negroes were afraid to house them. With these incidents of violence and the absence of encouragement from the outside, few Negroes were willing to attempt to register in Tallahatchie County.

Fear of violence may not only deter registration but in rural counties may also prevent voting. Registration takes place at the county courthouse, while ballots are cast at polling places frequently located in isolated rural areas. The Commission heard testimony from several Negroes who were able to register but who were prevented from voting or afraid to vote.

One witness, Mr. James Rayburn, who had registered in 1963, attempted to vote in that year. He believed himself to be the only Negro registered to vote in his election district. As he approached the rural polling place at Dogwood Flats he was met by a white man who stopped him outside the building: "He asked me where I was going. I told him I was going to vote. The white man said, 'Well, you won't vote here,' and he begun to curse." The witness then entered the polling place. Inside another white man informed him that the election officer was absent.

MR. RAYBURN. He . . . walked back to the door and said, "you go out there and . . . wait out there under that tree." And I stood and looked at him and said, "Under the tree?" He said, "Yes, go out there and wait under the tree." And I walked off and the man that challenged me as I was going in, he challenged me again and this time he had a stick with a piece of iron on it.

He asked me where did I live. I told him. Asked me my name. I told him. He said "I'll make sure"—he cursed again—"that you won't vote no more. You vote now, you won't vote any more."

I would have voted if they would have allowed me, regardless of what he said. But see, the man in there told me to go out and get under the tree, and I knew out under the tree wasn't no place to vote, and I didn't sit around because he might have been building up to most anything. You could see he had a knife or pistol or something and I had just nothing but my hand, and that's just Negro bone.

When asked what he was told would happen if he voted, Mr. Rayburn replied: "They would kill me." He left the polling place without voting and said he did not dare return to vote in November 1964.

VICE CHAIRMAN PATTERSON. You said you didn't want to go alone to Dogwood Flats to vote. Would you go alone now?

Mr. Rayburn. I would. I believe I would, but I would seek better protection, or some protection.

Vice Chairman Patterson. Where would you go to get that protection?

Mr. Rayburn. Possibly I [would] have to pull several different strings. I might not go directly to the law, but I might pull the strings with some fellows who would have influence over the law.

Vice Chairman Patterson. A white man?

Mr. Rayburn. Yes.

Another witness, Mrs. Adlena Hamlett, a retired school teacher, was one of the first Negroes to register in Tallahatchie. She had registered to vote in 1962. When her name was published in the newspaper pursuant to State law, she returned home to find a life-sized effigy of a woman hung above her mail box. Asked why she thought this was done, she testified, "to scare me." Although she did go to the county seat to register, she said that fear of violence made her unwilling to go to her polling place to vote in the elections which followed.

In Jefferson County, located in southwest Mississippi, the voting age Negro population is approximately 3,500—more than double that of the white. Yet only a single Negro is registered. The Commission heard testimony of an attempt to register by two Negro families which resulted in a visit from the Ku Klux Klan. Mrs. Dorothy Mae Foster stated that she, her husband, brother-in-law, and sister-in-law took the registration test in September 1963. A few weeks later she and her sister-in-law were each visited by a party of five men who warned them to withdraw their names. They handed her a card.

Mrs. Foster replied, "Those names are signed in ink and they are there to stay." One of the men answered that someone would return. None of their group succeeded in passing the test and they were not visited again. Since that time, no Negroes are known to have attempted to register in Jefferson County.

The Legacy of Violence

Violence in reprisal for registration or voting has an immediate impact upon the willingness of Negroes to attempt to register or vote. A history of violence may have a similar impact even in the absence of recent incidents. In a county with a history of repeated episodes of brutality by law enforcement officers or where night riders have engaged in violence, Negroes may be expected to approach the registration process with great hesitation. Their apprehension is magnified when recent incidents of violence or reprisal in other areas in Mississippi or in neighboring States suggest that past practices in their county may be revived. The feeling of fear has become so ingrained that one witness described it as, "an inherent pattern, . . . [a] reluctance to come forward on all matters . . . something that is handed down . . . from one generation . . . to another."

A history of violence appeared to be an important contributing factor preventing Negro political participtaion in Carroll County. This county lies in the hills at the eastern edge of the Delta. While Negroes make up roughly half the voting age population of 5700, only five were registered to vote at the time of the hearing. Four had been registered in 1959 following the voiding of a murder conviction on the ground that Negroes had been systematically excluded from the jury rolls. Because Mississippi law at that time required jurors be drawn from among registered voters, the sheriff requested the four to register and the registrar assisted them.

One of the Negro farmers who had been registered in this way, Mr. Jake Cain, subsequently asked the former registrar who had helped him to register, whether he would be allowed to vote. He was told that there might be trouble and that he should see the sheriff. This Mr. Cain was unwilling to do:

> But I wanted him since he guided me in the registering. I wanted him to guide me through the voting. I wanted him to go like he did when he registered me, for some protection. But, he wouldn't go, didn't go. He told me to go alone.

He never attempted to vote. Asked why, Mr. Cain replied, "Well, we was raised kind of on the atmosphere that kept us under the fear of even asking, going up to vote."

The atmosphere of danger in Carroll County is rooted in a history of violence by its white community against local Negroes. The incidents, which are part of the county's folklore, began with a mass killing of Negroes attending a trial in the county courthouse in 1886. Mr. Cain, who is 78 years old, described in testimony how his father had been wounded and his uncle killed at the courthouse on that occasion:

> MR. CAIN. Well, my father was in that riot or mob or whatever they would call it because the white people said that it was a riot, but the older folks said it was a mob, I know my father was shot through and through. He was shot back under his left breast there and it came out under his shoulder blade there, the bullet hole; I mean the scar showed on his, just under his left shoulder blade, and his brother were killed on the steps of the courthouse at the same time. My father said he jumped from the upper stair, upper deck, down and ran until he ran to the corporate limits of the town, and thereby he fell, but he did recover, God knows it.

Continuing violence has reinforced the tradition. As William Eskridge, a former school teacher described it:

Now, mind, this continues; this didn't stop there. We had less violence, but it continued throughout the years. Whenever a colored person was killed, nothing done about it. Whenever a white man got ready to hit one over the head, he hit him over the head and asked him if he liked it, and he had to tell him that he did.

Both Mr. Eskridge and Mr. Cain agreed, however, that the situation in Carroll County was improving. Recent sheriffs had stopped violence by subordinate law enforcement officials and there was less fear in the Negro community. Encouraged by what seemed to be some change in attitude, Mr. Cain asked his grown daughter, the only one of his seven children remaining in Carroll County, to attempt to register.

MR. CAIN. I spoke to my daughter there a few months ago, . . . it seems to have softened up some. I asked her if she would go and she said "I about make up my mind but everytime I go to the courthouse something tells me not to go in." But this time she says when she went in to pay her tax, something told her to go in, so she went in and took the test, but how she came out I couldn't tell you.

Her fear in making an attempt to register was reflected in Miss Cain's testimony.

MR. TAYLOR. Miss Cain, did you attempt to register this time?
MISS CAIN. I did.
MR. TAYLOR. Have you ever gone to the courthouse before to try to register?

• • •

MISS CAIN. Yes, I have, but that was my first time to attempt to register.
MR. TAYLOR. You had gone to the courthouse before but had not gone in to register?
MISS CAIN. I was afraid.
MR. TAYLOR. But, this time you decided to?
MISS CAIN. I decided.

• • •

COMMISSIONER RANKIN. Miss Cain, you have talked about registering; haven't you?
MISS CAIN. Yes, I have.
COMMISSIONER RANKIN. And, it is fear that keeps them from trying to register? Is that correct?
MISS CAIN. That's correct.

• • •

COMMISSIONER RANKIN. Do you agree with your father that it's better to go one by one than for a group to go down?

MISS CAIN. Well, I agree maybe more than one by one, but I wouldn't——

COMMISSIONER RANKIN. You would like to have had somebody with you; is that right?

MISS CAIN. Well, I wasn't alone because I had prayed, and I believed that Somebody was with me. That's why I had the courage that I had when I went there. . . .

12c.   Registration Tests and Poll Taxes

The county registrar is the official charged by law with the duty of administering the registration test. Mississippi law requires the State Board of Election Commissioners to appoint, as registrar, the clerk of the circuit court, who is an elected county official with a four-year term. As indicated in the previous chapter, registration laws allow him broad discretion in determining who shall qualify as an elector. The Commission sought information on the way in which registrars were exercising this discretion. . . .

The Humphreys County registrar, G. H. Hood, testified that in administering the test he followed the practice of choosing constitutional sections consecutively. When he reached the end of the 286-section constitution, he would begin again. Mr. Hood stated that he did not draw any distinction between hard or easy sections. Each section was given in turn. This testimony was supported by records he submitted in response to the Commission's subpena.

While Mr. Hood did not appear to discriminate in choosing sections, he did not eliminate very difficult sections, such as section 182, concerning the power to tax corporations, which the registrar of Issaquena County had reserved for Negro applicants. By using these sections he imposed a test which neither he nor the majority of white Mississippians had been required to take when they registered. When asked at the hearing whether he could interpret this section, the following colloquy ensued:

COMMISSIONER GRISWOLD. I hand you a copy of section 182 of the Mississippi constitution. Would you please make a reasonable interpretation of section 182 for the Commission?

(Pause.)

MR. HOOD. You say 182?

COMMISSIONER GRISWOLD. Yes.

MR. HOOD. I'm sorry, sir. I've been reading 183.

(Pause.)

MR. HOOD. Well, it means that the power to tax corporations, their property, shall never be surrendered or abridged by any contract. And——

COMMISSIONER GRISWOLD. I didn't ask you to read it, Mr. Hood. I asked you to interpret it.

MR. BRIDGES (Aside to Mr. Hood).

COMMISSIONER GRISWOLD. Mr. Chairman, I think it should be the witness' interpretation; not his counsel's.

MR. BRIDGES. If you please, gentlemen, the conference between the witness and his attorney had nothing to do with the question. It was a question whether he was to answer it or not.

MR. HOOD. Which I will not.

MR. BRIDGES. Which he will not.

COMMISSIONER GRISWOLD. You decline to interpret section 182?

MR. HOOD. On pressure being put on me before a Committee like this.

COMMISSIONER GRISWOLD. On the ground that it may incriminate you?

MR. HOOD. That's right.

• • •

COMMISSIONER GRISWOLD. I find it a little hard to see how citizens of Mississippi are expected to interpret the section if the registrar is unable to do so and he is the person who grades the interpretation which is made by a citizen of Mississippi.

MISSISSIPPI VOTER REGISTRATION APPLICATION FORM
SWORN WRITTEN APPLICATION FOR REGISTRATION

(By reason of the provisions of Sections 241, 241-A and 244 of the Constitution of Mississippi and relevant statutes of the State of Mississippi, the applicant for registration, if not physically disabled, is required to fill in this form in his own handwriting in the presence of the registrar and without assistance or suggestion of any person or memorandum.)

1. Write the date of this application ....
2. What is your full name? ....
3. State your age and date of birth ....
4. What is your occupation? ....
5. Where is your business carried on? (Give city, town or village, and street address, if any, but if none, post office address.) If not engaged in business, so state. ....
6. By whom are you employed? (Give name and street address, if any, but if none, post office address.) If not employed, so state. ....
7. Where is your place of residence in the county and district where you propose to register? (Give city, town or village, and street address, if any, but if none, post office address.) ....
8. Are you a citizen of the United States and an inhabitant of Mississippi?
....
9. How long have you resided in Mississippi? ....
10. How long have you resided in the election district or precinct in which you propose to register? ....
11. State your last previous places of residence. (Give street address, if any, but if none, post office address.) ....
12. Are you a minister of the gospel in charge of an organized church, or

the wife of such a minister? If so, what church? (Give address in each instance.) . . . .

13. Check which oath you desire to take: (1) General . . . . . . (2) Minister's: . . . . . . (3) Minister's wife: . . . . . . (4) If under 21 years at present, but will be 21 years old by date of general election. . . . .

14. If there is more than one person of your same name in the precinct, by what name do you wish to be called? . . . .

15. Have you ever been convicted of any of the following crimes: bribery, theft, arson, obtaining money or goods under false pretenses, perjury, forgery, embezzlement, or bigamy? . . . .

16. Have you ever been convicted of any other crime (excepting misdemeanors for traffic violations)? . . . .

17. If your answer to question 15 or 16 is "Yes", name the crime or crimes of which you have been convicted, and the year, court, and place of such conviction or convictions: . . . .
. . . .
. . . .

18. Write and copy in the space below, Section . . . . . . of the Constitution of Mississippi: (Instructions to Registrar: You will designate the Section of the Constitution and point out same to applicant). . . . .
. . . .

19. Write in the space below a reasonable interpretation (the meaning) of the Section of the Constitution of Mississippi which you have just copied:
. . . .

20. Write in the space below a statement setting forth your understanding of the duties and obligations of citizenship under a constitutional form of government.
. . . .
. . . .

21. Sign the oath or affirmation referred to in question 13, and which is:
    NOTE: Registrar give applicant oath selected under question 13. Mark out that portion of oath that is not applicable.
    NOTE: Registrar. In registering voters in Cities and Towns not all in one election district, the name of such city or town may be substituted in the Oath for the Election District.
    (a) GENERAL and/or SPECIAL OATH:

I, ... , do solemnly swear (or affirm) that I am twenty-one years old (or I will be before the next election in this County) and that I will have resided in this State two years, and . . . . Election District of . . . . County one year next preceding the ensuing election, and am now in good faith a resident of the same, and that I am not disqualified from voting by reason of having been convicted of any crime named in the Constitution of this State as a disqualification to be an elector; that I will truly answer all questions propounded to me concerning my antecedents so far as they relate to my right to vote, and also as to my residence before my citizenship in this District; that I will faithfully support the Constitution of the United

States and the State of Mississippi, and will bear true faith and allegiance to the same, So Help Me God.

....
Applicant's Signature to Oath

(b) OATH OF MINISTER and/or MINISTER'S WIFE:

I, ..., do solemnly swear (or affirm) that I am twenty-one years old (or I will be before the next election in this County) and that I am a Minister, or the wife of a Minister, of the Gospel in charge of an organized church, and that I will have resided two years in this State and in .... Election District of .... County six months next preceding the ensuing election, and am now in good faith a resident of the same, and that I am not disqualified from voting by reason of having been convicted of any crime named in the Constitution of this State as a disqualification to be an elector; that I will truly answer all questions propounded to me concerning my antecedents so far as they relate to my right to vote, and also as to my residence before my citizenship in this District; that I will faithfully support the Constitution of the United States and of the State of Mississippi, and will bear true faith and allegiance to the same. So Help Me God.

....
Applicant's Signature to Oath

....
Applicant's Signature to Application
(The Applicant will also sign his name here)

STATE OF MISSISSIPPI

County of ....

Sworn to and subscribed before me by the within named .... this the .... day of ...., 19.....

....
County Registrar

(SEAL)

Is applicant of good moral character? ....

If not, why? ....

Does applicant qualify? ....

Passed .... Failed ....

....
County Registrar

12d. Findings and Recommendations

Preliminary Statement

The 15th amendment to the United States Constitution commands that no citizen shall be deprived of the right to vote by reason of race or color. This requirement of the Constitution which is binding in every State has, in substance, been repudiated and denied in

Mississippi. Since 1875 Negroes in Mississippi have been systematically excluded from the franchise by legislative enactment, fraud and violence.

For many years the Federal Government failed to take any action to enforce the 15th amendment in Mississippi or in other Southern States where similar practices existed. But since 1957 Congress has acted three times in an effort to eliminate discrimination in voting, and the Civil Rights Division of the Department of Justice has vigorously exercised the authority conferred by Congressional enactment.

In Mississippi these efforts have proved largely unavailing and few Negroes have been registered to vote. The barriers of unjust tests and discriminatory administration have remained all but insurmountable while a deep-seated fear of economic or physical reprisal has acted as a significant deterrent for Negroes who would otherwise wish to register.

Legislation is now pending in Congress which will go far to solve these problems by eliminating the tests and by authorizing the appointment of Federal examiners to register voters. Since 1959 the Commission has recommended such legislation as the only solution and its recent experience in Mississippi which is reflected in this report has confirmed this view.

At the same time the Commission has received evidence of the beginning of a change of attitude in Mississippi towards Federal law. At the hearing, Governor Paul Johnson appeared before the Commission and stated that Mississippi would obey the Civil Rights Act of 1964 "as the law of the land." The Mississippi Economic Council, the State chamber of commerce, issued a statement urging, among other things, "that registration and voting laws, should be administered fairly and impartially for all." Similar statements have been made more recently by other groups.

The Commission is gratified by this evidence of acceptance of the requirements of the Constitution. In this state of affairs, it is worth emphasizing that there is nothing in existing or pending Federal legislation which will in any way detract or interfere with local efforts to eliminate discrimination. While the pending voting bill, if enacted, may result in the appointment of Federal examiners in Mississippi, it would not prevent State officials from registering voters. The State in fact could do much to undo past acts of discrimination by taking affirmative action to encourage citizens to register and vote. State officials might consider, for example, the adoption of procedures, already utilized in a number of other states, to facilitate registration by providing local or precinct registration units or even door-to-door canvassing. They might further consider positive steps to assure Negro teachers that registration and voting will not result in the loss of their jobs.

Under the leadership of President Johnson, the Federal Government is now making a new and full commitment to assure all citizens the right to vote. If this commitment is enacted into law and the law is implemented vigorously, Negro Mississippians may finally enjoy the right to participate in the processes of self government. If the State of Mississippi joins in this commitment and assumes its share of the responsibility, places now suffering the consequences of racial strife can become communities of understanding and progress in which all citizens have a stake.

Findings

1. The State of Mississippi, for the purpose of preventing registration by Negroes, has enacted over the past 75 years a series of laws establishing a constitutional interpretation test, and other tests for registration, and has vested broad discretion in county registrars to administer these requirements. The stringency of these tests was increased at a time when most whites were already registered and few Negroes were registered.

2. Registration records indicate that county registrars in a large number of Mississippi counties have discriminated against Negroes in the administration of these tests primarily by (a) giving Negroes more difficult constitutional sections to interpret than whites; (b) disqualifying Negroes for insufficiencies in the completion of the application form or in the interpretation of the selected constitutional section when comparable or greater insufficiencies failed to disqualify white applicants; and (c) affording assistance to white applicants but not to Negroes.

3. The Mississippi poll tax was established and made a qualification for voting for the purpose of preventing the exercise of the franchise by Negroes. In some counties local officials have refused to accept payment of the poll tax from Negroes, or have encouraged white electors to pay such tax and have failed to encourage, or have discouraged, Negroes from doing so. The poll tax was adopted on the belief that Negroes as a class would find it more difficult to pay than whites as a class. In 1890, when the poll tax was adopted, this belief was justified and it remains so today. In light of actual economic conditions, the payment of a poll tax is a significantly heavier burden for most Negroes than it is for most whites.

4. Negro applicants for registration, Negroes seeking to vote, and civil rights workers have been harassed and intimidated by local officials in connection with registration and voting activities. On occasion such persons have suffered violence from private persons.

5. Negro applicants for registration, Negroes seeking to vote, and civil rights workers have, on occasion, suffered acts of economic intimidation and reprisal in connection with registration and voting, both from public officials and from private persons.

6. There is widespread fear in many Negro communities that an attempt to register or vote would result in economic or physical reprisals. Such fears have been increased by the provisions of Mississippi law which require newspaper publication of the name and address of any applicant, and by the practice of requiring the applicant to return to the office of the registrar to determine whether he has passed the test. Fear of reprisal is a major factor inhibiting attempts by Negroes to register or vote. In counties where fear is great, Negroes will not attempt to register in significant numbers without assistance or encouragement.

7. Most Negro Mississippians now of voting age have been educated in segregated public schools which were and still are inadequate and greatly inferior to public schools provided for white children. Public education of Negroes has been so poor and so inferior to the education afforded whites that any test of skills taught in the public schools is inherently unfair as a prerequisite to voting.

8. Existing Federal remedies have not proved adequate to eliminate discrimination and to prevent reprisals for voting. Law suits against registrars have proved too slow and too cumbersome a device to remedy discrimination. Recent judicial approaches promise more speedy relief but are still inadequate in that the registration machinery will remain in the hands of State officials who have demonstrated an unwillingness to enforce Federal law. Law suits aimed at acts of reprisal have been filed in only a few cases and do not appear to have provided an effective remedy.

9. As a result of the foregoing, it is estimated that in Mississippi less than 7 percent of the Negro voting age population but more than 70 percent of the white voting age population are registered to vote. Mississippi has by far the lowest rate of Negro registration of any State in the South and has shown virtually no increase in such registration as the result of the enactment of Federal legislation designed to eliminate discrimination in voting.

Recommendations

Recommendation No. 1: In past reports to the President and Congress, the Commission has recommended a variety of corrective measures to eliminate discriminatory denials of the right to vote. Prime among these recommendations have been proposals calling for the elimination, as a prerequisite for voting, of any test or requirement of literacy, and the establishment of a system of Federal registrars to provide an effective administrative procedure for securing the right to vote in areas where racial discrimination exists.

The Commission wholeheartedly supports the legislation now pending in Congress which would accomplish these objectives. For the legislation to be fully effective in securing the right of citizens to vote, we make the following recommendations:

(a) All literacy tests, including any requirement that the applicant complete any form, should be abolished in view of the fact that such tests and requirements have been established and used for discriminatory purposes.

(b) In areas where Federal examiners have been appointed, applicants should be free to seek registration with such examiners without prior recourse to the State registration process.

(c) The requirement of any poll tax payment as a prerequisite to voting in any election should be abolished, in view of the fact that poll taxes have been intended and utilized as a means of discrimination. In the opinion of the Commission, there can be no reasonable doubt of the power of Congress to enact such a provision as an exercise of the power expressly granted to Congress to enforce the 15th amendment.

(d) Provision should be made for the assignment of Federal poll watchers at election places (in districts where Federal examiners have been appointed) to determine whether persons entitled to vote are being permitted to vote and have their vote counted.

Recommendation No. 2: The Commission recommends to the President that the resources of the Executive branch be explored for the purpose of establishing an affirmative program to encourage persons to register and vote. Such a program should:

(a) Assure better dissemination of information concerning the right to vote and the requirements of registration. (In this connection consideration should be given to the use of branch facilities and personnel of such agencies as the Post Office and the Department of Agriculture.)

(b) Provide training and education to foster better understanding of the rights and duties of citizenship and the significance of voting, and to encourage persons to register and vote. (In this connection consideration should be given to the use of programs of adult education, literacy and community action which are administered by the Department of Health, Education and Welfare, the Department of Agriculture, or the Office of Economic Opportunity.)

Concurring Statement of Vice Chairman Patterson and Commissioner Rankin on Recommendation No. 1: We cannot defend the poll tax in view of its use as a means of discrimination, and we concur in the recommendation that it be abolished. However, we take no position on the validity of the proposition stated in the second sentence of paragraph (c).

Concurring Statement of Commissioner Hesburgh on Recommendation No. 1: I am aware that some are concerned that in acting upon our strong conviction that literacy tests must be removed as a discriminatory impediment to voting, we may somehow impair the foundations of good government based upon an informed electorate. While I can appreciate this concern, I do not think that this legislation will produce such a result.

In an era when citizens can and do inform themselves by means of television and radio, literacy no longer seems an important qualification for voting. There are some 30 States which do not impose any literacy test for voting. No one has claimed that the quality of government in these States has suffered in comparison with States which have such tests.

During the Mississippi hearing, we heard scores of witnesses who had little formal education and who did not meet all of the traditional standards of literacy. Nonetheless, these were people who by their interest and awareness were eminently qualified to participate in responsible democratic government. Their concerns for good citizenship and good government have been sharpened by years of deprivation and denial. When they are permitted to register and vote, democracy will be stronger for their contribution.

Selection 13

THE SUPREME COURT: TERRY *VS*. ADAMS*

The Fifteenth Amendment declares that the right to vote shall not be denied or abridged on account of race, color, or previous condition of servitude. Southern states tried to get around this amend-

* *Terry* vs. *Adams*, 345 U.S. 461 (1953).

ment in a number of ways. To deprive the Negro of his right to vote, a number of methods were used: literacy tests, poll taxes, the "Grandfather clause" (declared unconstitutional in 1915) and the "white primary" (declared unconstitutional in 1927 and in 1932).

The next attempt took the form of laws which turned over the responsibility of nominating candidates to political parties. It was argued that since political parties are private, not public agencies, they could admit anyone they wanted. This was declared unconstitutional in Smith *vs.* Allwright *in 1944. Then Texas tried to revive the "white primary" idea by creating the Jaybird Association, a private club for white people only, which would have the power to select political candidates.*

The following selection gives the opinion of the Supreme Court on the constitutionality of this move in 1953.

Mr. Justice Black announced the judgment of the Court and an opinion in which Mr. Justice Douglas and Mr. Justice Burton join:

In *Smith* vs. *Allwright,* 321 U.S. 649 (1944), we held that rules of the Democratic Party of Texas excluding Negroes from voting in the party's primaries violated the Fifteenth Amendment. While no state law directed such exclusion, our decision pointed out that many party activities were subject to considerable statutory control. This case raises questions concerning the constitutional power of a Texas county political organization called the Jaybird Democratic Association or Jaybird Party to exclude Negroes from its primaries on racial grounds. The Jaybirds deny that their racial exclusions violate the Fifteenth Amendment. They contend that the Amendment applies only to elections or primaries held under state regulation, that their association is not regulated by the state at all, and that it is not a political party but a self-governing voluntary club. . . .

There was evidence that:

The Jaybird Association or Party was organized in 1889. Its membership was then and always has been limited to white people; they are automatically members if their names appear on the official list of county voters. It has been run like other political parties with an executive committee named from the county's voting precincts. Expenses of the party are paid by the assessment of candidates for office in its primaries. Candidates for county offices submit their names to the Jaybird Committee in accordance with the normal practice followed by regular political parties all over the country. Advertisements and posters proclaim that these candidates are running subject to the action of the Jaybird primary. While there is no legal compulsion on successful Jaybird candidates to enter Democratic primaries they have nearly always done so and with few exceptions since 1889 have run and won without opposition in the Democratic primaries and the general elections that followed. Thus the party has been the dominant political group in the county since organization, having endorsed every county-wide official elected since 1889.

It is apparent that Jaybird activities follow a plan purposefully designed to exclude Negroes from voting and at the same time to escape the Fifteenth Amendment's command that the right of citizens to vote shall neither be denied nor abridged on account of race. These were the admitted party purposes according to the following testimony of the Jaybird's president:

Q. . . . Now Mr. Adams, will you tell me specifically what is the specific purpose of holding these elections and carrying on this organization like you do? A. Good government.

Q. Now I will ask you to state whether or not it is the opinion and policy of the Association that to carry on good government they must exclude Negro citizens? A. Well, when we started it was and it is still that way, I think.

Q. And then one of the purposes of your organization is for the specific purpose of excluding Negroes from voting, isn't it? A. Yes.

Q. And that is your policy? A. Yes.

Q. I will ask you, that is the reason you hold your election in May rather than in June or July, isn't it? A. Yes.

Q. Because if you held it in July you would have to abide by the statutes and the law by letting them vote? A. They do vote in July.

Q. And if you held yours at that time they would have to vote too, wouldn't they? A. Why sure.

Q. And you hold it in May so they won't have to? A. Well, they don't vote in ours but they can vote on anybody in the July election they want to.

Q. But you are not answering my question. My question is that you hold yours in May so you won't have to let them vote, don't you? A. Yes.

Q. And that is your purpose? A. Yes.

Q. And your intention? A. Yes.

Q. And to have a vote of the white population at a time when the Negroes can't vote, isn't that right? A. That's right.

Q. That is the whole policy of your Association? A. Yes.

Q. And that is its purpose? A. Yes.

The District Court found that the Jaybird Association was a political organization or party; that the majority of white voters generally abide by the results of its primaries and support in the Democratic primaries the persons endorsed by the Jaybird primaries; and that the chief object of the Association has always been to deny

Negroes any voice or part in the election of Fort Bend County officials.

The facts and findings bring this case squarely within the reasoning and holding of the Court of Appeals for the Fourth Circuit in its two recent decisions about excluding Negroes from Democratic primaries in South Carolina. . . . South Carolina had repealed every trace of statutory or constitutional control of the Democratic primaries. It did this in the hope that thereafter the Democratic Party or Democratic "Clubs" of South Carolina would be free to continue discriminatory practices against Negroes as voters. The contention there was that the Democratic "Clubs" were mere private groups; the contention here is that the Jaybird Association is a mere private group. The Court of Appeals in invalidating the South Carolina practices answered these formalistic arguments by holding that no election machinery could be sustained if its purpose or effect was to deny Negroes on account of their race an effective voice in the governmental affairs of their country, state, or community. In doing so the Court relied on the principle announced in *Smith* vs. *Allwright,* that the constitutional right to be free from racial discrimination in voting ". . . is not to be nullified by a state through casting its electoral process in a form which permits a private organization to practice racial discrimination in the election."

The South Carolina cases are in accord with the commands of the Fifteenth Amendment and the laws passed pursuant to it. That Amendment provides as follows: "The right of citizens of the United States to vote shall not be denied or abridged by the United States or by any State on account of race, color, or previous condition of servitude."

The Amendment bans racial discrimination in voting by both state and nation. It thus establishes a national policy, obviously applicable to the right of Negroes not to be discriminated against as voters in elections to determine public governmental policies or to select public officials, national, state, or local. . . .

The Amendment, the congressional enactment and the cases make explicit the rule against racial discrimination in the conduct of elections. Together they show the meaning of "elections." Clearly the Amendment includes any election in which public issues are decided or public officials selected. Just as clearly the Amendment excludes social or business clubs. And the statute shows the congressional mandate against discrimination whether the voting on public issues and officials is conducted in community, state or nation. Size is not a standard.

It is significant that precisely the same qualifications as those prescribed by Texas entitling electors to vote at county-operated primaries are adopted as the sole qualifications entitling electors to vote at the county-wide Jaybird primaries with a single proviso—Negroes are excluded. Everyone concedes that such a proviso in the county-operated primaries would be unconstitutional. The Jaybird Party thus brings into being and holds precisely the kind of election that the Fifteenth Amendment seeks to prevent. When it produces the equivalent of the prohibited election, the damage has been done.

For a state to permit such a duplication of its election processes is to permit a flagrant abuse of those processes to defeat the purposes of the Fifteenth Amendment. The use of the county-operated primary to ratify the result of the prohibited election merely compounds the offense. It violates the Fifteenth Amendment for a state, by such circumvention, to permit within its borders the use of any device that produces an equivalent of the prohibited election.

The only election that has counted in this Texas county for more than fifty years has been that held by the Jaybirds from which Negroes were excluded. The Democratic primary and the general election have become no more than the perfunctory ratifiers of the choice that has already been made in Jaybird elections from which Negroes have been excluded. It is immaterial that the state does not control that part of this elective process which it leaves for the Jaybirds to manage. The Jaybird primary has become an integral part, indeed the only effective part, of the elective process that determines who shall rule and govern in the county. The effect of the whole procedure, Jaybird primary plus Democratic primary plus general election, is to do precisely that which the Fifteenth Amendment forbids—strip Negroes of every vestige of influence in selecting the officials who control the local county matters that intimately touch the daily lives of citizens.

. . . We affirm the District Court's holding that the combined Jaybird-Democratic-general election machinery has deprived these petitioners of their right to vote on account of their race and color. . . .

[*Justice Minton dissented on the ground that what was done here amounted to private, not state, action.*]

Selections 14a–14b

CIVIL RIGHTS ACTS

After the Civil War, Congress enacted the Civil Rights Acts of 1866 and 1875 conferring citizenship on Negroes born in the United States, extending to them the equal benefits of all the laws relating to property rights, and the right of equal treatment in places open to the public. However, in a series of decisions, the Supreme Court restricted the meaning of these laws by declaring that these laws and the Fourteenth Amendment did not prohibit "individual invasion of individual rights." While state officials could not deny to Negroes the equal protection of the laws, there was nothing in the Constitution or the laws to prevent individuals from discriminating against Negroes.

Eighty-two years after the passage of the Civil Rights Act of 1875, Congress passed the Civil Rights Act of 1957. A Commission on Civil Rights was established to investigate and report cases of racial discrimination; the Attorney General was empowered to seek injunctions against interference with the right to vote; and obstacles to Negro service on federal juries were removed.

The Civil Rights Act of 1960, the second civil rights legislation to be passed during the Eisenhower administration, provided for federal voting referees to register Negroes when local officials would not do so.

In June, 1963 President Kennedy sent Congress the most sweeping civil rights bill in our history. This was the year when pictures of police dogs attacking Negroes in Birmingham shocked the American people, as well as the world. It was the year when Governor Wallace refused to admit Negroes to the University of Alabama. It was the year when a bomb exploded in a children's Bible class in a Sunday School in Birmingham and four Negro children were killed. The Civil Rights Bill became law in 1964, after the death of President Kennedy. The Senate debate on the legislation lasted eighty-three days, and cloture had to be invoked to end the prolonged debate and filibustering.

14a. Voting Provisions of the Civil Rights Act of 1960*

Title III

Required that voting records and registration papers for all federal elections, including primaries, must be preserved for 22 months. Penalties for failing to comply or for stealing, destroying or mutilating the records could be a fine of up to $1,000, and/or imprisonment for one year.

Directed that the records, upon written application, be turned over to the Attorney General "or his representative" at the office of the records' custodian.

Unless directed otherwise by a court, the Justice Department representative must not disclose the content of the records except to Congress, a government agency, or in a court proceeding.

Title VI

Provided that after the Attorney General won a civil suit brought under the 1957 Civil Rights Act to protect Negroes' right to vote, he could then ask the court to hold another adversary proceeding and make a separate finding that there was a "pattern or practice" of depriving Negroes of the right to vote in the area involved in the suit.

If a court found such a "pattern or practice," any Negro living in that area could apply to the court to issue an order declaring him qualified to vote if he proved (1) he was qualified to vote under state law; (2) he had tried to register after the "pattern or practice" finding; and (3) he had not been allowed to register or had been found unqualified by someone acting under color of law. The court would have to hear the Negro's application within 10 days and its order would be effective for as long a period as that for which he would have been qualified to vote if registered under state law.

State officials would be notified of the order, and they would then be bound to permit the person to vote. Disobedience would be subject to contempt proceedings.

To carry out these provisions, the court may appoint one or more voting referees, who must be qualified voters in the judicial district. The referees would receive the applications, take evidence, and report their findings to the court. The referee must take the Negro's application and proof in an *ex parte* proceeding (without cross-

* From *Revolution in Civil Rights,* Washington, D. C.: Congressional Quarterly Service, 1965, p. 34.

examination by opponents) and the court may set the time and place for the referee's hearing.

The court may fix a time limit of up to 10 days, in which state officials may challenge the referee's report. Challenges on points of law must be accompanied by a memorandum and on points of fact by a verified copy of a public record or an affidavit by those with personal knowledge of the controverting evidence. Either the court or the referee may decide the challenges in accordance with court-directed procedures. Hearings on issues of fact could be held only when the affidavits show there is a real issue of fact.

If a Negro has applied for a court certificate 20 or more days before the election, his application is challenged, and the case is not decided by election day, the court must allow him to vote provisionally, provided he is "entitled to vote under state law," and impound his ballot pending a decision on his application. If he applies within 20 days before the election, the court has the option of whether or not to let him vote.

The court would not be limited in its powers to enforce its decree that these Negroes be allowed to vote and their votes be counted and may authorize the referee to take action to enforce it.

The referees would have the powers conferred on court masters by rule 53(c) of the Federal Rules of Civil Procedure. (Rule 53(c) gives masters the right to subpena records, administer oaths and cross-examine witnesses.)

In any suit instituted under these provisions, the state would be held responsible for the actions of its officials and, in the event state officials resign and are not replaced, the state itself could be sued.

14b. Voting Provisions of the Civil Rights Act of 1964*

Title I: Voting

The purpose of this section is to provide more effective enforcement of the right to vote in Federal elections (for President, Vice President, presidential electors or members of Congress) without regard to race or color. It also speeds up the procedure by which voting rights suits may be decided.

The Act:

a. requires that the same standards be applied to all individuals seeking to register and vote;

* From *Civil Rights Digest*, Washington, D. C.: special bulletin by U. S. Commission on Civil Rights, August, 1964.

b. forbids denial of the right to vote because of some minor mistake or omission;

c. requires that only literacy tests that are written may be used as a qualification for voting; and that the tests and answers be available on request;

d. establishes that in voting rights law suits the court must presume that anyone who completed the sixth grade is literate, unless the State can prove otherwise.

In any voting suit brought by the Government charging that there is a "pattern or practice" of voting discrimination, either the Attorney General or the defendant may ask that a three-judge Federal court be appointed to hear the case. Appeals from the decisions of such a court may be taken directly to the Supreme Court.

Title VIII: Voting Statistics

The Secretary of Commerce is required to conduct a survey of persons of voting age by race, color, and national origin and to determine the extent to which such persons have registered and voted in such geographic areas as the Commission on Civil Rights recommends.

A similar survey must also be conducted on a nation-wide basis in connection with the 1970 Census. No person questioned during such surveys may be compelled to disclose his race, color, religion or national origin and everyone must be advised of his right to refuse to give this information.

Selection 15

THE GROWING IMPORTANCE OF THE NEGRO VOTE IN THE SOUTH*

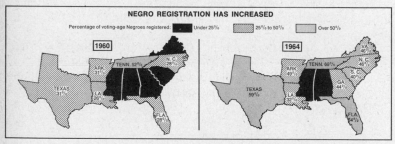

NEGRO REGISTRATION HAS INCREASED

Percentage of voting-age Negroes registered: Under 25% 25% to 50% Over 50%

1960 — ARK. 31%, TENN. 52%, N. C. 28%, TEXAS 31%, LA. 26%, FLA. 28%

1964 — VA. 46%, ARK. 49%, TENN. 69%, N. C. 46%, S. C. 40%, GA. 44%, TEXAS 59%, LA. 32%, FLA. 64%

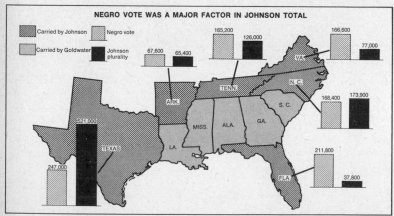

NEGRO VOTE WAS A MAJOR FACTOR IN JOHNSON TOTAL

Carried by Johnson   Negro vote
Carried by Goldwater   Johnson plurality

67,600   65,400
165,200   126,000
166,600   77,000
168,400   173,900
521,000
247,000
211,800   37,800

VA.   N. C.   TENN.   ARK.   S. C.   MISS.   ALA.   GA.   TEXAS   LA.   FLA.

The per cent of Negroes registered was lowest—under 45 —in the five states carried by Goldwater. Johnson's name was not on the ballot in Alabama. In four of the six states won by Johnson the Negro vote, almost 100 per cent of which was cast for the President, exceeded his plurality. Figures are from the Southern Regional Council.

* From *The New York Times,* January 22, 1965.

'Shucks! I'm just a nice peaceable feller!'

© 1965 Herblock in the *Washington Post*

Selection 17

THE RIGHT TO VOTE

L Y N D O N   B .   J O H N S O N *

In 1963 mass action by Negroes and their supporters aimed at de-segregating schools, eating places, beaches, hotels, and other places of public accommodation in the South. In 1964 the pressure was placed on the North to eliminate the social and economic injustices in the "black ghettoes." In 1965 the protest movement was directed against Southern barriers to Negro voting. Under the leadership of Dr. Martin Luther King, 1964 Nobel Peace Prize winner, members of the Southern Christian Leadership Conference, The Student Nonviolent Coordinating Committee, and other civil rights groups, launched a campaign to increase Negro voter registration in Selma, Alabama, the county seat of Dallas County. Violence and arrests followed and then a decision was made to lead a march from Selma to Montgomery, the state capital of Alabama, in order "to plague the conscience of the nation," in the words of Dr. King. Anticipating continued trouble, President Johnson federalized the National Guard and ordered units to protect the marchers.

On March 15th President Johnson addressed the nation, proposing a voting rights bill, which was passed several months later. This is considered one of the most important Presidential Messages delivered by President Johnson.

Message from the President of the United States

Mr. Speaker, Mr. President, Members of the Congress:

I speak tonight for the dignity of man and the destiny of democracy.

I urge every member of both parties—Americans of all religions

* From *House of Representatives Document No. 117*, 89th Congress, 1st Session.

and of all colors—from every section of this country—to join me in that cause.

At times history and fate meet at a single time in a single place to shape a turning point in man's unending search for freedom. So it was at Lexington and Concord. So it was a century ago at Appomattox. So it was last week in Selma, Ala.

There, long-suffering men and women peacefully protested the denial of their rights as Americans. Many were brutally assaulted. One good man—a man of God—was killed.

There was no cause for pride in what has happened in Selma.

There is no cause for self-satisfaction in the long denial of equal rights of millions of Americans.

But there is cause for hope and for faith in our democracy in what is happening here tonight.

For the cries of pain, and the hymns and protests of oppressed people, have summoned into convocation all the majesty of this great Government, the Government of the greatest Nation on earth.

Our mission is at once the oldest and most basic of this country: to right wrong, to do justice, to serve man.

In our time we have come to live with the moments of great crisis. Our lives have been marked with debate about great issues—issues of war and peace, issues of prosperity and depression. But rarely, in any time, does an issue lay bare the secret heart of America itself. Rarely are we met with the challenge, not to our growth or abundance, or our welfare or our security—but rather to the values and the purposes and the meaning of our beloved Nation.

The issue of equal rights for American Negroes is such an issue. And should we defeat every enemy, and should we double our wealth and conquer the stars and still be unequal to this issue, then we will have failed as a people and as a nation.

For with a country as with a person, "What is a man profited, if he shall gain the whole world, and lose his own soul?"

There is no Negro problem. There is no southern problem. There is no northern problem. There is only an American problem.

And we are met here tonight as Americans—not as Democrats or Republicans—we are met here as Americans to solve that problem.

This was the first nation in the history of the world to be founded with a purpose. The great phrases of that purpose still sound in every American heart, north and south: "All men are created equal" —"Government by consent of the governed"—"Give me liberty or give me death." And those are not just clever words and those are not just empty theories. In their name Americans have fought and died for two centuries and tonight around the world they stand there as guardians of our liberty risking their lives.

Those words are a promise to every citizen that he shall share in the dignity of man. This dignity cannot be found in a man's possessions. It cannot be found in his power or in his position. It really rests on his right to be treated as a man equal in opportunity to all others. It says that he shall share in freedom, he shall choose his leaders, educate his children, provide for his family according to his ability and his merits as a human being.

To apply any other test—to deny a man his hopes because of his color or race or his religion or the place of his birth—is not only to do injustice, it is to deny America and to dishonor the dead who gave their lives for American freedom.

Our fathers believed that if this noble view of the rights of man was to flourish, it must be rooted in democracy. The most basic right of all was the right to choose your own leaders. The history of this country in large measure, is the history of the expansion of that right to all of our people.

Many of the issues of civil rights are very complex and most difficult. But about this there can and should be no argument. Every American citizen must have an equal right to vote. There is no reason which can excuse the denial of that right. There is no duty which weighs more heavily on us than the duty we have to insure that right.

Yet the harsh fact is that in many places in this country men and women are kept from voting simply because they are Negroes.

Every device of which human ingenuity is capable has been used to deny this right. The Negro citizen may go to register only to be told that the day is wrong, or the hour is late, or the official in charge is absent.

And if he persists, and if he manages to present himself to the registrar, he may be disqualified because he did not spell out his middle name or because he abbreviated a word on the application.

And if he manages to fill out an application he is given a test. The registrar is the sole judge of whether he passes this test. He may be asked to recite the entire Constitution, or explain the most complex provisions of State law and even a college degree cannot be used to prove that he can read and write.

For the fact is that the only way to pass these barriers is to show a white skin.

Experience has clearly shown that the existing process of law cannot overcome systematic and ingenious discrimination. No law that we now have on the books—and I have helped to put three of them there—can insure the right to vote when local officials are determined to deny it.

In such a case our duty must be clear to all of us. The Constitution says that no person shall be kept from voting because of his race or his color. We have all sworn an oath before God to support and to defend that Constitution.

We must now act in obedience to that oath.

Wednesday I will send to Congress a law designed to eliminate illegal barriers to the right to vote.

The broad principles of that bill will be in the hands of the Democratic and Republican leaders tomorrow. After they have reviewed it, it will come here formally as a bill.

I am grateful for this opportunity to come here tonight at the invitation of the leadership to reason with my friends, to give them my views, and to visit with my former colleagues.

I have had prepared a more comprehensive analysis of the legislation which I had intended to transmit to the Clerk tomorrow, but which I will submit to the Clerk tonight. But I want to really discuss with you now, briefly, the main proposals of this legislation.

This bill will strike down restrictions to voting in all elections—Federal, State, and local—which have been used to deny Negroes the right to vote.

This bill will establish a simple, uniform standard which cannot be used however ingenious the effort to flout our Constitution.

It will provide for citizens to be registered by officials of the U.S. Government if the State officials refuse to register them.

It will eliminate tedious, unnecessary lawsuits which delay the right to vote.

Finally, this legislation will insure that properly registered individuals are not prohibited from voting.

I will welcome the suggestions from all the Members of Congress —I have no doubt that I will get some—on ways and means to strengthen this law and to make it effective. But experience has plainly shown that this is the only path to carry out the command of the Constitution.

To those who seek to avoid action by their National Government in their home communities—who want to and who seek to maintain purely local control over elections—the answer is simple.

Open your polling places to all your people.

Allow men and women to register and vote whatever the color of their skin.

Extend the rights of citizenship to every citizen of this land.

There is no constitutional issue here. The command of the Constitution is plain.

There is no moral issue. It is wrong—deadly wrong—to deny any of your fellow Americans the right to vote in this country.

There is no issue of States rights or National rights. There is only the struggle for human rights.

I have not the slightest doubt what will be your answer.

But the last time a President sent a civil rights bill to the Congress it contained a provision to protect voting rights in Federal elections. That civil rights bill was passed after 8 long months of debate. And when that bill came to my desk from the Congress for my signature, the heart of the voting provision had been eliminated.

This time, on this issue, there must be no delay, or no hesitation, or no compromise with our purpose.

We cannot, we must not refuse to protect the right of every American to vote in every election that he may desire to participate in.

And we ought not and we cannot and we must not wait another 8 months before we get a bill. We have already waited a hundred years and more. And the time for waiting is gone.

So I ask you to join me in working long hours, nights, and weekends if necessary to pass this bill. And I do not make this request lightly, for from the window where I sit with the problems of our country I recognize that from outside this Chamber is the outraged conscience of a nation—the grave concern of many nations—and the harsh judgment of history on our acts.

But even if we pass this bill, the battle will not be over. What happened in Selma is part of a far larger movement which reaches into every section and State of America. It is the effort of American Negroes to secure for themselves the full blessings of American life.

Their cause must be our cause too, because it is not just Negroes but really it is all of us, who must overcome the crippling legacy of bigotry and injustice. And we shall overcome.

As a man whose roots go deeply into southern soil I know how agonizing racial feelings are. I know how difficult it is to reshape the attitudes and the structure of our society.

But a century has passed—more than 100 years—since the Negro was freed. And he is not fully free tonight. It was more than 100 years ago that Abraham Lincoln, a great President of another party, signed the Emancipation Proclamation. But emancipation is a proclamation and not a fact.

A century has passed—more than 100 years—since equality was promised. And yet the Negro is not equal.

A century has passed since the day of promise. And the promise is unkept.

The time of justice has now come. And I tell you that I believe sincerely that no force can hold it back. It is right—in the eyes of man and God—that it should come. And when it does, I think that day will brighten the lives of every American.

For Negroes are not the only victims. How many white children have gone uneducated and how many white families have lived in stark poverty—how many white lives have been scarred by fear because we have wasted our energy and our substance to maintain the barriers of hatred and terror.

And so I say to all of you here and to all in the Nation tonight that those who appeal to you to hold on to the past do so at the cost of denying you your future.

This great, rich, restless country can offer opportunity and education and hope to all—all black and white, all North and South, sharecropper and city dweller. These are the enemies—poverty, ignorance, disease—they are our enemies, not our fellow man, not our neighbor. And these enemies too—poverty, disease, and ignorance—we shall overcome.

Now let none of us, in any section, look with prideful righteousness on the troubles in another section or the problems of our neighbors. There is really no part of America where the promise of equality has been fully kept. In Buffalo as well as in Birmingham, in Philadelphia as well as Selma, Americans are struggling for the fruits of freedom.

This is one Nation. What happens in Selma or in Cincinnati is a matter of legitimate concern to every American. But let us look within our own hearts and our own communities, and let each of us put our shoulder to the wheel to root out injustice wherever it exists.

As we meet here in this peaceful, historic Chamber tonight, men from the South, some of whom were at Iwo Jima, men from the North, who have carried Old Glory to far corners of the world and brought it back without a stain on it, men from the East and from the West, are all fighting together without regard to religion or color or region in Vietnam. Men from every region fought for us across the world 20 years ago.

And now, in these common dangers and these common sacrifices, the South made its contribution of honor and gallantry no less than any other region of the Great Republic, and in some instances—a great many of them—more.

And I have not the slightest doubt that good men from everywhere in this country—from the Great Lakes to the Gulf of Mexico, from the Golden Gate to the harbors along the Atlantic—will rally now together in this cause to vindicate the freedom of all Americans. For all of us owe this duty, and I believe that all of us will respond to it.

Your President makes that request of every American.

The real hero of this struggle is the American Negro. His actions and protests—his courage to risk safety, and even to risk his life— have awakened the conscience of this Nation. His demonstrations have been designed to call attention to injustice, designed to provoke change, designed to stir reform. He has called upon us to make good the promise of America. And who among us can say that we would have made the same progress were it not for his persistent bravery and his faith in American democracy?

For at the real heart of battle for equality is a deep-seated belief in the democratic process. Equality depends not on the force of arms or tear gas, but depends upon the force of moral right—not on recourse to violence but on respect for law and order.

There have been many pressures upon your President—and there will be others as the days come and go—but I pledge you tonight that we intend to fight this battle where it should be fought, in the courts and in the Congress and in the hearts of men.

We must preserve the right of free speech and the right of free assembly. But the right of free speech does not carry with it, as has been said, the right to holler "fire" in a crowded theater. We must preserve the right to free assembly, but free assembly does not carry with it the right to block public thoroughfares to traffic.

We do have a right to protest and a right to march under conditions that do not infringe the constitutional rights of our neighbors. And I intend to protect all those rights as long as I am permitted to serve in this office.

We will guard against violence, knowing it strikes from our hands the very weapons with which we seek progress—obedience to law, and belief in American values.

In Selma, as elsewhere, we seek and pray for peace. We seek order. We seek unity.

But we will not accept the peace of stifled rights, or the order imposed by fear, or the unity that stifles protest. For peace cannot be purchased at the cost of liberty.

In Selma tonight—and we had a good day there—as in every city, we are working for a just and peaceful settlement. And we must all remember—after this speech I am making tonight, after the police and the FBI and the marshals have all gone, and after you have promptly passed this bill—the people of Selma and the other cities of the Nation must still live and work together. And when the attention of the Nation has gone elsewhere they must try to heal the wounds and to build a new community. This cannot be easily done on a battleground of violence, as the history of the South itself shows. It is in recognition of this that men of both races have shown such an outstandingly impressive responsibility in recent days—last Tuesday, and again today.

The bill that I am presenting to you will be known as a civil rights bill. But, in a larger sense, most of the program I am recommending is a civil rights program. Its object is to open the city of hope to all people of all races.

Because all Americans just must have the right to vote. And we are going to give them that right.

All Americans must have the privileges of citizenship regardless of race. And they are going to have those privileges of citizenship regardless of race.

But I would like to caution you and remind you that to exercise these privileges takes much more than legal right. It requires a trained mind and a healthy body. It requires a decent home, and the chance to find a job, and the opportunity to escape from the clutches of poverty.

Of course people cannot contribute to the Nation if they are never taught to read or write, if their bodies are stunted from hunger, if their sickness goes untended, if their life is spent in hopeless poverty just drawing a welfare check.

So we want to open the gates to opportunity. But we are also going to give all our people—black and white—the help that they need to walk through those gates.

My first job after college was as a teacher in Cotulla, Tex., in a small Mexican-American school. Few of them could speak English and I could not speak much Spanish. My students were poor and they often came to class without breakfast—hungry. And they knew, even in their youth the pain of prejudice. They never seemed to know why people disliked them, but they knew it was so because I saw it in their eyes.

I often walked home late in the afternoon after the classes were finished wishing there was more that I could do. But all I knew was to teach them the little that I knew—hoping that it might help them against the hardships that lay ahead.

Somehow you never forget what poverty and hatred can do when you see its scars on the hopeful face of a young child.

I never thought then in 1928 that I would be standing here in 1965. It never even occurred to me in my fondest dreams that I might have the chance to help the sons and daughters of those students—and to help people like them all over this country.

But now I do have that chance and I will let you in on a secret— I mean to use it.

And I hope that you will use it with me.

This is the richest and most powerful country which ever occupied this globe. The might of past empires it little compared to ours.

But I do not want to be the President who built empires, or sought grandeur, or extended dominion.

I want to be the President who educated young children to the wonders of their world.

I want to be the President who helped to feed the hungry and to prepare them to be taxpayers instead of tax-eaters.

I want to be the President who helped the poor to find their own way and who protected the right of every citizen to vote in every election.

I want to be the President who helped to end hatred among his fellow men and who promoted love among the people of all races and all regions and all parties.

I want to be the President who helped to end war among the brothers of this earth.

And so at the request of your beloved Speaker and the Senator from Montana, the majority leader, Mr. Mansfield, and the Senator from Illinois, the minority leader, Mr. Dirksen, and Mr. McCulloch and others, Members of both parties, I come here tonight not as President Roosevelt came down one time in person to veto a bonus bill; not as President Truman came down one time to urge the passage of a railroad bill. But I come here to ask you to share this task with me and to share it with the people we both work for.

I want this to be the Congress—Republicans and Democrats alike—which did all these things for all these people.

Beyond this great Chamber—out yonder in the 50 States are the people we serve. Who can tell what deep and unspoken hopes are in their hearts tonight as they sit there and listen? We all can guess, from our own lives, how difficult they often find their own pursuit of happiness; how many problems each little family has. They look most of all to themselves for their future.

But I think that they also look to each of us.

Above the pyramid on the great seal of the United States it says in Latin, "God has favored our undertaking."

God will not favor everything that we do. It is rather our duty to divine His will. I cannot help but believe that He truly understands and that He really favors the undertaking that we begin here tonight.

LYNDON B. JOHNSON

The White House, March 15, 1965

Selection 18

THE VOTING RIGHTS ACT OF 1965*

The Voting Rights Act of 1965 became law on August 6, 1965. As in the Civil Rights Act of 1964, there had been a long debate in the Senate which lasted twenty-four days, and cloture had to be invoked.

On March 7, 1966 the Supreme Court upheld the constitutionality of the new law.

Voter Requirements Outlawed by This Act

No State or political subdivision (counties, municipalities and parishes) covered by the Voting Rights Act may require the use of any test or device as a prerequisite for registration or voting.

Tests or devices included in this Act are those which require:

1. A demonstration of the ability to read, write, understand or interpret any given material.

2. A demonstration of any educational achievement or knowledge of any particular subject.

3. Proof of good moral character.

4. Proof of qualifications through a procedure in which another person (such as an individual already registered) must vouch for the prospective voter.

Coverage

The Voting Rights Act of 1965 states that no person shall be denied the right to vote in any Federal, State or local election (including

* From *Voting Rights Act of 1965*, Washington, D. C.: U. S. Commission on Civil Rights, 1965.

primaries) for failure to pass a test if he lives in a State or political subdivision which:

1. Maintained a test or device as a prerequisite to registration or voting as of November 1, 1964, *and*

2. Had a total voting age population of which less than 50 percent were registered or actually voted in the 1964 Presidential election.

If the above two factors are present, the State or political subdivision is automatically covered by the 1965 Act. If an entire State meets these qualifications, all of its counties come under the provisions of the Act. If only one county in a State meets them, the single county is subject to the requirements of the law.

States covered by the Act include Alabama, Alaska, Georgia, Louisiana, Mississippi, South Carolina, Virginia, and approximately 26 counties in North Carolina.

Cessation of Coverage

A State or political subdivision may be removed from coverage by filing a suit in a three-judge District Court for the District of Columbia. The State or political subdivision must convince the court that no test or device has been used for the purpose or with the effect of denying the right to vote because of race or color during the five years preceding the filing of the suit.

However, if there has been a previous court judgment against a State or political subdivision determining that tests or devices have been used to deny the right to vote, the State or political subdivision must wait five years before it can obtain an order from the District Court for the District of Columbia removing it from the coverage of the Act.

A judgment may be obtained more quickly if the Attorney General advises the court that he believes that the tests have not been used to discriminate on the basis of race or color during the five years preceding the filing of the action. He may also ask the court to reconsider its decision anytime within five years after judgment.

Changes in Voting Laws

When a State or political subdivision covered by the Act seeks to change its voting qualifications or procedures from those in effect on November 1, 1964, it must either obtain the approval of the U.S. Attorney General or initiate a Federal Court suit. If the Attorney General objects to these changes, or if they have not been submitted to him for his approval, the new laws may not be enforced until the District Court for the District of Columbia rules that the changes will not have the purpose or the effect of denying the right to vote because of the race or color of any person.

Federal Examiners

Once it is determined that a political subdivision is covered by the Act, the U.S. Attorney General may direct the U.S. Civil Service Commission to appoint Federal examiners to list voters if:

1. He has received twenty meritorious written complaints alleging voter discrimination, *or*

2. He believes that the appointment of examiners is necessary to enforce the guarantees of the Fifteenth Amendment.

The times, places and procedures for listing will be established by the Civil Service Commission.

Authority of the Examiners

The Federal examiners will list (that is, declare eligible and entitled to vote) those who satisfy state qualifications that have not been suspended by the Voting Rights Act. Examples of valid qualifications would be those of age and residence.

The examiners will prepare a list of qualified voters and send the list each month to State authorities who must register them—that is, place their names in the official voting records. This list must be available for public inspection. Each person on the examiner's list will be issued a certificate by the examiners as evidence of eligibility to vote in any Federal, State or local election.

No person listed by the examiner will be entitled to vote in any election unless his name has been sent to local election officials at least 45 days before that election thereby allowing the State election machinery to run without complication.

Enforcement of Action by Federal Examiners

At the request of the Attorney General the Civil Service Commission may appoint poll watchers in counties where Federal Examiners are already serving to observe whether all eligible persons are allowed to vote and whether all ballots are accurately tabulated.

If anyone who is properly listed or registered is not permitted to vote in any political subdivision where examiners are serving, a complaint may be made to the examiners of this denial within 48 hours after the polls close. If the examiner believes that the complaint has merit, he must inform the Attorney General immediately. The Attorney General may seek a district court order that provides for the casting of the ballot and suspends the election results until the vote is included in the final count.

Challenge of Listed Persons

A formal objection challenging the qualifications of a person listed by the Federal examiner may be filed (at a place to be designated by the Civil Service Commission) within ten days after the list of qualified voters has been made public and must be supported by at least two affidavits. The validity of the challenge will be determined within fifteen days after filing by a hearing officer appointed by the Civil Service Commission. The U.S. Court of Appeals may review decisions of the hearing officer.

Until the final court review is completed, any person listed by the examiner is still eligible and must be permitted to vote. If a challenge is successful, the name of the registrant will be removed from the examiner's list.

Withdrawal of Federal Examiners

Examiners may be withdrawn from a political subdivision when the names of all persons listed by the examiners have been placed in the official records and when there is no reason to believe that persons in the subdivision will be prevented from voting.

The removal may be accomplished by action of:

1. The Civil Service Commission after it receives notification from the U.S. Attorney General, *or*

2. The District Court for the District of Columbia in a suit brought by a political subdivision after the Director of the Census has determined that more than 50 percent of the nonwhite voting age population in the subdivision is registered to vote.

A political subdivision may petition the U.S. Attorney General to end listing procedures and to request that the Director of the Census conduct a survey to determine whether more than 50 percent of the nonwhite voting age population is registered.

Poll Taxes

The Act contains a Congressional finding that the right to vote has been denied or abridged by the requirement of the payment of a poll tax as a condition to voting.

The U.S. Attorney General is directed to institute suits against Alabama, Mississippi, Texas and Virginia which require the payment of poll taxes in order to determine if such taxes violate the Constitution. While a suit is pending, or upon a finding that the poll tax is constitutional, persons registered or listed for the first time in areas covered by the Act need only pay the tax for the current year. The poll tax may be paid up to 45 days prior to an election regardless of the timeliness of the payment under State law.

Voting Suits

The Voting Rights Act of 1965 gives new enforcement powers to the courts in voting cases. When the court finds that there has been a denial of the right to vote in a suit brought by the U.S. Attorney General, the court must:

1. Authorize the appointment of examiners by the Civil Service Commission unless denials of the right to vote have been few in number, they have been corrected by State or local action, and there is no probability that they will reoccur.

2. Suspend the use of tests or devices in an area where it has been proved that at least one such requirement has been utilized to deny the right to vote because of race or color.

When examiners have been authorized by court order, they may be removed by an order of the authorizing court.

Language Literacy

If a person residing in a State where tests or devices have not been suspended has completed at least six grades in an "American-flag" school (a school in the United States or its territories), his inability to speak the English language shall not be the basis for denying him the right to vote. For example, a person who completed six grades of school in the Commonwealth of Puerto Rico but who now resides on the mainland of the United States would satisfy literacy requirements.

Criminal and Civil Penalties

Public officials or private individuals who deny persons the right to vote guaranteed by the Voting Rights Act of 1965 or anyone who attempts to or intimidates, threatens, or coerces a person from voting are subject to criminal penalties. It is also made a crime to attempt to or to intimidate, threaten or coerce anyone who urges or aids any person to vote. Criminal penalties are provided for applicants who give false information about their eligibility to vote or who accept payment to register or vote in a Federal election. The U.S. Attorney General is also authorized to bring action for injunctive relief to restrain violations of the Act.

NEGRO REGISTRATION IN THE SOUTH HAS INCREASED DRAMATICALLY*

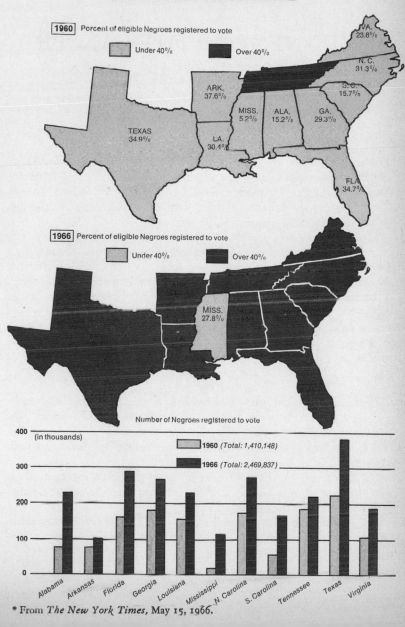

1960 Percent of eligible Negroes registered to vote

Under 40% Over 40%

VA. 23.8%
N. C. 31.3%
ARK. 37.6%
S. C. 15.7%
MISS. 5.2% ALA. 15.2% GA. 29.3%
TEXAS 34.9%
LA. 30.4%
FLA. 34.7%

1966 Percent of eligible Negroes registered to vote

Under 40% Over 40%

MISS. 27.8%

Number of Negroes registered to vote

400 (in thousands)

1960 (Total: 1,410,148)
1966 (Total: 2,469,837)

300

200

100

0

Alabama Arkansas Florida Georgia Louisiana Mississippi N. Carolina S. Carolina Tennessee Texas Virginia

* From *The New York Times*, May 15, 1966.

Selection 20

THE NEGRO VOTE CAN BE POTENT, IF—

TOM WICKER [*]

Washington, May 14—In Newark, N. J., this week, in the Democratic primary, Mayor Hugh Addonizio failed to win a majority. The Mayor faces a runoff against his principal opponent, Leo P. Carlin, primarily because a third candidate, Kenneth A. Gibson, polled just under 20 per cent of the total vote.

Mr. Gibson is a 33-year-old Negro, and he was running in a city where Negroes make up almost 50 per cent of the population. In a larger field, and polling a few more votes than Mr. Gibson, another Negro, Calvin West, won election as a city councilman-at-large.

These results did not attract as much national attention as the Alabama Democratic primaries last week, and Newark is not really analogous to the South because the city's Negro community is a higher proportion of its total population than Negroes ever will achieve in any Southern state.

"Poor" Majority

But some political analysts here believe that, as more and more Negroes vote and reach political sophistication in the South, the Southern political order will develop somewhat like Newark's. They were influenced by the following realities of Southern politics:

(1) In the South, the dominant majority in the region as a whole and in every state is white—and the Negro proportion of the population is generally declining.

(2) Another majority exists in the South that is not, so far, dominant. It is the majority of the less advantaged, of whatever race—

* From *The New York Times*, May 15, 1966.

of those from the middle income groups ranging down to the poverty-stricken.

(3) For nearly a century, the white majority of the South has dominated the "poor" majority because the issue of race has been used to unite white men of whatever economic class—all too often for the benefit of the Bourbons.

The smashing victory of Mrs. Lurleen Wallace, running as a stand-in for her husband, Gov. George Wallace of Alabama, disclosed these underlying realities once again.

Resistance

There now are, in Alabama, 235,572 registered Negroes—and about 115,000 of these have been put on the polling books since the passage of the Voting Rights Act of 1965. Yet, the total is only 16 per cent of Alabama's registered voters, and in the period since the voting act was passed, so many whites were also registered that Negroes succeeded in "closing the gap" between their vote and the white vote by a net of only 12,000.

Moreover, the whites of Alabama were sufficiently united—no matter what their other interests—by two factors. Governor Wallace had made himself a symbol of white resistance to Federally imposed Negro gains. His wife's principal opponent, Attorney General Richmond Flowers, openly campaigned for the Negro vote. The race issue, however soft pedaled in speeches, was central to the election.

Mr. Flowers got an estimated 90 per cent of the Negro vote—suggesting that only about 150,000 Negroes voted in the gubernatorial race—but even with eight other candidates in the field, Mrs. Wallace won a majority of about 52 per cent and avoided a runoff. She is estimated to have received more than 60 per cent of the white vote.

Political Realities

Negroes did win Democratic nominations for some local offices, in electorates where their numbers were in higher proportion. In the Texas primary in the same week, three Negroes won nominations for the State Legislature.

All this suggests that astute Negro political leadership in the South will grasp two overriding facts: that the Negro in that region is a political minority and will remain so, and that when the issue of race is raised either by white bigots or by obvious Negro bloc voting, the white majority will unite at the ballot box, at least in the foreseeable future.

That is why the Newark results become relevant to the South.

Newark showed that Negroes can influence important elections without trying to dominate them; that they need no longer be ignored or ridden over by white leaders. It showed that factors other than race—for instance, Mayor Addonizio's City Hall organization and powers—can influence the Negro as well as any other voter. It showed that important local offices can be won by Negroes—not only improving their present political power but building up experienced politicians (not merely Negro politicians) for the future.

New Order

Such an approach in the South appears numerically necessary, because of the Negro's permanent minority position. And it is the only route that offers any real hope anytime soon of uniting that other majority in the South—the vast body of whites and Negroes whose economic interests are identical.

Wherever the issue of race is openly raised, by whites or by Negroes, that majority is likely to be split, as it always has been before; where the race issue can be kept in the background, a new political order might be built in the South.

Democratic analysts appear to be particularly impressed by this long-term possibility. They believe their party offers the economic and social program upon which a big majority of the less advantaged—white and black—could agree, if racial politics could be avoided on both sides.

As Alabama showed, it is a big if.

PART III

JUSTICE FOR
THE NEGRO

Justice is supposed to be blind. Sculptors who create a blindfolded figure as the symbol of justice try to convey the idea that our courts and our law-enforcement agencies are not influenced by a person's wealth, religion, color, or nationality. All persons are entitled to the equal protection of the law and to due process of the law.

Charges of injustice toward Negroes and other minority groups are found in Northern and in Western cities, as well as in the South. These complaints often declare that Negroes are the victims of police brutality and "third degree" methods of prolonged questioning.

The selections which follow suggest some problems relating to the treatment of the Negro, mainly in the South.

Selection 21

SOUTHERN JUSTICE IN THE EARLY 1900s

RAY STANNARD BAKER*

This distinguished journalist offers us a view of Southern justice at the turn of the century.

One thing impressed me especially, not only in this court but in all others I have visited: a Negro brought in for drunkenness, for example, was punished much more severely than a white man arrested for the same offence. The injustice which the weak everywhere suffer—North and South—is in the South visited upon the Negro. The white man sometimes escaped with a reprimand, he was sometimes fined three dollars and costs, but the Negro, especially if he had no white man to intercede for him, was usually punished with a ten or fifteen dollar fine, which often meant that he must go to the chain-gang. One of the chief causes of complaint by the Negroes of Atlanta has been of the rough treatment of the police and of unjust arrests. After the riot, when the Civic League, composed of the foremost white citizens of Atlanta, was organized, one of the first subjects that came up was that of justice to the Negro. Mr. Hopkins, the leader of the League, said to me: "We complain that the Negroes will not help to bring the criminals of their race to justice. One reason for that is that the Negro has too little confidence in our courts. We must give him that, above all things."

* From Ray Stannard Baker, *Following the Color Line: American Negro Citizenship in the Progressive Era*, New York: Harper & Row, 1964, pp. 49, 51. [Originally published in 1908 by Doubleday, Page & Co.]

In accordance with this plan, the Civic League, heartily supported by Judge Broyles, employed a young lawyer, Mr. Underwood, to appear regularly in court and look after the interests of Negroes.

Convicts Making a Profit for Georgia

One reason for the very large number of arrests—in Georgia particularly—lies in the fact that the state and the counties make a profit out of their prison system. No attempt is ever made to reform a criminal, either white or coloured. Convicts are hired out to private contractors or worked on the public roads. Last year the net profit to Georgia from its chain-gangs, to which the prison commission refers with pride, reached the great sum of $354,-853.55.

Of course a very large proportion of the prisoners are Negroes. The demand for convicts by rich sawmill operators, owners of brick-yards, large farmers, and others is far in advance of the supply. The natural tendency is to convict as many men as possible—it furnishes steady, cheap labour to the contractors and a profit to the state. Undoubtedly this explains in some degree the very large number of criminals, especially Negroes, in Georgia. One of the leading political forces in Atlanta is a very prominent banker who is a dominant member of the city police board. He is also the owner of extensive brick-yards near Atlanta, where many convicts are employed. Some of the large fortunes in Atlanta have come chiefly from the labour of chain-gangs of convicts leased from the state.

Fate of the Black Boy

As I have already suggested, one of the things that impressed me strongly in visiting Judge Broyles's court—and others like it—was the astonishing number of children, especially Negroes, arrested. Some of them were very young and often exceedingly bright-looking. From the records I find that in 1906 one boy six years old, 7 of seven years, 33 of eight years, 69 of nine years, 107 of ten years, 142 of eleven years, and 219 of twelve years were arrested and brought into court—in other words, 578 boys and girls, mostly Negroes, under twelve years of age!

"I should think," I said to a police officer, "you would have trouble in taking care of all these children in your reformatories."

"Reformatories!" he said. "There aren't any."

"What do you do with them?"

"Well, if they're bad we put 'em in the stockade or the chain-gang, otherwise they're turned loose."

Selections 22a–22b

THE SCOTTSBORO CASE

The following selection is the famous first Scottsboro case, one of the most important decisions concerning the rights of an accused person.

Although the Scottsboro defendants had won a great legal victory in 1932, they had to use the courts for a second time in 1935, in order to secure their rights. Selection 22b gives the opinion of the Supreme Court in this second Scottsboro case.

22a.   Powell *vs.* Alabama*

Mr. Justice Sutherland delivered the opinion of the Court:

These cases were argued together and submitted for decision as one case.

The petitioners, hereinafter referred to as defendants, are Negroes charged with the crime of rape, committed upon the persons of two white girls. The crime is said to have been committed on March 25, 1931. The indictment was returned in a state court of first instance on March 31, and the record recites that on the same day the defendants were arraigned and entered pleas of not guilty. There is a further recital to the effect that upon the arraignment they were represented by counsel. But no counsel had been employed, and aside from a statement made by the trial judge several days later during a colloquy immediately preceding the trial, the record does not disclose when, or under what circumstances, an appointment of counsel was made, or who was appointed. During

* 287 U.S. 45 (1932).

the colloquy referred to, the trial judge, in response to a question, said that he had appointed all the members of the bar for the purpose of arraigning the defendants and then of course anticipated that the members of the bar would continue to help the defendants if no counsel appeared. Upon the argument here both sides accepted that as a correct statement of the facts concerning the matter.

There was a severance upon the request of the state, and the defendants were tried in three several groups, as indicated above. As each of the three cases was called for trial, each defendant was arraigned, and, having the indictment read to him, entered a plea of not guilty. Whether the original arraignment and pleas were regarded as ineffective is not shown. Each of the three trials was completed within a single day. Under the Alabama statute the punishment for rape is to be fixed by the jury, and in its discretion may be from ten years imprisonment to death. The juries found defendants guilty and imposed the death penalty upon all. The trial court overruled motions for new trials and sentenced the defendants in accordance with the verdicts. The judgments were affirmed by the state supreme court. Chief Justice Anderson thought the defendants had not been accorded a fair trial and strongly dissented. . . .

In this court the judgments are assailed upon the grounds that the defendants, and each of them, were denied due process of law and the equal protection of the laws, in contravention of the Fourteenth Amendment, specifically as follows: (1) they were not given a fair, impartial, and deliberate trial; (2) they were denied the right of counsel, with the accustomed incidents of consultation and opportunity of preparation for trial; and (3) they were tried before juries from which qualified members of their own race were systematically excluded. These questions were properly raised and saved in the courts below.

The only one of the assignments which we shall consider is the second, in respect of the denial of counsel; and it becomes unnecessary to discuss the facts of the case or the circumstances surrounding the prosecution except in so far as they reflect light upon that question.

The record shows that on the day when the offense is said to have been committed, these defendants, together with a number of other Negroes, were upon a freight train on its way through Alabama. On the same train were seven white boys and two white girls. A fight took place between the Negroes and the white boys, in the course of which the white boys, with the exception of one named Gilley, were thrown off the train. A message was sent ahead, reporting the fight and asking that every Negro be gotten off the train. The participants in the fight, and the two girls, were in an open gondola car. The two girls testified that each of them was assaulted by six different Negroes in turn, and they identified the seven defendants as having been among the number. None of the white boys was called to testify, with the exception of Gilley, who was called in rebuttal.

Before the train reached Scottsboro, Alabama, a sheriff's posse seized the defendants and two other Negroes. Both girls and the Negroes then were taken to Scottsboro, the county seat. Word of their coming and of the alleged assault had preceded them, and they were met at Scottsboro by a large crowd. It does not sufficiently appear that the defendants were seriously threatened with, or that they were actually in danger of, mob violence; but it does appear that the attitude of the community was one of great hostility. The sheriff thought it necessary to call for the militia to assist in safeguarding the prisoners. Chief Justice Anderson pointed out in his opinion that every step taken from the arrest and arraignment to the sentence was accompanied by the military. Soldiers took the defendants to Gadsden for safe-keeping, brought them back to Scottsboro for arraignment, returned them to Gadsden for safe-keeping while awaiting trial, escorted them to Scottsboro for trial a few days later, and guarded the courthouse and grounds at every stage of the proceedings. It is perfectly apparent that the proceedings, from beginning to end, took place in an atmosphere of tense, hostile, and excited public sentiment. During the entire time, the defendants were closely confined or were under military guard. The record does not disclose their ages, exept that one of them was nineteen; but the record clearly indicates that most, if not all, of them were youthful, and they are constantly referred to as "the boys." They were ignorant and illiterate. All of them were residents of other states, where alone members of their families or friends resided.

However guilty the defendants, upon due inquiry, might prove to have been, they were, until convicted, presumed to be innocent. It was the duty of the court having their cases in charge to see that they were denied no necessary incident of a fair trial. With any error of the state court involving alleged contravention of the state statutes or constitution we, of course, have nothing to do. The sole inquiry which we are permitted to make is whether the federal Constitution was contravened . . . ; and as to that, we confine ourselves, as already suggested, to the inquiry whether the defendants were in substance denied the right of counsel, and if so, whether such denial infringes the due process clause of the Fourteenth Amendment.

First. The record shows that immediately upon the return of the indictment defendants were arraigned and pleaded not guilty. Apparently they were not asked whether they had, or were able to employ, counsel, or wished to have counsel appointed; or whether they had friends or relatives who might assist in that regard if communicated with. That it would not have been an idle ceremony to have given the defendants reasonable opportunity to communicate with their families and endeavor to obtain counsel is demonstrated by the fact that very soon after conviction, able counsel appeared in their behalf. This was pointed out by Chief Justice Anderson in the course of his dissenting opinion. "They were nonresidents," he said, "and had little time or opportunity to get in touch with their families and friends who were scattered throughout two other states, and time has demonstrated that they could or would have been represented by able counsel had a better opportunity been given by a reasonable delay in the trial of the cases judging from the number and activity of counsel that appeared immediately or shortly after their conviction." (*Powell* vs. *State,* 224 Ala. at pp. 554–555, 141 So. 201.)

It is hardly necessary to say that, the right to counsel being conceded, a defendant should be afforded a fair opportunity to secure counsel of his own choice. Not only was that not done here, but such designation of counsel as was attempted was either so indefinite or so close upon the trial as to amount to a denial of effective and substantial aid in that regard. This will be amply demonstrated by a brief review of the record.

April 6, six days after indictment, the trials began. When the first case was called, the court inquired whether the parties were ready for trial. The state's attorney replied that he was ready to proceed. No one answered for the defendants or appeared to represent or defend them. Mr. Roddy, a Tennessee lawyer not a member of the local bar, addressed the court, saying that he had not been employed, but that people who were interested had spoken to him about the case. He was asked by the court whether he intended to appear for the defendants, and answered that he would like to appear along with counsel that the court might appoint. . . .

It thus will be seen that until the very morning of the trial no lawyer had been named or definitely designated to represent the defendants. Prior to that time, the trial judge had "appointed all the members of the bar" for the limited "purpose of arraigning the defendants." Whether they would represent the defendants thereafter, if no counsel appeared in their behalf, was a matter of speculation only, or, as the judge indicated, of mere anticipation on the part of the court. Such a designation, even if made for all purposes, would, in our opinion, have fallen far short of meeting, in any proper sense, a requirement for the appointment of counsel. How many lawyers were members of the bar does not appear; but, in the very nature of things, whether many or few, they would not, thus collectively named, have been given that clear appreciation of responsibility or impressed with that individual sense of duty which should and naturally would accompany the appointment of a selected member of the bar, specifically named and assigned.

That this action of the trial judge in respect of appointment of counsel was little more than an expansive gesture, imposing no substantial or definite obligation upon any one, is borne out by the fact that prior to the calling of the case for trial on April 6, a leading member of the local bar accepted employment on the side of the prosecution and actively participated in the trial. It is true that he said that before doing so he had understood Mr. Roddy would be employed as counsel for the defendants. This the lawyer in question, of his own accord, frankly stated to the court; and no doubt he acted with the utmost good faith. Probably other members of the bar had a like understanding. In any event, the circumstance lends emphasis to the conclusion that during perhaps the most critical period of the proceedings against these defendants, that is to say, from the time of their arraignment until the beginning of their trial, when consultation, thorough-going investigation and preparation were vitally important, the defendants did not have the aid of counsel in any real sense, although they were as much entitled to such aid during that period as at the trial itself. . . .

Nor do we think the situation was helped by what occurred on the morning of the trial. At that time, as appears from the colloquy printed above, Mr. Roddy stated to the court that he did not appear as counsel, but that he would like to appear along with counsel that the court might appoint; that he had not been given an opportunity to prepare the case; that he was not familiar with the procedure in Alabama, but merely came down as a friend of the people who were interested; that he thought the boys would be better off if he should step entirely out of the case. Mr. Moody, a member of the local bar, expressed a willingness to help Mr. Roddy in anything he could do under the circumstances. To this the court responded: "All right, all the lawyers that will; of course

I would not require a lawyer to appear if—." And Mr. Moody continued, "I am willing to do that for him as a member of the bar; I will go ahead and help do anything I can do." With this dubious understanding, the trials immediately proceeded. The defendants, young, ignorant, illiterate, surrounded by hostile sentiment, hauled back and forth under guard of soldiers, charged with an atrocious crime regarded with especial horror in the community where they were to be tried, were thus put in peril of their lives within a few moments after counsel for the first time charged with any degree of responsibility began to represent them.

It is not enough to assume that counsel thus precipitated into the case thought there was no defense, and exercised their best judgment in proceeding to trial without preparation. Neither they nor the court could say what a prompt and thorough-going investigation might disclose as to the facts. No attempt was made to investigate. No opportunity to do so was given. Defendants were immediately hurried to trial. . . . Under the circumstances disclosed, we hold that defendants were not accorded the right of counsel in any substantial sense. . . .

The prompt disposition of criminal cases is to be commended and encouraged. But in reaching that result a defendant, charged with a serious crime, must not be stripped of his right to have sufficient time to advise with counsel and prepare his defense. . . .

Second. . . . The question . . . which it is our duty, and within our power, to decide, is whether the denial of the assistance of counsel contravenes the due process clause of the Fourteenth Amendment to the federal Constitution. . . .

. . . The fact that the right involved is of such a character that it cannot be denied without violating those "fundamental principles of liberty and justice which lie at the base of all our civil and political institutions" (*Hebert* vs. *Louisiana,* 272 U.S. 312, 316), is obviously one of those compelling considerations which must prevail in determining whether it is embraced within the due process clause of the Fourteenth Amendment, although it be specifically dealt with in another part of the Federal Constitution. Evidently this court, in the latter cases enumerated, regarded the rights there under consideration as of this fundamental character. That some such distinction must be observed is foreshadowed in *Twining* vs. *New Jersey,* 211 U.S. 78, 99, where Mr. Justice Moody, speaking for the court, said that ". . . it is possible that some of the personal rights safeguarded by the first eight Amendments against national action may also be safeguarded against state action, because a denial of them would be a denial of due process of law (*Chicago, Burlington & Quincy Railroad* vs. *Chicago,* 166 U.S. 226). If this is so, it is not because those rights are enumerated in the first eight Amendments, but because they are of such a nature that they are included in the conception of due process of law." While the question has never been categorically determined by this court, a consideration of the nature of the right and a review of the expressions of this and other courts, makes it clear that the right to the aid of counsel is of this fundamental character.

It never has been doubted by this court, or any other so far as we know, that notice and hearing are preliminary steps essential to the passing of an enforceable judgment, and that they, together with a legally competent tribunal having jurisdiction of the case, constitute basic elements of the constitutional requirement of due process of law. . . .

What, then, does a hearing include? Historically and in practice, in our own country at least, it has always included the right to the aid of counsel when desired and provided by the party asserting the right. The right to be heard would be, in many cases, of little avail if it did not comprehend the right to be heard by counsel. Even the intelligent and educated layman has small and sometimes no skill in the science of law. If charged with crime, he is incapable, generally, of determining for himself whether the indictment is good or bad. He is unfamiliar with the rules of evidence. Left without the aid of counsel he may be put on trial without a proper charge, and convicted upon incompetent evidence, or evidence irrelevant to the issue or otherwise inadmissible. He lacks both the skill and knowledge adequately to prepare his defense, even though he have a perfect one. He requires the guiding hand of counsel at every step in the proceedings against him. Without it, though he be not guilty, he faces the danger of conviction because he does not know how to establish his innocence. If that be true of men of intelligence, how much more true is it of the ignorant and illiterate, or those of feeble intellect. If in any case, civil or criminal, a state or federal court were arbitrarily to refuse to hear a party by counsel, employed by and appearing for him, it reasonably may not be doubted that such a refusal would be a denial of a hearing, and, therefore, of due process in the constitutional sense. . . .

In the light of the facts outlined in the forepart of this opinion —the ignorance and illiteracy of the defendants, their youth, the circumstances of public hostility, the imprisonment and the close surveillance of the defendants by the military forces, the fact that their friends and families were all in other states and communication with them necessarily difficult, and above all that they stood in deadly peril of their lives—we think the failure of the trial court to give them reasonable time and opportunity to secure counsel was a clear denial of due process.

But passing that, and assuming their inability, even if opportunity had been given, to employ counsel, as the trial court evidently did assume, we are of opinion that, under the circumstances just stated, the necessity of counsel was so vital and imperative that the failure of the trial court to make an effective appointment of counsel was likewise a denial of due process within the meaning of the Fourteenth Amendment. Whether this would be so in other criminal prosecutions, or under other circumstances, we need not determine. All that it is necessary now to decide, as we do decide, is that in a capital case, where the defendant is unable to employ counsel, and is incapable adequately of making his own defense because of ignorance, feeble-mindedness, illiteracy, or the like, it is the duty of the court, whether requested or not, to assign counsel for him as a necessary requisite of due process of law; and that duty is not discharged by an assignment at such a time or under such circumstances as to preclude the giving of effective aid in the preparation and trial of the case.

The United States by statute and every state in the Union by express provision of law, or by the determination of its courts, make it the duty of the trial judge, where the accused is unable to employ counsel, to appoint counsel for him. In most states the rule applies broadly to all criminal prosecutions, in others it is limited to the more serious crimes, and in a very limited number, to capital cases. A rule adopted with such unanimous accord, reflects, if it does not establish the inherent right to have counsel appointed at least in cases like the present, and lends convincing support to the conclusion we have reached as to the fundamental nature of that right.

The judgments must be reversed, and the causes remanded for further proceedings not inconsistent with this opinion.

Judgments reversed.

22b. Norris *vs.* Alabama*

Mr. Chief Justice Hughes delivered the opinion of the Court, saying in part:

Petitioner, Clarence Norris, is one of nine Negro boys who were indicted in March, 1931, in Jackson County, Alabama, for the crime of rape. On being brought to trial in that county eight were convicted. This Court reversed the judgments of conviction upon the

---

* (294 U.S. 587; 79 L. Ed. 1074; 55 Sup. Ct. 579. 1935.)

ground that the defendants had been denied due process of law in that the trial court had failed in the light of the circumstances disclosed, and of the inability of the defendants at that time to obtain counsel, to make an effective appointment of counsel to aid them in preparing and presenting their defense. (*Powell* vs. *Alabama,* 287 U.S. 45). . . .

After the remand, a motion for change of venue was granted and the cases were transferred to Morgan County. Norris was brought to trial in November, 1933. At the outset, a motion was made on his behalf to quash the indictment upon the ground of the exclusion of Negroes from juries in Jackson County where the indictment was found. A motion was also made to quash the trial venire in Morgan County upon the ground of the exclusion of Negroes from juries in that county. In relation to each county, the charge was of long continued, systematic and arbitrary exclusion of qualified Negro citizens from service on juries, solely because of their race and color, in violation of the Constitution of the United States. . . . The trial . . . proceeded and resulted in the conviction of Norris who was sentenced to death. On appeal, the supreme court of the state considered and decided the federal question which Norris had raised and affirmed the judgment. . . . We granted a writ of certiorari.

First. There is no controversy as to the constitutional principle involved . . . this Court thus stated the principle in *Carter* vs. *Texas,* 177 U.S. 442, 447, in relation to exclusion from service on grand juries: "Whenever by any action of a state, whether through its legislature, through its courts, or through its executive or administrative officers, all persons of the African race are excluded, solely because of their race or color, from serving as grand jurors in the criminal prosecution of a person of the African race, the equal protection of the laws is denied to him, contrary to the Fourteenth Amendment." . . . The principle is equally applicable to a similar exclusion of Negroes from service on petit juries. . . . And although the state statute defining the qualifications of jurors may be fair on its face, the constitutional provision affords protection against action of the state through its administrative officers in effecting the prohibited discrimination. . . .

The question is of the application of this established principle to the facts disclosed by the record. That the question is one of fact does not relieve us of the duty to determine whether in truth a federal right has been denied. When a federal right has been specially set up and claimed in a state court, it is our province to inquire not merely whether it was denied in express terms but also whether it was denied in substance and effect. . . .

Second. The evidence on the motion to quash the indictment. In 1930, the total population of Jackson County, where the indictment was found, was 36,881, of whom 2688 were Negroes. The male population over twenty-one years of age numbered 8801, and of these 666 were Negroes.

The qualifications of jurors were thus prescribed by the state statute . . . : "The jury commission shall place on the jury roll and in the jury box the names of all male citizens of the county who are generally reputed to be honest and intelligent men, and are esteemed in the community for their integrity, good character and sound judgment, but no person must be selected who is under twenty-one or over sixty-five years of age, or who is an habitual drunkard, or who, being afflicted with a permanent disease or physical weakness is unfit to discharge the duties of a juror, or who cannot read English, or who has ever been convicted of any offense involving moral turpitude. If a person cannot read English and has all the other qualifications prescribed herein and is a free-holder or householder, his name may be placed on the jury roll and in the jury box." . . .

Defendant adduced evidence to support the charge of unconstitutional discrimination in the actual administration of the statute in Jackson County. The testimony, as the state court said, tended to show that "in a long number of years no Negro had been called for jury service in that county." It appeared that no Negro had served on any grand or petit jury in that county within the memory of witnesses who had lived there all their lives. Testimony to that effect was given by men whose ages ran from fifty to seventy-six years. Their testimony was uncontradicted. It was supported by the testimony of officials. The clerk of the jury commission and the clerk of the circuit court had never known of a Negro serving on a grand jury in Jackson County. The court reporter, who had not missed a session in that county in twenty-four years, and two jury commissioners testified to the same effect. One of the latter, who was a member of the commission which made up the jury roll for the grand jury which found the indictment, testified that he had "never known of a single instance where any Negro sat on any grand or petit jury in the entire history of that county."

That testimony in itself made out a *prima facie* case of the denial of the equal protection which the Constitution guarantees. . . . The case thus made was supplemented by direct testimony that specified Negroes, thirty or more in number, were qualified for jury service. Among these were Negroes who were members of school boards, or trustees, of colored schools, and property owners and householders. It also appeared that Negroes from that county had been called for jury service in the federal court. Several of those who were thus described as qualified were witnesses. While there was testimony which cast doubt upon the qualifications of some of the Negroes who had been named, and there was also general testimony by the editor of a local newspaper who gave his opinion as to the lack of "sound judgment" of the "good Negroes" in Jackson County, we think that the definite testimony as to the actual qualifications of individual Negroes, which was not met by any testimony equally direct, showed that there were Negroes in Jackson County qualified for jury service. . . .

The state court rested its decision upon the ground that even if it were assumed that there was no name of a Negro on the jury roll, it was not established that race or color caused the omission. The court pointed out that the statute fixed a high standard of qualifications for jurors . . . and that the jury commission was vested with a wide discretion. The court adverted to the fact that more white citizens possessing age qualifications had been omitted from the jury roll than the entire Negro population of the county, and regarded the testimony as being to the effect that "the matter of race, color, politics, religion or fraternal affiliations" had not been discussed by the commission and had not entered into their consideration, and that no one had been excluded because of race or color. . . .

We are of the opinion that the evidence required a different result from that reached in the state court. We think that the evidence that for a generation or longer no Negro had been called for service on any jury in Jackson County, that there were Negroes qualified for jury service, that according to the practice of the jury commission their names would normally appear on the preliminary list of male citizens of the requisite age but that no names of Negroes were placed on the jury roll, and the testimony with respect to the lack of appropriate consideration of the qualifications of Negroes, established the discrimination which the Constitution forbids. The motion to quash the indictment upon that ground should have been granted.

Third. The evidence on the motion to quash the trial venire. The population of Morgan County, where the trial was had, was larger than that of Jackson County, and the proportion of Negroes was much greater. The total population of Morgan County in 1930 was 46,176, and of this number 8311 were Negroes.

Within the memory of witnesses long resident there, no Negro had ever served on a jury in that county or had been called for such service. Some of these witnesses were over fifty years of age and had always lived in Morgan County. Their testimony was not contradicted. A clerk of the circuit court, who had resided in the county for thirty years, and who had been in office for over four years, testified that during his official term approximately 2500 persons had been called for jury service and that not one of them was a Negro; that he did not recall "ever seeing any single person of the colored race serve on any jury in Morgan County."

There was abundant evidence that there were a large number of Negroes in the county who were qualified for jury service. Men of intelligence, some of whom were college graduates, testified to long lists (said to contain nearly 200 names) of such qualified Negroes, including many businessmen, owners of real property and householders. When defendant's counsel proposed to call many additional witnesses in order to adduce further proof of qualifications of Negroes for jury service, the trial judge limited the testimony, holding that the evidence was cumulative.

We find no warrant for a conclusion that the names of any of the Negroes as to whom this testimony was given, or of any other Negroes, were placed on the jury rolls. No such names were identified. The evidence that for many years no Negro had been called for jury service itself tended to show the absence of the names of Negroes from the jury rolls, and the state made no effort to prove their presence. . . .

For this long-continued, unvarying, and wholesale exclusion of Negroes from jury service we find no justification consistent with the constitutional mandate.

. . . That showing as to the long-continued exclusion of Negroes from jury service, and as to the many Negroes qualified for that service, could not be met by mere generalities. If, in the presence of such testimony as defendant adduced, the mere general assertions by officials of their performance of duty were to be accepted as an adequate justification for the complete exclusion of Negroes from jury service, the constitutional provision—adopted with special reference to their protection—would be but a vain and illusory requirement. . . .

We are concerned only with the federal question which we have discussed, and in view of the denial of the federal right suitably asserted, the judgment must be reversed and the cause remanded for further proceedings not inconsistent with this opinion. . . .

Selection 23

"A Guy's Entitled To A Jury Of His Peers, Ain't He?"

© 1965 Herblock in the *Washington Post*

Books

FEDERAL LAW

STATE LAW

STUDENTS' PLIGHT

SANCTUARY

Selection 24

JUSTICE: REPORT OF U. S. CIVIL RIGHTS COMMISSION, 1963*

This selection from the 1963 Report of the United States Commission on Civil Rights points up the problem of injustice to the Negro in communities throughout the country.

The rights of citizens to speak freely, to assemble peaceably, and to petition government for the redress of grievances are guaranteed by the First Amendment to the Constitution. These rights are protected against State encroachment by the Fourteenth Amendment. Official actions taken to stop recent civil rights protest demonstrations in the name of peace and order often have infringed upon these protected rights.

To determine the extent of these infringements, and to study the dilemma often caused by the need to guarantee private rights while maintaining public order the Commission focused its administration of justice study on five cities where protest demonstrations have taken place. They are Birmingham, Ala.; Cairo, Ill.; Baton Rouge, La.; Jackson, Miss.; and Memphis, Tenn. In its study, the Commission found that existing legal remedies for blocking official interference with legitimate demonstrations are insufficient and that protests against civil rights deprivations are being frustrated. The study also demonstrated that effective legal remedies must be fashioned if unwarranted official interference is not to result in the total suppression of constitutional rights to protest.

During its current term, the Commission also investigated the participation of Negroes in the administration of justice. The Commission found that in many places, Negroes have been discrimi-

* From *Report of the United States Commission on Civil Rights—1963*, Washington, D. C.: pp. 107–14, 123–25.

nated against as lawyers; as law enforcement, court, and prison employees; and as prisoners. The results of this study also are presented in this chapter.

Civil Rights Protests and State Action

On February 1, 1960, four college students in Greensboro, North Carolina entered a variety store, made several purchases, sat down at the lunch counter, ordered coffee, and were refused service because they were Negroes. They remained in their seats until the store closed. In the spring and summer of 1960, young people, both white and Negro, participated in similar protests against segregation and discrimination wherever it was to be found. They sat in white libraries, waded at white beaches, and slept in the lobbies of white hotels. Many were arrested for trespassing, disturbing the peace, and disobeying police officers who ordered them off the premises. Thus began the sweeping protest movement against entrenched practices of segregation.

Since the equal protection clause of the 14th Amendment prohibits State-enforced segregation, it is clear that convictions under a statute or ordinance requiring segregation cannot be sustained. In general, officials who acted to suppress demonstrations in the cities studied did not attempt to apply such laws directly. But any arrest, even without a conviction, operates as a sanction, since the imprisoned protester still must stay in jail or post bail, retain counsel, and defend himself.

The Supreme Court, following the *School Segregation Cases,* has consistently held that State and local governments may not segregate publicly owned or operated facilities. It has recently held that a municipality may not arrest and prosecute Negroes for peaceably seeking the use of city owned and operated facilities. But in both Jackson and Memphis, police arrested protesters seeking desegregated use of public facilities. The charge in most of these cases was breach of the peace or disorderly conduct. In finding the protesters guilty, a city judge in Jackson found that, while they had been orderly, their conduct could have provoked a breach of the peace by others. However, the mere "possibility of disorder by others cannot justify exclusion of persons from a place if they otherwise have a constitutional right (founded upon the Equal Protection Clause) to be present." The exercise of the First Amendment freedoms of speech and assembly cannot be abridged "unless shown likely to produce a clear and present danger of a serious substantive evil that rises far above public inconvenience, annoyance, or unrest."

The right to use vehicles and terminal facilities in interstate commerce on a nonsegregated basis is another right that has been established by Federal court decisions and specific orders of the Interstate Commerce Commission. In Baton Rouge, Memphis, Jackson, and Birmingham, when protesters sought to use such facilities, they were arrested. They were charged, not with violation of segregation laws, but with breach of the peace. In Jackson, more than 300 demonstrators were arrested during the 1961 Freedom Rides. Local authorities claimed that they committed a breach of the peace by refusing to obey police commands to leave the interstate bus terminal's segregated waiting rooms. The riders claimed their Federal rights peaceably to seek and obtain unsegregated service as did protesters in the other cities. An early application to the Supreme Court for an injunction to stay the State criminal prosecutions in Jackson was denied. The lengthy route through the Mississippi courts is still being pursued some two and a half years later.

The constitutionality of arrests and prosecutions of those who seek desegregated service at privately owned facilities open to the public has also been questioned. These protests have included lunch counter sit-ins, which have occurred throughout the country and in four of the five cities studied by the Commission. While this type of demonstration has formed only a part of the total civil rights protest movement, it has presented one of the most difficult constitutional problems arising from protest activities. The question these cases raise is whether the arrest and conviction of protesters peacefully seeking such desegregated service represents unlawful "State action" under the 14th Amendment.

Having disposed of the first sit-in cases on other grounds, the Supreme Court in May 1963 approached the question in a series of sit-in cases from Greenville, S. C.; New Orleans, Birmingham, and Durham. The protesters had been convicted, not for breach of the peace, but for trespass on the private property of those who operated restaurants and lunch counters. Confronted with an apparent conflict between the proprietors' property rights and the protesters' right to be free from State-enforced segregation, the Court found that State action was involved and reversed the convictions.

The Greenville and Birmingham cases involved ordinances requiring operators of eating places to segregate. Although not directly invoked, these ordinances were found to have left such operators no choice but to segregate. The Court held that the use of the State's criminal processes to arrest and convict the protesters had the effect of enforcing the segregation ordinances and was consequently prohibited State action in violation of the Equal Protection Clause of the 14th Amendment. In New Orleans, where there was no law requiring segregation in eating places, the Court ruled that city officials' public statements that attempts to secure desegregated service would not be permitted had the same effect as segregation ordinances.

These decisions have removed virtually all doubt about the validity of trespass convictions in situations such as Birmingham, where there are laws requiring segregated eating facilities. Moreover, the principle of the New Orleans case apparently applies to situations such as the Commission found in Baton Rouge and Jackson, where city officials were publicly committed to using State criminal processes to maintain segregation. But the applicability of the 1963 sit-in decisions to situations such as Cairo is not clear. Here, the voice of the State has clearly spoken for desegregation. The Mayor of Cairo has personally urged proprietors to obey the Illinois law prohibiting discrimination, in places of public accommodation. Yet students were arrested for trespass when they sought service at a private restaurant.

Many cities either do not have or have repealed segregation ordinances. Many officials either have never made or have stopped making public statements committing the State to maintenance of segregation. This has brought to the Court the broad question of whether the State has any right to arrest and prosecute protesters for seeking equal access to places of public accommodation.

In these situations, the protesters acted to secure immediate desegregated use of a facility. But different problems may be presented when protesters engage in street demonstrations against discrimination in general. One such incident occurred in March 1961, when 187 Negro students marched on the South Carolina State House to make their grievances known to the public and the legislature, which was then in session. Refusing to disperse, they were arrested and convicted for breach of the peace. Their appeals were decided by the Supreme Court in February 1963. The Court found that the protesters had been orderly, that they had not obstructed pedestrian or vehicular traffic, and that there had been no clear and present threat of violence by bystanders which the police were unable to control. Reversing the convictions, the Court held that "in arresting, convicting, and punishing the petitioners under the circumstances disclosed by this record, South Carolina infringed the petitioners' constitutionally protected rights of free speech, free assembly, and freedom to petition for redress of grievances."

Application of this Supreme Court decision to events in the five cities is difficult because the material facts differ in each case. On many occasions Memphis and Cairo officials did not interfere with mass demonstrations on public streets. Cairo police arrested protesters under an ordinance requiring parade permits which was enacted after the demonstrations started. The Illinois attorney general joined in an NAACP suit challenging the constitutionality of the ordinance. State and local officials and protest leaders later consented to dismissal of the suit on the understanding that the charges against the arrested protesters would be dismissed and the ordinance would not again be invoked against peaceful street demonstrations. Baton Rouge officials did not interfere with mass street demonstrations during the 1960 protests. In 1961, official policy changed. Conduct that had been permitted in 1960 resulted in arrests.

The official policy in both Jackson and Birmingham, throughout the period covered by the Commission's study, was one of suppressing street demonstrations. While police action in each arrest may not have been improper, the total pattern of official action, as indicated by the public statements of city officials, was to maintain segregation and to suppress protests. The police followed that policy and they were usually supported by local prosecutors and courts.

Discrimination in Processes of Justice

Denials of equal protection may arise not only from attempts by officials to enforce segregation but also in the processes of justice when an official treats a person differently because of his color, race, religion, or national origin.

In civil rights demonstrations, the role of the policeman has been significant; his actions often speak for the community. When a policeman acts to deprive a person of his constitutional rights, he violates Federal law. Moreover, police inaction which results in a failure to provide adequate protection to persons asserting their constitutional rights may also constitute a violation of Federal law. When Montgomery police failed to provide protection for the Freedom Riders in 1961, a Federal district judge declared, "The failure of the defendant law enforcement officers to enforce the law in this case clearly amounts to unlawful State action in violation of the Equal Protection Clause of the Fourteenth Amendment."

Testimony at the Commission's Memphis hearings disclosed that none of the protesters there was subjected to physical mistreatment by the police. Nor were there any allegations of lack of police protection for demonstrators. On one occasion in Cairo, protesters complained of police beatings and the use of tear gas. They also charged that State police and sheriff's deputies failed in another instance to protect demonstrators against a crowd of violent whites. Commission investigations found some evidence to support these allegations; however, such instances were not part of a pattern of action by law enforcement officials in those cities.

There have been few complaints of police mistreatment of protesters in Baton Rouge. In fact, a leader of the 1960 protests praised the police for their conduct. But in 1961, students complained of police misconduct in dispersing a protest assembly and of mistreatment of arrested demonstrators by jail guards.

The situation was different in Jackson and Birmingham. There, the Commission found a pattern of police abuse of civil rights protesters. In Jackson, there were continuing police efforts to disperse by force many forms of demonstrations and there was evidence of mistreatment of students, both in the county jail and State penitentiary.

Evidence also showed there was continuing abuse of protesters by Birmingham police. In 1963, dogs, clubs, and firehoses were used to disperse mass demonstrations. Violent reaction by Negroes followed. The reaction was directed not against white bystanders, but against the city police.

Prosecutors claimed that Negro students received the same treatment in the criminal process as anyone else. But in October 1962 the district attorney in Baton Rouge told Commission investigators:

> I'm going to make it just as hard on these outside agitators as I can. And I don't know a judge or official [in Baton Rouge] who doesn't agree with me.

His statement was addressed primarily to the fixing of bail requirements for arrested demonstrators. Discriminatory use of bail requirements raises a question of denial of equal protection.

In neither Memphis nor Birmingham did bail requirements present a serious problem, although the aggregate bond cost was high when mass arrests were made. In Cairo, most students were released on their own recognizance. The 1961 mass arrests of Freedom Riders in Jackson presented a serious bail problem. Surety bonds were required, and exhaustive efforts by protest leaders were unsuccessful in finding a company anywhere in the country to tended periods in the county jail and State penitentiary. . . . write the bonds. The result was that most of the Riders spent ex-

Summary

The right of citizens to assemble freely and to express grievances is a fundamental guarantee of the Constitution. In recent years persons concerned with civil rights have exercised their First Amendment rights to assemble and protest against segregation and discrimination. In some circumstances, demonstrations may exceed the boundaries of free speech and interfere unduly with public peace and order. In the cases studied by the Commission, however, protests with few exceptions have been peaceful and orderly and well within the protective guarantees of the First Amendment.

Where protests such as sit-ins involve entry into places of public accommodations, other issues may arise. The Commission's study reveals that breach of peace and trespass ordinances, on their face unrelated to the preservation of segregation, have been employed by local officials to maintain it. That this use of breach of the peace and trespass ordinances may be prohibited by the 14th Amendment has now been recognized by the Supreme Court in a series of cases decided in 1963.

The Commission's statistical survey establishes that law enforcement agencies throughout most of the Nation are staffed exclusively or overwhelmingly by whites. This fact may influence the administration of justice, but, whether it does or not, the attitude of the Negro toward local law authorities is affected.

Recommendations

Recommendation 1: That Congress empower the Attorney General to intervene in or to initiate civil proceedings to prevent denials to persons of any rights, privileges or immunities secured to them by the Constitution or laws of the United States.

Recommendation 2: That Congress enact a program of grants-in-aid to assist State and local governments, upon their request, to increase the professional quality of their police forces. Such grants-in-aid should be conditioned upon nondiscriminatory administration by the recipient and might apply to the development and maintenance of (1) programs to encourage applications by qualified persons for appointment as police officers; (2) recruit selection tests and standards; (3) training programs in scientific crime detection; (4) training programs in constitutional rights and human relations; (5) college level schools of police administration; and (6) scholarship programs that assist policemen to receive training in schools of police administration.

Recommendation 3: That Congress amend Section 1983 of Title 42 of the United States Code to make any county government, city government, or other local governmental entity that employs officers who deprive persons of rights protected by that section, jointly liable with the officers to victims of such officers' misconduct.

Recommendation 4: That Congress amend Section 1443 of Title 28 of the United States Code to permit removal by the defendant of a State civil action or criminal prosecution to a district court of the United States in cases where the defendant cannot, in the State court, secure his civil rights because of the written or decisional laws of the State or because of the acts of individuals administering or affecting its judicial process.

Selection 25

RECOMMENDATIONS OF U. S. CIVIL RIGHTS COMMISSION, 1965*

Following are the recommendations of the United States Commission on Civil Rights on expanding Federal law enforcement in the South. The commission's report was released on November 13, 1965.

I. Criminal Remedies

Failures of state and local law enforcement officials to prevent or punish crimes of racial violence and the inadequacy of the current Federal criminal statutes urgently require additional legislation to protect persons exercising rights guaranteed by the Constitution and by Federal statute.

The commission recommends, therefore, that Congress consider enacting a criminal statute based on its powers to regulate interstate commerce and to enforce the 14th Amendment by appropriate legislation.

Part I of the statute, based on Congressional power over interstate commerce, would make criminal any act of violence, threat, intimidation, or punishment against a person engaging in certain protected activities if the perpetrator used or was using the mails or any facility of interstate commerce or if the victim was using a facility of interstate commerce.

The protected activities would include the lawful exercise (or attempted exercise) of any right created or secured by a Federal statute relating to equal or civil rights, or any peaceful and orderly activity which is protected by the First Amendment, when undertaken for the purpose of obtaining equality for individuals of a particular race or color.

Violation of the statute would be a felony and the penalties for

* From *The New York Times,* November 14, 1965.

its violation graduated according to the seriousness of the unlawful act.

Part II, based on the Equal Protection Clause of the 14th Amendment, would permit the prosecution in Federal court of cases of racial violence that violate state law where the failure of local officials to act, or the nature of their action, constitutes a denial of equal protection in the administration of justice or where it is determined that justice is administered in the community involved in a manner so as to deny equal protection of the laws. The statute could set forth various standards, such as the extent of racial discrimination in the selection of juries, to be evaluated in making the latter determination. Punishment should be the same as if the case had been prosecuted in state court.

To minimize interferences with state criminal procedures, the determination of whether a Federal prosecution is justified could be made by a three-judge Federal court. If the three-judge court determines that a Federal trial is appropriate, the trial should proceed before a single judge sitting with a jury.

II. Civil Remedies

1. To increase the authority of the Attorney General to initiate and intervene in civil rights cases: Title IX of the Civil Rights Act of 1964 provides that the Attorney General may intervene in any case of general public importance brought in Federal court where relief is sought "from the denial of equal protection of the laws under the 14th Amendment to the Constitution on account of race, color, religion, or national origin. . . ." The commission recommends that Congress consider amending this statute to empower the Attorney General to initiate, as well as to intervene in, such proceedings and to initiate or intervene in proceedings to protect persons exercising First Amendment rights directed at obtaining equal treatment of all citizens regardless of race, color, religion or national origin.

2. To provide relief to private persons against unlawful state court proceedings: Although private persons may seek relief against prospective prosecutions under state statutes unconstitutional on their face which abridge First Amendment rights or where state statutes are applied for the purpose of discouraging protected activity, such relief is not available once a prosecution is instituted.

The commission recommends that Congress consider amending Section 1983 of Title 42 to permit injunctive relief, notwithstanding the anti-injunction statute, where state prosecutions are brought against persons for exercising First Amendment rights directed at obtaining equal treatment of all citizens regardless of race, color, religion, or national origin.

3. To strengthen civil remedies against unlawful official conduct:
In 1961 the commission recommended that Section 1983 of Title
42 of the United States Code be amended "to make any county government, city government, or other local governmental entity that
employs officers who deprive persons of rights protected by that section, jointly liable with the officers to victims of such officers' misconduct." The commission again recommends that Congress consider the need for this revision. The commission also recommends
that Congress consider amending Section 1983 to provide that in
all cases brought under this section—actions for injunctions, as well
as for damages—the court, in its discretion, may allow the prevailing party reasonable attorney's fees as part of the costs.

4. To extend the Equal Employment Law to public employment:
In order to help assure that justice is administered in a nondiscriminatory manner, employment in law enforcement agencies
should be available to all persons, regardless of race, color, religion
or national origin. Title VII of the Civil Rights Act of 1964, providing for equal employment opportunities, does not cover public
employment.

Although discrimination in public employment can be challenged
in private lawsuits, administrative and judicial remedies also should
be provided. The commission recommends that Congress consider
amending Title VI to extend its coverage to public employment.

III. Executive Action

1. Methods of Federal law enforcement: The employment of Federal force to curb racial violence should not be limited to situations
involving a Federal court order. Federal protection should be accorded where local authorities fail to protect persons exercising constitutionally guaranteed rights or where general racial violence, un-
checked by local law enforcement officials, deters individuals from
exercising such rights.

• • •

The commission recommends that the President direct that Federal law enforcement officers be stationed at the scene of likely violence, that increased numbers of Federal officials be assigned to
communities where violence has occurred, that more extensive investigation and surveillance activities be undertaken by these officials, and that Federal law enforcement officers be authorized to
make on-the-scene arrests for violations of Federal law. In addition,
the commission recommends that the staffs of Federal law enforcement agencies, particularly the United States marshals, should be

strengthened and that their training and organization be designed to carry out these functions.

2. *Assistance to local law enforcement agencies:* Congress has enacted the Law Enforcement Assistance Act of 1965 which provides Federal funds to assist in training state and local law enforcement officials and to improve techniques, capabilities, and practices in local law enforcement in order to prevent and control crime. The Attorney General administers this act. The commission recommends that in administering this act particular attention should be paid to assisting communities with problems of law enforcement raised by crimes of racial violence. Efforts should be made to develop techniques for recruitment, selection, screening, and training procedures which will improve the quality of local law enforcement.

Selections 26a–26b

TWO VIEWS
OF THE JURY SYSTEM

The following selections refer to the jury system, the bulwark of American justice.

The first selection, written by New York Times reporter Fred P. Graham, describes discrimination in the selection of juries in some areas of the South.

The second selection, written by James J. Kilpatrick, warns against tampering with the jury system.

26a. "Jim Crow Justice" on Trial in South

FRED P. GRAHAM*

In three hours and five minutes, two all-white juries in Hayneville, Ala., have given the civil rights movement a prime target for next year—"Jim Crow justice."

* From *The New York Times*, October 31, 1965.

It took one jury an hour and thirty-five minutes to acquit volunteer deputy sheriff Thomas L. Coleman of the shotgun killing of young Jonathan Daniels. Last week another jury beat that record by five minutes—it acquitted Collie Leroy Wilkins of murder charges in the slaying of Mrs. Viola Gregg Liuzzo in an hour and a half. Both victims were white civil rights workers.

Dr. Martin Luther King rushed home from Europe to organize protests, and Negro leader James Farmer called for a new Federal law "to prevent the Southern jury system from continuing to deprive Negroes and whites of justice."

The Justice Department jumped Monday into a private suit against exclusion of Negroes from the Hayneville jury rolls, and it became quickly clear that a key goal of the civil rights movement during the next session of Congress will be legislation to get more Negroes on Southern juries.

No Prosecution

But how? The one existing U. S. law against jury discrimination is so puny that the Justice Department has yet to prosecute any official under it in this century. Attorney General Nicholas deB. Katzenbach threatened last week to invoke the 1875 criminal law, but privately Justice Department officials said it could serve only as a prod to local officials.

Since the law punishes only past offenses, and allows only fines and not jail penalties, and since the official himself would get a trial by a Southern jury, the criminal statute is considered almost worthless.

The Federal courts have held for years (and the Mississippi Supreme Court agreed last week) that Negroes' convictions cannot stand if members of their race have been systematically excluded from the grand and petit jury rolls. This doesn't require that Negroes actually serve on the jury, and one Federal court has struck down a Negro's conviction because a Negro was deliberately put on the jury.

That these case-by-case appeals of convictions have little effect is shown by Carroll County, Miss., where Negroes comprise more than half the population. In 1959 the murder conviction of a Negro was reversed because of jury discrimination. Yet the Civil Rights Commission heard testimony last spring that Negroes still don't serve on juries there.

But civil rights advocates have been embarrassed to learn that, even when Southern officials stop excluding Negroes from jury lists and attempt to seek them out, few Negroes actually serve on juries. When the American Civil Liberties Union sued to remedy the dearth of Negroes on Birmingham juries, its own brief confessed that jury officials had sought Negro jurors by mail and by knocking on Negroes' doors.

Few Negroes answered the letters, the brief said, and many were afraid to answer the door.

The common practice of picking jurors at random from telephone books, voter registration lists, club and church membership lists, automobile owners and real property taxpayers' lists results in the exclusion of poor persons.

The A.C.L.U. has asked the Court of Appeals for the Fifth Circuit to outlaw all lists and to require that prospective jurors be picked as the Gallop Poll is conducted—by scientific surveys that seek out an accurate cross section of the community.

Aside from the trouble and cost of this proposal, it raises an important policy question—should jury panels represent a cross section of the community (including, presumably, illiterates)? Or should it be enough that no groups are deliberately excluded?

Some civil rights advocates are pressing for the "cross section" theory because in communities such as Hayneville it would amount to a quota system on Negroes. Seven Negroes were on the jury panel in the Liuzzo murder trial last week—yet none of them made it through the selection process to serve on the jury. Since the Hayneville community is 60 per cent Negro, a quota system would have placed so many Negroes on the panel that some of them would necessarily have gone on the jury.

Whether this could have resulted in a conviction, or even prevented the acquittal, is a moot question. But indications this week were that the Justice Department would not consider a quota system.

Sources within the department confirmed that an anti-jury discrimination law will probably be submitted to Congress with other civil rights proposals next year. It will probably give the department the power to bring suit to bar local officials from excluding prospective jurors because of their race. It might also lay down some guidelines for use in selecting prospective jurors (now many officials just pick the friends of employes in the court house). It could prohibit discrimination in hiring court personnel.

In the meantime, the Justice Department was expected to spotlight the problem soon by indicating a few of the most discriminatory Southern jury officials, and by joining in other private suits by Negroes complaining about jury exclusions.

26b. The Jury System

JAMES J. KILPATRICK*

This is the year of Runnymede, and alas, it is the year of Hayneville, too. Martin Luther King is calling upon Congress for laws that will make federal cases of state offenses. The Supreme Court is being pressed all over again to toss out convictions returned by biased juries. And all of a sudden, the local jury system itself, as an institution of American jurisprudence, has caught the innovator's eye.

As a good many scholars have pointed out, Magna Carta's famed Section 39 ought not to be taken as the fountainhead from which the jury system emerged. Juries were known in the days of the Carolingian kings; in a rudimentary form, a jury system came to England with the Norman conquest; long before John put his seal to Magna Carta, the right of a free man to be put to "the lawful judgment of his peers" was beginning to have a significant meaning.

Nevertheless, it is to Magna Carta that we look for the roots of our own Fifth, Sixth, and Eighth Amendments. The Great Charter of 1215 dealt with fair punishment, stable courts, the necessity for witnesses, speedy justice, and administration of "the law of the land" by competent judges. Out of these medieval beginnings came the whole precious system we cherish as "due process of law," and no component part of that system, until quite recently, had been regarded as more important than the ringing phrases that begin the Sixth Amendment: "In all criminal prosecutions, the accused shall enjoy the right to a speedy and public trial, by an impartial jury of the state and district wherein the crime shall have been committed . . ."

It is not a bad idea, in the angry aftermath of the Hayneville trials, to reflect upon the antiquity of the jury system. No one was really amazed when the 12 good men and true, all white, came back into their Alabama courtroom on Sept. 30 and found Tom Coleman not guilty of killing Jonathan Daniels. Neither was anyone astounded, three weeks later, when another jury, equally white, found Collie Leroy Wilkins Jr., not guilty of killing Viola Liuzzo. As Holmes once remarked, juries are "extremely likely to be impregnated by the environing atmosphere." The environing atmosphere of Lowndes County, in the autumn of 1965, had precisely the result Holmes had in mind.

Now the cry is being raised that the two trials were fiascoes, travesties, miscarriages of justice, and the word is out that civil

* From *Newsday*, November 2, 1965.

rights groups will unite in demanding new federal legislation to make such acquittals more difficult. In King's description, it would become a federal crime "to brutalize, murder, or otherwise intimidate persons in pursuit of their constitutional rights and civil rights workers aiding them in this pursuit." With the unwitting help of a few more Hayneville juries, the Congress might even be persuaded to adopt such a law.

At the risk of seeming to condone the Alabama verdicts, a voice should be raised in behalf of the long view. The federal system that has left predominantly to the states and the localities the definition and punishment of crime has served this nation well. Over the years, it is true, a number of "federal crimes" have been created, but in each case the Congress has gone to some pains to base its enactments upon a constitutional foundation. Robbery of the mails, transportation of stolen automobiles, kidnapings across state lines, the illicit distilling of whisky—all of these federal offenses arise rationally from some federal power.

The frustrated civil rights leaders, understandably chagrined at the freeing of Coleman and Wilkins, offer no such justification for the federal intervention they are seeking. The slaying of young Daniels, the cowardly assassination of Mrs. Liuzzo, were in every sense local crimes. A federal interest in "persons in pursuit of their constitutional rights" is a tenuous interest at best, and it could not be invoked without a major upheaval in the federal structure.

Perhaps the trials of Coleman and Wilkins might have ended differently in a federal court, before a jury chosen from wider horizons than those of Lowndes County. This is idle speculation. The defendants have been tried and acquitted and cannot be tried for these crimes again. The important thing, now, is to preserve faith in the system itself: local crimes, local juries.

Surely there will be times, as Mr. Justice Black remarked in the Quarles case 10 years ago, when prejudiced jurors will betray the cause of justice. But it is equally true that many times in our history, juries of plain men, strong men, have resisted hysterical pressures to convict or to acquit the guilty. The system is not perfect; but in the 750 years since Runnymede, it is merely the best that man has devised.

PART IV

EMPLOYMENT FOR THE NEGRO

A man's job adds dignity to his life or reduces him to the level of a slave. The Negro's protest against job discrimination springs from his realization that a man without a job is a man who cannot support himself, a wife, and children. The unemployed begin to lose the dignity associated with financial independence.

The following selections highlight the problem as it exists today and the steps that have been taken to open the job market to Negroes.

Selection 27

JOHN HENRY

This is a famous and familiar Negro work song.

John Henry was just a l'l baby
Settin' on his daddy's knee
He p'int his finger at a little piece of steel, Lawd
"Steel gon' be the death of me
Steel gon' be the death of me."

Cap'n told ol' John Henry
"I believe this mountan's sinkin' in"
"Stan' back, captain an doncha be afraid, Lawd
It's nothin' but my hammer catchin' wind."

Captain told John Henry
"Gonna bring my steam drill around.
Gonna take my steam drill out on the job, Lawd, Lawd
Gonna beat John Henry down."

John Henry told his captain
"A man ain't nothin' but a man
And before I'd let your steam drill beat me down Lawd
I'd die with this hammer in my hand."

John Henry hammerin' on the right-hand side
Steam-drill drivin' on the lef'
John Henry beat that steam drill down, Lawd, Lawd
But he hammered his fool self to death.

Selections 28a–28b

PRESIDENTIAL EXECUTIVE ORDERS

With the outbreak of World War II in 1939 and the conversion of American industry to war production, it was believed that Negroes would at long last find employment. But this was not so. The tendency was to absorb the unemployed whites.

Dissatisfied with the slow rate of Negro employment, A. Philip Randolph, president of the Brotherhood of Sleeping Car Porters, proposed a March on Washington of 50,000 to 100,000 Negroes. This, he hoped, would bring to public attention the plight of the Negro and would lead, hopefully, to their increased employment in defense industries. Government officials were disturbed by this

March planned for July 1, 1941. Although there had been similar marches before—by Coxey's Army of Unemployed in 1894, and by the Bonus March of American veterans in 1932—it was felt that such a march at this time, even though we were not officially at war, would create an unfavorable picture of our nation. President Franklin D. Roosevelt persuaded Randolph to call off the March with a promise to issue "an order with teeth in it," prohibiting discrimination in employment in defense industries and in the government. On June 25, 1941, the President issued his famous Executive Order 8802.

28a.   Executive Order 8802[*]
June 25, 1941

Whereas it is the policy of the United States to encourage full participation in the national defense program by all citizens of the United States, regardless of race, creed, color, or national origin, in the firm belief that the democratic way of life within the Nation can be defended successfully only with the help and support of all groups within its borders; and

Whereas there is evidence that available and needed workers have been barred from employment in industries engaged in defense production solely because of considerations of race, creed, color, or national origin, to the detriment of workers' morale and of national unity;

Now, Therefore, by virtue of the authority vested in me by the Constitution and the statutes, and as a prerequisite to the successful conduct of our national defense production effort, I do hereby reaffirm the policy of the United States that there shall be no discrimination in the employment of workers in defense industries or government because of race, creed, color, or national origin, and I do hereby declare that it is the duty of employers and of labor organizations, in furtherance of said policy and of this order, to provide for the full and equitable participation of all workers in defense industries, without discrimination because of race, creed, color, or national origin;

And it is hereby ordered as follows:

1. All departments and agencies of the Government of the United States concerned with vocational and training programs for defense production shall take special measures appropriate to assure that

[*] Selective Service System, Monograph No. 10, *Special Groups* (Washington, 1953), II, 3.

such programs are administered without discrimination because of race, creed, color, or national origin;

2. All contracting agencies of the Government of the United States shall include in all defense contracts hereafter negotiated by them a provision obligating the contractor not to discriminate against any worker because of race, creed, color, or national origin;

3. There is established in the Office of Production Management a Committee on Fair Employment Practice, which shall consist of a chairman and four other members to be appointed by the President. The Chairman and members of the Committee shall serve as such without compensation, but shall be entitled to actual and necessary transportation, subsistence, and other expenses incidental to performance of their duties. The Committee shall receive and investigate complaints of discrimination in violation of the provisions of this order and shall take appropriate steps to redress grievances which it finds to be valid. The Committee shall also recommend to the several departments and agencies of the Government of the United States and to the President all measures which may be deemed by it necessary or proper to effectuate the provisions of this order.

FRANKLIN D. ROOSEVELT

The White House, June 25, 1941

28b. Executive Order 10925
March 7, 1961

The following notice was sent to all Federal contractors as part of the program to enforce Executive Order 10925.

WE PLEDGE...
Equal Employment Opportunity

This employer is a Federal Government contractor and pledges to provide equal employment opportunities without regard to race, color, creed, or national origin. This pledge applies to all employees and applicants for employment in connection with:

* Hiring, Placement, Upgrading, Transfer or Demotion
* Recruitment, Advertising or Solicitation for Employment
* Treatment during Employment
* Rates of Pay or Other Forms of Compensation
* Selection for Training, Including Apprenticeship
* Layoff or Termination

Inquiries or complaints should be addressed to:
PRESIDENT'S COMMITTEE ON EQUAL EMPLOYMENT OPPORTUNITY
Washington 25, D.C.

Section 301 (1) of the Executive Order 10925, dated March 7, 1961, states:

The contractor will not discriminate against any employee or applicant for employment because of race, creed, color, or national origin. The contractor will take affirmative action to ensure that applicants are employed, and that employees are treated during employment, without regard to their race, creed, color, or national origin. Such action shall include, but not be limited to the following: employment, upgrading, demotion or transfer; recruitment or recruitment advertising; layoff or termination; rates of pay or other forms of compensation; and selection for training, including apprenticeship . . .

FEDERAL CONTRACTORS ARE REQUIRED TO POST THIS NOTICE AT CONSPICUOUS PLACES AVAILABLE TO EMPLOYEES AND APPLICANTS FOR EMPLOYMENT.

Selection 29

NEW YORK STATE LAW AGAINST DISCRIMINATION IN EMPLOYMENT*

The New York State Law Against Discrimination is an example of how some of the states have tried to handle the issue of job discrimination.

Sec. 125. Purposes of article: This article shall be known as the "Law Against Discrimination." It shall be deemed an exercise of the police power of the state for the protection of the public welfare, health and peace of the people of this state, and in fulfillment of the provisions of the constitution of this state concerning civil rights; and the legislature hereby finds and declares that practices of discrimination against any of its inhabitants because of race, creed, color or national origin are a matter of state concern, that such discrimination threatens not only the rights and proper privileges of its inhabitants but menaces the institutions and foundation of a free democratic state. A state agency is hereby created with power to eliminate and prevent discrimination in employment because of race, creed, color or national origin, either by employers, labor organizations, employment agencies or other persons, and to take other actions against discrimination because of race, creed, color or national origin, as herein provided; and the commission established hereunder is hereby given general jurisdiction and power for such purposes.

Sec. 126. Opportunity for employment without discrimination a

* March 12, 1945. State of New York, Executive Department, State Commission Against Discrimination, *Compilation of Laws Against Discrimination because of Race, Creed, Color or National Origin,* New York: 1948, pp. 1-A-1-H.

civil right: The opportunity to obtain employment without discrimination because of race, creed, color or national origin is hereby recognized as and declared to be a civil right. . . .

Sec. 131. Unlawful employment practices: It shall be an unlawful employment practice: 1. For an employer, because of the race, creed, color or national origin of any individual, to refuse to hire or employ or to bar or to discharge from employment such individual or to discriminate against such individual in compensation or in terms, conditions or privileges of employment.

2. For a labor organization, because of the race, creed, color or national origin of any individual, to exclude or to expel from its membership such individual or to discriminate in any way against any of its members or against any employer or any individual employed by an employer.

3. For any employer or employment agency to print or circulate or cause to be printed or circulated any statement, advertisement or publication, or to use any form of application for employment or to make any inquiry in connection with prospective employment, which expresses, directly or indirectly, any limitation, specification or discrimination as to race, creed, color or national origin, or any intent to make any such limitation, specification of discrimination, unless based upon a bona fide occupational qualification. . . .

Sec. 134. Penal provision. Any person, employer, labor organization or employment agency, who or which shall willfully resist, prevent, impede or interfere with the commission or any of its members or representatives in the performance of duty under this article, or shall willfully violate an order of the commission, shall be guilty of a misdemeanor and be punishable by imprisonment in a penitentiary, or county jail, for not more than one year, or by a fine of not more than five hundred dollars, or by both; but procedure for the review of the order shall not be deemed to be such willful conduct. . . .

Selections *30a–30c*

CIVIL RIGHTS ACT OF 1964

Title VII of the Civil Rights Act of 1964 was designed to improve the opportunities for Negro employment.

30a. Employment Provisions of Civil Rights Act of 1964*

Title VII: Equal Employment Opportunity

This title establishes a Federal right to equal opportunity in employment. It creates an Equal Employment Opportunity Commission to assist in implementing this right.

Employers, labor unions and employment agencies are required to treat all persons without regard to their race, color, religion, sex, or national origin. This treatment must be given in all phases of employment, including hiring, promotion, firing, apprenticeship and other training programs, and job assignments.

When this title goes into full effect employers will be subject to its provisions if they have 25 or more regular employees in an industry that affects interstate commerce. Generally speaking, labor unions will be subject to the Act if they either operate a hiring hall for covered employers, or if they have 25 or more members who are employed by a covered employer. Employment agencies are also included if they regularly undertake to supply employees for a covered employer.

(Enforcement of the nondiscrimination requirements for employers and unions is postponed for one year. Employers and unions with 100 or more workers will be covered beginning July 2, 1965 and coverage will be extended each year until July 2, 1968 when employers and unions with 25 workers will be covered.)

* From *Civil Rights Digest*, Washington, D. C.: special bulletin by U. S. Commission on Civil Rights, August, 1964.

Not covered by this title are (1) public employers, (2) bona fide private clubs, (3) educational institutions with regard to employees working in educational activities and all employment in religious educational institutions, (4) employers on or near an Indian reservation with regard to preferential treatment of Indians; and (5) religious corporations, institutions, etc., with regard to employees working in connection with religious activities.

When someone believes he has been discriminated against because of race, color, religion, sex, or national origin in any phase of job placement or employment, he may bring his complaint within 90 days to the Equal Employment Opportunity Commission or to the Attorney General.

The Commission will handle his complaint directly, unless the State or locality where the alleged discrimination occurred has fair employment laws. If so, the person complaining must allow the State or local officials no more than 120 days to resolve the matter. If there is no satisfactory conclusion within this time or if the State or locality rejects the complaint before the time is up, the complainant may then go to the Commission, which is authorized to settle valid complaints by conciliation and persuasion. Nothing said during the conciliation proceedings may be made public or used as evidence without the consent of the parties.

If the Commission fails to secure compliance within a period of no more than 60 days, the individual may take his case to a Federal court. This court may appoint an attorney and may exempt the complainant from payment of certain costs. The court, in its discretion, may allow the Attorney General to enter the case.

A worker who thinks he has been discriminated against may take his complaint directly to the Attorney General, who may bring the case before a three-judge court if he believes there is a pattern or practice of resistance to this title.

If the court in either action finds discrimination, it will order the employer, employment agency or union to take corrective action, which may include hiring or reinstating employees with or without back pay.

30b. Bans on Job Bias Effective Today

JOHN HERBERS*

Washington, July 1—The first national law prohibiting discrimination against minority groups in private employment goes into effect tomorrow.

* From *The New York Times,* July 2, 1965.

The prohibition, contained in Title VII of the Civil Rights Act of 1964, has the potential of opening vast new employment opportunities for Negroes, other racial groups, religious minorities and women.

The extent and time of its effectiveness, however, are in doubt for several reasons. Chief among these is the fact that the law is cumbersome, possibly riddled with loopholes, and gives the agency administering it, the Equal Employment Opportunity Commission, no enforcement powers.

Also, President Johnson waited so long to appoint the commission —until May 10—that it cannot be in full operation for several months. It now has only a skeleton staff operating out of temporary offices and has yet to formulate its policies.

. . .

Title VII is one major provision of the Civil Rights Act, which was signed by President Johnson last July 2. Congress delayed the effective date of Title VII for one year to give all concerned time for orderly compliance and to enable the commission to be appointed and begin functioning.

The enactment of Title VII culminated two decades of effort by civil rights advocates to make fair employment practices a statutory requirement. In 1941, President Roosevelt, father of the commission's chairman, established by executive order a Fair Employment Practices Commission. He acted after Negroes had threatened to march on Washington to protest discrimination in defense jobs.

That F.E.P.C. died in 1946. Since then the Government has had a series of agencies at work to prevent discrimination in connection with Government contracts. But it was not until the civil rights breakthrough of 1964 that the Government attempted to forbid employment discrimination throughout the entire economy.

Title VII forbids discrimination in hiring, dismissal, promotion or any other term or condition of employment on the basis of race, color, religion, sex or national origin on the part of employers, unions and employment agencies.

For the first year, until July 2, 1966, the law applies to employers and unions with 100 or more workers or members; the second year, 75 or more; the third year, 50 or more; and thereafter, 25 or more.

There are a number of exemptions in the law. These include cases in which religion, sex or national origin is a genuine occupational qualification necessary to the operation of a business or school. Discrimination against Communists is permitted.

Racial Balance Not Needed

Reverse discrimination is outlawed. That is, an employer is not required to maintain racial balance in his place of business. On the other hand, a business operating on or near an Indian reservation may give preference to Indians. Existing preference laws for veterans remain in effect.

Discrimination is not defined in the law and lawyers concerned with it say this will be done over a period of time through the commission and the courts.

Any individual or a member of the commission may file a complaint. If the complainant lives in one of 27 states that have a fair employment practices law he must act first under the state law and wait 60 days to begin action under the Federal commission.

If the commission finds discrimination exists it must try to end it by conciliation. If conciliation fails, the complainant may bring a civil suit in a Federal District Court, which may appoint an attorney for him and permit him to proceed without cost.

The Attorney General may intervene for a complainant if he considers the case of general public importance—a pattern of discrimination, for instance.

Mr. Roosevelt appeared before a Senate Appropriations subcommittee today and said the commission would stress conciliation.

"We have no intention to persecute or interfere with the rightful prerogatives of any employer, labor union, or employment agency," he said.

He requested $3.2 million to run the agency its first year. He said a staff of 190 was foreseen. Regional offices will be established by the end of the year in New York, Los Angeles, Chicago, Cleveland, Dallas and Atlanta.

Preparing the Way

Even before the law took effect, civil rights groups began attacking it as too weak and started a campaign to give the commission more enforcement power. They believe it should have power to order an end to discrimination rather than conciliate and wait on the courts.

Civil rights organizations, however, have promised to seek relief under the present law.

Herbert Hill, labor secretary for the National Association for the Advancement of Colored People, said he would give the commission a few days to organize, then file a substantial number of complaints against both employers and unions.

"We are basically concerned with elementary patterns of discrimination," Mr. Hill said. "We hope the commission will be pattern oriented rather than a passive, complaint taking bureau."

Although complaints are expected to come from throughout the nation, a large portion of them are expected to come from the South, where there are no F.E.P.C. laws.

30c.   Rights Landmark Seen by N.A.A.C.P.

M. S. HANDLER*

Denver, July 1—In the view of civil rights leaders meeting here, a landmark will be established tomorrow when Title VII of the Civil Rights Act of 1964 goes into effect.

This section of the law, which prohibits racial discrimination in employment, was assessed today by members of the National Association for the Advancement of Colored People, here for the group's 56th annual convention.

Yet officials of the association said that they believed the law represented more of a promise than a reality. Much strife and litigation will ensue before the law is enforced to the satisfaction of Negroes, they predicted.

The labor department of the N.A.A.C.P. is expected to submit within 30 days scores of complaints against major industrial corporations, banking institutions and labor unions charging them with an established pattern of discrimination against Negroes in employment.

Herbert Hill, director of the department, said that the association was determined to make Title VII an effective instrument.

Wilkins Receives Threat

The convention continued to run its quiet public course today. Many caucuses were being held in the Denver Hilton Hotel to gear the 1,800 branches of the association to help the Government implement the Civil Rights Act and the Federal antipoverty program.

A threat to Roy Wilkins, executive secretary of the N.A.A.C.P., was reported to have been telephoned to his apartment at 3 A.M. today, but it hardly caused a ruffle at the convention.

A male voice identifying the speaker as "Kelly" was reported to have said that Mr. Wilkins would be killed if he did not get out of town. The police assigned more plain-clothesmen to the hotel.

Meanwhile, Negroes attending the convention were agreed today

* *The New York Times,* July 2, 1965.

that they felt more at ease in Denver than in almost any other city in the United States. They said that the white people of Denver were not behaving as if they were doing the Negroes a favor by treating them courteously.

Leadership by Mayor

Discussions with persons identified with racial problems in Denver appeared to confirm the feelings of the Negro delegates. They said that the city and the state of Colorado, whose political lives were dominated by the Ku Klux Klan in the nineteen-twenties, had radically changed in their treatment of Negroes.

In part, this change was attributed to the leadership of Mayor Tom Currigan and his administration.

Mr. Currigan and his top officials have been intimately identified with the problems of race relations and have taken the initiative in organizing efforts to solve these problems.

The size of the Negro community, estimated at 47,000 in a population of a million in the metropolitan Denver area, was said to have reduced the Negro problem to manageable proportions.

Many Hold Federal Jobs

A third factor is that the many Federal agencies in Denver serve as the principal employers of Negroes. The estimated rate of Negro unemployment here is put at 8 per cent, compared with rates as high as 20 per cent in other urban centers.

Although a Negro slum area exists in Denver, many Negroes live in integrated sections, a situation that has been favored by the buyer's market in real estate here in recent years. It was also said that public accommodations were not a problem for Negroes here.

De facto segregation in the schools follows the housing patterns, but the Board of Education is credited with making a determined effort to improve the quality of instruction in Negro schools.

Sebastian Owens, the Urban League's representative in Denver, said today that the league had received strong support from business and industry in testing Negro candidates for jobs.

Mr. Owens and others said that the principal racial problem here, and a very serious one, concerned the large concentration of Spanish-speaking people who occupy the lowest economic status in the community. This segment has not yet been able to produce a leadership so effective as that of the Negro movement.

The Spanish-speaking group is composed of Mexican immigrants and people descended from the colonial Spanish. Tension between this group and the white majority at times becomes rather sharp.

Selection 31

THE JOB GAP

HERMAN P. MILLER[*]

*This article by Herman P. Miller, Special Assistant to the Director
of the Census Bureau, explores the reasons why the Negro in the
ghetto does not share our country's prosperity.*

The United States is now well into the sixth year of uninterrupted
economic expansion. This is the longest upsurge in our history and
the end is nowhere in sight. Unemployment is below the 4 per cent
level and economists are predicting a near-record growth in the
national income this year. The President did not exaggerate when
he told Congress in January that American incomes are higher than
ever before, profits are bigger and jobs are better. "Our nation's
industries, shops and farms," he said, "prosper today far beyond the
dreams of any people, any time, anywhere."

How has the Negro fared in this growth? Prosperity may be unrelated to some of the Negro's major complaints against this society
—segregation, discrimination and the denial of basic rights. But it is
closely related to the demand for better jobs, higher pay and greater
regularity of employment.

There can be no question that the economic status of Negroes
has improved during the past few years, though the *gap* between
whites and Negroes has not changed much, if at all. The unemployment rate for Negroes is still twice that of whites, and they
earn about half as much. The economic *level* of both groups, however, has risen considerably.

Since 1961 (the current expansion started in March of that year),
family incomes have risen proportionately as much for Negroes as
for whites. The average for Negroes was about $3,800 in 1964 and

* From *The New York Times Magazine*, May 8, 1966, p. 30.

was probably over the $4,000 mark last year. Unemployment has also dropped proportionately as much for Negroes as for whites. The Negro unemployment rate declined from 12.5 per cent in 1961 to 8.3 per cent last year. During the same period, the rate for whites dropped from 6 per cent to 4.1 per cent. Finally, there has been some upgrading of jobs for those Negroes who are employed. Negro women in particular are breaking into professional, technical and white-collar employment in growing numbers. There has been a marked decrease in the proportion employed as domestics—the most despised of all jobs in the Negro community.

Despite these gains, significant trouble spots remain. They have caused some Negro leaders to deny that any real progress has been made. Adam Clayton Powell, for example, commenting on the announcement of a 12-year low in the unemployment level in March, declared: "I seriously doubt this statistic will gladden the hearts of Appalachian and other rural youngsters trudging hopelessly over the barren soil in search of a job, or Negro teen-agers wandering aimlessly in Harlem or Los Angeles. To date, the war-on-poverty impact on unemployment has been more along the lines of a feather pillow than a machine gun."

This pessimistic view is supported by the results of the recent census in the Watts district of Los Angeles, which showed that the economic status of Negroes in that area has deteriorated in the past five years in sharp contrast to the experience of the nation as a whole. In Watts and similar Negro neighborhoods around Los Angeles, family income has declined, the number of poor people has risen, housing has deteriorated, there has been no improvement in unemployment and no change in the job opportunities available to Negroes. This evidence suggests that, despite the national improvement, places like Watts are losing ground because they are becoming gathering places for persons deeply imbedded in poverty and unlikely to get out of it—unwed mothers, deserted wives, the physically and mentally handicapped and the aged. Successful families tend to move out of such economically and socially depressed areas, leaving behind the incompetent, the uneducated and the unfortunate. As a result, there is a piling up of concentrated and explosive misery in the Negro ghetto which is hidden by the overall national statistics.

Unemployment is, of course, a sensitive indicator of economic change. As a rule of thumb, the unemployment rate for Negroes is about twice that of whites, regardless of the age or sex of the group that is compared or the general economic climate at the time of the comparison. The 2:1 ratio is particularly stable for adult men and women. Among teen-agers, however, there has been a growing disparity between the rates for whites and Negroes since the recession of 1957–58. Currently, nearly one-fourth of Negro teen-agers are unemployed, as compared with 10 per cent for the whites.

The fact that unemployment rates have dropped sharply—and that they have dropped proportionately as much for Negroes as for whites during the current expansion—is a sign of progress. It must also be noted, however, that the unemployment rate for Negroes at the height of prosperity is greater than the rate for whites during any of the past three recessions. The high rate of youth unemployment is particularly distressing not only because of the immediate frustrations and hardships it causes for the youngsters and their families, but also because it undermines training programs and the attempts to prevent school dropouts. If one-fourth of Negro youths are unable to find jobs after five years of continuous prosperity, they have a right to join the chorus when Bayard Rustin asks: "What is this foolishness about training? You can't train any segment of the population unless there's a demand for their work."

NONWHITE UNEMPLOYMENT RATES
(Annual averages)

	20 and over		18- and 19-yr.-olds	
	Men	Women	Boys	Girls
1960	10%	8%	25%	25%
1961	12	11	24	28
1962	10	10	22	31
1963	9	9	27	32
1964	8	9	23	29
1965	6	8	20	28

In contrast to the favorable trends in the data for the nation, the census for Watts shows that, in this ghetto, unemployment rates in the peak year of 1965 were nearly as high as they were in the recession year of 1960. About 13 per cent of the men and women are currently unemployed. The situation in several neighboring ghettos, like Avalon, Central and Green Meadows, is not much better.

As significant as the high unemployment rate in Watts is the sharp rise in the proportion of men who have dropped out of the labor force (stopped working or looking for work) during the last five years. In 1960 about 70 per cent of the men in Watts were in the labor force, as compared with only 58 per cent in 1965. (Nationally, about three-fourths of the Negro men are in the labor force.)

This change largely reflects a rise in hidden unemployment among men who have simply stopped looking for jobs.

Five years is perhaps too short a period in which to expect changes in occupational distribution. But the past five years are particularly significant because they represent a period of continuous economic expansion combined with new legislation and vigorous efforts to reduce discrimination in employment. Although the results show some improvement, they can hardly be called spectacular. Among Negro men, the most significant change was a drop in the proportion employed as farm workers (from 14 to 10 per cent) and an increase in the proportion employed as professional and technical workers (from 4 to 6 per cent).

The other occupations showed little change. The drop in farm workers is not particularly connected with events of the last few years. It is part of the historic movement from the farm to the city, which must soon come to an end because of the small size of the farm population.

The increase in professional and technical employment among nonwhite men is small proportionately but it translates into about 100,000 additional Negro families that have their feet firmly on the bottom rung of the middle-class ladder. These are the families that can make the break from Harlem to Long Island and from the District of Columbia to Bethesda. These are the new faces that show as TV announcers, government officials and business executives.

It was not so very long ago that Negroes graduating from college could look forward to careers as preachers, teachers or social workers and little more. That situation now seems to have changed. Negroes are now being admitted to the better white colleges in growing numbers and white employers seem to be willing and even anxious to hire qualified Negro professional workers. Many personnel managers claim that the demand for Negro professionals far exceeds the qualified supply. If this is so, the numbers employed in the better-paid professional jobs might be expected to increase more rapidly in the future as more young Negro men complete college.

Despite the small signs of progress, the most striking fact about the occupational distribution of nonwhite men remains their very heavy concentration in low-paid jobs. Despite all the fuss and fury of the past few years, nearly half of the Negro men still work as laborers, janitors, porters, busboys and in similar service jobs.

The progress for women has been much more striking than that for men. Cleaning up white people's homes is still the most common type of job among Negro women. About 30 per cent do this kind of work. The proportion has dropped since 1960, but it is still very high, especially when consideration is given to the fact that an additional 10 per cent or more do the same kind of work as domestics (chambermaids, charwomen, janitors, etc.), but are employed by hotels, restaurants, hospitals and similar service establishments rather than by housewives. Thus, even today, after years of progress, conservatively 40 per cent of the Negro women are doing unskilled and menial housework in one form or another.

Yet there has been a sharp increase in the number of Negro women employed in white-collar jobs. The proportion has risen from 18 to 24 per cent for the three job categories—professional, clerical and managerial sales. But even this movement by women into better-paying jobs is not an unmixed blessing. It reinforces the dominant role of women in the Negro home and is not conducive to stable family life. So long as most Negro men work at dead-end jobs that provide neither economic security nor regularity of employment, little improvement can be expected in the Negro home. Changes in employment patterns during the last five years provide little cause for optimism in this respect.

Negro family purchasing power has increased at the rate of about $120 per year since 1960, as compared with a growth rate of $220 per year recorded by white families during the same period. Here again there has been progress, but not enough to make more than a small dent in the reduction of Negro poverty. Since 1960 about one-quarter of a million Negro families have been removed from the poverty category (the equivalent of a $3,000 annual income, or less, for a nonfarm family of four). This is no mean accomplishment, but the fact remains that nearly two million Negro families—39 per cent of the total—are in poverty today, at the height of economic expansion:

NONWHITE FAMILIES

	Total Number (millions)	Number of Poor (millions)	Pct. of Total
1964	4.8	1.9	39
1963	4.8	2.0	43
1962	4.6	2.1	47
1961	4.5	2.1	48
1960	4.3	2.1	49

The Negro ghetto goes by different names in different places— Harlem, Watts, Cardozo in Washington, Hough in Cleveland—but it is basically the same everywhere: a decaying part of the central city that has been largely deserted by white residents and those Negroes who can get out. These ghettos have no walls as in medieval European cities and the inhabitants wear no special uniform. Most of them, however, are just as surely locked in as were the Jews in Central and Eastern Europe a century ago. The important point, with respect to poverty, is that nearly half of the poor in the big cities of the United States live in these ghettos. Whereas the white poor in the big cities are dispersed, and a large proportion (25 per cent) are aged, the Negro poor are concentrated and young—nearly 60 per cent are under 21. The heavy concentration of deprived and frustrated Negro youth in urban slums can only spell trouble.

Historically, Negroes in the United States have made their greatest economic gains during periods of wartime. Under these conditions, full employment in industrial centers has simultaneously increased the flow of migrants from the farm to the city and from the South to the North; it has led to an improvement in the occupational structure of Negroes by providing job opportunities that might otherwise be filled by whites, and it has raised the pay of Negroes relative to whites by forcing up wages in the lower-paid occupations. In the light of previous experience, a prolonged war in Vietnam would probably accelerate the rate of improvement in Negro economic status, at least of those Negroes and their families who were not directly involved in the fighting.

We certainly do not want to rely on war to achieve goals that we are now seeking by other means. Such gains are not only undependable but are tainted as well. Although the Negro has been helped by some of the programs now in operation, the progress has been slow and there are many gaps. An acceleration of progress would require far greater commitments of funds and resources than have been made to date, and would increase the inflationary pressures which now threaten economic stability. Yet even if we cannot move boldly forward in our attempt to reduce the economic disparities between Negroes and whites, there are steps that can be taken to strengthen current programs. Although these measures will solve no basic problems, they may help avert the catastrophes of the last two summers.

Perhaps the most urgent need at present is to find work for unemployed youth in the central city. The gutted buildings in Watts still stand as ugly reminders of the damage that can be done by youthful idleness, despair and hate. An expansion and redirection of the Neighborhood Youth Corps could immediately provide several hundred thousand jobs for unemployed young Negroes. Enrollment in this program reached a peak of 278,000 last summer, but has since tapered off to about 150,000 per month because of a limitation of funds. About three-fourths of the participants are students, the remainder are dropouts or graduates who can find no other work.

This program has been criticized as unadulterated work relief, and recommendations have been made for its "enrichment" with counseling and other services. The criticism is valid, particularly for the out-of-school youngsters, but the program does provide work for idle hands and money for empty pockets. Sar Levitan of the Upjohn Institute for Employment Research, who is currently making a study of the antipoverty program for the Ford Foundation, has pointed out that "unemployment decreases as youths mature. It may therefore be wiser policy simply to provide as many unemployed youths as possible with jobs to tide them over the critical years when they find it most difficult to secure employment in the market place."

The training and work-experience program for unemployed parents on relief might also be redirected so as to get more people directly into jobs in the private economy where they are needed. The program now attempts to increase the employability of these parents by providing education, training, counseling and other supportive services prior to, or simultaneously with, job placement, which is largely in government and nonprofit institutions. With job shortages in many fields that require relatively little training, there may be advantages in using funds earmarked for rehabilitation and supportive services to place these relief recipients directly into private jobs.

The manpower training program (M.D.T.A.) has now been in existence for four years. Most of those chosen for training have had 12 or more years of schooling. The policy of selecting the best-qualified applicants was followed largely because they are the ones most likely to succeed. In the current tight labor market it should be possible to take greater risks in selecting persons for training and to let the more qualified fend for themselves in the labor market. The social gains that might come from using this program as a vehicle for helping the very needy and uneducated instead of those who are somewhat higher in the social and economic scale might easily offset the inefficiencies that come from "wasting training on poor risks."

The military draft is the last way in which a democratic society should try to solve its social problems. But we are at war and men are being drafted. Many young men are now being rejected for service because of minor physical defects, low scores on intellectual attainment tests and petty criminal records. There has been talk from time to time about changing the draft and enlistment standards so as to make it possible for these men to enter the armed forces, where they might receive special training before being assigned to regular units.

One recent advocate of this kind of change is Selective Service Director Lewis H. Hershey. In recent testimony before a House Merchant Marine subcommittee he stated: "The services can be a rehabilitating force. They can do moral and intellectual as well as physical rehabilitation. . . . I think we are going to have to induct more people and I think we will have to get into correctional procedures the armed services might not like."

These are very modest proposals. Their chief virtue is that they can be made without any appreciable increase in Federal expenditures, but they will solve no basic problems and are at best a holding action. It will take time, money and imagination to bring the Negro into the mainstream of American economic life. Expenditures high in the billions may be required for many years to provide housing, education, medical care, employment and training and a host of other services.

Whether or not we can afford these outlays is a matter of choice, not necessity. The war in Vietnam is expensive, but not so expensive as to preclude a modest expansion in welfare programs. Unless there is an escalation of military activities in Vietnam during the next year, we will spend only 8 per cent of our output on defense. We spent more than that in every year between 1951 and 1963, and did not regard the situation as catastrophic.

The threat of inflation is also serious, but not insurmountable. By recouping some of the tax dollars that were so generously given to middle- and high-income families several years ago, it might be possible to finance the war in Vietnam and to expand welfare programs. As Sar Levitan aptly points out: "Those who oppose expansion of welfare legislation find it convenient at this time to substitute for ideological objections the patriotic grounds of 'helping the boys.' For them, every military cloud has an inflationary lining."

Our progress in helping the Negro during the last five prosperous years has not been outstanding. If we are to do better in the future, we shall have to try harder.

The decision to hold the line in expenditures on most of the Federal programs in aid of the poor during the next fiscal year can only mean that we are again postponing improvements in housing, employment and living conditions of Negroes. Next summer we will probably be working as frantically as we are this summer in trying to find jobs for Negro youth as a form of riot control. This approach to the problem is demoralizing as well as self-defeating.

As Bayard Rustin has pointed out, it teaches "impoverished, segregated and ignored Negroes that the only way they can get the ear of America is to rise up in violence."

There are other ways. The President had a noble vision in his concept of the Great Society—perhaps the most noble vision of any President since Lincoln. The vision will become a reality only if we are willing to invest the time, money and effort that is required. A cautious, "prudent" man would never have conceived the Great Society; a cautious, prudent man will never make it work. Bold, new, expensive programs will be required. Some will fail as they inevitably must. In the end, however, it will be a better America for the Negroes and for everyone else.

Selection 32

THE NEGRO FARMER

GENE ROBERTS*

This selection by Gene Roberts, New York Times reporter, summarizes the problems facing the Negro farmer.

Sharecropping Doomed

Atlanta, July 15—Keever Suit pulled a pencil stub from the bib of his overalls, totaled the money he had earned as a day laborer during the last week and said it came to "just under $16."

"Where I ought to be is back in the country," said the 44-year-old former sharecropper who has moved to Durham, N. C., from a tobacco farm, "but I can't find me enough crop to tend."

Mr. Suit's employment dilemma has been faced by many of the three million persons who have left Southern farms since 1940. Hundreds of thousands of others will face it within the next decade.

* From *The New York Times*, July 19, 1965.

Some farm population experts are now predicting that "virtually all" of the 1.5 million Negroes now in Southern and Border state farms will have to look elsewhere for employment within the next 10 to 25 years.

The prospect of increased migration to cities and towns in both the South and the North is alarming civil rights leaders who already consider the lack of jobs the chief civil rights problem.

Selz B. Mayo, chairman of the department of rural sociology at North Carolina State College—the University of North Carolina at Raleigh—offers them little encouragement. He expects a major wave of off-farm migration within the next five years and predicts that "within 10 years there will not be any Negroes left on Southern farms."

Calvin Beale, head of a farm population analysis section of the Department of Agriculture in Washington, agrees that the Negro farmer will "virtually disappear," but says the process will take 20 to 25 years.

The beginning of the end for the Negro, they both agree, will come with the development of a mechanical tobacco harvester.

Will Slash Man-Hours

This will cut the man-hours involved in tobacco farming by more than half, they say, and will speed the departure of the Negro from the bright-leaf tobacco belt, the last stronghold of the Southern sharecropper.

The belt begins in Virginia and stretches through the Carolinas into Georgia and Florida.

Dr. Francis J. Hassler, head of the department of agricultural engineering at North Carolina State, predicts that the mechanical harvester will be available commercially within the next five years —a semi-mechanical one is already on the market—and will come into widespread use soon after in the bright-leaf belt.

A bulk curing process developed by Dr. Hassler is already coming into use and is cutting about 125 man-hours off the 400 normally required to grow and harvest an acre of tobacco. The mechanical harvester would cut the total man-hours required to "little more than 100," Dr. Hassler says.

Deep South Picture

Mechanical cotton pickers and grain harvesters have "all but erased" the sharecropper in the Deep South, Mr. Beale reports, leaving only about 500,000 Negroes on farms there as day laborers. Most of the million other Negroes on Southern and Border state farms are tobacco sharecroppers and their families.

Sharecropping, which has been widespread in the South since the end of the Civil War, is being replaced by a new system that sociologists are calling owner-renter.

Junius Evans of Fremont, N. C., near the heart of the bright-leaf belt, is typical of the new breed of farmer (almost all of them white because of the capital involved) who owns tractors, other mechanized equipment and a small farm and rents additional land to take maximum advantage of the equipment.

"A Reasonable Living"

Mr. Evans owns a farm with 50 cultivated acres and a Government tobacco allotment of 4.7 acres. He rents enough additional acreage to raise his total commercial crop to 15.7 acres of tobacco, 70 acres of corn and 10 acres of soybeans.

With an average production of 2,200 pounds of tobacco an acre and at an average price of 60 cents a pound, Mr. Evans can expect to gross $20,000 from tobacco alone.

"Expenses are heavy," Mr. Evans says, "but you can make a reasonable living."

Before the tractor began coming into wide use 25 years ago, at least three farm families, possibly four, would have worked full time to cultivate the Evans acreage. Now Mr. Evans does it himself with tractors, mechanical grain harvesters and occasional day laborers from two families who live on his farm rent free.

Even the day laborers may go when the mechanical tobacco harvester is developed.

Public Works Urged

The Rev. Dr. Martin Luther King Jr., head of the Southern Christian Leadership Conference, sees little hope of stemming the off-farm migration. He believes instead that public works and "other imaginative, job-producing programs are necessary" to aid those leaving the farms.

Another civil rights leader, Bayard Rustin of New York, also sees public works as an answer. "The machine," he says, "has become as great an enemy of the Negro people as segregation and discrimination ever were."

James Farmer, the national director of the Congress of Racial Equality also favors public works but says his organization is studying "the type of collective farm in use in Israel" as one possible way of keeping some of the Negroes on the farm.

Mr. Beale of the Department of Agriculture expects many Negroes, perhaps one family in three, to remain on the farm and commute to jobs in the city.

He says such a trend is already pronounced among whites. Although Southern white farmers and their families have declined from about eight million in 1940 to slightly more than two million, they are continuing to live in rural areas in large numbers.

Selection 33

THE CAT WITH THE SILVER SPOON

CHARLES SILBERMAN *

The following selection from Charles Silberman's Crisis in Black and White *examines some of the problems which must be squarely faced if Negro employment is to be increased.*

. . . There are, indeed, an incredible number of factors which will operate to prevent any rapid increase in employment of Negroes unless a concerted and special effort is made. A formal policy of non-discrimination, of employing people "regardless of race, color, or creed," however estimable, usually works out in practice to be a policy of employing whites only. Hence Negroes' demand for quotas represents a necessary tactic: an attempt to fix the responsibility for increasing employment of Negroes on those who do the hiring (or in the case of trade unions, on those who control access to the job). As soon as we agree that special measures are necessary to overcome the heritage of past discrimination, the question of numbers—of *how many* Negroes are to be hired in what job categories—inevitably arises. Not to use numbers as a yardstick for measuring performance is, in effect, to revert to "tokenism." The point is not whether there is some "right" number of Negroes to be employed—obviously there is not—but simply that there is no mean-

* From Charles Silberman, *Crisis in Black and White,* New York: Random House, 1964, pp. 241–48.

ingful measure of change other than numbers. For all his opposition to quotas, for example, the late President Kennedy made it clear to the heads of all government agencies that he expected them to increase the number of Negroes in government jobs, especially in jobs at the middle and upper levels of responsibility. Wherever the number of Negro employees did increase, it was because administrative responsibility for hiring more Negroes had been fixed—not because the Kennedy Administration followed a policy of non-discrimination.

Unless responsibility is fixed in this way, policies of hiring more Negroes are likely to result in more talk than action. One reason is corporate bias. In the South, of course, discrimination is conscious and overt; employment of Negroes is limited by the tradition that Negroes not be permitted to work on an equal status with whites, and that they never be placed in a supervisory position over whites. In the North, exclusion of Negroes from the better jobs stems less from conscious corporate decisions to discriminate than from the conscious or unconscious biases of the personnel officers, the foremen, the executives—*i.e.,* all those involved in hiring and promoting. At the heart of this kind of unconscious discrimination is the concept of "place": the notion that certain jobs and certain situations are appropriate, others inappropriate, for Negroes: that is to say, in almost every company, whether through accident or choice, tradition has reserved some jobs almost exclusively for whites ("Negroes wouldn't be happy there"; "I'm not prejudiced, but my customers might object").

But prejudice is not the only factor tending to hold down Negro employment. "We would hire Negroes," the manager of Du Pont's sales office in Atlanta explained to a *Fortune* correspondent, "but we have no opportunity to do so. On the one occasion that we needed clerical help, we advertised, and our ad stated that we had signed the equal-opportunity agreement. But we had no Negro applicants. They just don't apply."

Of course they don't; the door has been closed too long. As we have seen, their own lives have given most Negroes reason enough to expect discrimination and prejudice, and to try to avoid it whenever they can; until they get positive reassurance to the contrary, Negroes are likely to assume that a firm discriminates, and they are likely to attribute any rejection to their race. Quite apart from their desire to avoid rebuffs, Negroes have no way of knowing when jobs are available. Virtually every study of how people find jobs has indicated that the most common method is recommendation by a relative or friend, usually one working for the same employer; relatively few people find jobs through newspaper advertisements, and even fewer through government or private employment agencies. But painfully few Negroes have relatives or friends working for corporations in anything but menial capacities; the most important means of finding a job in industry thus is not available, since Negroes are outside the web of job gossip.

Industry has to do more than just sit and wait for Negroes to come to their doors; it has to beat the bushes to find them, by recruiting at Negro colleges, at high schools in Negro areas, and at Negro employment agencies, by advertising in Negro newspapers and over Negro radio stations. At least a few corporations seem to be making a real effort to employ more Negroes. IBM now visits seventeen Negro colleges to recruit engineers, mathematicians, scientists, and sales and management trainees. McDonnell Aircraft of St. Louis, which has won praise from Negro militants for its employment policy (Negroes are employed in 127 job classifications) has developed a slide presentation picturing Negroes working alongside whites at every job level, and shows the slides at predominantly Negro high schools in the St. Louis area.

Recruitment is only the beginning. Corporations will have to revise personnel policies which, perhaps unintentionally, discourage Negroes from applying for jobs or from seeking promotions. When the Negro boycotts were under way in Philadelphia in 1962, for example, the president of one major corporation decided to take a look at his company's position in advance of any attack. He discovered that his Negro employees—two hundred out of two thousand—were all at the lowest level, although the company had no overt biases. Upon further examination, it developed that Negroes stayed at the bottom because they never took the written examinations the company used to measure qualifications for promotion; they simply assumed that the tests were designed to give the company an excuse for not promoting them. (Tests are frequently used this way in the South.) Since the tests in any case bore little relation to the job functions involved, the president ordered them replaced with job-performance tests and on-the-job training. As a result, seventy Negroes were upgraded.

If Negro employment is to be increased, firms will also have to find substitutes or shortcuts for the experience they now demand as a prerequisite in certain jobs. A large merchandising chain, for example, recently asked the National Urban League for help in hiring Negroes for a number of jobs, including store managers. But there was an unintentional catch: the firm required ten years of merchandising experience with the chain as a condition for promotion to manager. Since it had never employed Negroes in merchandising jobs before, the requirement obviously made it impossible for them to qualify for at least another ten years. The Urban League suggested that the firm develop methods for testing managerial ability in a shorter time.

It is not enough, moreover, for a firm formally to open jobs to Negroes on a non-discriminatory basis. At Hughes Tool in Houston, for example, the method of filling the skilled jobs that open up is to give existing employees a tryout. A few years ago, the company changed its policy to permit Negroes as well as whites to have a tryout. But since Negroes had been restricted to menial jobs like sweeping the floors, very few were able to qualify for better jobs. As *Fortune*'s Houston correspondent reported, "The past practice of keeping Negroes from running the machines has proved effective in continuing to keep them from running the machines."

All the recruiting in the world, however, and all the changes in personnel policies, would still leave corporations and government agencies short of qualified Negro applicants: Negroes have had neither the incentive nor the opportunity to acquire the qualifications now in demand. It is unrealistic to assume that Negroes *would* be qualified. "White folks seemed always to expect you to know those things which they'd done everything they could think of to prevent you from knowing," Ralph Ellison sardonically remarks in *Invisible Man*. The only solution, therefore, is to hire unqualified Negroes and to train them on the job.

It would be absurd to pretend that such a policy will not create serious difficulties for corporate managers and government officials. Granting more jobs to Negroes may mean fewer jobs for whites, particularly if total unemployment remains high, or at the very least, an end to the monopoly that whites have thus far enjoyed in many job classifications. Negro demands for preferential treatment thus are bound to set up counter-pressures from white workers— or white voters. One result is that businessmen, to their immense surprise, are likely to find that they actually *want* a strong FEPC law forbidding all businesses to discriminate in employment or in customer service; they will need such a law to protect them against employees, trade unions, recalcitrant employers, and hostile elements in their communities.

Efficiency may be lowered by the costs of hiring unqualified Negroes and training them on the job. Even more damage to efficiency may be done by the blow to the morale (and consequently to the productivity) of white employees when firms begin to discriminate in favor of Negroes. To be sure, no corporation is completely consistent in its adherence to the principle of merit; all kinds of subjective and irrational judgments enter into the selection and promotion of employees. But deliberately departing from the merit principle is something else again, and there is no point in pretending the corporations will not pay a heavy price for doing so. The cost of not discriminating in favor of Negroes, however, will be considerably greater, both to business and to the community at large. It will be considerably cheaper for business to subsidize Negro employment for a time than to pay it out in welfare—or in the cost to the community of racial violence.

It will be far easier to do these things, of course, if the present business expansion continues and the economy returns to full employment. During the labor shortages of World War Two, and again during the Korean conflict, business learned that it can put "unqualified" men and women to work by teaching them on the job, or by reorganizing the work where necessary to require less skill.

During World War Two, for example, American optical manufacturers assured naval procurement officers that it was impossible to manufacture more than a few thousand prism binoculars annually; there was a shortage of lens grinders, and it took a number of years to train one. By breaking the lens-grinding operation into several steps, however, the Navy was able to cut training time to a few weeks—and to increase output to a half-million binoculars a year. More recently, industry has had to meet its need for engineers through on-the-job training and upgrading. Between 1954 and 1957, for example, industry increased its employment of engineers by 100,000, or 27 per cent. In the same period only 70,000 engineers were graduated by all American colleges, and not all of them went to work for industry. Clearly, corporations supplied the difference through upgrading, promotion, and transfers from other work.

Some American corporations that operate in the underdeveloped nations have had to be even more ingenious in upgrading unqualified workers, since employing native workers may be the price of staying in the country for any length of time. Aramco, for example, used to import virtually its entire labor force from the United States; it seemed "obvious" that illiterate Saudi peasants could never cope with the complex technology of oil drilling and transportation. Faced with the long-range danger of expropriation, however, Aramco discovered that the Saudis could be taught after all. The company now uses Saudi drilling crews directed by Saudi foremen; roughly one-quarter of the labor time Aramco pays for is spent in education and training of some sort.

Most Negro Americans, needless to say—even those from the rural South—are quite a few notches above the Saudi tribesman in education and training. Given the chance, they can learn as well as whites; the expense of training them represents a cost of broadening the labor pool. There are present or potential shortages in many skilled jobs partly because of rising demands, but in good measure because union training regulations artificially restrict the supply. The pressure to hire more Negroes for skilled jobs may give industry the opportunity to take a fresh look at obsolete training requirements.

There may be a touch of hypocrisy, moreover, in some of the expressions of alarm over what may happen to job standards when more Negroes are employed. No one, after all, has suggested that unskilled Negro laborers be turned into brain surgeons or corporate presidents. What has been suggested is that Negroes be allowed to become plumbers, or electricians, or steam fitters, or carpenters; and, as David Danzig suggested, no one who lives or works in a recently built New York City building is likely to be impressed with the sincerity of the New York building trades unions' concern over maintaining the standards of their craft. Nor is anyone who has had difficulty keeping a new car or a new washing machine in working order likely to be overawed by Detroit's devotion to workmanship.

The way in which business responds to Negro pressures, perhaps more than any other single factor, will determine the character and tone of race relations over the rest of this decade. Businessmen like to think of themselves as conservatives; they have a rare opportunity to conserve American society by repairing what has to be repaired and changing what has to be changed. As we have seen, Negroes have become increasingly cynical about the efficacy of law and the integrity and good faith of white leadership. If they act on their own initiative to create jobs for Negroes, businessmen may be able to convert that distrust and cynicism into some degree of confidence and so, in the phrase of Edmund Burke, "make the Revolution a parent of settlement and not a nursery of future revolutions." If they are to do this, however—if they are to play a truly constructive role—businessmen will have to look beyond the rules and canons of business management. They will need to learn the art of politics in the highest sense of that term, for they will be engaged in what has been called "the politics of repair."

There is a precedent for what businessmen are being called upon to do. In many ways, the current racial conflict resembles the conflict over trade-unionism during the 1930s; businessmen then resented the unionists' demands to share in managerial power, and they were concerned over what would happen to efficiency if extraneous considerations—union membership or seniority, for example—were made a condition of employment or of promotion. The analogy can be pressed too far, of course; there are important differences, the main one being that trade unions could purport to speak for most of a firm's employees, whereas Negro organizations speak only for a minority. The fact remains that the United States averted class warfare in the 1930s because large corporations gradually came to accommodate themselves to trade union power—that is, to negotiate with it. Business has a similar role to play today in averting race warfare.

PART V

HOUSING FOR
THE NEGRO

Food, clothing and shelter are prime necessities, and a good job generally means a good home, good food, and fine clothing. But for the Negro this has not usually been so. Even if he earns a high salary, he finds it difficult to move into decent neighborhoods. Agreements among white homeowners have kept Negroes out of so-called better neighborhoods for a variety of reasons.

The following selections examine several aspects of the problem of discrimination in housing.

Selections 34a–34b

SUPREME COURT RULINGS

The two Supreme Court decisions which follow indicate how our highest tribunal looks at the problem of residential discrimination.

Buchanan vs. Warley deals with a law enacted in Louisville, Kentucky which segregated Negroes in the location of their homes.

Shelley vs. Kraemer is concerned with restrictive covenants or agreements that property will not be sold or rented to people of a certain race, color, or national origin. The case of Buchanan vs. Warley dealt with city action favoring discrimination in housing. Shelley vs. Kraemer deals with private action or private agreements restricting Negroes from moving into a white neighborhood.

34a. Buchanan *vs.* Warley*

Mr. Justice Day delivered the opinion of the court:

Buchanan . . . brought an action in the chancery branch of Jefferson circuit court of Kentucky for the specific performance of a contract for the sale of certain real estate situated in the city of Louisville. . . . The offer in writing to purchase the property contained a proviso:

> It is understood that I am purchasing the above property for the purpose of having erected thereon a house which I propose to make my residence, and it is a distinct part of this agreement that I shall not be required to accept a deed to the above property or to pay for said property unless I have the right, under the laws of the state of Kentucky and the city of Louisville, to occupy said property as a residence.

This offer was accepted by the plaintiff.

To the action for specific performance the defendant, by way of answer, set up the condition above set forth, that he is a colored person, and that on the block of which the lot in controversy is a part, there are ten residences, eight of which, at the time of the making of the contract, were occupied by white people, and only two (those nearest the lot in question) were occupied by colored people, and that, under and by virtue of the ordinance of the city of Louisville, approved May 11, 1914, he would not be allowed to occupy the lot as a place of residence.

In reply to this answer the plaintiff set up, among other things, that the ordinance was in conflict with the 14th Amendment to the Constitution of the United States, and hence no defense to the action for specific performance of the contract. . . .

The title of the ordinance is:

> An ordinance to prevent conflict and ill-feeling between the white and colored races in the city of Louisville, and preserve the public peace and promote the general welfare by making reasonable provisions requiring as far as practicable, the use of separate blocks for residences, places of abode, and places of assembly by white and colored people respectively. . . .

We pass . . . to a consideration of the case upon its merits. This ordinance prevents the occupancy of a lot in the city of Louisville by a person of color in a block where the greater number of residences are occupied by white persons; where such a majority exists, colored persons are excluded. This interdiction is based wholly upon color; simply that, and nothing more. In effect, premises situated as are those in question in the so-called white block are effectively de-

* 245 U.S. 60 (1917).

barred from sale to persons of color, because, if sold, they cannot be occupied by the purchaser nor by him sold to another of the same color.

This drastic measure is sought to be justified under the authority of the state in the exercise of the police power. It is said such legislation tends to promote the public peace by preventing racial conflicts; that it tends to maintain racial purity; that it prevents the deterioration of property owned and occupied by white people, which deterioration, it is contended, is sure to follow the occupancy of adjacent premises by persons of color.

The authority of the state to pass laws in the exercise of the police power, having for their object the promotion of the public health, safety, and welfare, is very broad, as has been affirmed in numerous and recent decisions of this court. Furthermore, the exercise of this power, embracing nearly all legislation of a local character, is not to be interfered with by the courts where it is within the scope of legislative authority and the means adopted reasonably tend to accomplish a lawful purpose. But it is equally well established that the police power, broad as it is, cannot justify the passage of a law or ordinance which runs counter to the limitations of the Federal Constitution; that principle has been so frequently affirmed in this court that we need not stop to cite the cases.

The Federal Constitution and laws passed within its authority are, by the express terms of that instrument, made the supreme law of the land. The 14th Amendment protects life, liberty, and property from invasion by the states without due process of law. Property is more than the mere thing which a person owns. It is elementary that it includes the right to acquire, use, and dispose of it. The Constitution protects these essential attributes of property. . . .

True it is that dominion over property springing from ownership is not absolute and unqualified. The disposition and use of property may be controlled, in the exercise of the police power, in the interest of public health, convenience, or welfare. Harmful occupations may be controlled and regulated. Legitimate business may also be regulated in the interest of the public. Certain uses of property may be confined to portions of the municipality other than the residence district, such as livery stables, brickyards, and the like, because of the impairment of the health and comfort of the occupants of neighboring property. Many illustrations might be given from the decisions of this court and other courts, of this principle, but these cases do not touch the one at bar.

The concrete question here is: May the occupancy, and, necessarily, the purchase and sale of property of which occupancy is an incident, be inhibited by the states, or by one of its municipalities, solely because of the color of the proposed occupant of the premises? That one may dispose of his property, subject only to the control of lawful enactments curtailing that right in the public interest, must be conceded. The question now presented makes it pertinent to inquire into the constitutional right of the white man to sell his property to a colored man, having in view the legal status of the purchaser and occupant.

Following the Civil War certain amendments to the Federal Constitution were adopted, which have become an integral part of that instrument, equally binding upon all the states and fixing certain fundamental rights which all are bound to respect. The 13th Amendment abolished slavery in the United States and in all places subject to their jurisdiction, and gave Congress power to enforce the Amendment by appropriate legislation. The 14th Amendment made all persons born or naturalized in the United States, citizens of the United States and of the states in which they reside, and provided that no state shall make or enforce any law which shall abridge the privileges or immunities of citizens of the United States, and that no state shall deprive any person of life, liberty, or property without due process of law, nor deny to any person the equal protection of the laws. . . .

That there exists a serious and difficult problem arising from a feeling of race hostility which the law is powerless to control, and to which it must give a measure of consideration, may be freely admitted. But its solution cannot be promoted by depriving citizens of their constitutional rights and privileges.

As we have seen, this court has held laws valid which separated the races on the basis of equal accommodations in public conveyances, and courts of high authority have held enactments lawful which provide for separation in the public schools of white and colored pupils where equal privileges are given. But, in view of the rights secured by the 14th Amendment to the Federal Constitution, such legislation must have its limitations, and cannot be sustained where the exercise of authority exceeds the restraints of the Constitution. We think these limitations are exceeded in laws and ordinances of the character now before us.

It is the purpose of such enactments, and it is frankly avowed it will be their ultimate effect, to require by law, at least in residential districts, the compulsory separation of the races on account of color. Such action is said to be essential to the maintenance of the purity of the races, although it is to be noted in the ordinance under consideration that the employment of colored servants in white families is permitted, and nearby residences of colored persons not coming within the blocks, as defined in the ordinance, are not prohibited.

The case presented does not deal with an attempt to prohibit the amalgamation of the races. The right which the ordinance annulled was the civil right of a white man to dispose of his property if he saw fit to do so to a person of color, and of a colored person to make such disposition to a white person.

It is urged that this proposed segregation will promote the public peace by preventing race conflicts. Desirable as this is, and important as is the preservation of the public peace, this aim cannot be accomplished by laws or ordinances which deny rights created or protected by the Federal Constitution.

It is said that such acquisitions by colored persons depreciate property owned in the neighborhood by white persons. But property may be acquired by undesirable white neighbors, or put to disagreeable though lawful uses with like results.

We think this attempt to prevent the alienation of the property in question to a person of color was not a legitimate exercise of the police power of the state, and is in direct violation of the fundamental law enacted in the 14th Amendment of the Constitution preventing state interference with property rights except by due process of law. That being the case, the ordinance cannot stand. . . .

Reversed.

34b.   Shelley *vs.* Kraemer*

Mr. Chief Justice Vinson delivered the opinion of the Court:

. . . It is well, at the outset, to scrutinize the terms of the restrictive agreements involved in these cases. In the Missouri case, the covenant declares that no part of the affected property shall be "occupied by any person not of the Caucasian race, it being intended hereby to restrict the use of said property . . . against the occupancy as owners or tenants of any portion of said property for resident or other purpose by people of the Negro or Mongolian Race." Not only does the restriction seek to proscribe use and occupancy of the affected properties by members of the excluded class, but as construed by the Missouri courts, the agreement requires that title of any person who uses his property in violation of the restriction shall be divested. The restriction of the covenant in the Michigan case seeks to bar occupancy by persons of the excluded class. It provides that "This property shall not be used or occupied by any person or persons except those of the Caucasian race."

It should be observed that these covenants do not seek to proscribe any particular use of the affected properties. Use of the prop-

* 334 U.S. 1 (1948).

erties for residential occupancy, as such, is not forbidden. The restrictions of these agreements, rather, are directed toward a designated class of persons and seek to determine who may and who may not own or make use of the properties for residential purposes. The excluded class is defined wholly in terms of race or color; "simply that and nothing more."

It cannot be doubted that among the civil rights intended to be protected from discriminatory state action by the Fourteenth Amendment are the rights to acquire, enjoy, own and dispose of property. Equality in the enjoyment of property rights was regarded by the framers of that Amendment as an essential pre-condition to the realization of other basic civil rights and liberties which the Amendment was intended to guarantee. Thus, . . . 8 USCA § 42, . . . derived from § 1 of the Civil Rights Act of 1866 which was enacted by Congress while the Fourteenth Amendment was also under consideration, provides: "All citizens of the United States shall have the same right, in every State and Territory, as is enjoyed by white citizens thereof to inherit, purchase, lease, sell, hold, and convey real and personal property." This Court has given specific recognition to the same principle. . . .

We conclude, therefore, that the restrictive agreements standing alone cannot be regarded as violative of any rights guaranteed to petitioners by the Fourteenth Amendment. So long as the purposes of those agreements are effectuated by voluntary adherence to their terms, it would appear clear that there has been no action by the State and the provisions of the Amendment have not been violated. . . .

But here there was more. These are cases in which the purposes of the agreements were secured only by judicial enforcement by state courts of the restrictive terms of the agreements. The respondents urge that judicial enforcement of private agreement does not amount to state action; or, in any event, the participation of the States is so attenuated in character as not to amount to state action within the meaning of the Fourteenth Amendment. Finally, it is suggested, even if the States in these cases may be deemed to have acted in the constitutional sense, their action did not deprive petitioners of rights guaranteed by the Fourteenth Amendment. We move to a consideration of these matters. . . .

The short of the matter is that from the time of the adoption of the Fourteenth Amendment until the present, it has been the consistent ruling of this Court that the action of the States to which the Amendment has reference, includes action of state courts and state judicial officials. Although, in construing the terms of the Fourteenth Amendment, differences have from time to time been expressed as to whether particular types of state action may be said to offend the Amendment's prohibitory provisions, it has never been suggested that state court action is immunized from the operation of those provisions simply because the act is that of the judicial branch of the state government.

Against this background of judicial construction, extending over a period of some three-quarters of a century, we are called upon to consider whether enforcement by state courts of the restrictive agreements in these cases may be deemed to be the acts of those States; and, if so, whether that action has denied these petitioners the equal protection of the laws which the Amendment was intended to insure.

We have no doubt that there has been state action in these cases in the full and complete sense of the phrase. The undisputed facts disclose that petitioners were willing purchasers of properties upon which they desired to establish homes. The owners of the properties were willing sellers; and contracts of sale were accordingly consummated. It is clear that but for the active intervention of the state courts, supported by the full panoply of state power, petitioners would have been free to occupy the properties in question without restraint.

These are not cases, as has been suggested, in which the States have merely abstained from action, leaving private individuals free to impose such discriminations as they see fit. Rather, these are cases in which the States have made available to such individuals the full coercive power of government to deny to petitioners, on the grounds of race or color, the enjoyment of property rights in premises which petitioners are willing and financially able to acquire and which the grantors are willing to sell. The difference between judicial enforcement and non-enforcement of the restrictive covenants is the difference to petitioners between being denied rights of property available to other members of the community and being accorded full enjoyment of those rights on an equal footing.

The enforcement of the restrictive agreements by the state courts in these cases was directed pursuant to the common-law policy of the States as formulated by those courts in earlier decisions. In the Missouri case, enforcement of the covenant was directed in the first instance by the highest court of the State after the trial court had determined the agreement to be invalid for want of the requisite number of signatures. In the Michigan case, the order of enforcement by the trial court was affirmed by the highest state court. The judicial action in each case bears the clear and unmistakable imprimatur of the State. We have noted that previous decisions of this Court have established the proposition that judicial action is not immunized from the operation of the Fourteenth Amendment simply because it is taken pursuant to the state's common-law policy. Nor is the Amendment ineffective simply because the particular pattern of discrimination, which the State has enforced, was defined initially by the terms of a private agreement. State action, as that phrase is understood for the purposes of the Fourteenth Amendment, refers to exertions of state power in all forms. And when the effect of that action is to deny rights subject to the protection of the Fourteenth Amendment, it is the obligation of this Court to enforce the constitutional commands.

We hold that in granting judicial enforcement of the restrictive agreements in these cases, the States have denied petitioners the equal protection of the laws and that, therefore, the action of the state courts cannot stand. We have noted that freedom from discrimination by the States in the enjoyment of property rights was among the basic objectives sought to be effectuated by the framers of the Fourteenth Amendment. That such discrimination has occurred in these cases is clear. Because of the race or color of these petitioners they have been denied rights of ownership or occupancy enjoyed as a matter of course by other citizens of different race or color. The Fourteenth Amendment declares "that all persons whether colored or white, shall stand equal before the laws of the States, and, in regard to the colored race, for whose protection the amendment was primarily designed, that no discrimination shall be made against them by law because of their color." . . . Only recently this Court has had occasion to declare that a state law which denied equal enjoyment of property rights to a designated class of citizens of specified race and ancestry, was not a legitimate exercise of the state's police power but violated the guaranty of the equal protection of the laws. *Oyama* vs. *California,* 332 US 633 (1948). Nor may the discriminations imposed by the state courts in these cases be justified as proper exertions of state police power. . . .

The historical context in which the Fourteenth Amendment became a part of the Constitution should not be forgotten. Whatever else the framers sought to achieve, it is clear that the matter of primary concern was the establishment of equality in the enjoyment of basic civil and political rights and the preservation of those rights from discriminatory action on the part of the States based on considerations of race or color. Seventy-five years ago this Court announced that the provisions of the Amendment are to be construed with this fundamental purpose in mind. Upon full consideration, we have concluded that in these cases the States have acted to deny petitioners the equal protection of the laws guaranteed by the Fourteenth Amendment. Having so decided, we find it unnecessary to consider whether petitioners have also been deprived of property without due process of law or denied privileges and immunities of citizens of the United States.

For the reasons stated, the judgment of the Supreme Court of Missouri and the judgment of the Supreme Court of Michigan must be reversed.

Selection 35

"IF GOD HAD MEANT FOR THEM TO LIVE NEAR WHITES HE WOULDN'T HAVE MADE SO MANY BIGOTS"

© 1965 Fischetti and Publishers Newspaper Syndicate

Selection 36

THE COLOR LINE IN
NORTHERN SUBURBIA*

The following episodes, which were reported by sociologists, disclose techniques used to restrict Negro movement into the suburbs.

Over 95 per cent of Suburbia's youthful population are white, native-born Americans. The remainder are white, foreign-born.

Why, in the light of the desirability of Suburbia for young families, is there this conspicuous absence of Negroes and orientals?

In the light of this challenging question, two teams of sociologists made a survey of Suburbia's realtors. Each team was composed of two Caucasians and one Negro, attempting to discover what devious means, if any, are used by realtors to continue restrictive housing. What myths, if any, are perpetuated by realtors to exclude minority groups from private housing? What devious means, if any, are used by professional sellers of real estate to continue to restrict the freedom of residential movement by minority racial and ethnic groups?

The Negro, serving as the follow-up, made a request for housing comparable to that of the Caucasian couple. The follow-up had more effect on the study, since the Negro would be observing the attitude of the realtors to a Negro prospect and would learn what reasons, if any, were given or techniques were used in discouraging sales to Negroes.

Realtor 1: He offered to show the couple around. The couple was in a hurry, but accepted listings and the realtor's card. They prom-

* James H. Kirk and Elaine D. Johnson, report, *Hearings before the U.S. Commission on Civil Rights, San Francisco, California, January 27–28, 1960,* in *Freedom Now!* Alan F. Westin (editor), pp. 178–82.

ised to call the realtor later for an appointment to go house hunting. They were also given assurance by the realtor that there were many other homes available.

Negro Follow-up: The realtor hedged about twenty minutes. Then he started giving excuses: Realtors will not sell to Negroes; real-estate association won't allow it; their office once tried to sell a home to a Chinese family and nearly lost their license.

NEGRO: How can you enforce the restrictive covenant when it isn't legal?

REALTOR: We have a fifty-year covenant.

NEGRO: I would like to live in the Suburbia area.

REALTOR: You are the first Negro who has approached me in the eight years I have been in Suburbia. The tract offices might have some listings, and they are FHA. Why don't you try them?

NEGRO: Do you mean to tell me the tract offices will sell them without discrimination as to race?

REALTOR: There is no Negro living in the Suburbia area. You could buy in the Jonestown area. If you will come back, I will be glad to show you houses in the Jonestown area.

Realtor 2: The realtor offered to show the couple around the Suburbia area. When his offer was refused because of the pressure of time, he gave several listings in the area requested, with down payments as low as $1,000 to $1,650.

NEGRO (The realtor was very tense): Do you have any houses with a $2,000 down payment?

REALTOR: We have nothing for less than $3,000 to $4,000 down.

NEGRO: Do you have any tract houses, GI, available?

REALTOR: Yes, for $3,000 or more down. If you will call me for an appointment, I will show you around. Is there any particular reason why you want to live in the Suburbia area?

NEGRO: Yes; I work in this area and we have all our charge accounts here. Yet we live in Smithville.

(Negro interviewer felt very sympathetic with the realtor, who was very tense and uncomfortable, and assumed it was the realtor's first contact with a Negro prospect. Then, too, there were women employees in the office who were giggling in the background and listening to the conversation. Interviewer heard one remark, "I wonder what the Negro is up to." The realtor didn't seem free to talk, as if he were afraid of ridicule from the women employees.)

REALTOR: Do you have enough money for a down payment?

NEGRO: I have $3,500.

REALTOR: I would discourage your looking for homes in this area. (On two walls of this real-estate office were listings with addresses in the Suburbia area.)

Realtor 3: Listings for houses in the Suburbia area were requested by and were given to the couple.

It was found that the young salesman, who gave three listings, was very friendly and cooperative. The cooperation of the young salesman was so sincere that the interviewer questioned the possibility of any difficulty arising.

REALTOR: I have just come from a section of the country where the problem of segregation in housing is not acute. I will speak to my associate about you, for he is an officer of the realty association in Suburbia and may be able to help you. We have had no Negro inquiries about housing before. (The realtor shook hands, gave his card, and invited the Negro to return.)

. . .

Realtor 9: The realtor stated that he had many houses available in the area at the price mentioned. He brought out a mimeographed list similar to the one shown by realtor 8. He stated there were many GI resales, and gave the couple a number of listings.

NEGRO (The realtor was very evasive at first): I notice that you have a three-bedroom home for sale with a small down payment. You have it listed on the board in front of your office.
REALTOR: The people who owned that property have changed their minds, and withdrew the listing. I would suggest you look in the Metropolis and Smithville areas. You would be unhappy in the Suburbia area.
NEGRO: Why?
REALTOR: Because there are no Negroes here.
NEGRO: That would make no difference to me as long as the house was desirable. (When the realtor was asked for his card, the realtor walked away, entered his office, and placed a call. As he was telephoning, he fumbled in his desk drawer, drew out a card and waved it at the Negro, which the latter "failed to see." When the call was completed the realtor handed the interviewer his card.)
NEGRO: Would it be possible to buy a house in this area?
REALTOR: The people living in the neighborhood would object.
NEGRO: Do the people listing a home for sale stipulate that it be sold to Caucasians only?

REALTOR: Of course not.

NEGRO: Is it the policy of all the realtors in the Suburbia area to refuse to show or to sell property to a Negro?

(The realtor did not answer this question. During the entire time he appeared, first, nervous, evasive; then adamant; then antagonistic because of the last question.)

Realtor 10: The procedure was reversed in this interview and the one following, with the Negro making his call before the Caucasian couple, which resulted in more information—unsolicited.

NEGRO: I would like a home from $12,000 to $14,000 with a $2,000 down payment.

REALTOR: We have no listings for less than $3,400 to $4,200 down.

(The realtor didn't act cordial, nor offer a chair. However, the interviewer sat down. No listings were given; however, the realtor gave the assurance that he would take the Negro house hunting on the next visit. As the Negro stepped out the door, he heard the realtor remark in a low tone, "—— ——!")

Couple (as husband and wife): The two realtors in the office, a man and woman, treated the couple graciously. They were assured there were many houses for sale to meet their requirements, and a large listing sheet was leafed through. The woman realtor said it included 550 listings in this area.

HUSBAND: Before you look any further, you should know that I have a criminal record. Would that have any effect on our getting credit to buy a home?

WOMAN REALTOR (gesturing with arms raised): Goodness, no; none at all. The realtors can't refuse to sell property to anyone. Your past record won't be investigated—it isn't the same as an employer checking your record.

HUSBAND: What if my wife had been a dope addict; would we have trouble getting a home here? (As wife tugs to roll sleeves below elbow as though trying to conceal needle marks.)

WOMAN REALTOR: That wouldn't make any difference; as long as you have the money required for the down payment and make this much a month, you qualify. (She figured four times the monthly payment.) I am writing out a number of listings, and here is my card. However, I would be glad to show you around.

WIFE: Dear, we had better hurry. Aren't you to report for work at noon today?

HUSBAND: Oh, well, what if I do lose this job—there are others.

WIFE: You are always so optimistic about finding work.

WOMAN REALTOR: A job is a job.

HUSBAND: Oh, well, what the hell! What's a job?

WOMAN REALTOR (aside to realtor): How did you get rid of that Negro?

REALTOR: I just yessed him to death.

HUSBAND: Any chance of Negroes moving into this area?

REALTOR: No. You won't have to worry about colored neighbors here.

WIFE: Don't you have to sell to them, though, according to law?

REALTOR: Yes; we can't refuse to show them property. But we can get people to withdraw listings. If Negroes would move into this area, the people would get up in arms and make it hot for them. They couldn't stay.

WIFE: What would happen to you if you sold to Negroes?

REALTOR: If it were known by other realtors that our office sold to Negroes, we'd be out of business.

WOMAN REALTOR: We'd be blackballed. . . .

Selection 37

SPEECH BY THE ATTORNEY GENERAL*

This speech by the Attorney General of the United States, Nicholas deB. Katzenbach, was delivered on June 15, 1965.

We meet this evening on the anniversary of an event of momentous and seminal significance in the development of Anglo-Saxon law and government. On June 15, 1215—750 years ago today—"in the meadow which is called Runnymede between Windsor and Staines" King John affixed his seal to the Magna Carta.

* Remarks by Attorney General Nicholas deB. Katzenbach at the St. Louis Conference on Equal Opportunity in Housing, St. Louis, Missouri, June 15, 1965.

The rebellious barons who forced the King to grant the charter were not much concerned with its effect in the distant future. They were practical and selfish men who demanded redress for specific grievances. Nor did the tyrannous John probably know or care that in granting redress he was setting precedent for the limitations of governmental power. Until that time, the power of the King, so far as anyone knew, was absolute.

The language of the charter is still remarkably acute. It set down a guarantee of freedom under law:

"No free man shall be taken, imprisoned, disseised, outlawed, banished, or in any way destroyed, nor will We proceed against or prosecute him except by the lawful judgment of his peers and by the law of the land."

And it guaranteed impartial administration of justice.

"To no one will We sell, to none will We deny or delay, right or justice."

These are words which have filtered down the centuries with enormous impact. The principles of the Great Charter were carried by the colonists to the New World. The Constitution and the Bill of Rights are its direct descendants.

This link was dramatically, if poignantly, underscored at the recent ceremonies in which an acre of ground at Runnymede was deeded in perpetuity to America by the British people in honor of President Kennedy.

We are, in the United States, today, still working to guarantee the impartial administration of justice written into the Magna Carta. We are still fighting to assure that "to none will We deny or delay, right or justice."

Equal justice before the law is, after centuries of denial, finally being won for Negro citizens.

This has been a decade of struggle and a decade of great achievement. The courts have made it clear that separate but equal has no meaning in any area of the law. The 1957 and 1964 Civil Rights Act gave the government tools to eliminate publicly sanctioned segregation. The Voting Rights Bill of 1965, which I am confident will be passed by Congress with dispatch, will further hasten the end of official discrimination.

The work is not complete. There will continue to be difficulties in enforcing legal guarantees. Loopholes may develop in the laws and mopping-up action will be required. But the legal principle is now established; the system of officially sanctioned segregation is in its death throes in the United States. The legal rights guaranteed to the American Negro have existed for a century. Now they are being put into effect.

We have thus, as President Johnson noted at Howard University ten days ago, reached the end of the beginning. For as the President said, "it is not enough just to open the gates of opportunity" unless everyone can walk through the gates.

We seek, in the President's words "not just equality as a right and a theory but equality as a fact and equality as a result."

Moving from the area of theory and law to the area of fact means that we must now confront all the mean realities of inequality, of deprivation, and poverty right at home in our own communities.

These problems will be even more difficult to dissolve because they represent the sum total of our neglect and failure as a whole society.

Unemployment, poverty, bad health, inferior schools, rat-infested slums—these are not just Negro problems—they are American problems. This conference is concerned with what is probably the most crucial and the most important problem of all. Segregated housing is the cause—direct and indirect—of many other kinds of segregation.

Almost three out of four Negroes in America live in a city, and most Negro city dwellers are forced by discrimination into slums. Segregated housing creates segregation in schools and hospitals and most other areas of everyday life. It creates a separate community that might as well be walled in like a medieval ghetto, so effective is the division.

These walls will not be made to tumble by law alone, but by persuasion and action on the community, neighborhood and individual level.

Conferences like this already have proved their value. Last November I spoke at a similar meeting in Baltimore. Following that Conference the local board of realtors revised its listing contract to contain a clause saying: "The Seller agrees to offer his property to all qualified purchasers regardless of race or color."

Not stopping with a simple statement of nondiscriminatory policy, the Baltimore board has developed an educational program to acquaint salesmen with ways to overcome seller resistance to prospective Negro buyers.

Promising steps of a similar nature have been taken in other cities. In Cincinnati, for instance, the housing industry has joined civil rights groups in setting up a city-wide fair housing council. Such action has not been restricted to cities, but has been growing rapidly, even in white, middle-class suburbs.

In the past five years, fair housing committees affiliated with the National Committee Against Discrimination in Housing have increased from 18 to about 1,000.

The fact that three levels of government—city, county, and state

—are co-sponsoring this conference with the President's Committee on Equal Opportunity in Housing, says much about the interest in finding solutions here in St. Louis.

I have no need to stress to this group, however, that despite all these positive beginnings, the great bulk of the work lies ahead. We have barely scratched the surface of accomplishment in truly integrated housing.

The first job is to clear away the fables and fears that block progress in this field. The causes of discrimination rest, at bottom, in the human mind. It is there where discriminatory attitudes must first be undermined. It is there where the fantasies about what will happen if a Negro moves into the neighborhood must first be broken.

These myths do not come as sharply into play when their falsity is theoretical—when they are to be tested in someone else's backyard. But they may be the dominant cause of resistance when the question is not theoretical equality, but Negroes moving to one's own street.

You know what these myths are—they are as much a part of American folklore as Paul Bunyan:

"If we let one in they will all come in."

"They will take over."

"All the whites will move out."

"The neighborhood will deteriorate."

"Property values will go down."

Statements of this kind are so common and so mesmerizing that it is easy to forget that they are just myths. But that is what they are—myths—untrue assumptions.

"I cannot comprehend how any man can want anything but the truth," wrote Roman Emperor Marcus Aurelius. "It is our false opinions of things which ruin us."

The only way to counter the mythology of race relations is with facts and knowledge. And facts and knowledge are becoming increasingly available as starts toward integrated housing are made in many cities. Evidence is now piled high that the parade of horrors evoked by the prospect of a Negro family moving into a white neighborhood is a mirage.

Hundreds of white communities, both urban and suburban, throughout the country, have been quietly and successfully integrated. Apartment developments in dozens of major cities have adopted equal opportunity policies. And they have done so without financial calamity, disorder, or disruption of any sort.

The towns, cities, and developments where integration occurred are not freaks. The white families who accepted Negro neighbors were not all "do-gooders" or "firebrand liberals." The builders and owners were not possessed or suicidal. They were serious businessmen, not afraid to make a change which was both sound business and the right thing.

Little progress will be made in opening equal opportunities in housing until more real estate dealers and housing industry executives emulate them. One of the most dismaying things about the myths I have mentioned is that so many real estate people—men and women who should be better informed—either subscribe to them or are convinced that every prospective white customer believes them.

In either case, by preserving the misconceptions and misapprehensions of a passing age, they are damaging the nation's interests in general, and their own in particular. All prospective customers are not bigots. Impartiality toward Negroes does not mean financial ruin or social ostracism.

Lending institutions, home builders, and real estate dealers who insist on believing the opposite are fighting what is essentially a rear-guard action, and in so doing, are endangering their own long-range business prospects.

For, above all, segregation is really not practical. It is not practical because trying to preserve it in the face of the overwhelming trend of history, of opinion and of moral influence, will be costly and ultimately self-defeating.

With the Voting Rights bill nearing passage civil rights leaders have already indicated that housing is their next major goal for advancement.

I hope that leaders in the housing industry will work with them to bring about progress. Early and constructive action can obviate the kind of hostility and conflict that which help none and hurt all.

This conference and others like it can help to smooth the path. It can facilitate communication between the groups. And it can spread the understanding that in North as well as South, in St. Louis as well as Selma, national interest is self-interest.

The confirmed existence of ghettoes, whether they be of Negro poor, or Puerto Rican poor, or Irish poor, endangers and deprives and deprecates not only those in it, but the entire community.

If our central city areas increasingly become empty cores in fat doughnuts of suburban prosperity, we do damage not only to our democratic vision, but also to the prosperity of downtown businessmen. If welfare costs mount ever higher, the price is paid by all citizens. If crime continues to increase in slum areas, its effects reverberate through all levels of society.

In stressing the impracticality of continuing segregated practices in housing, I have not meant to ignore the even more fundamental consideration. For aside from the fact that it is economically unsound, and aside from the fact that it is opposed to public policy, segregation is basically immoral.

I am happy to note that St. Louis religious leadership has been active in the fight on segregation and is participating in this conference. The significant role the clergy has played in recent civil rights developments underlines the fact that this revolution is as much moral as it is social, and as much spiritual as it is secular.

There is a rising tide which recognizes that our prosperity is not complete and our promise as a nation not fulfilled until all can partake of it, and all can contribute to it.

This is a hope and an idea as old as man, and we are today working to attain it.

"Your abundance," says the New Testament, "may be a supply for their want, that their abundance also may be a supply for your want; that there may be equality."

Selection 38

HOUSING COLOR LINE UPSET BY CALIFORNIA HIGH COURT

LAWRENCE E. DAVIES*

The following newspaper article summarizes the story behind California's attempt to prevent discrimination in the selling of property.

San Francisco, May 10—The California Supreme Court today prohibited racial discrimination in the disposal of property. In a 5-to-2 ruling, the justices held invalid an amendment to the State Constitution that permitted such discrimination. It held that the amendment violated the 14th Amendment to the Federal Constitution.

The state amendment, which appeared on the ballot as proposi-

* From *The New York Times,* May 11, 1966.

tion 14 in November, 1964, was approved by the voters by a margin
of 2 to 1, after one of the bitterest campaigns ever mounted in California.

One result of the court's decision is expected to be a flow of Federal money into California for redevelopment projects that have
been held up because of the discriminatory provisions of the state
law.

U.S. Rejected Brown's Plea

Gov. Edmund G. Brown announced in March that the Federal
Government had rejected his request to free at least $200-million in
urban renewal funds for California.

The Supreme Court based its decision primarily on a case on
appeal from the Superior Court of Orange County, involving a
Negro postman in Santa Ana and his wife. But six companion
cases, including one filed by the Fresno Redevelopment Agency,
were also covered.

Mr. and Mrs. Lincoln W. Mulkey had sued Neil Heitman and
apartment owners and managers in Orange County, charging that
rental of available apartments had been denied to them solely because they were Negroes. The trial court had ruled for the apartment owners and managers on the ground that "the passage of
Proposition 14 has rendered Civil Code Sections 51 and 52 upon
which this action is based null and void."

Proposition 14 specifically provided that "neither the state nor any
subdivision or agency thereof shall deny, limit or abridge, directly
or indirectly, the right of any person, who is willing or desires to
sell, lease or rent any part or all of his real property, to decline to
sell, lease or rent such property to such person or persons as he, in
his absolute discretion, chooses."

14th Amendment Cited

But the State Supreme Court, in overturning this provision, declared in the majority opinion by Justice Paul Peek:

"It is now beyond dispute that the 14th Amendment, through the
equal protection clause, secures, without the discrimination on account of color, race [or] religion, 'the right to acquire and possess
property of every kind.'"

In a dissenting opinion, Justice Thomas P. White, retired, sitting
temporarily for Justice Stanley Mosk, who had disqualified himself
as a former Attorney General involved in the Proposition 14 fight,
protested:

"Nothing in the Federal Constitution gives one citizen the right to acquire property from another citizen who does not wish to sell it to him even if the refusal is based on race or religion."

Two Acts Restored

In effect, the decision puts back in force the Unruh Civil Rights Act of 1959, which prohibits racial discrimination by business concerns, including real estate of dealers, and the Rumford Fair Housing Act of 1963, which forbids racial discrimination in the sale or rental of private dwellings containing more than four units.

The two acts are named for their sponsors, Jesse M. Unruh, Speaker of the Assembly, and W. Byron Rumford, an Assemblyman from Berkeley. Both are Democrats.

Federal Appeal Forecast

Governor Brown, a Democrat seeking a third-term nomination in the June 7 primary, said that the decision would undoubtedly be appealed to the United States Supreme Court.

The Governor, a strong advocate of open housing, said that until the Federal tribunal acted he would "continue to enforce this law [Proposition 14] as I do all other California laws." He said he would instruct the State Fair Employment Practices Commission not to enforce the Rumford Act until the Federal Court ruled.

Attorney General Thomas C. Lynch declined to comment directly on Governor Brown's statement. But he declared that the antidiscrimination laws wiped out by the passage of Proposition 14 now were back on the books and that he planned to start enforcing them immediately.

If the F.E.P.C. began action under the Rumford Act, the Attorney General said, he will represent the commission.

Justice Peek was joined in the majority opinion by Chief Justice Roger J. Traynor and Justices Raymond E. Peters, Mathew O. Tobriner and Louis H. Burke. Justice Marshall F. McComb also wrote a dissenting opinion.

PART VI

THE NEGRO AND THE MILITARY

Selection 39

A FRENCH DIRECTIVE ON THE TREATMENT OF AMERICAN NEGRO TROOPS IN WORLD WAR I*

May, 1919

To the French Military Mission stationed with the American Army. August 7, 1918. Secret information concerning the black American Troops.

It is important for French officers who have been called upon to exercise command over black American troops, or to live in close contact with them, to have an exact idea of the position occupied by Negroes in the United States. The information set forth in the following communication ought to be given to these officers and it is to their interest to have these matters known and widely disseminated. It will devolve likewise on the French Military Authorities, through the medium of the Civil Authorities, to give information

* From Martin B. Duberman, *In White America*, Boston: Houghton Mifflin Company, 1964, pp. 110–12.

on this subject to the French population residing in the cantonments occupied by American colored troops.

1. The American attitude upon the Negro question may seem a matter for discussion to many French minds. But we French are not in our province if we undertake to discuss what some call "prejudice." American opinion is unanimous on the "color question," and does not admit of any discussion.

The increasing number of Negroes in the United States (about 15,000,000) would create for the white race in the Republic a menace of degeneracy were it not that an impassable gulf has been made between them.

As this danger does not exist for the French race, the French public has become accustomed to treating the Negro with familiarity and indulgence.

This indulgence and this familiarity are matters of grievous concern to the Americans. They consider them an affront to their national policy. They are afraid that contact with the French will inspire in black Americans aspirations which to them (the whites) appear intolerable. It is of the utmost importance that every effort be made to avoid profoundly estranging American opinion.

Although a citizen of the United States, the black man is regarded by the white American as an inferior being with whom relations of business or service only are possible. The black is constantly being censured for his want of intelligence and discretion, his lack of civic and professional conscience, and for his tendency toward undue familiarity.

The vices of the Negro are a constant menace to the American who has to repress them sternly. For instance, the black American troops in France have, by themselves, given rise to as many complaints for attempted rape as all the rest of the army. And yet the [black American] soldiers sent us have been the choicest with respect to physique and morals, for the number disqualified at the time of mobilization was enormous.

Conclusion

1. We must prevent the rise of any pronounced degree of intimacy between French officers and black officers. We may be courteous and amiable with these last, but we cannot deal with them on the same plane as with the white American officers without deeply wounding the latter. We must not eat with them, must not shake hands or seek to talk or meet with them outside of the requirements of military service.

2. We must not commend too highly the black American troops, particularly in the presence of [white] Americans. It is all right to

recognize their good qualities and their services, but only in moderate terms strictly in keeping with the truth.

3. Make a point of keeping the native cantonment population from "spoiling" the Negroes. [White] Americans become greatly incensed at any public expression of intimacy between white women with black men. They have recently uttered violent protests against a picture in the "Vie Parisienne" entitled "The Child of the Desert" which shows a [white] woman in a *"cabinet particulier"* with a Negro. Familiarity on the part of white women with black men is furthermore a source of profound regret to our experienced colonials who see in it an overweening menace to the prestige of the white race.

Military authority cannot intervene directly in this question, but it can through the civil authorities exercise some influence on the population.

Selection 40

EXECUTIVE ORDER 9981*

July 26, 1948

Whereas it is essential that there be maintained in the armed services of the United States the highest standards of democracy, with equality of treatment and opportunity for all those who serve in our country's defense:

Now, therefore, by virtue of the authority vested in me as President of the United States, by the Constitution and the statutes of the United States, and as Commander in Chief of the armed services, it is hereby ordered as follows:

1. It is hereby declared to be the policy of the President that there shall be equality of treatment and opportunity for all persons in the armed services without regard to race, color, religion or national origin. This policy shall be put into effect as rapidly as possible, having due regard to the time required to effectuate any necessary changes without impairing efficiency or morale.

* From *Freedom to Serve* (Washington, D.C.: 1950), pp. xi–xii.

2. There shall be created in the National Military Establishment an advisory committee to be known as the President's Committee on Equality of Treatment and Opportunity in the Armed Services, which shall be composed of seven members to be designated by the President.

3. The Committee is authorized on behalf of the president to examine into the rules, procedures and practices of the armed services in order to determine in what respect such rules, procedures and practices may be altered or improved with a view to carrying out the policy of this order. The Committee shall confer and advise with the Secretary of Defense, the Secretary of the Army, the Secretary of the Navy, and the Secretary of the Air Force, and shall make such recommendations to the President and to said Secretaries as in the judgment of the Committee will effectuate the policy hereof.

4. All executive departments and agencies of the Federal Government are authorized and directed to cooperate with the Committee in its work, and to furnish the Committee such information or the services of such persons as the Committee may require in the performance of its duties.

5. When requested by the Committee to do so, persons in the armed services or in any of the executive departments and agencies of the Federal Government shall testify before the Committee and shall make available for the use of the Committee such documents and other information as the Committee may require.

6. The Committee shall continue to exist until such time as the President shall terminate its existence by Executive Order.

HARRY S. TRUMAN

The White House, July 26, 1948

Selection 41

THE GREAT SOCIETY—
IN UNIFORM*

"You might say I'm military all the way," Air Force Capt. Randolph Sturrup, a 27-year-old Negro, said briskly as he fitted a white technical sergeant with a set of false teeth in his dentist's office at Ellington Air Force Base near Houston. "I hope to make it for 30 years. It's a chance to improve yourself professionally . . ." A world away from Captain Sturrup's air-conditioned clinic, First Sgt. Ollie Henderson Sr. shrugged out of his flak jacket after returning from a combat patrol in a steamy jungle near the headquarters of the Army's First Division at Di An, South Vietnam. Henderson, a gentle, 40-year-old father of four, has fought in three wars during his 22 years in the Army. If he survives Vietnam, he'll stay in for eight years more. "It's a place where a guy feels he's wanted," Sergeant Henderson said softly. Off the coast of Vietnam, Lt. (j.g.) Harold Roberts Wise Jr. was stopped short when a NEWS-WEEK reporter asked about racial discrimination in the Navy. "I never thought about it . . . until you came aboard," he said. "I'm just one of the guys, out here."

Haven: Captain Sturrup went to Fisk, Howard and Columbia universities. Lieutenant Wise is a 1964 graduate of West Chester State College in Pennsylvania (with a distinctly unmilitary degree in music education). Henderson's formal education stopped at 16 when he left the hardscrabble coal fields of Perry County, Kentucky. But like thousands of other Negroes of differing dreams and attainments, they have found a haven of regimented democracy in the U.S. armed forces, where the color of a man's uniform counts more than the color of his skin. "In the service," summed up Staff Sgt. Seman Jenkins, a thirteen-year Air Force veteran now stationed at Ellington AFB, "I have felt more a real part of the Great So-

* *Newsweek*, August 22, 1966, p. 46.

ciety. I have been recognized as a man in every sense of the word."

That recognition is now eighteen years old. Master Sgt. Ralph Tann, 43, a recruiting supervisor at the Boston Army base, remembers the "old" army, which he left in disgust in 1946 (only to be recalled during the Korean War). "Negro units were getting the worst quarters and the worst equipment and were considered a necessary evil by most commanders," he recalls. "They weren't permitted to fight; they were thrown into service and supply units." But, with the sweep of a pen, President Truman desegregated the armed forces on July 26, 1948. And while the Negro in service must still contend with an occasional bigot as a commander—and suffer most of the humiliations of a Negro civilian once he leaves the base—his life in uniform is immeasurably better.

"In the Navy," declares Chief Petty Officer Joseph Jones, who supervises a crew of 50 Negro and white enlisted men at Da Nang, "promotion is as fair as it is possible to make it. You have to take written exams for promotion, and they're graded by machines that can't be programed to know your color." And indistinct as the on-base color line may be in the States, it is almost totally obscured by the smoke of battle in Vietnam. Pfc. Claude Weaver Jr., 22, an assistant squad leader in the First Cavalry Division, summed up his view of battlefield brotherhood: "You get shot at, you get hit equally out here . . . and everybody knows it."

Off the battlefield there is a sort of separation of the races—in Saigon where the Negroes tend to seek out their own bars, or in rest areas where whites and blacks often congregate in separate groups. But this is personal choice rather than imposed segregation. As one Negro GI chuckles: "We sometimes segregate ourselves from those white guys. We don't like their hillbilly music."

Disproportion: Negroes—who constitute 11 per cent of the nation's population—currently make up 9.5 per cent of the armed forces. But last year Negroes accounted for a disproportionate 13.4 per cent of the draftees inducted. And the disproportion is even more evident in Vietnam. The last Defense Department study available shows that at the end of 1965, 12.5 per cent of all U.S. servicemen in Vietnam—and 14.6 per cent of the battle dead—were Negroes.

In the Newsweek poll, civilian Negroes agree by a margin of 47 to 26 per cent that a young Negro stands a better chance in a military uniform than in civilian clothes. "In the armed forces, they really look at your ability," says Mary Oakley of Springfield, Mass. "In civilian life, it's your skin."

Yet a sizable number of Negroes have doubts about the fairness of the draft, or even whether Negroes should be fighting in Vietnam at all. Among rank-and-file Negroes in the NEWSWEEK survey, 25 per cent think the draft is unfair to their race, and this feeling rises to a hefty 58 per cent among Negroes in the NEWSWEEK leadership sample. For example, Jackie Robinson protests: "They're drafting people that have a lack of opportunity." Similarly, 35 per cent of the rank-and-file Negroes and 22 per cent of the leadership group agree that the Negro should be against the war in Vietnam because he has less freedom to fight for. "What are we fighting for? I don't know," snaps a San Francisco housewife. "Communists? We should be fighting the white folks in Mississippi." Another 44 per cent object that the war in Vietnam means less money for poverty and civil-rights programs at home.

'We Love Her': Perhaps because of their disaffection, 29 per cent of the Negroes (compared with 12 per cent for the nation as a whole) would like to see the U.S. withdraw from Vietnam. But 54 per cent approve of the way President Johnson is handling the war and—while less hawkish than American whites—Negroes proudly feel by 3 to 2 that their men make better combat soldiers than whites. And if the U.S. should become involved in another world war, there is no question about Negro loyalty. Fully 87 per cent (compared with 81 per cent in 1963) say their country is worth fighting for. "America is the Negro's country too," says a college graduate from Cartersville, Ga. "She's not perfect . . . but we love her."

What does the Negro serviceman think? Probably his patriotic fever chart would run a few points higher than the civilian's 87 per cent. To get a firmer fix on his feelings about more specific questions—the draft, the war and civil rights—NEWSWEEK reporters talked to dozens of servicemen in Vietnam and at Stateside points in Massachusetts, Alabama, Texas and California.

'All Americans': Surprisingly, there seems to be little resentment of the draft. "A higher proportion of Negroes to whites is drafted because of a lower educational level," says Sam Steele, a 26-year-old Conroe, Texas, native who just finished a two-year hitch as an Army medic. And at Fort Ord, Calif., First Lt. Donald L. Holmes, 30, an Army career man, said the draft is not only fair—but might do some of the complainers some good in the long run. "If a young man is in college, and his grades are at a certain level, he should be allowed to finish his education," Holmes says. "A lot of these guys who just hang around poolrooms and street corners might get something out of the Army, anyway. Most of them wouldn't take an education if you offered it to them."

Assignment to Vietnam is hardly coveted by any GI—Negro or

white. But most of the Negroes see nothing sinister in the fact that, proportionately, they are carrying a heavier share of the American load—and consequently suffering a larger share of the casualties. "Somebody's got to be here," shrugs Aircraft Maintenance Helper Second Class Walter Foster, on the carrier Intrepid. "We're all Americans." Other military sources point out that bonus pay (such as the $55 a month extra paid paratroopers) attracts poorer Negroes to volunteer; and these outfits are most often in the thick of the Vietnam fighting. From Saigon, NEWSWEEK's John Berthelsen adds another point: "Negroes tend to volunteer for tough duty in disproportionate numbers, as if they feel the need to prove their valor to themselves and to their race."

As to the war itself, most of the Negro soldiers, sailors and marines want to fight through to victory. But they don't feel—as do many Negro civilians—that America's shortcomings on civil rights should affect its role in Vietnam. "I've got a lot of friends who have been wounded and killed over here for America," says the Army's Sgt. Joseph Conner in Saigon. "The main thing is to do our job and get out of this damned country. Civil rights can wait, as far as soldiers are concerned." Added Navy Chief Joe Jones: "Most fighting men don't want to be here—not just Negroes. The only way you can look at it is that it is my country I am fighting for . . . whether you are black or white." Whatever his motive, the Negro's fighting quality has won a tribute from Gen. William C. Westmoreland, the U.S. commander in Vietnam. "One of the great stories to come out of this war," he has said, "is the magnificent job being done by the Negro soldier."

Don't Rock the Boat: As men trained to fight, most Negro servicemen sound surprisingly nonviolent when it comes to the civil-rights struggle at home. The Rev. Martin Luther King is universally admired as the leader with the right technique; black power and black nationalism are just as universally scorned. "My people have been told all their lives they are inferior," says Chief Petty Officer Jones. "Now to have someone tell them they are superior is a little silly. I don't think the movement [black power] will get far; most Negroes I know don't like it." Navy man Foster sums up even more succinctly: "Black power is a bunch of nuts."

Part of the Negro serviceman's seeming malaise on civil rights at home stems from the fact that he's out of touch. And for some who have found a home in the service, there is a certain don't-rock-the-boat attitude. "During the Emmett Till case," recalls Sgt. Maj. Garland Alston, 39, a Negro career man at Fort Ord, "I went around to all the day rooms and collected copies of a magazine that had a big story on the lynching. It was a good balanced story, but it might have stimulated some racial conflicts. That's something you can't afford to have in a military establishment."

Status: For all of them—career man and draftee—military service will end some day, and the Negro protectively colored in Army khaki, Marine green and Air Force or Navy blue will be just another black civilian face. Some, such as Lieutenant Holmes, have suffered through this humiliating shift in status once before. He enlisted in 1958 after two years of college, and in 1961 was discharged and started looking for a job. "I'd call for an appointment about a job I knew was open and when I'd get there they'd say, 'I'm sorry, sir, this job is no longer open. But we have something in the janitorial field.' At 25, I saw no reason why I should accept a job as a garbage man." Holmes re-enlisted. Re-enlistment, in fact, has been the obvious answer for many Negroes; in 1965 the re-enlistment rate for whites was 17.1 per cent, for Negroes 45.7 per cent.

But one thing is clear: those Negroes who do leave the service—and especially those who have fought in Vietnam—are not going to be satisfied with second-class citizenship when they get home. "I feel right now I've qualified myself for anything anybody else has," says Sergeant Henderson, yearning to be home. "I've exposed myself to the same dangers." Navy Chief Jones, sweltering in Da Nang's 110-degree heat, declares: "I don't think I'm going to have as much patience as I had before when I go home. Why should I? There are some things due me and I want them." And M/Sgt. Frederick Robinson, resting at a Special Forces camp in the Mekong River Delta, puts it bluntly: "When I get back I am as good as any son of a bitch in the States."

BOOK FOUR

The Negro Today: Balance Sheet

INTRODUCTION

The balance sheet—successes and failures in the crusade for equality —is not an easy thing to compute. When we are dealing with the minds and hearts of human beings, it is difficult to make a list of credits and debits upon which most people will agree. Some point to progress toward equality in areas such as laws and court decisions. Others argue that laws and court decisions mean nothing unless they are carried out and accepted by the people.

Sometimes a humorous note can cast some light on a serious problem. One is reminded of the story about the optimist and the pessimist. The optimist looks at a glass containing some water and concludes that it is half-filled. The pessimist sees it as half-empty. As we review the civil rights movement of the twentieth century, each of us will have to decide what has been accomplished and what still remains to be done. Regarding the unfinished business of race relations, we ought to keep in mind that in this area no man or woman is a bystander.

ON PROGRESS—TWO CONTRASTING VIEWS

Selections 1a and 1b are a half-century apart. The little boy's message was in the early 1900s. James Baldwin's is a selection from his popular book, The Fire Next Time.

1a. Little Coloured Boy's Famous Speech

RAY STANNARD BAKER*

I was at Macon while the first State fair ever held by Negroes in Georgia was in progress. In spite of the fact that racial relationships, owing to the recent riot at Atlanta, were acute, the fair was largely attended, and not only by Negroes, but by many white visitors. The brunt of the work of organisation fell upon R. R. Wright, president of the Georgia State Industrial College (coloured) of Savannah. President Wright is of full-blooded African descent, his grandmother, who reared him, being an African Negro of the Mandingo tribe. Just at the close of the war he was a boy in a freedman's school at Atlanta. One Sunday General O. O. Howard came to address the pupils. When he had finished, he expressed a desire to take a message back to the people of the North.

"What shall I tell them for you?" he asked.

A little black boy in front stood up quickly, and said:

"Tell 'em, massa, we is rising."

Upon this incident John Greenleaf Whittier wrote a famous poem: and at the Negro fair, crowning the charts which had been prepared to show the progress of the Negroes of Georgia, I saw this motto:

"WE ARE RISING"

* From Ray Stannard Baker, *Following the Colour Line: American Negro Citizenship in the Progressive Era*, New York: Harper & Row, 1964, p. 92. [Originally published in 1908 by Doubleday, Page & Co.]

1b. The Negro Problem

JAMES BALDWIN*

It is a fact that every American Negro bears a name that originally belonged to the white man whose chattel he was. I am called Baldwin because I was either sold by my African tribe or kidnapped out of it into the hands of a White Christian named Baldwin, who forced me to kneel at the foot of the cross. I am, then, both visibly and legally the descendant of slaves in a white, Protestant country, and this is what it means to be an American Negro, this is who he is —a kidnapped pagan, who was sold like an animal and treated like one, who was once defined by the American Constitution as "three-fifths" of a man, and who, according to the Dred Scott decision, had no rights that a white man was bound to respect. And today, a hundred years after his technical emancipation, he remains—with the possible exception of the American Indian—the most despised creature in his country. Now, there is simply no possibility of a real change in the Negro's situation without the most radical and far-reaching changes in the American political and social structure. And it is clear that white Americans are not simply unwilling to effect these changes; they are, in the main, so slothful have they become, unable even to envision them. It must be added that the Negro himself no longer believes in the good faith of white Americans— if, indeed, he ever could have. What the Negro *has* discovered, and on an international level, is that power to intimidate which he has always had privately but hitherto could manipulate only privately —for private ends often, for limited ends always. And therefore when the country speaks of a "new" Negro, which it has been doing every hour on the hour for decades, it is not really referring to a change in the Negro, which, in any case, it is quite incapable of assessing, but only to a new difficulty in keeping him in his place, to the fact that it encounters him (again! again!) barring yet another door to its spiritual and social ease. This is probably, hard and odd as it may sound, the most important thing that one human being can do for another—it is certainly *one* of the most important things; hence the torment and necessity of love—and this is the enormous contribution that the Negro has made to this otherwise shapeless and undiscovered country. Consequently, white Americans are in nothing more deluded than in supposing that Negroes could ever have imagined that white people would "give" them anything. It is rare indeed that people give. Most people guard and keep; they suppose that it is they themselves and what they identify

* From James Baldwin, *The Fire Next Time*, New York: Dell, 1964, pp. 114-19.

with themselves that they are guarding and keeping, whereas what they are actually guarding and keeping is their system of reality and what they assume themselves to be. One can give nothing whatever without giving oneself—that is to say, risking oneself. If one cannot risk oneself, then one is simply incapable of giving. And, after all, one can give freedom only by setting someone free. This, in the case of the Negro, the American republic has never become sufficiently mature to do. White Americans have contented themselves with gestures that are now described as "tokenism." For hard example, white Americans congratulate themselves on the 1954 Supreme Court decision outlawing segregation in the schools; they suppose, in spite of the mountain of evidence that has since accumulated to the contrary, that this was proof of a change of heart —or, as they like to say, progress. It all depends on how one reads the word "progress." Most of the Negroes I know do not believe that this immense concession would ever have been made if it had not been for the competition of the Cold War, and the fact that Africa was clearly liberating herself and therefore had, for political reasons, to be wooed by the descendants of her former masters. Had it been a matter of love or justice, the 1954 decision would surely have occurred sooner; were it not for the realities of power in this difficult era, it might very well not have occurred yet. This seems an extremely harsh way of stating the case—ungrateful, as it were—but the evidence that supports this way of stating it is not easily refuted. I myself do not think that it can be refuted at all. In any event, the sloppy and fatuous nature of American good will can never be relied upon to deal with hard problems. These have been dealt with, when they have been dealt with at all, out of necessity—and in political terms, anyway, necessity means concessions made in order to stay on top. I think this is a fact, which it serves no purpose to deny, *but, whether it is a fact or not, this is what the black population of the world, including black Americans, really believe*. The word "independence" in Africa and the word "integration" here are almost equally meaningless; that is, Europe has not yet left Africa, and black men here are not yet free. And both of these last statements are undeniable facts, related facts, containing the gravest implications for us all. The Negroes of this country may never be able to rise to power, but they are very well placed indeed to precipitate chaos and ring down the curtain on the American dream.

This has everything to do, of course, with the nature of that dream and with the fact that we Americans, of whatever color, do not dare examine it and are far from having made it a reality. There are too many things we do not wish to know about ourselves.

People are not, for example, terribly anxious to be equal (equal, after all, to what and to whom?) but they love the idea of being superior.

Selection 2

A TALE FROM NEGRO FOLKLORE

The Fox and the Goose

One day a Fox was going down the road and saw a Goose. "Good morning, Goose," he said; and the Goose flew up on a limb and said, "Good morning, Fox."

Then the Fox said, "You ain't afraid of me, is you? Haven't you heard of the meeting up at the hall the other night?"

"No, Fox. What was that?"

"You haven't heard about all the animals meeting up at the hall! Why, they passed a law that no animal must hurt any other animal. Come down and let me tell you about it. The hawk musn't catch the chicken, and the dog musn't chase the rabbit, and the lion musn't hurt the lamb. No animal must hurt any other animal."

"Is that so!"

"Yes, all live friendly together. Come down and don't be afraid."

As the Goose was about to fly down, way off in the woods they heard a "Woo-wooh! Woo-wooh!" and the Fox looked around.

"Come down, Goose," he said.

And the dog got closer. "Woo-wooh!"

Then the Fox started to sneak off; and the Goose said, "Fox, you ain't scared of a dog, is you? Didn't all the animals pass a law at the meeting not to bother each other any more?"

"Yes," replied the Fox as he trotted away quickly, "the animals passed the law; but some of the animals round here ain't got much respec' for the law."

Selections 3a–3b

PESSIMISTIC VIEWS

The following selections present the pessimistic side of the civil rights effort.

3a.

'DEAR SON — I'M PROUD THAT YOU'RE DEFENDING
THE FREEDOM WE'RE TRYING TO GET...'

© 1965 Fischetti and Publishers Newspaper Syndicate

'WHAT'S THE SECRET OF YOUR SUCCESS?'

© 1965 Engelhardt in the *St. Louis Post-Dispatch*

3b.   Urban Lag Found in Desegregation
BEN A. FRANKLIN*

Washington, Aug. 7—There is little hope in the next few decades of ending the de facto segregation of Negroes in the nation's major cities, a sociologist has concluded after an extensive survey.

This is so, the sociologist said, because the segregation is not the result of factors commonly cited as the cause—such as poverty, lack of education, or other factors that could be altered by the courts, government programs or national policy. Instead, he said, the segregation results from unchanging and apparently unchangeable human prejudice.

This forecast on the nonassimilation of most urban Negroes by the "white culture" of American cities was published this week as the leading article in the magazine "Scientific American," a periodical usually given over to the physical and biological sciences.

Dr. Karl E. Taeuber, author of the article, is an associate professor of sociology at the University of Wisconsin. In his survey he used a new method of statistically analyzing detailed census data from more than 200 cities. His conclusions challenge a number of beliefs, widely held by white and Negro integrationists.

Discrimination the Key

Basically, Dr. Taeuber concludes that "discrimination is the principal cause of Negro residential segregation, and there is no basis for anticipating major changes in the segregated character of American cities until patterns of housing discrimination can be altered."

He sees little possibility that such patterns will change in the next few decades.

Almost the whole civil rights effort since the school desegregation decision of the United States Supreme Court in 1954, Dr. Taeuber believes, has been directed at altering such factors such as cultural deprivation, lack of education, poverty and denial of employment, voting and other rights among Negroes. In comparison, little has been done about segregated housing patterns.

However, Dr. Taeuber asserts, in the cities these factors are either irrelevant or much less important to the cause of urban racial assimilation than is "outright discrimination" against Negroes by whites and members of other non-Negro ethnic groups.

In a telephone interview, he said:

"If you are talking about a way out of the urban segregation trap in 10 years, there is no evidence of a workable program now that

* From *The New York Times*, August 8, 1965.

will do it. But if you are talking about 30 or 40 years, I don't know.

"What is needed is radical social change, but radical change is a threat to many people and there are a lot of pressures operating now against it."

Leaders Not Surprised

Dr. Taeuber's pessimistic short-run view was not surprising to many urban civil rights leaders, questioned about his findings. From a less statistical basis, many of them shared his unhopeful outlook about ending urban de facto segregation.

Using Census Bureau reports for city blocks in some cases and for census tracts in others, Dr. Taeuber found that the most striking feature of the life of Negroes in cities was "the segregation of their residences from the residences of whites."

Yet, his article reports, "a higher percentage of Negroes than whites live in cities."

Ten large cities in the North and West, the article says, contain "the overwhelming majority of Negroes in those regions, which in turn contain 40 per cent of the nation's Negro population."

In these cities, as in cities in the South, he found that "this ghetto situation is one of the most pronounced and most tenaciously maintained forms of segregation the Negro American faces."

Translated into a so-called segregation index—a statistical tool developed by Dr. Taeuber—census figures indicate that residential segregation in Northern and Western cities is gradually, almost imperceptibly declining while steadily increasing in Southern cities.

Under this segregation index, a reading of 80 indicates that 80 per cent of the Negroes in a city would have to be "redistributed to predominantly or exclusively white blocks if the city were to achieve an unsegregated pattern of residence."

None of the 207 cities for which Dr. Taeuber calculated the index scored lower than 60 (San Jose, Calif.), and the median index number of all the cities was 87.8. The highest index was 98.1, in Fort Lauderdale, Fla.

After having dismissed poverty and a "choice" by Negroes to remain segregated as the primary causes of urban residential segregation, Dr. Taeuber said that "even if Negroes gained full economic equality in the distant future, their residential segregation from whites would be considerable."

The index also provided a statistical basis for projecting in several cities the "expected segregation"—the amount of residential segregation that would prevail if economic factors such as Negroes' ability to pay for housing in all-white areas were the sole, or even the major inhibitor working against integrated housing.

These projections showed that in Atlanta, where the segregation index based on census data of 1960, was 85, the "expected" index—based on economic ability of the city's Negro population—would be 25. In Washington, Dr. Taeuber's index figures was 68 for actual residential segregation, but the "expected" index was 14.

In New York City, Dr. Taeuber calculated that the 1960 segregation index for Negroes was 80—a decline from 87.3 in 1950.

Dr. Taeuber and his wife, Alma, who is also a sociologist specializing in population studies, have written a book, "Negroes in Cities."

Selections *4a–4c*

OPTIMISTIC VIEWS

*These selections, in contrast to the preceding ones, see bright hope
for the future of the drive toward equality.*

4a.

"It's A Hell Of A Note — No Accommodations For Me!"

© 1965 Herblock in the *Washington Post*

4b. Civil Rights: Decade of Progress
ANTHONY LEWIS[*]

Washington, Dec. 19—The scene in the Supreme Court as the Civil Rights Act cases were decided this Monday was not one of obvious emotion. Justice Tom C. Clark, reading the opinions he had written for the Court, seemed almost deliberately subdued.

Yet anyone with a sense of history had to recognize that here was a great occasion, a symbolic watershed for both the civil rights issue and the Supreme Court. After a decade in the front lines of the racial struggle, the Court was passing the burden on to Congress, and generally to political and social mechanisms beyond the law.

A passage quoted by Justice Clark from the great Chief Justice, John Marshall, was interestingly relevant. Marshall was speaking of the great breadth of the power given to the Federal Government to regulate interstate commerce. One could not look to the courts to supervise the exercise of that power, he warned.

Restraints

"The wisdom and discretion of Congress," Marshall wrote, "their identity with the people and the influence which their constituents possess at elections . . . are the restraints on which the people must often rely solely . . ."

How different from the characteristic posture of the last 10 years it was to have the Supreme Court advising opponents of the nation's civil rights policy to take their argument to Congress. For the Court over much of that decade had to carry on alone, without real support from Congress or the President, the effort to eliminate racial discrimination in this country.

Probably there has never been anything like it before: A court leading a country and its political leaders into awareness of a fundamental social problem and a determination to do something about it.

With all the tragedies that have occurred in race relations, and all the remaining difficulties, it is sometimes hard to remember how much progress has been made. The change has been remarkable, overwhelming, in the decade since the Supreme Court's school desegregation decision set the process in motion.

Gunnar Myrdal's "An American Dilemma," the great study of race relations first published in 1944, was reissued in paperback this year by McGraw-Hill. In a "postscript 20 years later," Prof. Arnold Rose of the University of Minnesota remarks that the changes that

* From *The New York Times,* December 20, 1964.

have occurred in our racial situation "appear to be among the most rapid and dramatic in world history without violent revolution."

For much of the last 10 years the underlying issue has been respect for law itself—willingness to abide by the word of this country's final source of law, the Supreme Court. In that struggle the Court was gravely handicapped for a time by the hands-off posture of President Eisenhower.

When Autherine Lucy was driven off the campus of the University of Alabama by a mob in 1956, university authorities appealed to the Justice Department for help in carrying out the desegregation orders of the Federal courts. They got no answer. When troops barred Negro children from Central High School in Little Rock, Ark., in 1957, President Eisenhower's first public comment was that "you cannot change people's hearts merely by laws" and that the South saw "a picture of mongrelization of the race."

Moral Commitment

But when the integrity of Federal law was inescapably challenged at Little Rock, General Eisenhower stood firm. His use of force to carry out Federal court orders there really settled the issue of resistance, although more turmoil and bloodshed had to be suffered at Oxford, Miss., and elsewhere.

The moral commitment of the Presidency was secured in John Kennedy's brief term. It was symbolized by his speech to the nation on the night of June 11, 1963—in the opinion of many, his greatest speech, and much of it extemporaneous.

"If an American, because his skin is dark," Mr. Kennedy said, "cannot eat lunch in a restaurant open to the public; if he cannot send his children to the best public school available; if he cannot vote for the public officials who represent him; if, in short, he cannot enjoy the full and free life which all of us want, then who among us would be content to have the color of his skin changed and stand in his place? . . ."

"Moral Crisis"

"We face, therefore, a moral crisis as a country and a people."

President Kennedy spoke in the wake of the Birmingham riots, which had touched the nation's conscience with their brutal police repression of demands for equal service. Moved by that emotional crisis, and seizing that sympathetic moment to go to Congress, the President eight days later proposed the broadest civil rights legislation ever seriously suggested.

The proposals became law a year later, after Mr. Kennedy's death and the accession of a Southerner committed to carry on the fight for racial justice—President Johnson. Now the most debated provision of the Civil Rights Act of 1964—Title II, outlawing discrimination in hotels, restaurants and places of amusement—has the unanimous constitutional imprimatur of the Supreme Court.

That a corner has been turned is evident not only from this week's decisions but also from the actual racial situation in the country. Resistance to law is no longer the basic consideration, even though it remains an anguished factor in such matters as the attempt to bring to book the killers of the three civil rights workers in Philadelphia, Miss., last summer, or the effort to register Negro voters in Mississippi.

Complaint

Ollie McClung Jr. of Birmingham, whose barbecue restaurant was the subject of one of the test cases in the Supreme Court this week, said after the decision:

"We have practically no legal recourse left. . . . Therefore we will begin complying with the law just as nearly every other restaurant in the country. . . . We are simply joining ranks with all the rest of the restaurants."

Indeed, Ollie's Barbecue was the only eating place in Birmingham that refused to serve Negroes when civil rights groups carried out a test last summer. Burke Marshall, chief of the Justice Department's Civil Rights Division, concluded in a recent speech about acceptance of the new statute:

"Instead of the resistance to change that we had seen in the past, we have had massive compliance as befits a nation governed by law and a people who respect and comply with the law."

President Johnson announced Mr. Marshall's resignation yesterday, effective shortly after the new year. In their exchange of letters there was further evidence of the new phase into which Federal civil rights activity must move.

"Now that the Civil Rights Act of 1964 has become law," Mr. Marshall wrote, "and the nation has overwhelmingly endorsed your leadership and ratified the decision of the Congress, I believe that the policy direction of the Department of Justice is clear beyond question.

"Compliance with the law has been general. The task of eliminating discrimination in voting, education and those places of public accommodation that are engaged in a pattern of resistance to the law is now a straight-forward matter of litigation, requiring primarily administrative skills, hard work and good lawyers."

Mr. Marshall added that the "policy focus of Federal civil rights efforts" should now move outside the Justice Department—especially in relation to the fair employment title of the act, which goes into effect next year. It is for similar reasons that Mr. Johnson has asked Vice President-elect Humphrey to coordinate all Federal efforts in the area.

Warm Praise

The President's letter, warmly praising Mr. Marshall, said that "during the past four years the nation has at long last come to grips" with the racial problem. One remembers Mr. Marshall mediating in the Birmingham riots, or planning the first desegregation break-through in Mississippi. But those dramatic tests of the resources of a lawyer are, hopefully, now mostly past us.

Of course there is still much for the law to do. Justice Department lawyers will still have to plough doggedly through Mississippi voting records and fence with Mississippi Federal judges. President Johnson assured continuity of effort by appointing to succeed Mr. Marshall his assistant, John Doar. But it is clear that the legal job from here on should be more administrative—and that it will surely depend less on statement of new principles by the Supreme Court.

The fact is that the Court has taken legal principle just about as far as it will go in the racial field. It is clear that any official, overt discrimination on the ground of race cannot stand.

But the country has come painfully to realize in the last few years that the Negro carries a burden much heavier than that of open discrimination. The racial unrest in Northern states where discrimination has long been unlawful speaks for itself.

Mopping Up

And so, as the mopping-up operations of the law continue in the South, the whole country faces up to the larger social problems of race. They are problems of poverty of education, of delinquency. Jack Greenberg, director counsel of the N.A.A.C.P. Legal Defense and Educational Fund, predicted this week:

"All of us concerned with race relations will become increasingly occupied with those most difficult economic and social issues which transcend racial status but are also completely bound up with it."

As long as Negro unemployment runs twice the rate of white, as long as central cities continue to become Negro ghettos surrounded by white suburbs, as long as the slum child enters school with his capacity for learning already severely damaged—so long as these facts are unaltered, law will not solve America's race problem.

That is why the focus is leaving the Supreme Court. That is why civil rights groups are especially interested in President Johnson's prospective aid-to-education legislation and his antipoverty program.

It has been an extraordinary decade, a revolutionary one in fact if not in Professor Rose's sense of political upheaval. Some of those who sat in the Supreme Court courtroom on Monday wondered whether the country's political and social institutions would deal as effectively with the new aspects of the racial problem in the next decade as the Supreme Court had dealt with the legal aspects in the last.

4c. Civil Rights: South Slowly Yields
JOHN HERBERS*

Atlanta, Dec. 19—In 1963, when Robert F. Kennedy, then Attorney General, was pleading with Congress for passage of a public accommodations bill, he cited the plight of the widow of a Negro serviceman.

She could see her husband buried in Arlington National Cemetery with full military honors, he pointed out, but on the journey from and to her home in Mississippi she and her children would be turned away from motels, restaurants—even service station rest rooms.

Today, because of the new Civil Rights Law, she would find the vast majority of those doors open to her, although it might require considerable courage to try them.

The Supreme Court decision upholding the public accommodations section of the 1964 act was received so quietly in the South this week that one might wonder what all the uproar had been about.

Detachment

In contrast to earlier predictions that the law would be detrimental to both commerce and race relations, the unanimous decision was met with a degree of detachment in many areas.

"Nobody has to like this law," The Raleigh News and Observer said in an editorial. "But the time of resistance is clearly past. The time for as painless adjustment to it as possible has arrived. Its existence may mean little to the multitude of American Negroes. It may prove much less disturbing than many American white people feared.

"The law is here," the paper concluded. "That fact may be far less disruptive than the fears."

Where there was opposition it was generally mild and in some areas the decision was accepted with a degree of relief.

* From *The New York Times,* December 20, 1964.

The Community Relations Service headed by former Florida Gov. LeRoy Collins has played an important part in achieving peaceful compliance with the law. The service, which was created by the law, has a staff of conciliators who go into communities where there is likely to be trouble.

They work with local officials and leaders in an advisory capacity to prepare the community for the change. In many cities bi-racial committees were formed to assist in the transition.

Kept Secret

Although the law requires that the specific role of the conciliator be kept secret it is known that they have worked with success in some Deep South areas—McComb, Miss., for instance—where resistance is greatest and where there is hostility toward Federal intervention.

"We have been received with much more hospitality than we had anticipated," a spokesman for the service said. "In one community they were so beset with problems that we were welcomed with open arms. One of the officials told us, 'I never thought I would be glad to see a Federal agent.'"

Another factor that contributed to the smooth transition was the wide margin of victory for President Johnson in the Nov. 3 election. To many, this dispelled a belief prevalent in the South that the Civil Rights Law would soon be repealed.

There had been widespread compliance even before the law was tested in the courts. The Community Relations Service conducted a survey in October, three months after passage of the law, in 53 cities of more than 50,000 population in the 19 states which had no public accommodations statutes.

In virtually all of these cities it found that desegregation had been accomplished in more than two-thirds of the hotels, motels, chain restaurants, theaters, sports facilities, public parks and libraries.

Subsequently, desegregation was carried out under the law in some "hard core" areas such as McComb and Natchez, Miss. The decision brought further compliance.

Ollie's Barbecue of Birmingham, Ala., one of the two establishments involved in Monday's decision, served five Negroes two days after the Supreme Court ruled. "We have practically no recourse left," said Ollie McClung Jr., a co-owner.

The amount of non-compliance is yet to be determined, but it was apparent that many establishments would continue to try to circumvent the law.

Lester Maddox, the Atlanta restaurant owner who has used force to keep Negroes from his property, announced he would continue to screen his customers, but not on the basis of "race, color, creed or national origin" as prohibited by the law.

"My discrimination is based on political beliefs," Mr. Maddox said. "There's nothing in the language of the law about political beliefs. I do not admit integrationists into the Lester Maddox cafeteria, regardless of race, color or creed. If a person's political beliefs are that he is an integrationist, then I don't want him."

Forgotten Symbol

Mr. Maddox, however, may find himself the forgotten symbol of defiance, according to civil rights leaders here. Negroes, they said, do not want to eat in his restaurant, which has become a gathering place for segregationists, and the civil rights organizations prefer to leave him alone now that the law has been upheld.

The major resistance to equality in public accommodations remains in the smaller cities, the towns and rural areas of the Deep South. Even here there has been a degree of compliance. Negroes from Atlanta were surprised to find they were accepted in motels in small towns of South Georgia.

This does not mean, however, that Negroes who live in these areas will find the public accommodations open to them. The old patterns of segregation are maintained more by economic pressures and subtle means of persuasion than by the law.

To the Negro of the rural South, there are things more important than the right to eat in the white man's restaurant. And in many areas there is no active civil rights movement to lead the way.

Since the enactment of the law, many restaurants and some hotels and recreational facilities have become private clubs. The legality of these is yet to be tested in the courts.

Some, however, seem to constitute a clear evasion of the law. The North Louisiana Restaurant Association has issued, without cost, membership cards for use in a number of restaurants in the area open to "members only."

Membership Fees

A restaurant in Norfolk, Va., has a membership fee of five cents.

The cafeteria in Little Rock, Ark., which had denied service to Negroes, was turned into a membership club requiring no dues.

Although the new private clubs are found chiefly in the Deep South, the Community Relations Service said they exist in other areas as well, as a means of avoiding desegregation.

A number of cities which have accomplished desegregation after long and bitter resistance have found that once the testing period is over most of the establishments, particularly the more expensive ones, have few if any Negro customers thereafter.

"Desegregation of public accommodations does not basically alter the pattern of social life anywhere," a Mississippi restaurateur said. "That is why it has been accomplished as easily as it has."

Nevertheless, Southern whites are becoming accustomed to seeing Negroes in restaurants, theaters and motels that formerly excluded them. And in most instances desegregation has resulted in little, if any, loss of business.

There have been some isolated hardship cases. Some theaters which had been marginal operations were forced to close. A theater owner in a small town in Georgia reported his revenue dropped to $12 a week after he desegregated.

For the Southern Negro, the Supreme Court decision was the crowning victory in a struggle that began on Feb. 1, 1960, when four students from North Carolina Agricultural and Technical College staged a sit-in demonstration at a Woolworth lunch counter in Greensboro.

This was a new concept in the civil rights movement—direct action against segregation on private business property—and it quickly spread to other areas of the South. It led by successive stages to the Birmingham, Ala., crisis in the spring of 1963 when harsh police tactics were used to break up civil rights demonstrations, and the subsequent decision by President Kennedy to submit the civil rights bill.

For almost five years the public accommodations issue has been at the forefront of the Negro movement. The Negro protest in this field has been directed against real grievances. At times it has been directed against barriers simply because they were there.

Public accommodations has been an issue around which Negroes could rally and create interest in the overall movement. Leaders could always interest someone in going down to the dime store lunch counter for a sit-in.

Even before the law went into effect, however, civil rights leaders were saying that other issues were more basic to the Negro cause. The major civil rights groups are now planning to put more emphasis in the future on housing, job opportunity and voting and less on public accommodations.

While there will continue to be pockets of discrimination and de facto segregation in this area the day of the sit-in seems to be over.

"We are going to keep these business places open by testing them," one leader said. "But there won't be demonstrations. We have a law now and we will simply take the businessman to court."

Selection 5

STATISTICAL DATA*

The following chart and graphs pinpoint the problems to be faced in the future by those who are working to achieve equality for all Americans.

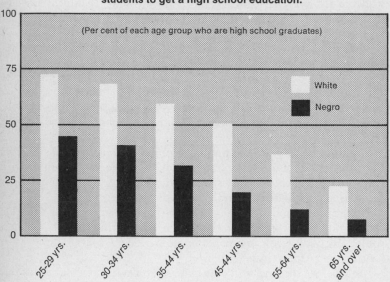

Negroes have less chance than white students to get a high school education.

(Per cent of each age group who are high school graduates)

* From *The New York Times*, June 13, 1965.

They are concentrated mostly in occupations with low wage scales.

Chart shows per cent of each work force

WHITE-COLLAR WORKERS

WHITE 46.5%

NEGRO 18.4%

BLUE-COLLAR WORKERS

WHITE 36.4%

NEGRO 41.9%

SERVICE WORKERS

WHITE 10.8%

NEGRO 31.4%

FARM WORKERS

WHITE 6.3%

NEGRO 8.3%

They are paid less than whites when they do equivalent work.

Chart shows life-time earnings

TEACHERS

WHITE $256,000

NEGRO $183,000

CLERICAL WORKERS

WHITE $218,000

NEGRO $162,000

CARPENTERS

WHITE $190,000

NEGRO $112,000

LABORERS

WHITE $157,000

NEGRO $105,000

Their current rate of unemployment is more than twice as great.

(Per cent of each work force unemployed)

WHITE 4.3%

NEGRO 9%

Selection 6

HOW WHITE VIEWS OF THE NEGRO HAVE CHANGED*

The 1966 Newsweek *Poll presents the following summary of the change in the attitudes of whites between 1963 and 1966.*

WHITES WOULD MIND	All Whites		Southern Whites	
	1963	1966	1963	1966
Sitting next to Negro in restaurant	20%	16%	50%	42%
Sitting next to Negro in movie	24	20	54	46
Using same rest room as Negro	24	21	56	56
Trying on same clothing Negro had tried on	36	28	57	54
Sitting next to Negro on bus	20	16	47	44
If teen-age child dated a Negro	90	88	97	94
If a Negro family moved next door	51	46	74	69
If a close friend or relative married a Negro	84	79	91	92

* From *Newsweek*, August 22, 1966, p. 26.

Selection 7

PROGRESS MADE—
AND PROGRESS WANTED

* *This chart appeared in the 1966* Newsweek *Poll.*

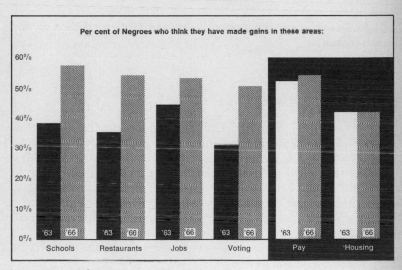

Per cent of Negroes who think they have made gains in these areas:

* From *Newsweek*, August 22, 1966, p. 23.

Selections 8a–8b

EFFECTS OF INTEGRATION TROUBLES ON OUR FOREIGN RELATIONS

The following newspaper accounts describe foreign reaction to our racial dilemmas.

8a.   Dulles Says U. S. Damaged Abroad*

Secretary of State John Foster Dulles said today that the Little Rock integration trouble and other integration problems in the South "are not helpful to the influence of the United States abroad."

Dulles was asked to comment on reports that problems at Little Rock and other Southern cities were being broadcast widely not only by the Soviet Union but by the friends of the United States.

"I haven't read the reports but I have no doubt that this is true," Dulles said.

Radio Moscow has been chirping happily about the troubles of integration.

On September 4 a Moscow home broadcast stated: "A detachment of National Guardsmen, 250 strong and armed with rifles, guns, truncheons, and tear gas grenades, took up position yesterday in front of the building of Little Rock Central High School. Negro children came to the school. The governor of the state, Orval Faubus, sent troops to prevent these children from proceeding to the school when the governor's detachment lined up in front of the school. A crowd of racialists gathered in the street of the town and hoisted the Confederate flag under which their ancestors nearly

---

* From the *Arkansas Gazette* (Little Rock), September 11, 1957.

a century ago fought for the preservation of slavery in the United States."

8b.   U. S. Image in Africa Hurt by Selma Action

SEYMOUR FREIDIN[*]

Lagos, Nigeria—In Africa today Selma is no longer an exotic foreign name for a girl, but synonymous with stigma and shame.

The shock of brutality in Alabama, despite President Johnson's appeal to a joint session of Congress, has had a profound impact.

The public image on which the U. S. spends many millions is lop-sided in Africa. Those countries, prone to assail almost anything and anyone American, let out all the stops following the Alabama in-cidents—a kind of "We told you so."

The United States is much more fortunate in the reserved indig nation felt here. Nigeria—the largest African country, with a popu-lation of 38 million—remains generally patient and listens to ex-planations of how Negro rights are gradually won.

Many of its people, particularly the young intellectuals and junior officials, saw a television film of police assaults on marchers in Selma. They have read avidly all they could of events in the Alabama city. Their principal response to the crisis was to gesture to an American technical ship riding at anchor in the bay here. The vessel is to track the Gemini flight next week.

"So you can send vehicles and people to the moon, but you can-not peacefully regulate your own backyard," was their common observation.

The ups and downs of the outside world and all the nuances of policies and power pass over most Nigerians, as they do over most Africans. It will be a long time before names now in the headlines, like Viet Nam or Communist China mean something special.

But the sight of armed white troopers swooping down on Negroes needs no political explanation in any African nation, moderate or militant, especially in West Africa.

Ironically, the handful of Nigerians whose interest is gripped by events in the outside world has some special sentiment, too, for America. Many have acquired advanced education in the U. S. where they met and mingled with Negroes trained and educated far beyond the usual average here. These Nigerians ask why equal-ity should be stymied by brutal sheriffs in America's South.

Governor Wallace of Alabama may not care, but all his state did was to set the U. S. back in Africa a long way.

[*] From *Herald Tribune*, March, 1965.

Selection 9

VIEWS OF THE WHITE HOUSE CIVIL RIGHTS CONFERENCE*

The following selection consists of excerpts from the recommendations of the Council on the White House Conference on Civil Rights, in 1966.

Economic Security and Welfare

There is no single, simple or quick solution for the economic problems of Negroes but nothing less than a broadly based "crash" program can significantly improve the life-chances of hundreds of thousands of Negro Americans now trapped in joblessness and poverty.

I. *Establish metropolitan jobs councils in all major urban areas:* Metropolitan jobs councils should be established in each major urban area with a substantial Negro population. Membership should include organized labor, metropolitan governments, education and training institutions and other appropriate community organizations.

II. *Create a rural jobs task force:* The council recommends the appointment of an emergency rural jobs task force whose first report, with action recommendations, should be due no later than Sept. 1. Local and regional rural jobs councils will be needed to implement the action program.

III. *Develop a comprehensive human resource program:* The recommendation will provide a flexible basis for creative action; serve as a guide in developing new manpower, economic, or related legislation; help to alert local and national planners to emerging

* From *The New York Times,* May 25, 1966.

problems or trends, and provide guidelines for manpower program actions by business, organized labor, local and state governments and other agencies.

IV. *Develop guaranteed jobs programs:* Jobs must be provided without delay to solve the Negro unemployment crisis. And these jobs must be made available for Negroes at their existing level of skill attainment.

The tasks assigned to workers on a proposed government employment program, far from being "make work," are essential to fill the very real and pressing needs for public works and services that have accompanied population growth, urbanization, and increasing demands on the nation's physical resources.

V. *Mount year-round programs for Negro youth:* Young Negroes need especially intensive vocational counseling to determine their best occupational prospects, and to plan the most effective educational and training programs tailored to their individual needs.

VI. *Affirmative actions by private employers, labor organizations, and Government to provide more and better jobs:* Employers need to look, think, and act beyond simple nondiscrimination and pro forma or passive equal employment opportunity programs. Active and deliberate efforts to increase and improve jobs for Negroes are necessary. The Government itself needs to become a model employer in every respect and set the example for affirmative action. State and local governments should also become model employers.

Management must devote as much thought and effort to this as it does to other major functions of administration.

Labor organizations have failed to take affirmative action commensurate with the problems faced by Negro job seekers.

Churches, educational institutions, health and welfare groups, and associations can undertake affirmative action through technical assistance and through the example of their own practices.

Title VII of the Civil Rights Act of 1964 should be strengthened by expanding its coverage, authorizing "cease and desist" orders, and providing back pay to persons suffering financial loss.

The Equal Employment Opportunity Commission's technical assistance and education programs should be greatly expanded to help employers, labor unions, and others develop capabilities for providing equal employment opportunities and to reduce employment prejudice and discrimination.

VII. *Initiate and reinforce supportive services:* There is a crucial need to make available occupational training and related basic and remedial education to help prepare jobless Negroes for employment.

There is also a need for training to upgrade employed Negroes who are working below their skill potentials.

There is a need to federalize the public employment service.

VIII. *Strengthen income maintenance and labor standards programs:* The strengthening of income and labor standards programs is of special importance for Negroes, who are heavily concentrated in occupations and industries which pay low wages, provide only intermittent employment, and are excluded from protective labor standards legislation.

IX. *Restructure public assistance and related welfare programs:* The nation's welfare programs fail to provide welfare recipients and other impoverished people with maximum opportunity to move from dependency to self-sustaining employment.

The Federal Government should establish and enforce national standards.

State and local governments and community organizations should make available supplemental services to needy people, consumer education, legal assistance, vocational and personal counseling, health information, home management services, free family planning services, day-care centers for working mothers, and expanded school lunch programs.

Housing

For 15 million Negroes congested slums have constituted their homes and ghettoed isolation has been their environment. In housing, as elsewhere, there have been and continue to be two Americas.

The only program aimed at their housing needs was low-rent public housing. After nearly 30 years, however, that program has accounted for only 1 per cent of the nation's housing inventory.

I. *Freedom of choice—the open market:* A firm and vigorous policy on the part of the Administration to utilize all the programs and resources of the Department of Housing and Urban Development and other agencies to promote and implement equal opportunity and desegregation is needed.

Enforcement under the executive order and Title VI of the Civil Rights Act of 1964 must be more affirmative and vigorous.

A comprehensive Federal antidiscrimination law is urgently recommended.

State licensing authorities should require that all licensed brokers, builders, etc., show that they are serving the entire public without distinction as to race as a condition of the issuance or reissuance of the license.

The National Association of Real Estate Boards (N.A.R.E.B.), the National Home Builders Association, the several banking and saving and loan associations, and insurance companies engaged in housing finance, are urged to adopt and prominently publish policy statements advocating equal opportunity in housing guaranteed by law.

N.A.R.E.B. and all state and local real estate boards are urged to admit all licensed real estate brokers of all races to membership.

Fair housing councils or their equivalent should be organized in every urban area. Housing information and service centers should be established at convenient locations in each urban area.

II. *Housing supply for low- and moderate-income families:* More than one million new houses per year are required to take care of the housing needs of the expanding population. At least half, preferably more, of the new stock should be made available to low- and moderate-income families.

The Federal Government should invest as extensively in promoting research and development in housing as it has in, for example, agriculture.

Federal legislation designed to increase the rate of production of new houses to 2,000,000 units per year is urged.

The rent supplement bill as submitted to Congress in 1965 is strongly endorsed as a model until a more comprehensive program can be devised.

The Department of Housing and Urban Development should request funds necessary for a vastly enlarged program of research and development in housing and urban development.

Consultation of experts on all aspects of community development and housing should be called.

F.H.A. 221 (D) (3) below market interest program, which benefits moderate-income families, requires greatly increased funding.

The authorization of federally chartered rural housing development corporations to build homes in rural areas for either the elderly or for agricultural labor, migrant or otherwise, is urged.

A housing industry program, patterned after the plans for progress program in employment, should be launched under the leadership of the President.

III. *Suburban communities and new towns:* The Federal Government bears a large share of the responsibility for the dual market—new housing in the suburbs for white families with sufficient incomes, and old housing in the central city for Negroes regardless of their incomes.

Federal assistance to any local governmental unit should be conditioned on the submission of a metropolitan-wide plan providing for the desegregation of housing and promotion of communities inclusive of all races and incomes.

In areas in which local governing bodies are not meeting their responsibility to provide housing for all segments of the population, the nonwhite and the poor, the Federal Government should take direct action to provide the housing needed.

In locating, transferring or expanding governmental agencies, departments, and other operations, the Federal Government should require racial and income inclusiveness of the community.

H.U.D. should be empowered to purchase, lease, and sell land to assure that its development and occupancy, now and in the future, will provide housing, facilities and services for persons of all races and incomes.

Local public housing authorities should be enabled to function on a metropolitan basis.

State governments should either regulate the zoning activities of municipal and township governments, establish state land banks for housing purposes, or create district authorities to reserve land in all parts of each metropolitan area for housing for lower-income families.

State governments should create housing development corporations comparable to the industrial development corporations which have come into common use in recent years.

IV. *Revitalizing and integrating the Ghetto:* Thirty years of public housing experience and 15 of urban renewal have taught us that the problems of the American slums are far too huge and complex to submit to the piecemeal, uncoordinated attacks of separately conceived and administered programs.

The elimination of the segregation pattern of residence from the American urban scene, the affirmative implementation of equal choice and freedom of movement for all Americans and the revitalization of existing ghetto areas should be made the cornerstone of Federal housing policy.

The proposed demonstration cities program is strongly endorsed in its principle and its general design.

A realistic plan for promoting racial desegregation in the city and metropolitan community should be a basic and mandatory element of all workable programs for urban renewal.

The practice of locating large public housing projects in areas of racial concentration must be changed.

Education

More than 90 per cent of our children are educated in racially segregated schools. Segregated Negro schools, almost without exception, are inferior in quality to white schools.

Federal courts, the Congress, and the executive branches have made almost no affirmative contribution to solving problems of de facto segregation in the North and West, which has become more, rather than less rigid.

State governments have defaulted in their obligation to achieve adequate and equal educational opportunity for all.

I. *Equalizing educational investment:* The present average of per pupil public expenditure is $533. A reasonable goal would be $1,000 per child.

States must commit themselves to a public policy of equalization, educate their citizens on revenue needs, and devise formulas in allocation of financial and human resources that will remedy past inequities.

Individual local school districts must also take the initiative in achieving equality of educational opportunity.

The Federal Government should increase the allocations under Title I of the Elementary and Secondary Education Act.

II. *Reduction of racial concentration:* The Federal Government should proclaim that it is national policy to reduce racial concentration in the schools—racial concentration of pupils, teachers, and other school personnel.

Proposals to deal with problems of de facto segregation should not eclipse the size of the job still to be done to eliminate the dual system prevailing in the South.

The Federal Government should enlarge the scope of present provisions for demonstration centers.

Specific efforts must be made to promote integration in teacher and other school personnel assignments.

The sanctions already enacted in the Civil Rights Act of 1964 are failing in their purpose and must be strengthened.

It is time that the burden of desegregating the Southern schools be removed from the Negro parents and children where it now resides, and placed squarely as the responsibility of school boards and administrators.

III. *Quality education for all:* Communities must realize that built-in inequities cannot be compensated for by an effort of a year or two, in effect shaking an educational Aerosol can over our nation's slums.

Individuals and organizations, school boards and school administrators, civil rights groups and government officials, private foundations and other private resources must take on the hard task of reorganizing local education to establish flexible, healthy educational centers that belong to the community and to the children.

School boards must, as far as possible, be constituted so as to support a policy of equal opportunity, reduction of racial concentration, and improvement in the quality of education.

Consideration should be given to a major reorganization of the school system.

School systems should make kindergarten a regular part of the school program in the many areas where it does not now exist, with curriculum, teacher-pupil ratios, and enrichments patterned after successful experimental programs.

Rural communities need to investigate curricular innovations which will prepare their children not only for probable migration elsewhere, but for different kinds of vocational and technical skills.

Vocational education has not kept pace with the rapid changes in technology and work, and has not involved sufficiently the efforts of industry, labor, schools, agencies and organizations to make it relevant.

Negro students in present agricultural programs have little opportunity to participate in work experience in local agri-business.

Two years of postsecondary education should be made available at public expense for all high school graduates.

Predominantly Negro colleges should be adequately supported and strengthened.

Administration of Justice

Effective legislative and executive measures are needed to combat the deplorable condition, found in some parts of the Deep South. where Americans are murdered, beaten, and subject to other forms of intimidation because they exercise constitutional or other Federal rights or aid others in the exercise of such rights.

The threat to the personal security and rights of Negroes and civil rights workers in the South warrants the attention of the country and the Congress. There must be adequate Federal protection for those asserting Federal rights.

There is a need to secure equal justice for Negroes in the South. Negro citizens and civil rights workers must be free to exercise their constitutional rights free from harassment, intimidation and discrimination by courts, court officials, law enforcement agents, and unfairly selected juries.

Police-minority group community relations is an urban problem most pronounced in the North and West but with grave implications for the entire nation. Positive steps must be taken to deal with them. Fairer and more professional police departments will be far more able to cope with the rising incidence of street crime.

I. *Protection of Negroes and civil rights workers from intimidation:* There should be broad support of Title V of the Administration's civil rights bill, which would provide greater Federal protection to Negroes and civil rights workers from intimidation.

Legislation should be enacted giving persons who suffer physical injury or property loss as the result of exercising rights protected by the criminal provisions of Title V, or as the result of urging or aiding others to exercise such rights, an opportunity to receive compensation for the injury or loss.

Any county, Government, city government, or other local government entity that employs officers who deprive persons of rights should be jointly liable with the officers to persons who suffer injury or loss from such officers' misconduct.

More Federal agents should be made available to increase the effective enforcement of civil rights laws.

II. *Equal justice:* Title I and II of the Administration bill which provide for nondiscrimination in the selection of Federal and state jurors should be supported.

Federal legislation should be enacted to provide for the removal of civil rights cases from state to Federal trial courts in order to assure a fair trial.

Federal legislation should be enacted to permit private persons to obtain injunctive relief where state prosecutions are brought against persons for exercising First Amendment rights directed at obtaining equal treatment for all citizens.

Federal legislation should be enacted to afford more adequate criminal sanctions against state and local officials who deprive citizens of constitutional rights.

Law schools and bar associations, including the American Bar Association, should take steps to assure zealous representation by local counsel of Negroes and civil rights workers.

Legal aid centers should be established by the Federal Government to provide adequate legal representation to Negroes and civil rights workers.

III. *Improvement of police-community relations:* The Federal Government should seek to improve police-community relations by establishing assistance programs in the areas of recruitment, testing, selection, training, organization and pay.

The states and localities themselves must take action in those areas in which success will depend upon their initiative. The states should take the following steps:

1. Initiation of a positive and aggressive campaign to recruit and hire qualified minority group personnel.
2. Establishment of minimum state standards for all police officers.
3. Provision for periodic training programs.
4. Assist localities in developing better police forces.
   The major burden for improving police-community relations rests on the local government. They should undertake the following steps:
1. Upgrade police organization, equipment and facilities.
2. Establish adequate complaint procedures.
3. Define the role that the police department is expected to play in the community.
4. Establish a community relations unit in the police department.

Selection 10

THE CITY AND THE NEGRO

CHARLES   SILBERMAN*

"The approved way to talk about cities these days," Paul Ylvisaker of the Ford Foundation has observed, "is to speak solemnly, sadly, ominously, and fearfully about their problems. You don't rate as an expert on the city unless you foresee its doom." Doom is easy to foresee in the spreading slums, the increasing crime rates, the public disaffection of almost every large city. And yet the city can survive, as it has survived for a century and a half. Indeed, American cities today have a chance to achieve their greatest success and their greatest glory.

For this to happen, however, city planners and civic leaders will have to understand better than they now do what their cities' greatest problem is. It is not, as so many assume, to bring the wandering middle class back from the suburbs. The large city, as Jane Jacobs of *Architectural Forum* has put it, cannot import a middle

* From *Fortune*, March, 1962.

class; it must manufacture its own. And, indeed, most of the huge middle class that dominates American life today was manufactured in the big-city slums of yesteryear. Cities always have had to create their own stable, cultivated citizenry out of whatever raw material lay at hand. For the American city during the past hundred and fifty years, the raw material was the stream of immigrants pouring in from Britain, Ireland, Germany, Norway, Russia, Italy, and a dozen other lands. The city needed these immigrants to build its streets and offices, to man its factories, service its homes and hotels and restaurants. (Many well-intentioned Americans to underestimate this difficulty.) Some people see the Negro problem as purely legal and social and assume that it will be solved automatically by desegregating schools, restaurants, bus terminals, and housing developments. Other people see it as purely economic, to be resolved by upgrading Negro jobs and incomes. And a good many Americans believe the problem would be solved if the Negroes would just decide to adopt white middle-class standards of behavior and white middle-class goals of economic success.

There are no cheap or easy answers to the Negro problem, however; it involves all these elements and a good many more besides. The problem's roots go back to slavery, whose impact is still being felt in the disorganization of the Negro family, and to the Negro's systematic exclusion from American society since slavery ended a century ago. These are sins for which all Americans are in some measure guilty and for which all Americans owe some act of atonement. Those who hesitate to act because of the magnitude of the problem should remember the stricture of Edmund Burke: "The only thing necessary for the triumph of evil is for good men to do nothing."

But the triumph of "good" in this instance (as in most others) requires a lot more than good will. To solve the Negro problem will demand difficult and occasionally heroic decisions on the part of civic and political leaders, and changes in the behavior of Americans in every walk of life: teachers and students; trade-union leaders and members; employers and employees. This article—the sixth in *Fortune*'s series on "The Public Business"—will document what is being done across the country, and what needs to be done, to speed the Negro's advance and thereby save the large city.

Filling the Vacuum

The Negro has come to the big city because it needed his labor, especially after the cutting off of European immigration created a vacuum in northern labor markets. The Negro population outside the Deep South has increased fivefold since 1910; it has nearly

The Negro Migration from South to North and from Country to City

One of the great population changes in modern history is depicted in the maps above, which show the Negro population of the U. S. by state and city of residence. Each dot represents 10,000 Negroes; major city concentrations are shown by clusters of dots. (A single dot is used in states like Nevada, which have fewer than 10,000 Negroes.)

As the maps reveal, Negroes are involved in two shifts: from South to North, and from country to city. Half a century ago, in 1910, eight out of ten U. S. Negroes resided in one or another of the eleven states of the Old Confederacy. Over 90 per cent of these Negroes, moreover, lived in rural areas. Negroes began moving to the North during World War I and continued to move during the 1920's, when restrictive legislation slowed down the flow of immigrants from southern and eastern Europe. By 1940 the Negro population in the Old Confederacy had increased only 12 per cent, whereas in the same period the Negro population elsewhere in the U. S. had more than doubled, from 1,900,000 to four million. But the Old Confederacy still contained more than two-thirds of all U. S. Negroes.

The Negro migrations got under way again during World War II, and have continued since then. Between 1940 and 1960 the Negro population outside the Old Confederacy increased two and one-quarter times, going from nearly four million to over nine million—48 per cent of the total U. S. Negro population. In the eleven states of the Old Confederacy, by contrast, Negro population grew a scant 9 per cent. Most of the increase outside the South occurred in the central cities of the twelve largest U. S. metropolitan areas—New York, Los Angeles, Chicago, Philadelphia, Detroit, San Francisco-Oakland, Boston, Pittsburgh, St. Louis, Washington, Cleveland, Baltimore—which now hold 31 per cent of all U. S. Negroes. In the last decade, however, Negro migration has diffused somewhat from big to smaller cities, such as Buffalo, Rochester, Newark, New Haven, Fort Wayne, San Diego.

Within the Old Confederacy, meanwhile, Negro population was shifting from country to city. The number of Negroes declined in the rural areas, as the proportion living in cities jumped from 21 per cent in 1940 (and 7 per cent in 1910) to 41 per cent in 1960. The Negro population of Dallas and Houston, for example, went up two and a half times, and rose 75 per cent in Atlanta and Miami.

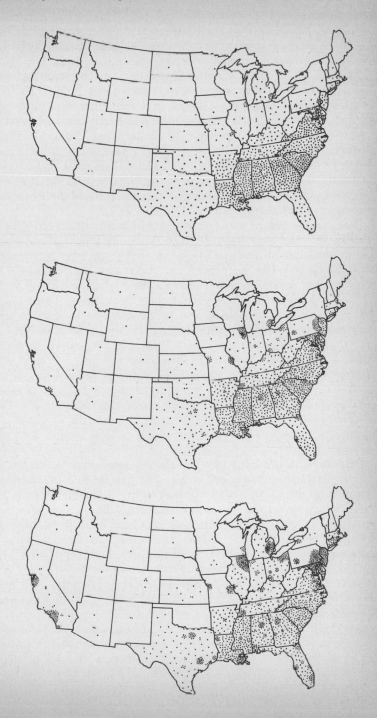

tripled just since 1940. (See maps, pp. 509.) Part of this expansion, of course, has come from natural increase rather than migration; but it is the migration of Negroes in the childbearing ages that enabled the natural increase to occur outside the South.

Most of the Negroes moving to the North have crowded into the slums of the twelve largest cities, which today hold 60 per cent of the Negroes living outside the Deep South. Since 1940 the Negro population of New York City has increased nearly two and one-half times, to 1,100,000, or 14 per cent of the city's population. In Philadelphia, Negroes have doubled in number since 1940, to 529,000, or 26 per cent. The Negro population of Detroit has more than tripled, to nearly 500,000, or 29 per cent of the city's population. And the Negro population of Los Angeles County has jumped a phenomenal sixfold since 1940, from 75,000 to 464,000.

The Negroes, to be sure, are not the only disadvantaged peoples coming into the large cities. In New York the Puerto Rican population swelled from perhaps 100,000 in 1940 to over 700,000 in 1960. And Cincinnati, Baltimore, St. Louis, Columbus, Detroit, and Chicago, among others, receive a steady stream of impoverished white hillbillies from the southern Appalachian Mountains. These Appalachian whites—of the oldest and purest U.S. stock—have at least as much initial difficulty adjusting to the city as do the Negroes and Puerto Ricans. But the Puerto Ricans and Appalachian whites affect only a limited number of cities, usually in only a limited way. There are a good many other city problems besides the Negro problem, in short. But the Negro problem is what city planners and officials are really talking about when they refer to The City Problem.

The Crucial Difference

Migration to the large city has always involved a heavy cost in family dislocation, pauperism, crime, delinquency, and urban blight. Immigrants bring with them housekeeping and other habits that clash with city standards; and the impersonality of city life tends to erode the social relationships that regulated behavior in "the old country." Hence the U.S. middle class has always had the sense of being engulfed by uncultivated newcomers, and has always been on the move. As early as the 1840's, for example, New York City's Fourth Ward—the district in which George Washington had lived when he was inaugurated President—had become a slum so overrun by violence that even the police dared not enter except in parties of six or more. And by the 1870's New Yorkers were already lamenting the exodus of men of "moderate income to the suburban towns." With its "middle classes in large part self-exiled, its laboring population being brutalized in the tenements, and its citizens of the highest class indifferent to the common weal," a journalist commented at the time, "New York has drifted from bad to worse and become the prey of professional thieves, ruffians, and political jugglers." Measured against the backdrop of history, therefore, the gangs and crime and squalor of today seem almost benign, and some historians and sociologists have concluded that time and patience are almost all that's needed.

It will take more than that. The Negro is unlike the European immigrant in one crucial respect: he is colored. And that makes all the difference. The Irish, to be sure, faced job discrimination a century ago as severe as the Negro faces today. But the Irishman could lose his brogue; as soon as he was "Americanized," his problem was resolved. But the Negro cannot escape so easily. "All other slum dwellers, when the bank account permits it," James Baldwin has written, "can move out of the slum and vanish altogether from the eye of persecution." Not so the Negro.

There are other differences. The European peasant, no matter how depressed his position, had roots in a "whole society" with a stable culture and stable institutions and above all a stable family life. The Negro does not. Slavery made a stable family life (and a stable culture) impossible. Husbands could be sold away from wives, children from parents. Such family life as did exist centered almost entirely around the mother.

What slavery began, prejudice and discrimination have helped perpetuate. Family disorganization is endemic. Negro women frequently find it easier to get jobs—e.g., as domestics—than Negro men, thus making them the financial center of the family. The inability of Negro men to find jobs that confer status and dignity, together with the servility required of them in the South, have led Negro men to sexual promiscuity, drinking, and violence as means of asserting their masculinity. Embittered by their experience with men, Negro mothers seem to take more interest in their daughters' than in their sons' upbringing. Twice as many Negro girls as boys go to college. (Among white college students, the reverse is true.) And family disorganization is compounded by the overcrowding and dilapidation of Negro housing.

Hence the Negro, all too often, is trapped in a vicious circle from which he cannot extricate himself. Little in the Negro boy's environment is likely to give him any sense of aspiration or any direction; he has no male model to follow and little reason to assume that education offers a way out of the slum. His lack of education and aspiration, in turn, makes it virtually impossible for the Negro youth to find a job with dignity and status, even where discrimination is absent. All too often, therefore, he decides that there is no point to trying, and he loses the capacity to take advantage of such opportunities as do arise. In the jargon of the social worker, he "develops a self-defeating mode of living" that keeps him trapped in the slum forever.

To make matters worse, the gap is widening between Negro education and training, on the one hand, and the requirements of the labor market, on the other. The Europeans immigrated during periods of rapidly expanding U. S. demand for unskilled labor; no great transfer of skill was needed to enable an Irish or Italian peasant to find a job on a construction gang. But in the U. S. today, the demand for unskilled labor is shrinking relative to the total labor force. Since 1947, employment of white-collar workers—executives, entrepreneurs, professional and scientific employees, clerks, and salesmen—has gone up 43 per cent, compared to only a 14 per cent gain in blue-collar and service-worker employment. By 1970 a substantial majority of workers will be in white-collar or highly skilled blue-collar jobs—in jobs that characteristically require real training and thought. Three out of four nonfarm Negro male workers, however, are in unskilled or semiskilled occupations, compared to only one in three among white workers.

In this new world of specialized skills, Negroes have more and more trouble finding and holding jobs. The unemployment rate among Negro men is more than twice that among white men. In some cities as many as one Negro male in three is out of work. The problem is particularly acute among Negro youths; in one northern Negro slum area surveyed by Dr. James B. Conant, 70 per cent of the young men who had left school were out of work; in another the ratio was over 50 per cent.

The Other Side of Jordan

It would be a serious mistake to equate the Negro's apparent apathy and lack of motivation with a sense of contentment. It is a lot harder for today's Negro to bear his poverty and lack of status than it was for the European immigrant, who arrived at a time when the great majority of the population was poor. The Negro migration, by contrast, is occurring in an affluent society. Like the underdeveloped peoples everywhere, American Negroes have been fired by the revolution of rising expectations. In Harry Ashmore's phrase, Negroes have seen "the other side of Jordan"; they are in a hurry to cross. Among a good many Negroes, especially the college students involved in the sit-in movement, impatience with their rate of progress has conquered apathy and led to direct, disciplined, and frequently courageous action to improve the Negro position in

American life. But among the great mass of working-class Negroes and a large part of the middle class, apathy exists side by side with a growing, festering resentment of their lot. These Negroes are more and more convinced that they should have a better life; they are less and less convinced that they themselves can do anything about it.

Impatience is greatest, perhaps, in the area of civil rights; the Supreme Court decision on school segregation raised expectations of a new era in race relations that has been painfully slow in coming. But Negroes are also impatient over their economic progress. During World War II and the early postwar boom, Negroes did make remarkable economic strides; the median income of urban Negro males shot up from less than 40 per cent of white income in 1939 to 60 per cent in 1952. Negroes have not been able to improve their relative position since 1952, however; the slowdown in the economy during the 1950's bore most heavily on the durable-goods industries, where many Negroes are employed. Thus the income of the average Negro male city dweller, which was 60 per cent of the average white income in 1952, had gone up only to 61 per cent by 1960. Outside the cities, average Negro income has actually declined since 1952.

As a result, impatience is turning into bitterness, anger, and hatred. The danger is not violence but something much deeper and harder to combat: a sense of permanent alienation from American society. Unless the Negro position improves very quickly, Negroes of whatever class may come to regard their separation from American society as permanent, and so consider themselves permanently outside the constraints and the allegiances of American society. The Negro district of every large city would come to constitute an American Casbah, with its own values and its own controls—and a deep hostility to the white community. In such a situation, communication between the races would become impossible. And life in the large city would become unbearable.

But the Negro advance depends on changes within the Negro community as well as within the white community. Understandably, Negroes have been reluctant to recognize this fact. They have assumed that an end to discriminatory practices will by itself solve the Negro problem. It will do nothing of the sort, although an end to discrimination certainly is a prerequisite to any solution. "If the color barrier could be eliminated overnight," Professor Eli Ginzberg of Columbia put the matter baldly in *The Negro Potential,* "that fact alone would not materially improve the position of the Negro."

The truth is that too many Negroes are unable—or unwilling—

to compete in an integrated society. Because of the shortage of professional and technical personnel in industry and government, just about any qualified Negro can get a good job, but employers willing to hire Negroes have trouble finding Negroes to hire. Colleges and medical and professional schools eager to admit Negroes (and to give them scholarships) cannot find as many qualified Negroes as they are willing to admit; the National Scholarship and Service Fund for Negro Students reports that there are five times as many places available in northern colleges as there are Negroes to fill them. Nor have Negroes been taking advantage of the professional and business opportunities that the growth of the big-city Negro population has offered. The number of Negro physicians in the U. S. has been static for fifty years. As the U. S. Commission on Civil Rights sadly concluded, a principal reason for continued Negro poverty is "the lack of motivation on the part of many Negroes to improve their educational and occupational status."

The Negro community also lacks the sort of self-help institutions through which the European immigrants climbed out of their slums. Negros, as Professor James Q. Wilson of Harvard put it in *Negro Politics,* are "the objects rather than the subjects of civic action. Things are often done for, or about, or to, or because of Negroes, but they are less frequently done *by* Negroes." There is no tradition of Negro philanthropy. Because the Negro has no indigenous culture to protect, the Negro community has not seen the same need to organize itself that European ethnic groups felt. The paucity of Negro self-help organizations may also be due to the tremendous growth of public assistance during the past quarter-century. The fact that help now comes from the city or state or federal government, sociologist Nathan Glazer suggests, has tended to channel "social energies" into the formulation of demands for new governmental programs rather than into the establishment and financing of voluntary organizations among Negroes.

The Need for Excellence

This institutional vacuum must be filled. For one thing, charitable and social-welfare programs organized, staffed, and supported by Negroes are likely to have a much greater impact on Negro behavior than programs administered by government or by private white agencies, both of which tend to be viewed with suspicion and hostility. Then, too, as Professor Ginzberg has been reminding Negro audiences, freedom is only the precondition for equality, not its equivalent. The more Negroes get what they want in terms of formal rights—voting, education, desegregation, etc.—the more responsibility they will have to assume for their own well-being.

This fact is now beginning to get its due. Perhaps the most important single factor making for solution of the Negro problem is the emergence of pride of race among Negroes. This new pride is the product of many factors: the Negro gains during World War II, the independence of the African nations, the courage and dignity shown by the sit-ins and Freedom Riders. Pride, to be sure, is always a two-edged sword; among the Black Muslims it leads to hatred of everything white and to threats of anti-white violence. But overall, the new sense of pride is serving to raise the level of Negro aspirations and behavior; even the Black Muslims stress the importance of work, sobriety, chastity, and self-discipline.

A growing number of Negro leaders and spokesmen, moreover—particularly at the national level—are encouraging Negroes to assume more responsibility for their own fate. "All the intellectual arguments and sociological explanations in the world," the distinguished Negro journalist, Carl Rowan, now Deputy Assistant Secretary of State for Public Affairs, has written, "do not meet fully the need to do something about the fact that people are being killed and maimed, street gangs are spreading terror in big cities, young girls are bearing an increasing number of illegitimate children, and dope and gin mills are flourishing in our urban centers." Negro leaders must recognize, Rowan argues—and in fact, they are beginning to recognize—"that it is not enough to blame every Negro misdeed on segregation, or to pretend that integration will be a cure-all for every social problem in sight."

Significantly, Rowan's view is shared by the man who has given the most dramatic leadership in the fight against segregation and who, more than any other leader, has captured the imagination of the Negro rank and file, the Reverend Martin Luther King Jr. "We have become so involved in trying to wipe out the institution of segregation, which certainly is a major cause of social problems among Negroes," Dr. King says, "that we have neglected to push programs to raise the moral and cultural climate in our Negro neighborhoods." Negroes, in Dr. King's view, must learn to strive for excellence in every field of endeavor—"not excellence as a Negro doctor or lawyer or a Negro craftsman, but excellence per se." He is urging his Southern Christian Leadership Conference to emphasize what he calls "the constructive program" of raising Negro standards as much as the program of "creative protest"—i.e., the sit-ins.

The National Urban League, moreover, is shifting its emphasis from opening up new job opportunities to preparing Negroes for the job opportunities that are opening up. "It's one thing to eliminate barriers," Dr. Whitney Young Jr., the league's dynamic new executive director, observes, "and quite another to get a previously depressed people to take advantage of the new opportunities." Dr. Young believes that Negro family life must be stabilized if Negroes are to be able to take advantage of these opportunities, and he's looking for funds to finance an ambitious new program in which the league would recruit a number of settled, well-adjusted middle-class Negro families to "adopt" a newly settled family and facilitate their adjustment to urban life.

"More Powerful Than Apathy"

There is reason to think that Negroes, even those living in the worst sort of slum, can be mobilized to help themselves. In many ways the most impressive experiment affecting the Negro anywhere in the U. S. is going on now in Chicago's Woodlawn area, an oblong slum running south of the University of Chicago campus and containing about 100,000 people, almost all Negro. Woodlawn's physical decomposition is more than matched by its social disorganization. It is the principal port of entry for Negroes coming to Chicago from the South, and so has had a large transient population. It also contains a flourishing traffic in gambling, narcotics, and prostitution. Woodlawn, in short, is a social chaos of the sort that social workers have always assumed can never produce a large, active organization.

It's producing one now. The guiding genius is a highly controversial Chicago sociologist and criminologist, Dr. Saul D. Alinsky, executive director of the Industrial Areas Foundation. (No one else in the city of Chicago, as two Woodlawn ministers have written, "is as detested or as loved, as cursed or blessed, as feared or respected.") Alinsky was one of the principal architects of Chicago's much-admired Back of the Yards Neighborhood Council, which has turned a white slum area that had been the locale for Upton Sinclair's *The Jungle* into one of the most desirable working-class neighborhoods in Chicago. Alinsky was asked by three Protestant ministers and a Catholic priest to organize Woodlawn; the project is being financed by grants from the Catholic Archdiocese of Chicago, the Presbyterian Church, and a private philanthropy, the Schwartzhaupt Foundation.

If Alinsky succeeds, it will be the first time a large, broadly representative organization will have come into existence in any Negro district in any large American city. Alinsky is trying to create an organization that, as one local leader puts it, "will be the most powerful thing in Woodlawn—more powerful than the political party . . . more powerful than the apathy that holds the community in its grasp." He eschews the usual appeals to homeowners' interests in conserving property values or to a general neighborhood spirit or civic pride—appeals, in his view, that apply only to middle-class neighborhoods. Alinsky, instead, uses the classical approach of trade-union organization. He appeals to the self-interest of the local residents and to their resentment and distrust of the outside world, and he develops a local, indigenous leadership.

"They're Paying Attention"

The issue that is principally animating Woodlawn now is the University of Chicago's proposal to annex a strip a block wide and a mile long adjacent to the campus. The Negro residents have no particular attachment to the strip in question, but they suspect that its annexation will be the prelude to bulldozing a large part of the area for middle and upper-income apartment houses. There is ample basis for their fears; urban-renewal projects have been going on for some time under university sponsorship in the Hyde Park–Kenwood district north of the university, designed in good measure to clear Negroes out. To force the university and city-planning officials to bargain with the Woodlawn residents, Alinsky is mobilizing the residents into a group called the Temporary Woodlawn Organization; he had 8,000 Woodlawn people enrolled in the T.W.O. within six months of the project's inception. The T.W.O. organized an impressive campaign to get the usually apathetic Woodlawn residents registered and voting; during the registration period last August, a caravan of forty-six buses took some 2,300 members down to City Hall to register.

What makes the Woodlawn experiment significant, however, is not what it is doing *for* its members but what it is doing *to* them. "The most important thing to me about the forty-six busloads of people who went to City Hall to register," Alinsky says, "was their own reaction. Many were weeping; others were saying, 'They're paying attention to us.' 'They're recognizing that we're people.'" What is crucial, in short, is not what the Woodlawn residents win, but the fact that *they* are winning it. This fact seems to make the Woodlawn members see themselves in a new light, as people of substance and worth. While Alinsky's methods create a sense of militancy that could be misused, they create a sense of responsibility as well, and this is their most important product so far.

The Twenty-Point Drop

The Negro problem is not just the responsibility of the Negro community, of course; its resolution requires drastically changed policies by a variety of governmental agencies. The social institution that touches the Negro problem most directly is the public school, which since the 1890's has been the principal means by which new-comers to the city, or their offspring, have been able to move out of the slums. The public school offers the greatest opportunity to dissolve the cultural barrier that blocks the Negro's advance into the mainstream of American life.

The opportunity is being muffed. Admittedly the problems encountered in the Negro (or for that matter, the white) slum school are enough to discourage the best-intentioned. Children entering school are ill-prepared, poorly motivated, and badly behaved; teachers must spend inordinate amounts of time maintaining order, and they are occasionally in danger of physical harm. Because families move from tenement to tenement with great frequency, pupil turnover is incredibly high—more than 100 per cent in some New York slum schools; the standard quip has it that if a teacher is absent a week, she won't recognize her class when she returns. Under these conditions one might reasonably expect that cities would spend more per Negro pupil than they do per white pupil. The reverse is generally true; the schools in Negro slum areas are the most overcrowded, are manned with the least-experienced teachers, and have the highest ratio of students to teachers.

The results are predictably poor. Coming from semiliterate or illiterate backgrounds, which not only offer no incentive to learn but rather frequently regard the school as a hostile force, many children never learn to read properly. Their inability to read at grade level in turn makes them fall behind in every other subject, even vocational courses; for example, shop students can't learn carpentry if they can't read blueprints or calculate fractions of an inch. The result is that their learning ability itself becomes atrophied; I.Q. typically drops twenty points as the Negro child progresses through school. By junior or senior high, it is almost impossible to reach him or teach him; three out of five Negro youngsters drop out of school before completion—uneducated, seemingly uneducable, and virtually unemployable. And yet these children can be educated; New York City and St. Louis, in particular, as we shall see, have demonstrated the fact beyond doubt.

The question first is, what kind of education can they—and should they—be given? Unfortunately, the current discussion is being shaped by Dr. James B. Conant's recent *Slums and Suburbs,* which has been accepted blandly and uncritically by almost everyone concerned with the problem, Negro or white. Dr. Conant has performed a great public service in calling attention to the dimensions of the problem and to the need for immediate action. But he has prescribed the worst possible remedy: a great expansion of vocational education for Negro youth.

If Conant's advice were followed, it would doom the Negro permanently to the bottom rung on the economic ladder. "A generation or two ago," as Professor Eli Ginzberg put it in *The Negro Potential,* "a man with negligible formal education could become a skilled worker. Today, participation in the industrial process requires of the worker not only basic literacy but a fairly high level of ability to deal with words and figures." The worker must be able to follow written instructions, to read the bulletin board, to keep various kinds of records, to master considerable technical knowledge. And he must be able to learn new skills, for nobody knows what job skills will be needed ten years from now.

What the Negro child needs, in short, is the same kind of education the white child needs and is beginning to get: an education that teaches him how to learn, that gives him the intellectual discipline and depth of understanding that will enable him to meet new conditions as they arise. But it will take more than a return to the three R's to give Negro children this kind of education. To penetrate the environmental and cultural curtain that keeps the Negro child from learning, the school must take on a whole range of functions that lie outside its normal sphere.

A Success Story

The most spectacular demonstration of what can be done to raise the aspirations and performance of Negro slum children is occurring in St. Louis, in the "Banneker group"—twenty-three elementary schools enrolling 16,000 children, 95 per cent of them Negroes living in the city's worst slum. Dr. Samuel Shepard Jr., the assistant superintendent in charge of the Banneker district, decided to take action four years ago, when the city's high schools instituted a three-track system of ability grouping. Only 7 per cent of the Banneker graduates were able to make the top ability track; nearly half were put in the bottom track. In three years Dr. Shepard has been able to triple the proportion of Banneker graduates admitted to the first track, from 7 per cent to 21 per cent, and to cut the number going into the bottom group to 21 per cent. Last June, in fact, Shepard's eighth-graders actually exceeded the national norm in reading; three years before the Banneker eighth-graders had been a full year behind.

The results largely reflect the impact of Shepard's powerful personality and dedicated leadership. He has changed teachers' and principals' attitudes toward their students from one of condescension to one of sympathy and challenge. More important, he has changed the Negro community's attitude toward the school. He keeps up a steady fire of meetings and of assemblies, field trips, pep talks, contests, and posters, designed to inculcate a respect for learning. For the children, he sets up a very competitive athletic-like atmosphere, in which the kudos goes to "the achievers." For the parents, Shepard uses an extremely blunt approach. He shows them by slides, charts, and film strips exactly how poorly their children are doing and warns them that unless the children do better in school they'll be no better off than their parents. He explains that things *can* be different for children, he shows in great detail the relation between education and employment, pointing to specific jobs now open to Negroes in St. Louis for which no qualified Negroes can be found. He also explains at length how the school operates at each grade, what the parents should demand of their children, and how they can help. And through all of this he emphasizes reading as the key to academic—and vocational—success.

Shepard has achieved these results without the use of extra resources; the greatest strength of his program is the fact that it depends on the ordinary classroom teacher. But remedial-reading teachers, guidance counselors, psychologists, and social workers can also be used to good effect, as New York City has shown with its Demonstration Guidance Project and its Higher Horizons program. In the first year of the Higher Horizons program the city was able to cut third-graders' retardation in reading from six months to only one month. Under grants from the Ford Foundation's Great Cities School Improvement Project, other cities are experimenting with a variety of techniques. Detroit and Philadelphia, for example, are employing "school-community agents" in slum schools to try to break down parental suspicion and hostility and persuade parents of the importance of education.

The programs now in operation, however, affect only a minute fraction of the children needing special help. What must be done is to put these programs into effect on a mass scale. To do so will cost money, of course. But the cities will get the money back—and a lot more besides—in lower relief costs, decreased juvenile delinquency and crime, and increased income for its residents—not to mention a radical improvement in the whole quality of city life. "A community which made its schools rather than its central business district the tender object and physical center of its urban-renewal operations," Paul Ylvisaker recently suggested, "would be taking one of the noblest and shrewdest steps forward in the civic progress of this century."

The Underdeveloped Country

The city, in short, must exercise "positive discrimination" in favor of the Negro if it is to enable the mass of Negroes to compete with whites on equal terms. The U. S. must learn to look upon the Negro community as if it were an underdeveloped country.

One thing that must be done—by industry and labor, as well as by government—is to develop long-range programs to educate workers who are already out of school, and whose lack of education makes them particularly vulnerable to technological unemployment. Armour's experience in trying to retrain workers made idle by automation has shown clearly that crash programs can provide only limited help. Of the 170 employees who applied for retraining when the company closed its Oklahoma City meat-packing plant, for example, 110 could not be given any training because they lacked the minimum skills in reading and mathematics.

There must also be a broadening of job opportunities for Negroes. There has been a significant reduction in job discrimination against Negroes in recent years, largely because of government prodding, but Negroes still find it very difficult to obtain jobs in the skilled trades, where union prejudice is a big stumbling block, and in clerical and sales jobs. It isn't enough for employers to make jobs formally available to Negroes; as a result of generations of discrimination, Negroes tend to assume that prejudice exists even where it has ended. A special effort must be made, therefore, to publicize the new job openings; Negroes must be brought within the web of job gossip through active recruitment.

Meanwhile, cities must try to alleviate some of the disorganization of Negro family and community life. The city has a vast panoply of services designed to prevent, relieve, and cure problems of individual and family behavior and circumstance. But each service deals separately with the individuals involved, sometimes in bureaucratic competition with the others. As often as not, the Negro—or the white slum dweller, for that matter—sees the bewildering array of police, school, and welfare agencies as enemies to be played off one against another.

It is possible to close the distance between the individual and government, and to coordinate the activities of the agencies affecting him. Wayne Thompson, the young city manager of Oakland, California, has pulled together seven public agencies representing four levels of government into something called the Associated Agencies. Fortnightly meetings of the A.A. workers in each section of the city are held to coordinate their work. In dealing with one school marked by frequent violence, for example, the school superintendent allowed the police to seal off the school area and then clean out the guns and knives in the school lockers. The school, police, recreation, probation, and welfare workers then culled a list of troublemakers, letting each agency take responsibility for the children it already knew, or upon whom it had some particular claim. Out of 2,800 pupils, only fifty-four turned out to be real troublemakers; when the whole job had been finished, only two had to be moved out of school and into detention. Since the Associated Agencies program started in late 1957, Oakland has been relatively free of trouble. The city recently received a $2-million grant from the Ford Foundation to extend the program.

New York City is trying to accomplish somewhat the same thing through its Neighborhood Conservation Projects. The coordination is not as complete, and the emphasis is fairly heavy on conservation of real estate rather than of human beings. But several projects have gone beyond physical rehabilitation—e.g., in the Bloomingdale district on Manhattan's West Side. The projects, in a sense, are designed to create a modern-day (but honest) counterpart to the old Tammany district leader, who served a very important function for the European immigrant, in effect locating him in the city and providing a channel to its government.

The Housing Dilemma

More must also be done about Negro housing. Despite a remarkable improvement in the condition of Negro housing since the end of World War II, nearly half of all the houses and apartments occupied by Negroes are still classified as "dilapidated" or "deteriorating" in the census rolls, compared to only 15 per cent of white homes. And Negroes live under far more crowded conditions. While good housing doesn't guarantee good behavior, bad housing does contribute to family disorganization and hence to delinquency.

The deterioration and overcrowding of Negro housing are due in good measure to the poverty of Negroes as a group. A study of the Philadelphia housing market by Chester Rapkin and William Grigsby of the University of Pennsylvania, for example, disclosed that only about 5 per cent of all Negro households had incomes sufficient to buy houses costing $12,000 or more—about the minimum price at which private builders were able to erect houses in that city. But discrimination as well as income robs the Negro of freedom of choice. Housing, as the U. S. Civil Rights Commission puts it, with only slight exaggeration, is "the one commodity in the American market which is not freely available on equal terms to everyone that can afford to pay."

Because economic and social factors bar Negroes from the market for new construction—and because Negro population is growing at an explosive rate in most large cities—Negroes are constantly looking for homes in the older, less expensive areas of the city. This pressure is as unsettling for the white community as it is for the

Negro, for it leads to unstable and rapidly changing neighborhoods. To most white persons, as Eunice Grier of the Washington Center for Metropolitan Studies puts it, "there is no such thing . . . as a stable and permanent integrated neighborhood." Hence, when Negro demand appears in a neighborhood, the community either resists Negro entry—sometimes with violence—or it abandons the neighborhood completely. The latter usually occurs in any case. As Negroes start moving in, the whites start moving out—some because of prejudice, others because they fear that if they remain they will rapidly become a minority. Integration, as Saul Alinsky sardonically observes, "is usually a term to describe the period of time that elapses between the appearance of the first Negro and the exit of the last white."

There is considerable evidence to suggest that whites *will* live in integrated neighborhoods if they have some assurance that they will not be swamped. For that reason a number of housing experts now advocate the use of "benign quotas" as the best—or only—means of solving the Negro housing problem. New York City's Housing Authority, for example, is using a quota system to try to integrate its low and middle-income housing projects, with fair success.

But the benign quota is no panacea and will work only where there is some authority able to decide how many Negroes will be admitted, and to determine which Negroes will be admitted. The authority must be powerful enough to enforce compliance after the quota has been filled. Enforcing a quota, moreover, frequently involves a painful conflict between two laudable objectives—housing integration and an increased supply of housing for Negroes. In order to maintain the desired racial balance, a housing authority frequently has to turn down qualified Negroes in desperate need of housing in favor of whites whose need is far less acute.

It's doubtful, in short, whether any simple, dramatic approach can solve the Negro housing problem. So long as the great majority of Negroes have slum incomes, they are going to live in slums. In the long run, therefore, the only way to solve the problem of Negro housing is to solve the problem of Negro people—to raise the economic and social level of the Negro community.

The Cost of Delay

A new pride in self that is developing among Negroes is a powerful lever to raise Negro aspirations and achievements. The Negro's growing political activity is a powerful lever to force cities to face up to the problem; the Negro vote was decisive in last fall's mayoralty elections in Atlanta, Detroit, and New York.

And the U. S. economy itself should facilitate the Negro's advance during the 1960's. In a rapidly expanding economy employers will have to end job discrimination and upgrade unskilled and semiskilled Negro workers if they are to produce all their markets will demand. The training programs developed during World War II show what industry can do when the stakes are high enough. And with a shortage of skilled labor likely, unions will have far less incentive to restrict entry into the skilled occupations.

These trends will make solution of the Negro problem less difficult; but they will not solve it. If the Negroes are to take their proper place in U. S. society, millions of hard decisions will have to be taken by people of both races. And the longer the U. S. delays those decisions, the more painful this most urgent piece of public business will become.

Selection 11

THE SOUTH LOOKS AHEAD

RALPH MCGILL *

The writer of the following article, which first appeared in Ebony *magazine, is Ralph McGill. As editor and publisher of the* Atlanta Constitution, *he has won the Pulitzer prize, as well as an international reputation.*

Ebony magazine is to publish a centennial edition of the Emancipation Proclamation . . . will you contribute an article under the title, 'The South Looks Ahead' . . . ?"

Before beginning work one sat down to think.

Memory recalled the summer of 1959 and the journey to Russia and Warsaw with Vice President Richard M. Nixon. The publisher of *Ebony,* John H. Johnson and Mrs. Johnson were members of the press party. We had become friends and had had many talks. At

* From Era Bell Thompson and Herbert Nipson (editors), *White on Black,* Chicago: Johnson Publishing Co., 1963, pp. 220–30.

Sverdlovsk (where Francis Gary Powers and the U-2 plane not long thereafter were to meet disaster) the Soviet journalists invited the visiting press corps to dinner with dancing. The day had been long, hot and exhausting, and we sat gratefully down to a good dinner. The courteous, competent young women whom Intourist had sent along as interpreters were present, neat and attractively clad for a dinner dance.

One of the Russian-speaking United States staff members sought me out and said: "I thought you might like to know that I have heard the Soviet newsmen talking. They are waiting to see if you, from that South about which they have heard so much and know so little, will ask Mrs. Johnson to dance. If you do, they won't mention it in their dispatches. If you don't it may well be a featured part of the news from here."

So, I sought out Mrs. Johnson. "Mrs. Johnson," I said, "I haven't danced in perhaps twenty years. I was never any good at it and, with general approval, gave it up. But I think we must dance for the honor of our country." I then told her the story. "I am exhausted," she said, "and my feet are, as the saying goes, killing me. But we mustn't disappoint them." So, later, when the music began, I went to Mrs. Johnson and asked if she would dance. She would. Indeed, we were the first on the floor. There was no feature story from Sverdlovsk that night.

The harmful impact of America's racial injustices and the outbreaks of defiance, such as Little Rock had presented, were subjects of frequent discussions on that journey in Russia. But as I sat before the typewriter to do this article memory recalled that many conclusions of 1959 seem far, far back in time in the light of the swift-moving transition. In 1963 some eighteen million Negroes have broken through the major barriers that for some two hundred years have separated them from equal participation in American life. Within the foreseeable future the system of segregation will be wiped out.

The acceleration of pace in pursuit of that objective will intrigue historians of the future. The ugly, murderous mob at Oxford, Mississippi, created by the folly of a Mississippi long withdrawn from the American dream and purpose, was a therapeutic event in that it shocked the national conscience. After all, those who had before Oxford remained aloof from decision could not say, "I approve of Ross Barnett and the policies of the White Citizens Councils." The fact that the government sent troops there to establish and maintain the constitutional rights of one man was reassuring. (In a trip to six West African countries and the Congo early this year I found that the prompt action of sending troops to enforce the decision of the United States courts had made a really profound impression.) It remained for Birmingham, Alabama, its police commissioner Eugene (Bull) Connor, the use of police dogs, the arrest of children, the brutal employment of high pressure fire hoses, and statements callous and coarse, to provide the catalyst, the quickening of will, the resolution to act from the grass roots of the Delta's rich soil and the ghettos of cities and towns, large and small.

So it was that by mid-summer, one could look ahead and see that New South—about which so many prophets have written and prophesied—coming over the horizon. There have been, of course, many new Souths in the long history of the region. But this one of freedom from the expensive and spiritually distorting bonds of a segregated system will be one really new . . . and the first one of truly free and great expectations.

But one could also look ahead and see that there was, and is a vast need of coordination of all agencies involved in the drive for full citizenship and a broadening of the base. This is not merely a movement of Negro citizens. It involves all those who are committed to the national principles, to all that is meant by the phrase Western civilization, to the meaning and strength of the Jewish and Christian ethics, and to all those sensitive to the human condition generally.

Such cooperation is of a first priority. There must be well thought out plans for what comes after the ending of segregated practices. (That these will hang on for a time in isolated rural pockets is a melancholy expectation, but not really important to the major need.) It is well understood today that lack of guidelines after emancipation and the end of slavery and the Civil War was disastrous. A hastily conceived reconstruction was concerned with immediacy, and not with the future. A new society might have been slowly and patiently constructed. But there were no plans to educate, to train, to communicate ideas or a philosophy of democratic development. Had there been, then and there, a blueprint, something along the lines of the Marshall plan that rehabilitated Europe politically and economically after the Second World War, the nation would have been spared much painful travail, and an accompanying human and economic loss. There was none. There were reaction and reunion in terms of the Rutherford B. Hayes sell-out.

After Birmingham, in the spring of 1963, had everywhere lighted a grass roots fire in America, the organizations at work in the field of human rights began to feel more sharply than before the need for coordination. It all had seemed to happen so quickly (though, actually, it did not), that no over-all plan of strategy or tactics existed. The Congress of Racial Equality (CORE), the Students Nonviolent Coordinating Committee, the Urban League, the NAACP, and individuals, led by Martin Luther King, had unity of objective. Yet, the more mature knew that even though civil rights were won after a long, hard fight, this, too, would be but a step. There would still be need for implementation. There were others who knew that because of the long isolation of the Negro from American life, a cultural and educational lag existed which would make it difficult for many Negroes—especially those in the rural South and those who had gone from it, untaught and unskilled, to the industrial cities of the East and West—to take advantage of the rights attained.

There were knowledgeable persons who were aware that for many Negroes in the North, jobs were of more immediate emotional appeal than civil rights. A poor, unemployed Negro can see that discriminations lie more heavily on him than on a skilled Negro wage-earner of the middle class or a successful professional man. In fact, the poorer Negro can look about him and see a certain economic kinship, at least, with the long-jobless white man, who, also, more often than not, is a product of the segregated educational system that has cheated both. The organizations and those who spoke for them soon were commonly agreed on the need for coordination.

As one looks ahead the NAACP comes strongly into focus. The direct action groups were invaluable. They worked in fields where, often, there was no "law." The student pickets and sit-ins, the freedom riders, and all those engaged in eyeball-to-eyeball confrontation with discrimination, telescoped time. They achieved in a relatively brief time what lawsuits could not have won in years. But the NAACP always was, as the legal arm, the great rock in a weary land. It is the organization that must bear the major burden of the future. The attainment of civil rights is not really the major objective. Once these rights are secured, then will come the exacting and demanding task of somehow closing the gulf in education and training, jobs and housing. Talents, skills and abilities unavailable to the nation because of segregation will be released for use in other fields of the nation's politically and economically complex life. The competitive erosion of that release will present many new problems, some as psychologically frustrating as those of a segregated society.

Ironically, as one peers toward the unfolding future, one sees that since only eighteen million of the roughly one hundred and eighty-five million Americans are Negro, it will be the white population—more especially that of the South, that will benefit most of all.

We know that the "Redeemer Democrats," after having sold out the Democratic candidate Tilden in 1877 for a promise by Republican President-to-be Hayes to remove troops and abandon the promise of civil rights for the newly-freed Negro, established the

one-party system. Commenting on that one-party system, the emi-
nent historian C. Vann Woodward said in *Origins of the New
South:*

"Had the white man's party of conservatism been democratically
organized, had the 'party line' been determined and criticized democratically, the one-party system might not have been stultifying. But
the organization and control of the party was anything but democratic. Issues, candidates, platforms—everything was the private
business of a few politicians known by the discontented as the 'ring'
or the 'courthouse clique.' The extent of their domination and the
nature of their machinery of control varied among the state rings,
but the ring was always present. . . ."

These "rings" or "courthouse cliques" still have considerable influence, but their grasp is being broken. The rings never voluntarily
gave up any power. Candor compels one to say that only the federal courts have initiated reform. Through the federal courts the
white primary was barred. Court attacks on the sometimes brutal,
always effective, restrictions on, and deterrents to, voting are having more and more success. Latest, and most important, was the
federal court orders to reapportion the legislatures so as to make
them more representative. In Georgia the iniquitous county unit
system, which long had made that state all but helpless against the
most corrupt and vicious elements in its politics, also was sponged
out by the courts.

There are signs of a developing two-party system, and of Democrats who do not approve of the racist views of senators and congressmen whose long political life and power in congressional committees have depended on the one-party politics of the region. President Kennedy was continually harassed and denied by this sort of
control of the rules committee in the House, and by other committees controlled by Southern Democrats who were subservient to the
extremist groups in their constituencies.

Most of the pragmatic business of looking ahead in the South
fell to the white Southerner. As the Negro's image of himself
changed, the image of the region inevitably took on a different
aspect. This reached deep into the rural regions. Almost overnight
the Negro farm tenant, cropper, or small land owner, seemed to be
(and was) "different." He was not, as some said, a new Negro.
But in the new climate of things he could publicly say and express
thoughts and feelings long suppressed. One month, for example,
the Mississippi planters and mayors of cities in that state could, and
did, speak of contented Negroes who were being disturbed by outsiders. The next month many of these same Negroes were in the
demonstration of discontent in Jackson, the state's capital. It is fac-

tual to say that in the rural South the white man was certainly astonished, bewildered, and usually resentful of this change. The trumpets of a new era had blown down the walls of the old Jericho. It was less easy for the rural Southerner to look ahead. His whole economy and society was based on the old ways. But, change being relentless, this Southerner had to look forward, and even if he closed his eyes against what he saw, he nonetheless had to open them now and then.

In the urban areas, and the South is largely urban, there was looking forward. It needs to be said that well before the pickets and the sit-ins there were some few industries and businesses which had looked ahead and begun to upgrade Negro employees and to hire more than before. By 1960 this number had increased, though, comparatively, it was small. By 1963, most of the large corporations and businesses had begun—or had plans ready to put into operation—to upgrade Negro employees who were ready for promotion, and to send others to training schools. Looking ahead, one could see a steady, accelerated improvement in job opportunities for Negroes.

In looking ahead, Negro and white began to understand they had to look back at the low quality of most of Southern education and admit that a segregated system, in a region lacking the income to pay for one good system, had penalized all children with an inadequate dual set-up. The penalty, to be sure, was heaviest on the Negro children, particularly those in the poorer rural areas. Many of those who came from the tenant cabins and the small farms were, therefore, neither prepared psychologically nor technically, for an industrial society. But they were there—and more were coming. This made looking ahead by the white leadership even more imperative.

Looking ahead one may see that it is in the field of voting rights that the real revolution will come. Voting strength will quickly win better schools, will end discriminations in relief benefits, jobs, housing and other aspects of life. The South, free of its burdens of taxes wasted in supporting two systems, and maintaining all the other financially and morally costly trappings of a segregated society, should become the great boom area. The South has sacrificed its children, colored and white, to inferior education, and has, across a hundred years, discriminated, in one degree or another, against all its people. A free South will be, in fact, a New South. The human condition always has had at least three yearnings . . . to be treated as a human being, to have an equal, fair chance to win respect and advancement as an individual in the economic environment, and freely to seek spiritual and cultural happiness.

All this means that attainment of civil rights is only a means to the more distant end—the long-term harvest of social, political, and economic reforms made possible by the possession and use of those rights.

Planning and foresight, which will enlist all Americans, of whatever racial background, to build a stronger nation of commitment and belief is the opportunity offered by the days and nights that move toward us. If we miss this second opportunity—100 years after the first—it is unlikely we will have another.

Selection 12

THE TASK AHEAD*

Alexis de Tocqueville, a young French nobleman of thirty, heralded in 1835 the development of "two great nations in the world, which started from different points, but seem to tend towards the same end. . . . the Russians and the Americans." "The conquests of the American are . . . gained by the plowshare; those of the Russian by the sword. The Anglo-American relies upon personal interest to accomplish his ends and gives free scope to the unguided strength and common sense of the people; the Russian centers all the authority of society in a single arm. The principal instrument of the former is freedom; of the latter, servitude."

Turning his discerning gaze to the domestic problems of the United States, a country which he had visited in 1831–32, Tocqueville recognized the paradox of a free society's dependence upon a system of slave labor. The presence of millions of enslaved Negroes was the "most formidable of all the ills that threaten the future of the Union," and confronted Americans with a problem which appeared to defy solution.

He defined the alternatives available to the slave-holding States with simplicity. They might emancipate the Negroes and treat them with some degree of civility, or perpetuate their serfdom for

---

* From *Freedom to the Free*, A Report to the President by the United States Commission on Civil Rights, Washington, D.C.: U.S. Government Printing Office, 1963, pp. 202–07.

as long as possible. Emancipation, he saw, would solve few problems in the immediate future. The evidence suggested that freedom for the Negro intensified rather than alleviated the prejudice on the part of the whites:

Thus it is in the United States that the prejudice which repels the Negroes seems to increase in proportion as they are emancipated, and inequality is sanctioned by the manners while it is effaced from the laws of the country.

Slavery might recede, Tocqueville said, "but the prejudice to which it has given birth is immovable."

But although emancipation would not automatically solve the problems resulting from slavery, efforts to perpetuate slavery would create the danger of racial conflict "likely to terminate, and that shortly, in the most horrible of civil wars and perhaps in the extirpation of one or the other of the two races."

Tocqueville was correct in his assessment. Slavery precipitated civil war, but it was a war fought between North and South, not between Negro and white. He also was correct in his judgment that emancipation was not a panacea—its immediate effect was to intensify prejudice, and to bring the Negro a freedom more fictional than real. To the end of the nineteenth century and well into the twentieth, the legally-free Negro citizen was denied the franchise, excluded from public office, assigned to inferior and separate schools, herded into ghettos, directed to the back of the bus, treated unequally in the courts of justice, and segregated in his illness, his worship, and even in his death.

Up to this point in time and history, Tocqueville's predictions were confirmed. His view that whites and Negroes could exist together on the American continent only as masters and slaves or as armed combatants seemed confirmed by failure of the United States to pass its first major post-Emancipation test—the reconciliation of the two races in the Reconstruction era. By the time that emancipation had been achieved, the venom of racism had so infected the body politic that the Government had become incapable of enforcing the new civil rights legislation. Moreover, the gap in Federal enforcement had only in rare instances been filled by the States. This was the long, dark night for civil rights in America, a period in which the American people refused to commit themselves to the principle of equal protection under the law.

Yet if Tocqueville was accurate in predicting that slavery would precipitate armed conflict, he was wrong in his judgment that the only alternative to slavery was the "extirpation" of either race. Not only have both white and Negro survived; they have shown a remarkable capacity to work together for their common benefit. A significant factor in creating this capacity has been the Negro's demonstrated ability to rise from slavery and become an educated contributor to himself and the community.

The first decades of the twentieth century saw profound social and economic changes that were to have a significant impact on the struggle for equal rights. The migration of the Negro from farm to city, and from South to North presented him with new opportunities but it also confronted him with new problems. In an atmosphere of indifference or even hostility, the Negro assumed a greater part of the burden in the struggle for equal rights. He formed his own private organizations to champion the cause of civil rights; he sought higher education and entered the professions; he used the political process as a tool for the achievement of economic and social gains; and he fought for his country on foreign shores. Yet the presence of qualified Negroes in ever increasing numbers often only heightened the unwillingness of many Americans to grant the Negro that equality to which the law said he was entitled, and which the Negro increasingly asserted he deserved.

Important gains were wrought out of the crucibles of depression and world war with government support for private initiative, but they did little more than set the stage for more insistent demands by a minority group which had been called upon for equal sacrifice, but had continued to receive unequal rewards.

Another major factor in the reawakening of Americans to an interest in civil rights has been the Nation's profound involvement in international affairs and the realization that America's prestige in a world torn between ideologies often rests heavily on its performance in living up to its avowed principles of democracy. This new external pressure has brought about a searching reconsideration of the meaning of the Declaration of Independence and the Bill of Rights.

America's new position of world leadership has encouraged action by private groups and government at all levels. It has similarly heightened the interest of the American business community in the condition of the Negro. The interest has been expressed in several divergent ways. One involves the potential of the Negro as buyer to generate a substantial increase in consumption of goods and services.

The business community is also conscious of the studies which show that slum sections of the city yield only about six percent of its total tax receipts but absorb about 45 percent of the total cost of municipal services. And the businessman is growing increasingly aware that refusal to hire qualified Negroes for positions of responsibility is a waste of manpower resources and talent.

As the century following emancipation draws to a close, more forces are working for the realization of civil rights for all Americans than ever before in history. Government is active in every branch and at every level, if not in every region. Voluntary associations in the field have multiplied at such a rate that it is difficult to catalog them. In this swirl of social change, a new pattern is emerging. While it does not reveal solutions to the problems it poses, it offers an increasingly clear portrait of the differing character of civil rights problems which must be met in different regions of the country.

In the South, the problem may be characterized generally as resistance to the established law of the land and to social change. The irresistible force is moving the object which was thought to be immovable; progress is slow and often painful, but it is steady and it appears to be inevitable. In the North, the issue is not one of resistance to law. It is here that segregation and discrimination are usually *de facto* rather than *de jure,* and it is here that the last battle for equal rights may be fought in America. The "gentlemen's agreement" that bars the minority citizen from housing outside the ghetto; the employment practices that often hold him in a menial status, regardless of his capabilities; and the overburdened neighborhood schools, which deprive him of an adequate education, despite his ambitions—these are the subtler forms of denial and the more difficult to eliminate.

Beyond these factors, which are largely ones of public attitude, there is the increasing problem of physical change. The minority person has been anxious to flee the confines of rural life for the promise of the city. In the rural areas, change often comes slowly and customs may linger beyond their validity. The city, by contrast, provides a climate for the generation and acceptance of new ideas. Yet contemporary history has demonstrated that the growing city becomes a significant menace to minority rights when its physical facilities, public services, and private opportunities fall behind the demands generated by the population.

As a city dweller, the Negro seemingly should gain from efforts to replace dilapidated housing and neighborhoods, to achieve efficient transportation systems, and to make the city a center of community and culture. Instead such projects have often exacerbated the problems of minority residents. The fixing of highway routes and selection of sites for large-scale housing projects, parks, and civic centers historically follow the path of least resistance. This path frequently leads across the depressed neighborhood of the minority person. When old housing is eliminated without providing adequate replacement units for its residents, the result is more overcrowding of the remaining minority neighborhoods. And there, because of the custom of assigning pupils to the schools in the neighborhoods in which they live, the minority child receives an inferior education in a crowded and segregated school.

Thus one paradox gives rise to another. The Negro suffers from the denial of his rights in the rural area because it refuses to change. He suffers from denials in the city because it must change. In the South, he has struggled to get into the neighborhood school. In the North, he is fighting to get out of it. While he seeks and has largely found identification with the mainstream of American life, he has suffered more than others from its occupational and technological dislocations.

As a Nation, we have solved Tocqueville's paradox of a free society's dependence upon a system of slavery. In doing so, we have been presented with new paradoxes for which we have not yet evolved solutions. We have come a far journey from a distant era in the 100 years since the Emancipation Proclamation. At the beginning of it, there was slavery. At the end, there is citizenship. Citizenship, however, is a fragile word with an ambivalent meaning. The condition of citizenship is not yet full-blown or fully realized for the American Negro. There is still more ground to cover.

The final chapter in the struggle for equality has yet to be written.

Selection 13

CRISIS AND COMMITMENT

The following statement was issued as a memorandum from the NAACP and appeared in the New York Times. *Dr. Martin Luther King expressed his approval on the following day.*

Crisis and Commitment

No one can any longer doubt or ignore the depth of crisis which today confronts Negro Americans struggling to enjoy full and equal citizenship in their native land. The year's events have piled confusion and uncertainty on underlying racial prejudices in the majority population. The consequence has been intensified resistance to change at a time when the need for change is greatest. We consider it imperative, therefore, to make crystal clear to Americans of every origin and of every degree of commitment to justice the principles upon which the civil rights movement rests.

There is nothing new about these principles. What is new are the conditions which compel us to re-state them—not the least of which is their abandonment by some individuals and groups whose positions are nevertheless frequently interpreted as representing the civil rights movement.

I. *We are committed to the attainment of racial justice by the democratic process.* The force of law and its fulfillment in the courts, legislative halls and implementing agencies, the appeal to conscience, and the exercise of the rights of peaceful assembly and petition are the instrumentalities of our choice. We propose to win genuine partnership for all our people in the United States, within the framework of this nation's constitution.

II. *We repudiate any strategies of violence, reprisal or vigilantism, and we condemn both rioting and the demagoguery that feeds it,* for these are the final resort of despair, and we have not yielded to despair. Defense of one's family, home and self against attack is not an issue; it is a basic American principle and must not be perverted into a cover for aggressive violence.

III. *We are committed to integration, by which we mean an end to every barrier which segregation and other forms of discrimination have raised against the enjoyment by Negro Americans of their human and constitutional rights.* We believe that a sense of personal worth and a pride in race are vital to integration in a pluralistic society, but we believe that these are best nurtured by success in achieving equality. We reject the way of separatism, either moral or spatial.

IV. *As we are committed to the goal of integration into every aspect of the national life, we are equally committed to the common responsibility of all Americans, both white and black, for bringing integration to pass.* We not only welcome, we urge, the full co-operation of white Americans in what must be a joint endeavor if it is to prosper. It should go without saying, that, in seeking full equality for Negroes, we cannot and will not deny it to others who join our fight.

The reaffirmation of these principles must do more than simply distinguish between those who accept them and those who, for one reason or another, no longer choose to operate under them. For us, these principles are inextricably joined with obligations to which we have consistently devoted our meagre resources and our energies. We call upon the nation as a whole to assume the same obligations; its failure to do so will not only extend and perhaps complete the sabotage of our efforts, but will ultimately undermine domestic security and United States leadership in the world of nations.

It is not condoning riots to cry out against the conditions in the Negro ghettos which render some Negroes susceptible to the emotional gratification of pillage, looting and destruction. It is not condoning riots, but demanding the means to end them, that compels us to note the steady worsening of the average Negro's lot in the face of unprecedented general prosperity. It is not turning our backs on the need for education to note that the average Negro college graduate can expect a lifetime's earnings no greater than those of a white high school graduate. It is not an abdication of responsibility, but an affirmation of it, to say that society cannot perpetuate discrimination against Negroes and then blame the victims of their leaders for the outbursts of those who have been made desperate.

It is an obligation of the whole of American society to take the massive actions which alone can turn the downward tide of Negro economic status with its concomitant growth of frustration and bitterness. It is the special obligation of those who can see more clearly and feel more keenly than the rest to assume their own leadership burden and to spare no effort to bring their fellows to an equal comprehension. It is the obligation, in particular, of the mass media to moderate their obsession with sensation and conflict and to help create a climate of genuine knowledge and understanding in which perspective is restored.

The near-total absence of this perspective is reflected in the survey figures showing declines in public sentiment favoring civil rights. Has the nation forgotten, for example, that for every Negro youth who throws a brick, there are a hundred thousand suffering the same disadvantages who do not? That for every Negro who tosses a Molotov cocktail, there are a thousand fighting and dying on the battlefields of Vietnam? It is a cruel and bitter abuse to judge the worth of these larger numbers, the overwhelming preponderance of the Negro population, by the misdeeds of a few.

We cannot ignore the signs of a retreat by white America from the national commitment to racial justice. The inadequacies of enforcement of this commitment, which has been hammered out over long years of judicial, legislative and administrative pronouncement, have been a scandal; yet we have seen the United States Senate scuttling enforcement of antidiscrimination law and refusing to act on legislation to protect Negroes against racist assault. We have seen the appeal of bigotry elevated to a major political instrument, with votes being sought and won across the nation, by exploiting the so-called "white backlash." We have seen sometime friends pulling back in full retreat and yielding to the battlefield scavengers ground which could have been held if it had been fought for.

This trend can be disastrous to the nation's, as well as the Negro's, welfare if it is not checked, if our forces are not rallied and if the hard, demanding job of building lasting public support is not pressed forward now. It can be worse than disastrous for the generation of younger Americans, white as well as black, who would then indeed face a future without viable idealism. Thousands of them have been personally involved in the civil rights movement over the last few years, many in situations involving hazardous confrontations. They are needed now more than ever before, in work which, while seeming more routine and less adventurous, is in many ways harder and more vital. They can be effectively drawn to these new tasks only if they have assurance that the adult world is solidly engaged to the same purpose.

Ninety years ago, this nation permitted the democratic promise of Emancipation to wither and die before a rampant reaction which condemned the Negro to segregation, disfranchisement, peonage and death. Then, as now, the voices of temporary liberalism sounded discouragement and disillusionment with the capacity of the freedmen for full citizenship. Then, as now, the South capitalized on Northern weariness with the "race problem" and was enabled to shut off the hope of freedom. But the "race problem" remained, and today we are paying for yesterday's default.

We are determined that this history shall not repeat itself and we call upon all our countrymen, black and white, of all faiths and origins, to move with us.

[Signed:]

DOROTHY HEIGHT, *Pres. National Council of Negro Women;*

A. PHILIP RANDOLPH, *Pres. Brotherhood of Sleeping Car Porters, AFL-CIO;*

BAYARD RUSTIN, *Director, A. Philip Randolph Institute;*

ROY WILKINS, *Exec. Director, Nat'l Ass'n for the Advancement of Colored People;*

WHITNEY M. YOUNG, JR., *Exec. Director, National Urban League;*

AMOS T. HALL, *Exec. Sec'y Conference of Grand Masters, Prince Hall Masons of America;*

HOBSON R. REYNOLDS, *Grand Exalted Ruler, Improved Benevolent and Protective Order of the Elks of the World.*

BIBLIOGRAPHY

In recent years, as if to compensate for past neglect, an unusually large number of books of varied quality have been published on the Negro in American history. The following list of recommended reading represents a sampling of those volumes which are especially useful. Some of the more specialized works are particularly relevant to one section of *The Negro in Twentieth Century America,* in which case that section is indicated by a Roman numeral after the listing. Books available in paperback edition are preceded by an asterisk.

Baldwin, James, *The Fire Next Time.* New York: Dell Publishing Co., 1962. (I)

    A searing book, brilliantly written, on what it means to be a Negro in America.

*Bardolph, Richard, *The Negro Vanguard.* New York: Random House, 1959.

    A history of the achievements of outstanding American Negroes from 1770 to the present.

*Bennett, Lerone, Jr., *Before the Mayflower: A History of the Negro in America, 1619–1964* (revised edition). Maryland: Pelican Books, 1966.

    A popular survey which includes a special section in "Landmarks and Milestones."

*Broderick, Francis L., and Meier, August, eds., *Negro Protest Thought in the Twentieth Century.* Indianapolis: Bobbs-Merrill Co., 1965. (II)

    A valuable collection of historic expressions of Negro thought, illuminating the present crisis in race relations.

*Butcher, Margaret J., *The Negro in American Culture.* New York: Alfred A. Knopf, Inc., 1964.

    Based on materials left by Alain Leroy Locke, the volume discusses the Negro's role in music, dance, folklore, poetry, fiction, drama, painting, and other cultural fields.

Carter, Robert L., *et. al., Equality.* New York: Pantheon Books, Inc., 1965 (II)

    Four essays by legal authorities on the issue of quotas and compensatory treatment for Negroes.

*Cash, W. J., *The Mind of the South.* New York: Random House, 1941.

    A critical interpretation of the customs, virtues, and faults of the South.

*Dorman, Michael, *We Shall Overcome.* New York: Dell Publishing Co., 1965. (III)

    An eye-witness account by a reporter of racial troubles during the years 1962–63 with special emphasis on integration of the Universities of Alabama and Mississippi.

Clark, Kenneth B., *Dark Ghetto: Dilemmas of Social Power.* New York: Harper & Row, Pubs., 1965.

    A dissection of the nature of the ghetto accompanied by a strategy for change.

*Duberman, Martin B., *In White America*. Massachusetts: Houghton Mifflin Co., 1964. (I)
A documentary play which seeks to describe what it has been like to be a Negro in this country.

Franklin, John Hope, *From Slavery to Freedom: A History of American Negroes*. New York: Alfred A. Knopf, Inc., 1964.
A comprehensive text in the history of the American Negro.

Friedman, Leon, ed., *Southern Justice*. New York: Pantheon Books, Inc., 1965. (III)
Nineteen lawyers describe their experiences in handling civil rights cases in the South.

*Ginzberg, Eli, *The Negro Potential*. New York: Columbia University Press, 1965. (IV)
An analysis of the Negro potential and a strategy for developing it.

*Golden, Harry, *Mr. Kennedy and the Negroes*. New York: Crest Books (Fawcett World Library), 1964. (II)
A well-known humorist writes a serious book about President Kennedy's concern for the Negro.

*Handlin, Oscar, *Fire-Bell in the Night: The Crisis in Civil Rights*. Boston: Little, Brown & Co., 1964. (IV)
A discussion of strategy (equality versus integration) and tactics (moderation versus racism) in the civil rights movement.

Hays, Brooks, *A Southern Moderate Speaks*. Chapel Hill: University of North Carolina Press, 1959. (II)
The author was congressman from Arkansas for sixteen years; many ascribe his defeat in 1958 to his position on the Little Rock school integration controversy.

*Hentoff, Nat, *The New Equality*. New York: Viking Press, Inc., 1964. (IV)
A discussion of the economic and social changes that are prerequisites to achieving the new equality.

Hill, Roy L., *Rhetoric of Racial Revolt*. Denver: Golden Bell Press, 1964. (II)
A collection of speeches by distinguished Negroes on the struggle for equality.

*King, Martin Luther, Jr., *Why We Can't Wait*. New York: New American Library of World Literature, Inc., 1964. (II)
One of the leaders of the civil rights movement discusses his philosophy and his vision of the future.

Lewis, Anthony, and the *New York Times, Portrait of a Decade: The Second American Revolution*. New York: Random House, 1964. (III)
Based on articles from the *New York Times,* this volume is a comprehensive chronicle of events in the civil rights revolution from 1954–1964.

*Lincoln, C. Eric, *The Black Muslims in America*. Boston: Beacon Press, 1961. (II)
An exhaustive study of the origins, doctrines, and leaders of the group.

*Logan, Rayford W., *The Betrayal of the Negro: From Rutherford B. Hayes to Woodrow Wilson*. New York: Crowell-Collier Pub. Co., 1965. (II)
An historical study of developments in the period 1877–1918, which es-

tablished segregation and placed the Negro in the status of a second-class citizen.

*————, *The Negro in the United States: A Brief History*. Princeton: D. Van Nostrand Co., Inc. (Anvil Original), 1957.

This brief history is accompanied by a set of useful documents.

*Lomax, Louis E., *The Negro Revolt*. New York: New American Library of World Literature, Inc., 1962 (II)

A report on the racial crisis, its past history and its current implications.

Marshall, Ray, *The Negro and Organized Labor*. New York: John Wiley & Sons, 1965. (III)

A comprehensive and scholarly summary of the subject.

*Mendelson, Wallace, *Discrimination*. New Jersey: Prentice-Hall, Inc., 1962. (III)

A summary of the 1961 five-volume *Report of the United States Commission on Civil Rights* which examined discrimination at the polls, in education, in employment, in housing, and in the administration of justice.

Miller, Loren, *The Petitioners: The Story of the Supreme Court of the United States and the Negro*. New York: Pantheon Books, Inc., 1965. (III)

A scholarly examination of the subject from 1789–1965.

Morris, Willie, ed., *The South Today: 100 Years After Appomattox*. New York: Harper Colophon Books, 1965.

Essays by writers, historians, and journalists—all native Southerners with one exception—which attempt to present a portrait of the present-day South.

Myrdal, Gunnar, *An American Dilemma: The Negro Problem and Modern Democracy*. New York: Harper & Row, Pubs., 1944.

Regarded by many scholars as a classic study of the problem. (A one-volume summary of this book is *Negro in America,* Arnold Rosen, New York: Harper & Row, Pubs., 1948.)

Newby, I. A., *Jim Crow's Defense: Anti-Negro Thought in America, 1900–1930*. Baton Rouge: Louisiana State University Press, 1965. (II)

An examination of the scholarly and popular sources of anti-Negro attitudes.

Parsons, Talcott, and Clark, Kenneth, eds., *The Negro American*. Boston: Houghton Mifflin Co., 1966. (II & IV)

A collection of scholarly articles originally published in Daedalus, 1965 and 1966, on many aspects of the racial crisis.

*Pettigrew, Thomas F., *A Profile of the Negro American*. New York: D. Van Nostrand Co., Inc., 1964. (IV)

A comprehensive study of the social and psychological aspects of the Negro problem.

*Quarles, Benjamin, *The Negro in the Making of America*. New York: Crowell-Collier Pub. Co., 1964.

A brief, well-written, general history.

*Redding, Saunders, *On Being Negro in America*. New York: Bantam Books, Inc., 1964 (II)

A personal document by a distinguished writer.

*Silberman, Charles E., *Crisis in Black and White*. New York: Random House, 1964. (II, III & IV)

An analysis of the various facets of the Negro problem and a warning that concrete action cannot long be delayed.

*Silver, James W., *Mississippi: The Closed Society,* 2d ed. New York: Harcourt, Brace & World, Inc., 1966. (II & III)

A professor of history at the University of Mississippi from 1936–1965 analyzes the nature of Mississippi society and its relation to the racial problem.

Smith, Frank E., *Congressman from Mississippi: An Autobiography.* New York: Pantheon Books, Inc., 1964. (II)

Outspoken autobiography of a man who spent twelve years as a congressman from Mississippi.

Sutherland, Elizabeth, ed., *Letters from Mississippi.* New York: McGraw-Hill Book Co., Inc., 1965. (II)

A collection of some of the letters written in the summer of 1964 by the young men and women who went to Mississippi to work in Freedom Schools and in community centers, and to help in the voter registration drive.

Thompson, Era Bell, and Mipson, Herbert, eds., *White on Black.* Chicago: Johnson Publishing Co., Inc., 1963. (II)

Twenty-two prominent white Americans present their views on the American Negro.

*United States Civil Rights Commission, *Enforcement: A Report on Equal Protection in the South.* Washington, D.C.: U. S. Government Printing Office, 1965. (III)

Warren, Robert Penn, *Who Speaks for the Negro?* New York: Random House, 1965. (II)

A transcript of conversations with Negro leaders with commentaries by the author.

Waskow, Arthur I., *From Race Riot to Sit-In: 1919 and the 1960's.* New York: Doubleday & Co., 1966. (II & IV)

A comparison of the racial crisis in the summer of 1919 and the early years of the 1960's, with a proposal for achieving racial justice.

Wilson, James Q., *Negro Politics: The Search for Leaders.* New York: The Free Press, 1960. (II & IV)

An analysis of Negro politics in the North, with Chicago as a case study.

*Wish, Harvey, ed., *The Negro Since Emancipation.* New Jersey: Prentice-Hall, Inc., 1964. (II)

A collection of readings from Douglass to Elijah Muhammed on the injustices of racial discrimination.

*Woodward, C. Vann, *The Strange Career of Jim Crow,* 2d revised ed. New York: Oxford University Press, 1966. (II)

An important book on the emergence of the Jim Crow system in the South.

Zinn, Howard, *SNCC: The New Abolitionists.* Boston: Beacon Press, 1964. (II)

The story of SNCC, told by an historian and advisor to the organization.

VINTAGE WORKS OF SCIENCE
AND PSYCHOLOGY

VINTAGE HISTORY—AMERICAN

VINTAGE BIOGRAPHY AND AUTOBIOGRAPHY